THE DIARY OF
Benjamin Robert Haydon

Volume One

1 8 0 8 – 1 8 1 5

BENJAMIN ROBERT HAYDON
by David Wilkie, 1815. From the drawing in the Ashmolean Museum, Oxford.

THE DIARY OF

Benjamin Robert Haydon

Edited by

WILLARD BISSELL POPE

HARVARD UNIVERSITY PRESS

Cambridge, Massachusetts

1 9 6 0

Distributed in Great Britain by Oxford University Press, London

*Publication of this book has been aided by a grant from the
Ford Foundation*

Typography by Burton Jones

*Printed and bound by the Colonial Press Inc.
Clinton, Massachusetts, U. S. A.*

Library of Congress Catalog Card Number 60–5394

CONTENTS

Contents

ILLUSTRATIONS

Preface

Benjamin Robert Haydon began his diary in 1808 and ended it with a prayer for forgiveness a few minutes before he killed himself in 1846. These thirty-eight years of war and peace, depression and prosperity, constitute an interesting period of great importance to students of English history, fine arts, and literature.

The diary begins at the time of the Peninsular War; six years later, with the temporary defeat of Napoleon, Haydon could visit Paris to see the treasures of conquered Europe which were then in the Louvre. The victory at Waterloo in 1815 brought only short-lived stability; soon Haydon was recording disputes among the allies and deploring what he considered a dangerous tendency to build up France until again she threatened the peace of Europe.

With the development of industrialization, the chief domestic political issue during the reigns of George IV and William IV was the Reform Movement, which finally triumphed in 1832. All the major Whigs sat to Haydon for their portraits in his great picture of the banquet held to celebrate passage of the Reform Bill; thus he had an unusual opportunity to converse with the political leaders of the period, for he was also well acquainted with many celebrated Tories.

Shortly before Haydon started his diary, he first saw the Elgin Marbles, recently brought from Greece. Immediately he recognized them as superb works of art and defended them and their owner against widespread defamatory attacks. Although he exaggerated his role in persuading Parliament to purchase the Marbles for the nation in 1816, he contributed valuably to the establishment of their reputation.

Haydon commented extensively on the founding of the National Gallery, the establishment of government schools of design, and the construction of the present Houses of Parliament. He knew the artists, sculptors, and architects associated with these events, and described in detail his friendships and enmities, notably with the Royal Academy and individual Academicians.

As for literature, Haydon was a close observer of the culmination of the Romantic Period and a valuable influence on at least one of its poets — Keats. Byron is the only major writer of the time with whom Haydon was not acquainted, but the diary contains much interesting material even on him, as well as on the galaxy of Romantic and early Victorian authors.

Haydon wrote his diary in twenty-six nearly uniform vellum-bound folios, approximately eight by thirteen inches, and in three smaller notebooks. A few days before his death he sent most of these volumes to Elizabeth Barrett for safekeeping, with the hope that she would prepare them for publication. Following the advice of her future husband, she declined and returned the diary to Mrs. Haydon; she bequeathed them in 1854 to her elder son, Frank Scott Haydon, who locked the volumes in two specially constructed metal chests.

After Miss Barrett's refusal, Mrs. Haydon and Longman, the publisher, commissioned Tom Taylor, a barrister, dramatist, professor of English Literature at London University, and contributor to *Punch*, to edit the diary. In 1853 he issued *Life of Benjamin Robert Haydon, Historical Painter, from his Autobiography and Journals*, in three volumes. The only surviving holograph of an *Autobiography* is a volume supplementary to the diary entitled "Vita"; comparison with Taylor's text suggests that it was a rough first draft of the "Autobiography" or "Memoirs," which Haydon first recorded that he was writing on July 7, 1839. The "Vita," like the "Autobiography," is incomplete, the former ending with 1825 and the latter with 1820.

Taylor made no pretensions to publication of the entire diary. Through 1820 his text is the *Autobiography*, and thereafter he wrote of Haydon in the third person, with copious, long, but by no means verbatim quotations from the diary. Using his discretion and taking all liberties of a Victorian editor, he silently deleted or altered passages at will, and the result is a very greatly Taylorized Haydon, a version of the diary "full of blunders," as Frank Scott Haydon wrote to H. Buxton Forman on September 8, 1882.

With minor changes and trifling additions, Taylor issued a second English and first American edition later in 1853. This provides the text for all later editions, which should more properly be called reprints, since no writer on Haydon had access to the manuscripts of the diary, with the exception of Frederic Wordsworth Haydon, who borrowed the volumes from his brother Frank to compile *Benjamin Robert Haydon: Correspondence and Table-Talk* (2 vols., 1876). This book consists of a very subjective biographical memoir, of letters to and from Haydon, and of "Table-Talk," which contains many rewritten excerpts chosen at random from the diary.

The two chests seem to have been locked most of the time until the 1930's; few scholars obtained access to the contents, and inquiries in *Notes and Queries* concerning the location of the manuscript diary were apparently unanswered by either Frank Scott Haydon or his daughter, Ellen Mary Middleton Haydon, who inherited the volumes in 1887.

The owner, however, assisted William I. Knapp as he prepared his *Life, Writings and Correspondence of George Borrow* for publication in 1899; she is described in his acknowledgment as "Miss Ellen Haydon of Eastbourne." This was the latest allusion to the manuscripts which I had found when I was conducting research in the British Museum on Haydon in 1931 for my doctoral dissertation. I wrote a letter to the Eastbourne *Gazette*, explaining my interest in Haydon and requesting information concerning Miss Haydon and the diary. I had received no reply when I completed my research and left London for a ten-day vacation in Ireland before returning to America. Mail addressed to me in London was forwarded to the ship; as I sailed down Galway Bay bound for New York, I read a letter from a firm of solicitors in London saying that their client Miss Ellen Haydon had seen my letter in the *Gazette*, that the complete diary was in their custody, and that I might inspect it whenever I cared to call.

The call was necessarily delayed until I could return to London in 1932, and during these months the cordial attitude of Miss Haydon and her solicitors changed to one of complete hostility. Because her lawyer refused to give me her address, I could deal only with him; he told me frankly that his duty was to protect his client from meddlers who wished to consult private family papers from mere curiosity, and he remained unimpressed by my arguments that scholarship could be served only by reference to the manuscripts, since Taylor's text was corrupt and abridged. My efforts were obviously futile so long as Miss Haydon owned the diary.

I described my frustrations to my friend M. Buxton Forman, who at that time was preparing his second edition of *The Letters of John Keats.* He wished to collate the texts of the sixteen letters from Keats to Haydon with the holographs, which he correctly assumed were attached to the diary. In approaching Miss Haydon he referred to the friendship of her father and his father, H. Buxton Forman, who had received useful assistance from Frank Scott Haydon in the preparation of his four-volume *Poetical Works and Other Writings of John Keats* (1883). Since Mr. Forman's interest was solely in the Keats-Haydon correspondence, Miss Haydon and her solicitors granted his request; he warmly thanked her in his preface and mentioned with deep regret her death on March 25, 1935.

Mr. Forman purchased the two chests and their contents from Miss Haydon's estate and took them with him to Pretoria when he moved to South Africa in 1946. He sold them to me in 1951.

The diary is far more than a record of Haydon's daily activities. Many pages contain spirited pen-and-ink sketches; to others are pasted or wafered newspaper cuttings and letters from his friends, and many are devoted to drafts of letters and articles which he wrote, as well as random thoughts on diverse subjects. It is sometimes difficult to determine whether these "essays" are authentic entries, but I have deleted only those which I believe obviously form no part of the diary. Letters and newspaper cuttings attached to the diary are similarly deleted unless they pertain to an entry.

In Haydon's will, written immediately before his suicide and invalid because his signature was not witnessed, he clearly expressed a desire for the publication of his memoirs "to 1820 — my journals will supply the rest. The style, the individuality of Richardson, which I wish not curtailed by an Editor." Following Haydon's desire in this matter, I have attempted to reproduce his text as closely as is possible. The transcript was not easy to make, for his penmanship at best is hardly caligraphy and at worst is illegible. He seems to have written very rapidly, and sometimes, in attempting to make his hand keep up with his thoughts, let his pen

run dry. Phrases crowded between lines as additions are often difficult to read, and I am therefore occasionally obliged to indicate
passages which are illegible to me and others. I have standardized
his method of dating entries, and have silently corrected his punc-
tuation when I believe that a change clarifies his meaning, but I
have not altered his capitalization and spelling.

My annotations attempt to identify all people whom Haydon
saw and many about whom he wrote, books to which he referred
and passages which he quoted, and current events that require
elucidation. With such a wide objective my search has not always
been successful. Names are identified only at their first appearance
in the diary. The place of publication of books cited is London
unless otherwise stated.

The present edition will present the complete text of the entire
diary. The first two volumes, which cover the period from 1808
through 1824, will be followed by other volumes for the years
from 1825 through 1846.

Many institutions, libraries, and individuals have contributed
so much to the preparation of this book that my thanks, deep as
they are, can never adequately express my gratitude. Acknowledg-
ments of specific aid are frequently made in footnotes, but here I
wish to record my gratitude: to the trustees of the Ford Foundation and of the University of Vermont for granting generous sub-
ventions for publication; to Mrs. Helen Oustinoff and staff members of the University of Vermont Library, the British Museum,
the Courtauld Institute of Art, the Frick Art Reference Library,
the New York Public Library, the Boston Public Library, and the
libraries of Harvard University, where Miss E. Louise Lucas of the
Fogg Museum Library, Miss Mary Reardon of the Theatre Collection, and Miss Mabel A. E. Steele of the Houghton Library have
assisted me enormously; and to dozens of learned and helpful
friends in this country and in Great Britain.

In a letter written with all the spirit of her grandfather, Mrs.
Lina Boyd-Carpenter of Doncaster, daughter of Frederic Wordsworth Haydon, granted her full permission for publication. My
correspondence with this charming octogenarian has given me
great pleasure, as well as immeasurable assistance in genealogical
matters, supplementing information provided by the late Henry

Haydon, Esq. Professors John H. Kent and Walter A. Stultz have read and clarified quotations from the classical languages and passages pertaining to anatomy. Professors Herschel Baker, Jack Stillinger, and Alvin Whitley have identified quotations for me and consulted sources in places which I could not visit, as have Mr. and Mrs. Norman Kilgour and Miss L. Simpson. Professor Francis Colburn helped me choose the illustrations from the hundreds of sketches in the diary. I am grateful for the encouragement and assistance I received from the late M. Buxton Forman, Esq., during the early stages of this work, when he owned the diary and I worked from microfilm, which he kindly permitted me to make in 1936. Dr. Evan Turner read my entire manuscript and gave me many useful ideas derived from his profound knowledge of fine arts. My final encouragement and greatest aid, from both tangible suggestions and the example of his impeccable scholarship, came from the late Professor Hyder E. Rollins, who read two-thirds of the present book before his fatal illness. My last and largest thanks are to my wife, who has aided and abetted every scholarly procedure and, as it were, welcomed the residence of Benjamin Robert Haydon in our house for many years.

Through ignorance or carelessness, Haydon's spelling of the following words frequently differs from the standard practice of his day:

Ades (for Hades)
Aegystus ⎱
Agystus ⎰ (for Aegisthus)
Affaganistan ⎱
Affaghanistan ⎰ (for Afghanistan)
affects (for effects)
agonising
aidecamp
Air (for Ayr)
anticks
apellation
Aristeides (for Aristides)
Arithmathea (for Arimathea)
artizan
asmatic
atticks
attrack

Baily (for Baillie)
Bailey ⎱
Bayley ⎰ (for Baily)
batcheler
batchelor
bear (for bare)
Basheba (for Bathsheba)
Beechy (for Beechey)
Beerhing (for Bering)
believe (for belief)
Belvidere (for Belvedere)
benefitted
Bennock (for Bennoch)
Berkley ⎱
Berkly ⎰ (for Berkeley)
betwix
Billinsgate (for Billingsgate)
Bing (for Byng)
Boccacio (for Boccaccio)

Bonifacio (for Bonifazio)
Boon (for Boone)
born (for borne)
Bourienne (for Bourrienne)
bow (for beau)
braceletts
brawney
brouze
browness
Brown (for Browne)
Busaco (for Bussaco)
Buonaroti (for Buonarroti)
bye (for by)

Calcott (for Callcott)
callendar
Cammucini (for Camuccini)
Canaletti (for Canaletto)
Caractatus (for Caractacus)
Carel (for Karel)
caterwhawling
Castilione (for Castiglione)
Catholick
Chappel
characterise
Chatam (for Chatham)
Chauntrey (for Chantrey)
chear
chimnies
chowl (for jowl)
chrystal
citidal
cleaness
clentched
Clerke (for Clarke)
cloathes
cloaths

cloride
cobling
cocknies
Colysaeum
commisseration
connoiseur
cooly (for coolly)
Corregio (for Correggio)
Corruna (for Coruña)
council (for counsel)
croky
cryed
crys
crysalis
X (for Christ)
Xrist
Xtianity

Dalilah (for Delilah)
Dalmeney (for Dalmeny)
damdest
dappled (for dabbled)
defacated
Delawar (for De La Warr)
descrimination
devellope
disabille (for dishabille)
dissappoint
dout (for doubt)
drewled
drunkeness
Dugal (for Dugald)
dyspeptick

easil
Eclesiasticus (for Ecclesiasticus)
ectasy
Edingburgh (for Edinburgh)
effect (for affect)
enterance
erisipelas
erruptions
Eschylus (for Aeschylus)
Ester (for Esther)
examplifying

excressencies
ercrutiating
exstatic
extacies
extasy

Farrington (for Farington)
fidler
figitted
Fontainbleau (for Fontainebleau)
forboding
forgetfullness
forlorness
fortelling
Frank Halls (for Frans Hals)
Frazer (for Fraser)
Fuzeli (for Fuseli)
Frederick (for Frederic)

gaity
Ganimede (for Ganymede)
gaters (for gaiters)
Georgione (for Giorgione)
glittring
gogle
gossipping
greaze

hacknied
Halam (for Hallam)
Hambden (for Hampden)
Harlowe (for Harlow)
harrassed
Harrington (for Harington)
heigth
Herenhausen (for Herrenhausen)
Hobbima (for Hobbema)
Hodson (for Hodgson)
Hopner (for Hoppner)
horne
Hougomont (for Hougoumont)
Humphrey (for Humphry Davy)

Ilyssus (for Ilissus)
imbecil

imbecillity
immoveable
interprise
intollerable
Iphegenia (for Iphigenia)
Irvine (for Irving)

Jennings ⎱ (for Jenyns)
Jennyns ⎰
Johnson (for Jonson)
Julio (for Giulio)

keeness
knashing (for gnashing)
knat (for gnat)
knawing (for gnawing)
knifes (for knives)
Kolback (for Kaulbach)

lightening (for lightning)
Lionard ⎱ (for Leonardo)
Lionardo ⎰
liquour
Littleton (for Lyttelton)
Lock (for Locke)
Lockart (for Lockhart)
loose (for lose)
Lopez de Vega (for Lope de Vega)
lopp
Lorenzo di Medici (for Lorenzo de' Medici)
lye (for lie)
lyme
Lyndurst (for Lyndhurst)
Lysymachus (for Lysimachus)

Macauley ⎱ (for Macaulay)
Macauly ⎰
Mahamet (for Mahomet)
macgylp (for megilp)
manouvred
marshall (for martial)
maratime
Marybone (for Marylebone)

Massaccio (for Masaccio)
Massachusets (for Massachusetts)
Mathew (for Matthew)
mawl stick (for maulstick)
McClise (for Maclise)
meaness
merchandize
Methusalem (for Methuselah)
mishapen
mislead (for misled)
Murillio (for Murillo)
muzzel
mysentery (for mesentery)

Newisham (for Newsam)

openess
opthalmia
oreids
Otley (for Ottley)
overated
oxigen

panygeric
paralise
parallized
parallysed
paroxism
past (for passed)
patriarcal
Petersburgh (for Petersburg)
Phillip ⎱ (for Philippe)
Phillipe ⎰
Phillips (for Philips)
physionomy
Pinturrichio (for Pintoricchio)
Pizano (for Pisano)
Plunkett (for Plunket)
poling (for polling)
pommade
Pompei
pouring (for poring)
pray (for prey)
preferr

Prentice (for Prentis)
principals (for principles)
principle (for principal)
profets (for prophets)
proofed
prophane
prophligacy
protagé
protogé
pruved
Punjaub (for Punjab)
puppeism
pye ball'd

quinzey
quoirs (for choirs)

Rafaell ⎫
Raffael ⎭ (for Raffaello)
rapp
Rawleigh (for Ralegh)
rediculous
Rembrant (for Rembrandt)
ressussitation
rhinocerous
Richlieu (for Richelieu)
Romily (for Romilly)
rotteness
rubb
ruff (for rough)
Russel (for Russell)

sadler
Saltmarsh (for Saltmarshe)
Sampson (for Samson)
satyre (for satire)
satyrs (for satires)
scepticle
Scobell (for Scoble)
Scotts (for Scots)
scurrillity
Sharpe (for Sharp)
sheperd
Shiel (for Sheil)
Sibil

Sibyll
sleave (for sleeve)
Snorr (for Schnorr)
sollicitor
sonnetts
soul (for sole)
Southwall (for Southall)
Spencer (for Spenser)
squallid
staid (for stayed)
Stern (for Sterne)
Steven (for Stephen)
stimullated
stopt
Stotard (for Stothard)
sulfurous
sulleness
superseed
Sybil
Sybill
Syren

tastless
Tholouse (for Toulouse)
Thompson (for Thomson)
throtled
Thuilleries (for Tuileries)
topled
Totness (for Totnes)
trajedy
Trelawney (for Trelawny)
trowsers
twylight

underate
undully
unparralleled

Vandervelde (for Van de Velde)
Van Eyk (for Van Eyck)
Van Omburg (for Van Amburgh)
vigourous
villany
Vimiero (for Vimeiro)

wantoness
wastcoat
Waverly (for Waverley)
Wellesly (for Wellesley)
welnigh
Werter (for Werther)
Westmoreland (for Westmor-
 land)
wetting (for whetting)
whigs (for wigs)
White (for Wight)
wholy
wicket (for wicker)
Wickliffe (for Wycliffe)
wifes

Wigs (for Whigs)
Winchelsea (for Winchilsea)
Windham (for Wyndham)
Wirtemberg (for Würtemberg)
wisper (for whisper)
wit (for whit)
withold
Witsun (for Whitsun)
Wolf (for Wolfe)
wrisled
wrack (for rack)
wrote (for wrought)

yat

In the footnotes I abbreviate the names of Haydon and his sons: BRH means Benjamin Robert Haydon, FSH means Frank Scott Haydon, and FWH means Frederic Wordsworth Haydon. For concise reference, I use the following short titles:

Autobiography. The Autobiography and Memoirs of Benjamin Robert Haydon, ed. Tom Taylor. A new edition with an Introduction by Aldous Huxley, 2 vols., New York [1926].

Boswell. James Boswell, *The Life of Samuel Johnson, LL.D.,* ed. G. Birkbeck Hill, revised by L. F. Powell, 6 vols., Oxford, 1934–1940.

Britannica. The Encyclopaedia Britannica, 11th ed., 29 vols., New York, 1910–1911.

Correspondence. Benjamin Robert Haydon: Correspondence and Table-Talk, ed. Frederic Wordsworth Haydon, 2 vols., 1876.

Cunningham. Allan Cunningham, *The Life of Sir David Wilkie,* 3 vols., 1843.

D.N.B. Dictionary of National Biography, ed. Leslie Stephen, 76 vols., New York, 1885–1901.

Farington. Joseph Farington, *The Farington Diary,* ed. James Greig, 8 vols. [1922–1928].

George. Eric George, *The Life and Death of Benjamin Robert Haydon,* 1948.

Hazlitt. *The Complete Works of William Hazlitt,* ed. P. P. Howe, 21 vols., 1930–1934.

L'Estrange. *Life of Mary Russell Mitford, Related in a Selection from her Letters to her Friends,* ed. Alfred Guy L'Estrange, 3 vols., 1870.

Letters of Keats. The Letters of John Keats, ed. Hyder Edward Rollins, 2 vols., Cambridge, Massachusetts, 1958.

Lectures. Benjamin Robert Haydon, *Lectures on Painting and Design,* 2 vols., 1844 and 1846.

Lockhart. John Gibson Lockhart, *Memoirs of the Life of Sir Walter Scott, Bart.,* 7 vols., Edinburgh, 1837–1838.

Muirhead. *London and its Environs,* ed. Findlay Muirhead, 1922.

Olney. Clarke Olney, *Benjamin Robert Haydon, Historical Painter*, Athens, Georgia, 1952.

Pigot. *Pigot's Commercial Directory, 1823–24.*

Thieme-Becker. Ulrich Thieme and Felix Becker, *Allgemeines Lexikon der bildenden Künstler von der Antike bis zur Gegenwart*, 36 vols., Leipzig, 1911–1947.

Vasari. Giorgio Vasari, *Lives of Seventy of the Most Eminent Painters, Sculptors, and Architects*, ed. E. H. and E. W. Blashfield and A. A. Hopkins, 4 vols., New York, 1923.

Waagen. G. F. Waagen, *Treasures of Art in Great Britain*, tr. Lady Eastlake, 4 vols., 1854–1857.

Whitley, *1700–1799*. William T. Whitley, *Artists and their Friends in England*, 1700–1799, 2 vols., 1928.

Whitley, *1800–1820*. William T. Whitley, *Art in England, 1800–1820*, Cambridge, England, 1928.

Whitley, *1821–1837*. William T. Whitley, *Art in England, 1821–1837*, Cambridge, England, 1930.

Unless otherwise noted, the Loeb editions of classical authors have been used, with the following translators: *The Aeneid*, H. Rushton Fairclough, *The Iliad*, A. T. Murray, *The Odyssey*, A. T. Murray, and Pliny's *Natural History*, H. Rackham. Quotations from Milton and Shakespeare are cited from *The Poetical Works of John Milton*, ed. H. C. Beeching, 1928, and *The Complete Plays and Poems of William Shakespeare*, ed. William Allan Neilson and Charles Jarvis Hill, Boston, 1942.

THE DIARY OF
Benjamin Robert Haydon

Prologue

With characteristic vanity, Haydon attempted to prove that his direct ancestor of the seventeenth century was Gideon Haydon of Cadhay House, an estate near Ottery-St. Mary, which he visited in September 1828. His son Frank Scott Haydon examined the genealogical "evidence," dismissed it as mere wishful thinking, and began the family tree which he prepared in 1872 with his great-great-grandfather, one "——— Haydon, ob. in 1724." His son was Robert (1714–1773), who "began life as a Sign & Fillet Painter" and died "a Bookseller & Printer" in Plymouth. He married Mary Baskerville, probably a sister of John Baskerville, the great printer. Robert Haydon bequeathed his establishment to his only son, Benjamin Robert (1758–1813), described as "Printer to H. R. H. William, late Duke of Clarence." In 1782 he married Sarah Cobley, daughter of the rector of Dodbrooke, Devon. On January 25, 1786, their son, the diarist, was born at Plymouth.

From 1793 to 1799, Benjamin Robert Haydon attended a grammar school conducted by the Rev. Dr. Bidlake, acquiring what he later considered a very superficial education. His interest in drawing began at this period and was fostered by a Neapolitan employee in his father's shop. At the age of thirteen, the boy was sent to a boarding school in Plympton, where his classical knowledge and proficiency in drawing increased. Wishing to start his son's career in the family business, his father sent him to Exeter for training in accounting, and then, when he was fifteen, bound him as an apprentice for seven years.

Although the elder Haydon's bookshop prospered, the apprentice became increasingly unhappy with the growth of his love for drawing and his hatred of trade. His father thought that he would relinquish his hope to become an artist after a serious illness in 1803 had temporarily blinded him; from that time onward his sight was seriously impaired but his determination increased. At the age of eighteen he gained his father's reluctant permission to break the indenture and to enroll as a student in the Royal Academy's school.

He reached London on May 15, 1804, and immediately became a most diligent, ambitious, and confident art student, studying at the Academy under Henry Fuseli, and presently developing warm friendships with two other young students, David Wilkie and John Jackson. Early in his career Haydon became interested in anatomy and studied it far more extensively than the curriculum required, since he felt that a thorough knowledge was necessary to create historical paintings of "high art," the only sort of pictures which he wished to paint.

Through Wilkie, Haydon met Lord Mulgrave and Sir George Beaumont, who introduced him to others as a young artist of great promise. They admired his first picture, "Joseph and Mary Resting on the Road to Egypt," which he successfully exhibited at the Royal Academy in 1807, and Lord Mulgrave commissioned him to paint a picture of "The Assassination of Dentatus."

In January 1808, while planning the composition of this picture, Haydon first saw the Elgin Marbles and, responding at once to their beauty and anatomical accuracy, determined to incorporate their principles in all his painting. He studied them closely until summer, when he took a vacation — and started his diary.

Volume IIIa

JULY 1808

Although Haydon's consecutive diary begins in Volume I with a fragmentary entry made before September 7, 1808, the last fourteen pages of Volume III, read from back to front, are headed "Journals of my little Country Excursions. 1808" and contain the following account of his trip to Dover, from which he had returned to London by August 9, when Wilkie noted in his diary: "Was surprised by a call from Haydon, whom I believed to be at Dover" (Cunningham, I,187).

Volume IIIa

JULY 1808

July 23. I left Town for Dover [on] the mail and arrived there
the next morning. I walked about in the Town and about evening
wandered away to Shakespeare's clift; here perhaps, I said, Shakespeare has stood, here Lear defied the Storm, there, as I looked
towards the Castle, Cordelia died; how many Kings of England
have embarked from Dover to France? For the first time in my
life I saw the white cliffs of England, beating back the murmuring surge, and as the Sun shot a last gleam athwart the ocean, I
caught a glitter of the distant coast of France — how I felt.
There, I thought, is France, the proud enemy of England; what
a feeling two thousand years hence, when England & France
shall have long sunk into silence, like Carthage & Rome; when
those straights, now covered with shipping, shall then be as silent
as the desarts of Egypt; at such a period, for some traveller, who
from his infancy has been feeding his fancy and storing his mind
with the history of the wars of these Nations, at such a moment,
for some being after an anxious night, as the day dawned, the
Star glittered, and the Sun rose, the white cliffs of England, and
France, should burst on his sight. Standing as it were as they always stood, proudly defying each other, regardless of Centuries,
ages, and events — who will not hereafter, as the breeze wafts
him between, contemplate with awe England & France. "There's
England — and that's France," will be the usual exclamation, —
and then till they are lost in air, Silence will ensue, every man
wrapt up in his own feelings & meditations — I staid on the clift
of Shakespeare till twilight was far advanced, and as I moved
down, towards Town, and turned round to take a last look for
that night of the clift that towered in the Sky and was almost lost
in the *embruno* tint of twilight, how grand it would be, it flashed
into my mind, if there [were at] the top a Colossal Statue of
Britannia, with her Lion at her feet, surveying France with a lofty

3

air. If this remained alone when England becomes a desart, how poetical would this and its White cliffs be when light[ed] up by the rising or engoldened by the setting Sun.

It would be a mark at Sea — Some person to whom I mentioned this said, "Why, it must be 20 feet high." — "20 feet!! 150." — "Who would you get to undertake such a thing?" — Who would I get? is this a question that an Athenian would have asked? —

This shews how little diffusion of taste there is yet in England — so little are the people acquainted with the great purposes of Art, that any mention of any colossal, great, or Public [undertaking] is literally a source of ridicule. — I recollect once I happened to say a great colossal Statue of Neptune at the Admiralty, one foot on one side & one foot on the other, holding in one hand the telegraph, towering in the air so as to be visible for miles, would [be] an ornament worthy of such a city. "You had better," said a collector of Dutch Pictures, with a sneer, "propose it to Parliament." "That I would," said I, "were there the least chance of success." It may be a source of amusement to you, whose ideas of art are circumscribed within a Dutch pitcher — but it's a melancholy thing for those whose whole ambition is the advance of the National taste — to see all the faculties of men, squeezed into an inside of a tasteless dutch Room, with a woman clouting a child — all the delight English men feel is in cocking their nose close to the Picture, and let its intellectual qualities be what they may, condemn or praise in proportion to its mechanical excellence. They talk of Raphael & the Cartoons,[1] but they merely talk — for God knows they feel e'en little enough — Wherever I dine — what is the conversation — if it turns to art? Is it on Milton, Homer, Michel Angelo or Raphael, is it the moral effect of Art, is it the source of intellectual delight great efforts afford, is

1. Seven cartoons by Raphael for tapestries on subjects pertaining to the lives of St. Peter and St. Paul, formerly kept at Hampton Court, and now in the Victoria and Albert Museum. The Royal Academy obtained copies of the cartoons made by Sir James Thornhill about 1730. "As long as Somerset House was the home of the Academy [i.e., until 1837] it was the custom to hang the copies in the Great Room when it was not engaged for the annual exhibitions; and it was a common thing for the Professors of Painting, whose addresses were delivered in the Great Room, to point out and descant upon passages in the compositions of Raphael" (Whitley, 1800–1820, p. 14).

it where is London deficient in great works, and how can England rival Greece, do men seem sensible of the respect due to the higher walks? Wherever I dine, wherever I go, a string of technical phrases that are for ever on the tongue, without effort or reflection, are perpetually uttered — how that floor is imitated, what a colour that turnip is, how delightful is that cabbage, look at that herring — wonderful — what could you expect from infants if you talked to them about art — but that they would be enchanted at the imitation of their doll, or their bells, so with the People of England, all their ambition and all their delight, and all their ideas of art go not beyond their immediate object of their senses; the exact copy of a pound of butter, or a capitally touched china cup — an effort of intellect can certainly be shewn in the arrangement of a pound of butter or china cup — it requires intellect to do any thing with reference to a whole. I am not ridiculing the Artists, but the people; they see only the individual likeness to the thing and there their delight ends and there their notions of art are confined — they care nothing — uneducated People might be forgiven — but Noblemen, refined, educated, classical Noblemen, the ministers of the Country, the government of England, instead of standing at an awful distance, and surveying with dread great works, uttering with admiration "what a conception, what a fancy, what an Idea," instead of being ambitious of having their Souls elevated, and their minds expanded, instead of this, to see them rush, with their heads jammed as if in a wedge, clap up their glasses before a Picture, "three feet long, and two feet wide,"[2] and uttering exclamations of ravishment and rapture, at a smutty crock, or a brass candlestick — even in my friend W[ilkie]'s Picture.[3] What do they admire in it? The character or the mind? No, the dutch part, the touching, the knifes, the pewter plates, and tin saucepans — this is all they

2. As Professor Hyder E. Rollins informed me, the third stanza of Wordsworth's "The Thorn" concluded, in the 1798 edition, with these lines describing a mountain pond: "I've measured it from side to side:/'Tis three feet long, and two feet wide."

3. David Wilkie (1785–1841) left Scotland in 1805, becoming a fellow student of BRH at the Royal Academy. By 1808 he had achieved considerable fame, with his leading pictures, "The Blind Fiddler" and "The Rent Day," purchased by Sir George Beaumont and Lord Mulgrave. BRH probably refers to the latter picture, which shows glasses, decanters, and table utensils.

comprehend — this is what they look for, and this is what they see —

The Noblemen of England have not strength of mind to relish grand, terrible subjects; they like to lie on their sofas and indolently admire a Landscape by Glover;[4] they like to put down small Pictures on a chair by the window and wonder at trifles —

I've seen C——, M——, D——, L——, and all the Ministers of England,[5] squeeze to a small P—— of W—— of a Servant washing a child's face with her hand,[6] while one eye being only seen is squeezed up in agony —"look at that eye," said D——, "look at that eye; good God, how extraordinary that he could express so much in an eye" — This is a specimen of the government of England, these are the People to whom dejected Painting looks for assistance — Poor Painting, Poor Painting, you may talk till you are Hoarse of the effect of Public works — But the Nobility of England will take more delight in brass saucepans. I have watched them at Lord Elgin's.[7] Was every English Nobleman to put his hand to his heart, and say what he really thinks of those exquisite remains, he would say he thinks they are not worth preserving.

4. John Glover (1767–1849), president of the Old Water-Colour Society from 1807 to 1817. "Putting Turner out of the question, [he] had been for some years the most prosperous artist of his kind in England. A writer of 1817, when speaking of his 'much merited success,' estimated that he had already accumulated a fortune of £30,000 by his professional labours" (Whitley, 1800–1820, pp. 269–270).

5. The administration under the Duke of Portland (March 1807 to October 1809) contained George Canning, Lord Castlereagh, Lord Camden, Lord Mulgrave, Robert S. Dundas, and Lord Liverpool.

6. Wilkie's "Sunday Morning," painted in 1806, depicts such a scene.

7. The seventh Earl of Elgin (1766–1841) was appointed envoy extraordinary at the Ottoman Porte in 1799. In 1801 he received permission to make plaster casts and to remove any Greek sculptures which he desired, chief of which were the fragments from the Parthenon in Athens. In 1803 he shipped the first part of his collection to England in the Mentor, which was wrecked on the island of Cerigo or Kythera. Salvage of the sculptures occupied three years, and other delays prevented Lord Elgin from arranging his collection in London until the summer of 1808, when he had returned from Turkey. The marbles were exhibited in a temporary building attached to Lord Elgin's house in Park Lane. Immediate and vituperative controversy developed, with accusations of vandalism and denial of the artistic importance of the sculptures, refuted by BRH as one of the first champions of the Elgin Marbles. Canova's strong endorsement in 1815 influenced Parliament to purchase the collection for the British Museum in 1816; Lord Elgin, who had spent more than £50,000 on the marbles, received £35,000 from the nation.

I have lately refused every invitation to dine out, I prefer the delights of Virgil and Homer, to the imbecile, tiresome, technical nonsense of dutch connoiseurship, "how cleverly that is painted," &c, &c, — after dinner one takes a candle and walks over to an insipid Jan Mieris, of a Woman and a Boy, with cabbages, Potatoes, & red herrings, a cat, a brass pan, and some carrots, — then all are in raptures, "what an exquisite imitation, look at the carrots, look at the herrings, well we must take that down" — down it's taken — put on a chair; then My Lord & My Lady, and Master & Miss, all crowd round this inimitable carrot Picture, lost in rapture & delight. God, I wish for the spectre of Michel Angelo to frown them into grandeur, but even his spectre, and a vision of the Capella Sistina at his heels, would stand a poor chance, with such an opponent as Jan Mieris, at the Table of an English Noble Connoiseur. With broken spirits and a harrassed mind, after having all day spent in dwelling on Homer and Achilles, I kneel down, in torture, and join in their acclamations; it cuts me to the soul to be obliged to listen to such applause, on a Dutchman; while Poor Raphael, or Michel Angelo, or Phidias are never mentioned or thought of.

To hear terms that would be applicable to the highest beauties of Art applied to a tame, insipid, smooth, flat, mindless imitation of carrots — Good God, is this the end of Art, is this the use of Painting? Mere mechanic deception; can Painters really excite pity or terror or love or benevolence or lift your soul above this world by sublime, heavenly fancies, or carry your mind to Hell by grand furious conceptions? Can Painters really stimulate a Man to Heroism, or urge a Man to Repentance, or excite a Man to virtue? No, certainly, not in such minds, it never can; Pictures with such properties would pass unheeded by, if they should unluckily stand by a Jan Mieris — O God, why was I not born to be known to Pericles or Lorenzo di Medici? O God, how would I acknowledge in Gratitude thy kindness, could I but find such Patrons, such Protectors, could I but find some one of rank who would relish grand fancies and promote grand art — In thee I trust still — Amen —

This fancy of the Statue of Britannia was a source of great delight to me, for when I saw Shakespeare's Clift, my mind instantly supplied what was wanting — I used to wander about evenings along an extended shore, far from human habitation, & sometimes disturb the sea birds in their holes, who with their screaming added grandeur to the scene, of murmuring waves, "Quum venti posuere," [8] and contemplate France, as for a moment the "setting sun" would, against it, "level his evening rays" [9] — there is the country that overran Europe, I thought; not 100 miles from that coast is Buonaparte, the wonder and detestation of the World; there, as I turned towards Boulogne, he has stood and perhaps with disappointment and malice surveyed the distant cliffs of England. I took a boat, and went over as near as was prudent, about half-way, and saw the windmill where Buonaparte had his little Iron house, & where his troops were encamped for invasion[1] — I never saw any coast so exactly answering the feeling excited by Homer's description & scenery; here was the Place to read Homer, here was the place for the πολυφλοίσβοιο θαλάσσης.[2]

What different scenery there is in Homer & Milton, one has all the rich rural dingle dong or dell of wild woods, and "twilight meadows," [3] and the other all the sublime terrors, and melancholy soothings of a Sea shore — when Achilles (among a thousand instances) Σμερδαλέα 'ιάχων,[4] would it be half so much like a sounding voice, in any other place, as on θῖνα θαλάσσης[5] — would any other place give such scope to voice, such room for fancying echo — I almost thought I saw Achilles in naked majesty moving his "mighty thighs" along the Shore, and with raised hand shouting to the Grecians as he passed — in every battle description of Homer, you always associate the sounding shore, which makes the uproar more horrible & thundering. From being so compleatly

8. Identified by Professor Herbert McArthur as *Aeneid*, VII,27. "When the winds fell."

9. *Paradise Lost*, IV,543.

1. The coast near Boulogne was heavily fortified during the period from 1803 to 1805, when Napoleon hoped to invade England. A pavilion or "Baraque" was built for him "100 feet in length and 22½ feet in width; the extremity which overlooked the harbour was shaped like a rotunda, and was 30 feet in diameter. It was built entirely of wood, like the wooden huts of a fair, only the planks were carefully finished off, and painted light grey" (Fernand Nicolay, *Napoleon at the Boulogne Camp*, tr. Georgina L. Davis, New York, 1907, p. 17).

2. *Iliad*, I,34, *et passim*. "Loud-resounding sea."

3. *Comus*, l. 844.

4. *Iliad*, XIX,41, *et passim*. "Cried a terrible cry."

5. *Iliad*, XIX,40. "The shore of the sea."

alone, I began to conceive some new subjects for Pictures, and one night, after reading with eagerness Macbeth, he in terror in the act of murdering the sleeping Duncan, and his wife listening & grooms sleeping, darted into my brain — I made several other sketches, nor did I so compleatly enjoy myself in all the delight of solitude as at Dover. Every body stared on the beach, no person knew my name or where I came from, I was always wet, alone, on some solitary shore or silent meadow — at last having enquired of the bathing man for Lodgings, some lady left directions of whom he enquired, and away I sallied; I was shewn into a Room, where stood an old harpsichord, miserably out of tune, a pair of dirty ladies' gloves lay on it, with a parasol, a torn lace veil, there was an appearance [of] profligate poverty, struggling to disguise all by an effort at gentility, which I did not like. At last in came the mistress, a flattering, a chattering, polite, cunning thing, that wore the look of once being a beauty, and after making several efforts to get out of me how long I was to stay, &c, her daughter entered, & in bad French told her Mother the room was ready upstairs; she was a fine, tall, dashing girl, to whom I suppose the dirty gloves, torn veil, and miserably toned harpsichord belonged, and with which, I supposed, she had charmed the hearts of half the coxcombs of the garrison. I did not like the appearance of the people; I could have nothing, I found, to myself. I found they thought they would be doing me a favor by intruding themselves upon me at all hours. "You'll never want Society, Sir; there is always me or my daughter," and when I was going, [she] offered her daughter to accompany me and shew me to some other friend who might perhaps suit me — I begged to decline the offer, feeling when I got clear, as if for an hour I had been breathing in a stew, of vice & debauchery — I could not help observing while here, the respect and awe every person had for the military, as if they were tinctured by the opposite coast. "You mustn't walk there, or here, or to this place" was in every body's mouth, and I daresay I was charged ten times with the bayonet for doing what appeared to me perfectly innocent; by night I was only allowed to walk on the beach from sentry to sentry — and then not without every time I approached each being always challenged. The windows of the Inns were scribbled

9

with the feelings of People leaving England, or returning to it; every thing in the place was new and excited in me new Ideas; half the People talked some sort of French or other; they appeared altogether of a different character; they seemed the *half tint* between England & France, hardly Frenchmen and not altogether Englishmen —

One evening a tremendous thunder storm came on, and away I sallied to the heights. Nothing could be more awful than the rumbling echo among the heights, and the illumined sea at intervals, where for an instant you would see ships labouring in surge, and then again they would be buried in darkness. "Things that love night, love not such nights as these," [6] I thought, "since I was man Such sheets of fire, such bursts of horrid crashing Thunder," [7] such groaning of roaring wind and rain, I never remember to have heard — The wind blew as if 'twould blow its last, the rattling shower rose on the blast, the speedy gleams the darkness swallowed, loud, deep, & long the thunder bellowed — I returned drenched with rain, and exhausted with walking — I fancied Lear with his White hair, which the impetuous blasts caught in their fury and made nothing of uttering imprecations on his fiend-like daughters, and defying the lightening to singe his white head, and spent the whole evening in reading it — before the Storm began, I observed a black cloud gathering and sailing towards the town; as it approached it encreased, and at last rushed over the town, which it enveloped in Darkness, followed by a stream of rushing wind which swept up every thing; all the People & animals darted into the Houses & Horses reared with fright in their eyes and pawed the ground, and a cat I saw that could not get in rose its back, enlarged its tail, and hissed with terror, till the cloud was passed, pregnant with fluid.

I met by accident on the beach one morning Mr. Watson, a gentleman of amiable and affectionate manners who had behaved politely to me in London — being a commissioner of excise he had the Cutter under his orders and gave me many pleasant excursions; we went to Hythe and saw the Martello Towers; the one

6. *King Lear,* III,ii,42–43.
7. *King Lear,* III,ii,45–46. "Since I was man,/Such sheets of fire, such bursts of horrid thunder."

we were in they made the passage to go out in the front, instead of behind, so that instead of presenting the strongest front to the enemy, they presented the weakest. I mentioned this to the engineer whom I met with afterwards and he said it was the only one that was so — we saw the castle. I could not help laughing at the Artilleryman who to shew the infallibility of his stink pots assured me he nearly smothered the Duke of York, and his Royal highness did not recover till carried into the air — there was a place of retreat for the inhabitants &c. Mr. Seguier,[8] another [friend] of Mr. Watson and mine, came down — how compleatly a Londoner is out of his element, when not walking on flat stones — we went to the light of the Goodwin Sands — where Gen. Phipps[9] told me Mr. Pitt and he had been together and saw Calais Plainly —

We shortly left Mr. Watson and returned to London — every inch was classical ground — Rochester — Gadshill — I saw the very place where Falstaff robbed the exchequer — we came to London in the evening — and I was soon again vigourously pursuing my Studies —

8. William Seguier (1771–1843), who had known BRH since 1806 (*Autobiography*, I,36). Although he was an artist, Seguier's chief influence in the realm of art was advisory. He became the first keeper of the National Gallery after its establishment in 1824 and was conservator of the royal art collections under George IV, William IV, and Victoria.

9. General Edmund Phipps (1760–1837), Lord Mulgrave's brother. He served as M.P. for Scarborough.

Volume I

SEPTEMBER 1808—DECEMBER 1808

The first thirty pages of Volume I of Haydon's diary are largely devoted to Greek exercises, vocabularies, and grammatical rules. Rough pen and ink sketches of classical figures are found in the inner front cover and two other pages, and on the tenth page is a sketch of a fist, endorsed by Haydon "July 3rd, 1808 — my own hand." Eight pages are blank. The diary itself begins with a fragmentary entry, following a page which has been torn out.

Volume I

SEPTEMBER 1808—DECEMBER 1808

. . . that I may truly say I have been purely Idle — when shall I be purely industrious? God only knows — my conscience is so burthened with vice & irreligion & Idleness that I am afraid to think, afraid to look into myself; — O God, that I with a thorough conviction and experience of the happiness bestowed by virtue, should ever plunge with this conviction in my mind, into the misery attendant on vice — I never retire to bed but with a new scheme of life and I arise only to exemplify its futility — I close this day a little happier to think that I have not wholly lost it — laus Deo — Hours 5½ drawing.

September 7. Wednesday. Arose at ½ past Six, made sketches from the Scull of a Horse, the anatomy of which I learnt (i.e. the bones), Drew at Lord Elgin's again from ten till two, and from three till six — walked & came home, drank tea & passed my time laxly in reading Boswell's Johnson, — I shall certainly draw every day at Lord Elgin's this week and do as much as I can as when the winter comes, it will be too cold. Is not this a mere excuse to be Idle & put off painting? — However I have been more pure and calm to day than for some time — O God grant every day of my future life I may encrease in purity, piety & energetic exertion — listen to me, O Merciful Father, thro Jesus Christ my Redeemer, — Amen, with all my soul —

Went to bed ½ past ten, — 7 hours drawing.

September 8. Thursday. Arose at eight — washed myself from top to toe with water. Drew at Lord Elgin's from ten till ¼ past two, and from three till ¾ past five, — walked about and looked at those matchless productions. I consider it truly the greatest blessing that ever happened to this country, their being brought here; the principles they are executed on I am truly ignorant of, yet I begin to relish them with a right feeling, and God grant I may be able to do something before I die that may stand in competition and raise the honor of my Country — I have been more

15

pure in my thoughts this day, than during the whole year, I hope it's a prelude to the remainder of my life, could I be always so industrious, so pious & so pure, O Almighty being, I should have no one thing to wish for — in the intent and hope I may be daily more worthy of thy mercy and assistance — Amen. hours 6¾ drawing. went to bed XI —

September 9. Friday. Awoke at Six with my night cap off, put it on to keep my head warm for a minute or two, and then I resolved to get up, but alas during that minute or two, I dozed away into a Sleep, and never awoke till eight!! — drew at Lord Elgin's again from ten till two, and from three till ¼ past six, & finished the best drawing I have made yet, marble fell down and cut my leg — went to bed at XII — am much improved this week in the knowledge of Horses. How the Greeks attended to every alteration in the body produced by the slightest movement! The more I study them the more do I feel my own insignificance. God grant I may rival them yet — equally pure to day and free from disturbing thoughts as yesterday — Thanks to God — Amen — may I encrease in virtue & purity & industry, to absolute perfection, let me admit of no degrees of excellence, nothing but indisputable greatness, on solid scientific principles — the House built on the Rock[1] — read Boswell's Johnson. There is no resisting this book — Hours 7¼ drawing.

September 10. Saturday. Arose at Seven, washed myself as usual — did not begin drawing until ½ past ten, drew on with some interruption till five o'clock, then dined, came home and read Boswell — What has affected me to day I cannot tell but I have drawn with evident weakness and on looking at my yesterday's drawing I was truly astonished to see such vigour and spirit; I cannot tell what has ailed me. I have been disturbed in my thoughts and have not been able to apply myself so acutely — it is no use altering my present drawing but I will begin a fresh one on Monday, and I hope to give a better account of myself on Monday night — I lay abed after I awoke, and this always weakens me, relaxes me and shatters me for the day. I find the method to preserve my health is to lie on a hard mattress, sleep

1. Matthew 7:24. "A wise man, which built his house upon a rock."

6 hours, jump up out of my first sleep, wash myself in cold water, Study 8 hours, drink nothing but water and weak tea, eat nothing but simple food, no suppers, no hashes or Stews. When I do this I always feel braced, healthy, inclined to Study, and strong enough for great exertion, whenever I break in to the slightest degree on this plan I am sure to suffer, to feel relaxed, incapable of energy, and the day is given up, without a struggle — to bed ½ past ten. Subtracting every time I got up and figetted about & Idled, which as I work at home by an eight hour glass I have a habit of instinctively reproaching myself whenever I do it. I have worked this day about I think 5½ hours drawing.

September 11. Sunday. Arose at ½ past Seven — Breakfasted out — came home and passed the day in calmness, purity, & reading — my leg has been painful — I have been free, totally free, from disturbing thoughts — O God Almighty grant I may every day encrease in purity, let me not arise, but to do that which will render me more worthy of everlasting happiness, let me end each day with a silent conviction of having passed it with thy approbation, let me master & controul every Idle habit, and every vicious propensity and have my passions in perfect subordination. O God in mercy grant my prayer for Jesus Christ's sake, amen.

September 12. Monday. Passed the day in reading & writing, not able to walk, obliged to put my leg on a chair, could not paint — Turlington's Balsam did not agree with me at all —

September 13. Tuesday. My leg still painful — read & was excessively affected at the account of Johnson's Death; to those who have been used to a sick room, when it says in the morning he asked the hour, they told him six, he answered, all went on regularly, he felt he had but a few hours to live,[2] every thing rushed into mind, all the accompaniments, the expiring rush light, as day begins to break, the attendants stalking about gently after sitting up all night, whispering to each other and now & then drawing back the window curtain to see how near the day, the Stars twinkling like gems, as if they were doing their utmost be-

2. See Boswell, IV,419.

fore they are extinguished by the Sun — and Johnson with proven energy in his expiring awful voice begging mercy at intervals of the Almighty. This brought my dear Mother's[3] death, with its dreadful circumstances to my recollection, and after fearing my impetuosity in hastening her on to London might have aggravated her complaint, I was consoled at the reflection that all the little happiness she enjoyed for the latter part of her anxious life was occasioned by my success and exertions — Thank Thee O God I never gave her one moment's sorrow by any vice — My dear dear Mother, forgive me for all my unkindness, forgive me for any inattention, if you are now sensible to my present feelings — I have never felt so pious, so pure, & calm as this day for this last twelvemonth. O could it last, but I trust in thee, assist me, let not Sin conquer me, Almighty Being — O God —

My Mind has been in a compleat state of suspension between Greek, Latin & French. But after mature reasoning, I am determined to go on again with Greek; French is fit only to be spoken, and Latin is more the language of a Critic than a Poet or a Painter, — Homer I will read. God bless my exertions.

September 14. Wednesday. Read Homer, in English, to stir up my fancy, that I may conceive and execute my Hero's head with vigour.[4] My leg better.

3. A genealogical chart prepared in 1872 by FSH shows that BRH's father, Benjamin Robert, was born on March 8, 1758, and died on June 25, 1813. He is described as "Printer to H. R. H. William, late Duke of Clarence." In 1782 he married "Sarah, eldest daur. of Rev. Benjamin Cobley, Rector of Dodbrooke (Dev.). . . . Died 21st November 1807. Burd. at Ide near Exeter. Tablet inside church to her & her father." The Reverend Anthony D. Coleridge, vicar of Ide, informed me in 1949 that the memorial tablet no longer exists, since the present building replaced the original church in 1833; the Ide burial register describes Mrs. Haydon as the second daughter of Benjamin Cobley and does not give the date of her birth.

During BRH's visit to his parents in Plymouth in 1807, his mother developed angina pectoris. To consult a specialist, he and his sister started to take their mother to London, but she died at an inn at Salt Hill (*Autobiography,* I,58–63), Bucks., between Slough and Maidenhead, only 21 miles on the coach road from Hyde Park Corner. She doubtless died at the Castle Inn.

4. In a letter dated September 9, 1806, Wilkie transmitted to BRH the commission of the third Baron Mulgrave (1755–1831) to paint the assassination of Lucius Sicinius Dentatus, as described in Hooke's *Roman History* (*Autobiography,* I,39).

About the year 448 B.C., during the Third Decemvirate, Sicinius Dentatus angered the decemvirs by accusation of military mismanagement. Although he was

September 15. Thursday. Read — 8 hours.

September 16. Friday. Read — 9 hours.

September 17. Saturday. Read Virgil; understand it and can make it out pretty well, but the Idea of the bird, "Decidit exanimis, &c." [5] not so beautiful and true as Homer's, who makes the feathers fly out and quiver away in the air. Got quite into the feeling for Latin & Greek, — I hope it always continues so. 13 hours reading — my right eye a little strained.

September 18. Sunday. Read Homer; any fine passage I went to the Greek immediately and made it out but with great bungling, yet I hope by accumulation to do it at last.

Nothing can exceed the description of Achilles arming for Battle — how Pope has missed this exquisite sentiment —

$$\dot{\epsilon}\nu\ \delta\dot{\epsilon}\ o\dot{\iota}\ \hat{\eta}\tau o\rho$$

$$\delta\hat{v}\nu'\ \ddot{a}\chi o\varsigma\ \ddot{a}\tau\lambda\eta\tau o\nu.^{6}$$

Grief and revenge his furious heart inspire.

Pope.[7]

---

a veteran of 120 engagements, he was sent out again, with a hundred soldiers instructed to assassinate him. "Sicinius having led them into the narrow passages of some mountains, they took that opportunity to fall upon him. He no sooner perceived their base design, but setting his back against a rock, that he might not be attacked behind, he received them with a courage that struck terror into the boldest of them. Calling up all his ancient valour, he slew several of the assailants, and wounded others: And now not one of them durst venture near him: They stood at a distance and threw their darts at him. But as even this did not effect their purpose, the villains climbed up to the top of the rock, and thence knocked him on the head with stones. They then went back to the camp, and gave out that they had fallen into an ambush, in which they had lost their captain, and part of their comrades" (Nathaniel Hooke, *The Roman History,* 1757, Book II, Chapter 28, I,355).

Lord Mulgrave was created first Earl of Mulgrave in 1812; the picture, reproduced by George, is in the possession of his descendant, the Marquess of Normanby, at Mulgrave Castle, Whitby.

5. *Aeneid,* V,517–518. "Decidit exanimis vitamque reliquit in astris/aëriis fixamque refert delapsa sagittam." "Down she [the dove shot by Eurytion] fell dead, left her life amid the stars of heaven, and, falling, brought down the arrow that pierced her." Cf. *Iliad,* XXIII,875–881, "High up beneath the cloud he [Meriones] spied the timorous dove; there as she circled round he struck her in the midst beneath the wing, and clean through passed the shaft, and fell again and fixed itself in the ground before the foot of Meriones; but the dove, lighting on the mast of the dark-prowed ship, hung down her head, and her thick plumage drooped. Swiftly the life fled from her limbs, and she fell far from the mast."

6. *Iliad,* XIX,366–367. "Into his heart there entered grief that might not be borne."

7. *Iliad,* XIX,394.

this gives one an Idea of a furious beast but Homer's conception is full of pathos; he says Achilles was arming, grinding his teeth, his eyes flashed fire, but his heart was full of intolerable grief. This mention of grief brings the mind back again to his affectionate Friendship for Patroclus and anguish at his Death and gives a pathetic feeling to the bloody scene which you anticipate in his going to battle. Nothing can be so refined. 10 hours reading.

September 19. Monday. Wrote several letters. Idle day. My leg very weak.

September 20. Tuesday. Began my Picture once again. Wilkie Breakfasted with me on his return from Lord Lansdowne,[8] a portrait of whose Lady he has brought home, which is truly exquisite. I had no Idea of his being capable of so much, it gives me real pleasure. God Bless our exertions, and let Death only put an end to our improvement. We dined with Lord Mulgrave in Private, quite free from restraint, his little family all playing about us — he talked about the late treaty at Lisbon,[9] &c — nothing can exceed his liberal attentions, I hope I shall every day be more worthy of them — 4 hours painting.*

[*The next page of the diary has been torn out. FSH attached the following note to the stub of this missing page: "Unchastity — Broke his oath 'never to touch another woman' in two days!"*]

October 9.[1] Sunday. Was more pious but not recovered from yesterday's shock.

October 10. Monday. Arose calm & pious but not quite pure; prayed as sincerely as I was able, painted little this day, repelled

* I remember my tremendous struggles against vice at this period with wonder — it was useless — I was totally unable to remit my burning appetites in spite of all my efforts. 1816.

8. The third Marquis of Lansdowne (1780–1863), statesman and art collector. Wilkie was at Southamption from September 1 to 14, painting the portrait of Lady Lansdowne. He returned to London on September 20 (Cunningham, I,192–197).
9. The Convention of Cintra, seventeen miles from Lisbon.
1. This date is verified by comparison with Wilkie's diary, which describes the events of October 15 and 23 mentioned by BRH (Cunningham, I,202–204).

lascivious fancy that hovered round me, drew at the Academy, spent the evening after with Fuzeli[2] who in the course of his conversation, which is always pointed & instructing, said that a subject for a Picture should astonish, surprize, or move, if it did neither it was not fit — a long argument about Xtianity; both agreed that its exquisite morality proved its divinity — came home, prayed sincerely, and am now going to bed, in a pious, resolute, & pure state of mind. O God may I encrease and go on without one single Deviation to the end of my life. Let me recollect how fallible I am, and never trust myself a day without prayer, O God forgive me, for Jesus Christ's sake, Amen.

October 11. Tuesday. Arose ½ past Seven, — went to the Institution,[3] — came home, made a sketch of Brutus seeing his evil Genius — did nothing to my Picture, no Academy — O God I begin again to breath in virtuous conceptions, strengthen them; grant me a clear view of my Indolence & idleness, and resolution to conquer, and resist them, O God let every hour & every moment render me more worthy of eternal happiness. A day passed negatively, free from vice, I shall account nothing, — I must be actively exerted, to say this day I deserve more than yesterday Thy approbation, O Merciful Father — a negative day may save me from punishment, but will never render me worthy of reward — O God bless my intentions, banish lasciviousness from my fancy, let me daily feel the consequence of virtue and the delights resulting from it, O God make me sensible, convince me — Amen. A negative day.

October 12, 13, and 14. Wednesday, Thursday, Friday. Industrious days, pure & virtuous. Thank God.

October 15. Saturday. Wilkie breakfasted with me & away

2. Henry Fuseli (1741–1825), R.A., born in Zurich but a resident of England after 1763. A student of Greek sculpture and of Michelangelo, he was professor of painting at the Royal Academy from 1799 until his death.
3. The British Institution was founded in 1806. Its purpose, as stated in the by-laws, was "to encourage the talents of the artists of the United Kingdom. . . . With this view the British Gallery is appropriated to the Exhibition and sale of the productions of British Artists and also to the Exhibition of Pictures by the Old Masters." The British Institution's School of Painting encouraged artists to study and copy the Old Masters borrowed from private collectors for the exhibitions, which were held from 1806 to 1867.

we went to Sir William Beechey's[4] to endeavour to get his vote, for Charles Bell,[5] as Professor of Anatomy to the Academy. Sir William made Wilkie sit for his head, while this was performing I went to call on Smirke[6] and left Wilkie to break the matter; came back & found it as hopeless a matter there as at Smirke's. Carlisle[7] is the man, he knows the effect good dinners have on half starved Academicians. Sir William as well as Smirke gave us no hopes, and I went to Bell to tell the truth, however he was not to be discouraged and set off himself, — there is certainly no man so well adapted as Bell, what was I writing?[8] — he has given his mind to that part of the Subject we need; and the Students have attended his three courses of Lectures, and therefore know his qualifications, and have all derived the little knowledge we possess from him. Carlisle has always ridiculed Anatomy in Painting, and what can we expect from him? — in the evening I felt idly inclined and communicated my inclination to Wilkie, to go to the play; he, who was as Idly inclined as myself, only was cunning enough to conceal it, was agreed, and away we went — Idle day.

October 16. Sunday. Let me not reflect how sillily I passed this precious day, no Greek or reading in the Bible till the evening, and then I fell asleep and did not wake till one o'clock.

October 17. Monday. I felt in the evening an inclination to see Macbeth, Wilkie who has no relish for any thing of this sort, said I wanted firmness, but had it been Mother Goose, or any such stuff I have no doubt he would have had as little firmness as myself. I went, but whether it was that their performing in the Opera house gave the figures less effect, I fancied Mrs. Siddons[9] acted with very little spirit in the scene where she comes out

4. Sir William Beechey (1753–1839), R.A., portrait painter to Queen Charlotte.

5. Charles Bell (1774–1842), anatomist, surgeon, and author of numerous medical books, illustrated by his own anatomical drawings. He was knighted in 1830.

6. Robert Smirke (1752–1845), R.A., genre painter and book illustrator.

7. Anthony Carlisle (1768–1840), surgeon. On December 3, 1808, he defeated Bell for the Royal Academy's professorship of anatomy by a vote of twenty-five to four and held the position until 1824. He was knighted in 1820.

8. BRH refers to the fact that he inadvertently wrote "Carlisle"; he scratched it out and then wrote "Bell."

9. Lady Macbeth was a favorite role of Mrs. Sarah Siddons (1755–1831).

when Macbeth is in Duncan's chamber she says, "That which had them drunk, hath made Me bold," &c.,[1] she ought to have been in a blaze. I, who had been accustomed to read Macbeth at home, at the Dead of night, when every thing was so silent that my hair stood up, could not at this moment put up with such a laceration of feeling as to be roused from contemplation by the slamming of a box door, when I almost fancied Duncan was groaning — I grew quite enraged & disgusted and left the house before the third act — I will not go again to any of Shakespeare's plays; you always afterwards associate the actors with the characters. Thank God, Lear I can read with purity as I have never seen it, nor never will — No Academy — negative day.

October 18. Tuesday. Determined to obliterate the whole of my Principal Figure as by doing the parts separately they did not hang together; what time one loses from inexperience! I made up my mind and did it. I am happy it's over — at the Academy.

October 19. Wednesday. Had Sam,[2] he sat, and I sketched in the whole of my figure much better. I hope in God I shall do it at last — at the Academy — Wilkie and I had some words; he said I spoke harshly, I was insensible to it — soon settled. Greek an hour. Bell called and left me 5 guineas to begin any sketch I liked and when done 5 more.

October 20. Thursday. Breakfasted with Wilkie to please him against my own inclination, — I hate to go out Morning; it disturbs me — improved my figure, — too large I fear — At the Academy. Greek an hour.

October 21. Friday. Put in the head of my hero, not at all satisfied; not half so well as my sketch, there is always something in a sketch, you can never after get when your feelings are quiescent. I look forward to that time, the result of many years' incessant study when I shall be able to paint a Picture warm from my brain with fire, certainty & correctness. I must acquire through

1. *Macbeth*, II,ii,1. "That which hath made them drunk hath made me bold."
2. Samuel Strowger, a veteran of the Life Guards, porter, model, and friend of many Academicians and students from 1802 until at least 1821 (Whitley, *1800–1820*, pp. 84–86).

scientific Principles first, for facility without science is a knack, acquired by habit.

O God let me not be gratifying my fancy with visions of happiness, that are not to be realized, let them be realized, O God, and I shall die happy, I bless [Thee] for the purity of this week, I have never neglected my morning Prayers, and have had strength to resist temptation, O God let every hour add strength to my virtuous habits — pious resolution & energetic plans, through Jesus X. Amen. Greek an hour, at the Academy —

October 22. Saturday. Wilkie breakfasted with me, he as well as myself was not pleased with my head, after he was gone I went to Lord Elgin's to stimulate my conception, and saw some casts from moulds he brought with him. What productions! I made drawings of several legs, drapery, &c and came back with an eye correct, determined to obliterate every thing in my Picture that would not bear comparison. I found enough — and dashed out my head, without a moment's hesitation. I am again clear, and hope God will bless my exertions for excellence in my next attempt. O God think me not trifling or presumptuous, assist me for J. X., amen, amen — At the Academy, ½ hour Greek — This week has ended, and laus Deo I feel myself more inclined for virtue & Industry, more pure, pious & decided. O God let those feelings by this day week have gained strength & vigour, O God let no Sin or Lasciviousness break in, conquer or disturb me; let me tomorrow attend public Worship, and adore thee in purity & zeal, — have mercy, let me obliterate my innumerable Sins, by my future virtue. Amen — God bless my exertion & grant me health for Jesus X. sake, Amen, Amen.

October 23. Sunday. Wilkie and I breakfasted with Wilson,[3] our church was not repaired yet — we could not go to another of course!!! dined early & went to drink tea with one of the Porters, Sam, who is a very industrious, honest, Prudent man with a large family, he is the Academy Model, and has sat to me for my first

3. Andrew Wilson (1780–1848), landscape painter; he met BRH and Wilkie soon after his return from Italy in 1806 (Cunningham, I,130).

Picture many days without pay when I could not afford to pay
him a farthing, and had no prospect of being able to do it — this
I shall never forget, and shall be always happy to assist his family
in any way possible — I had long promised that Wilkie and I
would come down & drink tea with him & his wife, which seemed
to please him mightily, and this day we kept our promise. All his
little family were dressed out in their best, a fire in the parlour,
but Sam & his Wife were not returned from church; so we
walked in and were showed into the Parlour by the eldest Girl,
with a smiling countenance, who seemed to have been instructed
how to behave if we should arrive before they came back — at
last a rapp was heard, and away squeezed all the children out
into the passage to let in Father; Sam shooked hands with us and
welcomed us to his castle, which was a perfect model of neatness,
and order; his wife seemed a bustling managing woman; we soon
had tea, and he amused us with stories about the Academy for
some years back *and at present!!!* I don't know when I spent a
more innocent evening, every body seemed to anticipate all our
looks & wishes; we could not go of course without tasting some
beer *of their own brewing,* — as far as I have proceeded in this
World I have observed that prudence & piety are always rewarded by tranquillity & independence, and vice & dissoluteness
by misery & want; there cannot [be] a stronger instance of this
than in the two Porters at the Academy. They have both the same
wages, both the equal advantages; what 50£ a year can do when
managed with care, and how little when entrusted to imprudence.
The Porter we saw this afternoon has a comfortable little house,
virtuous little family & an active wife, all of which he keeps clean
& respectable by his prudence & diligence in his office. The other
in drunkeness & vice squanders his money in an ale house, has
married a woman whom he hardly knows where to find, when he
wants her, is always in want, always dependent, without a home,
a wife or a family and consequently full of misery, filth & immorality, this man will die in Gaol, or on a dunghill, without a
being to lament him or a wife assist him — the punishment of
vice is as certain as the reward of virtue; read the Bible, studied
my Greek.

October 24. Monday. Painted the chest of my dying figure[4] not at all well. Heard from my Father, with my monthly remittance of eight pounds. Went into the city and got Cevallos pamphlet, of the intrigues of Buonaparte.[5] Came home to superintend the casting of a Leg and in the same action as my Hero's, from a very fine model. The moulder was a bungling fool, as well as impudent & presuming. He broke the plaister all to pieces, the first as well as second time, when I turned him off. It was my own fault, I entrusted the model to get a man, when I should have obtained an experienced one myself. The model brought as great a fool as himself, naturally enough, and this is the result — something is to be learnt from every thing — I staid away from the Academy to superintend this affair, in hopes of getting a good cast. I am quite mad. Greek ¼ an hour.

October 25. Tuesday. Drew at Lord Elgin's; made a good study enough from one of the figures grappling the Centaurs, — at the Academy gained much as my own Picture looked very, very inferior when I came home. The Plaister man anxious to do it well. Tried another at his own house, but very bad. ¼ hour Greek.

October 26. Wednesday. The chest of my dying figure looked so miserably that I determined at once to take it out, it is now much better, — not advanced my Picture much this day, I shall draw the remainder of the week at Lord Elgin's, and then give it up till it's warmer. It is so dangerous to stay seven or eight hours on the ground this time of the year, tho Thank God I have not caught any cold — Greek ¼ a hour. At the Academy —

4. A Roman soldier stabbed by Dentatus. On April 5, 1845, Charles Eastlake wrote BRH concerning the death of his brother William, adding: "In calling to mind the length of time during which he was afflicted, your picture of Dentatus is one of the evidences of his sufferings many years since — sufferings which, though latterly much aggravated, never lessened his sympathy for others." On the second page of this letter, BRH wrote: "Poor William Eastlake! It is 7 & 30 years since about this very month I found poor W. Eastlake in a fit of asthma gasping for Breath. I said, 'You are the very model for my dying man.' I got a coach, took him out in a blanket, & painted the dying soldier in Dentatus! Poor Eastlake, he is gone — one of my early cheerers & Defenders."

5. Don Pedro Cevallos, *An Exposure of the Arts and Machinations which Led to the Usurpation of the Crown of Spain, and the Means Adopted by Buonaparte to Carry it into Execution.* Revised and edited by J. J. Stockdale, 1808.

October

O God Accept my unfeigned gratitude that I have by thy assistance kept clear of vice for these last 18 days, O God I am fallible, still assist me, leave me not to myself, or I shall certainly fall, O God still protect me & guide me, grant every day may add strength to my virtuous habits for Jesus Christ's sake, every hour I may get firmness in temptation and industry. O God in thee I trust, have mercy for Jesus Christ's sake. Amen, Amen.

October 27. Thursday. Drew at Lord Elgin's all day — at the Academy in the evening —

October 28. Friday. Went with Boswell a model to old Grant, a plaister man 80 years old, who was tradesman to the first Academy in Pall Mall,[6] to have a mold made of Boswell's thigh and leg; he began at eight in the morning, it being a painful position I did every thing to encourage Boswell to go through it, I went out for rolls, as he felt hungry and faint, being accustomed to take his Breakfast at that time. Mr. Grant began with caution and went on famously, made a joint before, but forgot to do one behind, which I in attempting to make for him pushed my head against the plaister on his thigh which . . .

[*The next two pages have been cut from the diary.*]

Spent the evening in reading —

October 31. Monday. Drew at Lord Elgin's from ½ past nine to five, without intermission, perhaps I got up twice, say I lost ten minutes or 15 — dined, at the Academy as usual from six to eight — 9 hours and a quarter absolute drawing without interruption, not at all fatigued, not at all sore, rather damp & cold. O God, protect me from injury, enable me to go through this week with firmness & energy, for Jesus Christ sake. This month is now ended, to-morrow I begin a fresh one; have mercy O God, enable me to begin it and end it as I ought, Almighty Father protect me, bless my endeavours to be good, let me by the end of this month to have finished my Hero in the grandest style, O God, think me not trifling & vain.

6. The Royal Academy occupied rooms in Pall Mall from 1769 to 1771, when George III assigned it rooms in Somerset House. Exhibitions continued to be held in Pall Mall until 1780, when the King made more space available in Somerset House.

What discrimination and judgement the ancient Sculptors possessed. I sketched the back of a Centaur, which has all that heavy, vulgar, porter like form you see in men used to carry burdens, which agrees with the character of a Centaur, which could not be very intellectual —

November 1. Thanks O God, I am this day free from Sin — I have began this new month by rising early, praying sincerely & Studying industriously, let this be the character of this month for Jesus X sake, and the character of the remainder of my existence. — Drew at Lord Elgin's from ¼ past nine to ¾ past 4 — at the Academy ½ past 6 to 8 — In the early part of the morning my mind was a little distracted, by so many exquisite things before my eyes. I had made sketches of some, which when I saw the originals, I felt a pain at the comparison, mine being so very inferior, I first of all resolved to begin new ones and do them correctly; I then thought I should be losing time. I had got the composition and that was the essential part — so I determined to relieve my mind from this excrutiating state and began correctly to do a fine trunk and legs which soon quieted me and I went on regularly the rest of the day — It has been the fault of all artists to put the markings of the antique into their figures without considering their own attitude, making the same marking serve for all; for instance I have seen that marking in the Torso,[7] a slip of the obliquus abdom[inis] — put into upright figures exactly as it is in the Torso, without reflection that the moment the Torso arose, that marking would unfold, and scarcely be perceptible; I should have marked it so myself had I not seen those exquisite things at Lord Elgin's, where it is shewn in every attitude with all the variety of nature — It is an appendage of the ribs and depends upon it for its form. 7½ hours drawing this day, 1½ less than yesterday.

November 2. Wednesday. Drew at Lord Elgin's from ten till ½ past four, 6 hours drawing, 1 hour less than yesterday; not at the Academy. Made casts from Rogers for the chest, and the hand

7. Later allusions in the diary identify this as the Belvedere Torso of a seated Hercules, inscribed by Apollonius of Athens and probably dating from the first century B.C. The original is in the Vatican; undoubtedly BRH had seen a cast.

of my dying figure; I was astonished when I took the hand from
the mold, at the similarity to the character of those alto relievo,
at the temple of Theseus, I have no doubt of the Ancients catch-
ing all the markings of instant exertion, by dashing something on
that took the impression, then casting it, and making their own
use of it, it is the only plan to attain certainty as you then have a
momentary action set for ever, and can draw it at leisure, while if
you attempt drawing from a model, instant action, the rascal gets
fatigued and plagues you by his awkwardness. You may [use] a
model to colour by but the cast will direct you to the form —

These Grecian figures are like Nature for you are never satisfied with your own imitation, till the originals are out side —

November 3. Thursday. Drew at Lord Elgin's from XI till five.
Then Wilkie and I went to see Henry VIII which I do not regret.
I gained many Ideas —

November 4. Friday. Drew at Lord Elgin's. 7 hours ½. Wilkie
and I went in the evening to see Henry VIII, last evening, which
interested me greatly. What absurd ambition that is which aims
at that greatness the power of a capricious Prince can destroy.
Went to see The Mourning Bride[8] — 'twon't do — after Shakespeare ranting declamation.

November 5. Saturday. Drew at Lord Elgin's — 6 hours. My
taste thank God is improved wonderfully.

[*The next six pages have been cut from the diary.*]

November 15. . . . put in the Head of my old Hero, God
grant I may make it a fine one — no more suffering, I am determined I was under an obligation to do it, but now there is an
end of it — dined at Lord Mulgrave's, it being Mr. Augustus
Phipps's birthday, Lord Mulgrave's brother,[9] a very elegant evening I passed — Missed the Academy, Wilkie also.

November 16. Wednesday. Painted the arm & Shoulders, &
altered the head — You cannot be too long about a Picture, pro-

8. Congreve's tragedy, in which Mrs. Siddons played Zara, at the King's
Theatre, Haymarket.
9. The Hon. Augustus Phipps, F.R.S., who was born November 15, 1762, and
died in 1826. He was a Commissioner of Excise.

vided you are applying your faculties during the time to the real difficulties of the Art, — if you suspend your exertions merely because you are not quite certain about the costume, because you have not ascertained whether the People you are representing wore a sandal with a heel, or a sandal without one, then I say you are Idle, under the mask of industry; if you are slow because you are unequal to execute your conceptions, if you are staggered at the difficulties of arrangement, and checked by unexpected obstacles, and desist, till you are more adequate or better qualified by deeper meditation, how slow soever you may be, if you proceed on this principle, every step you make will be a firm one, and you will ultimately execute with that facility, the result of science, instead of haste.

Remember this night ½ past ten Nov 16th, 1808.*

A Great Painter should make every thing bend to his art, if deviating from rule, costume, &c he can improve or produce finer feelings, *let him do it,* & bid defiance to antiquaries & connoiseurs; he does not paint for them but to effect the human heart for human feeling.

November 17. Past this day industriously, as well as friday & Saturday — & Dined at Lord Mulgrave's Friday again. I cannot perhaps say in all my life I have passed above 4 or 5 weeks, that is, weeks without intermission to Study, weeks of regular determined exertion, among them I can number perhaps, on consideration, this last, for tho I have not studied equally, I have regularly, I have fagged till I was exhausted and made great progress.

O God Almighty, grant me strength of mind next week not to presume on the industry of this last week to be idle, but calmly to consider where I have failed in my duty, and to pray to thee for additional caution & vigour to avoid those defects, so that I may have less to repent of at the end of the week; O God give me strength for Jesus Christ's sake — Amen.

My Hero's head, tho' nearly done, I see is not as it ought. I

* This night I remember *swearing* an oath I would never touch another Woman. I broke it with agonizing pangs in two days.

have made up my mind and out it comes again to-morrow — I am determined it shall be such as the greatest Painter that ever existed could have made it.

November 21. Monday. Painted about 3 hours this day, expected a model, he never came, kept me in a distracted state; however I began the drapery, and improved. Got a West Indian I picked up in the Street, a fine head — took out my Hero's head.

[The next page is torn from the diary.]

. . . life be but an aera in the art, let me but add to the stock of human virtue and human improvement and I shall die happy —

I pray thee O God I may deserve such happiness, but I fear it's more than such a Sinful wretch as I deserve in thee, Christ —

November 28. Monday. Arose at Seven — prayed — walked — set my Palette & breakfasted — as I had promised a very modest unassuming young Artist, at the Academy, to call yesterday and give him my opinion (as far [as] I am capable) of a Picture he is painting, and was prevented — I determined as he might be hurt, to go to day — I went — to Finsbury Square where he lived — and saw I fear a Picture that gives no hopes of future excellence, weak, tame, dry, hard & gaudy. I'll go no more to any young men, as I always have a higher opinion of myself.* Drew at the Academy 1½ hour; in other respects idled the day —

Wilkie changed his Lodgings,[1] I & Jackson[2] went to drink tea with him of course; it being always customary with us to do this with each other on such an occasion —

I daresay the dog will grow insolent on his new Lodgings — but I'll bring him down in a moment if I perceive the slightest variation.

* This Young Man has turned out as I foresaw. 1817.

1. Wilkie's diary of this date records that he moved from Sol's Row to 84 Great Portland Street (Cunningham, I,210).
2. John Jackson (1778–1831), portrait painter; he was instrumental in obtaining Sir George Beaumont's and Lord Mulgrave's patronage for BRH. He became an R.A. in 1817.

November 29. Tuesday. Sat to Jackson for my Portrait[3] — Painted little —

November 30. Sat again. Painted little — glazed the background of Mr. Lockyer's[4] Portrait with brown lake over brimstone & white — shadow Vandyke Brown — waistcoat with common red lake, over ultramarine & white — Tried orpiment with varnish on Brutus' shoulder — coat of Mr. L—— Indian lake — over blue black — one of my early things in Devonshire —

Thus ends this month, and one of more vice and wickedness — I recollect not. I have not been wholly Idle — my picture is advanced — and my mind improved & experienced — O God I dare not pray to thee — I humbly hope for every thing virtuous, pure, & energetic — through Jesus Christ my redeemer. Amen —

December 1. Last month. A Student who draws only outlines by parts from an Idea of being correct, deprives his mind of its only chance, effort in a drawing, which is in getting the whole together well, and then be as correct as you please —

December 2. Painted. Advanced my Picture —

December 3. Saturday. Improved the hand and arm of my Hero, put in the head but took it out again. O God grant I may do it right at last — Miss Phipps, Lord Mulgrave's eldest daughter, very ill, a sweet girl.[5] Called to know how she was — in a dangerous state — got the whole of my Picture more together. Walked at night & called on Wilkie — at XI. In Fuzeli's first edition of Pilkington[6] there being a prolix absurd life of that wretch

3. Taylor printed the entry thus: "Sat to-day to Jackson for a portrait for Lord Mulgrave" (*Autobiography*, I,77). H. C. Morgan, Esq. informed me in 1955 that the portrait is not in Mulgrave Castle and is apparently lost. It had not been finished by March 14, 1809, when Wilkie wrote in his diary: "To Jackson's, where I saw the portrait he is painting of Haydon" (Cunningham, I,229).

4. Probably Edmund Lockyer, who became mayor of Plymouth in 1811 (R. N. Worth, *History of Plymouth*, Plymouth, 1890, p. 385). BRH described his friendship with this family in his diary for September 25, 1829.

5. The Hon. Henrietta Sophia Phipps died on December 4, according to the *Annual Register* of 1808. On December 5 BRH wrote that she was "still very ill."

6. BRH does not refer to the first edition of Matthew Pilkington's *The Gentleman's and Connoisseur's Dictionary of Painters* (1770) but to another edition — *A Dictionary of Painters from the Revival of Art to the Present Period*, with alterations, additions, an appendix, and an index by Fuseli (1805).

Moreland,[7] he asked me if I would select the heads for him, or do as I liked if I gave him a new life — this was a request I would have refused any other man; but could not one from whom I have gained so much. I therefore selected one part of the old life — and made my own observations on his bringing on his Death by drinking — Such is the inveteracy of habit, and such our incapability of freedom, after having once gratified an abandoned appetite, under the impression that resistance is attainable when resistance is right — his pictures of familiar life have great merit in composition, he had great facility but certainly not power; it was a knack acquired by habit, independent of science or feeling — that the Public were so mad after his trash is not to be wondered at, admiration often proceeds from ignorance of higher excellence — up till two writing & reading Homer.

December 4. Sunday. Breakfasted with Wilkie; at church Sidney Smith[8] preached — he took his stand for Xtianity on St. Paul's conversion — if his vision & conversion were the effects of a heated brain or fanaticism; it was the first time that madness gave a new direction to a man's feelings — fanaticism is a want of fine perception of the different feelings and habits of mankind &c. I never heard a more eloquent man. Spent the evening in writing my ideas about art, at Mr. Hoare's[9] request, who is publishing in the encyclopedia — [1]

7. George Morland (1763–1804), a dissipated and unpopular genre and animal painter, frequently in financial difficulties.
8. Sydney Smith (1771–1845), cannon of St. Paul's from 1831 to 1845.
9. Prince Hoare (1755–1834), artist, dramatist, and author of books and articles on the fine arts.
1. The last fourteen pages of this volume of the diary contain an apparent draft of these ideas, which BRH continued writing on December 8 (see Appendix A). I cannot positively identify Prince Hoare's article in the fourth edition of the *Encyclopaedia Britannica* (Edinburgh, 1810, 20 vols.), but many of BRH's ideas are found in the essay entitled "Painting" (XV,626–695), for example, the following remark: "To ask if the study of anatomy is requisite to a painter, is the same thing as to ask if, in order to learn any science, a man must first make himself acquainted with the principles of it. . . . A man, who is unacquainted with the form and construction of the several bones which support and govern the human frame, and does not know in what manner the muscles moving these bones are fixed to them, can make nothing of what appears of them thro' the integuments with which they are covered; and which appearance is, however, the noblest object of the pencil" (XV,647).

December 5. Monday. Sat to Jackson from X till one, called at Lord Mulgrave's. Miss Phipps still very ill — obliged to go into the city as the armour I had from the Tower is getting rusty — and I went to the Armourer to know how to act. As I walked along Fleet Street, I felt hungry and went into Peele's coffee house[2] to have some soup, it was such an idle thing in the middle of the day, that I shrunk in, blushing, fearful to look up for fear of meeting the eyes of Michel Angelo's spectre, crying, "Haydon, Haydon, you Idle rascal, is this the way to eminence?" — in spite of such reflections in I went. Appointed to go with Wilkie to a friend of his against my will, but as he had bothered me to, I consented. I was to call [for] him at the Academy, not being able to go myself tonight, he was gone before I came and glad to find any excuse to get off, I returned home, delighted to have escaped the distraction of mind I should have experienced among a parcel of debating argumenting Scotchmen — Whitfield [3] called; he seems determined to study drawing fundamentally, I therefore lent him my drawings of the bones & Bell's bones & joints. I am glad he has sense & resolution to proceed so —

December 6. Tuesday. Finished the flying Drapery, Thank God at last, and I think it not badly arranged; enlarged the shield, which gives more irresistible weight to the figure, a more thundering air, & got in the head. I wish to express a lofty contempt among his other characteristics — how happy shall I be can I but finish the head this week — as it ought to be — Went to the Academy, came away early, my mind was so uneasy about my Picture; after a long struggle in my mind whether it was not idleness, I convinced myself it really was not, and came home, took out my Picture, put the candle on the floor, and began to think — Truth must not always be regarded; the object of Painting is to abstract the mind from sensual appetites, therefore the means of attraction must be considered. On this Principle I have acted in not making the assassins perhaps so assassin-like as they were. I have endeavoured to give as much beauty as is not quite

2. William Gurney was the proprietor of Peel's Coffee House and Hotel, 177 and 178 Fleet Street (Pigot).
3. Probably Edward Richard Whitfield (d. 1817), engraver.

34

inconsistent; if they had all had the faces of murderers it might have been more true, but what human being could have dwelt on it with pleasure? — It would have been avoided with disgust —

I observed last night in a sort of Deer brought from the Cape now at the Tower the characteristics of its extreme swiftness, the markings of the leg were clear, the points of bone, the origins & insertions could be traced, every thing sharp & braced; it is a good principle thus to survey nature and mingle the characteristics of one animal with those of another, to express any particular excellence, in a stronger degree.

S——[4] a friend of ours, has a good heart, but is perpetually on the stretch for ridicule, he never corrects an error, but in association with ridicule, and tho thus existing on Ridicule himself, is cut to the soul by ridicule from others; if he is so far in the wrong, as cannot be concealed under some pointed remark, he will take shelter and endeavour to make another more ridiculous; every thing serious, every thing not absolutely sacred, is to him a source of amusement.

December 7. Wednesday. I knelt down before my Picture last night before going to bed, and prayed God to give me strength of mind & vigour of body to go through it with a firm spirit, not to be daunted by difficulties however great, not to suffer my youth to be an excuse for inadequacy, not to think on that a moment but to consider how soon I may die, and if νὺξ ἄνεται[5] unexpectedly, that I may be taken doing all a human being can do and if I should be instantly judged after Death, to be ready for judgement —

People say to me, you can't be expected in your second Picture to paint like Titian, & draw like Michel Angelo but I do expect it, and I will try — and if I take liberties with Nature, and make her bend to my own purposes, consider you should not venture to do what Michel Angelo might, but I will venture, I'll dare any thing to accomplish my Purpose; if it's impudence & presumption without ability, I shall soon find my rank in the

4. Probably William Seguier.
5. *Iliad*, X,251, "The night is waning."

opinion of the world, but if it's the just confidence of science & genius, I shall soon find my reward. I have heard Nelson used to say, "never mind the justice, or impudence of any thing, let me but [be] successful." That is what no man, of the common timid feelings of mankind, would have dared say or feel, and what's the world's opinion of Nelson?

The danger is in putting these feelings off till you are older or more capable, that you will put them off till Death will interrupt the possibility of ever accomplishing them. It's very long in appearance to say,[6] "Stop till I am thirty," but thirty will so gradually approach, that your excuses will be habitual and every year & every hour will be more incapable of beginning — therefore whatever you feel, do, don't attend to the indolent, frivolous advice of people who live only to amuse themselves, who are little better than animals, the chief good & market of whose time is but to eat and live;[7] if I had the power I could spit fire at such insignificant wretches — I have not language to express my contempt — what Homer dared, I'll dare; if I have not ability & energy to the firm foundation for my daring, I'll soon find my proper level; if I have, I can never find it but by the trial. A man of Genius is sent into the world not to obey laws, but to give them; Nature to him is the field he must make his own use of — let this not be presumption, O God, let it be the firm conviction of experience.*

Would to God I could exist without sleeping, I would get my figure right this night, but as this is one of the conditions of my existence I must be content. If I did not fear my eyes being injured I would not think of it. Until I have settled it my mind is literally on the rack — & up will I be with the light if I awake. O God I pray thee grant me power to get it right, I pray thee grant it me.

* I was at this time twenty 2. I am proud to read it. 1817.

6. This is a doubtful reading but unquestionably nearer to the text than Taylor's "It is very easy to say" (*Autobiography*, I,81), though he probably interpreted BRH's meaning correctly.
7. *Hamlet*, IV,iv,33–35.
> "What is a man,
> If his chief good and market of his time
> Be but to sleep and feed."

December 8. Thursday. After a night of continual interruption and reflections literally excrutiating about my Hero, I arose quite in a fever of anxiety, and set about it. I hope I have it all right to go upon, but I cannot tell till to-morrow. O God grant it may be so. Sat up till one, writing some Ideas about the art[8] for Mr. Hoare as I promised him; it is not my business to write, old men should write and give the world the result of their experience.

December 9. Friday. Met a capital model; put in the head once again —

December 10. Saturday. Went on with my head; improved it; 'tis not the thing as it ought, there must be no delicacy of feeling & refined sentiment in the head of a man bred up in Camps in the stern heroic feelings of a Roman. Arranged the Rocks rightly.

On the helmet of one of my figures I have put some light, airy ostrich feathers, which give a more ponderous στιβαρόν[9] look to my Hero —

December 11. Sunday. Missed my church on purpose to meet a Gentleman called Hunt whom I promised to take to see Wilkie's Cut Finger.[1] He never came at the time; I never wait for any body so went out & made some calls — Idled this day. No church. No religious meditation.

December 12. Monday. Went to Mr. Henry Hope's[2] to meet Seguier, who was to take me to Lord Grosvenor's,[3] I waited a half hour, he never came — called on Fuzeli, staied three hours, talking of the Art, Italy, Michel Angelo, Homer, Virgil, Horace, enough to make a man mad. When Fuzeli dies, where shall I meet "his like again"?[4] I do not know any body I feel a greater

8. See Appendix A.
9. Strong, stout.
1. Painted for Samuel Whitbread, "The Cut Finger" was finished by April 4, 1809, and exhibited at the Royal Academy that spring (Cunningham, I,232).
2. Henry Philip Hope (d. 1839), like his brother Thomas Hope, who bought BRH's "Joseph and Mary," a collector of works of art and precious stones, valued at £150,000 at his death.
3. The second Earl Grosvenor (1767–1845), afterward first Marquis of Westminster, art collector.
4. *Hamlet*, I,ii,188.

affection or reverence for. From my first entrance into the Academy he noticed me in a particular manner, he said once to a friend of mine, as I used to draw there all day without intermission, "when the devil does he dine?" which I considered the highest praise; he happened to come in three or four times, on one or two days before it was my time for dinner* — Idle day.

December 13. Tuesday. Went to Lord Grosvenor's to see his Pictures. Idled and talked this whole day — tied up my specimens of Lake for Du Fresne,[5] who goes to India and is going to bring me home some —

December 14. Wednesday. Began again my head — improved it much, got in the neck & shoulder.

December 15. Thursday. Seguier called, liked my head much; thinks it will do, so do I in some measure, with a few alterations. Improved the position of my dying figure.

What are painters doing who from neglecting Nature have degenerated into Manner, and then say with contempt, she puts them out! but imitating her to the best of their recollection — but why does it put them out — why? because they find she is a perpetual check to indolence, by requiring skill & energy to select her beauties, & reject her defects — A man of real Genius will not suffer Nature to put him out, he will make Nature bend to him, he will make his own use of Nature, he will force her into his service — consult Nature for every thing, for tho she will not equal your wishes, she will often surpass, and where there is this chance she is certainly worth the trial — Young Students at first commencing acquaintance, not finding her yield them assistance in their present particular want, reject her, not considering that she can never be a substitute but an assistant, and therefore not to [be] discarded, but managed —

* I have since found Fuzeli a Traitor — mean, malicious, cowardly & debauched — Nov 27th, 1815.

5. By 1807 Wilkie had introduced BRH to Du Fresne, a member of a French family, who said he had witnessed the execution of Marie Antoinette. "He became a surgeon on a slave estate in the West Indies and died from yellow fever" (*Autobiography*, I,55). BRH learned of his death on September 16, 1824 (see II,496).

December 16. Friday. Went down among the Ruins of Athens, to consult about legs & feet; came home; it was so cold that I became benumbed in spite of my abstraction. I could stay there 8 or 10 hours in damp weather without inconvenience, but cold creeps insensibly upon you. Drew in the left leg & foot of Dentatus — took it out again. I observed in the feet [of the Elgin Marbles] the same exquisite system, the end of the toes are the parts that are press down, the upper joints not, consequently the flesh must rise all up about the nail and the top and the upper joint still keep its form.

This is a system of reasoning, this is sense; this gives motion, probability & truth. Can this be done in all the varieties that the Human body is capable of in each part without a constant, unremitting, incessant study of Nature — Can this be done by system, alone? — without Nature? — done by recollection? Will Nature put a Man out, who is on the continual watch for such beauties & niceties as these? It makes one melancholy to see Men satisfied with this excuse for their indolence and believing or willing to believe they are in the sure road to eminence, and every other man in the wrong — Made studies from a figure's feet in Fuzeli's room, a little Hercules — in a fine model there is always a slip of the Pectoral coming down in the ribs; it depends on the action to shew it; I observed it in the lying figure at Lord Elgin's, I am eternally obliged to Lord Mulgrave (poor dear little Miss Phipps is dead, I don't know when I was as effected; the sweetest & most acute little thing I ever met with; she always used to ask me how I got on with my battle Picture, pretty little Soul, she died while she was innocent). I shall be eternally grateful to Lord Mulgrave & Lord Elgin, the one for getting, the other for granting me permission to draw from the Ruins of Athens — It is impossible to say what knowledge I have gained — O God how thou hast protected, guided, & befriended me — I fear to dwell upon my happiness; I fear it may not last. O God grant I may deserve a continuance by my virtue & piety, my energy & industry — Amen with all my Soul.

December 17. Saturday. Did little.

December 18. Sunday. At Church — Wilkie and I breakfasted

with Seguier. Wilkie and I walked in the Park — at home in the evening —

Any man that says the sound being an echo to the sense[6] is absurd; read these two lines and see if the very sounds will not characteristically distinguish them:

'Εκ δ' ἄρα σύριγγος πατρώϊον ἐσπάσατ' ἔγος.[7]

καλὰ πέδιλα
'Αμβρόσια χρύσεια, τά μιν φέρον ἠμὲν ἐφ' ὑγρὴν.[8]

December 19. Monday. Glazed the drapery; made a sketch of an Idea that struck me while at Dover of a colossal Statue of Britannia and her Lion on Shakespeare's Clift right opposite the coast of France.[9] Went into the city for my allowance. Paid Mr. Perkins[1] 4£, which makes 12£ towards this quarter.

December 20. Tuesday. The Armourer came from the Tower to look at the Armour, as it was rusty; cleaned it. Altered the leg and thigh of my Dying Figure. After every victory and every exertion of Buonaparte,[2] the people of this country console themselves with finding fresh difficulties that must be insurmountable. What man of Genius thinks of difficulties? To indolent asses they may be difficulties, but to Buonaparte only stimulants. Nothing is difficult; it is we that are indolent. When you find People inclined to treat you with respect, never check it from modesty, from fancying you do not deserve it. You may be led to be familiar with them from an Idea that they will [be] gratified by your kindness and treat you with the same respect, but the moment you let yourself out of your shell that ought to suround you, their respect weakens into freedom and irreverant familiarity. Whenever you find people treat you with a sort of

6. Pope, *Essay on Criticism*, l. 365. "The sound must seem an Echo to the sense."
7. *Iliad*, XIX,387. "And forth from its stand he drew his father's spear."
8. *Iliad*, XXIV,340–341. "His beautiful sandals, immortal, golden, which were wont to bear him over the waters of the sea."
9. See I,3–4 and 7.
1. BRH's landlord, Henry Perkins, conducted a wholesale tea business at 40 Great Marlborough Street (Pigot). On July 6, 1842, BRH recorded that he was dead.
2. Napoleon received the surrender of Madrid on December 3, 1808.

awe, keep it up, and you will find it of great consequence. Took out the shield, as it was not large enough.

December 21. Wednesday. A man does not know his own improvement, or the difficulties he has conquered till some young beginner brings his first efforts for instruction; it is then you perceive the vast distance between his intellect and yours, and find you must carry your conversation back ten years to bring it on a level with his comprehension.

As you advance in life and reputation, you find the responsibility of your situation in society encrease; the eyes of the world are fixed on your conduct, the greater part with anxiety hoping some careless inattention or accidental deviation will enable them to lessen your rank and lower your estimation; any little inaccuracies of conduct while a youth are overlooked, and unheeded, but one single impropriety in manhood is never forgotten. You are arrived at a time of life when all hopes of amendment cease; you are in the Summer, not the spring of existence.

[The remainder of the page, about four lines, is torn away.]

December 22. Thursday. Began again my Shield; put it in all positions — the first the best.

December 23. Friday. Always appear thankful & gratified by just praise, for tho' it may be no more than you deserve, is there no merit due to those who acknowledge it? Some people if they hear their friends praised say, "well, it's no more than he deserved, what of that?" How few get what they deserve.

The Year is ended.

The remainder of the page is torn away, and the diary for 1808 ends. Volume I contains fourteen more pages discussing the necessity for an artist to understand anatomy, probably the "ideas about art [written] at Mr. Hoare's request" on December 4 and 8. See Appendix A.

Volume Ia

JANUARY 1809—JUNE 1809

The next volume of Haydon's diary, numbered Ia, begins as a commonplace book, with the first thirty pages devoted to quotations, maxims, and memoranda on anatomy and composition. The earliest entry, not in Haydon's handwriting, is dated "Sep. 1807," and the last "June, 1808." A list of subjects suitable for painting follows (see Appendix B), and then the diary continues from Volume I, on a page from which about four lines are cut out.

Volume Ia

What a fine broad fleshy colour you can get by mixing Indian Red & White & ultramarine White.

Eastlake[1] and his Brother spent the evening. Young Eastlake has determined on being a Painter, which he should never [have] thought of, he says, had he not seen my Picture.[2] I hope he may be eminent. If before I die I can but see the Art generally improved and all in the right road, I shall die happily.

January 4. Wednesday. A dreadfully dark day. Got on a little. In the evening read Churchill's "Ghost";[3] there are strong observations in it, a great deal of point. Recovered my purity & calmness, thank God with all my soul.

[About four lines have been cut from the diary.]

. . . agitation. Improved the background wonderfully. I wish to give a martial sounding air to it — tubae mugire per aethera clangor.[4] How Pope has missed the fiery independent vigour of this:

Αὐτὰρ ὁ βῆ παρὰ θῖνα θαλάσσης δῖος Ἀχιλλεὺς
Σμερδαλέα ἰάχων.[5]

1. Charles Lock Eastlake (1793–1865), who studied with BRH and at the Royal Academy school. From 1817 to 1830 he resided largely in Italy. He was elected to the Royal Academy in 1830; in 1850 he succeeded Sir Martin Archer Shee as president and was knighted. In 1841 he was appointed secretary to the royal commission for decorating the Houses of Parliament, and in 1843 he became keeper of the National Gallery, resigning the post in 1847.
2. As a note to this passage, BRH attached the following newspaper cutting: "December 3. The Queen has been pleased to appoint Charles Lock Eastlake, Esq., to be Secretary to the Commission for inquiring whether advantage might not be taken of the rebuilding of the Houses of Parliament for promoting and encouraging the Fine Arts." BRH added: "1841 — 32 years afterwards."
3. Charles Churchill, *The Ghost*, 1762–1763.
4. *Aeneid*, VIII,526. "The trumpet-blast pealed through the sky."
5. *Iliad*, XIX,40–41. "But goodly Achilles strode along the shore of the sea, crying a terrible cry."

He says in translating:

> Achilles to the strand obedient went,
> The Shores resounded with the voice he sent.[6]

Obedient! where is there any thing about obedient in the original? He did not go obediently, he went to revenge Patroclus's Death, not in obedience to the King. [In] his speech to the King he says, "whether it's your fault or mine is no difference." This is not much like obedience! Besides it [is] so unconnected with his character, it lowers his grandeur. The bare idea of the God-like Achilles obeying!!

January 7. Saturday. Idle the whole day & night.

January 8. Sunday. Breakfasted with Wilkie. Painted on the left leg & foot. Improved it. God forgive me painting on Sunday.

January 9. Monday. Idled. Wrote my Father a long letter. I painted Sunday to gain time and what I gained I have lost again today. It [is] really miserable.

January 10. Tuesday. Painted with energy. Improved my Picture. Studied it — had my eyes anxiously fixed on it 18 hours, including Painting.

January 11. Wednesday. Read Virgil & Homer with delight. Lord Mulgrave called; seemed satisfied. Painted vigourously; got in my right leg & foot. At night from ½ past nine till ¼ past eleven made drawings for the leg & foot against tomorrow. Not at all tired.

January 12. Thursday. Painted with energy. Got in the dead figure. First of all shewed his face in the agonies of Death, but this distracted the attention. There was no silence in the picture; all was passion & violence. I therefore determined to cover his face with his robe as if he had pulled it over (as the Romans generally did) and to keep it in shadow. This gave immediately a solemn feeling, a repose to all the bustle, and room for reflections which silent Death always excites.

January 13. Friday. Took out the hand, which I put in yester-

6. *Iliad*, XIX,43–44.

day, on his breast, it being too large. Made it the right proportion. Improved the whole figure. Wilkie & I enlisted three more and away we went to see Mrs. Siddons in "The Gamester."⁷ I had made up my mind to lose two hours. Was excessively affected — I'll not see it again. In one instance she was guilty of a gross stage effect, incompatible with true taste. It went mightily against my feeling. I always feel hurt when an actor or actress goes beyond the bounds of probability & truth.

January 14. Saturday. Painted and nearly finished my dead figure. Seguier called and liked it amazingly.

I am determined not to paint tomorrow. I felt unhappy at something today, and as I had neglected my church and daily prayer for some time, I know not where to seek relief. I always used to find satisfaction in Religious reflection. I hope tomorrow to atone for all my vice and all my folly tomorrow, in sincere repentance, and sincere prayer. God bless my wishes, for Jesus Christ's sake. Amen.

January 15. Sunday. Breakfasted with Wilkie. Went to Church and heard an excellent sermon from Sidney Smith. Prayed sincerely; from my Soul repented. Passed the evening quietly and elegantly. Whitfield called in. Why do we ever do anything but what will give us delight in reflection?

January 16. Monday. It became dark so shortly that I could not see; however, I drew in the left leg & foot again after pummicing out [the] first, which was heavy & a bad form. I was really in despair for about an hour, but I set to in a great passion, & my mind soon became tranquil. Paid Mr. Perkins. I have now paid him 16 £.

January 17. Tuesday. Expected a model to begin my leg from; he never came. Painted & scumbled in the rocks. Dined with a Gentleman from Devonshire. I found the company so grossly rude & ignorant that I left them shortly after dinner, and came home to study my old Hero.

7. A domestic tragedy by Edward Moore first produced in 1753. A playbill of January 12, 1809, in the Theatre Collection of the Harvard College Library, announces that the next night Mrs. Siddons would appear as Mrs. Beverley in *The Gamester,* at the Theatre Royal, Haymarket.

January 18. Wednesday. Painted at my Rocks & background. Lord Mulgrave & Sir George Beaumont[8] called. Liked my Picture much — put me quite in Spirits. Lord Mulgrave always kind. Decided I would come down and take a quiet dinner at the Admiralty with Sir George. Wilkie & Jackson were there also. Spent a very pleasant evening — conversation never lagged, always something new. What a contrast with the company yesterday. A man is always more at ease in society where he is sure he may expect nothing unpleasant, although his own vulgar propensities are under restraint, than in company where every thought or every joke has unbridled license, because you are in perpetual expectation of being disgusted or ridiculed yourself. Improved my Hero's head.

January 19. Thursday. Idle.

January 20. Friday. Did little.

January 21. Saturday. Did nothing.

January 22. Sunday. Nothing.

January 23. Monday. Less.

Went to hear Carlisle's first Lecture[9] — a very clever one — but if what he said last night is truth, what he wrote in "The Artist" [1] is a falsehood. He denied that the Greeks knew Anatomy, and then said there was a Grecian who boasted he had dissected six hundred bodies, and was called the butcher. Is not this a flat absurdity? If they dissected, no matter what disgust they excited, they dissected, and therefore must have studied scientifically. He

8. Sir George Howland Beaumont (1753–1827), seventh Baronet, a minor artist but a distinguished collector and patron of the arts. He was instrumental in the foundation of the National Gallery in 1824, to which he presented his collection.

9. Wilkie also attended this lecture, writing: "Heard a very sensible lecture from Anthony Carlisle, introductory to his Course of Anatomy. When this was concluded he began to demonstrate the general divisions of the human body on the living figure, for which purpose he had Gregson in the room, who is a well made man" (Cunningham, I, 222–223).

1. *The Artist, a Collection of Essays Relative to Painting, Poetry, Sculpture, Architecture, the Drama, Discoveries of Science, and Various Other Subjects,* edited by Prince Hoare. Anthony Carlisle's essay "On the Connexion between Anatomy and the Arts of Design" appeared in Volume I, Number 18, July 4, 1807, pp. 1–12.

said Genius without science could do little and the Greeks, he would have us believe, did all. He said the Greeks had names for all the cavities of the body, a good Idea certainly. He said the markings in a female should be only hints. Very true, but they should be hints of truth — there is no more doubt about the parts of the body on the Venus than the Hercules. I can find in the Venus every prominency of bone, every muscle, & every tendon as clearly as on the Hercules; but she must be investigated to be discovered. Here is the excellence of the Greeks — take their productions how you will, turn them in all lights and shadows, and what was not visible in some positions may be always found in others. This is Nature. If in a certain effect of Light & Shadow I see but a part of the markings of the Leg, if I put my hand to the parts not visible, I shall find them, and if I turn the light I shall see them. The most trifling exertion of the most trifling & insignificant muscle, the appearance of which can scarcely be seen, on the surface, yet in Nature if it is but hardly visible at any rate, there it is, and if you take trouble, there you may find it — it is there in the efforts of Greece. It is for this reason, I am convinced, they molded with something that would instantly set parts in instantaneous action, and by this method caught markings which no human mind could conceive would be indicated, and if he had seen them, it must have been the momentary beauties of a shooting star. This method in conjunction with science, genius cultivated by beauty, variety in the human formation, would be undiscovered or uninvestigated.

It has been the fashion to talk of the Greeks as beings above us, all attempts to reach whom were absurd, and a very proper way of talking, if we were contented with looking and not exerting, but how far did ever useless rhapsody advance human intellect? How far had Winckleman[2] or any other learned rhapsodist conduced to the improvement of modern art? Have they con-

2. Johann Joachim Winckelmann (1717–1768), German archeologist, probably the leading eighteenth-century authority on classical art. Before visiting Rome, Naples, Pompeii, and Herculaneum, in 1755 he published his *Gedanken über die Nachahmung der griechischen Werke in Malerei und Bildhauerkunst*, translated by Henry Fuseli as *Reflections on the Painting and Sculpture of the Greeks* in 1765. Winckelmann's masterpiece is *Geschichte der Kunst des Alterthums* (1764).

duced at all? As one method of Public improvement, they set out with abusing our Nation, and impudently attempting [to] establish that as a principle which was the result of local obstruction, they ridiculed our ever possessing the faculty of refinement, because our London atmosphere happened [to] be smoky and our days rather dark. Painting requires more protection & encouragement than Poetry, Philosophy, History, Law, or Music. An Artist must be employed, or there must be a prospect of a Protector, if he ventures without actual employment. An Artist can't be a secretary of men, and after being exhausted with Public duty, come home to relax himself on a great Picture, because he never can have such a command of the language of his Art as the Poet. It is for this we all fag, not to acquire conceptions, but to have the power of expressing them; if we could sit down indolently of an evening and pour out the conceptions of the day with as little manual exertion as the Poet, England would have many [of] the great Painters, because they would have been, as the Poets have all, independent of Public employment. Milton might very easily do the duties of a minister and at every interval of relaxation, add one vision or improve those already added, without any interruption to his duty, or his duty being an interruption to his Poem, for even in his duty he was acquiring power in the language of his art.

It never can be so with a Painter. He must rise with the Sun in Summer and before it in Winter; he must take his "librum cum lumine" [3] and let no day pass over without deep study & unexampled exertion. To do this presupposes having the means to existence. If doing this will not give him the means for it, [it] will [be] absurd to get such means of existence by any other method and in all intervals really persevere with Art; his language is a language that is only wanted in his Art, and being a language not learned till you have determined on being a painter, you spend your life in the acquirement and die just as experience has given you an adequate power.

Like the momentary beauties of a star — if, supposing his mind was thoroughly versed in anatomy, he would not be able to give the shape by mere knowledge, if it remained in action so

3. Horace, *Epistles*, I,ii,35. "A book with a light."

short a time, what method can be [a] surer one than molding it instantly, casting it, and at leisure studying it? How could he perceive it if he was ignorant of Anatomy? Any man that has watched the progress of his own intellect knows how beauties have past unheeded before him, when his feelings were uncultivated, and his judgement uncertain, knows how these very beauties have afterwards affected and how he has been astonished at his own former stupidity. Why is this? Because he has added science to his ability.

Carlisle said that Aristotle's Son dissected 600 bodies at Alexandria. Any Sculptor of any energy would have gone to Alexandria then, if his Countrymen objected to his doing it in Greece.

Mr. Carlisle perhaps might think his being called butcher that dissected might be rather [an] obstacle. What man of Genius would attend to the ridicule of ignorance? What man of Genius? What, can a feeling at being called butcher or hangman if dissecting or hanging a man would contribute [to] his attaining higher excellence in his profession — these are all the notions of indolence & imbecility.

This week — a week of Idleness and walking about.

January 29. Sunday. At Church.[4] A dreadful fire in Conduit Street;[5] the wind being high it was excessively grand. Studied the fire so thoroughly and the forms of flame and colour, that I made a sketch this morning, Monday, [January 30].

All last week I spent days & nights in excrutiating anxiety about Sir John Moore[6] and our brave army in Spain. Thank God he beat the French; it's pretty clear now that our Soldiers are as great as our Sailors. What would I have given to have been in the Battle of Corruna, and to have finished my Picture afterwards. O

4. On this day Wilkie wrote: "Sir William Beechey, and Haydon, and I, went to church, where we had a very good sermon from Sydney Smith, on the use and abuse of time" (Cunningham, I,223).

5. "Sunday, Jan. 29. This afternoon, about five, a fire broke out in the kitchen of Warren's Hotel, in Conduit-street, Hanover-square, which communicated to every part of the house. The flames next consumed another large house in front of the street, and extended to two others lying towards George-street. The Hotel being quite full of visitors, every exertion was made by the firemen and servants to save the moveable property; such as writing-desks, portmanteaus, &c" (*Gentleman's Magazine*, January 1809, 79:83).

6. Lieutenant-General Sir John Moore (1761–1809), killed in action in the Peninsular War, January 16, 1809, during the defeat of the French at Coruña.

God, grant I may astonish mankind as a great Painter and then die in Battle, and I shall die as I sincerely wish, and let me not die undistinguished, let me die in "the blaze of my [*an illegible word, possibly* name *or* fame]." [7] I fear it will be impossible for me to die in Battle — how can it be brought about I don't see, but I live in hopes as these are strange times.

January 31. Tuesday. Why should the Greeks be so peculiarly gifted or do all they have done in the Arts without Study or Science? They had the vices and the follies we have, and why should not they be liable to the same imbecilities of intellect? Not coolly examining why, and endeavouring to set us right, but at once with bare faced impudence & French volatility setting us down Asses, we who had produced the greatest Poets, Historians, Moralists, Mathematicians, & Philosophers, and with the greatest sang froid, given us up to eternal darkness.

February 1. Wednesday. Painted vigourously.

February 2. Thursday. Painted with energy.

February 3. Friday. Painted with energy. Advanced my Picture. Drew from ten o'clock till one in the morning. Retired to bed about two having on my knees thanked God for my industry and energetic application this day.

February 4. Saturday. Painted with energy. Advanced my Picture. Kept my model for 5 hours nearly in one position — poor fellow, his leg was nearly stiff.[8] Thank God I have been to-day industrious & energetic. Studied my Greek again, which I had neglected for some time.

February 6. Monday. Saw a fine collection of Sir Joshuas at Caleb Whiteford.[9]

7. Professor Herbert McArthur suggests that the source of this quotation is "For what is glory but the blaze of fame" (*Paradise Regained,* III,47).

8. On October 3, 1812, BRH referred to his "old and faithful model, Salmon, Corporal Horseguards. . . . From him I painted Dentatus's hands, as well as Macbeth's." Signing his name "John Sammons," he witnessed an agreement made on January 1, 1820, between BRH and George Robertson, by which, in consideration of £210, BRH agreed to instruct Robertson for three years. After this date, BRH spelled his name "Sammons," writing on June 18, 1836, "My poor old rascal of a Servant, Sammons, of the 2d Life Guards, dead."

9. Caleb Whiteford (1734–1810), diplomatist. Reynolds painted his portrait.

The Greeks seemed to have considered the general character of the line of any character and then to have left out all accidental interruptions to [it] — I suppose the way they distinguished characters was by lines, & full scientific knowledge of what lines were in harmony with others; for instance, the tendon of the [semi-]membranosus is seen at the knee in some, not in others. Now w[h]ere it is not seen, there must be a different formation of the other parts of the knee to prevent its want being perceived. What formation this is I am at present ignorant of; but I hope in God with a deep study of Nature, for this is every thing, to find out before I die — in conjunction why thy exquisite Productions, O Greece.

This morning[1] in Church I was thinking on the mystery of the Trinity and the Birth of Christ, and the general objection of indolent doubters. Why was mystery necessary, why not make every thing mathematically clear? What merit would there be in faith if that was the case? God seems to have said, "here is my doctrine, here are my moral principles, by which I wish mankind to regulate themselves. I choose Christ to be born of a virgin, which, if any of you doubt, reflect a moment on the divine principles of Christianity and your doubts will vanish, because why should I wish any thing absurd to be attached to such a system? If every thing was clear, what merit would there be in you, to believe that which could not be doubted? All that is necessary to be clear, all that regards your moral conduct in life, I have brought to the level of your understandings, but that which does not regard your moral conduct in life, that of which there was no necessity you should understand, I choose to keep in mystery, till you are worthy to understand it, by strictly adhering to that which you do understand." Any Men that take this as an objection of Xtianity, ask them this, "are you charitable, are you virtuous, do you love your friends and forgive your enemies, do you seek out the fatherless and widows, do you relieve their wants, and do you soften their afflictions, do you recollect that he who looketh on a woman to lust after her has committed adultery with her in his heart? [2] If you do not (as above), I say what

1. For the rest of February, BRH failed to indicate the dates of his entries.
2. Matthew 5:28.

right have you to dare object to that part of Xtianity which
depends on belief, by your following the other? You hypocrite,
you know the other part which with your brutal lusts & your
cursed propensities, you know if you owned you approved the
morals of Christ, it would be putting the root of your vices, your
own gratifications, therefore to satisfy your conscience, to quiet
your feelings, you dare doubt, because you are not in a frame of
mind to be capable of believing, as an excuse, also for not following the moral advice of our Saviour."

Perhaps we are not capable of understanding the mysteries of
God, in our present formation, and must undergo some change
first. You must be quiet, virtuous, and moral, with a heart void
of offence toward God & man, before you relish the sublime mystery. Ask any man when in this state of feeling if he ever doubted.

It appears to be the will of God, and that is sufficient.

Can any man doubt every thing mysterious will be one day
explained? When he contemplates the sublime, exquisite, divine,
heavenly purity of the moral doctrines of Xtianity, I say if he does
still doubt, he is a wretch, a being of insensibility & ingratitude.

Feby. has ended. I neglected to go on with my Journal. My
Picture is advanced, & I hope improved. Drury Lane Theatre
burnt down.[3] I ran down and got up on Somerset House leads.
Nothing could exceed the sublime Horror of the Scene. I saw
the whole South front, 450 feet, fall in at once; it sounded like a
distant crash of ten thousand rocks. When the explosion of gun
powder burst out, a column of fire expanded upwards at least a
mile and then vanished.

March 1. Every thing the Greeks did must have been on a
clear principle, which could be pointed out to all, of distinguishing characters, for in the lowest state of Roman Art they had
something of this. In the finest Greek works, the art and principles are compleatly concealed by being united with a feeling
for the simplicity & beauty & Nature. When the Art was sinking,
they still retained the System of their Predecessors, but not having their feeling & simplicity, their productions are all system,

3. On February 24, 1809.

art, and affectation. This is the characteristic of Roman Sculpture and one distinguishable in an instant from Greek.

Defend this nation from an inundation of half starved, systematized, ignorant, imbecile, ornamenting Room painting Italians.

Before Lord Elgin brought those heavenly productions into England, it was always a matter of caution to young Painters to beware of mixing the principles of Sculpture with Painting, to beware of making your figures like the Antique. Nothing could be more disgusting than to see young men square out their forms with all the Pedantry of knowledge, but now copy precisely any figure from the Temple of Theseus, and it will have all the probability & simplicity of inartificial nature and be adapted exactly for Painting, tho executed with as much art. There is nothing like Stone, nothing like regulated system apparent, all art lies hid. If you study them, you study Nature. Nothing is marked that ought not to be marked, for the mere purpose of shewing your skill, and nothing is left out that is essential. They are the accidents of Nature regulated, not rejected; it is nature methodised,[4] but yet with such fear of constraining her, such delicacy & such taste, and such a reverence for her will, that all improbability is sacrificed for the sake of truth, and nothing admitted that is incompatible or incongruous.

But having a system which could be explained to all, the Romans did every thing from this alone, without considering that it was only a directing post for investigation, a means by which beauties undiscovered might be brought [to] light, and not the end.

March 5. Sunday. Painted this day, God forgive me. Advanced my Picture lately considerably by energetic application.

Carlisle said in one of his Lectures that Anatomy was no use in a woman because it was merely hinted at; being only hints, knowledge is more necessary that you may hint with certainty.

[*About six lines are torn from the diary.*]

Raphael and Michel Angelo had less difficulties to combat, in

4. Pope, *An Essay on Criticism,* l. 89.

giving satisfaction than they that are born in the present age. Their works were alone the criterion, and the People's taste was as progressive as their improvement, but now the eyes of connoiseurs are so debauched by the works of Rubens and the Venetians, that form, which ought to be the first aim of youth, will not satisfy alone, without all that soft voluptuousness of pencil, which is the result and not the beginning of labour. March 21st, 1809.

[Eleven pages are torn from the diary.]

April 10. I am never daunted, frightened, or depressed at difficulties however great. All difficulties & dangers are to me stimulants for exertion; it is undeserved neglect or disappointment that tempts me to complain of life.

This I have never experienced yet, tho I fancy sometimes I have.

I mean by difficulties supposing I was a Soldier, privation of food, long marches, desperate battles ordered for the forlorn hope, losing my leg, sleeping on the ground, or bringing my troops in a situation where they would be all destroyed, unless relieved by an immediate conception of my own; or if a Painter, as I am, undertaking work which I find myself unprepared for being obliged to exert myself incessantly to render myself adequate, trying to express the most refined and difficult expressions, contending to extinguish all my Predecessors and contemporaries, burning for an opportunity to oppose myself personally with him who is considered the first Painter of the Age, painting one head, or any part, ten times before I can do it rightly — all these things are the delight of my very soul, but if after having accomplished these things, I find the World insensible to their excellence, I droop, am depressed, weary of my life, and then in a tumult of indignation, console myself with the Idea that one day their value will be understood.

Lord Mulgrave wished me to put his picture up for the Prize at the Institution. I told his Lordship if Mr. West[5] and all the

---

5. Benjamin West (1738–1820), who was born in Pennsylvania but moved to London in 1763 and soon became successful as a portrait and historical painter, under the patronage of George III. He became an original member of the Royal

Academicians were to be my competitors, nothing would give me greater delight, even if I lost it — less glory would be lost, and more won if I gained it. But to contend with a parcel of mannered, ignorant, illiterate boys, without science or principle, if I were successful would be no honour, and if unsuccessful, I should never hold up my head again. Besides, what do I care for prizes? I want public approbation and fame — this is the only prize I esteem.

Fuzeli said mystery and solitude were the two great engines of terror — a number destroys all terror. April 17.

I think an Epic Poet the greatest of all Poets because he is not confined like a Dramatic Poet to five acts. He has no need to hurry on his subject. This is just an unexamined thought that was excited by seeing Othello, and it struck me that Othello determined too quickly without examining the truth. Had he examined, it would [have] lengthened the play, which must not be done. April 22.

When Poets or authors illustrate any thing by Painting, they speak of it merely as an imitative art. From their ignorance they seem to forget it can raise the passions or excite sublime emotions.

They always say — *as a painter draws a likeness &c.* or some such inefficient, imbecile stuff. Apr. 23.

April 24. Passed the day in reading Shakespeare. Had a beautiful conception of Romeo leaving Juliet. Made a sketch. Also Lady Macbeth besmearing the faces of the pages with blood in dim half tint, while in the back ground Duncan murdered, stretched over the bed, and the door open, Macbeth seen leaning against the bannisters overpowered, looking round as if he heard something, into a dingy long passage.

Romeo & Juliet. In the garden the trees limpid and glistening with the dewy grey tone of morn; day just broke and shooting against the vault of Heaven, the moon fading at the approach of light, the morning star, with a liquid, lucid, agitated, trembling glitter, while the lark, "the herald of the morn," [6] in a tumult of fine delight, twittering, fluttering, bursting its throat, making the

Academy in 1768 and in 1792 succeeded Sir Joshua Reynolds to the presidency; he resigned in 1805 but was reëlected in 1806 and served until his death.

6. *Romeo and Juliet,* III,v,6.

skies ring "while upward springing blythe to greet the purpling east." [7]

In a balcony Juliet & Romeo; Juliet sinking, hanging on his neck, "utt'ring such dulcet and harmonious breath," [8] telling him it's not yet near day; "it was the nightingale and not the lark; believe me, love, it was the nightingale;" [9] her hair carelessly diffused about her heavenly neck, her delicate form appearing through her mantle. Romeo, a fine erect, heroic limbed youth, pressing her gently to his bosom, with a look of trembling tenderness, pointing to the east, unable to tell her what is really the truth, that day is beginning to break.

I feel my heart beat at the Idea of painting such a delightful subject. O God, grant I may execute it with "colours dipt in heaven"; inspire me, thrill my very soul with love — pure, unadulterated love. April 26.

How odd that such opposite conceptions should come into my head, almost at the same instant, as Lady Macbeth, smearing blood, and Romeo leaving Juliet. I cannot acct. for it; for a moment or two I dwelt with peculiar delight in fancying I saw her thrust her hand into the gaping wound of Duncan, yet warm, and steal, on tip toe, to the grooms. Almost at the same moment, I saw in my mind's eye Romeo pressing Juliet to his heart, the day breaking, the moon fading, the star glittering, and the lark singing; so vividly that I was lost in delight for an Instant, an inhabitant of another World, and then again all this died away, and I saw Lady Macbeth by the dim light of a shimmering lamp, gilding the faces of the spongy officers. [1]

April 28. Lord Cochrane [2] has had the order of Knighthood conferred on him. I could not read the ceremony without feeling an envy of his glory. Painters never can expect such honours.

7. Identified by Professor Herbert McArthur as Burns's "To a Mountain Daisy," l. 11.
8. *A Midsummer Night's Dream,* II,i,151.
9. *Romeo and Juliet,* III,v,2 and 5.
1. *Macbeth,* II,ii,56 and I,vii,71.
2. Lord Cochrane (1775–1860), later tenth Earl of Dundonald, created K.B. in 1809 for services in parliament and the navy — he distinguished himself in the engagement against the French fleet in Basque Roads, April 12, 1809. He was expelled from the order of the Bath in 1814 as a result of false accusations of fraud but was reinstated in 1847 as G.C.B. and became an admiral in 1851.

How I should have been delighted to [have] been in that battle with him. I am determined I will go out as volunteer one day or other some where, & try if I cannot get some glory in fighting as well as Painting. If I could but signalize myself in battle once before I die, as well as to be a great Painter, how happily shall I resign my existence. I like the Idea of fire, shot, shells, dying groans, tremendous explosions, enthusiastic huzzas, dying efforts, blazing fires, and all the horrors, terrors, fury, rage, & smoke of a thundering battle.

[*A sketch of a woman's head.*] I went to the play this evening.[3] Saw a beautiful creature in the boxes, which I have here tried to sketch from recollection. Just come home. XI o'clock. And another sweet girl with such a lustre in her eye as Juliet had.

As I was going to bed last evening and looked at my sketch of Macbeth, with a shock that shook my brain, in burst a fancy how grand & terrible it would be to look to see only the Shadow of Lady Macbeth's head & hand against the bottom of the Room, as if she was listening behind the door, with a lamp in her hand, her own head not appearing. I took my brush and painted out her head immediately and painted away con furore till one in the morning, when I thanked God that such an Idea came into my head. It gave such a mystery and silence to the whole scene, that I was terrified myself and dreamt about it all night. I thought also in the course of the evening what a beautiful subject Mary Queen of Scots' leading to execution would make. I would have her form feeble, & delicate, with a face of a refined sorrow & beauty, leaning on one of her maids, holding out her exquisite arm & hand to her Steward, who is on his knees bedewing it with his tears, her maids, their lips trembling with affection, looking on Mary, the Earl of Kent, Dean of Peterborough, & guards, standing round. In the background at the end of [the] passage, as if in an inner chamber, in dim, solemn half tints, should partly appear in "darkness visible"[4] the scaffold, block, & executioner leaning

3. Playbills of April 28, 1809, in the Harvard Theatre Collection, show that the Drury Lane company appeared at the Lyceum Theatre in Richard Leigh's *Grieving's a Folly* and Charles Coffey's *The Devil to Pay* and that George Colman, the younger's *The Iron Chest* and James Kenney's *The Blind Boy* were staged at the Theatre Royal, Haymarket.

4. *Paradise Lost*, I,63.

on his ax, all covered with black, and people & guards standing round at the foot. April 29.

I would rather make Mary looking towards Heaven, in sublime abstraction as if lost in angelic feeling for a moment. All human weakness should exclusively appear in her maids & servants. This will raise her character, and elevate the spectators' feelings as well, whereas if she appeared affected and weak, you would rather pity her than admire, and praise her conduct, but if this is done as it ought, it would excite feelings above this world altogether. 12 o'clock at night, 41 Gt. Marlborough Street, May 8.

May 13. How success or a prospect of success operates on men's minds. Two months since I dined at Lord M[ulgrave]'s with Sir G[eorge] B[eaumont] & W[ilkie]. L. M. & Sir G. B. were delighted with my picture. There was then every prospect of it being hung in a good situation in the Royal Academy and attracting public approbation, and every prospect too of the People being tired of W. and his falling in their estimation.[5] Of course every attention was paid to me. All their conversation was on the beauties of my Picture, on my perseverance, how fine this was or how fine that. Poor W. was literally not spoken to. Every body's attention, Ladies and Gentlemen, was directed to me. I finished my Picture,[6] sent it to the Exhibition, where by the rascality of

5. Joseph Farington's diary corroborates these opinions. On April 3, 1809, he wrote: "Haydon is now Sir George's *Hero,* who is with him every day. Wilkie is on the decline in favor." Sir George, apparently, was rather ruthless in exercising the prerogatives of a patron. Thomas Hearne told Farington in July 1809 that "Sir G. B. desires to be supreme Dictator on works of Art; gives opinions, — sweeps away those Artists who at the time are not His objects, & repeats these opinions to persons as if not given before." BRH was obviously not the docile protégé whom such patrons wished, as in May 1809 Farington heard that "Lord Mulgrave has recommended to Wilkie to advise Haydon to leave off His habit of swearing; and Sir G. Beaumont has done the same & also wished him not to put Himself forward in such a manner as to give offense to Artists His Seniors" (Farington, V,136,206, and 171–172).

6. Although "Dentatus" has few merits, it elicited extravagant praise from BRH's friends. One of them, probably James Elmes, writing under the strangely chosen pseudonym of Veritas, exclaimed: "Did Raffaelle at twenty put forth a more powerful picture than Dentatus? [BRH was twenty-two when he began Dentatus in 1808.] I have no hesitation in saying, No! and that in the essential qualities of heroic form, the figure of Dentatus alone will bear comparison with any figure Raffaelle ever executed in the heroic style. . . . I do not dare, Sir, to compare Haydon on the *whole* with Raffaelle on the *whole;* in fertility and num-

Mr. West it was hung so that nobody could see it. Of course every body pitied me, said it was a shame. Lord M. behaved to me like a noble fellow and expressed his feelings with indignation. Wilkie's Pictures were hung where they deserved, and still excited as much applause as ever, which they deserved also. I dined again at Lord Mulgrave's and with some company. Lord M. took me by the hand heartily, gave me a look as if to say "don't be discouraged," did every thing to keep up my spirits. I soon convinced him checks of this sort, tho they might hurt me, would not discourage me one instant from struggles to attain my object which I would die or accomplish. Still with all his wish to be kind, at table mark the difference. Wilkie, who two months ago was neglected, was now smiled on, spoken to, praised, flattered, while I, who when there was a prospect of success, was treated in a similar manner, was now unnoticed. Not a word about my Picture, no person but Lady Mulgrave[7] who sat next me, & Lady Beaumont,[8] who appeared interested for me, said any thing to me. Two months since, when I shewed an inclination to speak, every body turned towards me and listened with attention and smiles, but now my observations were drowned in clamour, and every ear and eye, with a gracious *oome* and a smile were directed to Wilkie. He that is successful is always welcome. Few men are bold enough to direct the public approbation, tho' all are cunning enough to acquiesce in it.

Fuzeli got my Picture a place in the Great Room, where my Joseph was hung in 1807. Mr. West, under pretence of doing me a service, told Fuzeli he thought he had not done me justice. Fuzeli then said, "get him a better place yourself," and went away. The next morning, in coming thro the Ante-Room, he was astonished to see my Picture hung there.[9] He asked who did this,

---

ber of works, Raffaelle is unequalled. I only wish to shew that the nature of Haydon's genius is not inferior to Raffaelle's, period by period, and picture by picture, as far as Haydon has gone" (*Annals of the Fine Arts*, 1817, 2:407–409).

7. Baroness Mulgrave (d. 1849), later Countess of Mulgrave.

8. Margaret, Lady Beaumont, the daughter of John Willes. She married Sir George in 1778 and died in 1829.

9. "['Dentatus'] had a central situation in a room where pictures by Reynolds and Gainsborough had often been placed, and where one of Lawrence's finest portraits was hung, when he was President of the Academy. Haydon says the ante-room had no decent light for a picture, which is untrue, for the light in which the 'Dentatus' was hung was as good as possible; nor can I acquit him

who ordered this. "Mr. West," was the reply. Mr. West met Sir George Beaumont at dinner, and told him that they had hung my Picture in a place where he could not bear to see it, and that he had it taken down, and hung it himself in the best light in all the Academy, in the centre of the Ante-Room. When Sir George asked him where it was hung before, he evaded it by saying it looked, &c. I dined at Sir George's next day and met Lord Mulgrave there. When he heard of it, "did ever Mr. West hang any of his own Pictures there?" was his question. I never saw such a piece of American finesse, he blamed Fuzeli for not doing me justice (who had done me ample justice), expressed a desire to hang it better, hung it where he knew the People would never look at it, told Sir George it was the best place in the Academy, and then actually lamented to another friend of mine, saying, "what a pity it is not in the Great Room, but, Sir, the Academicians will have their Pictures there," when the Academicians had hung it in the Great Room to oblige Fuzeli, and he himself took it from there, hypocritically abusing them for not doing me justice. He knew very well that had it remained there, it would [have] attracted the public attention and this he wished to prevent. Poor Opie[1] said once when West was down copying with the Students at the Institution, "West never does any thing but with some rascally motive, depend on that." This saying of Opie's gains ground the longer one knows West.

May 14. In an excrutiating state of mind the whole morning. I accused Wilkie of a want of warmth, in my interest, when I read to him from some paper where they said "I had added dignity to the Historical art of my country." Instead of expressing any joy, as I did when he first came out, he seemed mortified. This was so unlike a real friend that it hurt me excessively, and I told him of it after some time, and asked him if this was the way I treated him when they called him the Caledonian phaenomenon. I took him by the hand in a large company and told him he deserved

---

of wilful misrepresentation, when he says the ante-room had 'no window,' for this, though in one sense true, is substantially false, the ante-room being lighted by a sky-light, the best of all windows for pictures" (Charles Robert Leslie, *Autobiographical Recollections*, ed. Tom Taylor, Boston, 1860, p. 149).

1. John Opie (1761–1807), R.A., a successful portrait and historical painter, one of BRH's first acquaintances in London.

this and twice as much if possible. I read to them all the criticism on his Fiddler, and from my heart I can say I was sincerely happy. This was at a time too when my picture of Joseph was in the exhibition and no soul had noticed it, tho it hung in the same room. I felt no envy. I saw his merit and I was happy; the public saw it; and then when he knew with what difficulties I had struggled, and how night and day I had fagged in Lord Mulgrave's Picture, and how I must have been hurt to find this Picture stuck out in the dark in the Ante Room, when my first Picture was thought worthy of a place in the Great Room; and Lord Mulgrave & every body had formed such expectations of its success — after all this came unexpectedly, notwithstanding its rascally place, some praise in the paper, which I instantly read to Wilkie, expecting he would be as much gratified as myself. But no, he seemed actually envious, said not a word, or tried to treat it with contempt. The first word that was ever mentioned of him, in 1806, I was so pleased, I recollect, I bought the Paper and marched up to him instantly. He was then sitting at breakfast in a dirty little parlour, where he eat, drank, painted, and slept. I read it to him so eagerly I could scarcely go on when I . . .

[*A page is torn from the diary.*]

I will not hurry it — do try" was his answer, "and rather than that you should not get it done, I would come and assist you myself," — in fun, merely meaning to express his strong wish I should exhibit. Yet when Sir George came to town and said the People were so unused to any thing of this sort, it might be ridiculed, in short it was a dangerous experiment, and I had better wait another year, &c., and all the feelings of timid imbecillity, but I told Sir George I had made up my mind to it, and therefore could not think of altering my determination. I would run the risk of ridicule, I did not mind that, comforting myself with the idea that Wilkie wished it as much as myself. Consider my astonishment at finding Wilkie, when I talked of it to him, advising me not, either not daring to disagree with Sir George, *after what he had said to me!!!!!!!* As many notes of admiration as would reach from here to Paris would never express sufficiently my indignation and surprise. I asked him what he could say for himself — nothing, of course, but only that I ought not to exhibit it because it was my first Picture. As I had taken the time of four about it, I answered I would. Seguier told me too it would do me credit, and yet he was fearful of Sir George, and advised me for my own interest not to disoblige. Prince Hoare was the only one who stuck by me. He told me by all means to send it, and then when it met with success, Lady B[eaumont] said, "it was lucky, Mr. Haydon, you did not follow our advice," and Wilkie joined them. Pshaw. If Satan and all his host had come from Hell to advise me not to do it, *I would have done it*. What a state of anxiety did I suffer, till the exhibition opened. If my Picture had been ridiculed, who would *have defended it?* If it had fallen, *who would have raised it?* I should have been told I was arrogant & conceited, to act so in opposition to older men. My Patrons would have left me, my Friends forsaken me, but now when Mr. Thomas Hope discovered the little merit it possessed, purchased, praised, & criticised it in "The Review of Art," [2] a quarterly publication, those who applauded my resolution, said "I told you it would do," those who opposed it, "I did not doubt its merit, but I was fearful the People might not feel it and it might have been ridiculed. However, it's very lucky it has turned out so." Give me the man that will struggle with ye thro' every storm, and waft with you in every breeze, like my friend Whitfield. I hate your interested, milk and water beings, who are your friends only as long as your friendship interferes not with their interest.

Some men cover their interested intentions by saying they wish not to be ungrateful. The Epic Poet when he has a poetical conception, can express it as coming from himself, and not make any of his heroes talk as if they were mad, whereas a Dramatic Poet must make some of his characters utter a fine strain of poetical rhapsody in the middle of the conversation, which is always strained and appears improbable — he has not other resource.

And yet I am attached to Wilkie; it is his way; he is a cold,

2. Thomas Hope (1770?–1831), art collector and connoisseur, purchased "Joseph and Mary Resting on the Flight to Egypt" and praised it anonymously in the *Review of Publications of Art*, 1808, 2:110–112. The picture was lot 59 in the Hope Sale at Christie's on July 20, 1917, and was bought by one Lee for seven guineas.

calculating, cautious, clear-headed Scotchman. Sunday evening [May 14].

I first thought of making Macbeth looking on Duncan, as if in a violent conflict of passion, Duncan, as it were, smiling in his sleep on his murderer, or Macbeth looking round in the dark as if he saw something, drawing the bed clothes off, Lady Macbeth leaning in behind the door in the background, her shadow against the wall, or Macbeth, in desperation, plunging the dagger into Duncan, or Macbeth grasping the clothes in one hand, the dagger in the other; at the instant he was preparing, he heard something; with terror and affright, he looks round, and sees the shadow only of Lady Macbeth glimmering in dim, half tints at the bottom of the room, the two grooms asleep at the foot of the bed, and Duncan as sound & tranquil as if dreaming of Heaven. This I have fixed on. I think it excites more horror, seeing only her Shadow. It was such a common Idea making him stabbing.

I began to study in London in lodgings in the Strand, 342, May 20th, 1804, and studied night [and] day, till I brought a weakness in my eyes, which obstructed me for 6 weeks. In January, 1805, I first entered the Academy. March, went into Devonshire, where I obtained bones from a Surgeon of Plymouth and drew nothing else for three months; returned to the Academy in July; met Wilkie there first time. Studied incessantly, sitting up many nights, shattered myself so much obliged to leave off. Went into Devonshire for the recovery of health. Began to paint after two years' application to Anatomy & Drawing, May, 1806. Commenced my first Picture, October 1st, and finished it March 31st, 1807. Went into Devonshire for 6 months. Studied heads from Nature. Came to town. My dear Mother died at Salt Hill. January 1st, 1808, commenced my second Picture, Dentatus. Went to Dover, for a month. At Lord Elgin's a month drawing.[3] Finished it March 31st, 1809, making 13 months actual employment.

3. It is not clear just when BRH made the drawings from the Elgin Marbles contained in a large sketchbook entitled "Haydon's Studies" now in the British Museum. In this volume BRH wrote: "1809. Sketched in Park Lane, in the Court Yard now built over Duke of Gloucester's, then Lord Elgin's, who bought the House of Lord Cholmondeley. The Elgin Marbles in the first Instance were in Richmond Gardens, then in Park Lane, & lastly Cavendish House."

May 23. Tuesday. Painted without resting once, from ten to four, with such vigour and spirit that I exhausted myself, and stretched myself out on the carpet and slept an hour. Another model came at 6, and I painted till near nine. Got in the whole of my subject in a sketch four feet long.

He that comes after, tho' he take advantage of his predecessors' labours if he add what they neglected, is certainly a greater man. May 23. at breakfast.

[*Five sketches of bats.*] Persons that lie with their feet exposed, they insinuate their sharp pointed tongue unperceived into a vein, and suck the blood till they are satiated; at the same time fanning their wings, and agitating the air, which in hot climates lulls the sufferer into a more profound sleep. Martyn Natural History. Madagascar Bat.[4]

June 16. Marshall Lannes,[5] Duke of Montebello, is dead. The Bulletin says Buonaparte passed an hour with him. What a fine scene this would [be] in [a] play, supposing Buonaparte's fortunes to be in the decline (as I suppose). I think this must give Buonaparte's mind a shock. This is the first friend he has lost, the first serious defeat he has met with; I should like to have been invisible at their meeting, Lannes dying, weak and nervous, advising Buonaparte must have made him think more seriously of his mortality than any thing that ever happened to him. I think I see the Ghosts of Enghien,[6] Palm,[7] Toussaint,[8] Palafox's[9] Friend, shot at Saragossa, hovering round their heads and smiling, as if the Age of horror, murder, and destruction was finishing. He that could hear & see thousands dying & groaning without a pang, would when he reflected that his Friend, the man who had shared

4. The excerpt is inaccurately quoted from the article on the Great Madagascar Bat in William Frederic Martyn's *A New Dictionary of Natural History*, 1785.

5. Jean Lannes (1769–1809), marshal of France, mortally wounded during the advance on Vienna.

6. Louis Antoine Henri de Bourbon Condé, duc d'Enghien (1772–1804), French émigré, seized and executed by Napoleon's orders on false charges.

7. Johann Philipp Palm (1766–1806), a German bookseller, executed for alleged participation in circulating an anti-Napoleonic pamphlet.

8. Pierre-Dominique Toussaint L'Ouverture (1743–1803), liberator of Haiti; he was captured by the French and died in the prison of Joux.

9. José de Palafox y Melzi, Duke of Saragossa (1775–1847), who led the Spanish resistance against the French at Saragossa in 1808.

his prosperity, who had executed his orders, who ridiculed perhaps the superstitions of mankind about religion, and who had no gaieté de coeur, thought perhaps they were never to die; when he saw this friend weak, miserable, helpless, in bed, wounded and dying, it must indeed have excited feelings. There is something tremendous in the Idea, Buonaparte.

I am convinced when I survey the state of Europe at this Period, and compare it with its state 2 years ago, that Buonaparte has lost ground, and the Historian hereafter may with propriety date his downfall from his invasion of Spain. Could any thing on Earth be more impolitic? He has not only lost the use of the Spanish Armies and fleets, but he divided his own forces, and gave a shock; his power he will never recover.

Ornament may be admitted with restrictions. Colour, Light & Shadow, Grace, Beauty, Form — all must be admitted as far as they assist expression & mind, where either attracts by superiority. No argument against perfection. A deficiency in the power of the Artist. Venetians not drawing at first — not beginning this way the result of accident, not principle. The Romans not colouring, not paying attention to colour, accident also — therefore absurd to fix principles — from their conduct — Artist excellent exclusively in any of the requisites, viz., colour. A defective painter — on this principle the Ancients and Raphael approach nearer perfection. Recapitulation — in Nature, when the face & body express any sentiment, or action, there is colour, form, light, & shadow, & grace, but they never interfere with the intention, they never attract, at first the passion is the attraction, the rest assist the passion to attract.

June 20. I was at Vauxhall last night, really excessively poetical. I observed in Hayman's[1] Pictures, tho' well painted, yet from their total deficiency in that inspired spirit, as it were, that pungent, acute feeling, which pervades the works of real genius. The People left them with indifference. Where this spirit is tho every thing else is neglected, it is sufficient. Others, you proceed with energy, certain that what you have done is right. On the

1. Francis Hayman (1708–1776), best known for his ornamental paintings at Vauxhall.

other hand it may be said that by laying open your Picture in its progress to be judged by all, you are liable to be distracted by the jarring, whimsical, and discordant opinions, that you lose sight of your first intention, that your life is [a] perpetual scene of uncertainty, that when your efforts are concluded, you are neither pleased yourself, nor do you please any other person. However, I think myself, and I think from experience, the most advisable plan is to steer between the two; to admit a few people at intervals. That is, if a man has an internal, invincible determination not to suffer his exertions to be weakened by praise or depressed by censure, if he has a decided firm notion of his own, to which all his efforts are directed, the opinions of his friends he can reject or adopt as they advance or deter him from accomplishing his notions. This on the whole he must have a decided object of his own, and then the admission of people at intervals will be an assistant. But when a man's opinions are hardened by experience, and his notions have been sanctioned by the world, so that he has authority for depending wholly on himself, a Picture certainly should never be shewn. Keeping it to himself entirely will then stimulate him not to disappoint what has been formed of him, and every effort will burst on mankind, with encreased & encreasing effect, but then, as in every thing else, he must depend on his own judgement.

Volume A

JUNE 1809—AUGUST 1809

The diary continues with seven unbound quarto sheets, entitled "Journal of a jaunt into Devonshire in company with Wilkie 1809" (Volume A).

Volume A

JUNE 1809—AUGUST 1809

Wilkie and I left London 22 June, 1809, for Portsmouth, with a letter of recommendation to Sir Roger Curtis,[1] the Port-Admiral, from Gen'l Phipps (Lord Mulgrave's Brother) telling him if an opportunity occurred to send us on board a man of war for Plymouth. He behaved very politely to us, invited us to dine with him, shewed us the Dockyard, and as unfortunately for us the Grand Expedition[2] drew every thing from Plymouth to Portsmouth instead of vice versa, he was obliged to put us on board a King's Cutter, the only vessel bound in that direction.

While we [were] there one morning at breakfast, the alarm bell rang with agitated quickness, and People appeared rushing towards the beach in crowds. At first I thought it a fire, but we heard Gunpowder had exploded on the beach; away we went and found on our arrival all appearance of some dreadful convulsion. The glass in the windows was shivered to atoms; here lay one poor Soldier, blown compleatly in two; there another lacerated, his jaw fixed and rolling on his back in excrutiating agony, while the crowd were thunderstruck, as if the whole was enchantment. We could get no satisfactory information from any soul. All were enquiring, and nobody answering. We found afterwards it was occasioned by a woman striking the contents of her pipe against some baggage that lay on the beach, of a regiment just disembarked, near where lay some loose powder, and not far off a barrel. The loose powder flashed, and the barrel instantly exploded.

After contemplating this melancholy, interesting scene, we set

1. Admiral Sir Roger Curtis (1746–1816), G.C.B., appointed commander-in-chief at Portsmouth in 1809.
2. The expedition against Walcheren, the westernmost island in the mouth of the River Schelde, led by the Earl of Chatham. He failed to take his major objective, Antwerp, and finding his position on the island untenable, withdrew his forces with nothing accomplished. Controversy over the Walcheren Expedition led to the duel between Viscount Castlereagh, secretary for war and the colonies, and George Canning, foreign secretary.

sail to see the Caledonia, 120 Guns, then at Spithead. There is in our Navy a sublime, terrible simplicity; nothing admitted but what is absolutely useful. The cannon, the decks, & the Sailors wear the appearance of a stern vigour, constituted to resist the elements. No beautiful forms in the gun carriages, no taste or elegance in the cannon, the ports square, & the cannon iron, and the Sailors muscular. Every thing inspired one with awe & admiration. I felt as if I could have stood like a rock on such a deck and braved the fiercest battle. I could have drifted into the fight biting iron, such inspired, energetic vigour did every thing I saw excite in me. There was nothing elegant or tasteful that would excite indolent, luxurious delight; every thing was rough, terrible, & firm, that roused the fiercer passions. There was a grandeur in the sight of 350 Sail at anchor at Spithead, destined for some great enterprise. We rowed about amongst them & returned to Portsmouth, where the People were not yet recovered from their panic.

After waiting three days we became quite hopeless, and calling on Sir Roger to take leave, we obtained two places in the packet-boat. Just as we were on the point of embarquing, Sir Roger came puffing in to desire us to delay our present plan as he could get us something better than the packet. He would recall the officer who was under weigh by signal, which he did immediately, & introduced him to us. We were soon on board, and soon again under weigh. The transport we convoyed shortly followed us, and we dwelt with delight as we floated by the shores of the Isle of Wight. We passed through the Russian fleet. The sailors stared at us. How unlike English Sailors they appeared, their lips covered with nasty, sandy coloured mustachios, some in hairy caps, some in green jackets. When they laughed it was like the grins of Jackalls or Apes. Their ships appeared strongly built ships.

Evening approached, the Sun set, and as we wafted with the breeze, the Moon, apparent queen, unveiled her peerless light, and glittered on the sails of the distant shipping. Every thing now seemed hushed, except the rippling and bubbling of the waters as we gently divided them. I could not help saying,

Adspirant aurae in noctem, nec candida cursus
Luna negat, splendet tremulo sub lumine pontus.[3]

As we passed through the Needles, every Soul was on Deck, and I could perceive, as they faded from us, the Star-like glimmer of the distant light house. I now retired to the cabin and stretching myself on the seat, wrapped up in signal flags, while Wilkie crept into their cupboard beds. Every three hours I heard the Whistle for a fresh watch and the measured step of the Master, as he walked the deck over my head, approach and die away at intervals. Sometimes he would stop and mutter something to the men, which the wind carried from me, and would again begin his occupation.

Notwithstanding the creaking noises, I soon slumbered imperceptibly away, and when I awoke, went instantly upon Deck and found the Master still in silence, pacing, muffled up. I shivered. The day was just breaking, the moon fading, and with lurid, liquid, trembling agitation, glittered the star of morn.

There was a strong dewy breeze, and as I looked towards the north, I saw the white cliffs of Portland, standing as it were, alone & solitary, braving the dashing surge. Nothing could be more poetical. Every thing Homer, Shakespeare, Milton, & Virgil had said of morning rushed into my fancy, and put me in such a tumult of feeling as thrilled to my very soul. The beauties of day break, of Sun rise & Sun set, are certainly never felt with such exquisite acuteness on shore as at Sea; every thing here conspires to excite sentiment. You feel shut out from the world in a solitary little vessel. You feel attached to the crew. You would spend your life with them. The immense ocean around you, with not a being visible on it but yourself, excites a melancholy awe, which renders you more liable to impression than when you are distracted by the cares & anxieties, the hum and bustle of the land.

In the extreme distance, as I turned round, I perceived our companion, the transport, silently drifting on the dark blue Sea, while the dewy light of day lit up her sails like a vision. There

3. *Aeneid*, VII,8–9. "Breezes blow on into the night, and the Moon, shining bright, forbids not the voyage; the sea glitters beneath her dancing beams."

was something cheering in this; I never saw the sublime & the beautiful so imperceptibly intermingled.

All that day we were at Sea. Wilkie became very ill, obliged to keep his bed. I was slightly so for ten minutes and soon recovered. I found the Master an intelligent fellow and the Commander a compleat Seaman. They had seen a Ship almost in every situation a Ship could be in, and knew how to provide for every difficulty. What an advantage this must give them over the inexperienced French.

I relished their salt beef and biscuit, and never felt more vigourous and strong. As the Sun was setting we shortened sail, that the transport might come up to us. We then sent a boat on board for provisions, and while she passed us and the boat boarded her, while the Sun illumined her Sails, her masts seemed to tower in the illumined sky that was behind her, and cast a momentary deep-toned shadow over us. She then tacked, and again the Sun burst upon us, while the breeze rippled the waters, the boat returned, we hoisted Sail, and soon again left her in the distance. Nothing could be more exquisite than the variety of Scene. There was something poetical in visiting each other at Sea, out of sight of all land, at a place too where an hour afterwards there would be no vestige of any human being.

Poor Wilkie still continued totally unable to stand up. I pitied him lying on his back with his nose close to the deck, while they were scraping the decks, irons, brooms, brushes, mops, & scrapers all at work and making such an infernal noise as would almost split his head in two. Wilkie tried to come on deck, but such a figure! pale, hollow cheeks, blue, quivering lips, gummy, red, blinking eyes, and unshaved, that I took him for a spectre. As he slowly lifted his form up the hatchway, poor fellow, he tottered to the post, and after urging as if he would bring up his heart and Soul, tottered once more to his hammock.

The next morning [we saw] the Mew-Stone at the entrance of Plymouth Sound, and by three that afternoon we anchored.[4] The poor Sailors all were on the tip-toe to get on shore. One wanted to see his Mother, another had a bad hand, nor did they cease to

4. On June 28 (Cunningham, I,240).

importune their Commander till he thundered out "Silence." We landed at the Pier and soon reached home, where we were frankly received by my Father.

Moodie, the Commander, seemed a good seaman, but from what I gathered from him, he did not possess that spirit of determined enterprise I like. He said once, talking of something, "you may as well expect me to attack a frigate." I don't like that, when once a man believes himself incapable of attaining any thing. Such a supposition will paralise every effort he would otherwise make to attain it. There might be a situation where even in his cutter he might successfully attack a frigate, but if he set it down as a principle that attacking a frigate, because he was a cutter, was absurd, he would not of course be alive to seize the opportunity. A Hero should dare every thing and determine to do every thing. If a man does with a cutter what another man would hardly venture to do with a frigate, this man is the Hero. This is the system — no timid, cautious calculation for me.

We were soon invited to dine with a large party. The difference between a party in the Country and one in London! Here you meet men whom perhaps you never met before. All locality, all individuality, is at an end, but in the Country, you see only those who, grown up together from infancy, are acquainted with all the eccentric local characters that are always found in Country towns. Stories of them & their families are the only subject of conversation, and what they want in wit is made up by laughter.

We shortly went to Underwood, and spent a fortnight. We visited Sir Joshua's birthplace,[5] saw Saltram,[6] and spent our time agreeably with my dear Sister.[7]

I felt the want of my dear Mother; her bed, room, every place reminded me of her.

Nothing refined, I found, would do at a country table. Every thing must be broad & farcical to have any effect. We dined at

5. At Plympton-Earl. Wilkie and BRH went there on July 7 (Cunningham, I,240).

6. Saltram House, seat of the Earl of Morley, containing a distinguished collection of pictures, notably portraits by Reynolds.

7. Harriett Cobley Haydon (1789–1884); she married James Haviland of Bridgwater in 1815.

Sir William Elford's;[8] he told a pleasant story about Sir Joshua & himself. When Sir Joshua had finished his Picture for Plympton hall, he wrote Sir William requesting him to get it hung in a good situation, which Sir William attended to by hanging it between two old Pictures, and in his letter to Sir Joshua, said the bad Pictures each side of it acted as a foil and set it off to great advantage. Sir Joshua was highly diverted, as these very pictures were two early ones of his own Painting.

The People in Devonshire treated us handsomely, but in all their parties there was something wanting. From being all known to each other, brutality & ignorance are pardoned, and he that forgives it in his own house, expects the same indulgence in another's. The consequence is a regard for the comforts of another is neglected, and every man thinks only of himself. They are hospitable but unpolished. They will give you a good dinner and plenty of wine, but are deficient in that benevolent neglect of themselves that excites a belief your happiness and not their own is their object.

We bathed, and Wilkie learnt to swim at a place called Two Coves, near Plymouth, a delicious luxurious bathing place.

We left Plymouth the very day five weeks [after] we came out of London, and came to Exeter that night, after travelling the most delightful road in England. Every tree and every herb seem to sport in luxuriant wantoness. There was a rich full blown broad leaf on all the trees, that gave them an expanded appearance nothing could equal — it was on the Totnes Road to Exeter.

I felt a pang at leaving my Sister I never felt before, having no Mother to protect her. There was something orphan-like in leaving her. The first moment I can possibly afford to keep House, dear little Soul, she shall instantly come to me. Every encrease of affection is an encrease of anxiety, and as all anxiety is an interruption to study, I will strive to keep my heart untrammelled from love. God grant I may be an honour to my Country before I die and I shall die happy; to execute some great work ought to be every man's object, and every thing that will tend to interrupt my

8. Sir William Elford (1749–1837), banker, politician, and amateur artist. In 1814, with J. W. Tingcombe, he bought BRH's "Judgment of Solomon" for 700 guineas.

rendering myself adequate to execute it should instantly be dismissed. If I can but improve the moral art of my country and do that which will tend to abstract the mind from sensual gratification, if I can but add to the stock of human knowledge, how triumphantly shall I die. God grant me strength to be daunted by no difficulties, but to be stimulated. Let my exertions be always adequate, how great soever the object. I could drive my fist through the door when I think on it.

As it was the assize week every thing was bustling. I called on the Friends I depended on for a kind reception & bed, but they were all in confusion and misery. The House was worn out by sickness. These little checks to expected happiness serve to excite reflection and beget experience.

We took our places in the morning Coach, and arrived at Wells in the afternoon at three. I was excessively amused by a Sailor, who belonged to the Victory and was in Trafalgar. What he told me had all [the] simplicity of truth. He said as they were going down into action, Lord Nelson came round to them and told them not to fire till they were sure of their object. "When he came down," said he, "we were sky-larking, as every thing was ready & guns double shotted." "What d'ye mean by sky-larking?" said I. "Jumping over each other's head," he answered, "to amuse ourselves till we were near enough to fire." He was a robust, fine, stout, weather beaten fellow. At some House we stopped at there was a clean spindle legged local militia man smoking his pipe and besmeared with pipe clay. The Sailor and he soon quarrelled of course. "If I was thee," says the Militia man, "I would have put on a cleaner handkerchief about my neck." "Damn your eyes, what d'ye ask for your legs?" said the Sailor. No soul could help roaring with laughter, and Jack enjoyed a compleat triumph. The notion of asking a rough, sun burnt Tar why he did not put on a clean hand kerchief!!! Lord Collingwood [9] had written to the Admiralty to grant all the Victory's men 14 days' leave; they came home in the Ocean, after being in the Mediterranean 4 years.

I called on my Uncle John Cobley[1] and met with a most affec-

9. The first Baron Collingwood (1750–1810), vice-admiral, who took command on Nelson's death at Trafalgar, October 21, 1805.

1. BRH's maternal uncle, John Cobley (1754–1836), vicar of Cheddar from 1804 until his death.

tionate reception. We spent a very pleasant three days there. His eldest son was deprived of his intellects very early by fits. I saw he could relate every thing he observed with perfect accuracy but there it ended; he could make no deduction, nor draw a conclusion. I have always said to Wilkie there was no effort of mind in telling what happened, or what a man observed; the effort lay in drawing a result or forming a conclusion in laying down principles from what you saw. This is now exemplified by a man nearly an Idiot, observing but not thinking.

Here we visited the beauties of the Country, saw the tremendous Cheddar Rocks and Cavern. There was something terrific in their appearance, a wild, ferocious, sullen tone with a burst of light in the sky behind, which shewed their projections sharply — a place fit for Banditti.

Never was a mind more adapted for its purposes than Wilkie's. Among a thousand instances I select this: in the Cavern, which vault is a half mile, was a pure, silent stream of water, which vanished imperceptibly among the rocks. We fixed two bits of lighted candle to something that would float, and after hiding our own candles, sent them down the stream. Nothing could be more exquisitely poetical, the way they floated on, illumining the immense cavern, suspended as it were in the air, for the water was so clear its surface could not be seen. Then they would be lost behind some projection, and their effect only was seen. Then they would be again seen glimmering in the distance, and after streaming along for a little time, would float away into obscurity. This looked like spirits, on the Styx. We tried one more, but it upset and frizzed away in the water. Wilkie, who seemed unconcerned before, now burst forth in expressions of delight, and on my return, told me he had been thinking it would make a good subject, to have a number of people & children setting off those things and some of their lights frizzing & spitting in the water!!!

I recollect once when we [were] at Lord Elgin's, and I thought he was lost in admiration of those exquisite remains of Grecian art, on our coming out he said as usual, "I have been thinking of a capital subject, a parcel of boys, with one of those things they water gardens with spouting water on some others. I would make some," says he, "in a sort of Green house out of danger, laughing at the others; and one with his nose and lips squat flat against the glass." At first I told him I wondered at his being such a fool to think of such stuff in the midst of such refinement as he had just left. He did not mind me but went on laughing and saying what he would do; could any thing shew his bent in a stronger light, to be among productions that would create a soul under the ribs of Death,[2] and instead of feeling at all their excellence, or paying the least attention to their beauties, fancying boys spouting water & one squatting his nose against the glass. Nothing incongruous or incompatible with his powers ever enters Wilkie's head; nor can any thing refined or any thing grand ever draw aside his attention a moment from his own ludicrous conceptions.

We left Wells at Six next morning and breakfasted at Bath. I hate Bath. There is a stupid sameness notwithstanding the beauties of its Buildings. There was a confirmation at the Abbey Church, and as I looked on and saw the venerable Bishop lay his hand on the heads of two sweet beautiful girls about 15, who seemed lost in purity & piety, I felt the delight of virtue & devotion. I fancied I saw the Almighty and their Saviour, contemplating the scene, with sublime, heavenly complacency, while quoirs of cherubims and Angels, from their ever tuned harps,[3] uttered a swell or strain of breathing, dulcet, undulating symphony. O God, could I always feel so, who would be happier?

Wilkie employed himself at Plymouth in observing more the manners of the People than the beauties of the Scenery. Every thing being of course new to him provoked observation and thought, but to me nothing being new, nothing surprized me. In Scotland their manners will be as new to [me] as ours were to Wilkie. We left Bath again the next day and entered dear London after being abroad six weeks,[4] much renovated in health.

2. *Comus,* ll. 561–562.
3. *Paradise Lost,* III,366.
4. They returned to London on August 3 (Cunningham, I,243).

Volume II

SEPTEMBER 1809—JUNE 1810

A scrap of paper containing a lightly penciled profile is attached to the inner front cover of Volume II of the diary; it is labeled: "A Sketch of Wilson by Sir George Beaumont Aug. 1809 when I & Wilkie were staying a fortnight at his Seat, Leicestershire." Wilkie's diary shows that they remained at Coleorton Hall, near Ashby-de-la-Zouch, from August 14 to August 27 (Cunningham, I,246 and 250). Since Volume II begins with a fragmentary entry, we may assume that part of Haydon's diary has been lost.

Volume II

. . . did Nelson eat turtle soup, in his pursuit after Villeneuve[1] —
he never shaved for 8 days, such was his anxiety and in that time
formed 6 different plans of attack. What can be expected? —
Pshaw —

September 3. Things happen but once, I have often thought, in
this world — at the commencement of life, from Spring to Winter
appeared an inexhaustible length, and life appeared endless, but
now when I look back and find since that time five years have
rolled quickly on, I fancy 5 years more will roll as quickly — and
shortly my race will be ran —

How seldom is excellence which is the result of unexpected
spontaneous feelings ever acquired, by premeditated arrangement, or concerted association. Procrastination is from a supposition of having a greater power over futurity than you'll find you
have on experience. This is not to be wondered at in Youth, but
that men fully convinced of their incapacity — should persevere!!!
Here is the wonder. Always seize things as they are, never yield
to the wispers of indolence, which urge you to defer your exertions with a hope of supplying these defeats of things, and leaving nothing to obstruct you, heed not the obstructions, attend to
the possibilities, and of them make the most — Sep. 3rd, 1809.

What enthusiasm is excited by reading Homer, how many go
and survey with delight the plains of Troy and discover with rapture Simois & Scamander,[2] — but who alas, in this age, feels reverence or enthusism at our Saviour's character, who goes to Syria,
to contemplate with awe the place of his birth, who feels rapture
at the remembrance of his purity or who feels delight at the recollection of his goodness — he who expresses reverence for such a

1. Pierre de Villeneuve (1763–1806), French vice-admiral. Nelson's pursuit of
Villeneuve's fleet led from the Mediterranean to the Caribbean and back to
European waters, where it culminated in the Battle of Trafalgar, October 21,
1805.
2. Two rivers of Troas, celebrated by Homer.

being now is surveyed as if it were a weakness, or he was deficient [in] sense. Achilles, and blood, have now taken the place of Piety & Charity — I always fancy Our Saviour wandering in contemplation about the porches & porticos of temples; I have often thought he seldom slept, what a conception to suppose him when all the world were buried in sleep, on the mount of Olives or Garden of Gethsemane, lost in piercing reflection at the wickedness of human nature, and the treatment he foresaw. Angels wafting on the breeze would perhaps sooth his spirit by undulating breathing strains and as the morning Star glittered and day broke, would fade into air, and up to Heaven in many an airy wheel [3] — I then fancy our Saviour would wander again into cities, advising the wicked, healing the sick, and exposing the hypocritical till evening again approached, and he would again wander into solitude — and again be lost in meditation; if such a character as He is described existed now? Who could disbelieve him; that such a being did exist we have other evidence besides the Apostles and as he did exist, those who were always with him, must surely have known him best, can you wonder at their enthusiasm, to look at, to talk to, to listen to such a being — O my blessed Saviour — if he did not exist, a character so far from human frailty, could only have been conceived by a being, as free from defects as the character he described — but why suppose he did not exist? We have as strong historical evidence for his existence as for Caesar's — would it have entered into human conception to fancy such a being, so contrary to all, likely to attrack attention & applause in this world, humble and meek, charitable & forgiving, — if this really had not been his character, if they wished to recommend their darling one, this was surely not the easiest way? They told the truth, and left the World to judge — O thou great being, grant before I die I may be worthy to conceive and execute such a character for Jesus Christ's sake. Amen. How my heart rises at the thought, how my frame trembles — I fancy his fine, heavenly face, marked by grief & meditation. I fancy his erect form, his gentle commanding air, surveying the crowd, with complacency, & calmness, conscious of his own power, his own purity — O God — Sep. 1809. Tuesday.

3. *Paradise Lost*, III,741.

I went last night to see Hamlet,[4] what point, what sentiment,
I felt weary at first from the heat of the House, but my attention
became so compleatly engaged, that I forgot my misery in those
of Hamlet. How exactly, "how weary, stale, flat, and unprofitable
are to us the uses of this world" [5] — describes the feelings of one
after having lost a dear, affectionate parent, one who had anticipated every wish and realized every hope; you fancy that Shakespeare is full of points, which are the climax of a series of events
— as the Play proceeds, these points encrease in interest till the
whole ends — every point excites the association of every thing
that has before happened — The first point in Hamlet is the Play
Scene; your mind is pregnant with the Ghost, the murder, his
appearing on the watch, Hamlet's Grief — all this rushes into
your fancy during the scene — the next is Hamlet's conversation
with his Mother; what associations this excites!!! all that happened before the play; & the scene that occurred at the play also
— you see a youth, pierced with grief at the loss of a Dear Father,
come to upbraid a Mother who instead of drawing the link of
affection closer to her Son, snapped it by marrying her husband's
brother. You see his heart bursting with agony, knowing the
justice of feeling, checking his mother's attempts at superiority by
stern, cutting reproof — what a point. Again when the Ghost
rushes in — it is almost impossible to wind human feelings to a
higher pitch — I don't suppose Shakespeare did this from Principle but feeling — Everything is on the same Principle. You lopp
off all the little hesitations and repetitions, of common conversation in the language of a hero, as you leave out all the little accidental wrinkles in his form, — as you approach low characters,
those peculiarities are kept as the wrinkles & accidents in a form
of common Nature — Yet even this too requires selection —
There must [be] a selection in each. Sep. 1809.

When Lord Elgin was appointed ambassador to Constan-
tinople, he enquired of a Mr. Harris, an architect who was build-

---

4. The only performances of *Hamlet* at this time were on September 6 and
22, 1809, at the Theatre Royal, Haymarket, with Charles Mayne Young as Hamlet.

5. *Hamlet*, I,ii,133–134. "How weary, stale, flat, and unprofitable,/Seems to
me all the uses of this world!"

ing for his Lordship in Scotland,[6] whether he could be of any utility to Architecture & Painting, by procuring any moulds of the fragments at Athens. Mr. Harris said that we were possessed of all the measurements, but not having any thing that could give the Student an exact Idea of the Grecian style & grandeur, he thought it would be a most desirable thing if Lord Elgin could get moulds of the capitals, Frieze & basso relievos on the different Temples at Athens — he waited on Mr. Pitt & Lord Grenville,[7] but they with their usual frigidity, affected great love for the Arts, but declined using the Public money, without authority — they would have had no objection to pour thousands into La Vendée,[8] to urge human beings to cut each other's throats, but shrunk from advancing one penny towards their country in refinement and knowledge; he that could invent a destroying rocket by which defenceless towns might be burnt and innocent People murdered was much surer of patronage from such men than he that could lend his intellects to the moral improvement of mankind. Finding no encouragement from government, he determined to take it on his own Shoulders, and instantly endeavoured to procure some young Artist of enthusiasm who would visit and remain among the ruins of Athens, but alas, none could he find and almost in despair of success he sailed to Palermo; here the proposal was enthusiastically received, and he despatched his Secretary to Rome to procure artists; five were instantly obtained, and away they all went to Athens; for three years [they] were there drawing, measuring & moulding, contending with the prejudices of the People, who thought they merely got upon scaffolds to look at their women, who would if they saw them examining a bit of sculpture split it in pieces the moment their backs were turned, supposing it contained gold — about this Time Lord Elgin came down to Athens, where the Artists and his

6. BRH was in error. The architect of Lord Elgin's Broomhall, in Fifeshire, built in 1796, was Thomas Harrison (1744–1829).

7. In 1799, when Lord Elgin was appointed ambassador to the Porte, William Pitt (1759–1806) was prime minister, and the first Baron Grenville (1759–1834) was foreign secretary.

8. Doubtless in support of the Wars of the Vendée, a counterrevolutionary insurrection of 1793 in Vendée and adjoining departments of western France.

Secretary Hamilton[9] had been so long employed and found them going on comfortably enough, the People more reconciled from habit, and more awed from our late successes in Egypt — When Lord Elgin examined the Parthenon and saw several of the figures lying about, that had fallen from the building, it occurred to him, that many might be buried. He therefore bought the House of the Man that lived under the portico, pulled it down, and excavated the whole to the solid rock, and found a fragment of the breast of the Jupiter, & of the Minerva — he then thought he might be equally successful, at the other end, where several figures were wanting, he procured the House of the man that lived there also and dug down here as well, but found nothing — the Man then to whom the House belonged, told him he could have saved him all that trouble, for the figures that [had] fallen from this part of the temple, he had ground down himself into lime, as it made such excellent mortar to build his house with, and that the greatest part of the citidal had been built with mortar procured in the same manner — with such an example before him of barbarity, he thought himself fully justified in securing those that remained, for in all probability, were they to fall, they would share the same fate, — to this energetic resolution England is indebted for these exquisite productions, — for a moment what a state of excrutiating suspence his mind must have been in — such an opportunity might never again happen, — but then he was stripping Athens of all that rendered her ruins interesting, yes, but was he for the gratification of a few individuals who might visit Athens for a few years [to] neglect to seize the moment of bringing them to an enlightened part of the World where their future existence would be safe, and where by their beauty they might again renovate Art, to its purity & beauty? What would the World have said had they known Lord Elgin might have done so, and neglected to do so, from a squeamish fear of offending pedantic Antiquaries — Buonaparte would have had them the

9. William Richard Hamilton (1777–1859), antiquary and diplomatist. As secretary to Lord Elgin, he superintended the removal of the Marbles from Athens to London. He served as under-secretary for foreign affairs from 1809 to 1822 and was instrumental in restoring to Italy the stolen works of art which Napoleon had placed in the Louvre.

moment he had the power; the French had actually began to take them down before the revolution and there is one Choiseul had taken down now in the collection[1] — like a man of enterprise and decision, he determined not to neglect this happy moment, and immediately shipped the metopes and what remained on the frieze; what was so perfect on the Temple of Theseus, as would have been destroying the temple to touch, he moulded; behold his Secretary now after five years labour, embarqued, with the rewards of his toil, gratifying his fancy, with visions of the enthusiasm [with which] this country would receive these exquisite fragments of Athenian grandeur, Vela dabant laeti,[2] but scarcely had Greece melted into air, and in altum ruebant, when the Ship struck on a hidden rock, heeled, and almost instantly sunk; down went in a moment the labours of five years and all that remained of the once beautiful Athens, in "the deep bosom of the Ocean buried"[3] — this was enough to damp men of more than ordinary minds — but to men of great minds difficulties are stimulants; instead of standing still and bewailing his misfortunes, Lord Elgin directly determined, if possible to recover, and after two anxious years, all that that were again [were] ushered into existence and arrived in England without further disaster — and here may they always continue —

Where is the individual that would have had energy enough to persevere through so many obstacles; look at the marbles; the conception of moving such ponderous monuments requires a vigour of fancy few men are possessed of — posterity will do Lord Elgin ample justice, for their beauties will by that time have circulated through the Country, and their effects on English Art will be perceptible. Their landing in this Country will be con-

1. "Monsieur Choiseul Gouffier, the French ambassador, before Lord Elgin had applied for the same leave, did obtain it, actually removed a metope, which he left on the ground when the Revolution broke out, and which was brought away for him, and which metope I saw in Choiseul Gouffier's house in Paris, at the Champs Elisées" (*Lectures*, II,210). BRH refers to Marie-Gabriel-Florent-Auguste, comte de Choiseul-Gouffier (1752–1817), diplomat and antiquary; the metope in question is now in the Louvre.

2. *Aeneid*, I,34–35. "Vix e conspectu Siculae telluris in altum/vela dabant laeti et spumas salis aere ruebant." (Hardly out of sight of Sicilian land were they spreading their sails seaward, and merrily ploughing the foaming brine with brazen prow.)

3. *Richard III*, I,i,4.

sidered an aera in the Arts and the commencement of real Art will be dated from this period. Lord Elgin has done more for English Art [than] was ever done by any individual in any Country; he deserves indeed well of his Countrymen, and [instead] of affectedly lamenting, as some do, that he stripped Athens of what remained, we should rather lament he was not there to strip it sooner, and then perhaps the most beautiful productions in the World would not have been pounded into mortar.

These facts I heard Lord Elgin myself deliver to Mr. West, Nollekens,[4] and myself yesterday, Sep. 22nd, 1809, at his musaeum for the first time — It was after the company were all gone, and we remained behind. It was excessively interesting to hear him say "that I picked up myself at Eleusis," &c &c, "This I found outside the Acropolis," &c &c &c.

(if they have not the fate [of the] Houghton Gallery.)[5]

Let us suppose that some one in France had these things. Would Buonaparte permit them to lie neglected in his House? We should soon see [them,] I fancy, in a Salle Athenienne, a place worthy their reception — He that could order the Gladiator to be brought over the Alps, tho it took three months crossing St. Cenis, when he was fighting [the] battle of Austerlitz — would feel a little interested I think for the ruins of Athens —

West knows the figure but it is superficially — he does not know it deeply, & scientifically — he knows not where to lay the stress, when a limb is in action for instance, when he raises the arm, he always shews the serratus, strongly marked, which is never the case till the arm is moved above the horizontal position; and the serratus being attached to the end of the scapula, pulls it round, in conjunction with the acromion portion of the Deltoid, and enables the arm to rise — Refinements of this sort which the greeks knew, to a hair's point — he is totally unacquainted with — Mr. West is an eminent Artist but not a great Artist — he became too soon satisfied to arrive at perfection — Mr. West has never gone beyond a certain point in acquirements, for his intel-

4. Joseph Nollekens (1737–1823), R.A., sculptor.
5. Sir Robert Walpole (later first Earl of Orford) collected classical sculpture and paintings in the middle eighteenth century. His gallery at Houghton Hall, Norfolk, was sold to Empress Catherine II of Russia in 1779.

lectual powers go not beyond a certain point; he has no more power to express refinements of intellect, in human expression, than he has to acquire refinement of knowledge; he is refined in nothing — he paints expeditiously, he composes rapidly, he draws well, and colours without much trouble; I do not suppose a Picture ever cost him trouble — from his infancy — he is a Lopez de Vega in Painting —

I called upon him, Friday, to see the sketches he had made at Lord Elgin's and as I had also been drawing there, and as deeply as I could, investigating their principles and as I ventured to think with success — I was anxious to see whether he who talked with such confidence of their beauties and of what he had done — had discovered the same beauties, and the same refinements — When I once perceived their principle by a touch I could express the intended motions of the figure, and give it the exact roll of the original; for instance, a figure, giving himself up, relinquishing all his power as it were, to his horse, his legs stretching easily and indolently, each side his horse, his thighs grasping his back, as far as they could, without splitting himself, his hip then becomes the foundation for all the upper parts to roll upon; if then the figure had no wish to erect his body, but let [it] roll as it would, the ribs & chest would press indolently forward upon the hips, and the muscle between the ribs, and the hip, be folded — This is reason & common sense, and by making the Ribs appear to bend over the hips, and the legs to hang from the hips, and you would express this feeling by shaping the parts as they would be shaped in a figure in nature, so situated — A man thoroughly scientifically versed would express his meaning by the slightest touch, for he would put no touch but what conduced to the principal intention of the figure — therefore when you are acquainted with this principle you can discover in a moment, by the slightest sketch of another, whether he knows it — now in the Panathenaic procession, every action is difficult, and by being executed on the above principle, the parts are as variously shaped as the actions are varied; the ribs, hips, thighs, legs, knees, ankles, feet are all there, but all as altered by the particular action as Nature alters them. When a man bends, the ribs pressing on the hips, [the] muscle must be more acutely marked at its end, than when the Man is erect; this appears very simple, and so simple that no body could be silly enough to miss it but every body misses. Fuzeli marks his ribs and his muscles always the same way, and consequently every part being equally marked, no parts predominate and as no parts predominate, and all are equally marked, there must be no particular intention in the figure, and all motion towards a particular end, must be suspended — and always is in Fuzeli's figures — tho his figures appear by their direction to aim at something, yet by the parts being all equally prominent, their limbs look paralized — and like the Hindoos, as if they had made a vow never to move from a certain position.

The moment Mr. West took out his compositions from Lord Elgin I was satisfied he knew no more of this principle than I did, before I went down to study them. I saw instantly his figures were sketched in, in the Westian manner, — His figures were sitting on Horses to be sure, but with no more of the refined characteristics of sitting in various forms than that their legs were astride, and a Horse was between them —

He studied here as he has studied every where else — all his life; he came down with immense canvasses, sketched all the figures in an hour, put them into a composition, surveyed them, with the same superficial glance as he had surveyed nature, and all these hidden, deep seated exquisite beauties passed unheeded by — I have heard him talk of them in raptures, when I have been there with him, and wondered why he never talked to me scientifically about them or pointed out any particular beauties —

What an unfortunate thing it is to see an old Artist about forty walking about with a large sketch book under his arm, ugly, conceited & imbecil, a large nose covered with pimples, a dirty cravat, an old hat & never-cleaned boots, a rusty black coat and a torn silk waistcoat, living too, in a little miserable filthy house at the top of Tottenham court road, in a street that has never been paved, a foot deep in mud, with pigs, ducks, and Fowls sputtering up dirty stinking cabbage & putrid ashes — with a wife, too, and eight ragged children — puddling about among his plaister heads,

and dusty canvasses, one bedaubing himself with paint and another fighting with his dirty nosed brother[6] — Oct. 1809.

"Like another Sun risen at Noon Day"[7] is perhaps as gen-
uinely poetical an Idea, as ever entered man's head — What a
subject for a Picture —

Venus leaning on Aeneas and shewing him the Gods engaged
in the Burning of Troy — in foreground; in the Back ground, Troy
burning, Palaces tumbling & crashing, Women screeching; swords
clashing, men shouting, groaning & dying, Horses, having lost
their riders, galloping, in affright through the Streets, flames roaring, a whole Street just fallen, and red smothered fiery smoke
curling up in volumes to Heaven, in that Instant Aeneas' eyes
were cleared of the mortal film, and on the Highest Tower of
Troy, in the midst of the burning city, as the Black smoke and
red flame rolled on each side, and blazing illumined the Tower,
he saw Pallas, in a silvery cloud, with her dreadful Aegis flashing
lightening in one arm, and with her Spear in the other, shouting
terribly with prophetic fury encouraging the Grecians. The Sibil
shewing Aeneas the dreadful punishment of Hell, a Fury holding
back the door, in Shadow, her hand that holds the door, only enlightened — a large terrible door, grating harsh thunder as if it
had been instantly dashed back and in that Instant, all the
damned should Flash on the eye, Ixion rolling on the wheel,
Sisyphus in vexation rolling up his stone, Theseus sitting as if he
had sat *aeternumque*,[8] Tantalus, with a parched, agonized countenance, up to his chin in water — and he that had a large rock
suspended over his head looking up with terror expecting it to
fall —

I should wish to give the Idea as if the fury had dashed back
the door, and discovered the whole scene, at a flash; Aeneas
should start, the Sibil should survey the whole with silent solemnity, and the damned should appear to go on with their Labours,
as if they had always gone on and were insensible to being ob-

6. The description fits Benjamin West in no way. He was 71 at this time,
prosperous and respected, and he lived in comfort at 14 Newman Street.

7. *Paradise Lost*, V,310–311. "Seems another Morn/Ris'n on mid-noon."

8. *Aeneid*, VI,617–618. "Sedet aeternumque sedebit/infelix Theseus." (Hapless
Theseus sits and evermore shall sit.)

served and as if they would go on when the door was shut to all eternity.

I fancied another subject after which struck me as peculiarly fine — I would have Sin and Death, sitting, looking towards hell — which should glimmer. Death the nearest — Sin resting on a large key in Perspective further off — a long line of Horizon, fiery, with gleams of flame & dingy Smoke — wafting, sailing on his sail broad vans,[9] making for the Gate of Hell — I would have Satan, whom Sin & Death should be steadfastly observing — in silence.

Another and Death & Sin, sailing by the Planets, which at the blasted view are eclipsing — Sin in delight, pointing to Satan, whom she has discovered, betwix the Centaur & The Scorpion steering,[1] in likeness of an Angel bright, in the glimmering of a celestial, airy light, Sin & Death, in a dingy tone, with every thing wan around them.

What a string of subjects rushed into my head at the beginning of the week, Pallas shouting to the greeks, Aeneas surveying Hell, Sin & Death seeing Satan in like[ness] of an Angel bright, Sin & Death surveying Satan afar off as he ascends from Hell, and Maia impregnated by the wind — and the battalion of Youths at the Games —

Last night, Octo. 25, 1809, was kept the 50th Year of George the IIIrd.[2] I never saw a Mob in such good humour — they made every body that passed the Admiralty on horseback or in coaches take off their Hats. I walked about and then went to the theatre,[3] where the riot was greater than ever, — God grant them success

[The next page is torn from the diary.]

9. *Paradise Lost*, II,927–928. "At last his sail-broad vans/He spreads for flight."
1. *Paradise Lost*, X,328.
2. October 25, 1809, was the beginning of George III's jubilee year.
3. Playbills of October 25, 1809, in the Theatre Collection of the Harvard College Library, show that the Drury Lane company appeared at the Lyceum Theatre in George Colman, the younger's *Sylvester Daggerwood*, Samuel J. Arnold's *Britain's Jubilee*, and Prince Hoare's *The Three and the Deuce* and that Charles Macklin's *The Man of the World* and Thomas Dibdin's *The Jubilee* were staged at Covent Garden.

Every exterior accomplishment of Art should give way to the expression and intellect of a subject; if they interfere with it — they should be admitted as far as they do not interfere but no farther — expression, it is said, destroys beauty, there is a beauty in expression, because it excites association if the object of the expression &c, grace & form, contribute to beauty; grace is undulation of line; now if the expression requires this undulation to be broken, but then if in expressing the intention, grace was totally destroyed it might be softened, and made yield to grace, in as much as it would convey the intention to the spectator in a more delightful manner — this is the use of all the exterior accomplishments. They are assistants, they are the means and not the end, when they become the end, they usurp —

I wish to express in Duncan, an awful, sacred air, a regal, royal look — as if you would instinctively bow on approaching him, as if he was surrounded with an atmosphere that breathed the King in every breath — I'll bind his head with velvet, gold fringes shall dazzle from his sheets, and tassals from his Pillow, while the crown of Scotland shall repose in solemnity beside him, his fine, broad, naked, Kingly chest shall be exposed to the dagger of Macbeth, his fine old hand shall hang, in sleepy relaxation, on his bed, and even the moment his fate hanging over him, he shall smile like Heaven, in silence —

Charles Bell has the most easy, indolent, pleasant manner, of enchaining attention and communicating knowledge of any being I ever met with; an unaffected, even childish way he has, [so] that things the result of the deepest investigation come from [him] like a tale, and on reflecting, you are surprized at the intellect, discoverable in them — every thing he says appears attainable by any man. It seems to have cost him as little trouble in acquiring as in delivery; by this man sluggish indifference and wandering idleness are entrapped, enticed, and flattered into exertion — October 31st, 1809.

I recollect at present but [four] subjects that have all that beaming effulgence of fancy, that looks so much like inspiration — Raphael [4] like another Sun risen at noon day, — Satan having got in among his Peers, unperceived, at once bursts forth like a

4. The angel Raphael, sent to admonish Adam (*Paradise Lost*, V,310–311).

Star — Hector, thundering on covered with dust, smoke & blood, to attack Nestor; at that Instant the Sun breaks forth, on all the tumult of the battle; who does not fancy he sees, as the sun beam passes over the field, Horses panting, men groaning & gasping, others shouting, in all the enthusiastic fury of victory; whole battalions preparing to charge, Leaders encouraging, men struggling, thousands trampling to death, thousands rending the air with the clash and din of Shields and chariots — all this flashed for an Instant on the eye, and then again was obscured — and lost [in] dinginess. Aeneas discovering Pallas on a silver cloud shouting to the Grecians as Troy is burning —

Mengs[5] said fifty years ago, that perhaps the statues they then possessed were not the works the Ancients accounted their best, and had Mengs been happy enough to see the Elgin Marbles, he would have been convinced of the truth of his conjecture — it is a strong proof of his judgement to have said such a thing at a time when there was not the most distant conception that any thing superior to the Apollo was in existence — It appears extraordinary that no enthusiastic connoiseur should have thought of visiting Athens — that it should never have entered the head of that useless rhapsodist Winkelmann when Spon and Wheeler[6] had published their description of the beauties of the Parthenon —

Foreigners have said we have no English school; thank God we never have had one — as we now [have] such perfect examples to force us into excellence —

The Romans worked partly on the same system as the Grecians, but without that part of it which urged them to refer to Nature — with none of her accidental beauties to prevent their art being apparent — The old Antique (except the Gladiator and Laocoon) with the square methodized marble forms to be as compleatly overthrown by the exquisite beauty of the Athenian marbles as ever one system of philosophy was overthrown by another more enlightened — & when they are publickly seen and studied

5. Anton Raphael Mengs (1728–1779), German artist, critic, and friend of the archeologist Johann Winckelmann. He spent most of his life in Rome, where he served as director of the Vatican school of painting.

6. *Voyage d'Italie, de Dalmatie, de Grèce, et du Levant, fait és annéss 1675 et 1676 par J. Spon et G. Wheler,* 3 vols., Lyons, 1678–1680. Jacques Spon (1647–1685) and Sir George Wheler (1650–1723) were pioneers in Greek archeology and the collection of antiquities.

— the World will be of the same opinion — Time only is wanting
to confirm my opinion, which is the result of deep reflection, and
every hour's experience of their beauties will add to its stability — The English are slow of apprehension, but when once they
perceive — no nation is firmer —

What a constant examination of your habits you must keep up,
if you are anxious to avoid bad ones. I found latterly that I gave
up the day, without effort, after a certain hour, saying to myself
the day will be soon over, and I would then sit down, and look,
or Idle till the day really closed in — how often you will find Idleness, under a mask, creeping in into actions; she seems to be perpetually on the watch, and never to attack openly. I know an
Artist who has never began to paint, because he has never yet met
with a Room "that had a light worth a Farthing." He has been in
Italy where it seems the Rooms were as ill built as in England!!!
for he never began there. I had not seen him for some time when
I met him the other day in Bond Street. He instantly [said,] "I
have met with such a Room!" Of course I congratulated him and
hoped now he would delay no longer, but the next time I met him,
it seems it did not depend on the room; he poor fellow was still
in his delusion for with a very wise face he proposed that he and
I should take two large famous rooms he had just been looking at,
and keep a servant between us, — I really pitied him; I would
have laughed in his face but I saw his sincerity, and walked away
quite melancholy, fearing to ridicule him; it might be my lot, I
thought, when I saw a man of such good sense in other respects,
the perpetual dupe of indolence; every hour and every minute,
will bind him deeper in his dream* — Nov. 8th, 1809.

When the present Artists talk of feeling, they should say idleness — they make a mistake. I will allow a man in full possession
of the mechanism of his art, deeply versed in nature, who with a
dash of his pencil will give the exact form of a toe, or a thumb, to
talk of feeling, because the expression of his feelings will be the
instantaneous creation of things; by hitting at once their characteristics which supersedes high finish, — but to hear men deficient

* This man went to Italy, never began, & died there (1842).
B. R. H.

in every great principle, to hear men who can't draw a line, or make a vigourous stroke — excuse their indolence by talking of their feelings, — it is quite laughable — so when you see a sense-less, wiry splash of colour, instead of a hand, — hush — that's feeling — don't talk of these things — you'll hurt the Artist's feel-ings — Oh would there were a college of Artists to examine every man before he was allowed to practice the Art; to talk of feelings, and ruin taste. Nov. 1809.

No man has a greater delight in the real momentary expres-sions of feeling of great artists, Rembrant, Titian, Tintoret or Rubens, than I have; let them scrawl their brush in any way, you see by what they did they could do more, their splashes were never the splashes of ignorance — they were the splashes of minds in a heat that could not stay to express more than their meaning, who were possessed by the whole, and when that was hinted — rested — Certainly the present Pictures in the Exhibi-tion,[7] give you no such Ideas; it never occurs to any one that the Artist could not stay to express more than his meaning: — for half of them have no meaning at all —

So they talk of execution — you've no execution — if they see you lose facility by laboriously making out a limb — you are set aside — you have no execution — they forget, that by labouriously & studiously & carefully painting a limb in one Picture, tho' you should lose the facility of handling in that, you acquire the power of painting with the right sort of facility — in the next — talking sense as it were with fluency — putting the right touches at once, and no more or less [than] the right touches; not executing for the mere sake of executing — not scrawling about your brush — because you do not know what to do with it — but scrawl about your brush. He that lets his hand go before his head has began at the wrong end — I recollect seeing a dog's eye in an otherwise disagreeable picture of Rubens at Thomas Hope's, which [was] a perfect example of execution, here was the exact form of the lid, the brow, the eye, all expressed by as many touches only as they required to express them at once — here was sharpness & softness

7. An exhibition held at the British Institution of copies by students of the Old Masters lent by the Governors of the Institution (*Examiner,* December 3, 1809, p. 783).

and all the characteristics of nature hit out instantly — Rubens is full of these beauties, he is a perfect example of execution — but when you see an eye lid, which ought to be drawn with a dash, round at once, cut up by a dozen dashes of a hog's hair tool, at obtuse angles, and hear this praised for execution it makes one sick — Execution is expressing the right forms of things with facility — not expressing with facility any thing but the right forms — to see a head, without bone, sketchy, light, and flimsy, stuck on shoulders without a neck, enveloped in splashes of white, for a cravat, & a hand, dashed about [with] ostentation, is [as] much incapable of motion as one [that] is paralized, to me this is to see an example [of] Royal Academical execution — 1809.

What is their conversation, go into their painting Rooms, where they are surrounded with little bits of Rembrant, & every thing to mislead men who have not strength of mind to know what proper use to make of those exquisite effusions of colour — instead of discussions about motion, characters of limbs, beauty & form, what muscles are wanted, in such a position and what are relaxed, how to advance the art, and encrease the facilities of knowledge to the students or trying to investigate the principles of the greeks, the supreme vaunt of exquisite character in form, instead of this a senseless stream of macgylp, & tone, putty & wax, buttery touches, and fat colour, is all they are informed about, is all they know, is it any wonder the People are so ignorant when their teachers are little better? They have been blamed for not having any feeling for the Art, how were they to acquire it, at the Exhibition at that splendid effusion of colour without sense, by figures with no necks, bodies with broken arms, & legs with twisted feet, were they to be instructed by shoulders which when the head is covered, it is impossible to discover whether it's the back or the breast? Were they to be instructed, in the high departments of art, when the ambition of every Artist is to out glare his companion by red curtains & Lord Mayor's maces, instead of outdo him by fine outlines, fine forms, fine characters, & refined expression? When the People have their head so split, by pageantry & show, it is no wonder they have not yet been taught feeling for high Art. The Artists are the instructors of a Nation, and must create the taste by which they are to be admired. Did not Michel

Angelo & Raphael create the Roman feeling for art, did not Titian & Tintoretto & Georgione create the taste at Venice (It may be said that Artists conform to the People's wants, that the Venetians wanted Portraits, & Romans grandeur).

The deplorable state of this England is owing to the moderate praise where severe censure is more applicable, to saying things are very well when they are very bad, in hopes of encourag[ing] the Artist to produce better — the very reverse is the result from being praised for doing what did not cost much exertion; is he likely to make greater, when he has been praised for not making any? — To the ignorance too of those who influence the People, the critics in the daily papers, who are all swayed either by ignorance or pique, by interest or friendship, who misapply praise & censure, — survey the present Artists; are they men likely to produce a revolution in Art, is there one of them except West that can draw a foot — yet these are the men who ridicule the People for not having taste — who curse the government for not having employed them to bedaub St. Paul's, who struggle with all their might to smother rising genius, to prevent those who are taking a clearer & better road to excellence from opening the eyes of the World; exposing her deformities & pushing them headlong from their seats — But the day has dawned, the morning star of Art has risen and will usher in the rising sun, Thank God, the remains of Athens have fled for protection to England, the Genius of Greece still hovers near them, may she with her magic touch give new vigour to English Art, and cause new beauties to issue from English exertions —

W—— rotten & rank in art, a disease with veneral pungency spreads itself into every fibre of his brush and pollutes & contaminates every touch —

What delight I take in surveying a fine, tall English Girl about 20, firm & dignified, yet mild & gentle, surrounded with an atmosphere of chastity that refines & purifies every notion before it approaches her; with such a woman every lascivious idea, and every wanton fancy, would be refined & curbed, into virtuous, domestic, lawful delight; there is something English about the fancy of possessing the affection of such a woman — how Italian abandoned depravity, and Spanish wanton lasciviousness —

shrink before such a being — when you think of her, how firmly you could resist every allurement, and every excitement, which at other periods possess such power over you. —

M—— & F——[8] lectures are made of descriptions instead of deductions. The contrary is the character of Reynolds's — Nov. 1809.

Piety and virtue are the only true sources of happiness; in misfortune they console your affliction, and in success, temperate your joy. — Nov. 13, 1809.

Nature puts out young men & indolent men, as they say, because in every way she is beautiful, and her various beautiful effects draw off their attention, from their own intention, the consequence is they find themselves perplexed, & distracted, and give her up in despair, whereas if they have strength of mind to keep their own object in view, and not suffer themselves to be attracted from it, they will find her an assistant to that object, and inexhaustible source of delight & instruction — Nov. 1809.

Sir Joshua's Discourses are accused of contradictions, (very true) but they are not to be considered as a whole; they are separate discourses, delivered at separate periods, to Students who required different advice as they proceeded — Besides Painters & Poets are liable to the erruptions of different feelings —

O Divine, exquisite Raphael, thou painter of refinement, elegance, & intellect, I cannot express the delight, the rapture, thy conceptions excite in me; never shall I forget my feelings, at my first perception of thy intention, in the expression of the Youth, next to Archimedes, who is looking up to another over him, with a sleepy eye, an open mouth, and a head bent back in weariness, with all that appearance of lassitude one feels after an unsuccessful effort of thought, and as if relinquishing himself, entirely in despair, dulled by exertion, to the guidance & direction of another — with his hand pointing to the mathematical figure, which he has been trying to make out, he seems to say, *"what* is this, I *cannot* find it out." — Another Youth is still pondering, with his fingers sprawling about on his knees, as if left to their own fancy by the abstraction of their master. One above him has got it; it has

8. The name of no Royal Academy professor in 1809 began with M or F.

just flashed into his brain, and with a jirked up finger, and jirked out drapery, expresses an instantaneous perception,[9] — every bit of drapery, every bit of ornament in Raphael expresses in a stronger degree the characteristic of the character it adorns. Sometimes he clothes an elegant Youth in all the purity of white drapery fringed with gold; his feeling for character and expression was perhaps the most exquisite feeling ever bestowed on a human being, his head dresses, his hair, his drapery, his sandals, every ornament, every tassal, were in him vehicles of refinement, delicacy, & character; he did not cloak his women to conceal their beauties but to add interest, to encrease beauty, to excite love, in that lovely creature, in Heliodorus who extends her beautiful hand, her being covered, close about the neck, and to the wrist, while a sort of shawl encircles her arm, are parts of her character, and flowed from Raphael's exquisite feeling at the time he fancied her enchanting face[1] — O Raphael, if thy divine spirit is still sensible to this world, if thou art permitted to hover near those who relish thy beauties, instill thyself into my very soul, breathe on every touch, spread thy influence on every fancy, that I may add thy purity, thy modesty, & thy refinement, to the power providence has in goodness already given me — O God grant I may be good, great, and an honor to the World, — and I shall die happily — Amen — Nov. 1809.

O God grant I may not be satisfied with having prayed to thee for this but from my sincerity by my exertions — under thy blessing — Amen.

When one considers the purity, the perspicuity, the elegance, the grace, the divine refinement, the unaffected correctness of Raphael, how richness, splendour, & effect, the abuse of colour, and all the meretricious allurements attendant on its abuse, fade like ghosts at day break — what delight there is after having luxuriated in wanton voluptuousness on Titian or Rembrant, to lave one's fancy in the crystal fountain of Raphael —

This is the man whom brutality slanders with having died

9. These figures appear in the lower right corner of "The School of Athens," in the Vatican.

1. The figure appears in the lower left corner of "The Expulsion of Heliodorus from the Temple at Jerusalem," in the Vatican.

of disease; is it likely that a man like Raphael, courted by the nobility, caressed by Sovereign powers, living in the hea[r]t of elegance & [re]finement, beautiful & amiable, should be forced to engender with pestilential putridity; is it likely that a man, in the height of fame blooming with the lumen purpureum juventae,[2] should be totally uninteresting to refined beauty, would the man to whom Cardinal Bibiena offered his niece, Leo X a title,[3] would a man of such delicacy of love as Raphael, far removed from all lewdness — sate himself in a celestial bed, & prey on garbage?[4] These are the brutal insinuations of unfeeling ignorance, who rate every man's feelings by their own, who knowing Raphael's propensity to Women, think it must have been as destitute of selection and as deficient in sentiment as the merely animal impulse of a savage — Nov. 1809.

The first moment I awoke this morning Raphael and all his exquisite beauty & refinement flowed into my brain; elegant youths, beautiful women, flying drapery played about my fancy, and I lay an hour in bed before I arose, totally abstracted, in delicious musing. I arose in a steam of feeling, totally indifferent to every thing about me, the idea of having heard it insinuated he died of disease, so disgusted me, that I hope it may [never] again enter my fancy, — O Raphael, may I meet thy etherial spirit in the region of immortality; may I waft in thy society in boundless space — Tho there is such a distance in our existence here, I am he who was born to be thy friend; I am he who really estimate thy excellence, and I hope when I die shall be worthy to meet thee, on my entrance into a new existence; this fancy shall stimulate my exertions; may I be worthy to meet thee on equality. — Nov. 1809.

The cartoons are not the works of Raphael which give one the highest idea of his beauty & refinement; the School of Athens,

2. *Aeneid*, I,590–591. "Lumenque iuventae/purpureum." (And with youth's ruddy bloom).

3. Shortly before his death Raphael became engaged to the niece of Bernardo Divizio, Cardinal of Bibbiena. The marriage was delayed, as Raphael had reason to believe that Pope Leo X intended to make him a cardinal (Vasari, III,220).

4. *Hamlet*, I,v,56–57.

here is every species of educated classical sentiment, every turn of limb, every undulation of hair, and every floating fold of drapery, [which] bespeak the educated, subtilizing spirit of Plato & refinement. There is in the cartoons a rough, apostolic severity, — which shew the extent of his powers and the variety of his feelings, but if I had only seen them, I should not have loved Raphael as I do, nor have had such an Idea of his refinement & Grace —

They shew how compleatly Raphael entered into his subject — how he bent his feelings to propriety — There are exceptions in the Cartoons, but exceptio regulam probat; had beauty & refinement been the general characteristics of the Cartoons these would not have been exceptions —

Before Ananias[5] one trembles with awe. But before the School of Athens one longs to become an inmate of such an educated amiable assembly.*

It would have been a greater proof of Winckelmann's real candour, love for the Art, if instead of setting it down at once as one whose faculties were dulled by Northern foes, he had set about enquiring why the Nation who could boast the greatest Poets, Philosophers, Moralists, Seamen & Statesmen & Soldiers should be so deficient of Genius in Painting — This would have been rational & frank but to write such French impudence, to libel the Nation, and render all who visited Italy liable to such an imputation was unfeeling, brutal — Barry has proved it was owing to local obstruction,[6] — what could it be owing to else — poor thing, I don't wonder at his indignation when at Rome — It [is] hardly worth an answer.

I hope in God we shall all before long proof it in face of the World — No. 1809. Winckelmann is a useless, pedantic, ambiguous rhapsodist.

* But his Cartoons are his greatest Works. B. R. H. May 24, 1835.

5. "The Death of Ananias," one of Raphael's cartoons.
6. After visiting Paris and Rome, James Barry (1741–1806) published *Real and Imaginary Obstruction to the Acquisition of the Arts in England* (1775). He was an artist and professor of painting at the Royal Academy from 1782 until his expulsion from the Academy in 1799 for criticizing his fellow members.

I thought that the Apollo was the extreme of slenderness and length, but I should have recollected that it was united with manly vigour, which in unison with its long, slender, youthful proportions, produce a most exquisite character. What judgement & selection the Ancients had; every figure is of a different character and every character has different proportions, which difference in union with its contour, produces the variation —

The Apollo is two of its feet to the centre of the Patella, and two more to the apex of the Ilium, two feet from bottom of Pubis to insertion of [sterno-cleido-]mastoideus. As in a stronger figure and yet rendering the whole limb longer — In the Hercules, the calf is wider than half a foot and yet the foot bears the same proportion to the limb in length, four to apex of Ilium in Apollo. The principle that guided the Artist in the Paris, to prevent it from being lean & imbecil equally directed him here in the Hercules, that it might not degenerate into heaviness & ponderosity — in the one instance, he preserved the same width of the parts to the foot as in a stronger figure by lengthening the limb, that it might not be weak, and in the other the length of the parts to the foot as in a slender figure, in widening the limb, that it might not become heavy, not increasing the size of the feet & hands & bones, & Scull, where motion & power & strength do not lie, but preserving the parts to be moved, the general length, and encreasing the parts moving — in the one instance preserving the relative width of the limb, to the foot, where slender grace did not lie, and in the other preserving the relative length of the limb to the foot, where strength did not lie — the one having the width of strength and yet slenderly graceful, the other having the length of grace and yet strong — the slender is therefore preserved from being weak & [the] strong from being heavy. The Hercules and Paris are the two extremes, the Apollo is the medium.

The Hercules unites as much of the characteristics of slender grace as prevents his strength being heavy, by having the length of the Apollo's limbs, and the Paris as much strength as takes off the appearance of weakness from his slender grace by having its width — and the Apollo unites as much of the characteristics of either as serves to express manly vigour and youthful grace — as is not incompatible with the perfect union of the two qualities.

The union of the two extremes might produce a new and extraordinary character — Achilles —[7]

From bottom of belly in Apollo to mastoideus — insertion is two feet, in Paris two feet & half, now in Achilles by making the limbs the same length as those of Paris and the same breadth as those of Hercules, I should obtain a fine union of characteristic excellences — Achilles being πόδας ὠκύς,[8] graceful & strong, — the Proportion of the Slender graceful Paris in length would express that quality, the breadth of limbs his strength and his feet the thing to be moved, still keeping the proportion of Hercules, Apollo, & Paris, while his muscles, the things moving, were lengthened & enlarged, would express his swiftness, in short it must express it mathematically — The muscles of the Hercules being enlarged only express his greater power to move his feet with greater strength, and moderate degrees of swiftness, being the length of the Apollo — the length of Paris expresses swiftness, and his breadth of muscle his strength which is moderate, being the breadth of Apollo — now the Achilles having the breadth and strength of Hercules by broad muscles and length & swiftness of Paris by long limbs, and his feet being to be moved by the muscles must have a greater swiftness than Hercules & greater strength than Paris, and consequently be both swift & strong, the character of Achilles (and not being heavier or longer than Hercules & Paris).

Let it be granted length expresses swiftness; breadth, strength; breadth & length, power. A having only breadth will move the foot B only with strength, whereas C who has length & breadth too — will move it with strength & swiftness, and consequently with greater Power than A.[9]

Insertion of calf — a foot — inside a little more than two feet from heel to top of gastrocnemius. Navel a foot from bottom of belly, nipples half a foot wide from sternum, same in Paris — also a foot & half from Deltoid to Elbow — apex Ilium to navel half —

7. BRH illustrated his discussion by four anatomical diagrams, representing Hercules, Apollo, Paris, and Achilles. On the same page he also drew a rough sketch of a head, which he labeled "B. R. Haydon, thinking. 1810."
8. "Swift of foot," an epithet frequently used to describe Achilles; for example, *Iliad*, I,58.
9. No diagram accompanies this statement.

Clavicles half each to origin of the clavicular portion of Deltoid.

Extreme Greek character of head — Jaw three noses, Forehead, one — which is again divided, and at the half are the top of corrugators —

From nostril to the end of jaw, where ear begins, two noses exactly; from there to insertion of mastoideus, three noses exactly — the Forehead is one at its widest and half a one at its narrowest — eyes a third in width inside lid to top of other [lid] — a third from bottom of nose to the bottom of under lip (now in heads yet beautiful and not extreme Greek — it is a third to the end of upper lip —) from nostril [to] end of upper lip a third — from centre of chin to end of orbit two noses exactly — a nose from mouth to under eyelid (in the other heads which have their upper a third it is a nose from mouth to orbit, not eyelid — this generally accompanies that proportion of lip; yet the Meleager has an extreme Greek upper lip, which gives a beautiful character notwithstanding its eyes and other parts are not extreme Greek — this is a delightful combination) mouth three fourths — eyes two fourths & half [a fourth] — the ear seems invariably two noses from the nose sideway.

The Paris is smaller in relative size than the Apollo but larger in relative proportion. A figure may be ten heads high in itself tho only as tall [as a] figure 3 inches high in reality, and another may [be] 50 cubits high and only 6 heads in itself, and therefore a short figure. The figure three Inches [high] will have a more powerful look and taller than the other if it were as high & heavier with these proportions.

Fine hands are a third of the width of the Foot at Knuckles, Raphael's half —

Raphael has always kept his feet the general proportion (4 feet to apex Ilii) yet has made his heads & hands larger; his figures are therefore never more than six heads & half high, and yet by keeping his feet the proportion of taller figures in length, he has prevented them looking short, his figures are the same number of feet, but not the same number of heads, by this extraordinary union whether from principle or feeling, his figures never look short. They have always a natural, human look; they look like middle sized men for this is the principle on which middle sized men are built, and it agrees with Raphael's expressions and characters better than the long God-like limbs of the inspired ages of Greece —

Raphael often left his forms defective if he had hit an expression, as Rubens did, when he had dashed in a fine colour. This is not perfection; a brow is bent, a nostril opened, or a mouth extended, by muscles, attached to them for that purpose. When the expression requires a brow to be bent over the eye, you are not to content yourself by an inefficient scrawl which half covers the eye, and gives the expression, but you are to mark the brow in the exact shape it takes in nature in such a moment, as the Greeks did, to obtain the expression. These imbecil scrawls are excused from the intellect expressed.

A man ought to acquire the knowledge of the exact forms of things; the dashes of his brush would be the dashes of science, instead of imbecility; and having the same conception of the intellectual part, the expression of it would be the expression of truth, and of Nature —

A man in the early part of his existence should impregnate his mind with principles & science, and not suffer himself to do any thing but what he can account for or do again. Rather suffer the imputation of tedious anxiety and dull stupidity by carefully investigating, that you may one day be enabled to give vent to your feelings with furious certainty, than for the gratification of hastening before the Public; send them into the World, expressed with all the boldness & ignorance of imbecil inexperience, much of the spirit of a first fancy may certainly evaporate, and labour may be too apparent, let it be so; you are every day raising a fabric that ascending to the principles of things, will not easily fall, by choosing none but the strong bricks to lay at the foundation. Let your foundation be but strong, and you may give vent to your fancies in the upper stories without risk of falling. A man of Genius knows his powers; the world can only judge by what they see; never be frightened from your plan, if it be the result of principle & meditation by the remarks of folly & ignorance, or urged to haste, from impatience, to convince mankind of your talents, before he has perfected the arguments necessary to express them.

If you know & feel you have fancies & feelings and conception, and only want the power to express them as they ought to be expressed, be content to express fewer at first, that you so do it with a care; bear with firmness ridicule & slander, the time will come & the hour will arrive, when execution will rush like a torrent, and as fast as visions float on your fancy, your vigourous hand, steady from Practice, and your judgement sound from science, will be ready to shower them on your canvas with inspired profusion — and resistless impetuosity.

There are men who spend their lives in useless preparation, who all their life study nothing but anatomy because anatomy is useful. This is Idleness under a mask — this the abuse of acquirement — I allude to those who proceed, and not those who stand still; proceed ever so slowly, if you proceed you will arrive at last, you may be taken up on your journey, these are the chances of life. This chance surely is better to be taken after having executed two or three pictures, as finely as your powers permitted you, than as the middle of unexecuted projects & promised amendment —

You hear some men say of themselves "Study is no use; if I did not do it at once, I could never do it." If they *did* it at once, I would bow to their notions but do they do it at once? If you saw in their productions every variation of form, produced by the slightest variation of motion, if you saw proportions characteristic of every character, if you saw every muscle start forward, in its place that that action only requires to produce that action, and others in repose that ought to be so — if you saw fine refined expression, fine colour, fine arrangement, fine light & Shadow, Flesh with its peculiar characteristics of sharpness & softness, fine character of heads, fine hands, fine feet, fine ankles, fine elbows, fine backs, and heroic limbs, — if you saw these requisites of an excellence in the productions of those men of no Study, you would tremble at the inspiration and relinquish the art in despair — but do you see this is not the very reverse [of] the truth? Are not these Pictures the very essence of manner, affectation, falsehood, & absurdity; from knowing little they are anxious that that little should be obtruded on the ignorant world, that they might be supposed to know more —

One would excuse all this was it the affectation of knowledge, one may gain something by a foolish exhibition of real knowledge, but who ever became wiser from contemplating an affected display of ignorance? There is the absurdity.

Where this is then the character of the works, and you can point out fault after fault, without effort to hear them talk that unless they do it at once, study would never enable them to do it; — meaning of course that they have done it — is really laughable — all those who affect not to Study and investigate, I have always found do study and investigate in some degree; if investigation is absurd, why do it at all? If you do it at once without investigation, what occasion is there to examine any thing? You are an inspired man, you are pregnant with resources, you are full of beauties, why do you look at a limb, or a head, or Raphael or Michel Angelo, or the Greeks — why? — the answer is obvious — the faculty of receiving impressions is born with a man — this no Study can acquire — you do not study to acquire this feeling, if you have it not from Nature, no Study will acquire it, but you study to improve it, you study to impregnate this faculty, that it may produce; all Study will produce nothing, without this faculty and this faculty will be useless without Study — without investigation, you will do that which has been before done, investigation gives you a knowledge of the beauties as well as defects of your predecessors and enables [you] to avoid their defects and supply their deficiencies, if you have any original faculty from Nature —

(They know they don't do it enough, and therefore boldly say they don't do it [at] all that the little they do acquire may appear like inspiration) — and that the absurdities they are guilty of may be more readily excused — By investigating at all, you acknowledge it to be necessary and if necessary, why do it by halves, root out every thing to the bottom — dive through it and through it. You can always judge of any man from part of his conduct, if he be content, to skim the surface, in one instance, when he ought to plunge into Deep, he will do so in all.

I discovered another proof today at the Elgin Marbles of the exquisite judgement, Science and feeling of the Greeks. There are two figures in the collection with their left leg and thigh extended from their body. One thigh is supported upon its leg, and (consequently in perfect inaction), by the leg resting against the body of a centaur — the leg supporting the thigh below, and the arm & hand supporting the body above, the thigh being between them, hangs loosely, of course, and the muscles roll, in relaxation. The tensor vaginae femoris,[1] the glutaeus medius, the Pectorals, &c., Triceps, Rectus, all the muscles that arise from the pelvis and attach the thigh to it, by which the thigh hangs, are in quiet repose — Mark their descrimination in the other figure; the leg & thigh are jirked out, free in the air, unsupported, resting on nothing; these muscles must then exert themselves or the thigh would again fall back — they do exert themselves with vigour, and the thigh seems to need no support, it seems to support itself by its own power, even this has the appearance of vigour and activity.

The contour of the one is feeble & round, while that of the other is sharp, braced, and acute. Look at the hip 1, it seems supported below, while 2 has only the look of supporting itself, by its own strength — [2]

The slightest variation — even on the fleshy Pubis at bottom of rectus in first figure, the belly is protruded forward by the Action, thus fleshy Pubis is then drawn back on the bone and takes the above shape, but in the other when the belly is rolled in, the Pubis loses its shape, and is lost — the two spermatic cords being only apparent — every part having fallen back on them — is this accident — the Greeks were lucky fellows, always to hit the mark, blindfolded — !!!

This is not fancy, but actual truth. I can demonstrate it to be so, and there is an end — I could without much effort mention a man that would say how many *can* discover this? If you are defective, who will know it, if this was the principle of every man of genius, who would ever rise above ignorance — it is those refinements, imperceptible to unscientific inexperience, that distinguish great men from other human beings — It is by these delicate beauties the Greeks have reached the top, and the moderns will never equal or outstrip them, but by similar exhibitions

1. That is, the tensor fasciae latae.
2. Four rough diagrams illustrate these points.

of investigative & deep research — but no trouble need be taken
— sit still and this will come by intuition and if you don't do it
at once, you'll never do it by Study —

If a limb is extended, it is extended, and that would have been
enough, no matter whether it was supported below, or above, it
is extended, and this would have been a sufficient excuse for any
modern to tear up every muscle, and flea [*sic* for *flay*] every part
— who would have attended to this variation of form, — every
thing in them is reason, and good sense, this is their foundation —
who would have thus reasoned, on the cause — you made the
right use of science and knowledge, O Greeks, you made it subservient to truth, you brought it not into contempt, by superfluous exhibition.

Men are too anxious to let the world see what they know; let
them see it by looking for it but do not obtrude it on them, with
affected pomposity — how many beauties in nature peep unob-
served but to those who seek them, she is always modest & unassuming — yet take her more scientific —she never is hid. Dec.
9th, 1809.

I went to Covent Garden to night,[3] nothing could exceed the
vigour and alacrity of the O. P.'s.[4] The Duke of Gloucester[5] made
his appearance in his private Box, and was instantly greeted, by
repeated cheers, a good private character has always its weight
with the People — it had the grandest effect to hear one or two
thousand People stamp at once on the seats, and cry out in time
"O. P., O. P., O. P.," laying a vigourous emphasis on the P. — They
sung God save the King, in his Presence, and again gave him
three cheers, — when he retired — some constables made their
appearance, "turn them out," vociferated a thousand voices, and
about a hundred people in a body bore down like a torrent, on
them, and rolled them out of the Pit; at the conclusion the Gal-

3. A playbill in the Theatre Collection of the Harvard College Library shows
that BRH attended "a grand melo-dramatick opera" entitled *The Exile* and a
farce, *The Portrait of Cervantes, or The Plotting Lovers.*
4. When the new Covent Garden Theatre was opened in 1809, prices of admission were advanced. Public riots occurred at the theatre during December as a
protest, the rioters shouting "O. P.," meaning "Old Prices," and disrupting many
performances (*Annual Register*, 1809, pp. 404–408).
5. The second Duke of Gloucester (1776–1834), who married one of George
III's daughters in 1816.

lery proposed three cheers for the Pit, which was instantly agreed to, and the Pit in return cheered the Gallery. As I came home a drunken man ran against me — I caught him by the arm, and preserved him from falling. "God bless you," said he with his eyes glassy & fixed, — "O. P. for ever." — Dec. 9th, 1809.

Before I draw any conclusions, I shall simply write all the proportions I have attained from various Statues —

I shall begin with Elgin Marbles. One of the little heads of the Panathenaic procession — Four noses in the head — from the forehead to top of head is not quite a nose — angle of throat, corner of the mouth, is a nose, when the head is perfectly horizontal — Bottom and angle of nostril to top of eyelid, a nose. Bottom of mouth orbit, a nose. Mouth, a third, sideways. Tip of the nose to under lip, a third. Nostril, from thence a half of a third. From upper lip to where the nose ends to almost the end of under lip, a third. This is extreme Greek — and is generally accompanied by other beauties, which harmonize with this exquisite shortness of upper lip, so absent from all brutality — but this being the strong characteristic of human beauty, and the others, as it were, depending on this, and not solely expressing human beauty, without the aid of this shortness of upper lip, are often varied, or omitted, and this characteristic of extreme human beauty is united with other characteristics which belong to upper lips, not so exquisitely short — which is an exquisite union and perhaps puts one more in remembrance of nature and less of art, than this extreme shortness of upper lip when joined to its other extreme characteristics — for instance when the upper lip is a third of itself, from the angle of the mouth to the orbit of the eye is a nose, now when the upper lip is less than a third of nose and the third almost takes in both lips from the angle of the mouth to the under eyelid is a nose, instead of to the orbit — so that the eye is pulled down as it were and consequently enlarged. This is as far as Idea can go, to make the eye larger would be rediculous, in the other instance to make it smaller would be ugly, and when the eye is smaller, it is accompanied by a length of upper lip, short nose, and other usual characteristics of ugliness — the Ancients seem to have had a standard of beauty and every artist varied it according to his feelings or his wants — the Figures on Monte

Cavallo,[6] I should take as the Standard, and a correct knowledge of their characteristics of proportion would be a sufficient foundation to work upon to make your own use of as you wished to express any peculiar character of intellect, any peculiar beauty, or any peculiar characteristic of strength, swiftness, or agility, taking reason and reflection as a guide. As the characteristic of humanity is intellect, a perfectly human head & face, where the expression of intellect lies, should be in every respect removed from any thing animal or brutal; this should be the standard; in some characters you might wish to express any peculiar animal propensity, having this standard of what exclusively belongs to man to build upon, you would know where to lay the stress, to express this peculiarity, so having a standard of form as far removed from animal characteristics as possible, if you wanted to express any peculiar animal characteristic, in an eminent degree, having this standard to work upon, you would work with certainty and sense.*

The various characters, the various forms & beauties, the innumerable peculiarities of humanity must be left to the Artist's own observation, feeling, & research — This standard once fixed, and once seated in every man's mind, he will be able without error and without stumbling to vary it, according [to] his own fancies, feelings or visionary conceptions — This I think was the principle of the Greeks — and on this principle only can we account for the contradictory variety of proportions we find among them — As the head of the Figure of Monte Cavallo is so peculiarly human and consistent in itself, one may judge the rest of the Figure is so likewise. This is the reason I would choose that as the standard — the mouth, the nostril, the eyes, the neck, every part, is peculiarly beautified, unaffected, and so exactly the right forms of things cut out with so much power, nothing affected, nothing

* This was written as mere conjecture 1809; since, Thank God, I have proved my conjecture was founded in truth.

6. The Piazza del Quirinale in Rome (formerly known as the Piazza del Monte Cavallo) contains two large marble statues, now generally called the "Horse Tamers" but formerly believed to be the Dioscuri (not to be confused with the Castor and Pollux near the Piazza del Campidoglio). Inscriptions on the bases of the statues erroneously identify them as the work of Phidias and Praxiteles.

more or less than there ought to be, every thing on good sense
and science and nature —

This head, and the Elgin Horse's head, are a perfect example
of what the highest genius will do, when curbed & guided by
science. Here is the highest degree of fire. They are full of what
the World call genius & vigour, but this fire, vigour & animation
is not expressed at the expence of truth & correctness — every
thing is probable — These examples of the stupendous genius of
Antiquity are perfect examples of what art ought to be, and
what every man ought to struggle to attain — the most vigourous,
animated, momentary expression with the most perfect science,
the most perfect correctness — expressed with the most perfect
facility —

The moderns equal the Ancients in facility but they do not so
steep it in science that it may not be thrown away — here lies
the distinction — I never look at that horse's head but I fancy I
see the Artist in a fury fix his chisel at a point, and with a blow
rip round with the rapidity of lightning — and stop — he then
changed his direction and with another blow ran along on the
verge of incorrectness, with perfect security — again checked his
fire — where he ought. In an instant that furious eye started from
the stone — the next moment the nostril, the mouth, the jaw, and
every muscle that ought to move trembled on the marble. The
artist, overpowered by his feeling, would then rest exhausted &
contemplate in agitation — These are the moments of rapture
every Man of Genius sees as the reward, at the end of his disappointments and labour — till this delightful stupendous power is
acquired, what miseries, what anxieties, what checks, what struggles must he not undergo —

But if he has but the resolution to proceed firmly through
them and never be content till he has done what he wished, never
be daunted by difficulties however great, or danger however per-
ilous — then indeed will his reward be great, then indeed will his
faculty, hardened by practice & impregnated by science, enable
him to execute as furiously as he conceives and to conceive as
rapidly as he executes —

This almost looks like happiness too great for this World —
yet do I, presumptuously, I fear, O God, dare pray thee on my

knees to grant it may be my lot before I close my existence —
Amen — In humbleness and awe —

We all know how many fancies & visions, how many beautiful
arrangements & refined expressions pass into oblivion for the
want of this power in our youth. 'Tis this power we all fag for,
not Ideas. The sooner then this power is acquired, the happier &
greater is the artist — but this power can not be acquired but by
never suffering any atom to remain uninvestigated & unresearched
— till at last all nature is laid open, all animated being is at his
disposal and under his controul — I do mean, when I say every
atom ought [not] to remain uninvestigated, I do not allude to
those mindless investigations, those marks of idleness, consulting
records & antiquaries for costume &c — I do not mean that you
should perplex yourself about the shape of an Egyptian's beard,
or a Roman sandal — but what I mean by never leave one atom
uninvestigated refers to those permanent invariable beauties of
form, character & expression — if you can acquire an accurate
knowledge of the dress of nations, acquire it — do not go out of
your way for it — do not neglect the study of form, &c. to acquire
it; never hesitate a moment if you wish to shew any peculiar
human beauty of motion or form to strip the sandal from your
Roman or your Egyptian. Those beauties are as lasting as the
creation, but the others were as flax[7] and as changeable as the
fate of the Nation to whom they belong — but here as every
where else your own discretion must be your conductor.

I now refer to the peculiar character of various heads.

The Apollo is a singular figure; it is only four of its feet to the
apex Ilii, and two from Pubis to mastoideus — like the Hercules
— but the calf of the Hercules' leg is more than half its foot, the
thigh in proportion; while the Apollo is not so much and the
thigh is in proportion — the Apollo is slender by this means, but
the foot certainly has an extraordinary long look — by the calf &
thigh being reduced thus as it were — The first two feet of the
Apollo come to the center of the Patella — the first of the Hercules reach its top — the next two feet to the apex Ilii in the

---

7. Judges, 15:14. "And the Spirit of the Lord came mightily upon him [Sam-
son], and the cords that were upon his arms became as flax that was burnt with
fire, and his bands loosed from off his hands."

Apollo, so in the Hercules, so that the Apollo has no more in the whole than the Hercules, and the leg being thus lengthened, the thigh has a very short look — I cannot see any reason why it should be so — I don't know that short thighs or long feet express any of his peculiar characteristics — I should think the reverse — from the position of the Hercules, it is two feet from the penis to mastoideus, but was he erect & stretched like the Apollo, it would be two from Pubis, he certainly loses this in length by the sinking, bending position of his body — The Nipples are half foot from Sternum, so are the nipples of Hercules — this is a peculiar manly characteristic and is always a mark of fine, powerful forms — it is so in the Elgin Theseus and the finest Lapithae — and also from Nature — one might say it belonged exclusively to the Hercules & Theseus — and being mingled with the Apollo, and softened into harmony with his delicacies gives him a fine noble air — a head is generally as long as a foot — half a foot is then two noses or from forehead to end of nose — but the Apollo's head is by no means a foot and half; its head is considerably less than half its foot, so that supposing its foot to be according to its head, its limb would be an extraordinary length, which is counteracted by its foot being in length the proportion of shorter figures — instead of four feet only from apex Ilii to ground, it would be four feet, a half, and a third (taking the length of the foot from the head). The calf would then be more than half.

The head of the Apollo is to its body small in comparison with the heads of other figures to the bodies — The artist has built the figure from the foot certainly — not from the head — There is no saying the calf is the full size of manly vigour, supposing he made [it] from the head, and the chest is [of] this character supposing he formed it from the foot — it is useless & uncertain how he did, such the figure is —

Insertion of its calf a foot from ground. Two feet & a little more from ground to top of gastrocnemius. The calf is not a half a foot wide — navel half foot from bottom of belly, nipples a foot asunder —

The Apollo certainly is a singular combination — and by no means in the highest style — it has a systematic awkward look, when one looks at it, and recollects for a moment, the suppleness, activity, length of limb, and God like activity of the first Lapitha grappling the centaur or the lofty grandeur of the figures on Monte Cavallo — it won't stand the comparison with all its majesty —

I should be happy if I could produce such a figure as the Apollo but I should be much happier to produce the Theseus, the Lapitha, the Monte Cavallo figure, or the Elgin Woman — This is my exact feeling. The Apollo is a fine production, but these are finer — ten thousand times finer.

According to its Head, the width and height are extreme but to its Foot, the general proportion, to that tho' length predominates, it's so tempered by the foot that it predominates not in the extreme. It is the striking characteristic of the figure, majestic tallness kept in check by the foot relating only the right proportion. The artist could not have gained his point on another principle or in any other way.

The one is all vigourous activity, beauty, & nature, the other all poverty, system & ugliness — large ankle, large knee, & bow legged, actually the Apollo has a Roman air — the other, all the beauty & Style of Grecian refinement. Very likely had the feet been made in proportion to the head, its extreme length would have compared with the breadth of its calf, the foot being the general proportion to the body & limbs. The extreme length of the body & limbs to the head is not too apparent, tho it affects you, but is kept from striking you too strongly, as a defect, which it would do was it not that the foot is in general proportion to the limb — This [is] the only view I see there, viz. that the foot is larger than the head. — Dec. 1809.

A man ought to acquire a knowledge of the exact forms of things not before he begins to express his Ideas, but in the act of expressing them — thus if when he is painting a limb or head of any character, he is ignorant, stop & survey art & Nature and then proceed again; by thus doing you put instantly in practice what you acquire, fix it in your memory, and perfect theory & practice at once — you must gain a certain degree of mechanical power before you begin certainly — but when once you can draw with tolerable correctness, it is time to commence —

Painting is Ideas conveyed by forms. An exact knowledge of these forms by which Ideas are conveyed is therefore requisite to express them clearly — and the compleat power of representing those forms on canvas, constitutes the painter — the only method of acquiring this power is by never suffering any part to pass uninvestigated or without being rooted out, and never at the same time suffer them to remain unexpressed — never mind how tamely soever you express them at first, but express every thing distinctly and on the same principle as a child runs, after a little time walking, will your hand & brush fly over your canvas, and hit out Ideas by forms — This power comes of itself, if a man is perfectly ignorant of every principle — from mere mechanical repetition makes a man [*an illegible word*] than ignorant execution. It is then objected to by all, who underate it from its abuse — this is no argument against it — common feeling tells us nothing is more delightful than to see Ideas expressed with facility — the only thing is to regulate and educate your mind & impregnate it with knowledge at first that when facility pours in on your hand from habitual exercise, your mind may know where exactly to direct the fury of your hand — This is the great principle of Painting — to acquire this rapturous Power are the efforts of Genius directed — Application brings this out but does not nor ever will supply the deficiency.

A Singer must have a voice, a Hercules muscle, a Dancer a leg, and the powers of the mind are not from nature, no — all men [are] equal in powers of intellect, forsooth any man can be a man of genius who tries!! but no men sing or dance or pull down a house but who have powers from Nature — What is this against reason, to say that Michel Angelo was born with powers to paint as Catalani[8] was to sing — application only can bring them out —

What do the Rooms of the English Nobility exhibit but inefficient sources of imbecil intellects? What books do you see on the tables? Do you see Homer, Milton, or Johnson? No, these are [too] powerful for their enervated faculties, Histoire secrèt de court de Berlin, Lettres de Sévigné, les exiles de Sibérie and such trifling efforts of French puppeism and effeminacy — to these

8. Angelica Catalani (1780–1849), Italian soprano, considered England's leading prima donna after her debut in London in 1806.

puny contemptible frivolities they turn for relaxation; they take more delight in studying court intrigue [than] in being roused to Heroic action by a passage of Homer, than to rejoice in the hymns of Milton's angels or have taken delights in having their minds excited, to the investigation of moral truth by Johnson's vigourous meditations. They take more pleasure in perusing the puny letters of wanton maids of honor. It [is] more gratifying to their effeminate voluptuous ineffective souls to weep, but a foolish form of purest sensibility.

December 17. There was something extremely soothing and tranquillizing to me after I had been spending weeks in the solitary gloom of my Study, sometimes distracted at the discovery of how little I knew, and sometimes acutely miserable at the reflection of my past Idleness, there was something very delightful in the illuminated gay splendor of Lord Mulgrave's apartments, which together with his affable manners and amusing conversation, spread a calm over my troubled soul I had not felt for months. I returned better pleased with myself, and the World, and passed the night in such quiet repose as had not lately fell to my Fortune*—

I this day commenced Macbeth on a new canvas — I proceeded with the other but was compleatly checked by the difficulties I experienced — I then stopped in misery. I felt I was ignorant — I knew so much of the art as shewed me what I wanted, but not what I should do — I looked at Raphael, Antique, surveyed all the collections I had access to — came home evenings, and dwelt with agony on my inefficiency. At my age Raphael was perhaps, I thought, versed in every principle of art, but here am I just emerging from ignorance — every hour new notions dawned on me. I saw beauties that I had before passed over with indifference; I felt excellencies I had before no concep-

* This was written when I was agitated by the apparent neglect of Lord M[ulgrave], who I am sorry to say thought less of Dentatus because it was hung in the dark, till the year after it won the prize at [the] Gallery—[9]

9. On May 17, 1810, "Dentatus" received the British Institution's prize of one hundred guineas for the best historical picture (*Autobiography*, I,104–105).

tion of — I rejoiced at my being checked, I was delighted I had met with opposition which tho it produced misery, excited enquiry, and knowledge was the result — I once more relinquished despair, Hope stimulated me again to exertion. I ordered another canvas, and renovated by converse with the greatest minds, began with better prospects, and sturdier determination — Dec. 17th, 1809.

This must be the progress of him who struggles after unattainable excellence, and let no man be soothed, by indolent imbecility, into a notion that he can approach it by roads less frequented by danger or opposition.

I think the faculty of Genius is distinguished from mere susceptibility in this way. A man of mere susceptibility is violently & entirely impressed by external circumstances, the impression dies away, and there is an end — But he who has the faculty of Genius is as acutely impressed, which impression excites his faculty to work, and something original is the result, is the produce — in the former it produces mere expressions, delight or rapture — there can be genius without susceptibility — the power may exist but nothing will get at it — it will be useless, — susceptibility is the door by which Ideas enter — the faculty of Genius is like a mill which may go on grinding to all eternity and you may wait at the bottom with your bag in anxious expectation, but no flour will fill it, unless corn is thrown in at the top — the Ideas of others come in to the men of no Genius, and come out again, as they come in, untouched, unaltered — but they make their exit from the mill of genius reground, refreshed & regenerated —

This principle will account for imitators who, having no faculty of their own, send forth their masters' ideas, manners, and absurdities, uninvestigated; some there are who having a portion, refine the notions of others, tho they have not the power to obliterate all traces of the fountain from which they draw up. He is not the greatest genius who is most unlike others, but he who combines what others have done with what he himself has from Nature, and something the world never before saw is the result.

The Artist has sometimes chosen the head, as his guide and sometimes the foot. The calf has the width of strength, as to [the] head — the chest the width of strength as to the foot — the calf is thus slender in extreme according to foot, and chest wide in extreme according to head — as slender grace is spread over the Apollo — the width of parts is generally from the head and the head being small tho the width is the full width of strength, is measured from it — yet the width as to the length of parts is not the feet width of strength — but the proportion of slenderness — The Slenderness is kept in check by the length being the common proportion to the foot and the width being the common proportion to the head — In common the head & foot are the same length, but here the head is smaller than the foot — slenderness and manly vigour are exquisitely united by the head being smaller as to the height — and the foot being the right length as to the height —

Slenderness is produced by length of limb, manly vigour by breadth of limb. The head ought to be the same length as the foot —

If then you build a figure from the foot and make it [the] right length, if you make the head smaller, the length according to the head will be longer than according to the foot — your figure then according to the head will be a slender figure; if you make the breadth of limb the manly breadth, from your head, yet the head being smaller than the foot, and manly figures have the head the same size — still your figure will be a slender one — because the head is smaller than the foot — and you have taken your breadth from your head & not from the foot — the figure then according to the head is a slender figure in length, and in breadth according to the foot, is a slender figure also — and yet according to the foot it is not a slender figure, in length — and according to [the] head it is not a slender figure in breadth either, so that it is a manly figure according to the head in breadth, and to the foot in length, and a youthful slender figure according to the head in length and the foot in breadth — the proportion of slenderness and manliness are therefore united — and yet, to obtain a peculiar manly beauty, he has made the breadth of every part according to the head and not to the foot in all the breadth of the limbs.

The nipples ought to be a foot asunder; this is the characteristic of manly strength. The head is the length of the foot — but in this figure [the] head [is] not the length of the foot — therefore had the nipples been broad from the head according to the foot, they would not have been [the] breadth of manly vigour, but of slenderness — yet as the limbs are the breadth of manliness according to the head, why not the chest too — if the breadth of the chest had been proportioned from the head — like the limbs — it would have a decided character of slenderness throughout, and no part being in breadth according to the foot, the foot would apparently and decidedly would have been out of place, and too long for its breadth, but by making the breadth of the nipple from the foot — you sanction the length of the foot as there is some part in the body that bears its breadth from it and carries it off, as it were — and by making one of the parts manly breadth from the foot, as the whole length is manly from the foot — you compleatly intermingle the opposite beauties of slenderness & manly vigour — it is the link of the union —

Had the figure been the proportion of manly vigour in length only according to the foot and in breadth only according to the head, the line would have been too strongly drawn — there would have been a division — the foot would have been decidedly too long for its breadth or the head too small for its length — but by making manly vigour one part here in its breadth from the foot as all the other part of manly vigour is this length, you prevent the length of the foot from being out of place, and sanction its appearance in a figure the proportions of which according to its head are the proportions of extreme slenderness — and by enabling it to maintain its place as a figure of such a character according to its head — you prevent its being that character wholly and from an exquisite & delightful union of two characters — the head is therefore prevented from look[ing] too much from the foot, and foot too long by the breadth of the nipples — The head is small to express slender youth, and the foot long, manly vigour, the nipples being broad according to the foot unite the two — as the link by which they can unite — this intermingles them —

The result is the Apollo, a composite of manly vigour & youthful slenderness — It is the proportion of manly vigour from its foot, and youthful slenderness from its head — If the foot was the same size (as in other figures) as the head is, it would [be] a figure of youthful slenderness only. — If the head was the proportion the foot is, it would [be] a figure of manly vigour only, but by making the foot and head different, the one bearing the proportion to the whole of manly vigour and the other to the whole of youthful slenderness, a composition of the two characters is affected —

This is the last night of the year 1809 — a year perhaps of greater Idleness & folly, disappointment and anxiety I have not experienced since I commenced my Studies — such is my irregularity, & folly, that I dare not, O God, conclude it with one hope of amendment, in trembling awe, I trust in thee through Jesus Christ my Saviour, my mind is pregnant with hopes, & wishes, plans and schemes of virtue & industry & ambition. O God I humbly ask thee to pardon my past wickedness, on condition of future virtue — on this condition only I ask it thro Jesus Christ — my Blessed Saviour — O God listen to me, listen to my last prayer, uttered in the sincerity of pungent repentence. Amen — Amen — Amen —*

* This Folly & Idleness was the result of the bitter and acute disappointment, from the ill treatment of the Academy — who took Dentatus on which my Future hopes hinged — & placed it in the *dark* — I lost my Patrons — & sunk into a species of despair & embarrassment from which I have had occasional gleams of Sunshine but never permanent fortune — The conduct of Phillips,[1] Howard,[2] Shee,[3] & Flaxman[4] — who composed the Council 1809 — to a picture built on such everlasting principles, & to a young man like myself of most extreme enthusiasm & uprightness of feeling at that time, a young man wanted in fact — threw a cloud on the whole of my life — embarrassments, exasperations followed — I attacked & exposed the conduct of such men — I lost all employment & sunk to a Prison — but I will live to

1. Thomas Phillips (1770–1845), R.A., portrait painter, professor of painting at the Academy from 1825 to 1832.
2. Henry Howard (1769–1847), R.A., portrait and historical painter.
3. Martin Archer Shee (1769–1850), portrait and historical painter, one of the founders of the British Institution in 1807. He was knighted on becoming president of the Royal Academy in 1830; he held the position until his death.
4. John Flaxman (1755–1826), R.A., sculptor.

It is now three years since I first became acquainted with Sir George B[eaumon]t. I was at first fascinated by his affability, his smiles, his flattery, his advice expressed and uttered with all the warmth of sincerity and regard — in the fervor of my youthful heart I believed no man had any intention but that of benevolence — I believed none could have such fundamentally wicked propensities as to be gratified with seducing youthful inexperience, for the mere purpose of abandoning it at the first blast of unsuccess. He called on me, liked my Picture, about a day or two afterwards he again called, and expressed a wish to have a sketch, when I had concluded my Joseph and Mary; tho' approving it he advised me not to exhibit it; this first excited a doubt in my mind of his sincerity; from this moment I examined his character with wary suspicion. Sir G. B[eaumon]t is a man who wishes to have the reputation of bringing forward Genius without much expence, if a young man promises any thing, he immediately procures a slight sketch for a trifle; if this youth succeeds he has something to shew, to prove he first employed him, he first had acuteness to discover his talents — if on the contrary he fails, the sketch passes into oblivion, he denies all knowledge or recollection of him, and every thing relating to him is forgotten —

This being Sir G.'s principle of action, this being his profession, only, unconnected with any real love for the Art, or very sincere wish for its advancement, it follows from human principles he must be jealous of any rival — and when he objected to

---

triumph completely yet — O God grant it genocchione. B. R. Haydon. May 24, 1835.

I have triumphed — I have had the pleasure to see Howard, Phillips & Shee before a Committee 1836 [5] — & could not help thinking as I looked at them — waiting for examination about their coats & candles — There was a Providence that shapes our ends rough hew them how we will [6] — B. R. Haydon. Jan. 19, 1837.

5. BRH outlined their evidence in his diary for June 25 through July 16, 1836.
6. *Hamlet*, V,ii,10–11.

my exhibiting Joseph & Mary, it was not from any fear lest it might injure me, but from a fear that this Picture might attract some other person's attention, and I might plunge into notice before I was employed by him — and some other person might have the credit of bringing me forward; that this was his real reason was evident enough from his desiring me not to mention he had requested me not to exhibit it. Why should he wish to conceal it, if he feared not his motive would immediately be discovered by those who better knew his character than he suspected I did myself —

Sir George never comes to Town, but he brings Doubt, Irresolution & Misery in his train, to let loose upon every Artist, as his whim directs or his fancy excites — he is one who has been unsettled always himself, is unsettled now, who unsettles every body else, and settles nobody, whose specious, fascinating, syren advice will bewilder, enchain and distract the firmest mind, with whom it was impossible to resolve, or determine, till you were without the magic circle of his manners, and if you had then brought your mind to a point and were again to venture with vigourous confidence within this influence, you would soon find your resolution fade and your whole mind shook by such perplexing distraction, by his refined, artful, and pungent attacks, that it was only by a sudden paroxism of violent exertion you could prevent your "prison'd soul" [7] from yielding paralised to his controul, and with effeminate relinquishment bowing, in fascination to his bewildering fancy.

Sir George is always under the influence of some fancy, and this he has the power of communicating to others with such fascination, that no man can resist him, — While this fancy lasts, he acts with real warmth, and sincerity, but it is soon succeeded by a new one which sets things before him in a new light, and he then thinks it no dishonour or immorality to act and speak as this directs him, tho it be in compleat contradiction to his former opinions. This is I think the principle of his conduct and not from any diabolical wish of pulling a man down after he has set him up, — but that if one year he is in raptures, and the next in horrors — that he really feels what he says in both years — such a

7. *Comus*, l. 256.

man of rank is a dangerous character, for when the feeling is not regulated by principle of him who has power, what misery can he not produce?

Time could tell a tale of many a Man of Genius elevated & depressed, harrassed & ruined, the Victim of Sir George's seduction, who either distrusted their own powers from his ridicule, and sank, in despair — or despised his weakness, and relinquished, in indignation — As so few think for themselves and so many are fools, and Sir G. is surrounded by shoals of both, and as he who has resolution to give opinions be they what they may, is always listened to by those who have neither opinion or resolution, the influence Sir G. has had among the nobility is not to be wondered at.

I looked up to Sir George Beaumont when I first knew & heard of him, as one sincerely anxious for the advancement of the Art of his Country, as one who if he saw a young man struggling with the difficulties of art, struggling to improve the taste of his country, would put forth his hand and exert his power and influence to second his exertions, who would as it were make common cause, for the Public advance of art — whose sole anxiety and wish was to bring forward young men, and to support and nourish old ones, — but alas, this cloud of delusion soon dissolved before my sight — in a short time I saw through the inmost recesses of his heart. I penetrated his plans, his intentions.

Sir G. B. is a man whom I consider as playing a deep game, and all the World his opponents, he is a man of rooted meaness of heart, who would as soon have Blood wrung from him as money — and this he tries to conceal from the world, by wishing to appear a liberal patron of Art. One cannot help admiring the skill with which he manages this, tho' one detests the motive — Lord M[ulgrave] is a liberal fine hearted unsuspicious man, ignorant of Pictures and ignorant of Art, wishing to have the reputation of being a connoiseur and caring not for his money — Sir G. B. then has fixed his talons on Lord M. whom he makes buy while he only praises — he brings forward young men while Lord M. employs them. They are therefore playing on each, Sir George through Lord Mulgrave's means appears a liberal patron and Lord M.

even by the Picture which Sir George must recommend has the reputation of being a connoiseur.

There is room yet I think for some great dramatic author to appear with sentiments that breath more true English liberty, established at the revolution; sentiments to put us in mind oftener of our Freedom, and set the Theatre in an enthusiastic shout like those of ancient Greece, than are found in Shakespeare, or any one — Feb. 1810.

Was this man a Patron of Taste? — was this like one anxious for the improvement and advance of Art, to permit a youth to go on in security for four months, gratifying his fancy, and stimulating his exertions by the wish to please his employer and then telling him he should like a smaller Picture as his house was not adapted for large ones? — why did he not tell me this before I began — but more of this when I have time —[8]

[The next two pages are torn from the diary.]

8. "One day [in August 1809], while I was riding with [Sir George] at Coleorton, he said to me: 'What size do you intend to paint Macbeth?' I replied: 'Any size you please, Sir George.' He said: 'Would a whole length be large enough?' 'Certainly,' I replied; 'it is larger than I had contemplated, and I should be highly gratified at being allowed to paint the picture such a size'" (*Autobiography*, I,98).

Farington says, however, that Sir George wished the figures to be considerably smaller than life-sized but that BRH soon asked for permission to make them full scale. Sir George complied and was most displeased, when he first saw the picture, to find that BRH had made his figures of a size which Sir George "particularly disliked — something less than the life & looking like a race of little men. He then objected to them, but at Haydon's desire, He was to finish the picture thus begun & shd not Sir George like it, He was to paint another of the size which Sir George preferred" (Farington, May 7, 1810, VI,58).

Wilkie, as the friend of both partisans, heard the two sides of the discussion and endeavored to win BRH to acquiescence with Sir George; his diary for January 1810 contains almost daily references to the controversy. Wilkie believed that "it would be of great advantage to Haydon to paint small, from the much greater demand there would be for his pictures" (Cunningham, I,272). Although he felt that BRH was obligated to Sir George, when he saw a small-scale sketch for a new "Macbeth" which BRH grudgingly executed, Wilkie was obliged to urge him to proceed with the original picture in preference.

The correspondence between BRH and Sir George which developed was couched in amicable enough terms, but each disputant was determined, and BRH's repeated comparisons of his figures to those of Titian and other artists never shook Sir George's conviction that they approached "too near the natural height of man witht. being it" and were therefore "dwarfish" (Farington, March 1, 1810, VI,17).

I have for this last fortnight been dissecting, drawing, and studying the Lion — the amazing power of the animal was visible in every arrangement of muscle, in every origin and insertion — the immense temporal muscle which fills the whole cavity from the occipital process to the end of the jaw — many muscles slip into each other so that they can add strength to the one they unite with, and in their turn be assisted by it — the principle of the lever runs throughout — there were two extensors of the fingers — which crossed each other at their insertions — and only one extensor Radius — but it had two tendons inserted in the same way as the brevior and longior in Man — the Supinator longus was fleshy to its insertion — I did not see much of an Anconaeus — the triceps was a flat muscle — the Deltoid had only two heads — the spinal portion and acromion portion — the clavicle is so insignificant I did not see any portion attached to it. The Brachian internus was strong & round, was very visibly marked in Nature, I perceived in the evenings I went to Pidcock's[9] and studied their motions — the Deltoid was flat — the biceps long & thin — the Pectorals instead of going into the middle of the arm, went from the Sternum to the same insertion as the Biceps and in union with it to the Radius and the Biceps slipping into the trapezius and acting as it were from the occipital process — must enable the animal to bend his limb with extraordinary power — the Deltoid flat, the biceps long & the triceps flat, the Supinator (not ending suddenly in a beautiful short round belly as in Man), the Anconeus hardly visible, and two large extensors of the fingers, the great projection of olecranon marked the difference of form from Man — gave a squareness totally opposite to the exquisite variation of line, in a human being — there was very little pronation or supination — the little finger had an abductor like man exactly — the paws looked exquisitely graceful — the claws were placed between the joints tho each attached to its joint outward; the thumb claw antagonised the other — not exactly, between, they slipped on one side, — tho when the skin

9. "In the rooms over Exeter 'Change, in the Strand, is a collection of divers beasts and birds, the property of Mr. Gilbert Pidcock" ([John Feltham], *The Picture of London for 1810* [1810], p. 287).

was on, they looked compleatly between — a tuft of black hair marks their situation when drawing in — tho in living Nature they always hang out — when walking &c — or in eager anxiety or agitation or anger — a rim of white was each side each joint, and the hair stood up — a rim of this colour streaked the center — the white hair followed the toe — the black hair stood out and bits of hair squeezed down between the toes under the paw, stood out like antipodes — this gives a perpetual variety of touch — and makes it so difficult, without thoroughly understanding them — to do paws rightly — Rubens — from prints has made the claws come out directly in the center thus [*a sketch*] which takes away compleatly from that tufty beautiful look a paw has in Nature — and yet when angry — the claws being out, the shape of the toe being seen and yet hairy — looks more dreadful than this chiselled sort of form — The savage character of the head was marked by hanging of the corner of the mouth — the pointing upward of the eyes, the hairy ear, the immense round cheek, the snarling look of the upper lip.

A Painter who had argued on the absurdity of studying Anatomy — one who is reputed for his painting Lions — exclaimed on seeing the dissection — "I always thought the claws were in the center of the toes!!!" This comes of trusting to other men — this comes of not investigating yourself — of not going to the fountain head — Nature — when you know how things are under the skin, you will find them outside the skin, tho ever so gently indicated — and then with gentlest touch you will give a truth, a grace, and beauty that he wanting this knowledge can never attain to —

The arrangement of the soles of the feet as it were are thus [*a sketch*] — a large sole from the end of metacarpal bones to the end of fingers. One at bottom of each claw, one at Pisiform, one at thumb claw. The trapezius, complexus and splenius capitis form an immense mass of neck and give a powerful gigantic look to the animal —

The hind limb, the Vastus externus, is a powerful muscle — internus very trifling; Sartorius thin, fascilia powerful — going side of knee — the Semitendinosus semimembranosus — & Biceps femoris all arise from tuber Ischii like Man, but are inserted by strong tendons with tendo Achilles into os calcis — The biceps fibratis to the head of fibula and acts in that way too but their use here is to enable the animal to spring with greater power — by pulling the os calcis back, and straightening the limb, and raising him up, the Peronei and extensors rising from the fore part of the head of the thigh bone, instead of Tibia & fibula as in Man, all contribute perhaps to this action, truly animal — the Peronei all go behind the ankle — the largest, which is the longus in Man, has here the same insertion as brevis in Man — root of metatarsal bone of little toe — the next in size which is brevis in Man goes to place of the longus — root of great toe under the foot. The tertius goes a little farther over this in man but arises behind the outer ankle [*a sketch*] whereas in man it arises halfway up, the fore part of fibula —

Every muscle in the Lion seems arranged for activity and power; they all arise as far as possible from the center of motion so that they may not only move their own particular objects with greater vigour, but serve other purposes in other actions — they are so inserted, and so melt into each other in many instances that they decidedly act two ways — The digastrics and all the muscles of the throat were quite visible in Nature. In the Tail also a part of the fascialis slips back to it and so acts as an abductor and lying united with the fascialis acts the whole way from the head of thigh bone, which enables the animal to strike with such amazing force with his tail; again the fascialis acts from the tail —

I have gained great knowledge of the animal, — to which I am indebted to Charles Bell, as I am for many other opportunities of information, and knowledge; he bought it of Pidcock, where it died. The Artists will one day know the extent of the loss in not selecting him for their professor at the Royal Academy. A man so adapted, so delighted with the art, with such a picturesque mind, so anxious to acquire and to communicate what he acquires, with such an exact estimation of what an artist wants — that his failure of success is in my estimation a Public misfortune to the Art — He is truly the Painter Anatomist — I never go in there but there is something new, some new animal, some new scheme

— or some new arrangement that stimulates enquiry and investigation. —

March 1. The muscles are amalgamated & mixed together that you may say when one part is in action, every muscle in the body assists — what a proof of design; this accounts compleatly for so great a power in so small a shape.

What are the academic honors become but the substitute of talent, the last refuge of mediocrity to obtain business; on whom do the academicians bestow their honors; do they bestow it on those who are likely to become an honor to the Art, or improve the taste of their country, do they bestow it on Students of interprise or vigor — do they bestow it on those who they fear? No — no — no — he that has not Genius to excite envy, he that has not industry to provoke emulation — and he that [has] not courage to resist being the tool of the party who brings him in — he is the man with whom Michel Angelo would unsuccessfully contend for the honors of the Royal Academy.

A Patron of Art is one who seeing the deficiency of his countrymen, endeavours by his protection and encouragement to attract the Genius that is always floating among the people to this particular point. He is anxious only to advance the Art, to raise it to the highest pitch of excellence for the intellectual gratification of the world — he grapples a man of real talent to his soul [1] the instant he discovers him, as one suited to his purpose, as one who in conjunction will have in effect his intentions — he is not swayed by caprice, novelty has no effect on him, his only wish is the public improvement of taste, and for this end only he exerts his influence, and extends his protection.

Such were the Patrons of Ancient art and without such patronage Art would never have reared her head from slumber & obscurity — and the consequences would be the same in this country and in others, were the Patrons of Art to act in the same noble spirit with the same extension of view and the same liberality of protection it would be rediculous to enquire. Such ought to be the Patrons, that such is not the Patron of this Country, the

---

1. *Hamlet*, I,iii,63. "Grapple them to thy soul with hoops of steel."

following narrative will exemplify. Sir George Beaumont has the reputation of being the great connoiseur, the great Patron, and kind protector of the Genius of this country — we shall see whether his reputation for connoisance be the result of real knowledge, his fame for Patronage of real extension of view — and that for protection, of real benevolence the following narrative will exemplify — or whether the whole be not acquired by political management and pitiful trick.

Sir George called on me during the Winter of 1806 and after seeing my sketches and Picture invited me to dine the Sunday following. This appeared odd, on so short an acquaintance; however I went, and met several amusing men; a day or two afterwards he again called and said in an undetermined manner, he believed he must have a sketch of me — In a little time he believed it must be a picture — I proceeded with my Joseph; he left town, and shortly to my surprise [I] received a most friendly letter — About April he arrived in Town. I had finished my Joseph, he liked it but advised me not to exhibit it — why, if he so much admired it he advised not to exhibit it, I knew not; however a suspicion darted across my mind, at his saying which [*sic* for *when he*] found I was determined — "don't mention I advised you not to exhibit it" — I exhibited Joseph — I was successful at his own Table full of company — It was talked [of] in a high strain — I was praised & admired for my industry and my energy in accomplishing so much in two years — Sir George joined the company, with I verily believe a heavy heart — I was now known & should be soon noticed — as I arose in the esteem of others, I should rise also in my own — My [*sic* for *the*] demand for my works would be greater — and Sir George was engaged to me for a Picture, irrevocably engaged, by every tie that would bind an honourable man — he soon began to talk to Wilkie and I about the impropriety of asking large prices, that it was the ruin of young artists, that Milton got but ten pounds for Paradise lost — that Artists were paid a great deal too much — and in short, that liberality of reward, in the Patron, instead of stimulating to Genius was its ruin — this from an Artist, the person to be paid, would have worn the appearance of sincerity & enthusiasm — but from a Patron — the person to pay, — had rather a suspicious look

— and I began to suspect Sir George rather repented of having engaged one whom he could so little controul — who was so likely to wring a little of his money — and who there was every prospect would rise into reputation, & improvement — From this moment I watched him with a wary eye — the first thing he proposed shortly after again roused fresh & confirmed my former suspicions — he one morning thought it by far the best plan for me to paint his Picture before Lord Mulgrave's — and asked me what I thought.

That the vices of men of rank oftener attract attention; that the virtues of men of rank excite more praise, and their vices more reprobation.

I cannot expect that by this exposition that artists will avoid communication with him as they ought, I cannot expect they will have heroic firmness enough to resist the allurements of his rank or the fascination of his manners, all that I can hope for is that having laid open the secret of his quackery and exposed the hollowness of his intentions — inexperience will be on its guard against his plausibility and the Public will not allow for the future his word to elevate or depress, as his caprice or his avarice direct or excite him —

I said I would mention it to Lord Mulgrave and he went on in his hesitating manner, as if afraid to commit himself and yet wishing to gain some object — the next time I saw him, having I suppose considered the dishonor of wishing me to put by Lord Mulgrave's commission to begin his — he told me, he thought I had better go on with Dentatus, the subject Lord Mulgrave wished, but advised me by all means to do it; small figures about the size of Lord Ashburnham's Salvator[2] were quite sufficient for all the purposes of art — I went with him to Lord Ashburnham's that morning — and how were all my enthusiastic fancies of the fiery energy & power of Dentatus shocked, at finding Salvator's figures 4 Inches high!!! what an elevated conception of the Purposes of Art Sir George must have had. I without the slightest hesitation told Sir George I could not possibly do what I wished so small. I said my object was to paint great Pictures, that the

2. Salvator Rosa's "River Scene, with Apollo and the Sibyl," owned by the third Earl of Ashburnham (1760–1830) and now in the Wallace Collection.

133

sooner I did this the better, that I totally differed with respect to the belief that equal power could be shewn in small when so many tricks could conceal defects — From the first moment Sir George saw me, I openly expressed my intentions — I never led him to engage me by arguing with his notions of size, for when he said he thought Joseph quite large enough — I said at once I should wish to paint as large as possible and that I did this so small as a mere picture of trial. Sir George was compleatly in a fever, he had engaged me, after Lord Mulgrave, he saw I was determined to exert myself on Lord Mulgrave's Picture — if I made a fine Picture of Lord Mulgrave's and he paid me handsomely, he must do the same, and the idea of giving 200 Guineas to an artist for a Picture, I have no doubt prevented his sleeping the whole season. I was perpetually attacked before Lord Mulgrave, who never said a word; wherever I went in the carriage, in the street, every small Picture in collections was pointed out to me, as being quite large enough — and the deplorable appearance, & agitated face of Sir George whenever he mentioned it, so astonished me, that I could not conceive what all this agitation was about — I fixed on Lord Mulgrave's size, began it, he saw it, made no objections — liked what I had done — and let me proceed, unshackled and like a man; some times he would harrass me a little, with ideas of improvement, but after their adoption really proved so, sometimes he would suggest arrangements, but always with that deference & politeness that left it to my own feelings of their propriety, and my own notions of their excellence —

As I proceeded with Dentatus, Lord Mulgrave would now and then at Table ask me before Sir George what Subject I had thought of for Sir George — he would then turn to Sir George — who never said a word, went on with his dinner, or turned off the conversation — and if I told Lord Mulgrave any subject that I had been thinking of, Sir George with hesitation & perplexity, would quiver out "ah, yes, indeed, ah" or some such unmeaning observation; he never in his life talked about his Picture before Lord Mulgrave or said any thing by which Lord Mulgrave could hereafter relate as a proof of his believe that he had engaged me.

I became now uneasy. I began to suspect Sir George repented engaging me and as I was determined not to be insulted with impunity, I feared I might injure myself in the struggle. I finished Lord Mulgrave's Picture; things were now drawing to a close. Lord Mulgrave at table again asked; Sir George again was silent — and I now mentioned my suspicions to Wilkie who thought them groundless — thrown again off my guard, by the advice of one whom I thought sincere — I proceeded with my sketch of Macbeth. About a day before the exhibition — they all called, and Sir George then before them all, asked what subject I intended for his Picture — I was now easy. I blamed myself for my former suspicions — and proceeded with the sketch — Wilkie and I went into Devonshire — and from thence I wrote to Sir George of some alterations I had thought of, and asked his opinion, expecting an explicit fair opinion & candid advice about the Picture, but a letter came acknowledging the receipt of mine, but not a single allusion was made to Macbeth — this appeared very odd — I began again to suspect and was again uneasy — We returned from Devonshire — went down to Coleorton, Sir George's seat, and spent a very agreeable fortnight — still whenever Macbeth was talked about before Wilkie Sir George was silent and only in private with me did he speak of it; it was one morning when I was riding with him, he asked me what size I intended his Picture — I said I did not know — he said "about a whole length" — I said "about a whole length, Sir George" — and I always gave him to understand I should do it as large as possible — I returned to Town, my suspicions at an end, quite delighted at the Idea of having my wishes with respect to size sanctioned by Sir George; full of fury, resolved to paint the finest Picture ever executed, to study form, as clearly as the Greeks, to colour it like Titian, to terrify like Michel Angelo — in short there was no end to my fancies! I thought the coach lagged on the road — I longed to be in Town, I longed to begin, I longed to conclude it — I soon arrived, the canvass was ordered, and I instantly commenced, but of course was soon checked by unexpected difficulties, and after some desperate unsuccessful struggles, a new arrangement darted into my mind. I determined again to recommence it, on another canvas, and get something ready against Sir George's arrival anticipating his approval of my resolution, his encouragement and satisfaction, at seeing my strength, my wish to do great things, to do something worthy his taste — and protection, I felt I was ignorant — I knew so much of the art, as shewed what I wanted, but not what I should do — I looked at Raphael, Antique, surveyed all the collections I had access to — came home evenings, and dwelt with agony at my inefficiency — at my age, I thought, Raphael was painting the Vatican — & versed in every principle of Art, whilst I am just emerging from ignorance — every hour new notions dawned upon me — I saw beauties that I had before [passed] over with indifference — I felt excellencies I had before no conception of, I rejoiced at being checked, I was delighted I had met with opposition, which tho it produced agony, excited enquiry, and knowledge was the result — I once more relinquished despair — Hope stimullated my exertions — I ordered another canvas, and renovated by converse with the greatest minds, began with better prospects and sturdier determination. This must be the progress of him who struggles after unattainable excellence, and let no Student be soothed by indolent imbecillity into a notion that he can proceed by roads less frequented with danger, difficulty or opposition.

Thinking it my duty to inform Sir George of what I had done, I wrote him and said that I had began his picture on a new canvas — that I had thought of a new arrangement, that I was indifferent to the sneers of ignorance, and that if it was necessary to its excellence I would begin twenty times but I would succeed — I received this most kind, soothing reply — he liked my new arrangement, he advised me by all means to act upon this principle through life that one perfect work would secure immortality — that the Lion produced few but they were lordly whelps — while the meaner animals filled the world with grunting reptiles — all this was very agreeable, and very encouraging, but still nothing decided about his picture — I could not shew any proof that I was painting one for him; he had never acknowledged it in a letter; in every instance except one he had avoided talking of it — and I now began to suspect afresh — in a week he arrived in Town. As the time approached for his arrival a Gentleman who knew Sir George well told me he would never have my Picture — that after Lord Mulgrave had paid me a hundred and sixty guineas he was perfectly convinced Sir George would shuffle off if he could — and that I might depend the moment he arrived in Town, he would begin to put his schemes in execution. Sir George arrived — the moment he saw my picture — he said, "why this is the full size of life." I told him it was rather less. He said, "this is larger than Lord Mulgrave's." I told [him] it was a whole length in length and a little broader — the size he himself mentioned at Coleorton. He thought it promised great things and went away apparently satisfied but I was roused; there was a hesitation, a nervous perplexity in his manner that shewed all was not right within. I went on with my studies, and two days afterwards after I had been fagging night and day, about four in the afternoon, when I was immersed in study, with a model before me, and in the midst of difficulties I had been struggling to conquer, Sir George & Genl. Phipps, his pupil and apprentice, entered. I was quite exhausted with application — Sir George must have seen it. I began to talk about the improvements I had made, full of enthusiasm at the hopes of succeeding at last — When Sir George, with quivering lips, and full of doubting, said he didn't know whether he should not like a smaller Picture — that Figures a little less than life looked dwarfish, that he had not room for such a Picture, that it was for my interest not to paint this size, that he defied me to shew an instance in the old masters of figures this size — I told him Titian repeatedly painted this size — "ah," said he, "then you may depend it was for some particular reason." Genl. Phipps of course supported his tutor — began with the greatest impudence to say Macbeth did certainly look dwarfish — that the groom was too much like Macbeth and other nonsense for no other purpose but to harrass & torment me — Sir George was determined I saw at all hazards to be displeased, for tho' the figures struck him at first as being as large as life and he never found out they were rather less till I foolishly mentioned it — yet he now used this as an argument against the Picture — an argument which I myself had inadvertently supplied him with — he left me, and I went back to my Picture, resolving that "come what come may" [3] I would conclude it as I began it — but I acted not consistently with my character. I ought in a firm tone to have told him at once I was resolved to conclude, and that when it was finished, it was time enough to make objections — the great requisites through life are decision and strength to act up to it — It is astonishing how every thing clears before a decisive character — had I once firmly resolved, I should never have been tormented into acquiescence, and frightened into concession by Wilkie's timidity and inclination for bowing — had I gone on firmly, adding something every day to what I had already, Sir George would soon have been bent to my notions and have yielded without opposition, but I had hesitated, my friends caught the moment — I yielded. And after walking about the Park an hour in agitation I went in and told Sir George I consented — from that moment my peace forsook me — I had lost my own esteem. I had not acted up to my principles and after excrutiating agony of mind and with a heavy heart, I relinquished all my schemes of rivalling Michel Angelo and the Greeks to make a pretty furniture Picture for the dining room of Sir George. I ordered a third canvas, and in disgust and indignation, commenced Macbeth the third time — as I proceeded my disgust increased, with contempt for Sir George and after nights of excrutiating reflection, and days of angry fury, I wrote Sir Geo. I could not paint Macbeth any other size, that had he not engaged me at Coleorton I should never have been induced to begin so large and that I was entitled to ask him to withold his decision untill it was concluded, that if the size of the figures was then disagreeable — far be it from me to express a wish repugnant to his feelings — that I should be proud to paint him any other subject, on any scale, at a future period but Macbeth I was determined to conclude [with] its present dimensions — by return of post I received an answer — telling me docility was a great requisite in early life, that magnitude was not grandeur, that he granted me he gave way to my wishes at Coleorton, directly contrary to his own judgement, but that his object was to serve me not to please himself — that the size he wished was quite

3. *Macbeth,* I,iii,146.

sufficient to express the passions — the three Maries of A. Carracci[4] was an example, that I surely should be content with the
reputation which has for centuries attended this picture, but that
if I was still determined to persist, he would withold his decision
untill it was concluded — I again wrote and proofed that the
dwarfish look of figures that he complained of did not depend on
their size, but on the relative proportion of one part to another —
that a figure reduced a degree with all its relative proportion of
parts exact — must have all the grandeur reduced only a degree
and Titian's repeatedly painting this size was a proof that neither
he or his employer thought it wrong — that if figures reduced one
degree look dwarfish, figures reduced two degrees must look
still more dwarfish — and on this principle if Titian's men were
dwarfs, Poussin's must be puppets — that such fame as Ananias
gained Raphael, and the Capella Sistina Michel Angelo was my
object, and I hoped God would bless my exertions — his next
letter began to open his character; he commenced with saying
that after the firm manner in which I had refused his request, he
should not have troubled me again, did I not seem to have mistaken some part of his letter — that I need no[t] be offended at
his mentioning the three Maries, for it was as much as I could
modestly expect at present, that he did not mean to hold it up
as the highest model — he only mentioned it to shew the passions
could be expressed in that size — that it was the first time he had
heard the works of Poussin compared to Puppets — that he hoped
I might succeed in rivalling Michel Angelo — that he totally
differed — &c and concluded as usual.

I wrote him to explain what he seemed wilfully to misunderstand, that I did not mean Poussin's figures were puppets in
reality — only from previous reasoning if Titian's were dwarfs,
Poussin's must be puppets in consequence — that I had no idea
of being offended at his mentioning the three Maries as a model,
that I begged with great deference to suggest whether I deserved the imputation of having refused to comply as if I had
done without proposal or concession, that I began the small pic-

4. Doubtless Annibale Carracci's picture known as "The Dead Christ; 'The
Three Maries,'" owned by the sixth Earl of Carlisle (1773–1848) and now in
the National Gallery.

ture at his request after I had been four months at work on a
large [one] at his request also — that I offered to paint a smaller
one at a future period — but that he did not do me the honor of
answering this part of my first letter — then came a letter as kind,
as affectionate as if I was his dear friend, saying he promised me
to withold his decision at my request and concluded with "dear
Sir, best wishes for my success, great regard, and faithful Servant" — that he did not think it necessary to determine what
should be done after but *"thus far* I *will* now say that *if you* paint
any thing for me it must be one third or half the size of life for
my house is not adapted for longer dimensions" — here the correspondence and here my narrative conclude. I will now survey
the whole and endeavour to illustrate by facts Sir George's real
meaning and intention —

That Sir George in the first instance really meant to engage
me to paint I have no doubt — but my succeeding beyond his
expectations in my first Picture, and Mr. T. Hope purchasing it,
and Lord Mulgrave's commission coming next and my succeeding
also in this gave a different turn to matters — I was now no longer
the unknown unnoticed Student; Sir George could have no hopes
now of being able to get a Picture of me for nothing — he saw I
was sincere in my intentions of trying to do great things tho' he
was not sincere in his of wishing to have great things done —
finding, therefore, that he must patronise in reality if he patronised me — and do that which it had been his great object through
life to avoid — reward liberally — his struggle now was to get
rid of the commission. If this was not his object — if he really
wished to have a picture of me after my other commission, why
not clearly and explicitly point [out] at once the size he wanted
at once, or if he wished not to have one, why not with determination tell me so, or with gentlemanly delicacy, of which he has
enough? It is to gain his end, withdraw his claim — this is not his
system, blame might have been imputable to him by some, had
he withdrawn after having engaged me, — he went a more cunning way to work, his object was [to] clear himself at my expence,
to throw out a bait about size which he knew I would grasp at,
to let me get deeply in with the work, and then to pretend to

have an insurmountable feeling of objection to either the size of
the figures, the canvas, the expression, or some part, by which he
could shift the blame on my shoulders; and that the world might
attribute his conduct to my inability. At Coleorton, his seat, he
began; to my surprise and delight he mentioned a whole length;
I told Wilkie with great pleasure of what had passed — I returned
to Town and began without sufficient grounds but I was thrown
[off] my guard, for whenever I mentioned my suspicions to any
of my friends, they assured me they believed them to be groundless, tho since one of them told me he always expected what has
happened, when all my friends thought I was wrong, and Sir
George himself with a full knowledge of my wishes specified a
size himself — I surely had nothing more to do than to begin
— It was not my place to doubt any longer — With respect to the
propriety [of] his objections to the size of the figures — that they
looked dwarfish and diminutive — I can only say Titian, Vandyke
& Corregio repeatedly painted this size and that the Greeks, the
highest authority in matters of design, did so also, in the exquisite metopes of the Elgin Marbles — that they or the Nation
did not think this size diminutive & dwarfish — is proved by their
doing it. As to the sincerity of Sir George, why if he really
thought so did he not mention it when I was painting Lord Mulgrave's Picture, why suffer his Friend to have a Picture with such
diminutive insignificant Heroes? Dentatus was the size of Macbeth — he says in his letter he gave way to my wishes contrary
to his own judgement, that his object was to serve me — not to
please himself — if his object was to serve me, he ought not to
have given way contrary to his own judgement. Why did he not
caution me, why did he not state all his fears, all his notions, all
his objections, before I began. If his object was to serve me, why
did [he] not tell me to finish my Picture before he judged of it,
why if he was sincere in his objections conceal any part of the
transaction, for what reason did he to all he mentioned it to, when
they said it might put me to great inconvenience after having
been so long at work on it, for what reason did he say I had only
began a week; why did he conceal I had been four months at
work, before I began this last — why be ashamed of telling all?

It was true I had only began a week the one he meant, but he took care to talk as if it was the only one I had began and such was the impression on all to whom he spoke of it.

That his object was to get off altogether is clear enough from his appointing to call on me on the evening of that morning I called, when I told him my mind was not made up and he requested me to consider of it and that he would call to know how I had settled — and then never calling — and when I went to him to say I would paint the small Picture — his appearing cool, and careless after being so very anxious before I had determined to other people and from when I offered to paint him a smaller Picture at a future period — his avoiding to answer me, and when I drove him to it still evading by "if you paint any thing for me"; why if he wished to have a Picture of me not agree to my painting a small one hereafter — surely after having been five months at work on the large one I was entitled to an indulgence of this sort —

A few more questions I wish to ask. Why, if he liked my first Picture, and thought it would do me credit, advise me not to exhibit it — and why if it was proper I should not exhibit it, and he was sincere and right in his advice, desire me not to mention he had so advised me — Why wish me to begin his before Lord Mulgrave's, as he knew Lord Mulgrave had engaged me first and why if he was right in wishing me to paint his first tell me afterwards I had better go on with Lord Mulgrave's — Why be silent when I offered to paint another subject, on any scale?

The best answer to these queries is some account of Sir George's character, but this is hardly an occasion after the previous narrative. — Sir George Beaumont is a man, then, who wishes to be considered the great Patron, the great connoiseur of English Art with as little expence as possible — To keep up this reputation he must have at his table a regular supply of Genius. If a young man promises any thing, he immediately procures a sketch, for a trifle; if this youth succeeds, the sketch is produced, to prove he first had acuteness to discover him; if on the contrary he fails, the sketch passes into oblivion, he denies all knowledge or recollection of him, and sets out in pursuit of better game, and happier talents. Sir George's principles of action being thus founded in meaness and vanity — his vanity took the alarm therefore at my wishing to exhibit my first Picture, lest some other person might purchase it, and have the [credit of bringing] forward a young man, and his meaness lest by selling it I might be induced to ask him a higher price for his commission that counter to his usual cunning he had without sufficient re- flection given me — but there is another part of his Character which is unaccountable; after having praised, flattered, seduced, & overwhelmed with attention a Youth, he will vilify, rap, and ruin him with delight & gratification, but this perhaps can be reduced to the same principle — having praised him from vanity, he then abuses him from meaness as an excuse for not employing him — the first moment he sees you he is your friend, you must dine with him, he invites you to his seat — he entangles you with obligations that if you should discover his character the world may reproach you with ingratitude at its exposure —

People will say "he has employed Wilkie — he has paid Wilkie" — yes, he has employed Wilkie, he has paid my poor Wilkie, but what — 50 guineas for that exquisite little thing the Blind fidler,[5] a Picture that took him nearly five months — and for which time 50 Guineas was hardly sufficient to obtain bread for his breakfast — I hear he did offer him 10 more, which Wilkie has refused — I considered Sir George as the clog of English Art — as one who hates Modern Art, as one who would rather have blood wrung from him than money, and who abuses both the Exhibition and Institution as an excuse for not buying — has he ever laid out a farthing at either? Every year you'll hear him say "it's really quite lamentable to see the things at the Exhibition & Institution" — with affected indifference and concern; all this should be only treated with contempt — did it not influence the ignorant [and] the good-natured who having no judgement of their own, depend upon Sir George and echo about his senti- ments.

Time could tell a tale of many a Man of genius elevated & depressed, harrassed and ruined, the victim of Sir George's seduc- tion, who distrusted his own powers from Sir G.'s ridicule and

5. Sir George presented "The Blind Fiddler" with the rest of his collection to the National Gallery in 1826. It is now in the Tate Gallery.

sank in despair, or despised his weakness and relinquished in indignation — will any one pretend to affirm Sir George to have a
kind benevolent heart, to let a youth like me, full of sincerity and
enthusiasm for the advance of art, go on four months with a Picture; to let him begin it twice, from his anxiety to do well, and
then come when I was in the midst of my study, and say he
should like a smaller Picture, not only say this but depreciate
with all his might his labours, as an excuse for his conduct, put
different constructions on his meaning, plausibly tell every body
he had only began it a week when he knew he had began it twice,
and when he asked to conclude what he had began himself at his
instigation, endeavour to hurt his feelings by sarcastic harshness,
then whom he avoided by brutal neglect.

If the Genius of English Art is to be at the mercy of such
Patrons what hope, what prospect has she of being able to rear
her head and exert her Nature — a real Patron is he who seeing
the deficiency of his country endeavours by his protection and
encouragement to attract the Genius that is always floating among
the people to this particular point; he is anxious only to advance
the Art for intellectual gratification — he grapples a man of real
talent the instant he finds him as one suited to his purposes — as
one who in conjunction with him can effect his intentions — he
is not swayed by caprice, his choice is not dictated by vanity; but
the result of a real estimation of talent from decided proof —
Such were the patrons of Ancient Art and without Patronage Art
would for ever have remained in eternal obscurity — I cannot
expect that by this exposition Artists will avoid communications
with him as they ought — I cannot expect they will have firmness
enough to resist the allurement of his rank and manners, all that
I can hope for is that having laid open the secret of his quackery,
and exposed the hollowness of his intentions, inexperience will
be on his guard against his plausibility, and the nobility and the
Public will not for the future, allow his word to elevate or depress, as his vanity, his meaness or his malevolence direct or
excite him —

I shall be perhaps accused of arrogance and ingratitude in
daring to attack a man of Sir G.'s rank. I have no enmity against

Sir G. I respect his rank, I respect also his influence, when a [man of] rank behaves dishonorably he becomes an example for thousands whom cowardice & timidity would for ever keep in awe, without such sanction.

I did hope, with excusable human partiality, when I was told of the many hearts you had cut by neglect, and of the many bosoms you had torn by caprice — that I had qualifications to avert such conduct. One might have been idle, another ignorant, you might have neglected both to stimulate them to exertion — But I thought my industry and sincerity, my talents and energy would secure me, and in my vanity I thought I was he, destined to convince the world of the falsehood of such assertion.

But I have done — a recapitulation of your meaness excites such disgust — my heart sickens. You are a lamentable instance, Sir George, how much cunning is an overmatch for sincerity — you never lay out a penny at either the exhibition or institution, and yet you have more the reputation of the patron of art than those Noblemen & Gentlemen who lay out thousands — in short such is your management that [you] have got and keep your reputation by never buying — by lamenting that there is nothing to suit your exquisite taste, &c — [you] thereby insinuate that those who do buy have no taste at all — Your getting Wilkie's fidler was a lucky hit, but do you deny the reputation for patronage you acquired by that picture — did you not attempt to trouble poor Wilkie as you have harrassed me — did you not evidently repent engaging him when you found he made such a name — did you not call on him, find fault, say you would call again, and then go out of town again without calling, leaving him in torturing suspence, uncertain what you meant and what were your intentions — Oh Sir George — I have no hope of putting a stop to your conduct — habit alone renders that impossible, I only wish to check its influence, by laying open the secret spring of its motions — did you not, to me [and] to many when you found you had paid him so little for it, attempt to damn the picture to excuse your own conduct, did you not say Wilkie did not [make his] colour quite the thing, that it was slaty, that you hung it out in your passage because it really looked so bad by your other pictures — that he must take care — novelty would soon go off — &c — and this is the one whom you are now courting, when you find he is too strong to be ruined —

A few words to Lord Mulgrave and I cannot with propriety again appear after this exposition of your Lordship's friend at your Lordship's Table — permit me in withdrawing to express my feelings of gratitude & respect for the happiness that for three years I have enjoyed at it — for the advantages of Study your Lordship's influence has procured me — advantages I shall feel to the last hour of my life — If I ever should do that, only by which I should be thought an honor to my country — If I can before I die advance the art one step — let my fate be what it may, I shall ever consider your Lordship's employing me when I was unknown and unnoticed, as a solid Patronage and disinterested benevolence —

I can expect nothing but that your Lordship's benevolence, and Lady Mulgrave's sweetness will be shocked at this harsh exposure of your Lordship's Friend. I cannot hope to be again admitted at your Lordship's — I wish it not, my Lord — I only hope the Public will do justice to my motive and not think I wish to gratify private malice, under the mask of public good. I have no malice against Sir George. I respect his rank, I only wish to weaken his pernicious influence — when a man of rank, my Lord, acts dishonorably, he becomes an example to thousands whom cowardice & timidity would for ever keep in awe without such a sanction —

Sir G. B. is perhaps an epitome of the world, mankind are pleased with the novelty of talent, they then praise without discrimination and without thought, in a short time they become jealous of the superiority to which they themselves have raised you, envy excites censure, your follies are exaggerated to vices, faults which you always possessed, but which were not seen till now, are criticised without mercy — and every effort is made to ruin, and overturn you, but if you proceed with firmness and steadily advance — in short hopeless at effecting your ruin they join in your praise, and you will find hundreds, who would have exulted in your fall, now loudly celebrate your success and claim praise to themselves in approving what it was not in their power to hinder —

Sir G. & Lady called, I should have thought after so much anxiety something would have been said about the subject, something to soothe my feelings, but no, they both talked and chattered as usual, and I saw they wished to let it die away — Every man will at periods, from indolence from different motives will be guilty of some trifling meaness, or some trifling dishonour, which he repents as soon as committed and endeavours to repair by apology or by reparation [which] from a previous tenor of his character, is accepted as soon as offered — but when a man goes on year after year & day after day, flattering, seducing, crushing, & oppressing — it must be either the result of propensity or habit, if propensity, exposition tends to weaken its influence, and if habit to check its progress — in either case, to expose such a man from whatever motive, is a public benefit — the motives that excite exposure therefore is no argument against the good the exposure may do, if truth only is told — resentment may urge a man to screen these events but I tell facts.

You hear the note "Historical painting will never do in this country" — but why won't it do — to whom is the fault imputable — Let the Nobility open their Halls and their Staircases, and have the deeds of their Ancestors illustrated, instead of purchasing trifles for the dining rooms and the parlours — and we shall soon see whether Historical painting will do — there is a perpetual argument, whether Genius is dependent on noble Patrons — whether if it exists it will not burst its way through all obstacles, whether employed or not — that it may exist independently of the Patron is true, but without his assistance that may be reduced to waste its fire on trifles — also as true, would the miracle of the Parthenon have started into existence had not Pericles employed Phidias? Pericles might [have] employed in vain had not Phidias existed — certainly — It can never be settled, the Patron and the Genius must exist together, and the rest must be left to a happy combination of coincidences. But yet in this Country, the Patron has never tried, every effort for great works has been the spontaneous feelings of the Artists — they offered to adorn St. Paul's for nothing — Barry painted the Adelphi — for nothing — The Shakespeare Gallery was a commercial speculation[6] and had nothing to do with enlightened Patronage — Nothing in this Country is ventured on without anticipating remuneration — the expence must be cleared by a set of Prints — or by the shillings of an exhibition!!! If Pericles had so calculated before Phidias was employed, the Parthenon would never have lifted its lofty head — if Julius had not ventured to employ Raphael before he had obtained subscribers for a set of prints — the beauties of the Vatican would have still been in oblivion — remuneration in profit is out of the question — the only remuneration a nation or a Patron ought to expect should be the excellence of the Work and the honor and fame it would bring the promoters — Patronage with any other view never has & never will produce any thing above brutal interested mediocrity.

April 21. I yesterday, 20th, Good Friday, for the first time since my birth, received the sacrament. I had put it off from year to year, and I was determined to delay no longer (I thank thee God I did not delay it). Tho burdened with Sin yesterday I ventured to approach the Altar; about two days before I had reflected on every thing with deep meditation — and conviction flashed on my mind at intervals — I never before felt the grandeur of the scheme of Christianity; when I considered this, the purity of the doctrine, the moral character of Christ, the originality of the miraculous conception — the probability that if God intended to reveal his will to us by a human being, it would be by a being not begot in lust, but by one conceived by spiritual influence, that would have our shape but not be liable to our Sins — when I thought on the impossibility of the whole plan of the law and the Gospel, being mere human invention — a plan of such comprehension, such grandeur, I dared not doubt, I felt as it were urged on to receive. I approached the Altar in trembling agitation — for some part of the morning I had felt extremely

6. John Boydell (1719–1804), a successful engraver and lord mayor of London in 1790, commissioned the leading artists of the day to paint scenes from Shakespeare's plays, which he exhibited in his Shakespeare Gallery in Pall Mall. Engravings were made from these pictures, but the venture was a financial failure.

agitated — I feared I might wander in my thoughts at the moment, but I thank God I never was more absorbed in my whole life. I eat the bread in awe, and drank the wine with firmness. I then tottered to my seat, flushed with the fancy of my Saviour in agony crying, "it is finished." [7] My God, I dropt on my knees, I felt a glow of pleasure, a delight at having obeyed the commands of my Saviour, and prayed with fervor it might be effectual to my redemption & reformation — as I returned home, the fancy of having drank wine & eat bread as our Saviour himself did 1800 years ago, and commanded us to do in remembrance of him, made me start — I have indeed done it, I thought, I am now a Christian — I shall begin tomorrow a new existence — I recollected all my Sins from my infancy to the moment, and hoped they were all expiated, by what I had done, if it was followed by effectual repentance and reformation —

I firmly believe in the Sacrifice of Christ, and I hope God will forgive me for ever daring to doubt it — if every young man was to bend his mind to receive the sacrament to consider the grandeur of our Saviour's sacrifice for the Sins of the world, to think only of the whole scheme and not particular petty objections, if young men were to do this, before they enter the World, they would find themselves effectually fortified against the ridicule of blasphemous infidelity. I cannot express the gratitude I feel to thee, O God, for enabling me to have strength to obey thy commands — I would not exchange the delight I feel, now I have drank & eat in remembrance of thee, My blessed Saviour, for the whole World — I feel as if I had now a right according to thy promise to be forgiven if I repent — before I was all doubt, distraction, and agony — I feel now assured, that if there ever was a revelation, it was through Christ, that if there ever was a perfect doctrine, it is Christ's, that if there ever was a prospect of a human being enjoying immortality, this prospect is only opened to him through Christ Jesus — tell me a purer doctrine, a purer character, a more simple system, or one more conducive to happiness — Christ Jesus have mercy on me, inspire me, purify me, grant I may every year approach thy altar with awe and delight,

7. John 19:30.

and every year with less to repent, & less to reform. O God, let me never neglect to commemorate thy birth, thy death, & thy ascension — and when I have done my duty in life, and my time for leaving it is near — But I cannot think of this without rapture — I have now entered the road thou hast directed those who wish to find thee; may I keep firmly in it without stumbling and without deviation — O God, protect me and bless me, thou Great, good, incomprehensible Being — for Jesus Christ Sake. Amen.

April 22. Easter Sunday. I again this day received the holy Sacrament, that I might compleat the reformation I had began — I received it to day with firmness and determination and renewed at the altar my resolution with a determined spirit, to avoid Sin, to rise early, to be industrious, to attend regularly my Church, never if possible to miss my morning and evening prayer, in short to struggle with all my might to do all a Christian who has obeyed his blessed Saviour's commands ought to do, to render himself worthy of his protection and blessing — may it be effectual. I have now appealed to the highest & holiest authority; if this has no effect on me, I am gone for ever — But I humbly [hope] in God through Jesus Christ that I shall have cause to bless my resolutions, instead of bewail them — It is a grand period of my existence — for the first time the truth of Christianity has beamed into my mind, I now comprehend with awe the grandeur, the vastness, and with delight & rapture, the love and goodness, displayed in Christ Jesus, redeeming human Nature by his yielding up the Ghost in agony on the cross — how every human amusement, every human pleasure sinks at the recollection, the conception only of a God, a Divinity — In the hour of temptation, or in the moment of vice, let this, O God, burst on my fancy and check me, in terror — "Come unto me all ye that travail and are heavy laden, and I will refresh you." [8] Till now I have read this exquisite passage without feeling, and as a part of the new testament, but never did I experience its efficacy till now, he is indeed refreshed who repents and approaches thee in penitence, and agitation, O God — he indeed retires, cleaned of doubts and re-

8. Matthew, 11:28. "Come unto me, all ye that labour and are heavy laden, and I will give you rest."

lieved of miseries who eats thy body & drinks thy blood in remembrance of thy propitiation —

Let him who dares disbelieve, discipline his mind in piety, and receive in humility; and if he believes not he must be unnaturally insensible — to the last hour of my existence shall I bless thee, for resolution to obey thee — for to that hour shall I feel its blessings — I feel strength enough to contend successfully with the world, if the whole world were to become infidels — I bless thee, O God, for thus opening my mind to conviction — may it every day become firmer — I conclude this blessed day of thy triumph over Death, O my blessed Saviour, in awe, rapture & gratitude, and will hope [to] begin my new existence to-morrow in prayer, industry and vigour. Amen, Amen, Amen.

After Sir G. and his Lady called, and seemed totally to forget that I had ever been painting a Picture for them, by their never hinting any thing about it — I sent the Picture the next day to be enlarged to do away all suspicion that I had any intentions of forcing them to take it (which was in my power) and to please Myself entirely, in every respect to prove to the World too the thorough contempt I entertained for them, and how little I cared about their patronage — I shewed the correspondence to everybody who wished it — and People soon began to talk how shockingly I had been used. I swore to all I would finish the Picture to the utmost of my power, and then publish the whole to the world —

I went on quietly for nearly a month and Sir George, who used to call every day and make me dine with him every week without any reason, for I had done nothing to deserve it, on the same principle deserted me, and let me proceed with as much indifference as if he never knew me — to my surprise about a month after he last called — I received a card requesting me to dine with him; after some hesitation, I determined to go, supposing that some proposition was to be made me about his Picture — I therefore sent to say I would attend his request — in this interval also something had happened that had materially altered the case with Wilkie; he had sent a small Picture to the exhibition and had been advised to withdraw it, because Bird his rival had such a superior one,[9] that his reputation would be materially injured by the comparison. Wilkie like a fool was frightened, and did withdraw it at the instigation of Sir George Beaumont, who was called on by W[est] for that purpose —

Wilkie, who now knew that Sir. G.'s tone would be altered to him now in some degree, degraded by being afraid to exhibit against Bird, advised me not to go — however as I always act as I please — I went —

On my entering the room, Sir George arose in evident agitation to receive me, while Lady B. instantly drew me off to the Window and kept me from observing him, which I did in a most determined manner — Sir G.'s attention to me was marked — my opinion was asked, about every thing — poor Wilkie absolutely neglected — company soon arrived, and they all trotted into his gallery — I followed, determined if Sir G. talked about Small Pictures or figures or hinted to me — I would have launched out directly with fury — not a word was said — and we shortly retired to dinner — here his attention to me was quite rediculous. Lady B. on one side and he on the other — Wilkie was not even spoken to — Sir G. begged I would drink wine with him — never asked poor Wilkie! who sat in awe watching his face and laughing at his wit before it was ready — however I was not thrown off my guard — As nothing had been hinted at Macbeth — I began to suspect he had heard of my intentions about publishing his letters — and had invited me to flatter or intimidate me out of it — I rather kept watching with care and thinking how I should act in case any thing should turn up —

After dinner in the course of conversation, Barry was mentioned — "talking of Barry," says Sir George, "I recollect something that Sir Joshua told me of him — that he once published something in the papers which he had entrusted him with in confidence — now you know," says he (while his face and his lips grew pale as he spoke it, and his eyes and head were turned

9. Wilkie sent "The Man with the Girl's Cap" (also known as "No Fool like an Old Fool" and "The Wardrobe Ransacked") to the Royal Academy's exhibition of 1810 but withdrew it since the Council considered "The Game of Put" and "Village Choristers" by Edward Bird (1772–1819) as superior pictures of the same type (Cunningham, I,289). Bird became an R.A. in 1815 and was appointed court painter to Queen Charlotte.

straight forward, without appearing to look at any thing), "now you know, nothing could be so shocking, to publish letters or any thing of that sort, nothing can be [so] shocking" — ah, ah, the whole at once beamed on my fancy. I appeared totally indifferent and agreed nothing was so shocking. The conversation took another turn, and I turned round and looked calmly at Sir George, who appeared ruffled, notwithstanding his forced smile and apparent gaiety — his character was now at stake before the world, he knew I had dived into his soul, that I had it in my power to expose him, in his real form and feeling and lay open his quackery; he knew the World well enough to foresee the reception of such an exposure, and the generous, the meek, the benevolent, the amiable Sir George — was in terror lest mankind might see that his generosity was affected to conceal meaness — his meekness to hide tyranny — and his benevolence, malice —

All the evening I was singled out by Lady B. "Don't you think so, Mr. Haydon, have you had time to read this or that, Mr. Haydon?" "Do sit," said Sir George — "how d'ye get on with Macbeth?" — !!! ha, ha, he now condescended to mention Macbeth, Bless my heart, it is very odd that length of time, which weakens the memory of every other human being, seems to refresh that of Sir George — does he indeed recollect Macbeth — he has not then quite forgot that he engaged me to paint a Picture at which I had worked 5 Months and began it three times — it is very odd, surely, that he be so lucky as to recollect Macbeth now, and to be unfortunate as to have entirely forgotten it when he arrived in Town — but some people have these convenient memories —

These were my reflections before I spoke, and I then told him that I was proceeding and hoped to get it finished — When we rose to take leave — "Good night," said they, "Mr. Haydon," and bowed to all the rest —

Wilkie, who knew very well what he must expect when we came out on the Street, seized an opportunity offered him and went home in the carriage of a Friend, who put him down at his own door — I could scarcely contain my indignation at their meaness — I looked round at the House when I came out — and thought "there live two of the most contemptible of human creatures — two, whose lives are a perpetual course of meaness &

duplicity, whose vices and villany are concealed beneath faces which always smile & tongues that always flatter" — My God, that such meaness, such cruelty, such hypocrisy should remain unexposed and unknown — They could flatter me now, now they feared me, but Lady B. could pass me at Lord S—— as if she had never seen me, when she thought I should have sunk from my unsuccess of my Picture being hung badly — and they might trample on me and shake off their commission — despicable wretches — I went home in a fever of contempt — I could scarcely [sleep] — and arose the next morning in a heat; the first impulse was to write — and I gave way to my feelings in such a strain of irony and energy as I verily believe would [have] killed him, and ruined me had I sent it — I wrote another and another and another. The next day I found Sir George's card upon the table — contemptible hypocrite — he could desert me, and leave me as he thought to be harrassed and oppressed by his neglect — when he thought I had not courage to oppose him — but the moment he heard of my intentions, and he found to his surprise that I reared up firmly against him, frightened out of his knowing the truth of my hate, he began to try if he could not lull me by his former flattery —

Then I was to dine there — then he talked of Macbeth — then he called, chattered, soothed, and flattered but had I shrunk in terror from the contest, then he would have slandered, vilified, trampled on, and crushed me — Thank God I was not terrified by slander, or staggered by his intimidations — Thank God I had a Father to support me — and a spirit not easily suppressed —

The day of private exhibition came. I went and there met Lord M. and his Brothers — Lord B. — and his beautiful wife — The moment Lord M. saw me he held out his hand to me and so did his Brothers of course — This he never did in his life before. This was a good omen — one of his Brothers said to me, "is it fixed what you are to paint for Sir George yet?" — "no Sir," said I, "he has never even hinted a word on the subject" — Sir George & Lady B. overwhelmed me with attentions — People were astonished to see me so intimate with *him* knowing how I had firmly refused to acquiesce in his caprice. They thought of course, I suppose to see me humble and cast down & waiting in anxious awe to catch his eye and cringe at his smile — they expected to see him walk into the academy as usual, enveloped in an atmosphere of consequence and me fall back in reverence as he passed — But after Sir George, with pale & harrassed countenance, appeared dejected & cast down, Lord M., whom he had been in the habit of ruling with an iron hand, now noticed me to his face in the most affectionate manner — every thing passed off as I could wish and I returned home more indignant at their meaness than ever — while I was passing down the Room, Sir G. turned to me and said "what do you think of Bird's Picture?" — I saw his object — the Academicians who had [been] concerned in decrying W.'s Picture which at their affected advice he had withdrawn, had surrounded Sir G. and were asking his opinion — Sir G. fearful of offending them — or of being decided before the Public had given the opinion, evaded the question, and seeing me, knowing I would have no hesitation in saying what I thought — and wishing to entangle me if possible — asked me — I said I thought it a very inefficient Picture and by no means so good as his last — this of course plunged me into a dispute — in which I held W. superior in such terms as made them stagger — Lady B. said she approved of W. withdrawing his Picture — I said I did not — it was a rascally thing to advise him so to do — &c — she said docility in early life was a great requisite &c — it certainly was, I answered, but one did not like to be trampled on — Sir G. shortly drove home — and W. & I retired to dinner. The Persian Ambassador was there in the Room — he looked at every thing with a vacant Stare like an infant and seemed to care little about Pictures — the Laocoon down stairs seemed to attract him —

It was evident now to all I had caught Sir G. & his Lady compleatly — they were in terror — they dreaded the exposure of their letters — they knew they stood on hollow ground — and it was in my power to plunge them through it. Every body who dreaded my encountering him now applauded my heroism — "go on — frighten him — harrass him — torment him — as he has frightened, harrassed, & tormented others." The Tuesday following as I was in the act of writing him — a thundering rapp at the door announced a carriage — and I had scarcely time to lock up my letter before he and his Lady entered — They walked into my

Painting room to look at Macbeth — and I followed determined now to bring them to a point — they witnessed an alteration in my manner and I saw a determination in theirs to keep me if possible from saying any thing about Macbeth — they kept chattering and chattering till they were exhausted and then I clearly asked Sir George if I was to paint this Picture of Macbeth or not for him — "I can answer that," said Lady B., "we have not room for such a Picture" — I took no notice of her impudence — and waited in silence for him — "ah — oh yes indeed — ah, ah — I thought it was to be as you mentioned in the Letter — that you were to go on with it but if I did not like it when done I was not to have it" — "certainly," said I, "I thought so too, Sir G. — but when You & Lady B. called on me on your arrival in London and never even hinted I had ever been painting for you — I thought and so did every one else that you wished to consider the engagement at an end" — "Oh no," said he turning like ashes — "we meant nothing — nothing — yes indeed — oh no — oh no — But then you have had it enlarged" — "certainly, Sir G. When I considered there was no prospect of your having the picture, I determined to please myself entirely — I should feel my mind greatly relieved if you would tell me decidedly whether you would have it or not — I should then begin it with energy — it would be a great stimulus." "Would it not be as great a stimulus if you were to paint it for me — but if when it is done I should not like it — I should not be obliged to take it?" — "But in that case I should consider myself engaged to you for a smaller Picture after Mr. Hope's — I assure [you] I would not have mentioned any thing to you was it not for your good — Will you agree to it? — I do not wish to force you to take it — I have no objection if you will agree to a stipulation of mine." — "What's that," said they. "Why," said I, "that neither you or Lady Beaumont shall see it till it is compleatly finished & in the frame." — "Why yes indeed — ah well — we have no objection — we'll agree to it" — "Very well, Sir G., I agree then — now then," said I, "we'll recapitulate — I am &c — &c. — to paint this Picture *the enlarged one*. Upon my honor I am sincere" — "upon my honor so am I," said he — we then shook hands — and by this time he was compleatly agitated — "now you need not mention this, you know — out of regard to you for fear if I should not like it — the sale might be injured" — "I won't promise, Sir G." — "I have no objection to W.'s knowing it" — "nor I to S[eguier]" said I — "Well, we wish you success, we wish you success — I am not to see [it] till you come for me" — "no" — "very well, good morning, we wish you success with all our hearts" — I attended them down stairs and bowed as they drove off — never did two People slink off as they did — instead of the chattering, impudent insolence that used to characterize her manner — Lady B. never spoke a syllable. Sir. G. trembled as he caught the bannister — and once more quivered out "good morning" —

Pitiful wretches — what falsehood — what meaness — she said she could answer my question — they had not room for such a Picture! How dare Sir G. to mention a whole length himself — how dare he to let me go on for five months — knowing when it was finished he had not room for it — how dare he say he had no objection to the size of the canvas — but the figures were the great obstacle — when his wife, the receptacle of his secrets, says it was the canvas that was too large —

To answer these question would be impossible — they wanted to get off, they cared not how —

(I expressly mentioned the *enlarged Picture was to be the one*, and made him understand it so; I write this here, I forgot it on the other page, and put it between the lines) —

When he was gone, wishing to mention it and knowing his only object was to conceal his meaness in not having it told — I wrote him — as he could have no object but my good — I would run the risk of that — that I must mention to Lord Mulgrave, a real patron — and Mr. T. Hope, another real patron of mine, that I was compleatly satisfied — but I must beg permission to write it.

He wrote again — that as his only object in concealment was to prevent the sale of my Picture being injured in case he *should reject*, according to my own proposal — I was at liberty to mention it not only to my *real* patrons or any other to whom I pleased — I again wrote the next morning saying that I was now going seriously to set down to Macbeth — that I should be obliged to him if he or Lady B. felt uneasy at being bound down by a bond

— to tell me and I would release him with the greatest pleasure — that it was certainly *my proposal* during the former agreement, but that I had considered that agreement at an end by his arrival in Town — and never hinting I had been ever painting a Picture for him — that if he recollected it was his proposal during the last agreement — for he asked me if it would not be as great a stimulus as painting it for him decidedly — that I merely mentioned it — I wished to state the truth — I was perfectly satisfied, — had never expressed myself other[wise] and never should — I said I should be much obliged to him if he was satisfied not to harrass and hurt me by talking of his fears of rejecting my Picture — That he should recollect, and I said it with deference, that it was *I* who had allowed him to withdraw from an engagement if it should be ultimately disagreeable out of regard to his feelings, an engagement unsought for on my part, and entered into by him with me — three years ago — without any stipulation on his — he first said no answer was required — and then shortly after said that he thought every thing was settled to my satisfaction — that enough & too much had been said on the subject — that he had no intention of hurting my feelings — that he requested me to proceed without further discussion — for he was resolved not to write another word on the subject —

I replied immediately — that I was now satisfied and should proceed without hesitation — that if he had let me proceed quietly six months ago nothing would have been said or written about it — that it was certainly at his own option whether he wrote the last letter, or any other I had the honor to receive from him — that I had now done — and should proceed with my picture that instant —

Here the correspondence ended — I have nothing now to do but strain every nerve and sinew to make a grand Picture — and God in heaven, as I sincerely promise amendment & repentance, grant me compleat success — O God bless this prayer — I humbly hope & only on condition of my effectual determined repentance — ask this — I will do all I can to be firm, energetic, & industrious — and on this only I ask thee to bless my exertion in every respect through Jesus Christ my Saviour. Amen.

June

[The next four pages are torn from the diary.]

June 18. How dare he say he thought it was to be as I proposed — (viz. I was to go on with it for him) when Lady B. said she could answer that question, they had not room for it —

I lost a great deal of time in this dispute, harrassed my mind, interrupted my studies, and then I develloped a character by my perseverance. Was I to do it over again — I would certainly have acted differently — In the first place I would never have began it smaller to please him after I had been at work six months on the first size, but finished it on that size — When once agreed, and employer and artist understand each [other], never let an artist worry but go on regardless of all caprice — and complete it — when done, if refused — let the law do the rest.*

* January 6, 1816. His great objection was want of room and *now* I am to paint him a Picture that will be *bigger every way* — He purchased this *very Macbeth* and it is at present hung up in the House 1816 where there was no room 1809 — but Sir G. did it from kindness & let the business rest — I repent the dispute and ever shall.

Volume III

JUNE 1810—SEPTEMBER 1811

With the beginning of a new volume, Haydon at last turned to consideration of other subjects than the denigration of Sir George Beaumont; yet sketches on the inner cover and the first two pages of Volume III may indicate subjective ideas on his trials and the triumph which he confidently expected as champion of British art — Sisyphus rolling his rock uphill, Ixion writhing on his wheel, and a savage lion killing his prey.

Volume III

JUNE 1810 — SEPTEMBER 1811

June 20. I went yesterday to see Angerstein's[1] collection and examined particularly the Sebastian del Piombo[2] — it is certainly finely put together as to the lines of composition; the characters of heads are various, too, and fine, but there is great want of effect and our Saviour is a mean affected figure. He seems too indifferent; he has no appearance of inspiration. I have heard this defended, as if the painter wished to make it appear as an easy matter to him as if it required no effort to raise the dead — this may be very true; it might require in him perhaps no other effort than stretching forth his hand, but as the Painter's object is to excite the greatest possible interest, every thing that will contribute to do this he should avail himself of — if you make [the principal figure] uninterested in your Picture, the Spectator will be equally uninterested while looking at it. I examined the Lazarus well, as Fuzeli says he is convinced Michel Angelo has gone over it[3] — I could perceive a visible difference in the manner of drawing & painting in the feet of Lazarus — and the thumb that presses the back of the man who is taking off the Linen is evidently painted by a more powerful hand than [his who] painted the other parts of the Picture. If Christ restored Lazarus to life, he would of course be instantly restored to his full powers, and therefore if shewn by the painter should have his form in full vigour. The chest is meagre, the Shoulder really badly drawn — and the feet have that peculiar squareness, in the toes, that characterise many of the Antique Statues found during that period — the leg that he is drawing out of the linen has certainly been repaired, for

1. John Julius Angerstein (1735–1823), merchant and philanthropist; he assembled one of the finest collections of painting of the early nineteenth century, which he frequently opened to artists. About forty of his works of art were purchased by the government in 1824 to form the nucleus of the National Gallery.

2. Sebastiano del Piombo's "Raising of Lazarus," now in the National Gallery; it was painted in 1517–1519 for Giulio de' Medici, in competition with Raphael's "Transfiguration," now in the Vatican.

3. "[Lazarus] was painted with the most earnest care, under the direction, and in some parts with the design, of Michelagnolo" (Vasari, III,323).

the foot of that leg and the leg itself are quite a different texture — and the leg poorly understood and not at all defined; the head of Lazarus has a fine expression, like a man just from the grave, as if he was astonished, and had not recovered his perceptions.

When I was looking at it I could not but compare it with the Style of Greece. It has an effected academical look — mannered — a useless display of anatomy — and the effort at abstracted form in the foot that presses the ground not at all carried through the figure — this foot has all the fleshiness and vigour of life, the shoulder all the bony meagreness of death. In the Shoulder instead of the trapezius coming down clearly between the two heads of the Deltoid to the acromion, and the middle head branching out where the Trapezius ends thus [a sketch] — there are a parcel of little unmeaning markings — the chest & neck are meagre and too skinny.

I had determined to examine this figure with care as it was done under Michel Angelo's direction and in competition with Raphael's Transfiguration and as I was warm from the exquisite productions of greece — I came with a correct eye — I am confident of the truth of what I have asserted and can prove it. Two years ago I would not have ventured to say a word whatever I might have thought — but now I venture to think myself adequate — and have a right to say in comparing one great man with others, where a difference & an inferiority is perceptible, as well for my own improvement as for the guidance of those who know less. —

The character of St. John behind our Saviour is very fine — The women have no pretensions to beauty — their hands are affectedly made out, with little lumps at all the joints as if they were padlocked — the foot of our Saviour is very poor, the toes meagrely drawn — and the whole flat — nothing of that exquisite system of reasoning that you perceive in every grecian foot — the fleshy parts pressing up round the bones, &c. — it looks as if there was no weight above it — no pressure — About the drapery of Christ there is a venetian look from its being glazed — The proportion too between the arms and legs is very bad — the Arm of the Man who is taking off the linen is as big as the leg of

Lazarus, and the arm of Lazarus is also too large for his leg — there is evidently no system of form, except accidentally in a foot, &c. There is a grand tone about the Picture which is very solemn, but to suppose that light and Shadow, handling, and keeping would take off from the grand Style is like supposing that to add a nose to a man born without one, would take off from the beauty of his face.

The arm of itself and the whole figure of the man in the corner is very fine — there is a great grandeur and originality in Style of it — evidently built on Nature but not far enough from it to be classed in the highest, and yet not too near to be ranked with the lowest — I think Rembrandt's[4] moment is the finer of the two.

There is great grandeur too in Christ directing the vacant stare of Lazarus to Heaven — to shew his gratitude there — but still it is not the dreadful moment of suspense. In composition and arrangement it will bear comparison with any thing — but in form it sinks beneath the grecian grandeur, truth, and simplicity.

Whoever is author of Lazarus could certainly not clear the essential from the superfluous — many parts of it are perplexed with useless anatomy, which takes off the simplicity of its contour, the great requisite of fine form.

The Grecian figures seem to say, as it were, Breast, Shoulders, arm, forearm, wrists, hands, ribs, hips, belly, thighs, knees, legs, ankles, feet, where Michel Angelo seems to say clavicle, a little slip of the Pectoral muscle which arises from half the clavicle, another little slip, insertion of the Pectoral between the triceps & Biceps along with Deltoid — &c. — and you are perplexed and distracted from the great motions and intention of the figure.

It is a grand Picture; a great acquisition to the country — and an honour to Mr. Angerstein's spirit and taste, in purchasing it[5] — Yet if God prolongs my life or cuts it not prematurely short, I hope I shall leave one behind me that will do more honor to my country than that has done to Rome — in Short, if I live — I will — I feel I shall (God pardon me if this is presumption.)

4. Rembrandt painted two pictures of "The Raising of Lazarus" and made two etchings of the subject.
5. Angerstein bought the picture in France at the Orléans sale in 1792.

June 21. The Theodosius by Vandyke[6] is an exquisite Picture; the grey tone of the Sky & building eminently contribute to the brilliancy & brightness of the flesh — the clearness of this Picture is really delightful — it is in wonderful preservation.

I could not help observing the other day on looking at a head of Giotto, saved from the Carmelites' Church at Florence, the exact resemblance it bore to the heads of the Panathenaic procession, as if (and it is certainly evident from this) he had been instructed by the poor Grecian Artists who fled to Italy during the invasion of their country and carried with them what they had seen at Athens.

The head has the character — dividing the head by the hair, &c. — as the heads of the Youths on horseback at the Elgin Musaeum — brought from Athens.

How little Raphael assists you in the complicated varieties and beauties of form — To Nature and to Greece if you want assistance, can you only recur to with any prospect of information —

Rubens' Lion Hunts appear and certainly are built on the Standard Struggle of Leonardo da Vinci[7] — that is the origin of all of them — the same system is apparent — it seems to have excited many of Rubens' finest compositions.

June 27. Such is Homer's impetuosity to rush again into the description of the Battle that no man can read the short energetic speeches of Achilles in council without partaking of his feelings, and thinking Ulysses, Agamemnon, & Nestor as tedious, drawling, old fools, even when Minerva descends by command of Jove to inspire vigour into the Breast of Achilles — Homer hurries her off with as much dispatch as possible, in a few lines, and having cleared the road, as it were, done every [thing] that is proper, he then bursts with vigourous energy into the preparation for the tremendous day — The Sun is rising — the troops are pouring out

6. "The Emperor Theodosius Refused Admission into the Church by St. Ambrose," owned by Angerstein and now in the National Gallery. It is a reduced copy by Vandyke of a painting by Rubens.

7. Rubens painted three pictures showing lion hunts. The first two resemble the copy by Edelinck(?) from Rubens' drawing after Leonardo da Vinci's "Battle of the Standard" in the Fogg Art Museum, Cambridge, Massachusetts.

as thickly as snow on the Shore, Achilles is arming, his eyes flashing fire, his heart full of grief, he takes his great, ponderous shield beaming like the moon, or like a flame upon a solitary hill, to mariners driven far off from their friends by Storms upon the fishy deep, he then drags forth his tremendous sounding spear, the death of Heroes, lifts his glittering helmet, which shone like a star, to his head, and burning for the battle, poises himself in his arms and feels a wing in every limb — his chariot and Horses gallop to the door of his tent, and are curbed in frothing with inspired fury, by Automedon, Achilles beaming like the rising sun springs into it and shouting, rushes into the field — who can avoid feeling his frame tremble at this unexampled description, who that reads does not long to burst into battle with Achilles — Jupiter instantly in a hurry assembles all the Gods and tells [them] to descend and mingle in the fight, on which side they may be each inclined, to check Achilles, lest in his furious inspiration he pass fate, and lay Troy in ruins — the Gods join the field, Discord arises and sets them in confusion, Minerva shouts horribly from the Walls, and sometimes along the Sounding Shore — Mars enveloped in terror and clouds roars from the Tower of Troy, and both armies are excited to the highest pitch at that moment, as if prophetic of the dreadful day; crashes of Thunder roll over their heads — a horrid earthquake shakes both armies, the Sea trembles, Troy totters, the woods of Ida are lifted — and Pluto starts from his horrid throne, and crys out lest in the uproar the Earth should open above him, and expose his dreary chambers and screeching Sufferers to the eyes of Gods & Men —[8]

I can never read this without being wound up to the highest enthusiasm, without wishing all the world to crash into confusion, and myself to be swallowed up in the uproar — without fancying the Alps and the Andes tumbling over each other and crushing all animated beings beneath their ruins — June 27th, 1810.

July 2. Every great man has two objects to gain, Immortality in this world and eternal happiness in the next — how happy is he who in struggling for the one by virtue here secures the other as

8. These events are described in the *Iliad*, XIX,309–XX,66.

well hereafter — Every man of great views should attempt to gain both by the same pursuit — July 2, 1810.

July 9. Neither Homer, Milton, or Virgil excite that dreary, sorrowful feeling by their description of Hell that Dante does. Such is Dante's Power that when reading him, you fancy the Italian language, peculiarly adapted to describe the infernal regions — and yet when reading Petrarch it seems purposely to talk love with —

There is nothing in Homer or Virgil to equal the "terra lagrimosa," [9] the "genti dolorose," [1] and the "aer senza stelle," [2] and "l'aer tenebroso" [3] of Dante — Dante's fancy seems to have been steeped in Acheron and to have so steamed with sadness and sorrow that every idea that entered came out dripping with misery and tinged with grief — I never think of that dreadful fancy (which must have shook his frame to the centre when he first fancied it)

> Per me si va nella città dolente,
> Per me si va nell' eterno dolore,
> Per me si va tra la perduta gente,[4] &c.

seeing these dreadful words in "colore oscuro" [5] written over the tremendous entrance to Hell at the end of a deep & woody way — and these too which totally overpower one, "Lasciate ogni speranza voi ch' entrate," [6] as he goes into the secret place and perhaps shuddered in awe as he passed the dreary eternal dreadful gate; sighs, moans, and deep groans resounded thro the air without a star, and he wept as he entered; then what had sounded like distant moanings & sighs, outside the gate, became now more distinct and dreadful inside, horrible tongues, unknown languages, accents of anger, moanings of grief, voices deep & hoarse, & clapping of hands, made a tumult in the eternal darkness like a whirlwind — you are more affected at this than

9. *Inferno,* III,133.
1. *Inferno,* III,17.
2. *Inferno,* III,23.
3. *Inferno,* VI,11.
4. *Inferno,* III,1–3.
5. *Inferno,* III,10.
6. *Inferno,* III,9.

Milton's sublimity & the warring atoms in chaos, because you see the suffering of your fellow creatures, it is pathetic — Virgil's "continuo auditae voces vagitus et ingens," [7] &c is certainly not so dreadfully grand, and pathetically terrifying as this — he does mention "infantumque animae flentes" [8] &c — but there it ends — Homer's ἀγείρετο μυρία νεκρῶν ἠχῇ θεσπεσίῃ[9] is not to be compared. To both Homer & Virgil I venture to think in their descriptions of Hell may be applied what Johnson said of Addison, "he thinks justly but faintly;" [1] certainly Virgil's Theseus "aeternumque sedebit," [2] and the Fury opening the door and shewing the damned at their labours is very grand — but you care nothing about Sisyphus or Tantalus or Theseus; you do not feel your mind clouded by grief, or your soul so strongly affected — Dante's descriptions and his scenery is more dreary — and his subjects more interesting; he must therefore affect you more strongly — and when you recollect he was a Christian — it is overpowering. What is there to equal the "luce muto," [3] the "misero vallone," [4] and the spirits whirled about by the "bufera infernal, che mai non resta" [5] — and the "abisso dolorosa," [6] which thunders with groans, "oscura, profond' era, e nebulosa" [7] — so that he could not perceive the bottom — Virgil & Homer don't go far enough; they don't make you shudder for yourself — Milton affects you with a sublime dreariness, but Dante harrows up your soul with melancholy — The three other great Poets have more taste, and don't disgust as Dante does in some parts, but comparing them in their efforts to affect the mind as they all struggle to do, with a dreary terror — Dante to my feeling beats them all —

7. *Aeneid,* VI,426. "At once are heard voices and wailing sore."
8. *Aeneid,* VI,427. "The souls of infants weeping."
9. *Odyssey,* XI,632–633. "The myriad tribes of the dead came thronging up with a wondrous cry."
1. "He thinks justly; but he thinks faintly." Samuel Johnson, *The Lives of the English Poets, — Addison (The Works of Samuel Johnson, LL.D.,* Oxford, 1825, VII, 452).
2. *Aeneid,* VI,617. "And evermore shall sit."
3. *Inferno,* V,28.
4. *Inferno,* XXXI,7.
5. *Inferno,* V,31.
6. *Inferno,* IV,8.
7. *Inferno,* IV,10.

Ibant obscuri &c. — very fine too.
Ibant obscuri sola sub nocte per umbram, &c.
Quale per incertam lunam sub luce maligna
Est iter in silvis, &c.[8]

Nothing can exceed Virgil's description of the Sibyll's inspired & labouring fury

"Poscere fata
Tempus" ait: "deus, ecce, deus!" &c. . . .
. . . Maiorque videri
Nec mortale sonans, adflata est numine, &c.[9]
. . . Cymaea Sibylla
Horrendas canit ambages antroque remugit, &c.[1]

This is the finest thing in all Virgil — or any body.

July 9. Spent a delicious morning surrounded with Homer, Virgil, Milton, & Dante —

Milton's sublime dreariness overpowers your mind but does not affect your heart.

When I am in company without Ideas or fancy, such as old People, my Father's friends whom I must some times visit — and they are talking about Mrs. Such a one, and lamenting the times, and drawling out imbecil stuff about boiling apple dumplings, &c., I always think of Achilles, leaping into his chariot like the rising Sun and shouting, rushing into the battle — [I] fancy Achilles glittering, his god-like form, his dreadful arm, his furious horses.

I recollect a connoiseur once looking at a Picture of Wilkie saying, "Gracious Heaven, look at that pincushion" — Achilles darted into my mind and I could have beat him to my feet with delight —

8. *Aeneid,* VI,268–271. "On they went dimly, beneath the lonely night amid the gloom, . . . even as under the grudging light of an inconstant moon lies a path in the forest."
9. *Aeneid,* VI,45–50. " ' 'Tis time to ask the oracles,' she says; 'the god, lo! the god!' . . . and she is taller to behold, nor has her voice a mortal ring, since now she feels the nearer breath of deity."
1. *Aeneid,* VI,98–99. "The Cumaen Sibyl chants from the shrine her dread enigmas and echoes from the cavern."

July

Sub pedibus mugire solum [et iuga coepta moveri
Silvarum,] visaeque canes ululare per umbram
Adventante dea.[2]

This is also very fine.

What more sublime than Priam seeing Achilles beaming
across the field like the Star Orion, which showers pestilence on
Mankind, Hector resolving to await his approach, firmly resisting his Father's and Mother's entreaties, stands like a serpent fed
with dreadful drugs, coiled up, and looks dreadfully, at the
approach of a Traveller — Achilles comes towering on like Mars,
balancing his terrible Spear on his right shoulder, his arms
gleaming like a burning flame, or like the rising Sun — Hector
looks at him as he comes on, beaming with Divinity — it overpowers him; he shudders — he dares not remain — he turns his
back on the gates — and terrified flies — Nothing can exceed
this[3] —

What a fancy it gives one of Achilles; even Hector could not
look at him without losing his usual firmness; he could not bear
his furious splendor. It makes one's own heart tremble at the Idea
— It awed him into terror — and Hector, the great κορυθαίολος[4]
Hector, fled, like a child — July 9th, 1810.

What a tremendous creature has Homer made of Achilles —
how truly sublime — It awes one into silence in reading this passage — nothing bombastical —

How grand too is the Agamemnon of Aeschylus — how every
thing [is] arranged; what beams of a poetic visionary fancy he
displays — The Idea of its opening with the Man who had been
watching for nine years for the signal from the nearest mountain
that Troy was taken lamenting his situation, anxiously looking out
for the long expected fire — on a sudden — the flame bursts thro
the night — It is the signal — in a tumult of Joy he rushes down
to tell the Queen — the whole city is in an uproar — preparations

2. *Aeneid*, VI,256–258. "The ground rumbled underfoot, the wooded ridges
began to quiver, and through the gloom dogs seemed to howl as the goddess
drew nigh."

3. The passage is found in the *Iliad*, XXII,25–176.

4. "Moving the helmet quickly," an epithet frequently used of Hector, for
example, *Iliad*, II,816.

are made for the reception of the King — a herald arrives — the King is landed — and in a short time enters the city in triumph with Cassandra. The chorus scream out that visions of horror are floating before their eyes, prophetic of some horrid event — one's heart beats at the fancy — Cassandra descends — and not speaking — the Queen leaves her in disdain — the Chorus ask her why she speaks not — she is still silent — she begins to foam at the mouth — and when the Chorus is exerted to a dreadful pitch of expectation, Cassandra screeches out with the fury of inspiration, 'Οτοτοτοῖ πόποι δᾶ Ἄπολλον Ἄπολλον.[5] The Chorus in terror ask her why she invokes Apollo with such accent of lamentation — Cassandra insensible to all but her own visions — again screeches 'Οτοτοτοῖ πόποι δᾶ Ἄπολλον Ἄπολλον, and to repeated questions cries out only Ἄπολλον Ἄπολλον. She asks the God to what house he has brought her. The Chorus tell the House of the Atridae — she tells them it is a House of Blood — she then has a vision of the murders that happened in it — she then sees in her prophetic fury what is to happen to Agamemnon, and tells them of the dreadful bath — she says, "O dreadful, dreadful παπαῖ, τί τόδε φαίνεται;[6] what is this that shines so in the net of Ades? — (nothing can give one a more dreadful feeling of a vision — the vision of the dreadful net appears to shine to her fancy — it so expresses those momentary flashes of terror — which rush into one's mind like sparks) — she again warns them of the bath — she seems rather exhausted, and foretells her own Death — the Chorus tell her that tho she has a terrifying sound in her voice, yet there is musick in it — Cassandra again says the furies are still in the House. She again has a vision and exclaims "What fire invades my body" — 'οτοτοῖ, Λύκει Ἄπολλον, οἲ ἐγὼ ἐγώ[7] — as she is entering the House, in a melancholy strain foretelling her own murder as well as the King's — she starts back with horror — "Why do you start," say the Chorus. These chambers breath blood & murder, φόνον δόμοι πνέουσιν αἱματοσταγῆ.

5. Aeschylus, *Agamemnon*, ll. 1072–1073. "Woe, woe, woe! O Apollo, O Apollo!" (Tr. H. W. Smyth.)
6. *Agamemnon*, ll. 1114–1115. ἒ ἔ, παπαῖ παπαῖ, τί τόδε φαίνεται; ἦ δίκτυόν τι [γ'] Ἄιδου. "Ha! Ha! What apparition is this? Surely 'tis some net of death."
7. *Agamemnon*, l. 1257. "Woe, woe! Lycean Apollo! Ah me, ah me!"

July

[Chorus.] Καὶ πῶς; τόδ' ὄζει θυμάτων ἐφεστίων.

[Cassandra.] Ὅμοιος ἀτμὸς ὥσπερ ἐκ τάφου πρέπει,[8]

such a smell as exudes from a tomb — says Cassandra, and enters — The audience must have been kept in dreadful suspense
after being worked up to such a Pitch of Horror and expectation
— in the midst of the awful silence that followed Cassandra's
departure — when every mouth was closed, and every heart beat,
and every frame trembled with terror — when in fact every man
must have fancied murder was committing in the house — Agamemnon groans forth from within, Ὤμοι, πέπληγμαι καιρίαν πληγὴν
ἔσω.[9] "Hush," say the Chorus, "who is it that groans, being struck
so near us mortally with a wound." Again Agamemnon groans —
Ὤμοι μάλ' αὖθις, δευτέραν πεπληγμένος.[1] "Ah, it is the King's cry,"
screech the Chorus; "they are about it" — and while they [are]
in doubt what to do, out rushes Clytemnestra glorying in the
deed, and bedewed with his blood — she then describes how she
struck him as he lay. The Chorus upbraid her — Δαῖμον,[2] who has
stirred the women of this House to commit such horrid deeds,
and art now sitting over the body croaking in savage delight thy
dreadful hymn, like a hateful crow — this dreadful speech is uttered by the Chorus — the play shortly afterwards ends. July 1810.

I was at Lord Elgin's today and studiously examined bodies,
legs, arms, and heads; the rectus muscle is beautifully and regularly divided by thin ribbons of tendon; this all painters have
always shewn in whatever position they put their figures — but
mark the beautiful attention of the Greeks in the Theseus. The
bowels fall in, the belly is therefore quite flat and all the markings
retain their form, but in the lying figure, the bowels falling out
destroys the regularity. What sense, what propriety in their making every thing bend to truth —

---

8. *Agamemnon,* ll. 1309–1311.
"Cassandra: The house reeks with blood-dripping slaughter.
"Chorus: What wouldst thou? 'Tis but the savour of victims at the hearth.
"Cassandra: 'Tis like a breath from a charnel-house."
9. *Agamemnon,* l. 1343. "Ay me! I am smitten deep with a mortal blow!"
1. *Agamemnon,* l. 1345. "And once again, ay me! I am smitten by a second
blow."
2. *Agamemnon,* l. 1468. "O thou Fiend."

In passing Piccadilly I observed in some horses galloping the various positions of their limbs — what was the position of the fore legs when the hind legs were in such a position, &c — it is astonishing how truly you get at their motions by thus scrutinizing; I made some sketches, after I arrived home, and they seemed to spring and had all the variety I could possibly wish — and such a look of Nature and activity! — July 11th, 1810.

I spent five hours with Fuzeli Sunday last spouting Homer, Virgil, Dante, & Milton; never shall I forget his recitation of Καὶ μὴν Σίσυφον ἐσεῖδον,[3] when he came to Λᾶαν ἄνω ὤθεσκε ποτὶ λόφον[4] he dwelt on ὤθεσκε so that I fancyed I saw him labouring to push it just to the top ἄκρον ὑπερβαλέειν[5] — then all was struggling to get over just as it came on the critical point, and the Countenance of Sisyphus began to brighten at the prospect of finishing his labours —

$$τότ' ἀποστρέψασκε κραταιΐς,$$
$$'Αὖτις ἔπειτα πέδονδε κυλίνδετο λᾶας ἀναιδής.[6]$$

Fuzeli rattled away these last lines in such a way that I thought I saw the stone suddenly leap & roll & crash down the Hill again, while Sisyphus in despair again began his labours — I learnt a great deal from him — his pronunciation of X & K had a grand sound — I never leave Fuzeli without a greater delight for my art, without being more full of grand Ideas, without being instructed by some observation, or delighted by a flash of wit — I flatter myself I can adopt so much of Fuzeli's fire & pungency as I find necessary for my own purposes, without suffering him to lead me astray, by his enthusiasm — I am firm in my own principles, as much as tends to advance or encrease the stability I imbibe — but the moment he advances any thing that won't bear investigation, I turn as deaf an ear to it as if it were uttered by [an] Idiot, such as his wishing me not to draw what I see in my studies &c — which I know to be erroneous — and which I never listen to. I thank God I always had from the first moment I com-

3. *Odyssey*, XI,593. "Aye, and I saw Sisyphus."
4. *Odyssey*, XI,596. "He thrust the stone toward the crest of a hill."
5. *Odyssey*, XI,597. "Be about to heave it over the top."
6. *Odyssey*, XI,597–598. "The weight would turn it back, and then down again to the plain would come rolling the ruthless stone."

menced studying a judgement of my own, a desired plan, which I felt an internal conviction of was the only right one — this I pursued with a dauntless intrepidity, in opposition to all, experienced & inexperienced — and was as little affected by their ridicule or their attacks as if I had had 50 years conviction of its excellence — That I did so God accept my gratitude; its excellence I now indeed perceive and can with a certainty of its success recommend it to others —

Enveloped as it were with these principles, I trusted myself fearlessly with all men, convinced of my ability to retain only as many of their notions as contributed to add firmness to my own. "Beware of Fuzeli" was the advice of all, but as this caution was necessary only to those who having no object of their own, were at the mercy of unsettled whim, I never let it operate on me an instant. I have now known Fuzeli five years — and consider his Friendship on the above principle a very, very great acquisition — no man has like Fuzeli the power of directing your fancies to a point — if you mention to him any conception, any subject, he sees instantly its defects and always (perhaps a little overstepping the modesty of Nature[7]) points out its capabilities. Tho' he may do this rather furiously — it is in the right road — tho' too far. Fuzeli is such a man as does not appear in two centuries — and that they'll think when he is dead.

[*About six lines are torn away.*]

Lawrence has too much execution.

The drawing an eye is thus [*a sketch*] — now proper execution would be to do it with as few touches as possible — that is, to give the right form at once and nothing more or less (as I have proved in my other journal). If then instead of thus [*a sketch*] drawing with your brush at once this form, you draw it thus [*a sketch*] for the mere purpose of shewing the dexterity of your Brush, you handle for the mere purpose of handling — which is a mean end — and beneath a great mind — but if you guide your brush with reference to the exact forms of things, dash as much as you please, it will always be delightful — it will be . . .

[*About six lines are torn away.*]

7. *Hamlet*, III,ii,21. "That you o'erstep not the modesty of nature."

Stotard [8] appears a very sensible man. He said (talking of poor Wilkie who was seriously ill [9]) that he thought a man of talent always imparted a portion of his respectability to his contemporaries and that one always partook of the disgrace that attends bad painters as well. There is always an angelic purity of character about Stotard's Women & Youths that marks a refined mind, but his men often border on effeminacy — and such a character as Achilles, it would be out of his powers to represent — flitting angels, elegant youths, and delicate women are his delight, and no man ever exceeded him in giving a look of innocence that is not of this world.

In Flaxman there is an affected pomposity of Christian virtue & humbleness that is quite laughable. At the same moment I could perceive he appeared gratified by scandal — and poured out insinuations with his eyes on the ground, as if from pity & compassion. In walking through his work shops, I was struck with immense public works he had in hand, and sighed to see Journeymen, chisseling without the least feeling things that might be made rivals to Ancient Greece. It is indeed little encouragement to Government to give the Public money to Painters, when their liberality to Sculptors has produced so little excellence. There are none deeply versed in form — Flaxman knows not rightly the shape of the knee — and as to the great essentials of motion — they are in total ignorance of. There is not amongst them a man of great genius — there is none who is anxious of the honor of his Country. They care not how their monuments are executed so long as they are once in [St.] Paul's and the cash in their pockets — ought they not to be ashamed to send out mishapen hands and twisted feet? Pshaw — there is neither nature or sense in their productions — they are a disgrace to the Country. It was lamentable to see their total deficiency in correctness — how they could

8. Thomas Stothard (1755–1834), R.A., painter and book-illustrator, best known for his "Canterbury Pilgrims" (1807).

9. On August 2, 1810, Wilkie wrote to Sir George Beaumont: "The accounts you have had of my indifferent state of health are but too true; I have been confined for these six weeks by a fever, which I am happy to say has now left me, though in a very weak state. As it was accompanied with a slight affection of the chest, I was induced by Lord Mulgrave to send for Dr. Baillie, who has attended me ever since, although, I believe, more from his own kindness than from any apprehension of danger" (Cunningham, I,306–307).

dwell as they did on their forms with such complacency is to me a dreadful proof of their conceit or their ignorance (I thank God that my eye is so acute. I hope I shall be always delicately alive to incorrectness and avoid it like Medusa's head — let me recollect never to dwell on it an instant. At present after dwelling with such rapture on the Elgin Marbles — without affectation such glaring ignorance gives me pain). I will think only on them, they shall be with Nature my only instructors — at present I tremble for fear I should be mislead. I hope not — industry and unremitting application are [my] only safeguard.

Among them all indeed, Painters & Sculptors, there is great want of that tremendous power, that overwhelming enthusiasm, the great characteristics of Genius. They are all married — the flattery of their wives, and their wives' friends blind them to their deficiencies — they are surrounded by a set — they are R. A.'s, they forget that every man is a Student till he dies, and longer too.

A man that begins to Study at Six in the morning will have gained 8 years when he has studied 50 years, over him who begins only at 8 — vice versa, he that lies abed till eight will have lost 8 years — 2 hours a day for meals — when you have lived 50 years you will have spent 8 years in eating.

$$\text{One hour a day} \quad \begin{array}{r} 365 \text{ hours in a year} \\ \underline{50 \text{ years}} \\ 18{,}250 \text{ hours — at one hour a day} \\ \underline{2} \\ 36{,}500 \text{ hours at two a day in 50 years} \end{array}$$

$$\begin{array}{r} 3{,}041.8 \\ 12\overline{)36{,}500} \\ \underline{36} \\ 50 \\ \underline{48} \\ 20 \\ \underline{12} \\ 8 \end{array} \qquad\qquad \begin{array}{r} 8 \text{ days} \\ 365 \text{ days in a year}\,\overline{)3041 \text{ days}} \\ 2980^{1} \\ \overline{61} \end{array}$$

1. As is frequently the case, BRH's arithmetic is incorrect.

In 25 years you will have lost 4 Years

12½	2 Years
6¼	1 Year
3 and Six weeks	½ Year
1 Six months & 3 weeks	¼ Year
9 Months 1 week 3 days ½	6 weeks
4½ — 5 days & ¼	3 weeks
2¼ — 2 days ½ ⅛	10 days ½
13 days ½ 1 day ¼ ¹⁄₁₆	5 days ¼
½ ½ day ¼ ½	2 days ½
¼	1 day

July 24. I arose at Six and painted with vigour two hours before breakfast and then painted on with encreased energy till dusk — I was going on doing this day after day with delight when a weakness attacked my eyes.

August 5. Sunday. I this day again received the Sacrament, and from my Soul I thank God I did so; I felt afterwards a veil of purity & cleanness of heart spread as it were over my mind. I listened in the afternoon to the Sermon, with real love, and felt a glow as every divine truth issued from the Clergyman — I never experienced finer sensations. I felt an enthusiastic delight at the fancy of pursuing with energy a religious life — I appeared eased of the burden of my Sin — I thought I was forgiven — and as I was abstracted in musing for a moment the sacred cup and wine beamed into my fancy with such an awful influence as made me tremble. The great scheme of my life is to be a great Painter, and to let the means by which I struggle to obtain this end be so virtuous at the same time to make me worthy when I die of obtaining eternal reward also hereafter — I will, if God permit me, receive the Sacrament monthly. No means are so effectual to me as constant employment, and constant Religion. There is indeed a delight in purity and Religion — nothing else bestows. How Good was Almighty God, not only to establish a covenant whereby Sinners might be saved on repenting, but to lay open also to the World a beautiful doctrine, by which, if they adhere to it, they may [be] prevented sinning.

That Religion and energetic exertion may be my only delight is my sincere prayer, O Almighty Father, thro' Jesus Christ my Saviour, Amen.

Impress me, O God, with awe at thy name; let thy greatness, goodness, so affect me as to prevent me wholly taking thy name in vain, let me tremble at the very notion — and grant my disgust at vice may encrease till I effectually conquer, for Jesus Christ sake — Amen.

My scheme of life, what I always arranged since I first came to Town, is what from my frailty and indolence I have never been able strictly to adhere to — when I first began I did however continue in it till stopped by sickness and having once done for some time, it begat a feeling in me so that I am never satisfied if I do it not and always feel irksome and uneasy. This I hope in God will never diminish, but rather encrease — and as long as I breathe I shall thank God that I did form such habits in the beginning of life — and which I hope will always influence my actions to the last hour of my existence. To rise at five, pray sincerely, to be in my painting room by Six, set my palette &c and begin at Seven, paint till nine, — breakfast, begin again at Ten — paint till five, with a quarter of an hour's intermission for some slight refreshment at two — at five dine — at Six make studies, for the next day, or if you are in no want of preparation, consider what you have been doing, or proceed with it — at eight clean palette & brushes and then walk — and [at] nine take tea, read, retire to bed shortly after ten; from ten to five is Seven hours rest, which will fit you for the next day's labour. This it is impossible to do regularly — business must be done, sickness will come, accidents will happen, difficulties will occur, which it will be impossible for human nature to prevent or provide for — but when you are settled with respect to your intentions, — when you are free from business, clear of accidents, and independent of sickness — what delight is it to put one's hand on one's heart by ten at night and be able to review a day of such employment & effort — how do one's wearied "limbs press the well known bed" — and with what vigourous alacrity does one spring, the morning following, from one's couch; again to struggle for eminence and fame — again to do that by which you hope to be immortal in this World, and receive the approbation of God in the next. This is indeed a happiness, and how often has he occasion to lament his human imperfections who has once relished the delight of this stimulus — August 5th, 1810.

But because business will happen & difficulties will occur, do not let me leave an opening to Idleness, as an excuse for inertion — no — I mean such business as it was impossible to arrange to happen otherwise — and such difficulties as are unexpected and unlooked for. But you must be firm never to suffer anything to interrupt if it depends upon you when it is to happen — you must be as jealous of your time as of your life; and bring your mind to such a habit of spontaneous feeling as to revolt at a lost hour or an indolent moment with as much horror as at the committing of a great Sin — when once you [have] thus trained yourself, you will fly to employment as the only resource from misery — as the only refuge from acute reflection and bitter remorse. Ag. 5, 1810.

It is comparatively easy painting what you see — the great effort is painting what you imagine — because you must combine so much truth only as will prevent your fancy being extravagant — no teaching, no study, will acquire the power of doing this to a point; it must be from Nature — it is a trait that cannot be expressed or explained — it is shewn in the first effort of a man — study will strengthen & improve it, study will enable you to do it with greater facility but will never give it — witness the efforts of those deficient in this feeling who have studied the Antique — or who have never seen the Antique — in the one instance, as they can do only what they recollect their figures are methodized marble — in the other brutal individuality — the power is knowing how so to unite these extremes as to produce elevated *natural* beauty — Augt. 7th.

I have often thought what a fine subject to exemplify the power of music Orpheus suspending Hell would be. The strains of his Lyre — Pluto as if moved — Persephone affected, concealing her face in her hand — a spirit in the fore ground looking up as if roused from her eternal slumber, with the look of ravishment and wonder, tears trickling down her cheek, Orpheus in the centre in an attitude of exquisite feeling, touching his lyre,

Eurydice flitting near him — shoals of spirits whisking about him, in the background Ixion's wheel stopped, Ixion lifting his head, his care worn pale languid cheek, and looking towards Orpheus, with the most melancholy sympathy, the furies agitated, Sisyphus resting on his stone &c, &c — would make an amazing [picture] I think that would touch one's soul and "lap it in Elysium." [2] August 8th, 1810.

September 2, Sunday. I received the Sacrament this day but not with that calm purity I had before received it; I was disturbed by the intrusion of improper thoughts. I promised amendment as sincerely as I could and I hope sincerely God will listen and bless my hope — I did not feel the influence of the virtue of the propitiation. I did not feel awed, but eat and drank in a sullen indifference of feeling — in the afternoon as I was returning and the organ was roaring through the vaulted roof — I felt as if I should be forgiven if from that moment I amended with energy all that was past — it is a refreshing fancy the notion of being forgiven, of being eased — what a blessed institution is the sacrament — God have mercy upon me, Amen.

September 9. As I looked toward a solemn corner of the Abbey just illumined by a rich painted Window, "casting a dim religious light" [3] in which stood the altar, embrowned as it were in shadow — I felt a dreadful influence awe me, and as a misty beam of light streamed through the glittering glass and gave a solemnity to the solitude of the corner, as the organ was roaring and the angelic voices of the boys were chanting, that one's sense was lost, in rapture; I fancied the spirit of God was reposing behind the Altar, and I thought I perceived its influence breathing, as it were, a purity around it. I had that sort of sensation as when in the dead of night, the whole house buried in sleep, you sit watching an innocent, beautiful & sleeping infant and listen to its little breathings, which is all that gives one an Idea of any thing living amidst the quiet and balmy repose that seems to hang over the World — I thought I heard the spirit of God breathing behind the Altar. I trembled from head to foot; for an

2. *Comus*, l. 257.
3. *Il Penseroso*, l. 160.

instant I was lost in a tumult of feeling that indeed belonged to another World, I hid my face in my hands, and prayed with more energy than I ever did before; for the remainder [of] the day, every roar of the organ, and every tone that came from the boys who chanted thrilled [me] to my Soul.

I can not look at this place without trembling — and I still have this feeling, whenever I turn my eyes towards it — I think there it was I saw the spirit of the great awful being reposing — it awes me into devotion in an instant. I thank thee, O God, for allowing me to have such a fancy.

I walked to see Wilkie yesterday to Hampstead;[4] as I returned about four o'clock the Sun was on the decline — and all the valley as I looked from Primrose hill wore the appearance of happiness & Peace. Ladies glittering in white, with their aerial drapery floating to the gentle breeze, children playing in the middle of the fields, and all the meadows were dotted with cows, grazing with their long shadows streamed across the grass engoldened by the setting Sun. Here was a mower intent on his pursuit, with his white shirt and brown arms illumined in brilliancy; there another, resting one hand on his Scythe, and with the other wetting it with tinkling music — some people were lying, others standing — all animate & inanimate nature seemed to enjoy and contribute to this delicious scene, while behind stood the capital of the World, with its hundred spires — and St. Paul's in the midst towering in the silent air with splendid magnificence.

What a change would Buonaparte make in such a scene of liberty and peace — could he but once set his withering foot on this dear island. The state of the rest of the World came into my mind as I stood abstracted, and every other country that my fancy pictured, I thought I saw a dingy lowering cloud hang over it — a beam of light burst through the cloud that enveloped Spain, but it appeared dripping with blood — England alone laid open her peaceful meadows, lit up by gaiety & innocence.

I arose this morning disgusted with my Macbeth and every [thing] about me after contemplating that exquisite form of the

4. Joanna Baillie had lent Wilkie her house in Hampstead (Cunningham, I,315).

black[5] — he is a perfect model of beauty and activity — small body & large limbs, with small joints — his contour was undulating and nature suffered nothing to interrupt this beauty in any position. Even when the arm was bent, the olecranon instead of making disagreeable angles, as in other meagre forms thus [*two sketches, numbered 1 and 2*] was buried as in 2 beautifully within the line — this seemed to be the principle; every thing was packed in.

Wilson was 3 noses to the top of his head, like the antique, but to his chin from the end of his nose is 1 nose and half — his was therefore shorter. Every part depends on its form from its action — the great beauty of the Antique and fine nature is the flexibility of the loins — that is the body in its motions to bend them instead of rolling on the thigh bones. The great error has been putting the markings of the antique into all actions — Wilson has all the markings of the antique in these actions, but they vary as he alters his position. This was the great system of the Greeks and this is the great system of nature. His fore arm is not longer than a European's, but his fore arm and leg are his feeble parts. His face is longer by ½ nose, that is his face is a half a nose longer of his own nose — but his own nose is shorter. He is not of the grandest Style; he is something of the Discobolus, yet his knees have a fine character — they are smaller as well as his hips.

Such is his flexibility and beauty that every attitude that one thought existed only in fancy could in him be realized. His pectorals were lengthened or shortened by raising or lowering his Shoulders.

He was 7 heads & ¾; his half below his pubis — the third head ends at his navel — and the other below his pubis so that his belly by the length of his navel from his breast was rendered small & beautiful — small joints (knees, elbows, & knuckles), small hips — twice his calf — his calf equal to his neck; broad shoulders — short body from the navel downwards — and long limbs — his

5. "About the latter end of [1810] the artists met with a black, a native of Boston, a perfect antique figure alive. On my getting a sight of him, I engaged him for a month, and proceeded to draw and cast him without a moment's loss of time in all the attitudes wanted for my picture." BRH's attempt to make a cast of his entire torso nearly resulted in his death (*Autobiography*, I,106–107).

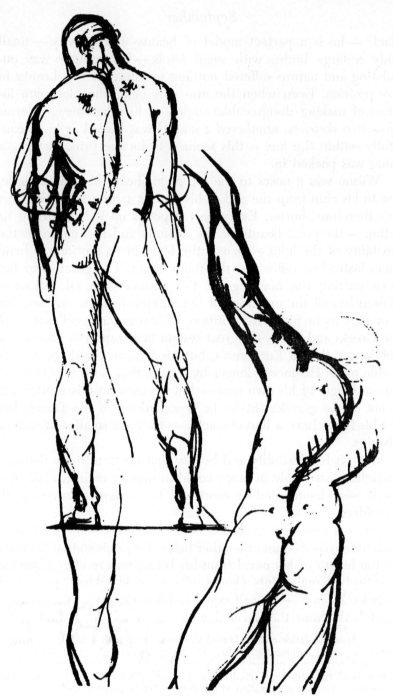

Wilson, the Negro model, September 1810.

thigh large — exhibiting his power to move his leg and foot — his arm powerful expresses the power to move his fore arm & hand. His great muscles — Trapezius — Pectoral and Deltoid — divided so as to comprehend all their actions. Shoulder 3 times the width of the back of his head.

Such was his beauty & power that whether in action or relaxation, his forms expressed either more perfectly than I ever before saw them in Nature — the moment he moved, his intentions were evident — this great principle was more strongly impressed than ever on my mind — *that the form of a part depends on the action* — he had that perfect suppleness that one felt but never before saw — his joints were exquisitely clear — every head of bone, having insertion of tendon — but marked by delicacy & feeling — in repose they became undulating beauties & in action vehicles of energy and refined activity — his body bent at his loins like whale bone; he sat upon his heel & put his foot over his neck — the motion of his wrist and ankles were flexibility itself — never was there any doubt as to his actions — the bony flatness of his joints & tendons and the fleshy fullness of his muscles produced that undulating variety of line — *I was now convinced from Nature that one great cause of action & strength as I had before observed in the antique was the parts to be moved always to be smaller and depending on the parts moving* — reverse this — large bones & small muscles are the general causes of awkwardness & deformity & want of vigour — it must be so.

Never were sharpness & softness seen in such perfection as in him [*two sketches*]. A low navel lessens the belly; raise the navel and the belly becomes long, full, & horrid [*two sketches*]. Therefore narrow shoulders, large joints, high navel, long body, & short limbs, large hands & feet & head & small neck are the characteristics of ugliness — there are some observations in this exercise to be arranged afterwards. 1810.

Make the figure 7 feet — the centre of the whole is the top of pubis — The Pectoral muscle is a foot from the thigh — the navel is the centre between the bottom of belly and Pecl. Muscle — and the Pectoral Muscle in the centre between the navel & clavicle — the head is a foot — and the space between the chin & clavicle in the throat — the acromions & crown of the head form an equilateral triangle — which is bisected by the line that bisects the head — the nipples are half a foot from the centre of Pectoral muscle — the hip muscle is half a foot from top of thigh.

As the navel is not the centre between the top of pubis and Pectoral muscle — and is the centre between the bottom of belly and Pectoral muscle, repeat the distance of navel from Pectoral and the bottom of belly is found — the clavicle from sternum is equal space of navel — the triangle at breast is equal space of pubis.

Great joints have a fine effect in such characters as Juno or Jupiter, where they encrease the great sweep and strength of the line, but in undulating, youthful beauty they should never be shewn to interfere [with] the flow and sweep.

His Deltoid was too short, which gave the arm a snapt appearance.* It should come lower than the insertion of the Pectoral.

The teeth and the belly are parts that are merely animal. The smaller the belly and the more receding the jaw, the farther it removes the man from the animal — reverse this, the consequence is obvious.

The inner ankle [in] the Lion and all animals [of] that species is lower than the outer one — this seems to be an animal character, for when Monkeys & Lions stand on the hind legs like man, their feet are flat. The Black's ankle inclining that way makes the feet flatter than the European's and is a link to and characteristic of animal Nature.

[*A largely illegible listing of "heroic," "lower," and "animal" anatomical characteristics occupies the next two pages of the diary.*]

The firmness and power of a limb should depend not on the joints and parts being hard and immoveable but on the internal vigour and power of the muscles to keep the limb firm; the joints should be all relaxation & suppleness. What more can shew the exquisite judgement of the ancients, than this distinction, in a *centaur* — that is a human body united to a horse — they have

* I had no idea of a system when I observed this. 1813. A mere observation.

marked the *depresscens* muscle which is the peculiar muscle of all graminivorous animals — and in a *Satyr* they have marked the [*an illegible word*] muscle which belongs peculiarly to all carnivorous animals.[6]

In the first place the great distinctions in the form of Man from Animals are his standing erect B on his feet — his feet alone supporting the whole weight of his body — the freedom of his arms from his body at the Shoulders A [*diagrams of a lion and a man explain these points*]. While animals walk on the toes of their four paws C C C C — and have their arms tied to the body at the elbows D — consequently that is the best shaped foot for a human being, which best enables him to stand firmly — and that the best shoulder which enables [him] to work his arm strongly. The length of the body of an animal in proportion to his limbs — in comparison to the length of a human in proportion to his limbs. If the body of a Lion was as short in proportion to its other parts, the hind legs would interfere with motions of the fore legs; it must therefore be so long as not to interfere, and not longer than will enable him when he springs forward to push the fore division (when it is up from the ground) with power — so that fore division may be not over and [*three illegible words*] or his fore legs — vice versa. The Deltoid muscle then enables a man to move his arms up — in front and behind, which requires these heads of the Deltoid. The Lion has no occasion in his motion to move his arm — he can't do it — he has the two feeble heads which arise to the Deltoid and which may assist in back motions of the arm.

A human foot is not formed for moving alone — it is only for support — the muscles of the leg move it — the four points on which a Lion runs all move individually — there are motions of animals that belong also to a man and which an animal has in

6. The illegible word looks like *ringlus* (an unknown word) or *singlus* (a possible misspelling of *cingulus*). Dr. Winfield Durrell, Department of Animal Pathology, the University of Vermont, Dr. J. F. Smithcors, Department of Anatomy, College of Veterinary Medicine, Michigan State University, and Dr. Malcolm E. Miller, Department of Anatomy, New York State Veterinary College, Cornell University, agree that by *depresscens*, BRH probably meant the depressor labii inferioris, common to herbivorous animals and absent in carnivores; however the illegible word may be read, it clearly indicates a sphincter or ring-like encircling muscle, such as the orbicularis oris.

more perfection; such qualities, if they degrade not a human being, may be added to make up a perfect composition of body and mind, such as springing, which is owing to the flexibility of the Loins — this tenuity is a great beauty.

The defective parts of Wilson, the black, were his Deltoid, his fore arm, his vastus internus, his calves, his ankles — and his feet — answering exactly to the defects of animals in comparison with a human form — which makes the gradation in approach.

The principle is to consider all animals as inferior human beings in the gradation of creation.*

All animals that have paws (which are an inferior species of hands & feet) I would consider an inferior class of human being because horses, pigs, cows, and all animals who have hoofs, single or double, have a different arrangement of bones and muscles, which in those parts have scarcely any resemblance to the human beings — therefore I would venture to consider them as further removed.

Intellect is the highest quality. He that has the highest intellect is the highest being — Man of all animals has the highest intellect, therefore he is the highest being. We may reasonably suppose that the parts subservient to his intellect are the best adapted to execute the suggestions of that intellect — therefore it may be granted that the form of man is the best form to wait upon and obey his intellect — and as man's intellect is the highest & most noble, we may infer that the form that contains it being the best adapted to it may also be the highest and most noble form.

We may then conclude that as the form of man contains the highest intellect, what distinguishes his form from the form of those beings who have less intellect are distinct characteristics of intellect — and where the form of other beings of less intellect differs, it is characteristic of a deficiency of intellect. Thus we find that Blacks in their form approach that of those who are deficient in intellect — their lobes of ear small, their teeth frequent, lower jaw retreats, the scull is diminished — they have longer bodies, longer fore arms, greater projection of elbows, deficient Deltoids,

* All animated creatures are but modifications of the human form — this is the gt. principle. 1815.

they are deficient in the great muscles which keep the form erect, vastus internus, &c. They have higher calves, greater projection of heels, flatter feet. Blacks then walk feebly, with a shuffling want of firmness — Monkeys have more of these characteristics and can neither walk or run, but only hop irregularly — and Lions are decidedly deficient in human characteristics of standing erect; [they] walk decidedly horizontally and cannot walk erect at all.

No doubt many high intellects are contained in many an animal form — but as Painting conveys intellect by forms, the forms by which she conveys intellect should be the most perfectly adapted to express it and as animals have inferior intellects and differ from man in form, every form that marks this difference in the form in animals should be avoided in a perfectly formed intellectual being, for how is a Painter to convey this difference of intellect but by the difference of form — form being his language?

December 26. It cannot be said certainly that because a man has a small lobe to his ears, because his body is long, or his legs short, because his feet are flat and his ankles inverted, it cannot be proved that deficiency of intellect must follow, or that because he is finely formed — intellectual greatness must necessarily be the consequence — from experience we find it occasionally otherwise — but exceptio regulam probat — the first man formed must have had all these qualifications of his class in perfection, intellectual and bodily, and every variation since, I should venture to call a deviation from the eternal principle, rather than a proof of its fallibility.*

This being ascertained, then, namely the form that best expresses intellect in Man — different characters of this form may be formed — such [as] the graceful & the strong, the delicate, the active, &c — always reflecting that the intellectual characteristic still bearing these proportions in the general variation to female

* Individual exceptions are nothing; where is the character of the class? The greatest part of cows have but one head but we know some are born with two — are we to say "you have no right to argue that one head is enough — because some have two"?

tenderness may be mingled with manly vigour — and even the peculiar qualities of any animals may be added to express any particular excellence in a stronger degree, provided it detract not from the human characteristics. The human characteristics must always be first placed — *man* must be first built — then any peculiar characteristic of any other creature may be mixed to express any particular intention. If an inferior character be wanted, this is another thing — but I mean when a graceful,* strong, active or beautiful intellectual being is wanted to be formed — if an inferior character, regularly degrade him first — and then add any animal quality to degrade him further, as you in the former instance added them to express any peculiar human quality in a more eminent degree.

As Nature varies the forms of intellect, so may a Painter; he may for variety put in intellect in the forms of idiotism &c — if any extraordinary end is to be gained.

Idiots come under another head. They are deficiencies in intellect, not in form. Animals have intellect — but on a lower scale. Idiots have none at all.

Grace, strength, slenderness & activity are inherent qualities of form — anger, love & horror, and all the passions &c are inherent qualities of the mind — affect all forms but for the moment they last. They have nothing to do with the character of the form — for the slender, the graceful, the active, & the strong may all be roused by anger, melted by love, or be paralized by horror — the passions of the mind act on the form, be the form what character it might, and act only occasionally — while the qualities of form are inherent, and act always in the man.

Small Loins, small knees, small ankles, & small wrists are notwithstanding animal characteristics — and according to the vulgar notions are beautiful — whereas they certainly give an appearance of weakness — and were *always avoided* by the ancients on that account — because the hip muscles, the glutaeal, all enable a man to keep erect and standing erectly being a grand intellectual distinction should be considered.

* Grace, strength, delicacy & acting in the man [are] inherent, delicacy & activity of an intellectual being always take care.

December

It would make a grand series of subjects, the different cere-
monies of all the superstitions of the Earth, and conclude with
the beaming purity of Christianity — Indian, Egyptian, Grecian,
Jewish, &c. The mysterious magical incantations of India, the
dismal dances of the Priests of Egypt about the blue furnaces of
their brutish Gods, the Pale eyed priests of Delphos uttering their
prophetic yells — the Solemn sacrifice of these Druids — the terrific descent on Mount Sinai — the birth of Christ — and his
bowing his head on the cross amidst the eclipse of the Sun, and
the thunder of the Almighty. The two latter would form a climax
that assuredly benefited the world and abolished all the other
superstitions, and opened the eyes of mankind to the truly divine
principle that conduct, not ceremony, was the only method of
obtaining approbation of the great being. Decemb. 28th, 1810.

The first thing to be settled — the distinctive characteristics
of an intellectual by his form — vary its character as often as you
please — only in whatever character you change it, let its intellectual marks bear the same proportion.

The three great distinctions are his standing erect — the great
power of motion in the scapula — and his moving his arms from
his shoulders — it follows that whatever contributes to his standing erect, and whatever contributes to the motion of the scapula
bone and what to the motions of his arm must be decidedly ascertained and must be decidedly characteristic of an intellectual
being.

It is found then that [in] an arched foot, the Inner ankles to
be the highest — the calves of the leg to be full, the three great
extensors, externus, internus, & rectus; the muscles that come from
the back internally, Psoas magnus, Iliacus internus, Triceps of
the thigh, Pectinalis &c, the obliqui, the rectus abdom[inis],
Longissimus & Sacrolumbalis, these combine to a human erection
of form. The motions of the scapula & arm are put in force distinctive from animals by the Deltoid supra-spin[atus], teres major, trapezius, Serrati, three divisions, the Lower and Levator
scapulae — Pectoral — mastoideus holds the head erect.

The parts necessary to enable a human being to stand erect,
and to move freely his arms & his scapulae (the great distinctive
marks of an intellectual being in form) being ascertained, the

various shapes & proportions of these parts form different characters — but the great thing [is] to fix this first human standard.

High narrowness of Pelvis are the characteristics of the
monkey — the ancients always avoided this — and for no other
reason I venture to think but because they found it in monkeys
and when they made the bones small they gave such amazing
power to the muscles that attach to it (on the principle of the
parts to be moved &c) as in the Torso, that the animal character
is compleatly lost — The Torso is a compleat standard of human
characteristics — all the muscles that contribute to the erection
of man are distinctly marked, so distinctly that it must have been
done on principle — (as there never was a human form compleat) all the muscles that enable him to move his arm & Shoulders, the consequence is that it has the appearance of being a
compleat human being — and truly might Michel Angelo say
that he could discover in that sublime fragment any principle of
art.* [7] The Torso seems to be a gentle admission of the animal
principles of activity — (leaping etc — which narrow hips ensure) combined with the principles of the human characteristics
of standing erect & walking firmly. This compleats a perfect
character.

The last night of 1810 — a year of success severely chastened
by misery & want — how little the World are acquainted with
the private miseries of their fellow creatures — God in Heaven
pardon the vice with which I have disgraced this past twelvemonth. I promise nothing — I humbly hope for all.

1 8 1 1

January 7. Painted faintly — raised my figure — a day on
which I can reflect with little pleasure.

January 8. Painted attentively about three hours, but not
conclusively — dined out. Did nothing from five till bed time — a
bad day.

* But it is inferior to Elgin Marbles in not having made its
forms subservient to the great laws of life. 1815.

7. "It was to this statue [the Belvedere Torso] that Michael Angelo declared
that he owed his power of representing the human form, and in his blind old
age he used to be led up to it, that he might pass his hands over it, and still
enjoy, through touch, the grandeur of its muscles" (Augustus J. C. Hare, *Walks
in Rome*, New York, 16th ed. [n.d.], p. 650).

January 9. Arose in a fever of anxiety about Macbeth — altered & advanced — not yet compleated the hanging together of my figure.

January 10. A thick dark fog obscured all light. I had my foot & knee cast in the morning in the action of Macbeth. The great principles of Nature are always apparent in the feeblest form — and will always assist. Did nothing the whole day — a third of the month is now gone.

January 11. Painted attentively — advanced my Picture — made Studies from Six to eight for the hand & arm of Macbeth.

January 12. Painted attentively — advanced my Picture — went to the Academy in the evening and saw the Laocoon placed out as it was four years ago — it excited immediately a train of thought of the many events that had taken place — and here it was still with all its excellencies — while the thousand effusions of indolence that disgraced the world & procured momentary applause were sunk into oblivion.

January 13. At the Abbey in the afternoon, and lost in delight at music of the organ.

January 14. Painted 5 hours with real vigour and determination the head of Macbeth. I think it is better now than ever it has been. Attended in the evening at a lecture at the Academy.[8] Made studies of the ear. I wish to give it a motion as if starting forward to catch the sound, like a horse's. I think this day has not been thrown away. I thank thee O God that I have this day exerted myself.

January 15. God grant I may express in this countenance terror, with a mixture of enthusiastic elevation at the Idea of possessing the crown. In Lady Macbeth, a malicious fury, while a triumphant flash of fire enlightens her eyes — & encrimsons her countenance.

8. Dr. Evan Turner suggests that this was the second lecture delivered by Joseph Mallord William Turner (1775–1851), who had held the professorship of perspective since 1807 but who did not begin his distinguished series of lectures until 1811.

Vigourously at work for 4 hours. Weak & exhausted from sitting up late last night.

January 16. Painted vigourously not more than 3 hours — advanced Macbeth. Studied till late. Wish the day were 48 hours instead of 24.

January 17. Painted vigourously — my Picture advanced. I feel the effects of confinement — four years ago my digestion was not so delicate as at present.

January 18. Painted not more than three hours — idled all the rest.

January 20. Painted faintly.

February 4. Painted vigourously for 6 hours. Got into Lady Macbeth.

February 5. Painted faintly.

February 6. At Lord Elgin's the greater part of day.

February 7. Drew at Lord Elgin's for 7 hours till I was benumbed with cold. Made a correct drawing of the two magnificent sitting women and sketches of different views under &c. I will make Lady Macbeth a fine creature — a bold, full, vigourously lovely form, flushed with wine, heated with fancy, with naked Shoulders half concealed by her jet black hair, which shall tumble in wild disordered luxuriance over her fine bosom heaving with anxiety for murder and a crown.

February 8. Drew at Lord Elgin's for 6 hours and half. One great cause of a flow of line is not to suffer the muscles to end suddenly on each other except in the most violent action.

It appears probable that the Artists of Greece may have been excited to study animals and mingle their characteristics with Man from the perpetual allusions of Homer — Homer is truly the Painter's Poet.

[*A page and a half are torn from the diary.*]

Drew at Lord Elgin's from 6 in the evening till eleven at night. The more I investigate those exquisite Productions, the more I am convinced they are produced on the Principle of selecting what is peculiarly human in form — first what is peculiarly human and then only what is only essential.

As the candle gloomed across and struck against backs, legs, & columns, I was peculiarly impressed with the feeling of being among the ruins of two mighty People — Egyptians and Grecians.

April 1. Raphael always seems to have made hair, like drapery & limbs, a vehicle of composition, tho always on a system in itself. It branches off from the sutures of the scull — this seems to have been the foundation.

Every figure of Raphael is a figure of prime intention, which is always clear — and the most essential — others having exceeded in the colour, light & Shadow, reflection & drawing, perhaps, but no one ever equaled him in expressing the sense of a thing and the harmony of lines in composition. Put the lines of any thing of Raphael's differently — and they come wrong. In short my admiration of Raphael encreases with my experience, tho he is not the Hero of my Soul; I recur to him for propriety, for elegance, for refinement, for arrangement, for the beauties of drapery & hair, of character & expression — he never awes me from sublimity or makes me shudder from terror — he has no being — Ἄρεϊ δὲ ζώνην, στέρνον δὲ Ποσειδάωνι,[9] with a tremendous arm, the death of Heroes — where shall I find a creature in Raphael who leaps into his chariot beaming like the rising Sun, and shouting dreadfully rushes into battle.

April. There cannot be a finer subject in the whole world than Macbeth the moment before he murders Duncan. In the fore ground are the grooms, drunken & drowsy; one has sunk down on his knees, oppressed with sleep, one arm crossed over and pressing on the other, the hand of which is hanging puffed up, red with wine and repletion, the veins enlarged & relaxed; the other has fallen back without power, his hands resting on the ground on each side, his face flushed, his jaw dropped, his hair disheveled, his frill and tunic tumbled up, in careless desolation, and everything about him denoting deep, drowsy, intoxicating

9. *Iliad,* II,479. "His waist like unto Ares, and his breast unto Poseidon."

slumber — immediately behind, between them and the bed, stands Macbeth, the victim of imagination and terror; he has just slid in, bursting with agitated horror, his chest heaved up with agony, his mouth gasping for breath with spasmatic effort, his nostril open, his eye glaring, and bending on vacancy, his lips blue, his cheeks pallid and sunk — and his hands fixed & grasping the daggers with supernatural clutching energy.

Behind lies Duncan the King, simply lying on his back, his breast bared, his sacred cheek flushed with sleep, unconscious and innocent of the horrid scene at that moment passing in his royal chamber; he is soundly sleeping as if surrounded with a breathing influence of sacred royalty. Beside him lies the crown of Scotland on a velvet cushion, pure white drapery covers his shoulders, and hangs from his breast. There is a pathetic look which excites the most intense feelings and forms a fine contrast to the guilty horror of Macbeth — while all the interest is exerted in the chamber, in dim obscurity without, the doors open and in an enthusiastic elevated fury, with a face heated by fancy, a bosom heaving with anxiety, and an eye glittering with delight at the anticipation of the crown, with a hand uplifted as if listening and the deep shadow of her form trembling on the wall and black hair tumbling in wild luxuriance over her fine form, is seen his dreadful wife. Her motion seems to have arrested Macbeth; her whole soul seems wrapped, in methodizing in imagination the murder of the King; her firmness and demoniac enthusiasm are opposed to the conscientious agitation of her heroic husband.

Macbeth's form is heroic — that such a being has fought & conquered at the head of armies is apparent, without shrinking, and his terror now at this moment shews how unworthy the present action is of his character — how unused his heroic soul has been to assassinate; he is in a scene of dreadful perplexity — if the grooms wake, if the King moves — all will be lost — your feelings are wound up to the most excrutiating pitch—and you are afraid even to move yourself, lest such should be the consequence.

The colouring is deep toned and high — Shadows awful — the terror is greatly encreased by the Shadow of Macbeth englooming across the royal bed.

April 7. An old Servant of my dear Mother & her Aunt called, who excited the most pleasing & melancholy associations — as such people cannot be talked to about Achilles, beaming like the rising Sun — I had some cold beef & Porter brought up for them and they appeared much better pleased than if I had attempted to amuse them in any other way.

Nothing can in pathos exceed Homer's exquisite description of the Phaeacians rowing Ulysses to Ithaca by night — after parting from Alcinous in the most affecting manner

'Αλκίνοε κρεῖον, πάντων ἀριδείκετε λαῶν
Πέμπετέ με σπείσαντες ἀπήμονα, χαίρετε δ' αὐτοί, &c., &c. &c. &c.[1]

May you delight in your wives, which you wed virgins & your children

θεοὶ δ' ἀρετὴν ὀπάσειαν
Παντοίην, καὶ μή τι κακὸν μεταδήμιον εἴη.[2]

Wine was poured out by Pontonoe; the noble Ulysses arose and put the cup into the hands of Areta the Queen.

Χαῖρέ μοι, ὦ βασίλεια, διαμπερές, εἰσ ὅ κε γῆρας
Ἔλθῃ καὶ θάνατος, τά τ' ἐπ' ἀνθρώποισι πέλονται.
Αὐτὰρ ἐγὼ νέομαι, σὺ δὲ τέρπεο τῷδ' ἐνὶ οἴκῳ
Παισί τε καὶ λαοῖσι καὶ 'Αλκινόῳ βασιλῆϊ.[3]

Having thus spoke he issued out of the Portal attended by Nymphs with presents; they spread carpets that he might sleep soundly; he then ascended and lay down in silence (κατέλεκτο σιγῇ),[4] the rowers cut the sable deep — slumber weighs down his lids — deep & delightful, even like death — they darted on, bearing a man equal to the Gods in wisdom, who had suffered such agony & misery in wars and passed so many changes, and now

1. *Odyssey*, XIII,38–39. "Lord Alcinous, renowned above all men, pour libations now, and send ye me on my way in peace."
2. *Odyssey*, XIII,45–46. "And may the gods grant you prosperity of every sort, and may no evil come upon your people."
3. *Odyssey*, XIII,59–62. "Fare thee well, O queen, throughout all the years, till old age and death come, which are the lot of mortals. As for me, I go my way, but do thou in this house have joy of thy children and thy people and Alcinous the king."
4. *Odyssey*, XIII,75–76.

this man of sorrow slept in dewy tranquillity, forgetful of all his misfortunes. To heighten this delightful scene of silence, the most glittering of Stars darts up — fortelling the light of the genial Aurora — they reach Ithaca — and land him still sleeping.

You see at last Ulysses reposing after all his toils, the Hero, the suffering Hero — it really affects one — the morning Star glitters, morning reddens, the rowers cut the deep, and Ithaca streaks the Horizon — Penelope's love, Telemachus's affection all associate — it goes to one's heart — I fancy Minerva in a silvery cloud stood at the Helm & watched him while he slept.

April 21. Neglected my Church — Θεω.

I have heard many people prefer Hector to Achilles, because, say they, he is more interesting — granted — Homer's object was to make Achilles only terribly sublime, hence his invulnerability, hence his invincible strength, his rapid motion, his glittering splendor, his awful height; to kiss your child who clings to her nurse's breast, to squeeze the hand of a beautiful, delicate, lingering wife are images of interest and gentleness, and excite love and pity for the amiable Hector. They spread a veil over, and diminish his warlike prowess — and certainly detract from his power to create terror in war — the Stormy Soul of Achilles was insensible to the delicate indolencies of domestic feeling (and Thank God they were so); his terrific arm, his gigantic breast, his mighty limbs, his heroic neck and beaming eye were made only for war, for destruction. Does any man wish, while his face is heated and his hand grasped in reading Homer's description of Achilles in fight — to have his tremendous sensations softened by the association of domestic tenderness? One tear, one tender look, one infantine smile crossing your fancy (as they do when Hector fights) and Achilles is no longer a moving engine of terror.

Hector has other qualities, Hector is amiable, Hector is gentle, Hector is tender; Achilles impetuous, unpitying, invulnerable. The qualities of Hector are more delightful, those of Achilles more terrific. The most delightful qualities are not the most useful in war. Homer's object was destruction, death, terror — and no such being but Achilles could have attained this object to such a degree — Hector might have spared the young, protected the feeble, defended the defenceless; Achilles by a blow of his gigantic arm would have swept them from off the earth and hurried on with a Lion's rapidity to fresh scenes of slaughter & destruction; had he been liable to wounds, a fear or a hope of his Death might have lessened the terror — rapid, fierce, invulnerable* — there is no hope, terror precedes, destruction follows, to meet is to be annihilated! — Hector, when tenderness & gentleness could not avail, fled before his terrific divinity — Homer's object was to excite fierce, awful terror — and in no other way could he have so compleatly accomplished it. April 21, 1811.

May 6. Last evening Rigo,[5] a French artist, member of the Egyptian Institute, and who accompanied Denon[6] to the Cataracts of the Nile — and remained in Egypt after his departure, and ascended again with the Savan[t]s[7] — who was at the dreadful battle of Sedimah with Desaix[8] — spent the evening with me. I was curious to get out every anecdote about Buonaparte, from one who had been with him repeatedly, seen him repeatedly, & was always at his table during the Egyptian expedition.

He said the night before the battle of Aboukir, where Buonaparte beat the Turks,[9] he lay on the ground in the same Tent with Buonaparte; about Midnight he told Berthier[1] and the rest of his Generals who were with him to go to sleep in their cloaks till the day break. (Rigo's brother was interpreter to Buonaparte with the Turks — they were all in the same Tent.) Rigo said he never was with or near Buonaparte but he was always attracted

* But he was not invulnerable. He was wounded in the hand in the Scamander. B. R. H.

5. Michel Rigo (d. 1815), genre and portrait painter.
6. Dominique Vivant, baron Denon (1747–1825), artist, diplomat, and author. He wrote *Voyage dans la basse et haute Egypte* (Paris, 1802, 2 vols.) after accompanying Napoleon to Egypt. He became advisor to Napoleon on collecting works of art for the Louvre from conquered countries.
7. Artists and archeologists who accompanied Napoleon's army and compiled *Description de l'Egypte* (Paris, 1809–1828, 20 vols.).
8. General Louis Charles Antoine Desaix de Veygoux (1768–1800). He commanded a division in Napoleon's Egyptian campaign of 1798–1799. After a victory at Sédimah, he subjugated Upper Egypt.
9. July 25, 1799.
1. Louis Alexandre Berthier (1753–1815), marshal of France and Napoleon's chief of staff.

by his Physionomy; there was something so penetrating, so acute, so thoughtful, so terrible, that it always impressed him, and that this night when all the rest were buried in sleep he could not avoid watching him. In a little time he observed him take the compasses and a chart of Aboukir and then measure and then take a ruler and draw lines. He then arose, went to the door of the tent and looked towards the Horizon. He returned to his seat, looked at his watch; after a moment he took a knife and cut the table in all ways like a boy — he then rested his head on his hand, looked again at his watch for some time, went again to the door of the tent, and again returned to his seat. There was something peculiarly awful — the time of night, his generals soundly sleeping, Buonaparte's strong features enlightened by a lamp, the association that the Turks were encamped near them, that before long a dreadful battle would be fought. Rigo said his feelings were so alive that he could not have slept. Buonaparte looked all round to see if all slept. Rigo shut his eyes in a moment, like all the rest. In a short time Buonaparte called to them all — they sprang up — ordered his Horse — and asked how long before day break. They told him an hour. The army were under arms. He rode round, spoke to the colonels & Soldiers, told them in his energetic manner that a mile from them there existed a Turkish army, and he expected by ten o'clock that they existed no longer.

Before ten they were annihilated. Kléber,[2] who commanded the reserve, did not join till after the Battle. About this time Buonaparte was surrounded with trophies, standards, cannon, trappings of the Turkish camp & Horses, when Kléber appeared suddenly at the door of the Tent. Kléber was Six [feet] two Inches high, and the handsomest man of his time. When Buonaparte came, he said, "Eh bien — qu'avez vous vu?" "Général," dit Kléber, "elle est la plus grande bataille du monde." He uttered it with furious enthusiasm. "Eh bien," said Buonaparte, "il faut que vous déjeunez avec nous."

Kléber had traversed the field of battle in forming his junction with the main body and had witnessed the dreadful effects of it.

2. General Jean-Baptiste Kléber (1753–1800), successor to Desaix as commander in Egypt. He was assassinated in Cairo on the same day (June 14, 1800) that Desaix was killed at Marengo.

Rigo said (after he returned from Egypt, at the Surrender of Menou[3]) [when] Buonaparte was Consul, he dined with him. He is never more than ten minutes at furthest at Dinner. His two valets, the moment he eat one dish, put another; he eat that, then drank a few glasses — and retired to his cabinet. They all arose when he got up, and then staid two or three hours.

Since he has become Emperor, he is not so easily seen, but about six months since, Marshal Bessières[4] called on him, by the Emperor's order. He carried down to Malmaison the sketch of what he was then about. The Emperor was in the Garden. The moment he saw him he smiled and said, "Vous engraissez." He shewed him the sketch. "Eh bien, what does David[5] say." &c. &c.

His private secretary is a young man about 29. He sleeps above the Emperor; the Emperor goes up to him at two & three in the morning and begins to work — he, the Emperor retires to bed at nine generally and is always up before day break.* He is grown very fat lately.

He said Buonaparte on the field of Battle was as cool & collected as in his Cabinet.

May. Painted 4 hours & ½, and went two hours and studied the Titians at Lord Stafford's.[6] Nothing can equal the exquisite lucid colours but the fleshy softness of the forms. Felt weak & relaxed; overslept myself — spent the evening in delight amid the ruins of Athens. Every day, every hour, these exquisitely delightful forms — I hope in God, for him I thank for being in existence when they arrived. Let [them] take deeper root in my nature. May they be interwoven about my soul. May their essence be mingled with my blood and circulate through my being. May I

* Bourienne's Memoirs prove that Napoleon seldom rose before 7 — and then often unwillingly (1829).

3. Jacques-François, baron de Menou (1750–1810), who succeeded Kléber. He surrendered to the English, August 30, 1801.
4. Jean-Baptiste Bessières (1766–1813), duc d'Istrie.
5. Jacques-Louis David (1748–1825), court painter to Napoleon.
6. The second Marquis of Stafford (1758–1833), later the first Duke of Sutherland, owned four important works by Titian: "The Three Ages of Man," "Venus Rising from the Sea," "Diana and Actaeon," and "Diana and Callisto." They are now in the collection of the Earl of Ellesmere in Bridgewater House, London.

never think of form, select from nature, draw a line or paint a touch without instinctive reference to these exquisite refinements. O God if there is a part of life I feel grateful to thee for more than any other, it is the part I have spent among those inspired productions.

June 1. Arose at half past six. Walked out and breakfasted with Wilkie at Chelsea[7] — home by a quarter after ten; began to paint at eleven; painted Seven hours, with vigour and attention. Was out in the evening from 8 till 11.

June 2. Sunday. Read.

June 3. Up late, at eight. Painted faintly — altered & improved.

June 4. Up late again, at eight — Painted faintly not more than two hours; out from 4 till nine — 5 hours lost — at Lord Elgin's 2 hours.

June 5. Arose late!! at eight — Painted two hours vigourously but not more. Called in an indolent raking humour on two Friends, and really laughed and idled the rest.

June 6. Arose [at] half past Seven — still late. Saw fine pictures — one of Vandyke, who had the power of keeping up that fine solid surface throughout more than any other man. Acquired great knowledge — tho put it not in practice today. Walked to Primrose hill with Hunt.[8] Read Alfieri's Memoirs.[9] Idle, idle.

The first six months of the year 1811 are now on the eve of closing. If I review them with rigour, what will they exhibit but

7. Wilkie was living at 4 Manor Terrace, King's Road, Chelsea (Cunningham, I,321).

8. Probably James Henry Leigh Hunt (1784–1859), editor of the *Examiner,* or his brother John (1775–1848), publisher of that weekly newspaper. BRH probably met Leigh Hunt in 1807 (see II,80); on May 11, 1808, Wilkie wrote in his diary, "With Haydon, called on Leigh Hunt" (Cunningham, I,172). BRH soon became "the artistic hope of the 'Examiner' group and Robert Hunt [another brother, who served as art critic] recommended Fuseli to study the 'property' of his 'hues, forms and expressions of passion' as exemplified in 'Dentatus'" (Edmund Blunden, *Leigh Hunt's "Examiner" Examined,* 1928, pp. 10–11). After BRH's father had withdrawn his financial support in 1810, BRH borrowed £30 from John Hunt (*Autobiography,* I,109).

9. *Memoirs of Vittorio Alfieri,* written by himself. Translated from the Italian. 2 vols., 1810.

one scene with few exceptions, of Idleness and vice, not either of absolute Idleness. I have been at times energetically employed, but I have not so conquered my habits as to have that invincible pertinacity of soul, to be so independent of circumstances, whatever they be, as to make them bend to me, as to proceed, tho' misfortune oppress me, tho' vice tempt me, tho' sickness overwhelm me. O God, can there be a finer spectacle than a human being steadily defying the accidents of life, and struggling in his last gasp for the object of his being, contemplating with rapture, while a drop of blood animates his soul, the efforts of his life for excellence — thinking that he has done all a human being could do, that he has fully exerted that talent which God implanted in him, and left not a moment unoccupied or a wish for excellence unattempted. God in Heaven grant that this may be my lot — when I lie in expectation of Death may my expiring eye glisten with delight at the reflection of my efforts from this moment — and may my senses close in silence here, to open to eternal harmonies in another existence.

June 18. The 21st will soon approach, and from that moment, the year declines with unheeded quiet.

January. The first week ill — the latter three, upon the whole vigourously employed.

Feby. The first week or ten days drew with vigourous application at Lord Elgin's, painted and advanced my Picture.

March. Certainly industriously employed at first; the latter part Idle.

April. Ill and weak — Idle the greatest part.

May. Painted faintly at first — vigourously about the latter end. Arose as I *always* ought at five and Six and drew two hours for a little time.

June to the 18th. Nothing to recollect but Idleness & folly.

June 19. Arose at ½ past five; in my painting room by Six — at work till eight; began again at ten. Seguier called, on whose judgement Wilkie & I so much depend — if Seguier coincides with us we are satisfied, and often we are convinced we are wrong if he disagrees with us.

He thought my Figure better than it ever has been — in short he congratulated me on its being right — Let me be in want — Let me be in misery — hungry & faint, and no money to relieve me (as I have been) — dispirited from sickness, and despondent from neglect — at the end of the day if my exertions have been successful — if my Picture is advanced, if my fancy has been expressed — if difficulties have [been] conquered — I can bear all, I can look with complacency on my miseries. I could regard the destruction of the world with firmness, and suffer destruction with it (at the notion of having done my duty) without a struggle.

I have not time to gain the affections of a woman; I have not time to suffer the petty interruptions of love, to be harrassed by the caprice of my mistress, or the jealousy of my own disposition — all this is delightful, no man on earth would enjoy it more than myself, but all this distracts attention and disturbs thought. I have not time to devote to it — and relinquish it I will.* June 26th, 1811.

July. I called last night on a Sister of my dear Mother's who married with every prospect of fortune & happiness but who by the carelessness of her husband has been reduced with 8 children to want and distress. My Father assisted them for some time — paid 80£ to bind out the eldest Girl — and the husband again altered his conduct and lived with & supported his wife. After innumerable changes and ruin, after living at Bath, Bristol, Worcester, and half the cities in England without any settled scheme — he is again in Town at 55 years of age with 8 children ignorant of to-morrow's fate or whether he shall be without a loaf for his next breakfast. It was a melancholy thing to see my dear Aunt lying [in] sickness in a little bed, up in a second floor with her family about her, I who recollect her in a splendid house with a curricle at her command and servants to anticipate every wish, I who have seen [her] laugh with joy and talk with rapture at the prospect of her family, and listen with delight to the flattery of guests — it was a melancholy thing to see her care worn cheek and expressive eye, her forehead knit into an acuteness of feeling from habitual sorrow, her depressed mouth and large full

* If I can. Note, 1835. Mary's eyes settled this! B. R. H.

and quivering lips, her nostril expanding at every breath — and her fine complexion mellowed into a faint rosiness of hue; to see her now bent with suffering whom I recollect erect with vigour and beaming with health — to see the tear start into her eye as I approached and took her hand — and to hear her tongue faintly falter "My dear Benjamin, I wish to die. My dear Sister is gone before me — I hope I am also going. At my time of life to be so harrassed, to have no settled home." I sat down by her and tried to keep up her spirits; sometimes a faint smile would lighten up her fine countenance — and the moment I was silent and she relapsed into abstraction, a tinge of pathetic grief would make her features tremble. The whole room had the silence and faintness of sickness. Her face was enveloped in a white bordered cap — a white bed-gown encircled her arms to her wrists with ruffles.

When I looked on and thought on her former splendour and health, and her present misery & sickness, "I will bring thy grey hairs with sorrow to the grave" [1] passed through my mind, with an awful sensation. I went home in silent reflection, and hoped to die before age had weakened me — or misfortune reduced me — I hoped to acquire the highest fame and to die like Nelson, when it blazed brightest. July 5th, 1811.

He that has elevated views is always at first stigmatised with selfishness or presumption till time has elicited his right to differ, and his reason for having a will of his own. Those who ridicule your intentions before they comprehend them are generally the first to applaud them when they do. Nothing is so injurious to a man's prospects as an *unseasonable* & early marriage — it hampers his attention and dulls his ambition. July 5th, 1811.

July 9. She is dead. My poor Cousin called on me this morning and told me she died quietly — with scarce a breathing heard. I declare I felt not regret — I had a sort of feeling come over me as if she was released from misery and trouble — God grant her spirit that calm repose that was denied it in this dim, groveling spot.

After the agony of mind I experienced at my Mother's death, no other trouble impresses me.

1. Compare Genesis, 42:38 and 44:31.

It gives great atrocity to a head when the Nose is equally distant from the Chin & forehead.

My principles of Art are these — the elements being professedly laid in imitation — every thing should be so true to Nature as not to excite attention individually — but only encrease the terror, beauty, or sublimity by its general resemblance, by having the great leading characteristics of things seized with truth — that is and ever will be my great principle of Study.

My Friends tell as a wonderful instance of my perseverance [that] after having finished Macbeth, I took him out again to raise him higher in my Picture, as it would contribute so much to improvement — the wonder in Ancient Athens would have been if I had suffered it to remain. In such a state is Art in this Country!!! July 20th, 1811.

I awoke about two and immediately putting on my hat issued out into the Garden. The day had just broke; with a streak the clouds of night were gradually breaking. The Morning Star glittered with beaming agitated refulgence. I inhaled the cool translucent dewy morning air, pregnant with the refreshing silent scent of new hay. I left the house and began to ascend the hill. The grass was long and glittering with dew, the cattle were still in indistinguishable obscurity, forming masses of dingy cool shade. When I reached the top, Day had shot up a beam to the Vault of Heaven; still Nature was buried in silence, still all animated being seemed buried in repose. I waited on the top of a rock surveying the scene of glittering obscurity with delight, when the village church bell at my feet toll'd the hour in rumbling solemnity; the clocks of the other villages of the valley answered in various harmony, intermingled with the shrill crowing of the cocks, till their mixed sounds died on the morning wind as it swept the vale with moaning stillness. The Horses rose, stretched and shook off the morning dew and began browsing on the side of the Mountains; the cows tumbled on their knees with awkward effort and sprung upon their legs; the sheep bell tinkled amidst the flock, and up they sprung in succession. At this moment the Star faded, light seemed to spread round the sky, a beam announced the approach of the Sun, the lark twittering rose rapidly, the fields spread out in vivid green, the distant hills appeared in misty blueness and masses of vapour rolled on in dispersion as the splendor of the Morning Sun glittered on their rotundity. Birds sung in the groves, dust announced travellers on the roads, all Nature seemed laid out in distinctness — every thing seemed ris'n into life and animation, while two hours before all seemed suspended by Death. I returned home refreshed, and found Wilkie still rapt in sleep, unconscious of the delicious scene that had passed in Nature. I stood lost in silence as day gradually approached. Day gradually encreased, and things began to shake off their supernatural drowsiness — the enchanted mists dissolved from plants, who lifted their heads with renovated vigour. July, 1809. Devonshire.

July 27. In a torrent of feeling about Homer the whole evening.

July 28. Breakfasted with Hunt — my spirits "light and airy from pure digestion bred" [2] — I am now convinced from experience depression of spirit is generally owing to repletion. I have curtailed my allowance of animal food and find myself adequate to study after dinner without interruption. My principle is to get as much health as possible, to be as free from disease as possible, to stretch it by the highest exertion possible, and yet without injury.

Hunt and I dined with Wilkie; spent a very pleasant evening. His Picture is nearly finished and a very fine thing he has made of it. [3] We began our Pictures together after our return from Devonshire. What a history would the events during their progress furnish to the inexperienced Student!!! How gaily we began them, how soon were we checked, he by disease and I by oppression. Notwithstanding Wilkie's [dis]interested treatment of me in many instances, yet I am attached to him, and so is he to me. God grant our lives may be an aera for the Arts of our country, he in his way, I in mine. May we go down to Posterity in an

2. *Paradise Lost,* V,4.
3. "The Village Festival," painted for Angerstein (who paid 800 guineas for it) and now in the Tate Gallery (Cunningham, III,525).

united blaze. I never think of him now but with this association.

July 29. Monday. An hour at French, from eight to nine. Went into the City for cash — came home exhausted — did not touch a brush.

July 30. Tuesday. Up at eight.

August 17. Up at seven. An hour at French. 3 hours drawing carefully from a model an accurate study for the chest of Macbeth — why could I not have done this at first? inexperience, wishing to find, as Sir Joshua says, shorter roads to excellence than those where energetic exertion is required.[4] Finished the hair of Macbeth. I am sick at heart when I recollect what I *have* done with what I *might* have done.

August 18. Sunday.

"An opinion has very generally prevailed that the flat noses of Africans is occasioned by the Mother pressing it down after birth. This is just as false as the notion that the curvature of the thigh bones is occasioned by the weight of the Child resting on the nurse's arms. Both are original formations, as they are seen in the foetus." Winterbottom's Sierra Leone, Page 201.[5]

Winterbottom begins very tremendously to attack White,[6] and quotes what he says about the different formations of the bones of Negroes, as if to knock the whole in the head, but what answer does he give? Does he prove assertion after assertion that White makes to be false? No. He begins by that terrible knock down

4. "[Young artists] wish to find some shorter path to excellence, and hope to obtain the reward of eminence by other means than those, which the indispensable rules of art have prescribed. They must therefore be told again and again, that labour is the only price of solid fame, and that whatever their force of genius may be, there is no easy method of becoming a good painter" (Joshua Reynolds, *Fifteen Discourses Delivered in the Royal Academy,* "The First Discourse," Everyman's Library [1907], p. 8).

5. Thomas Winterbottom, *An Account of the Native Africans in the Neighbourhood of Sierra Leone,* 1803, I,201.

6. Charles White, (1728–1813), surgeon, author of a treatise on evolution entitled *An Account of the Regular Gradation in Man and in Different Animals and Vegetables* (1799). Winterbottom attacked White's theories in Appendix III, II,254–274.

annihilating acknowledgement — that he never had an opportunity of examining skeletons — and it is very foolish to take a half dozen examples. In the first place what right has he to pretend to object to White when it turns out he never observed a Skeleton. Was there ever such imbecility? How does [he] know that a half a dozen were only taken as examples?

"The chief differences in Man are rather taken from the tincture of his skin than the variety of his figure; and in all climates he preserves his erect deportment and the marked superiority of his form." — Goldsmith.[7]

Here is the assertion of a Literary Man absolutely false. What, the chief difference in the tincture of his skin? — What absurdity, what absolute ignorance — and yet Goldsmith would be quoted by your literary men with the greatest conviction against Blumenbach[8] and Camper[9] or Bell & White, who had fundamentally & scientifically examined and proved to the contrary. Winterbottom says he saw a Youth whose features were regularly Greek and whose form might serve for the Apollo Belvidere.[1] What right has Winterbottom to such an opinion — is he a judge? has he studied the Apollo Belvidere? does he know its peculiar characteristics? does he know the principles on which the Figure is built? If he does not, he is not adequate to affect such a theory from the casual glance of his eye. Were Artists to talk about fever & wounds & fractures, would Surgeons listen to their unscientific nonsense — and why should surgeons talk about beauty & proportion? He says White asserts the fore arm to be longer — he never *observed* this, *he* says *he never observed it!* Did he ever measure it? If he never did, how does he presume to contradict a Man *who has?* I too have seen a Black of a fine form, but still all his peculiarities were there — his feet were flat, his ankles weak, his pelvis narrow, his calf high, &c. Can Winterbottom inform us were such were not the characteristics of this Youth in

7. Oliver Goldsmith, *A History of the Earth and Animated Nature*, 1774, Part II, Chap. XI, "The Varieties in the Human Race."
8. Johann Friedrich Blumenbach (1752–1840), German physiologist and anthropologist.
9. Peter Camper (1722–1789), Dutch anatomist and naturalist.
1. Winterbottom, *Native Africans*, I,200.

these parts — his trunk might have [been] full, his skin glorious, his thighs large, &c.[2]

How have the Greeks such reputation? Why are they always referred to as Standards? "Because they never suffered a fault to pass unamended with indifference or quitted it in Despair."

"The Angel of Death they name Duma, and say he *calls dying persons by their respective names at their last hour.*" — Sale's Koran, Page 95.[3]

When I reflect on the apparent inextricable difficulties I have been in, and the perpetual success of my attempts on extricating myself, I cannot help saying, "Fear thou not, for I am with thee; be not dismayed, for I am thy God. I will strengthen thee; yea, I will help thee; yea, I will uphold thee, even with the right hand of my righteousness."[4] With gratitude & reliance on thee, thou great being, did I ever apply to thee for assistance, even if wan from vice — without being listened to — never — never didst thou turn from me if I was in danger; never didst thou forsake *me* — tho' I have ever forsaken *thee* — but when I was in despair, O God, I am ashamed with gratitude. I am all repentance and humbleness, thou good, thou all merciful, tremendous, awful good being. I was in agony last night — opened the Bible and the above verse caught my eye. I got fresh energy — a means darted into my mind. I applied them today, have been compleatly successful, and am going to rest melted with a blushing grateful

2. BRH publicly stated his theory that the Negro race was the link between animals and men in a letter signed "An English Student" and published in the *Examiner*, September 1, 1811, p. 566. Hunt and several readers challenged his views, but he repeated his contention in the *Examiner*, September 29, p. 629. BRH was clearly swept away by the intoxication of seeing his name and ideas in print; he entered the controversy without due investigation, and later changed his ideas completely. After painting a picture of the Anti-Slavery Society's meeting in 1840 and becoming well acquainted with two Negro delegates, he wrote: "There was a time when I believed that the negro . . . was separated from the intellectual European irrevocably; when I believed his brain and bodily conformation were so inherently deficient, that no education and no ameliorated condition could ever improve them. I have lived, I thank God, to be convinced to the contrary. The head of this negro, Beckford, 27 years a slave, and the other, Barrett, 57, are as fine in physical construction of brain as any European in the picture" (*Description of Haydon's Picture of the Great Meeting of Delegates Held at the Freemasons' Tavern, June, 1840, for the Abolition of Slavery and the Slave Trade* [1841], p. 10).

3. *The Koran*, tr. George Sale, 1801, I,95. The italics are BRH's.

4. Isaiah, 41:10.

feeling — overpowered by his goodness, his benevolence, the abundance of his mercy. Aug. 27, 1811.

In consequence of the arm being pressed down close to the side the skin is rolled up under the arm pit. When the arm is raised this skin is stretched tightly over the body. I had observed this in Nature, but before I ventured to put it in Macbeth I went down to see if I could be authorised by the greeks. To my delight the first thing I saw in the fragment of the Jupiter's breast was this very thing. Even thus in the grandest of all abstract characters did the Greeks attend to these little *exquisite* truths of nature. Aug. 30th, 1811.

"Ah, but," said an Artist to me once, "every School has its character — the Roman School for drawing, the Venetian for colouring, the Lombard School for both, and the English School for *neither*. It is the character of the English School *not* to draw well, Sir; drawing won't do in this Country!" — or as a Patron said to me also, "if Michel [Angelo] & Raphael were alive now they would both die *in a prison*." Whose fault would it be if they died in a prison? Surely not theirs. If Artists of such transcendent abilities would have died in a prison, blame could not be imputable to them, but I don't believe they would have died in a prison. Genius will arise and make its way, if born at the bottom of the Indian Ocean.

There is nothing a Man cannot do, no difficulty from which he cannot extricate himself, if he be industrious, virtuous, & Religious. Industry, virtue, & Religion will elicit great talents, but not supply their want.

Let the Students consider every figure as if their existence depended on its excellence. Let them look and compare, scrutinize & alter. What they cannot perceive distinctly in shadow, let them take a candle and investigate, and not make a senseless mass like the sooty back of a chimney. Let them draw *exactly* what they see and nothing more or less. Let them get a correct and perfect knowledge of things as they are before they presume to alter a line, if but the thousandth part of a hair's point. I will venture to say it is the senseless, vicious, impudent, Academic squareness that has ruined or misled the hopes of all the Academies of Europe. You see those young puppies of art scrawl in a smutty outline with charcoal, then square away the features with chalk, then dissect the body into parts as if to shew their knowledge — when I have always observed it exemplified their perfect ignorance, for there was never a mark right; they make knees & ankles and feet, as ponderous & heavy & stoney as if they were building the Colossus at Rhodes. Get a perfect knowledge of Nature as *she is* before you presume to attempt to make her as she *ought to be.*

It makes me mad to see Sir Joshua write in his Lectures that the ancients had an easier task than the Moderns, because of the dress &c, &c.[5] If they had an easier task, it will be more to our honor if we equal them. Instead of giving this handle to indolence, he ought to hold it up as a stimulus, and say the Ancients had less difficulties to contend with, and therefore if we equal them or outstrip them, we shall be *greater men,* and not cant and whine about Modern Artists being obliged to remove a veil before they can see the state of things. Home went every student from his Lecture contented with his inefficient scrawls from round faces, and quieted his conscience by quoting Sir Joshua. Sep. 28, 1811.

Ah, but Socrates did not perceive at first the impropriety of his sensual appetites, and when he first gradully perceived it, he then by degrees also conquered them. This is no argument against him. When he perceived them, that power enabled him to perceive his sensual appetites & to conquer them at which period of his life was the intellectual power which negroes have not.

No diary entries are found in the remaining pages of Volume III. The next page begins a rough draft of the notes which Haydon copied in the margins of "Appendix A. Benjamin West, Esq., to the Earl of Elgin" of William Richard Hamilton's Memorandum on the Subject of the Earl of Elgin's Pursuits in Greece, (1811).

5. "[The manner in which statues are to be dressed] is a question which might employ a long discourse of itself: I shall at present only observe, that he who wishes not to obstruct the artist, and prevent his exhibiting his abilities to their greatest advantage, will certainly not desire a modern dress. . . . Working in stone is a very serious business; and it seems to be scarce worth while to employ such durable materials in conveying to posterity a fashion of which the longest existence scarce exceeds a year" (Reynolds, *Fifteen Discourses,* "The Tenth Discourse," pp. 169–170).

This book, now in the British Museum, contains two letters from West to Lord Elgin, dated February 6, 1809, and March 20, 1811, expressing gratitude for the artist's opportunity to study and sketch the Elgin Marbles, from which West adapted certain classical elements and under the influence of which, he contended, he painted the first modern picture based on the principles of the Elgin Marbles, "Christ Healing the Sick in the Temple." Purchased in 1811 by the directors of the British Institution for 3000 guineas (Whitley, 1800–1820, p. 189), and presented to the National Gallery in 1826, the picture is now in the Tate Gallery. For Haydon's marginal notes, see Appendix C.

The remaining pages of Volume III contain rough drafts of the series of letters which Haydon wrote "To the Critic⁶ on Barry's Works in the Edinburgh Review, Aug. 1810." *These appeared in the* Examiner *of January 26, 1812 (pp. 60–64), February 2 (pp. 76–78), and February 9 (pp. 92–96), under the signature "An English Student."* ⁷

6. Richard Payne Knight (1750–1824), archeologist and numismatist, who bequeathed his great collection to the British Museum. He was a governor of the British Institution, of which he had been one of the founders.

7. BRH acknowledged his authorship when the letters were reprinted in *Annals of the Fine Arts,* 1816 (1:155–172 and 269–294).

Volume IV

NOVEMBER 1811—OCTOBER 1812

Haydon scrawled five largely illegible maxims and memoranda on the inner cover of Volume IV, cut out the first page of the volume, and resumed his diary after a lapse of nearly eight weeks.

Volume IV

November 21. I am happy on beginning this new journal to reflect that my habits of industry and energetic application are steady & persevering — that my mind is constantly fixed on my delightful Art, and the great object for which I wish existence still animating me in my struggles, still supporting me under all trials; God in Heaven grant I may not close my eyes eternally till I have conquered all obstructions; and reached it — till I have made *all* the casualties of life bow to a spirit that will not bow to them & yield to assist my great design after having in vain attempted to frustrate it. Amen. In humbleness and gratitude.

First to select what is peculiarly human in form & feature & proportion.

Then what is peculiarly essential to motion or expression, & lastly what of those *essentials* to motion and expression are wanted for the particular action or expression given — again, to consider —

That the Machine is composed of bones & muscles and tendons, and

First, that the bones and tendons never alter their form tho' they do their position.

Second, that the muscles alter both, and when not in action take the form of that substance against which they are pressed by the action of others, or do press. This appears to me to be the principle of form of the Elgin Marbles.

Young men of "high Design" [1] are always sneered at with want of experience when they begin great works — as if this had not been the misfortune of all the greatest men at first setting out in life — but it is the capability or incapability of conquering the consequences that distinguishes the man of genius from the man of none. Nov. 22.

Great works in painting are as necessary to England's ranking with Italy & Greece as great works in Poetry & Architecture were

1. *Troilus and Cressida,* I,iii,102.

217

necessary to her ranking with them in Poetry & Architecture. Small works may be more fitted to our parlours & our fire sides, as Bell[2] in his Weekly Messenger last year mischievously tried to prove — and therefore Wilkie's art was more adapted to us — to our habits. This may be a very good argument for those who have small rooms & fire sides, but amounts to nothing regarding us as a great Nation. He might with as much justice have argued that the neat cottage & the snug little box were more adapted to us as a Nation than such buildings as St. Paul's or Covent Garden, that the little bronze figures for our chimney pieces & our side boards were more adapted to our habits than monumental Statues or colossal Heroes, that the snug little cutter & neat little brig were more consonant to our comforts than the 74 or the 98, and that therefore no Pictures as large as the Vatican ought to be painted in England — no buildings beyond three stories ought to be built, no Statues beyond three feet to be executed, and no Ships with more than 14 guns to be laid down, because we being a comfortable nation have no business with any thing that we cannot see while we sit with our legs across the grate or indolently suffer [in]digestion by a roaring fire. Granting all this for the fun of the thing, the question is how high should we have ranked when compared with other Nations had this delightful principle directed our energies. Should we have ever ranked beyond masons when talked of as architects, beyond versifiers when mentioned as Poets, beyond plastermen when cited as Sculptors, beyond mechanics when spoken [of] as Painters, or beyond privateering Pirates when thought on as Sailors? Certainly not — but by acting directly on the reverse we rank as the greatest Poets the World has ever seen, the [greatest] Philosophers the World has ever experienced, the greatest Sailors, &c, &c, &c, that ever existed, and it is because we have not acted on the reverse that we have not yet produced the greatest Painters, nor shall we ever till elevation of view [and] soul circulates among the Patrons, till we have made it our creed, that great works pregnant with sublimity of conception & great design are the only means of ranking us with our Poets or Philosophers, our

2. John Bell (1745–1831), proprietor of *Bell's Weekly Messenger*, a Sunday newspaper.

Architects & our Sailors. Magnitude is certainly not grandeur — if the execution be not proportionate to the conception. The conquest of England by the Armada was a mighty conception but became contemptible from its failure. Are we to argue that no Nations are to be conquered, no great battles to be fought because the mighty idea of conquering England from the ignorance of those who conducted it [failed]? If the plan had operated would Nelson have [won] the Battle of [the] Nile or thundered in triumph at Trafalgar?

[*The next page is torn from the diary.*]

Let the government purchase them [the Elgin Marbles]; let molds be executed and casts made from [them], let a set at the expense of government be sent down to Bath, Liverpool, Leeds, Dublin, & Edingburgh; this is the only way to circulate them through the Country, to impregnate the minds of the rising Students, with such notions of beauty & form as will make them revolt instantly at defect as at the commission of a heinous crime — with respect to multiplying the originals, lessening their consequences, [what] can be more absurd? Were they repeated till they out numbered the fishes of the Sea & birds of the air, yet would the original still be as sublime, as inspiring, and as unmixed in excellence, still would the People flock to see them and [stand] lost in feeling at [them as if] amidst remains of Athens. But then the usual complaint, the amount of our taxes and the approaching our destruction — stuff; don't they crowd to the theatres & churches and the more you can exchange their means of amusement, you do a moral good to them. If Government cannot afford to purchase them, let Patrons subscribe. The Students set them the example & began instantly. No doubt the poor Academicians will complain that I am mad — "don't listen to Haydon, a wild young man." I can only say if I am mad I wish I could as Genius bite some of them (as George the Second said to his Generals when they said Wolf was deranged—). Some will sneer because we urge it first. I don't want to be first on the list because I've suggested it first. Do you begin and we are ready to take our ranks in the middle or the end — where you please to marshall us, so long as the thing is done we don't care how. I fancy [I] see the faces of some the moment the thing is mentioned curdle & froth into gallstone envy, with the rapidity of boiled oil, and say "what stuff!"

I don't underate other branches of Art; let low life, water color painters, Portraits, & dogs all go on, but do put them in competition with the higher walks. We shall take the highest rank as a Nation in Art, if we go on succeeding in all. November 27.

December 2. Monday. Painted, but not the great difficulties. Trifled & amused myself with the light parts of my Picture. I have always found it a good plan when tired & wearied with the great difficulties to relieve your mind by painting the lighter parts, instead of giving up & idling with a sullen despair.

I am not one of those who wants to see one part of the Art encouraged at the expense of another; let all be encouraged; let the walls be covered every year at the Institution with Raphael, Titian, Poussin, & Claude, Teniers, & Ger[ard] Dou — but let the High Art be respected as high art and take that rank in the estimation of all to which its height entitles it.

"A performance indeed may be forced for a time into reputation, but destitute of real merit it soon sinks; time, the touchstone of what is truly valuable, will soon discover the fraud, and an Author (Painter) should never arrogate to himself any share of success till his works have been read at least ten years with satisfaction." Cit. of World, Page 74, Vol. 2.[3]

I exhort the rising Students to get a thorough, a compleat, a deep knowledge of what is under the skin, which will only enable them to mark with scientific firmness the beauties of energetic action or to hint with truth the delicacy of repose.

Let every Student be determined that Success shall encourage him, failure stimulate, misfortune rouse him, and oppression excite his indignation — and what is there within the scope of human ability that he cannot attain. December 20.

Let every Student invincibly determine that success shall encourage & not weaken his persevering efforts, that failure shall

3. Goldsmith, *The Citizen of the World*, Letter 81 (1774), II,77. In modern editions this is Letter 84.

stimulate and not depress them, that misfortune shall rouse him, and oppression excite his indignation, and what difficulty is there that "Grows in the veins of actions highest reared" [4] however great, he cannot conquer, what excellence within the scope of human ability he cannot attain.

I thought every man anxious for reform in Art — that the Academy being sanctioned by the King might be made a means of enlightening the public mind in Art more effectually than other institutions. This was my delusion till putting my name [down] [5] brought me immediately in contact with the members, and I instantly & with more clearness perceived & comprehended the views. It was not till then that I had an insight into the Souls, and ascertained that the advance or improvement of Art was of the most trifling importance, in comparison with paltry intrigues or petty cabals for superiority.

The only legitimate Artists of this Country are the Architects, men whose foundation is versed in their profession, and they are obliged to bow to the preponderating influence of splashing, dashing portrait painters. They could not indeed build a house without a foundation, slur over a window, or keep a staircase in shadow — the absurdity would be too palpable — but not more palpable would it be than painting a head without bone, putting dashes of senseless colour for a hand, or unmeaning scrawls for a wastcoat.

December 31. The last night of 1811, when I review the past. I certainly can dwell on it with more pleasure than any year since I commenced to study — tho' I am still at the mercy of vice whenever it attacks me violently, yet my habits of application have been energetic for at least 8 months of the twelve — I ought to be able to say all the twelve — but God grant me this power at the end of the next. I certainly have, I hope, got better habits — there is some consolation in knowing that however vicious I may be, I am always conscious that I am so — and never soothe

4. *Troilus and Cressida,* I,iii,6.
5. For an associateship in the Royal Academy in the election of November 5, 1810 (Whitley, *1800–1820,* p. 177). BRH received "not a single vote" (*Autobiography,* I,112). In his diary for May 11, 1845, BRH wrote that he had sought election in 1810, 1811, 1826, and 1827.

my mind by plausible excuses. My Picture is concluded,[6] by God's blessing, with a body still uninjured by application and a mind invigorated and refreshed for greater works and nobler undertakings — more experienced in all — and a degree, I hope, approached to that Idea of perfection I have formed to myself — as necessary to excellence — God in heaven on my knees I pray thee grant it may be my lot to realize my ideas of Art before I die and I will yield my soul into Thy hands with rapture — Amen with all my soul.

1812

January 1. I entered the year with a sort of indifference. Every thing in this world has an object; what then is [the] object of the existence of things of man to think & act. He has then a mind to think and a body to act — a mind to suggest and a body to execute its suggestions. Again the body has muscles to move it so that it may execute the suggestions of the mind; every suggestion immediately moves a number of those muscles sufficient only to enable the body to execute compleatly the intention, and none are moved but what are necessary, for if any were to move that

6. Early in 1812, BRH sent "Macbeth" to the British Institution, an organization sponsored in part by the Royal Academy, to compete for prizes of 300, 200, and 100 guineas. The Academicians, according to his account, wished to punish him for independence and "to cry up some novelty now Wilkie and I were old affairs." Henry James Richter's "feebly painted picture of Christ healing the Blind" was exhibited in June just before the British Institution was to make its awards. It was hailed as a triumph, declared the equal of Raphael's cartoons, and chosen at once for the Academy's permanent collection. To meet Richter's price of 500 guineas, the Academy withdrew the first and second prizes from the Institution's exhibition, and "bought this new miserably painted picture with the money thus literally stolen from us, voting the one hundred guineas left to a bad picture of a poor painter [George Francis Joseph's 'Procession to Mount Calvary'] and offering me thirty guineas!—that I might not be out of pocket for my frame which cost me sixty" (*Autobiography,* I,135–136).

As for the subsequent history of "Macbeth," it remained a frozen asset on BRH's hands until May 20, 1816, when Sir George Beaumont, after a reconciliation with BRH, gave him 200 guineas for the picture (*Autobiography,* I,244). Its unlucky destiny was not yet complete, however, for in 1823, when Sir George had lent the picture to BRH to be exhibited again, it was seized by sheriff's officers while BRH was imprisoned for debt in the King's Bench Prison, and Sir George seems to have paid again to redeem it from the law (Jared Bradley Flagg, *The Life and Letters of Washington Alston,* New York, 1892, p. 177). The unfortunate picture dropped from sight in 1830, when Sir George's heir sold it (Whitley, *1821–1837,* p. 202).

are not necessary, the body would do that that the mind intended it should not do, instead of what it intended it should, which would be an absurdity and produce confusion; therefore to express any intention of the mind, the muscles (the causes of motion) must be ascertained that are necessary for that action & nothing more or less be marked. This was the principle of the Greeks in form & in every thing. In their order of Architecture they first selected what was necessary to the support of the building and then ornamented that, but put no ornament for the mere purpose of ornament; and the figure must, on the principles of reason & common sense, appear to move to the given point and express the given thought.

January 15 and 16. Made a Sketch for Achilles rushing to Battle — brassy, gleaming, dreadful Armour against a dark blue sky — his spear a comet — Horses — blazes — in back ground Army shouting for miles.

The bones being what contains the intellect, the muscles are the means by [which] an intellectual being moves his form or his body to execute his thoughts. Therefore a thorough knowledge of them is a requisite to express ideas clearly in painting — as a thorough knowledge of a b c is necessary to express his ideas in writing. Therefore as a thought in Painting can only be expressed in painting by form & feature, the body & features should be in the Picture exactly as it would be in nature at such a moment excited by such a thought — and on the principles of association the thought that belongs to that action will be associated with it, and the action will excite association of the thought.

"The tendency of this religion, say they who are *better acquainted with it,* is to enlighten the mind with true wisdom; to banish superstition; to promote universal righteousness, charity & peace; to comfort us in adversity, and give *prosperity* its *highest relish;* to encourage the *most transporting hopes,* with *full assurance* that they *will not be disappointed;* to repress every malevolent and every evil passion; to make men, whatever their outward circumstances may be, *resigned* and *thankful;* and, in a

223

word, to promote happiness, both in time, and through all eternity." Beatty's introduction to the evidence of the Christian religion — Page 2.[7]

When a man becomes an Academician he suffers as great a change as if he had undergone chemical transmutation; however noble in feeling, however high his notions, however grand his ideas before his election, he instantly becomes cautious, timid, silent, politic, critical, effecting to know what he has never heard of, denying what he really knows, undervaluing his rivals and puffing those he need not fear, writhing in company from the praise of others, and never happy unless he can drop on the feelings of him that is praised a bit of that aqua fortis with which [he] boils. Academicians are like the elephants of the east, who are no sooner caught in the pits prepared for them than they become as eager as their masters, that their wild companions should be in the same predicament who are ranging the forest in boundless liberty.

The master of a family, when [an] Academician, suffers torture every evening after eight lest two should come at the same time. If they do, the children are dismissed to bed for fear that they might imbibe; the servants are ordered to deny all future visitors; coals are put on; and all draw closer to the fire in expectation of the commencement. No sooner does one open his mouth but the other snarls; if the mistress of the house looks two minutes longer at one than the other, the other is [in] a rage and is sure to recall her attention by some violent irony or cutting remark. If for an instant the one gets a momentary superiority on the other, if he is out in a date, then how his eyes sparkle, how he grins, how he hunts[?], how he strides. But let the other recover the ascendancy, and in as much as he was previously great, on the weakness of his friend, he is now contemptibly little on his own.

To be an Academician is [the] height of a young Student's ambition, and to qualify himself by cringing intrigue the object of his wishes, and those precious moments that should be spent in painting by day and drawing by night.

7. James Beattie, *Evidences of the Christian Religion*, 4th edition, 1795, I,2–3. The italics are BRH's.

February 3. His heart big with grief, the tear starting in his eye, that the sympathy may be excited in the spectator as if he were rushing out to revenge his Friend.

[*The next two pages are torn from the diary.*]

How Homer raises you by degrees to the fury of the battle. Every thing he describes has a beginning, a middle, & an end — as well as his whole poem. When the greeks first prepare for battle, they eat and refresh themselves, fall into rank clean, invigorated, refreshed, and beaming with the cool effulgence of the morning Sun. They meet, fight, kill each other till Mid day arrives, when the Sun is at its meridian, and the battle begins to rage. All is confusion, roaring, clashing, heat & perspiring. The Horses are panting, whitened by dust. The Heroes are fainting, exhausted with slaughter. Milton has perhaps a more elevated gloomy sublimity that belongs to hell and chaos — but no man equals Homer and Shakespeare in that *inspired spirit*, that raciness of nature, which animates and distinguishes every thing they mention. Every thing in Homer is enlivening and vigorous — you *fancy* all glittering in the heat of day, gilded by the setting or silvered by the rising Sun; but all Milton's mighty cherubin or seraphin seemed to draw their flaming swords, or clash their sounding shields, as if they shone through a darkened glass — dingy, red, solemn, terrible, interrupted by a groan of despair, or quivering sigh of anguish, the intervals of silence filled only with the dashing of the fiery surge which flings up at every roll on the burnt soil a battered arm or shattered ensign.

[*The next nine pages are devoted to quotations from Milton, Homer, Virgil, and Shakespeare.*]

The moment after Hector's effecting interview with Andromache, Hector bursts instantly into the field and kills a hero at the first throw of his spear. This gives one the exact feeling of Nature after yielding to sorrow for any time — you make up your mind with a desperate sort of vigour and get rid of your bursting feelings with a sort of wrench.

Homer says, Book VIII, line 425, "Thus saying the swift foot Iris went." Pope says, which in my opinion is much finer,

> Then mounting on the Pinions of the wind,
> She flew.

This gives one the feeling as if after having delivered her message she struck up perpendicularly and continued ascending & vanishing, glittering like a vision, with colours dipt in Heaven,[8] varying at every turn, when a sudden eddy of wind turned her off and whirled her out of sight in an *Instant*.

Can any thing on Earth compensate for the want of such feelings as these? Who would not bear starvation, destruction, and every misery this "dim Spot" [9] can heap on a man, when he has the power of abstracting himself from wretchedness and revelling, luxuriating, in such a world of delicious, beaming fancy. February 1812.

> Of able body, sound of limb & wind,
> Upright he walks, on pasterns firm and straight,
> His motions easy, prancing in his gait;
> *The first to lead the way to tempt the flood;* . . .
> Dauntless at empty noises; lofty neck'd,
> Sharp-headed, barrel-bellied, broadly back'd;
> Brawny his chest, and deep; his colour gray,
> For beauty dappled, or the brightest bay. . . .
> The fiery courser, when he hears from far
> The sprightly trumpet and the shout of war,
> Pricks up his ears, and trembling with delight,
> Shifts place and paws, and hopes the promis'd fight.
> Dryden, Georgics, III, [120–133].

March 7. In a torrent of enthusiasm, after [lying awake] in bed till three in the morning, about Achilles. The subject rushed into my head, in all its vigour. I was in doubt which to choose, Solomon or him. For a moment nothing would bear comparison — the army shouting, the sea roaring, Achilles beaming, his horses dashing, the God descending — this for a moment swept all obstruction. Solomon's fine heroic features, with his manly locks, conscious of his wisdom, half smiling at the anxiety of the young,

8. *Paradise Lost,* V,283.
9. *Comus,* l. 5.

beautiful βαθύκολπος[1] pathetic mother, who regarding only the safety of her offspring, had darted forward as the executioner lifted his sabre to divide it; the terror of a beautiful girl who imagined the deed was really to be done — the feeling of the [*an illegible word*] vanished before the beaming effulgence of Achilles — in a little time enthusiasm dies away and . . .

[The rest of the page is torn out.]

March 27. As I was lost last night in sullen meditation on my troubles, "Trust in God" said a voice within, and I shook with agitation. I had a feeling as if I saw "Trust in God" written in glittering letters in the midst of an awful misty darkness, like the "lasciate ogni speranza" [2] of Dante. I do, I will trust in God from the bottom of my Soul — God only give me strength compleatly to depend on him.

O God Almighty, thou who so mercifully assisted me during my last Picture, who enabled me to combat and conquer so many difficulties, who gave me strength of mind superior to all, desert me not now, O Lord, desert me not now. I forgot thy mercy and was vicious, I neglected my promises of amendment and fell into my abandoned ways — but O Lord, thy mercy is infinite, to thee I will again cry. Assist me then, O God; my difficulties are again accumulating and will yet accumulate. Grant me strength of mind and body again to meet, again to conquer them. Soften the hearts of those at whose mercy I am. Let them not harrass me, let them not interrupt me. Grant I may be able to proceed steadily unchecked by sickness or misfortune, with my present great Picture; and conclude it as it ought to be concluded. Let not the progress of this Picture be disgraced by the vice which disgraced my last. Let me be pure, holy, and virtuous, industrious, indefatigable, and firm. Enable me to conceive all the characters with the utmost possible acuteness & dignity, and execute them with the utmost possible greatness and power. O God, in every point let my intellectual power rise to the degree wanted for excellence and my vigour of body be proportioned to the fatigue. O God, grant me such purity & piety as may bring down on me thy bless-

1. Deep-bosomed.
2. *Inferno*, III,9.

ing and forgiveness, and grant me the power to make so fine a Picture as may create such a sensation and give such a shock to Art, that the nobility and the people may be roused and high Art have that assistance and that protection adequate to reward its difficulties and worthy of its grandeur. Grant these things for Jesus Christ's sake. Amen in humbleness and gratitude.

O God, in pecuniary emergencies thou hast never deserted me; still in such moments stretch forth thy protecting hand. Amen, Amen.

O God, spare the lives of my dear Father & Uncle till I am independent, and able to take my Sister, and much longer if thou pleasest to delight me, but till then I entreat thee, till then, thou great being and merciful God, Amen.

O God, let me not die in debt.[3] Grant I may have the power to pay all with honor before thou callest me hence, grant this for Jesus Christ's sake. Amen.

April 3. My Canvas came home (for Solomon) — a grand size. God in heaven grant me strength of Body and vigour of mind to cover it with excellence. Amen, on my knees.

April 4. Began my Picture — prayed God sincerely for Success — perspectivised the greater part of the day — felt a sort of check in imagination at the difficulties I saw coming, but, thank God, instantly a blaze of enthusiastic perseverance burst into my brain, gave me a thorough contempt for my timidity, and set me at rest.

April 5. At church.

April 6. Drew in my figures. Ascertained the perspective proportions of all the heads; squared in the pavement; oiled my ground. Thus I have advanced my picture, by God's blessing, more methodically than any I have yet done. Searched in the

---

3. BRH recorded that he began borrowing money in 1810, when his father withdrew his financial support. "*And here began debt and obligation, out of which I never have been, and never shall be, extricated, as long as I live*" (*Autobiography*, I,109). Discussing his situation at the end of 1811, he wrote: "I scrutinised my debts before beginning a new work and found they were £616, 10s., of which £200 was due to my landlord for rent" (*Autobiography*, I,124–125).

evening II Kings for hints as to architecture. I fancy my hand is more certain than it was from the schooling it has had from wading through the drudgery of Macbeth & Dentatus.

Let this not diminish but encrease my exertions. Let them, O God, end only with my existence. Amen.

I must endeavour to distinguish the effect of Solomon's order on different temperaments, some dull, just perceiving — others really alarmed, all wondering, &c., &c., &c., &c., &c.

April 7. Advanced my Picture.

April 8. Went to the London Institution[4] to search for manners of Israelites.

I wish to express in Solomon a fine youthful King of Israel, with delicate hands,[5] clothed in gold, with a sceptre, a crimson robe, [in] his face luscious youthful love mingled with profound wisdom. "The chains, bracelets, and mufflers, the bonnets, the ornaments of the legs, and the head bands, and the tablets, and ear rings, the rings, and nose jewels, the glasses & fine linen, the hoods and the veils," Isaiah, 3, 19. "Speak unto the children of Israel and bid them that they make them fringes in the borders of their garments throughout their generations and that they put upon the fringe of [the] borders a ribband of blue." [6]

The mother should be as if she had burst out of her usual modesty, and the moment she recollected herself would blush.

April 9. Breakfasted with Wilkie. Walked about the Regent's Park. Dined with Soane.[7] So has passed this present day without profit, and with bitter remorse of conscience.

4. The London Institution, established in 1806 "for the diffusion of useful knowledge." Its reference library has been transferred to the School of Oriental Studies, the British Museum, and the Guildhall Library.
5. Bewick said that Wilkie's delicate hands were BRH's models for those of the true mother (William Bewick, *Life and Letters,* ed. Thomas Landseer, 1871, I,62). Perhaps they served double duty and also appeared as Solomon's. BRH had also drawn Wilkie's hands for one of the figures in "Dentatus" (Cunningham, I,180).
6. Numbers, 15:38.
7. John Soane (1753–1837), R.A., professor of architecture at the Academy from 1806 until his death. He formed the Soane Museum from his collection of works of art. In 1831 he was knighted.

April 10. Worked hard, advanced my Picture, got in the architecture, sky, and part of the background, as well [as] Solomon. Certainly I paint with more certainty than I did. Got them in light & thin.

April 11. Worked vigourously; advanced my Picture. Got in the two mothers. At the Opera in the evening — the most delightful ballet I ever saw.

April 12. At church; at Montague's [?]; an idle day.

April 13. Idle.

April 14. Got in some heads; advanced my Picture.

April 15. Idle. Went to the Institution; looked at West's Picture;[8] hard, red, & mean, well-composed in some [parts]. Nothing can be more despicable than the forms. How the people have been duped. Upon the whole, it is one of his best. Looked at Macbeth after.[9] I must say there is an elevation of tone I find not in his, tho' there is a strawy crispness of manner which is not the right thing. The light spotty, the forms hard, the colouring fleshy, but too light. She is too near, not obscure enough — he too big. The mind cannot make allowance for their difference of size at once without an effort. The attitude of Macbeth certainly right, but the struggle to keep himself on his bent knee excites a painful feeling. But in spite of its numerous errors (which God in Heaven grant the Artist power & sense enough to avoid in the next), it is a grand picture. It excites awful feelings. There is an elevation of soul which makes one's heart expand.

Judith, Chap. X [3–4]. And braided [the hair of] her head, and put on a tire upon it, and put on her garments of gladness — and she took sandals upon her feet and put on braceletts and chains and her rings and her ear rings, and all her ornaments, and decked herself bravely, &c.

April 16. Worked.

8. "Christ Healing the Sick in the Temple." See Appendix C.
9. "Macbeth" was shown at this time in the British Institution's prize exhibition.

April

April 17. Advanced my Picture.

April 18. At Wilkie's private exhibition.[1]

April 19. Neglected my church.

April 20. At Wilkie's Public exhibition.

April 21. Industrious; got in the head of my landlord's child.

April 22. Made an accurate drawing for Solomon, from Salmon.

April 23. Breakfasted with Wilkie, who is in high glee, of course, about his exhibition — he heartily deserves all his success.

April 24. Two hours drawing from Salmon. Wilkie called and we had a grand consultation about the composition of my Picture.

April 25. Five hours drawing from Salmon. Finished my Study for Solomon.

April 26. Sunday. Idle.

April 27. Monday. Rode to Hampton [Court] on Wilkie's Horse. Spent a delicious four hours with the Cartoons. What an exquisite Heavenly, delightful mind Raphael had. Nothing can exceed the beaming love, the eager warmth of pure Devotion like St. John's head, in Christ delivering the keys. His delightful face seems to start forward from his hair with gratitude & rapture. His full mouth, unable as it were to utter from that sort of choaking one feels when the heart is full, his bare, youthful cheek, his long hair, his closed hands, bespeak the extatic sensations of rapturous piety, overflowing with gratitude & delight. Again in the Cartoon of Peter healing the lame Man; while the poor beggar is agitated with hope, and attempting to make an effort to rise, while St. Peter, with uplifted hand, is telling him in the name of Jesus Christ to arise, St. John looks down on him with such a mingled air of blushing, compassionate devotion, as if his heart glowed with feeling.

1. An exhibition of twenty-nine pictures and sketches by Wilkie, opening on May 1, according to Cunningham (I,351).

St. John seems to have been a character Raphael delighted in. It was in fact his own. Whenever he appears he has the same look of purity, piety, benevolence, meekness, and voluptuous rapture, with a glowing cheek enveloped in long heavenly hair.

What a beautiful creature is that in the corner, who is gracefully with a fairy's lightness supporting an elegant wicker basket of fruit, flowers, and doves, and holding a beautiful boy, who carries doves also, which are undulating their little innocent heads to suit his motion. She, as she glides on, turns her exquisite features, her large blue eyes, beautiful full nose, and little delicate breathing mouth, which quivers with educated refinement; the upper lip seems to tremble with feeling, and to conceal for a moment a little of the nostril. Never was there a more exquisite creature painted. It is impossible to look at her without being in love with her, without longing to press such an innocent creature to your bosom, and yet tremble for fear of offending her by such a conception. Raphael's flame has the steady, pure, divine, bland warmth of a silent lamp; Homer's the blazing, burning, furious strength of a heated, flaming furnace.

Several bye standers seem to regard the beggar with an ejaculation of "Poor man." One seems lost in abstraction as if reflecting on his helpless situation.

The whole picture excites the tenderest and most delightful sensations.

Think of Fuzeli's savage ferocity, his whorish abandoned women, the daughters of the bawds of Hell, engendered by lecherous, dusky demons, and then bring to your fancy this exquisite, graceful, innocent creature dropped from Heaven on a May morning or sprung up from the center of a rose spangled with dew, at the delicate, voluptuous, gentle kiss of a bending, pearly lily. Again think of Fuzeli's men, the sons of banditti, and contrast them with the rapturous innocence of St. John. It can't be born. The more I see of Nature, and the more I see of Raphael, the more I abhor Fuzeli's mind, his subjects, and his manner; let me root his Pictures from my fancy for ever, and banish them from my Soul. XI at night.

Thank God, I am capable of enjoying the sensations Raphael intended to excite. May they every hour interweave themselves with my being, and by mixing with the essence of the Elgin Marbles, produce such Art as the World has not yet seen. Grant this, O thou Great Being, and grant I may realize this conception before I die, and I will die content. Amen with all my Soul.

Raphael's faces are full of the "light within," [2] and truly is it a divine light; his eyes glisten, his cheeks glow, his mouths quiver; the soul seems bursting for utterance; the heads of every other painter are pantomimic puppets without Soul or sensation; but the heads of Raphael are the emblems of love & intelligence; his children are the germs of his Men & Women. The apellation of Divine indeed he deserves. In comparing his peculiar beauties with the beauties of the Elgin Marbles, the way I would distinguish them would be thus: their beauties are the beauties of form & flesh, the consequence of the Soul impelling the body; the beauties of Raphael are the beauties of the senses [and] features, the immediate external organs of the Soul. A body can only express action or repose compleatly; it can entreat, it can refuse, &c., but when it must shew the refinements of passion, how little can it do without the action of the senses [and] features; but a look can terrify, can delight, can oppress you with awe, or melt you with love, without a single corresponding assenting motion of the body. As then the end of painting is to express the feelings of men, and as the features alone can express more than the body alone, and as the body is subservient to execute the intentions of the Soul, and the features to express them, and as the office of the body is more material and that of the features more spiritual, and as spirit is more divine than matter, he that excels in the expression of the soul by the features is greater than he that excels by that only by the form* because they are capable of expressing more — of a greater compass.

April is ended, irregularly passed. The last week made drawings of heads.

* because the powers of the body are more simple and more attainable and less various than the powers of the senses. Reciprocity of feeling is stronger through the senses. The union of the two is certainly irresistible.

2. *Comus*, l. 381.

May 1. I cannot tell to this day how I passed [the month of April]. At the Exhibition,[3] some good Portraits, wretchedly off in the higher walks. Every year it will get worse — every year it will become more like a shop to get business.

May 9. Looked over a vast quantity of Stotard's designs — came home and began for [*a word written in cipher*] — 8 minutes past five.

May 27. Nothing but horror and idleness to reflect on for these last three weeks. January — attacked the Academy.[4] Feby. — ill, one Sketch. March — O. April — The first proof of a man's incapacity for any thing is his endeavouring to fix the stigma upon others.

June 1. I began, as last summer, to sleep at Wilkie's,[5] and walk in in the morning, which did me so much good.

We talked of the Cartoons last night, which I had been to see Saturday again. He said Rap[hael's] object was mind only, therefore he never shewed any parts but the heads & hands, because the face is never so much attended to when the body is visible, but I said, as the great organs of intellectual expression are the features, they will always keep their predominance, and as the body expresses the intention of the mind, tho in an inferior degree to the features, yet when they are both united the expression of mind will be more perfect.

> Ruddy as Gold his cheek, his bosom fair
> As Silver; the curl'd ringlets of his hair
> Black as the raven's wing; his lip more red
> Than eastern coral, or the scarlet thread. . . .
> Ivory with sapphires interspersed explains
> How white his hands, how blue his manly veins. . . .
> His stature all majestic, . . .
> Straight as the Palm-tree, strong as is the Pine.
>
> Prior's Solomon.[6]

3. The Royal Academy's exhibition, which opened on May 4, 1812 (Whitley, *1800–1820*, p. 199). BRH seems to have attended a "varnishing day."
4. See I,213.
5. Wilkie was living at 29 Phillimore Place, Kensington (Cunningham, I,349).
6. Matthew Prior, *Solomon on the Vanity of the World*, II,446–458.

Thy lips are a thread of Scarlet.
Thy Temples are like Pomegranite within thy locks.
Thy neck is like the tower of David.[7]

"My beloved is White & Ruddy, . . . his locks are bushy and black as a Raven." Sol. Song.[8]

"And the Lord magnified Solomon exceedingly in the sight of all Israel, and bestowed upon him such *royal Majesty* as had not been on any King before him in all Israel." I Chronicles, ver. 25, ch. 29.

"Moreover the King made a great throne of Ivory and overlaid [it] with pure Gold. And there were six steps to the throne, with a foot stool of gold, which were fastened to the throne, and stays on each side of the sitting place, and two lions standing by the stays.

"And twelve lions stood there on the one side, and on the other, upon the six steps. There was not the like made in any kingdom." II Chronicles. Ch. IX, Ve. 17, 18, 19.

The other Mother a grand tremendous creature, regarding the young one with a flushed sneer of malignant fury.

The highest style is to shew essence only. If you know not what is accident and what essence, how can you distinguish what is accident and what essence? How can you depend on your judgement clearing accident from essence, from its external appearance covered with skin, which varies in every individual, when if you know exactly the essence under the skin in which all which never varies except in one or two trifling instances, you perceive instantly the essential.

He is one who has never had his soul opened or his feelings tenderized by the endearments of a woman he loved. He is selfish & mean, tyrannical to the weak & cruel to the unfortunate, cringing to the successful and claiming the praise of foresight, let things turn out as they may.

A wild race of mountaineers appeared occasionally descending the heights into the defile or seated by the banks of the river, with sandals on their feet made of undressed bulls' hides bound

7. The Song of Solomon, 4:3–4.
8. The Song of Solomon, 5:10–11.

with thongs of the same materials around their ankles and in-steps. Such was the *caliga*, or military shoe, as we now see it represented in Grecian bronzes and medals. Page 122.

There is yet a singular appearance from the summit of this mountain, and as this is pointedly attended to by Homer, it seems to offer strong reason for believing that the poet had himself beheld it from the same place. Looking towards Lectum, the tops of all the Idaean chain diminish in altitude by a regular grada-tion, so as to resemble a series of steps, conducting to Gargarus, as the highest point of the slope. Nothing can therefore more forcibly illustrate the powers of Homer as a painter in the display he has given of the Country, and the fidelity with which he delineates every feature in its geography than the description of the ascent of Juno from Lectum to Gargarus, by a series of Natural eminences unattainable to by mortal tread, but present-ing to the great conceptions of poetical fancy a scale adequate to the power and dignity of superior beings. 138. Il. Ξ,285.[9]

The peculiar form of countenance exhibited by the Statues of Isis may yet be recognised in the features of the Egyptian Women, and particularly in those of Rosetta, when they can be prevailed upon to lay aside their veils. Vol. II, 305. Clarke.[1]

The features particularly of the women of Nicotia are regular and dignified, exhibiting that elevated cast of countenance so universally admired in the works of the Grecian Artists. 338.[2]

Never were maternal feelings more strongly pourtrayed than in the countenance of this woman. Not satisfied with having killed the criminal, she continued her blows, until she had re-duced it to atoms, unheeding any thing that was said to her and only abstracting her attention from its mangled body to cast occasionally a wild & momentary glance towards the child — it was entirely superb. 439.

Its eastern shore presents a sublime scene of mountains — Sea of Gallilee. 454.[3]

9. *Iliad*, XIV,283–291.
1. Edward Daniel Clarke, *Travels in Various Countries of Europe, Asia, and Africa*, 1812, Part 2, Section 1, pp. 304–305.
2. Clarke, *Travels*, p. 338.
3. Clarke, *Travels*, p. 454.

But its broad and extended surface covering the bottom of a profound valley, environed by lofty and precipitous eminences. — 462.[4]

Plain of Esdraelon. "The tribe of Issachar rejoiced in their tents." Deut. XXXIII, 18.

Judges, IV, 13, 14, and V, 19. Barach descended from Mount Thabor.

A preliminary sketch for "The Judgment of Solomon," June 1812.

2 Kings, XVIII, 29.

Warriors of every Nation under Heaven have pitched their tents upon the plain of Esdraelon and have beheld the various banners of their nations wet with the dews of Thabor and of Hermon. Legg.

Raphael entered the Vatican at 25, 1508, and began the first room. Finished it 1511 — he was 28. Completed the second, 1514 — he was 31; the third, 1517 — he was then 34.[5]

4. Clarke, *Travels,* p. 462.
5. The three "rooms" of the Vatican with frescoes by Raphael, to which BRH refers, are the Stanza della Segnatura, the Stanza d'Eliodoro, and the Stanza dell' Incendio.

August 3. Arose at five. In my painting Room by six. I thank
Almighty God that every hour and every day's encrease of knowledge tends to deepen my respect and exalt my adoration of
Michel Angelo, Raphael, & Greeks. No one can deny, I suppose,
the power of poetical conception, at least that part of Genius
which is most particularly considered as peculiarly its characteristic — imagination. This they possessed in the highest degree
and yet who more regulated by mathematical accuracy and design? They were all architects, all founded deeply in principles.
But in England principles of any thing but light & Shadow are
considered out of the question. Mathematics minus stupidity,
here Rembrandt & trowel paintings are the only proofs of talent.
How they all sink before the luminousness.

Michel Angelo's Genius is like the torrent of the desert, that
dashes and foams over craggy rocks and fathomless precipices,
that with its roar and its foam & its fury bears down all obstruction and blazes the soul to enthusiastic fury and awful adoration. A present Deity seems to animate his torrent and tumble &
direct the waves, as it splashes with thundering roar into dingy
obscurity. While Raphael's gentle genius is a smooth stream,
which oozes from a shining font and throws up at every [moment]
liquid bubble like stars. These shoot athwart the vault of heaven,
a delicious love, or trembling grace shaking their dewy wings or
skimming over its silver surface or winding with its crystal stream,
as it floats with limpid glitter, through its rosy banks, kissing
every flower that bends to pay it homage in its passage.

I left London outside the mail for Bristol, August 14th, 1812,
eight at night, and after a rapid journey arrived there at eleven
the next morning. I walked about the city, which I found dirty,
stinking, and disagreeable. The place seemed full of merchant
sailors and merchant captains. It had all the noise, confusion, &
pitchy stink of a sea port without the real grandeur. Merchant
sailors have not that air that the Sailors of the navy have. The
Exchange is a good building of the Corinthian Order. I saw a
beautiful specimen in the front of some office, of the Ionic order
& entablature. At the Inn where I slept, there was a manifest
difference in the spirit and activity of the People in comparison
with those of London — a sort of inclination to gape at every

trifle — to loiter. In the evening I walked to Clifton, which is a very sweet place, but there is a sulphurous heat about the air of this as well as Bristol & Bath, a muggy closeness which is extremely unpleasant.

August 16. The Mail arrived dressed with Laurels, bringing intelligence that Lord Clinton passed thro' Bath last night at ten o'clock, bringing dispatches from Lord Wellington, of the Victory.[6] Two Eagles, 2 Flags were hanging out of the Windows. The People were all rejoiced, all was bustle, longing for the gazette, cursing the French, & praising Wellington. I left Bristol on the Bridgwater coach outside for Cross,[7] and had a pleasant drive of three hours on the road. The Coach man pointed out Whitelock,[8] who it seems lived in the neighbourhood. I as well as all the passengers looked through him as he passed, and I could plainly perceive, by the quivering lip and timid countenance, he expected insult. I felt the utmost contempt — poor wretch — he was solitary, and I was informed generally about so, none but farmers and they very seldom, speaking to or accompanying him — see the different consequence of different conduct — Wellington by industry, energy, & activity, the theme of continual admiration for ever — Whitelock by cowardice, indolence, & dishonor, an object of universal contempt. It must be so — the consequences of industry were always the same if not destroyed by rashness.

I found my dear Sister on my driving to Cheddar had arrived a day before me. She was well and grown a fine Girl — happy enough to see me after so long an absence. My Uncle, Aunt, & Cousin all happy to see me also.

August 17. Recovered from the fatigues of my jaunt. Rode about the hills with my Uncle. Enjoyed the breezes, with a gust I had not experienced for some time. There is certainly nothing like fresh air.

6. The defeat of the French at Salamanca, July 22–24, 1812.
7. A hamlet, one mile west of Axbridge and about five miles from Cheddar, a well-known stop for stagecoaches.
8. Lieutenant-General John Whitelocke (1757–1833), court-martialed and cashiered in 1808 for his inglorious surrender to the Spanish in Argentina.

August 18. My Cousin & I rode to the Sea about 14 miles and after having been so long immured in London, the wide, expanded, dashing surge gave a spring to my mind that was delightful. All rivers, however great, sink before the immensity of the Ocean. I should suppose the first impression on one who saw it for the first time must be that of terror; there is such evident power in its appearance. The tide was dashing in with a strong breeze at S.W. and had an appearance of angry surf. We asked if it were possible to ride up Brean Down[9] and were answered "No, it was impossible." We tried and soon of course succeeded. When people get a notion into their heads that this or that is impossible, all exertion is parallysed. We, who were under no such impression, attempt and prove it the contrary. The prospect on it was very grand; we gallopped about — returned home in the evening after a round of more than 40 miles rather fatigued.

August 19. At home a little stiff. Stuck to my Italian. So far as I have read of Tasso's Aminta I think it a sweet thing full of refinement, and a sort of acuteness of feeling that reaches genius. Who but one with feelings of genius would have said so sweetly —

> Quella quercia, che pare
> Si ruvida e selvaggia,
> Sente anch' ella il potere
> Dell' amoroso foco: e, se tu avessi
> Spirto e senso d'amore, intenderesti
> I suoi muti sospiri.[1]

To the foggy dullness of common intellects this would appear *improbable!!*

August 20. Violent exercise in ringing up the tenor bell, which did me great good.

September. I am returned from the Country after a delightful month with my dearest Sister, much improved in vigour of body, and much in vigour of mind. The people in the Country are

9. A peninsula some five miles southwest of Weston-super-Mare.
1. Torquato Tasso, *L'Aminta*, I,i,157–162.

hospitable, but it proceeds as much from wishing to relieve the weariness of solitude as from a desire to oblige; from the constitution of our minds, variety is requisite to our continuance. The modes only are different. What is a relaxation to one man if his pursuit be great becomes an effort to another, whose faculties are lower.

[The next five pages contain Italian exercises.]

September 17. There seems to be a day about the end of the Summer when the Sun tries to make a last effort, as it were before Winter begins, to rise with vigour. Such a day was yesterday — a cloudless sky, a clear limpid, lucid, glittering Sun which darted a genial warmth into the vitals of nature; I walked into Kensington Garden. Every thing was quiet, trembling with a sort of misty heat. The birds in shade were singing; a falling leaf or the rustling of the waving foliage was all that disturbed the noontide silence of the scene. Here I read Tasso's Aminta with a rich sensation of delight, every thing in unison with his exquisite effusions, and for two hours I enjoyed his genius in delicious and dreaming abstraction. Sep. 17.

[The next two pages contain Italian exercises.]

August 20.[2] "Quel est l'homme qui peut gouverner sagement s'il n'a jamais souffert, et s'il n'a jamais profité des souffrances où ses fautes l'ont precipeté?"[3] says Fenelon. There is an exquisite beauty about him, in purity of thought and expression, that gives one an amiable idea of him as a Philosopher. At the same time now and then I venture to think, in attempting purity & chastity of sentiment, he falls into a child's drivelling, always talking about restoring *l'age d'or,* which any man who knows Human Nature, or who has had any experience in the World, laughs at. There is a want of Johnson's strength of thought about him. Perhaps Johnson from living & suffering in actual existence was too apt to

2. The position of this entry in the diary clearly indicates that this date is an error for September 20.

3. Identified by Professor Herbert McArthur as François de Solignac de La Mothe-Fénelon, *Les Aventures de Télémaque,* Book 18 (*Oeuvres de Fénelon,* Paris, 1835, III,152).

give a degraded & dreary notion, which still it is nearer the truth than the age of gold and impossible virtues.

[*The next forty-eight pages contain Italian exercises.*]

September 26. This week is now concluded and I have, thank God, got over the great mechanical difficulties of Italian. I have written out all that was essential and mastered all I have written out. In taking up Petrarch last night to my delight I found sense & intelligence beam on my fancy from words & tenses that before were the result of investigation and consequently lost half their force.

How one's first & early habits adhere to one with the tenacity of limpets. I have had with regard to languages always an early habit of carelessness to conquer, from not being placed with an energetic Master, from being suffered to attend an irregular and disordered day school, neglected by Masters, forgotten by my Father. I spent six years of mornings in planning schemes of mischief for evenings, passed whole days without saying a word, came in late, went out early, and found myself at 15 years with idle habits and abandoned inclinations, stumbling with difficulty and without a clear perception of what I wanted to do. What ever language I have studied since, I have had this weary, idle disgust to conquer, and tho the last 3 years of my education I passed with a man, Mr. Haynes of Plympton, whom it would have been my happiness to be placed under at first, yet I was snatched from him to study Merchants Accounts,[4] just as I was beginning to understand & relish the beauties of Virgil & Homer. My breast had begun to fire when the embers which three years afterwards burst out so irresistibly were for a time smothered by merchandize

4. In 1799 BRH was withdrawn from Dr. Bidlake's school in Plymouth and sent to Plympton Grammar School, under the headmastership of the Reverend W. Haynes. From Plympton he "was sent to Exeter to be perfected in merchants' accounts" (*Autobiography*, I,11–12). The school may have been located in Honiton — see his diary for January 1, 1816, II,1). Joseph Farington stated that "the Rev. Mr. Hele" was BRH's master at the Plympton school, that he met this gentleman there in 1809, and that he was pleased to hear of his former student's success in London (Farington, V,284). J. Brooking Rowe stated that the Plympton Grammar School was sometimes known by the name of the founder as Elize Hele's School and that the Reverend William Hayne served as master from 1800 to his death in 1816 (*A History of the Borough of Plympton Erle*, Exeter, 1906, p. 330).

& bales & cotton. Thank God I have almost subdued the bad habits of my early life, and I hope ere long to say with a clear conscience that they [are] in chains of adamant.[5]

[*The next five pages contain Italian exercises.*]

October 2. All Painters, I venture to think, have erred in giving too much the appearance in Solomon's Judgement as if everything was in earnest — the Child is dashed up, the executioner is ranting as if he were going to cut down an ox — when Solomon says, "Bring me a sword and divide the child" — and immediately [?] the Mother cried out *before it was divided* and immediately as she fancied it was beginning. The delicacy is I think to give it the air of a trick without making it laughable, so that the spectators may see it was *not* meant, and yet feel interested for the lovely mother who thought it *was*.

[*The next page and a half of the diary are devoted to an unfinished rough draft of an article on the unfairness of withdrawing the first two prizes from the exhibition at the British Gallery in which Haydon had shown "Macbeth" (see I,222 n). The next four pages contain Italian exercises.*]

October 3. Made a[n] accurate study for Executioner for Solomon from my old and faithful model Salmon, Corporal Horseguards, who goes Wednesday next to Spain — perhaps it may be the last time he will sit — he said so himself with a melancholy tone. I hope he may return alive. I gave him and three more who had sat to me a bottle of wine to drink my health before they went and success to themselves — they are fine fellows and will do their duty; one of them is Shaw the pugilist.* I have always

* Poor Shaw was killed at Waterloo after doing deeds worthy of Ariosto's genius to adorn.[6] The other was Daikin, who sat for the inner groom in Macbeth & he was killed at Waterloo too, after killing several.

5. *Paradise Lost,* I,48. "In adamantine chains."
6. These deeds are described in the *Autobiography* (I,217–220) and in the diary for March 2, 1816 (p. II,10). John Shaw (1789–1815) enlisted as a private in the Life Guards in 1807. He achieved fame as a pugilist by defeating Burrows on July 12, 1812, and was a challenger for the championship of England when his regiment was sent abroad in 1815.

treated them well and they all seem attached to my service.

Tonight I had Salmon's wrists and hands in four different positions. He has the clearest joints of any man I ever saw. From him I painted Dentatus's hands, as well as Macbeth's.

Surely these tendernesses of separation, when one forgets and forgives all injuries, are feelings that belong to a purer existence.

Letters are attached to most of the remaining pages of this volume. The last nine pages, starting from the back, contain a rough, partially incoherent draft of a letter to the Examiner *concerning the injustices practiced by the Royal Academy.*

Volume V

OCTOBER 1812—JANUARY 1814

Volume V

OCTOBER 1812—JANUARY 1814

Il n'y a rien d'impossible à ceux, qui savent oser et souffrir. Fenelon.

October 4. "Vos fautes ne vous ont pas été moins utiles que vos malheurs; car quel est l'homme qui peut gouverner sagement s'il n'a jamais souffert, et s'il n'a jamais profité des souffrances où ses fautes l'ont precipité. Sur tout soyez en garde contre votre humeur; c'est un ennemi que vous porterez par tout avec vous jusques à la mort; il entera dans vos conseils, et vous trahira si vous l'ecoutez. L'humeur fait perdre les occasions les plus importantes, rend un homme inegal, faible, vil, et insupportable. Defiez vous de cet enemi." Fenelon.[1]

It may be laid down as a certainty that if wrists are clear, so are ankles, if elbows, so are knees. Thus, if the tendons that go from the Radius & Ulna to the hand are distinct and intelligible, that is, clear without be[ing] skinny, and yet full & fleshy without being fat (for this is the great characteristic of healthy activity & the Elgin Marbles), the tendons that go from the Tibia and fibula to the foot are clear also.

Perhaps the secret of Character in form and contour is repetition of being like colour. Thus begin with Deltoid, then repeat the form it makes when you can without violating truth. Thus you may repeat everything, till you have put your figure together like a map.

Salmon is that extraordinary character perceived in the reclining figure[2] at the Elgin Musaeum — that exact mixture of bone, tendon & muscle, which conveys a look of nature without poverty, and of elevation without manner, that exact composition of round, straight, and elliptical lines, joints tendonous, limbs fleshy, bones angular. This is the beauty of form, this is the just mixture of truth and refinement, that you look for in vain in the hard, marbly, puffed figure of the Apollo, the muzzy Antinous,

1. See I,241.
2. The Theseus, or Dionysus.

247

or the myriads of fragments that have inundated Europe for these last 300 years. To this are we indebted, as the World will be one day, to the inspired Elgin Marbles.

October 5. Kept down the principal figure, advanced my Picture. Hard work for the higher Art in this Country, when Painters, Patrons, & people set their face against great works.

October 7. "The Hand of the diligent shall bear rule; but the slothful shall be under tribute." [3]

The idleness, the wasteful idleness of this last year, I shall repent to my dying day. I have gained experience, but at a dear rate. Had I exerted myself as I ought, my Picture would have [been] well advanced; after attending the Academy, I should instantly have applied myself, but I loitered, got entangled with an infernal woman, which shattered my peace of mind, before I could extricate myself, and tho' I came off, thank God! without vice (for she was married), yet with my habits so broken and my mind so agitated that till now I have not had command of myself as usual. What a warning have I had! How has my presumptuous security been lowered! When I think out of what a hell I escaped, my head whirls.

With the exception of my attacking the Academy, which I glory in and ever will to my last gasp, my conduct has been abandoned, negligent, irresolute, contemptible. I nauseate myself. I have never had such a contempt of any being (except an Academician) during my existence.

After the delights of keen, eager, active employment, what are the horrors of ennui! none can tell but those who have felt both; and ennui to none is so horrible as to those whose minds have previously been for ever on the stretch. Abhoring my situation, anxious to retract and yet hankering to go on, fascinated by her deceitful tenderness, conscious I had no right to it, as she was married, determined to conclude when I was absent and forgetting every thing but her when present, jeered because I feared to commit a sin my soul abhorred, and yet stung to the

3. Proverbs, 12:24.

quick at her sarcasms on my unmanly timidity, knowing that my existence as a painter depended on my present exertions, and feeling when I attempted to commence my soul clogged, my mind shattered, my habits ruined — oh God, oh God, thou knowest the razor like cutting sensations of my broken heart, thou knowest my agony at the recollection of my former innocence, when I rose early, prayed sincerely, applied myself to my delightful art energetically, when I returned thanks to thee for the blessings of the day and slept as sweetly as if angels soothed me to slumber with their silver tuned harps undulating in the midnight air — now mark the contrast — a restless night, seeing *Ruin* blazing every where, like the "Lasciate ogni speranza" [4] of Dante to my disordered fancy, sighing as if to end my frame and break my being, dreaming in heated agitation, and starting with trembling agony, cursing the day light as it beamed on my weary eyes and bursting head, and walking miles before the Sun rose in senseless abstraction — it seemed a load, another day I thought, what a labour! Good God — when I recollected what I once was! Every thing that used to rouse my enthusiasm now excited not an emotion. My art had lost its relish! Nothing now gratified me but the anticipation of keen, galling, guilty pleasure. I began to look upon the restraints of Christianity as very well for School Boys — and certainly there could be [no] wickedness in a union of *kindred souls*. If such was my situation without the actual commission, what would it have been afterwards!!! When I recollected, when I saw an affectionate husband caressing his children and his wife!!! Whoever you are that read this, when I am dead, beware of the *beginnings* — fly from vice — think not it can be argued against in the presence of the exciting cause — nothing but absence & *actual flight* — beware of *idleness* which leaves you at the mercy of appetite — employment — employment — and you must be safe.

As I can now lay my hand on my heart and know I have escaped without compleat destruction, with what rapture do I again return to my art. I am yet young, I have had a severe, a nauseous, but an impressive lesson. I trusted in myself with too

4. *Inferno,* III,9.

fearless a security in my own infallibility. My pride is indeed lowered, and by vigourous industry, and temperate & full reliance in God, I may yet regain what I have lost and be rescued from that brink from which I am but now receding. God grant it *a ginocchione. XI at night October 7.*

I can never now look up at the bust of Michel Angelo without a detestation, a contempt, a horror of myself at my own insignificance. Such were not my feelings two years since. I then dilated at his presence and felt my cheek redden. How cowardly, how contemptible does Vice render the bravest — damnable, develish vice — what misery, what agony is concealed beneath thy artful, pathetic, interesting mask. However the Vicious may laugh at Religion as if in Defiance, how they shrink at the fear of detection, how alive are they to every innocent word, that their phosphoric souls kindle into meaning. With a guilty person you seek offence every instant. I should wish to ask them which is most pleasurable, the fears that Religion excites, that is, the fears of *doing* wrong, or the fears of Vice, that is, the fears of conviction, the horrors of guilt, the dread of the consequences of having been guilty. What are the feelings of Innocence when the first perception of vice darts into its mind? Where is tortured innocence? May those who are innocent never know.

October 8, 9, 10. Vigourously at work. Painted the head of Solomon. I doubt whether I should express any more in him than a general air of Royalty absorbed in his greatness. I have observed People that are not impatient are generally indolent. There is an impatience improper, and an impatience proper — impatience improper proceeds from a petty peevish disposition that cannot bear unavoidable troubles, where impatience can neither retard or remove them — impatience proper is an anxiety to be punctual, an angry uneasiness with those who have it in their power to be so and are not so.

October 11. I thank God, ginocchione, that my enthusiastic feeling for my art has again streamed into me. I now feel my frame burst at the idea of blaze, expand at the idea of pursuing to the utmost of my bodily & mental power my delightful Art.

God grant me strength & intellect to realize before I die my conceptions of Art, for Jesus Christ's sake, Amen, Amen, Amen. I hope I shall have no occasion to repent my vice this year; it may be my salvation; it has been such a warning, such a dreadful warning.

October 12. And he made the vail of blue, purple & crimson, and fine linen, and wrought cherubims thereon.[5]

And he took the King's crown from off his head, the weight whereof was a talent of gold with the precious stones, and it was set on David's head. II Sam. Chap. XII, [verse 30].

He sat upon his royal throne, and was clothed with all the robes of majesty, all glittering with gold & precious stones, and he *was very dreadful* — and lifting up his countenance which *shone with majesty*. Ester, Chaps. XIV, XV, v. 6–7.[6]

And so he held up his *golden sceptre* and laid it upon her neck and she said, "I saw there my Lord as an angel of God and my heart was troubled for fear of thy majesty, for wonderful art thou and thy countenance is full of grace." [7]

White, green, & blue hangings, fastened with cords of fine linen and purple to silver rings and pillars of marble. The beds were of gold & Silver upon a pavement of red and blue and white and black marble. Bring Vashti with the crown royal. 1st Ester, Ver. 6–11.

And the King *took his ring from his hand,* Chap. III, v. 10, *and sealed with the King's ring,* v. 12.

Let the Royal apparel be brought which the King useth to wear, and the horse that the King rideth upon. *Crown royal be set upon his head.* Ch. VI, verse 8.

And Mordecai went out from the presence of the King in royal apparel of blue & white and with a great crown of gold and with a garment of fine linen and purple. Chap. VIII, verse 15.

And the King held out the golden sceptre that was in his hand. Chap. V verse II.

5. II Chronicles, 3:14.
6. This sentence does not occur in the King James version of the Bible. The Book of Esther contains only ten chapters.
7. Compare Esther, 8:4–5.

A man who has a fixed purpose to which he devotes his powers is invulnerable. Nothing but sickness can affect him; melancholy & misfortune, vice & indolence may surround and beat on him like the waves of the sea [on] a solid rock that juts out into its bosom — but like the waves they will yield and split with harmless foam, imbecile & without effect. Oct. 20.

Young beginners are apt to obtrude all they know, not considering the first requisite is to please the mind through the eye; a multiplicity of parts distracts, disgusts, wearies; hence the origin of one thing subordinate to another, so that the mind may dwell on as much at a time as it can at once comprehend.

It came into my mind with such a blaze as if the Sun had burst up at the dead of midnight — never make Heroes or great characters with the peculiar characteristic of any Nation; they belong to Human Nature, and should be distinguished only by those general marks of elevation & beauty that belong to it.*

[*A sketch*] From recollection of a poor creature who saw her Son dashed in pieces by a Horse, near Temple Bar. Nothing could exceed her dreadful agony. Her nose & cheeks became a settled purple, a burning tear fixed, without dropping, on her lid, her livid lips shook with agony, while she screamed & groaned with agitated hoarseness on her dear boy! In passing an hour afterwards, I heard her dreadful screams, which had now become incessant, till they died away from senseless exhaustion into convulsive sighs. My heart beats at the recollection.

November 18. My colours in a most delightful State. Every thing floated on so exquisitely that I would not have exchanged my situation for Buonaparte's at Moscow, without a handsome remuneration, nor yet then.

November 20. Death is supposed to put a stop to all the prejudices of party, by which Merit is not fairly estimated during life. It does so, but let every Man desirous of greatness also remember that if it silence the injustice of enemies, it also weakens the prejudices of Friends. Many beauties elevated to transcendent

* Not true, 1843. B. R. H. Aegyptian, Greek, Roman, Negro Heroes must be distinguished.

excellencies by Friendly blindness, and many inadvertencies censured as degrading defects by malignant envy, bereft now of the
secret causes of either, take their true & proper level. Let this
reflection put a man on his guard; let them recollect that the
inaccuracies of indolence & idleness are never forgiven when his
own influence has ceased. He is then judged fairly by the number
of apparent excellencies without reference to the cause that there
are not more, or the reason that there are less than in others. Let
it also stimulate every Man to subdue at once procrastination.
Death may interrupt him before he has time [to] compleat his
intentions, & the World [will be] ignorant.

I now felt the purity of virtue as if my Soul had been melted
by floating undulations of harmony & saw a being glide through
the air in sunny light preceeded by such a blast as shook them
to prostration. After what I felt last night perhaps Death will
never be absent from my mind.

November 21. Advanced my Picture by rapid & successful
effort. My notions of colour are totally altered, and I hope for the
better. Glazing to such excess will certainly not do. It destroys
the natural solidity of things and gives the artificial clearness of
colours on glass. No Venetian Picture that I ever saw but had
the flatness of a coloured print and beside the magic solemnity
of Rembrandt looked like the Knave of hearts, spotty & gaudy.
There certainly is in Rembrandt tho' his light is too confused for
an extensive subject, a depth, a solemnity, a grandeur, a twilight
mistiness, a dawning coolness, a solemn richness that accords
with elevated subjects, and makes one feel like the tremendous
roar of an organ from the deep grey aisles of a Gothic monastery
— positive colour distracts.

November 22. Sunday. People called and interrupted my
going to Church as I fully intended — thus it is these things will
happen.

3 years ago, studying the form of Dentatus, I found that the
calf of the Gladiator was less than Hercules or other high characters, and that the Solaeus shewed all the way from its insertion,
which gave a meagre look.

Ignorant of the reason I avoided [this], as I had no principles of form but to select what was requisite for the great actions. But now [I] have established the principles of Greek form, first to select what is peculiarly human, &c., &c. The gastrocnemius is peculiarly human, and contributes to the great human distinction — standing upright. The more powerful it is, the more powerfully does it perform its function, and when powerful it swells over the Solaeus. Encrease the gastrocnemius, it swells over the Solaeus; diminish it, the Solaeus bursts out and gives a weak, animal look, because the calf is lessened like animals, and the calf being lessened, a muscle peculiarly human is lessened, and a limb that has a muscle peculiarly human lessened approaches the limb of an animal, who scarcely has any at all.

The senses are the organs of the brain or intellect. By them impressions are conveyed to it. When the eye sees, the nose smells, the ear hears, the tongue tastes, or the fingers feel, individually these organs express by their direction, or expansion, or whatever is the mechanical means of their acting that they do smell, see, or hear & touch & taste; so when the intellect has concluded any thing internally that sense or those senses to which the conclusion has reference is as much agitated & in action as if it was *externally* impressed. The senses are the means of knowing what passes in minds because they are means of enabling every thing to pass there as much as a soft substance being pressed will shew by the indentation something has pressed on it — so will a sense shew by its actions that something has affected it, either internally or externally.

There certainly are great traces in Homer of the simplicity and beauty of the Scriptures. In the Bible whenever a King or any man gives an order to a servant to carry a message, the servant delivers it in the very words it was delivered to him. It is always so in Homer, and, of course, Virgil and every imitator has it likewise. November 27.

Joseph is an exquisite story — "and he went in & wept and washed his face that it might not be seen." [8] What a piece [of] truth; it bears veracity in its very front.

8. Compare Genesis, 43:30–31.

November 30. Went to the House of Lords to hear the Prince[9] open Parliament in State. It was a very grand affair — the beautiful women — educated, refined, graceful, with their bending plumes & sparkling eyes — the Nobility, the Chancellor —

> the Sceptre and the ball,
> The sword, the mace, the crown imperial,
> The inter-tissued robe of gold and pearl,[1]

gave me a grand sensation; I could not help reflecting how long it was before society arrived at such a pitch of peace & quietness, that order & regulation such as I witnessed existed. What tumult, what blood, what contention, what suffering, what error, before experience had ascertained what was to be selected, or what rejected.

The Prince read admirably, with the greatest perspicuity, not the slightest provincialism, pure English. He appeared affected at the conclusion. I went down [in] the evening again to hear the debates. Lord Wellesly[2] made a fine energetic, noble speech, enough to "create a Soul under the ribs of Death."[3] It shewed him to be a man of grand, comprehensive intellect. He affirmed in a strain of energy almost amounting to fury, that Lord Wellington's[4] means were inadequate — that before the battle of Salamanca, so far from his retiring being to draw the enemy on, he was in full retreat, the 18th, 19th, 20th, 21st, & part of 22nd, and it was entirely owing to an error of Marmont[5] that the battle was gained. "But, my Lords, is this a ground to calculate upon? My Lords, if your hopes of success are grounded upon the errors of French generals, I fear they have a very shallow foundation." He said the Great General had not the means of transport for heavy

9. The Prince Regent (1762–1830), who succeeded to the throne in 1820 as George IV.

1. *Henry V*, IV,i,277–279.

2. The Marquis Wellesley (1760–1842), governor general of India from 1797 to 1805, eldest brother of the Duke of Wellington.

3. *Comus*, ll. 561–562.

4. The Duke of Wellington (1769–1852), at this time Viscount Wellington. The engagements at Salamanca occurred in July 1812.

5. Auguste-Frédéric-Louis Viesse de Marmont (1774–1852), marshal of France.

artillery, &c. I went away about the middle of Lord Liverpool's[6] futile answer, more a Wellesleyeian in heart than ever. I observed that Lord Wellesly in speaking put himself repeatedly in the attitude of Raphael's St. Paul at Athens, which is very interesting as it proves the truth of Raphael's feeling.

December 2. When we consider the great results of the books of Moses, that the Israelites were slaves to the Egyptians, that from their utility they must have been unwilling to part with them, that how like human nature is the vacillation of Pharaoh's mind, terrified at the instant by his sufferings, promising release, but the moment the terror was past reverting again to his predominant inclination, *then* trying to compromise by allowing the herds and cattle *only* to march, untill at last forced by the tremendous Passover in the dead of night to send for Moses, and while the impression of horror was on his soul urging them to leave him instantly with his people and his children — how likely, how apparently true, that the moment even this terrific event had passed, forgetful of the plagues, the locusts, and the rivers of blood, he should with all the petty littleness of a weak tyrannical mind, habituated to have his whims gratified, unused to contradiction, determined yet to make one effort more to regain them, and re-establish the belief of his infallibility in the minds of his enslaved people. When you reflect that the Israelites in number 600,000 did march thro' a barren desert, and establish themselves in a Country, that they became an illustrious people, under Solomon, that their laws & restrictions & commandments are found to contribute to the peace & happiness of Society to this day and have been the foundation of all the codes of the World since, when you reflect that at this early period of the World Mankind were overwhelmed with idolatry and that *they* only had a notion of a Great God, and that it is from them *we* owe our notions of one God — that they were told for their wickedness their city should be razed, their Temple destroyed & their nation scattered — and that the two first has been accomplished, and the last curse still existing; and lastly when you consider that from this

6. The second Earl of Liverpool (1770–1828), prime minister from 1812 to 1827.

very people proceeded Jesus Christ, who promulgated a system and a doctrine so exquisite as [to] be beyond the power of *human* invention, which if followed would make men angels and calm & tranquillize the World, which already has softened the cruelties of men. When you take these great results in consideration, in spite of two or three trifling unaccountable things, you must believe that these people were the most enlightened, or that they were made the instruments of God's will, and as their whole conduct shews they were not a virtuous & enlightened people but a barbarous & ungrateful nation, you must assent to the former proposition. They were *not* chosen by God because they had higher merits, but it was his pleasure to choose them; therefore their vices and follies are no arguments against the choice, but only against them as individuals. The revelation remains the same. They only are affected. Surely too the last curse being still in effect is a strong argument that all the other prophecies were equally previous to the event and equally founded in foresight as the present. Granting this, what is there to disbelieve? Christ's birth was foretold & did happen. The destruction of the Temple was foretold & did happen. The razing of the city was foretold and did happen, and lastly their dispersion among other nations, their becoming a bye word & ridicule was equally foretold, has equally happened, and is still happening. Allowing that the two first were inventions of Priests *after* the events had passed, still the latter could not be so because it has not yet done passing. Therefore it may fairly [be] argued that [the] two first were no more invention than the latter, and that all are equally founded in truth and that all had equally one origin. In short the more vicious, the more cruel [and] ungrateful were the Israelites, the stronger argument is it that their cause was divine revelation. Decem. 3.

If the books of Moses are inventions or fables, never were inventions so consistent or fables so likely. It is not the nature of inventions & fables, or poetic character, to tell what is likely to happen from the nature of a man but what ought to have happened or what a man ought to be, but in the Bible every thing is mentioned with the utmost simplicity, their moments of inspiration & their moments of weakness, the times when they were greater than human beings and the times when they were less; no impossible perfection, no attempt at imposition, all is told that all may be believed. But can men inspired by God do so & so & so? Certainly. Men inspired by God are not constantly inspired. When the inspiration is over, as when the heats of Genius are over, men are again men, and liable to the follies of their species. Here is the absurdity; you say men can never be inspired because they are sometimes vicious. You say no part that they deliver can be good because *all* is not equally excellent. With respect to the prophecies relating to Christ, the disbelievers (which is an important thing) are hopeless of proving their falsity, either at the time of their being written or their prophetic character not being able to get rid of these little objections from the known case of the Jews about their text and manuscripts. They affirm they related to something *immediately* subsequent; however we are quite easy about what they related to, when they acknowledge their antiquity & authenticity — grant these (which we defy them not to grant) and leave the rest in peace.

You talk of *trifling* unaccountable things! It may be said — was it trifling to slay 3,000 Israelites merely for dancing round a calf? Yet can you wonder at such proceeding from an ardent, ambitious, enthusiastic mind, as was the mind of Moses — descended from Sinai with the commandments of God delivered in terrors & thunders & lightenings in the sight of all the People — to find these people adoring a calf — after the miracles, after the manna, the water, the salvation from Pharaoh, to find this their return. The only thing I blame is, he did not mix Aaron with them in a general sweep.

With respect to the Midianitish women, had they not seduced the Israelites to debauchery & idolatry, it was a necessary example, but those who had been virtuous he should keep them for yourselves — that is for your wives, because in his parting Sermons he told them how to act about any beautiful captives, he expressly mentioned wives.

These are my excuses for this conduct. It was cruel conduct, but taking the temper of the man into consideration, his zeal, his eagerness, it is not to be wondered at, and its being related with the rest of his acts is a strong argument in my mind of the truth of the whole.

Do you expect, really expect, to raise British Art by encouraging Pictures "three feet long & two feet wide?" [7] Do you also agree with the Edingburgh reviewer that Raphael would have deserved *more* praise had he painted easel pictures of a moderate size? [8] He has done so and what are they? mawkish, flat, smooth, oily, & leaden, & he has painted easel pictures of a moderate size; therefore to prove it let us cut off his great works — and how high will he rank? Surely as high as Poussin, I grant, but of what value such rank?

But People can't afford. — People have not Room. — I know it. He must be a man of very moderate ambition who is contented to be stuck over a dining Room chimney piece, with a dull, yellow, foggy light oozing in from a narrow side window. We do not want private people to afford such assistance; — we want & expect you, who are assembled as the representatives of the taste of England as it regards Art, who are the Peers of taste, we want you who stand so highly in situation to act as it becomes it, as will grace it, as will give consequence to your situation and not let it give consequence to you. One of your own body has asserted that a great historical Picture, with a price adequate to its value, would be the one precisely to hang unsold on the walls of the British Gallery, and would not *he*, as one of the Patrons,

7. See I,5 n.
8. Payne Knight, in his review of *The Works of James Barry*, wrote: "We are so far from agreeing with him [Barry] in the notion of the vast space of the Vatican walls or Farnese ceiling being necessary to display the talents of a Raphael or Annibal Caracci, that we are convinced that both these great artists would have displayed more talent, and deserved more reputation, had they only been employed upon easel pictures of moderate size. . . . When the whole of a picture does not come within the field of vision, from the point of distance best adapted to show the beauties of particular expression and detail in the parts, it is too large; since its effect on the mind must necessarily be weakened by being divided, and the apt relation of the parts to each other, and to the whole, in which the merit of all composition consists, be less striking when gradually discovered, than when seen at once. That the great patriarchs of the art should have been so much employed upon such works, we much regret; not only because they might have been so much better employed, but because the skill and science displayed in them have given authority to false principles; and, by perverting laudable ambition from its proper objects, obstructed instead of promoting the expansion of succeeding talents" (*Edinburgh Review*, August 1810, 16:308–309).
For BRH's refutation of Knight's review, see I,213.

be equally censurable for suffering it? Certainly. He forgets he
implicates himself. If the Churches will not be opened, and why
St. Paul's should not be filled up as well as St. Steven's[9] — why
Pictures may not be admitted as well as Statues — no reason under Heaven can be given. Let their Public Halls be furnished
with subjects characteristic of their relations; let the Artists be
desired to send sketches, and let the best be chosen. At the same
time, for the support & encouragement of the rising Students, let
premiums still be given of one hundred & 50 guineas, which will
enable the best to advance on steady ground, which will afford
a prospect to Students in the first instance, and enable them to
look forward after being thus lifted for steady assistance if they
display equal improvement and equal industry in the Second.
Without such regular and systematic encouragement, nothing
will — nothing can — be done in England. Men of ardor & enthusiasm may risk their lives and ruin their health by privations,
may produce excellence, but if they are suffered to pass unheeded & neglected, what must be the end? Individual effort,
without support, can go but to a certain extent; its effect may be
great when enmity & prejudice are ceased. But they must be
sacrificed before the effect is produced. No man of Genius would
refuse or decline such a fate if necessary. He has not the proper
fire if he shrink from becoming the Decius of Art; but surely he
would prefer succeeding while alive, and confirming it by subsequent exertions.

December 5. I have always observed that effect of a cause is
always more awful when the cause is not visible. Thus in the
Passover, surely it was more dreadful when over, when they all
arose and found their children dead and saw nothing! than at the
moment the Angel was passing — because the cause being apparent would excite notions of the possibility of avoidance by
conquest, but what possibility was there here of avoidance or
conquest when the thing was done, the Angel passed, the children dead, beasts breathless — all must have been wonder, terror, horror, and nerveless silence.

9. Benjamin West's "Stoning of St. Stephen" hangs on the north wall of St.
Stephen's Church, Walbrook.

Give an equal opportunity to Painting. No. While you lavish yearly thousands upon thousands on Sculpture without effect, you refuse all assistance, all public support, all public opportunity to Painting. You load your churches, your halls & your Palaces with masses of unwieldy stone, and allow not one side or inch of your room for Pictures. Is this fair, is this just, is this liberal? You then complain Great Pictures will never do in this Country and great Pictures should not be painted. This really looks like infatuation — blind, prejudiced infatuation. In no country has sculpture [been] so favoured, fed, & pampered as in this country. In no Country under Heaven has such patronage been met with such shameful, disgraceful indolence as in this. Masses of marble scarcely shaped into intelligible boots, spurs, epaulets, sashes, hats, & belts huddled on to cover ignorance and hide defects. Why is this infatuated attachment to an art? Surely divide your favours and affections. If you shower thousands into the lap of Sculpture and fatten her to idleness with one hand, scatter hundreds into the lap of Painting also that her preternatural efforts without friends, without patronage, may be fostered & saved from being wholly without effect. No, year after year and day after day monuments & money are voted in ceaseless round without discrimination, without thought.

However the portrait painter may pretend that he is very welcome to be historical if he prefers starvation, &c., &c., &c.; when I call on them they always feel awkward & lament that they are obliged to do such damn things. They feel *little before a Student!* — on the brink of Starvation, without *money*, without friends, only because his objects are high & elevated. Will they with their country houses and their comforts know their insignificance of mind & body, and I have always observed through life that however gratifying the obtaining any immediate object may be to the senses for the time being, by any meaness there are moments when in the presence of nothing their quaking feelings amply pay them for their pleasure.

One of the Public Papers in speaking of the National monument said all the Genius of the Country should [be] called forth in Architecture & Sculpture & ultimately perhaps of painting —

ultimately perhaps — would this have been the language of Italy or of Greece?

Turenne used to say he never spent his time in regretting any mistake which he had made, but set himself instantly and vigourously to repair it.

December 14. Made a last application à mon Pére pour argent. He frankly tells me c'est impossible — that what J'ai eu is rather beyond ses moyens. I am au milieu d'un grand tableau, sans sous pour les necessaires de la vie, ou pour modeles; however I never felt more enthousiasme, more vigour, more resolution. This was my situation au milieu de Macbeth; being *new* it cut me deeply, but never checked or depressed me, but à present travaillé par misfortune, I can look at her without shrinking, pursue my intentions without fear, disguise my state by active, buoyant spirits, which I never want, and par la grace de Dieu, par vertu, et par industrie sans cessation, I have no doubt of subduing my Tableau with honour and come out of la bataille invigorated & ready pour les autres combats. En Dieu Je confie, qui a été toujours mon protecteur & mon ami. Amen, ginocchione.

Quand mes amis regardent mon visage toujours en santé, ma bouche toujours riante, how little do they think qu'ils tiennent secrets un coeur plain des troubles, not of *miseries,* car il n'y a rien qui cause la misère excepté le vice. Si votre conscience est sans reproche, what is there in the World qui peut rendre un homme miserable et sans l'espoir? Vicieux, et au plus haut point de succes, vous voyez été timide, inegal, infortune; vertueux, sans argent et sans amis, vous vous trouvez toujours invincible, toujours ferme. Je le connois bien, Je le connois bien.

Young men à l'amour de la vie believe not the dreadful effects of vice, think its miseries exaggerated, and that nothing can be worse than *want.* He that has advanced a little in the World and has been assailed & conquered by its temptations, knows well that want is a stimulant to your power, that you feel a cool, breathing, dewy morning vigour, if want be the result of great efforts or an extended design. While vice degrades, unnerves, paralyzes the faculties and tho it may procure the keenest delight for the moment, yet the intervals are dreadful and in desperation you rush again for forgetfulness, when forgetfulness can never be had. What is a more wretched spectacle than a young man seduced by a fascinating married woman to commit a sin he knows forbid by God, distracted by duty & passion, remorse & rapture. May he who knows not never know; may he be always in innocent & happy ignorance. No man will be convinced but from suffering & experience. The miseries of Vice & the delights of virtue may be preached to eternity, and no man will believe either till he has known both.

The last Edingburgh Review says, "we beg to recommend to these speculatists on the inferiority of Negroes the following, &c." [1] — and then as a specimen of their intellect, relates that they come down, get employment, get money, go back, dance with their friends, get drunk, spend their money, and march off again to get more. Certainly these are undoubted specimens of their high intellectual power!!! Now Sir, you call us speculatists; agreed, but are not you a speculatist also with your differing? You speculate on your hopes & your feelings, without the slightest foundation; *we* on facts — we find absolute, undeniable, bodily alliance to animals and therefore suspect in animals as they approach the body so do they the mind. You find they have heads, hands, & legs, & the power of speech — and then speculate that because they have this common thing, hence allow them the intellect. You acknowledge that nonsense of Bell that it may be laid down as an axiom inasmuch as the head differs with the characteristic of animals, it approaches the brutality, & why not [if] it be granted of the form also? Is there no reason in all this? Why cannot [an] animal stand upright? Because he is adapted to run on all fours, & why does he so? because it is better calculated to his character, vice versa of a human being — and if . . .

[*The ink is so faded that the last three lines of this entry are illegible.*]

December 19. I believe it can be proved that you are the *more*

1. *Edinburgh Review,* July 1812, 20:69, "Sixth Report of the Directors of the African Institution." The reviewer actually wrote: "The following passage we recommend to those speculatists who dream about natural and fixed incapacities of the Africans." BRH's "speculations" on Negroes were published in the *Examiner* of September 1 and 29, 1811 (see I,210 n).

speculatist; we speculate, certainly — but we speculate certainly, but however our facts [are] open to all who choose to investigate, while you sit at home & write on History and hope & wish with nothing to back you.

Why this infatuated attachment to Sculpture for monuments in spite of the neglect, idling, and the deformity with which your patronage is met? In all the Churches of the continent, Pictures are put up as well as Statues for monuments — give the Brush & pen an equal chance.

All the Historical attempts of the Country have been for nothing; Hogarth[2] & the rest adorned the Foundling for nothing, Barry painted the Adelphi[3] for nothing, Reynolds & West &c offered to grace St. Paul's without remuneration, and latterly Fuzeli,[4] how[ever] detested his style of art, made a gigantic effort in his Theatre Gallery without support, without Patronage. Had he not sold a few he would have been ruined.

While the Painters have been making such praeternatural effort without one smile, without a finger stretched forward to save them from destruction, the Portrait painter & the Sculptor have been nursed & pampered with splendid prices and every comfort & luxury. While great Nobles have thrown with a profuse hand to them, not only have the Painters in the higher walk of Art been neglected, but Patrons & Critics have taken the pains to prove that great Pictures are useless at the very time they are employing Sculptors on monuments of boundless extent without reason or restraint. I only beg to ask, is this just, is this fair? No doubt if the encouragement of Sculptors were left to the people, there would be the same cry against great Works, but as they are employed by government, it is the contrary. What can the People as individuals do, what have they ever done? Had Raphael been left to the People, what would he have done? If Phidias had been left [to] the People, what would they have done, what could he

2. William Hogarth (1697–1764) presented his "Adoption of Moses by Pharaoh's Daughter" to the Foundling Hospital. More famous pictures by Hogarth at the Foundling Hospital are his portrait of Captain Coram and the "March to Finchley."

3. James Barry painted six huge pictures representing "Human Culture" at the Society of Arts, Adelphi.

4. Henry Fuseli painted nine pictures for the Shakespeare Gallery established by John Boydell.

have done? This is the absurdity. The People or the Patron as an individual can do nothing. We don't want individual support only; we want public assistance, we want Parliament to vote Pictures as well as Statues to the Heroes or the Legislators of the Country — then indeed would a field be open, and from the industry of the Arts, then indeed would the Country spring to its proper station. Can any justice reason why Pictures should not be voted as well as Statues? None under Heaven. It may be objected that if Painters get such assistance as Sculptors, the same listless idleness, the same neglect, the same imbecility will begin to ooze into their feelings as has parallized their efforts lately. Why should you fear this? Soldiers who have been making forced marches without shoes are not likely to march slower when their feet are protected & their limbs strengthened by shoes & cloathes, are not apt to lose their energy when assisted. In the name of truth, let individuals at the Gallery purchase dead game & brass kettles and cabinet bits — let this go on, but at the same time afford that wholesome, sound assistance to the higher department, and it may proceed in the same ratio. No. Without reason, from mere caprice, great Pictures will never do. With the examples of all the nations, the Greek, Egyptian, & Italian, who have been illustrious in Art, staring them in the face, the Patrons of England set their face against great works, except it be for the purpose of elevating one man to destroy another; then indeed 300, 400, or even 500 guineas will be readily voted tho the Picture be as imbecil as Pompeo Battoni[5] [or] Raphael Mengs; tho it be without a single beauty in art or intellect, tho it be dry, mawkish, flat, hot, & earthy in colour, flimsy in substance, inharmonious in composition, & despicable in character, & absurd in conception, they may indeed find out they have disgraced themselves by the purchase, and fearful of hanging it up where it would ever be an existing monument of scandalous intrigue & bare faced ignorance, offer half the first intended price, and return it back to the poor painter, that he may hang it in his painting room, and hide their dishonour as well as his own. This then may be done, but these are trifles light as air, tho to the "discern-

5. Pompeo Girolamo Batoni (1708–1787), one of the most popular Italian painters of the eighteenth century.

ing mind as proofs of holy writ," [6] that they [are] incompetent by nature and despicable by habit to conduct encouragement, on a noble, an open and fair ground, without caprice or folly.

The great objects I oppose — Payne Knight & Sir G. Beaumont — are Men, no dout of fortune & taste. Of Mr. P. Knight — his judgement may be very easily estimated by his purchasing Westall,[7] saying his importance was in grace & dignity of attitude & character; & Sir G., tho' a delightful man certainly and capable of making an Artist's life very happy, yet his capacity for art goes not beyond a bit of Wilson[8] or a head of Vandyke. These are the men on whom the Nobility pin their faith — with a detestation in fact of great works, with a horror of any thing fine by Raphael, but pictures six inches long, with a sort of shrill at a large Rubens, and absolute apoplexy at a Cartoon — these are the men who rule Patrons & patronise Artists — and if such be the Patrons, what chance, what prospects for historic art?

Men are often incapable from mere nervous fancy, but while the impression exists, they are really so, tho not by nature. Thus it is with the Patrons & People of this Country, you find the impression every where that the Higher walk of Art will never do, that Starvation attends it, and destruction ends it. Thus they who are the causes of such effects by their own indifference and neglect tend by their belief in the natural impossibility to be otherwise, that they deprecate others to confirm it, and so they in whom the power of patronage lies are withheld by their own habitual fancy of incapability to do the good which they have the power to do, when by resolute reliance in their own power & in the ability, if properly fostered, of the Artists, the higher walk would at once

6. *Othello,* III,iii,322–324.
     "Trifles light as air
   Are to the jealous confirmations strong
   As proofs of holy writ."

7. On July 8, 1811, Farington reported a conversation with William Westall (1781–1850), who informed him that Payne Knight had ordered "The Grecian Marriage." "Mr. Knight said that He knew that such a picture would be a work of great labour (the size abt. 6 feet wide) and being sensible of it He would fix the price at *One Thousand Guineas*" (Farington, VII,12).

8. Richard Wilson (1714–1782), landscape and portrait painter and an original member of the Royal Academy. Sir George Beaumont owned his "Destruction of Niobe's Children," now in the Tate Gallery.

be released from its neglect and at once elevated to take its natural Station.

But thus from the want of a Minister of Taste, who would be above envy and have no petty interest to gratify in the talent of the Country at the mercy of meaness & ignorance, who knowing nothing and whose only object being the filling the vacant hour with something to hope and something to puff, cannot distinguish when they have hit on Genius or when on imbecility, and consequently desert either, when a new ignis fatuus starts up, clothed in novelty and beaming with freshness. There is a great fundamental error in the system of Exhibitions — a Picture is exhibited, bought or not considered, and it is perhaps huddled into obscurity for ever. No future opportunity is then ever given for candid judgement, nothing is left to time, its errors or its beauties are pressed on the people according to the interests or enmities of those who conduct or those who oppose the Society where it is hung. The consequence — every thing is in a heat, people are in a perpetual wilderness of feeling, papers puff or censure, Patrons praise or ridicule; just as it suits [them], and before a man has time to estimate with perspicuity, the Exhibition closes, and the Picture & the Painter are forgotten, or talked of like a new Teniers, and a new subject obliterates the recollection of both, while sound, fair, public encouragement, so that Works might be for ever [in the] public inspection of all the World, would give a man that reliance, that conscious comfort, that however his enemies might sneer, or his Friends damn by faint praise,[9] there the works would be; every man could judge for himself by a walk to the Public building where it hangs, and take others to judge with him. The consequence of such a system is that every opportunity is given to puffing of all descriptions; men who do not belong to a Society are at the mercy of those who do; nothing is open, candid, or fair.

December 21. Always recollect, the joints clear, boney, & tendonous; the limbs full, fleshy, & vigourous; the chest wide, the foot arched, the pelvis *not* narrow, the knees & ankles not small,

9. Pope, *Epistle to Dr. Arbuthnot*, l. 201.

the scull capacious, the face not large. [*Sketches of Adam and Eve.*] How clearly is it to be seen that the Man is from my own fancy and [the] Woman from a real object — the cut-up, hard-liney look of the one and the full broad look of Nature in the other is apparent. I have learnt a great deal by this accident.

At Nelson's death,[1] monuments & pillars were voted & erected at every considerable and every opulent Town by Parliaments of England & corporations of London. Neither the Parliament or the Corporation, neither Glasgow or Portsmouth, neither Noble or Gentlemen, ever employed or thought of employing one single Painter, in any way, large or small, to illustrate, to decorate or honour his illustrious Death of one of the greatest heroes; indeed such was the absolute indifference to the Painters' efforts that with the exception [of] little Pictures, which were a mere commercial speculation such [as] a set of Prints and Drummond's[2] clever sketch (neither Picture was bought), can there be a stronger proof of the public neglect of the higher Walk of Art in this Country than this? Good God! in Greece how would employment have showered on the Painters. Hardy & Nelson would have graced every Public Hall in the Country, like Miltiades & Themistocles at the battle of Men, Salamis — and yet nobody dies of a Public import, not even a port captain & a 20 gun Frigate, not even a commissary of a marching regiment, but monuments and tablets are instantly voted & "hear, hear" echoes from Whig, Tory, ministers, opposition, & reformists without hesitation.

Why this infatuated attachment to Sculpture for monuments? In all the Churches on the Continent, Pictures are put up as well as Statues to commemorate the Dead. You admit Mercury or Mars to illustrate the deeds of the Hero commemorated, but you refuse to admit St. Matthew or St. John! If you banish Painting, why not banish Music & Sculpture? Why not break the coloured windows? Why not expel the organ's solemn roar & the youths' angelic chaunt? Let us have it at once a barren desert. To be as great in Painting as we are in every other Art & Science, opportunity must be given for works as great as the works are in those

1. On October 21, 1805.
2. Samuel Drummond (1765–1844), A.R.A.; he painted "The Battle of Trafalgar" and "The Death of Nelson," both of which were engraved.

Arts & Sciences in which we already excel. That the Public Halls, Churches, & Cathedrals are the only places for such Works.

I repeat again, divide your favours. Let now a Picture & then a Monument be voted, or let both, and the Artists may not be confined to Fames, Victories, & Neptunes, with their crowns, their tridents, their trumpets, & let a subject of ancient history illustrative or applicable be painted which will as much honor the deceased as his own particular action by shewing that he is worthy of such an illustration. Let the artist be left to his own choice. Let him not be confined. What a cheering prospect would this be for Art, what a gratification for a Minister to be the first to propose it, for however great may have been our Chatams and our Pitts, yet a minister great in patronage of Art we have never yet seen — to this reputation — and all this might be done at half the expence too, which is no small consideration!!! Why are Pericles, Julius II, & Leo X so often in the mouths of all? I believe their patronage of literature and art will make them honored & remembered when their intrigue, and their propensity to war & dominion will be lost with the ferocity of an unchristian Nature. We are & have been great in every thing but in Art. Do not let us sink into oblivion without adding this necessary sparkling gem to the diadem of our greatness — it will surely be imperfect without it. There will always be a spot unfilled. Posterity will always wonder that in such a diadem, in which Philosophy, History, Poetry, Heroism by land & sea, had placed their richest ores, the polished diamond, Painting, should have been suffered to sparkle with a strength equal to all by its own innate vigour & brilliancy, unset & unnoticed, and then sink into darkness without being placed in fostering hand where it might have contended successfully in blazing with the brightest that glittered in the splendid circlet. Our notions of every thing but Painting are great; we have great Public Works of all descriptions — breakwaters, piers, churches, cathedrals, palaces, & prisons — our inventions of destructions, our notions of every thing [except] Painting are on an enlarged scale worthy a Nation eminent for its liberty & literature. The reason of all this is plain. There are but few of any pretensions to taste in this country. In them the Prince & the people put their dependence and every thing that relates to Art is consequently left to them. They are assembled with the avowed purpose of encouraging Art, but in truth more to have an occupation for the season, and an amusement for the day & dinner, than any sincere desire to advance the art of their Country; hence their perpetual changes of scheme, hence their perpetual inventions and perpetual plans that betray an ignorance of principle & a vacillation of system, that while it attracts by a perpetual hope, deserts with a continued caprice, that has at last opened the eyes and chilled the hearts of the most ardent & enthusiastic. *They* have only small houses, *they* want small pictures to adorn — small pictures are then the perpetual cry — great Works will never do, great Works are incompatible, great Works are not necessary. Yet as the virtue of perseverance had never visited their enfeebled intellects, to ensure success in any scheme, great works have been sometimes purchased for the sake of variety or the more villainous intention of crushing enthusiastic independence. As they cannot have great works themselves, and know that any Minister, or any Nobleman, becoming convinced of the necessity, would send them at once to their proper rank, idling & capricious connoiseurs with Raphael in their mouths & Ruysdael in their hearts. Till a Minister with the inclination & talent [arises] nothing will be done to foster the efforts of ardent individuals. The Public Halls & Public Palaces, the churches & the Cathedrals, the House of Commons & House of Lords, will be ever bare, cold, inanimate, will be for ever lasting proofs of a tastless government & an imbecile Prince. Let me for a moment indulge the privilege of Genius and revel with delights in the picture of my own Imagination. Let me conceive the House of Lords with its spacious & ample sides clothed with illustrious examples of Virtue & Heroism. Let me fancy — as [a] Nobleman of genius in the enthusiasm of debate illustrates his assertion with pointed finger to an example before his eyes — "My Lords, I refer you to the illustrious example of Virtue before you; let it stimulate you to do your duty to your Country & your King. Recollect, my Lords, that however imbecility may cloak its weakness by speciousness & power, however interest may blind the faculties or wilfully deaden the perceptions of all, 'time & the hour'[3] will lay open all to keen criticism of an unconverted posterity. Their faculties will not be blinded by intent, or their perceptions deadened by passion, their judgement weakened by affection. They will judge in the very teeth & forehead of your faults, they will strip off your power and your patronage, and lay you bare on the rack, torture you without mercy to force you, before you are allowed to take that station & cloak those feelings to which you so speciously aspire." Can it be possible to conceive any thing more likely to impress truth, virtue, & such examples & such allusions in the heat of debate & the fury of discussion? To give such an opportunity for reference would be worthy of a great Nation; it would be worthy an enlightened government, & honor and adorn the reign of an illustrious Prince.

The taste [of the] Nobility, People, and Prince is confined to the imitation of the immediate and common objects of their commonest perceptions — a copy of a turnip, or potatoes, or a round of beef excites the delight & enthusiasm of all. Naturally enough the things they see every day, and consequently have the capability to discover the resemblance. Every man with eyes can judge if a Portrait be like, but every man cannot judge of the truth of an expression, the beauty of a character, or the classicality of a scene; cultivation and a natural refinement must precede before any mind can relish these intellectual beauties either in Poetry or Painting. They are pure beauties of mind — the others beauties of senses — inasmuch as some are blind in their eyes, cannot judge of a resemblance, so others who are blind in their minds cannot feel an expression. It depends on the natural capability and cultivation of that capability in either case, for capability may exist in both cases, but without habitual cultivation, it would be useless. A man who has never seen light but lives in darkness would be equally as incapable to judge of a resemblance as he who was born blind. So of the intellectual powers, for the one always illustrates the other and ever will. The origin of this is a defect in education. In neither university is Painting ever thought of — of its relations, of its beauties, of its moral utility or the necessity of taste to perfect an accomplished character. Neither the public Tutors of the Nobility, nor the private Tutors of the

3. *Macbeth*, I,iii,147.

Prince ever feel themselves and ever impress on their pupils. Thus they grow up and issue out into the World, with a total ignorance of a feeling that has solaced & delighted the greatest princes, & the most accomplished men soon become conscious of this defect & soon [are] eager to supply it. They then profess a desire to protect artists & encourage art, but knowing nothing of its refinements and feeling nothing of its high claims, in the common course of things they fly to that which they *can* comprehend, and thus the powers of the nation & the protection of the nobility are devoted to foster mere imitation and common truth. Those who should know better from Travel & habit, the Dilettante & Connoiseur, either from wilful indolence or perverse inclination to check that of which they would not reap the praise, second the ignorance of the Nobles, and thus the necessity of great works is never thought of, or if considered, judged as the wild effusion of an enthusiastic youth, or the dream of a distempered imagination. These are the prejudices and these the rooted habits a Student in the high Art has to contend with in this Country, with a People uncultivated, a Nobility tastless, and a Prince unskilled, with a government cold, an Academy intriguing, & an Institution without honor — these, these are the stimulants and not the checks to enthusiasm & genius — to conquer these prejudices and subdue these misfortunes, accidental not natural, must the vigour of the rising Students be devoted, and were they once broken and but the slightest glimmer of dawn to break forth on the Horizon, all the clouds of ignorance & prejudice might be dispersed by the resistless blaze of the morning Sun, and the sky that has so long been darkened must then be lit with trembling glitter, and the fresh dewy, lucid effulgence of the Sky give prospect of a glorious blaze and burning evening — that the day of glory would last for ever. It would, from the natural imperfection of men, be useless to hope & impossible to promise, or that if it once breaks, it will pursue in breaking. In spite of all it would be futile to gaze in expectation; clouds may again rise, mists may again obscure, and the day of our glory may yet close in with its splendor and its brilliancy, unillumined & unsupported by the blaze of the Sun of Painting.

Management & not exposure, I believe, is the easiest and the

most useful way to conquer ignorance if united with power. It is
the only way effectually to direct that power to do good. If reaction is produced by attack, then power will be exerted however
wickedly, and the attacker who might be the man capable of
reformation may be crushed without effecting his purpose.

I fancy my fair readers will shrink with disgust at the mention
of turnips and a round of beef — but why, why should you
shrink at the mere mention of what you take the greatest delight
in seeing closely imitated? Surely the allusion cannot bring it to
your fancy so strongly as the absolute imitation or the imitation
as the reality — why then should you shrink?

What can be more absurd than admitting into the House of
God Statues to commemorate the arts of Warriors & Statesmen
and refusing to admit illustrations of the Divine acts of the divine Saviour of our pure & exquisite religion by which the heart
would be expanded and the moral feelings enlivened to keep &
revere the laws & regulations of the heavenly founder? Prima
facie, can any thing be so unreasonable, so infatuated, so absurd?
You admit the remembrance of men who have devoted themselves for the Country's temporary salvation as Englishmen, but
you refuse as Christians to admit any tablet, any relic, to remind
you of him who devoted himself for the salvation of the World to
all eternity. You refuse to admit illustrations by an Art of more
various capability, of more power, of more variety, than Sculpture, and consequently of more innate spirit to arrest, subdue,
and affect human feelings — you allow the Sculptor and the
Architect but exclude the Painter.

There is a morning purity in the feelings of virtue which those
who know the [*two illegible words*] confident, haughty, savage,
[*about four illegible words*] mean, unmanly sensations of vice —
feel how to value, how to estimate, how to enjoy.[4] Once you are
adequate to any exertion, or any misfortune in the latter, success
itself creates suspicions and misfortune gloomy, unamiable despair — for what consolation can that being have who cannot,
when Men have forsaken him, rely with conscious desert on God.

How strange is the blind infatuation of the Country. Nobody
refuses Portraits of themselves or their friends on canvasses 8,

4. A sketch of a crowned head, probably Solomon, covers the illegible words.

10, 12 feet long, but every one shuts their doors and locks up their hearts against the illustrious events of our own and other Nations being illustrated on a canvas larger than a half length, or a pocket port-folio. At the very time Sir G. Beaumont was harrassing me, after having engaged me on a whole length, about the size of it, Owen[5] was painting a portrait of his Mother on the very same scale, without remonstrance or objection. It is really so unjust, so short sighted — they like to see themselves the full size of life, but paint Achilles or Agamemnon, Macbeth or Lear on the scale of heroes, and they shrink with horror & disgust. What would Michel Angelo have said of the taste of the Country, when it was actually a question with the Patrons of it whether great works, or cabinet works, were the more essential [to] the greatness of the Nation? That it should ever have come to this!!! Could he lift his head from the grave and look round the World to observe the state of Art, how would he shudder and shrink, as he turns his face towards England, and huddle his shroud over him, to hide his anguish & remorse.

No man like Raphael fills without crowding, and yet has such breadth without emptiness. The face is his great object; to this he sacrifices every thing — drapery, hair, form, figure, nothing that is near it is ever suffered to come in competition. Dec. 29.

You admit Pagan Gods (arguing superstitiously), but you refuse to admit any thing relating to the one God Jehovah. If you banish some, why not banish all, why not break the coloured Window, which so encreases the solemnity of feeling, why not expel the organ & singing? Let us have it at once bare as a barren desert.

From what I have laid open, it is evident that to be as great in Painting as we are in every other Art, Science, or intellect, opportunities must be given for works as great as the works are in those Arts or Sciences in which we already excel — that the Public Halls & Churches & Cathedrals are the only places for such works.

That the expulsion of Painting (an Art of far greater power

5. William Owen (1769–1825), R.A., the principal portrait painter of the Prince Regent. His portrait of the Dowager Lady Beaumont, now in the National Gallery of Victoria, Melbourne, is 84 x 53¾ inches (T. S. R. Boase, *English Art, 1800–1870*, Oxford, 1959, p. x).

than sculpture or music), by which the perfection of the Christian religion as to morality might be delightfully & ably illustrated, and its divinity by the tremendous miracles of its founder, awfully and grandly impressed — that by such means the impression of the superiority of Christianity over other religions would be more strongly & vividly shewn, and the effect on those who attended Divine Worship, for the purposes of prayer or thanksgiving, more strongly & feelingly attained — that therefore to reject painting, the more powerful art, & admit music & sculpture, the weaker, is absurd, unreasonable, & infatuated, that therefore no just reason can be given why Sculpture should be admitted to illustrate the acts of Heroes in War, and why Painting should be rejected, and not suffered to illustrate the deeds of the great Martyr in Peace — that suffering Windows with painted glass of the Apostles & the Saints is a proof that Painting is allowed — and that if it be allowed, no just reason can be given why it be not allowed in its highest state of intellectual perfection to expand the heart and elevate the Soul by human feelings and divine acts, instead of being only suffered in its lowest to attract the eye & debauch the sense by transparent colour and glassy richness. That these two ways in which the powers of the Nation might be employed, either to commemorate our own deeds in our Public Halls, or the deeds of Christ in our Churches or Cathedrals — but that as our own deeds have been allowed admittance into the Houses of God by Sculpture, illustration by Painting also would not be incompatible or inconsistent.

That it is evident, tho' employment will not create genius if it does not exist, employment is necessary to call it out if it does. That there is no example of a Great painter existing without a great Patron or Patrons. That of course they must exist together, and the rest [be left] to less happy combination of circumstances. That if the distresses of this Nation were such that nothing was set aside for intellectual encouragement, surely the Painter would submit without a sigh to the fate of other Arts — but that as thousands are yearly devoted to Sculpture, the Painters only submit whether they have not a strong claim on the munificence of Parliament, both from the superiority of their Art, as well as from the insignificance of the sums required to foster them — that for this century thousands have been yearly devoted to Sculpture, and every opportunity given and that during that period not one single voice publickly has been raised in the favour of Painting — that all the historical attempts of the Country & by which the Country has been ornamented have been the result of the spontaneous efforts of enthusiastic artists, individuals — Hogarth, Reynolds, Barry, Fuzeli, West — and that not one single farthing on record has ever in this country [been] voted by Parliament either to purchase celebrated works in Paintings of the illustrious dead or to encourage the illustrious living, and that thousands have been voted to purchase Sculptures, a munificent place built for their reception, and encouragement held out in every way worthy of a great Nation.

With respect to those men with dull feelings & deadened perception who ask what is the use of Painting — let them answer me, what are the use of flowers? what are the use of birds? If the great Creator deprived the World of all that was not absolutely useful or barely sufficient for existence, how few would have been the objects [of] creation! We might have bowed in awful gratitude for being relieved from hunger or saved from sickness, but would our hearts have been so expanded with enthusiasm or our frames so have trembled with agitation & delight as they do when the day dawns with dozing silence, the sun gilds with cheery splendor, & the lark sings with fluttering delight, had we been confined & pinned down to life without ornament or ease; would the need [for] the procreation of Nature have been attained with the agitations & rapture that a bending beauty excites enveloped in plaits of hair floating in wild luxuriance, encreases the beauty it seems to conceal. As Men sink to animals, & animals to inanimation, utility & necessity without the ornament or beauty, are all that seem requisite to their pleasures, but the higher Nature rises till she ends in Man, the more refined & more numerous appear the sources [of] our pleasures, and as she goes in the scale of existence, sensations of which we are incapable, and objects of delight which we can never know are provided [by] the good and munificent Creator. It appears, as far as we can enter into the thoughts of God, to [be] the object of his goodness to cloathe utility and things necessary in delight &

beauty, in short, to instruct us by attractions to do Poetry & Painting; then this struggle to imitate [the] universal is possible — and endeavour to instruct by pleasing to clothe morality & virtue, illustrious acts & illustrious actors, in all the variety of form & colour, light, darkness, magnificence, & splendor.

We only ask such protection for this delightful art as you have already afforded Sculpture & Architecture, only ask to admit us, where you have admitted our brothers into Cathedrals & Churches, Halls & Palaces. Stretch forth that fostering hand you stretch forth to other Artists & other Arts. Give us a similar opportunity, and if in ten years we do not prove ourselves worthy, stop your assistance; turn your backs on [us], and send [us] into disgrace & darkness without honor or reward.

We only beg to be allowed to try to honor our Country where it has not yet been honored. Such a trial cannot be made without your permission & assistance; you have afforded to others, afford it to us, and the result will then [be] that you will not afford it in vain, and when so much has been done without assistance as has rescued the Country from the stigma of imbecility, surely the effort is not likely to cease.

That the propensity to remuneration by a set of Prints is unworthy a great Nation, and that encouragement must be conducted on the same liberal scale, or it will be useless. Without one smile of Public support we have rescued the Nation from the stigma of Climate & dullness. Surely then when so much has been effected with so little support, we are not likely to do less with more.

Let us have a Public monument of Talent open to all, at all Seasons, & at all periods, to the Native & the Foreigner, and not yearly make gigantic efforts, which are dispersed & inefficient as soon as the summer ends, & huddled into an obscure country seat or a dingy drawing room, never seen by any one, and shortly forgotten by all.

What is there to rouse the blood by such a prospect? What to make the heart expand? What to rouse conception? and support effort? Surely nothing, nothing — & efforts are painfully made & painfully supported. The conception becomes dull & confused; the beating of the heart is scarcely perceptible, and the frozen blood, with difficulty, forces its passage through its obstructed and loaded vessels. While in a Public building, there could be no shuffling, no puffing inferiority by situation, and praise for a time before People have power to collect their perceptions. If it were puffed, a year's continued observation would soon open the eyes of all, and if it deserved praise, a year's study would confirm & not confute it.

December 31. The danger of Solitude is that a man centres every thing in himself. He fancies the World are watching him & the Heavens protecting him; he fancies that *he* only is employed, and that *he* only is ambitious. When he rushes out into Society he will find others occupied with wishes & efforts like his own, others who have been ambitious and are now humbled, others who have grandly failed in grandly struggling. This will subdue his own notions of his own importance and send him back to his Study prepared for the misfortunes & qualified for the miseries of life which would otherwise have come unexpectedly & while he was anticipating certain happiness & assured Success.

This [is] the last day of 1812. Alas, instead of having equalled my wishes of improvement in morals & mind, what have I to do at the end of every year but to recapitulate vices, repent, hope amendment, and before the new [year] has ushered in the spring, be as deep in abandonment as ever. I am weary, sick, & hopeless. Perfection in virtue & resolution in temptation, I begin to suspect, can never be attained here; I can only in awe & humbleness wonder that one such as I am with a clear & perfect knowledge of my duty, and the most correct Notions of Virtue, should while my heart is warm with admiration of it and my mind but just occupied with reflecting on it, be suffered to go out and before I return, to encrease the burthen of my iniquities.

Marriage is the only chance I have of attaining a composed deportment. I am now at the mercy of every sleepy and lustrous eye, of every bending & voluptuous hip. Sometimes, when I successfully contend & conquer, it is always at the expence of such agitations & agony that I am unnerved & reduced for a week. But I have never yet seen a woman unmarried to whom I would devote myself, who would enter into my views, my conceptions — when I do, if ever I do, how would I submit.

My feelings about the close of this year are dulled. Things happen but once in this World; as you enter life every thing is fresh & beautiful & impressing, but [in] a short time each recurrence is less noticed than the preceding one & perhaps when one leaves life a change is requisite from disgust & weariness.

O God, in thee I sincerely trust, desert me not, surrounded as I am with difficulties & dangers. Extricate me; let me not die, till I have paid all my debts with honor, till I have established my fame on an iron foundation, till I am worthy to be called to a purer existence. O God, listen to this prayer for Jesus Christ's sake. Amen. Amen. Amen.

Surely it is the feeling of human Nature, however depraved, rather to rejoice at the destruction of an object which we have taken from another when we find it will be otherwise returned, than to acquiesce to its restoration in sullen gloom and dark despair. The one is a general feeling, the other peculiar; it belongs to a singular temperament. She did not steal the child because [she] envied the other, but because she wished to have a child even at the expence of another's feeling. She loved children, she liked their amusement, their prattle, their innocence. These feelings are not incompatible with a Devil — it is not that she was always a Devil, but that at this particular moment the Devil burst out. You say Lear could even have been detest[ed] if it were not for Lear, inasmuch as Lear reconciles you to Goneril. So will I try to reconcile you by the real Mother — I don't put the other to be loved but to be detested, to contrast with the other; in the other instance she would indeed contrast but it would be at the expence of the other.

1813

January 1813. The people of this country are little better than children in matters of art. So unused are they to see grand forms of Heroes, so unprepared are they for great Art, that if a neck be full & vigourous like a pillar, "too thick" echoes through the Gallery, and down go all their cravats that they may feel their own skinny, meagre miserable necks, dwindled from confinement and distorted from binding. If a shoulder be full & round & bending, "how unnatural" says a petit-maître, with shoulders like a chicken

& the fine swell of the Trapezius flattened by braces. If a calf be energetically knit, or a knee firmly extended, if a hip be flowing or an arm sweepingly, irresistibly bent, away shrink Lords & Ladies to melt and die on the mawkish insipidity of Albano.[6] In my sleeping groom, where the veins of the neck were shewn, from intoxication & drowsiness, "no such in Nature," [they] exclaimed, "look at my neck!!!" "Drink," I could have answered, "till your brains become a limbeck[7] (which I suspect it now is without drinking), ramble into the King's room, fall asleep on the floor, sleep for an hour with your head thrown back, and then *feel* your neck — and if these veins do not start up, why then you have not got them!"

You say after all beauty is the thing. No, it is not the chief thing; intellect, the feelings of the heart, are the chief things. The more beautiful the garb that expression is dressed in, the better, but if you dress expression so beautifully as to overwhelm it, the object is not attained.

Beauty of form is but the vehicle of conveying Ideas, but truth of conveyance is the first object. If the vehicle attract on its own score, what it is intended to convey is lost, and the mind drawn to an object foreign. So with colour, light & shadow, and the means of the Art, for beauty is but a means.

This is the reason that tho many Painters have excelled Raphael in beauty they take their rank in an inferior station. Perfect beauty can only belong to beings not agitated by passion, such as Angels. But while human beings can be depressed or agitated, roused by terror or melted by love, perfect, composed, & regular beauty is incompatible to express such feelings, and the suffrages of mankind will always be in favor of him who conveys these feelings at once to their hearts, without weakening them by the mawkish interposition of regular beauty.

No doubt these feelings should agitate beauty, but then its sedate regularity is destroyed; and tho' it may be the expression of a beautiful countenance, yet the expression should predominate. Certainly a passion should not be torn in rags & tatters;[8] a line

6. Francesco Albani or Albano (1578–1660), a Bolognese painter of religious and mythological subjects.

7. *Macbeth*, I,vii,66–67. "The receipt of reason / A limbeck only."

8. *Hamlet*, III,ii,9–11. "O, it offends me to the soul to see a robustious periwig-pated fellow tear a passion to tatters, to very rags."

should be drawn, but it should be rather clear within the line of expression than risk weakening the expression by trespassing on the line of beauty.

People of no Practice sit still & refine themselves to impossible beings. They forget that we are made up of body & mind — such is our Nature — and an Art professedly laying its foundation in imitation of such nature, must remind us of it, or it will fail of its effect. [In] the highest Style the moment it departs from Nature, the moment the artist forsakes her, either in action, expression, or form, that moment does he cease to interest human beings.

All Homer's, all Shakespeare's characters have the elevations, & the failings of men. Do not Homer & Shakespeare interest human beings more than the other poets? No doubt the characters of Milton are higher characters, but I am talking of the dramatic human variety — of this and not the epic sublimity of another World. When you deal with human beings, they must remind [you] of human beings, when Heavenly, let this World and its failings be banished from their Souls, but mingling the perfection of Heavenly with the imperfection of human beings elevates them without heightening their interest and renders their effect futile and without strength.*

"Had I attended," says Nelson, "less than I have done to the service of my Country, I might have made some too; however I trust my name will stand on record when the money makers are forgot." Vol. 1, Page 176.[9]

"I am at this moment in the horrors I get from idling here; in short, I wish to be an admiral, and in command of the English Fleet. I would very soon do much or be ruined. My disposition cannot bear tame & slow measures. I went on board the Admiral and wanted him to pursue the enemy, but he, much cooler than myself, [said], 'We must be contented; we have done very well.'

* This is false — it does heighten the interest. No being is more interesting than Milton's Satan, and you are to convey expressions as beautifully as possible without weakening the expression. B. R. H.

9. James S. Clarke and John McArthur, *The Life of Admiral Lord Nelson, K.B.*, 1809, I,176.

Now, had we taken ten sail and allowed the eleventh to escape, I could never have called it well done." Letter to Lady Nelson.[1]

Page 36. "Captain Nelson, also during this march [in Nicaragua in 1780] had nearly experienced the same dreadful calamity. Being one day excessively fatigued, he had ordered his hammock, on one of their halts, to be slung under some trees. During his sleep, that extraordinary animal called the monitory lizard, from its faculty of warning persons of the approach of any venomous animal, passed across his face, which being observed by some of the attendant Indians, they shouted and awoke him. He immediately started up, and throwing off the quilt, found one of the most venomous serpents in that country curled up under his feet. From this providential escape, the Indians, who attended, entertained an Idea that Nelson was a superior being, under an especial protection; and this idea, which his wonderful abilities and unwearied exertions tended to confirm, was of essential service in gaining their confidence and prolonging their co-operation. See Shaw, Vol. iii, Part 1, 214." [2]

"It is no matter to me," say these refiners, "how expression is conveyed. I care not for the vehicle." They forget that the great Creator of the Universe has conveyed the profoundest system in the most delightful garb — the grace & colour of a tiger soften for a moment his ferocity & strength.

January 7. I wish I had thought of the following when I demolished Payne Knight. "The composition of the small Pictures in the loggia of the Vatican are equal to any thing of Raphael's. Here is a palpable instance of moderate sized Raphaels, and pray why do they not rank with the other works? Why are the School of Athens, the Heliodorus, & St. Peter talked of as his most important works? Why is not [the] loggia visited first? Why does it not divide the attention? The answer is evident from their insignificance as to scale — cut off his great works, and he will rank as high as Poussin; add them, and he becomes a greater Raphael." Jan. 7th.

1. Clarke and McArthur, *Nelson,* I,206–207. Not accurately quoted.
2. Clarke and McArthur, *Nelson,* I,36. Clarke and McArthur refer thus to George Shaw's *General Zoology,* 1802.

January 9. Drew at Lord Elgin's all day and evening till eight. How delightful is the exhausted faint feel after a day's hard work with an approving God within, in comparison with the listless horror after an idle day, and the stings of a reproachful conscience. Well I know, and sincerely do I thank God that I have compleatly recovered my tranquillity & conquered the agitation from that infernal woman, that wholly & undivided am I again devoted [to] my Art & my glory. I cannot sport on the borders of Pleasure without plunging within the circle. I will therefore keep off altogether as the only mode of salvation.

"Little measures," says Nelson in his Letter to the Queen of Naples, "can only produce little effects." Page 376. V.II.[3] "I do not think either in the last War, nor according to all appearances in the present, are our plans upon that grand scale which would bid fairest to keep France within due bounds."

"The weather on the 4th was variable & unsettled, light breezes, hazy, & drizzling rain, when *suddenly* the Phoebe, Hon. T. B. Capel, was discovered in the offing with *signal flying that the French Admiral was at sea!!*" To my feelings this is excessively poetical. B.R.H.

I have finished Nelson's Life, every syllable, with interest and delight. I had no idea of his powers of mind, of his knowledge of men and things, till I saw his correspondence. He was certainly a most extraordinary man, persevering in pursuing an object, restless & miserable if a chance of missing it, prompt & clear in his conception, yet cool & wary; after having conceived, rapid, energetic, unconquerable, keeping a steady eye, bending his whole soul, his whole body, his whole powers to compleat it. With all the simplicity and enthusiasm of a fiery Youth, he had all the wisdom & experience of suspicious age. He had the power of all great men of making others in his presence & society forget their own inferiority, of reconciling them with themselves & himself, whether a midshipman or mate, whether a lieutenant or a captain, whether an ambassador or an admiral, whether a Native or a Foreigner, all loved him, for all in his presence lost not their own respect. The Seamen adored, the officers loved, the admirals

3. Clarke and McArthur, *Nelson*, II, 376.

reverenced. He had the keen eager feelings of genius. Captives did not satisfy his soul. Annihilation was his object, and if in our being there was a further or deeper state of destruction, annihilation would have been insipid and absurd. "We have done well, we must be content," said Hotham.[4] "Content!" answered Nelson, with the true, the burning appetite of genius, "Content! and well done!! If we had taken 10 sail, and let the eleventh escape, I should not be content, or have called it well done."

This is the feeling of fiery vigour; this is the man who would not wait for opportunity, but make the most of what he had. This is the Hero who if he commanded a cock-boat would do something a cock-boat never did before.

Nelson is an illustrious example of what persevering, undivided attention to one Art will do; of how far a restless habit of enterprise will carry a man; to what a length never resting in indolent enjoyment after exertion, will go. He began the war unknown, a captain of a 60 gun ship, and concluded it famous throughout the World and the greatest Hero of his Country.

He had all the right feelings of the old school, and detested the Liberté & Egalité school, with philosophy in their mouths, & rapine, murder, & ravishment in their hearts.

I love him for this, and sign my name to all he wrote or said against this detestable, damnable set, French or English. Posterity will properly estimate the pure, honorable heroism of the English Admirals, in contrast with the ferocious, unbridled, tyrannical, & unprincipled bloody glory of the French. All his observations, all his views, all his notions, were fresh, vigorous, original, for they issued from a high, innate, & powerful faculty impregnated by experience; conscious without knowing what of something, he did every thing with a sort of authority from his infancy, and yet with the true feelings of a great mind, humble & willing to learn if ignorant.

The same eagerness, the same enthusiasm, the same powers, the same restlessness, the same determination to go on while in existence, in any art, will carry a man the same length, because such conduct begets a confidence in others, as well as yourself;

4. William Hotham (1736–1813), admiral and commander in the Mediterranean, under whom Nelson served as a captain.

opportunities are thus given, for dependence can be placed by those who have the power to give opportunities.

Nelson's life was a continued scene of glory & vigour, he is an example to all. May those who have similar views pursue them by similar methods. Amen, Amen, with all my Soul. January 9th, midnight.

Nelson's desire for glory was legitimate; it was for the honor of his Prince and salvation of his Country. It was not the turbulent love of fame like Catiline's, the unprincipled ambition like Caesar's, or the cold selfish & cowardly desire to conquer like that of Buonaparte. He died at the very moment he ought; if sympathy can be added to admiration, what stronger hold can you have on human Nature? When his voice was almost inarticulate, when his sight was dim, when his pain was excrutiating, as life was quivering on the borders of another World, and his gallant Soul was almost in the presence of the Almighty, he muttered, "I have done my duty, I thank God for it." What a glorious spirit! At such a moment if human beings are melted and forgive injuries & errors, will not a Being of perfect mercy, of perfect benevolence, of perfect purity, receive & forgive too? It must be so.

Nelson's life was such a continued scene of vigour & enterprise, and so compressed that one was continually forgetting his last glory in the splendor of his latest. He exerted himself in the greatest possible way, in the shortest possible time.

O God Almighty, pardon me pouring forth the enthusiasm of my Soul. Grant me such opportunities, grant me acuteness to perceive them, promptness, energy, health, & intellect to seize them, and genius & power to honor & immortalize them, for Jesus Christ's sake, have mercy on me and realize those conceptions, and grant me virtue & piety to deserve them. O God, I will relinquish life with delight, when thou pleasest to call me, but spare me till I have reformed the Art of my Country & roused Patrons & Students to a proper feeling — spare me till then, O God, O merciful, omnipotent being, & grant I may immortalize my name, do my duty as far as [a] human being ought to do, & honor & devote myself to my Noble Art. Grant these things, I humbly beseech, thou great, thou merciful Being. Amen. Amen.

January 11. The Theseus is a complete figure, not of the highest style, that is, not a figure of abstracted form, the essential only chosen, & nothing but. It is a figure of the second order as to style, but the first of its kind, indeed perfect of its rank. This Vertebra prominens [*a sketch*] which is uncovered by the branching off of the Trapezius each side, in the highest style is such an one, because [it] is enough, but in the Theseus agreeing with its other characteristics, two vertebrae are seen, which at once lower its character of form. A hard day's work.

January 12. Hard at work — seized in every part of my body with a pain. I take [it] I caught cold at Lord Elgin's last night, after painting in a warm room all day. I was literally frozen when I arrived home. Succeeded in my back.

January 13. The greater and more numerous the difficulties with which a man is oppressed the more he should be determined to exert his talents to the utmost, because, after all, if a Picture is so fine that no one can contradict it, it must have its effect. No man does his utmost.

January 14. Very ill, & consequently very miserable — tried to work, but so weak, uneasy, & uncomfortable, could not go on. How much serenity & energy of mind depend on health & vigour of body.

January 15. After every reflection on the state of historical Painting and my own particular difficulties, at every conclusion of thought, something seems to wisper "Paint a fine Picture, paint a Picture, like Titian, & express it like Raphael, and it must carry you through." It can't be resisted, no doubt of this — and this with God's blessing will I struggle for. God bless my exertions, God bless my exertions. Amen.

January 16. This week is ended — three days did I apply myself most indefatigably day & night, two days indifferently, and one day being ill and weak listlessly. This perhaps is an epitome of life, in this "dim spot." [5] How miserable it is that a darling object cannot be pursued without intermission, without sleep,

5. *Comus,* l. 5.

food, relaxation, & sickness, but did we make use of the time that is even left us, even with all these barriers & weights, how much more might we accomplish.

January 17. Dark day. Hard at work, but every now and then the light could hardly make its way "through the blanket of the Dark." [6] When I look round and recollect to my fancy the many and great apparently inextricable difficulties with which I have been surrounded, and the Friends that God has raised up to relieve me, my heart leaps within me with gratitude & joy. O thou Great Being, how merciful, how forgiving, how protecting hast thou been to me.

Drawing well what he sees every man who studies can do, and who has a correct eye, but it is having a poetical conception of character in form and being able to realize it that is the distinction from the mechanical draftsman. The drawing mechanically is drawing well & drawing poetically is drawing finely. Every fool can draw well if he apply himself, but every man cannot draw finely who has not a poetical imagination.

For God's sake, for the sake of Art, for the sake of your own character as Patrons, give great Works that significant, that important encouragement, which will give consequence to the higher Walk. Give Historical Art that protection as a Public body that Portrait has from individuals. Let us be great in every walk and every ramification of every walk. Let us go as far, or further, as Nature has hitherto allowed Man. Let us astonish the World & Posterity with a mass of power that shall sweep off all obstruction to immortality and leave future ages in hopeless gaze & desponding admiration.

I do not say "throw not away your time on dogs & fish." Dogs [and] fish well imitated are worthy encouragement; every part of this delightful [art] is entitled to protection; but I say, give that assistance to those who attempt to realize poetical & sublime conceptions that you give to those who imitate what they see.

January 27. Drew till two in the morning. What a delightful habit is the habit of work. How wretched, how miserable am I to have been out tonight five hours gabbling, idling, dining, when

6. *Macbeth,* I,v,54.

I had feet to prepare for to-morrow. However, before I sleep tonight it shall be done.

January 29. Spent the evening with Hunt, at Westend; walked out & in furiously after dinner, which has done me immense benefit. Hunt's Society is always delightful — I don't know a purer, a more virtuous character, or a more witty, funny, amusing, enlivening man. We talked of his approaching imprisonment.[7] He said it would be a great pleasure to him if he were certain of going to Newgate, because he should be in the midst of all his Friends,[8] and then we both laughed heartily at the idea of his being in the midst of all his Friends at Newgate!! and his being reduced to say it would be a great pleasure the idea of his going *there!!!*

January 31. January is ended — 10 days actually vigourously industrious, 12 days regularly employed, including Sundays, 9 days actually idle. This is a sorry account, but I am determined, however grating to my vanity, to put down a strict account at the end of every month, and at the conclusion of the year ascertain the amount of my exertion.*

Dined with Wilkie. Spent a pleasant evening.

February 1. The senses, the powers of expression are mechanically organised to act when influenced, and not else. We know this from habit & experience. The consequence is we associate the cause when we see the result; and on this principle it is we affect human feelings in Paintings.

Drawing and colouring are mechanical individually as rich tints, but the power of wielding them depends on the power of

* These plans of ascertaining the amount of exertion are all excuses — the best amount is the *production* — what have you to shew? What have you done? He that is energetic & industrious has no time for such futile plans. B. R. H.

7. Leigh and John Hunt were convicted of libeling the Prince Regent in the article entitled "Princely Qualities," published in the *Examiner* of March 22, 1812. Their imprisonments of two years, Leigh's in Horsemonger Lane and John's in Coldbath Fields, began February 3, 1813.

8. Edmund Blunden explains this reference by the fact that Hunt's old school, Christ's Hospital, was near Newgate (*Leigh Hunt,* 1930, p. 72).

conception and associations. The power of wielding them so as to excite great & delightful associations is expletive of the power of the man who wields them. Is colouring merely mechanical? Can no intellectual associations be acquired by it? Is the "lumen purpureum juventae" [9] nothing? Does not the peachy delicacy of a sweet woman excite associations of her character? Form and colour are a means, but the way they are used is expressive of the power of the user. The power of drawing & colouring are powers from Nature as much as conception. The degree to which they are carried depends on cultivation. Drawing & colouring cannot be acquired any more than a feeling for harmony.

Bird is a painter of fine intentions — nothing more.

All the greatest Poets have had the various excellencies of Raphael & Michel Angelo. It is astonishing to me they should ever be considered incongruous. What can be more opposite than the feelings of these two lines,

$$\text{Ἄρεϊ δὲ ζώνην, στέρνον δὲ Ποσειδάωνι}^{[1]}$$

[and]

$$\text{πρὸς κόλπον ἐϋζώνοιο τιθήνης?}^{[2]}$$

The one has the stern energy of Michel Angelo, the other the delicate voluptuousness of Raphael — the full, beautiful, beating, milky bosom of an exquisite, tender nurse, slightly, delicately girded about her shelving waist, separating by a zone her full shoulders & heaving breast from the sweeping flow of her hip; then mark the contrast — about the girth like Mars, that is, narrow, firm, contracted, & about the breast like Neptune — that broad, extended, heroic — like when Neptune lifts his awful head above the waves on a Summer noon, in the midst of the blue, fresh, & breezy ocean, till his manly God-like chest gradually rears itself above the waves, like a tower, and divides their sprayey foam as they dash against its energetic firmness. I fancy his chest, watery & cool from the perpetual washing of the waves

9. *Aeneid*, I,590–591. "Lumenque iuventae/purpureum" (and with youth's ruddy bloom).

1. *Iliad*, II,479; a description of Agamemnon, "his waist like unto Ares, and his breast unto Poseidon."

2. *Iliad*, VI,467; Hector bids farewell to his son, who shrinks "back into the bosom of his fair-girdled nurse."

— then he would dip down and the dashing surge would ripple over his shoulders, then he would again rear up, and expose his whole breast and then float on equally. Every now and then Nereids & Tritons would splash up & disappear.

February 5. Form, colour, & light & Shadow are but the means of exciting associations — the stronger, the more perfect they are, the more vivid will be the associations; consequently you may judge of a man's acuteness of feeling by the way he expresses it. Would feeble colouring, feeble arrangement, feeble expression, be born in a Poet? Certainly not. Then why should it in a Painter? Resemblances are more easily ascertained in Painting, the association sooner excited; therefore the World is more easily content. What is meant is easily seen in a Painting, however badly executed, but unless a Poet is clear & decided, one's attention is fatigued & disgusted. Let us for a moment affirm that no art or arrangement is necessary. What would be the consequence? It is obvious. Therefore, inasmuch as Poetry or Painting is feebly executed in any of its mechanical requisites, that is, in any of the modes of conveyance, so much will the impression be weakened, and the idea feebly conveyed.

"In those poets & other Artists, on the contrary, who have retained to the last all the powers of their genius, Imagination will be found to be one only of the many endowments and habits, which constituted their intellectual superiority; — an understanding enriched every moment by a new accession of information from without, and fed by a perennial spring of ideas from within; *a systematical pursuit of the same object through the whole life,* profiting, at every step, by the lessons of its own experience, and the recollection of its own errors; — above all, the steady exercise of reason and good sense in controuling, guiding, & stimulating this important but subordinate faculty; subjecting it betimes to the wholesome discipline of rules, and by a constant application of it [to] its destined purposes, preserving to it entire, all the advantages which it received from the hand of Nature." Dugal Stewart on Taste.[3]

3. Dugald Stewart, "On the Culture of Certain Intellectual Habits Connected with the First Elements of Taste," *Philosophical Essays,* Edinburgh, 1810, p. 523. The italics are BRH's.

I have [been] studying attentively these two last days the Bacchus & Ariadne of Titian, & [the Judgment of] Paris by Rubens.* The Bacchus & Ariadne, after all, is addressed to your acquired feelings, the result of education.⁴ I could not help observing in both Titian & Rubens the total want of fundamental principles of form. The opposite lines of a limb or body [are] the same, which is never seen, and physically cannot be; it always gives a weak, snapped look [*a sketch*].

There is a gentility in Titian that borders on insipidity, but give [me] the rich, racy, careless, teeming energy of Rubens, an energy that is driving after something beyond this dim spot, and tho it may carry him beyond bounds of *propriety*, who is there that would hesitate at being so carried?

Now from the action of Juno the left side being bent, the flesh must roll, not having its usual space; Rubens has made it straight [*three sketches*]. One side is as the other; such faults in Titian are more numerous.

Titian is careful, Titian is gentle, Titian is modest; Rubens, furious, teeming, & careless. Titian fears he may trespass on the bounds of Nature; Rubens seems weary of limits, and bursts out, depending on his powers, & heedless of failure. Titian attracts & never offends; Rubens fascinates & often disgusts. Tho Titian keeps longer on the wing, Rubens soars the highest. Who then would not soar with Rubens & risk destruction in the pursuit of other Worlds, than timidly & tamely keep in sight of this?

O God, on my knees I pray thee grant me the power to conclude my present Picture, Solomon, in every point of view grandly & magnificently. Let the scope of my intentions be greater than any other human being ever took. Grant me success, O God, grant me success. Grant I may rouse the Patrons to a feeling, a proper feeling, I humbly intreat thee. Before I die, O God, grant me a Patron worthy of my capacity, for Jesus Christ's sake, one who can give it full sway. Let me not leave the World, O Al-

* This Picture is the same purchased for the National Gallery at Penrice sale, 1844, by Eastlake, Secy. to R.A. B. R. Haydon.

4. Both pictures are now in the National Gallery. BRH saw them at Lord Kinnaird's house before the auction of his pictures and furniture early in March 1813 (Whitley, *1800–1820*, p. 213).

mighty Father, with the capacity with which thou has blessed me fruitlessly wasted and cruelly ruined. For Jesus Christ's sake, realize my notions of Art before I die, O God, O my Creator, Amen.

February 20. It is a delight [to] me to know I see & can prove errors, fundamental errors, in such men as Rubens & Titian — to know too that I have kept them to myself silently to benefit by them, and not obtruded them on others for the sake of shewing my skill. The Elgin Marbles have so refined my eye (I thank God daily) that errors strike it instantly. Neither had a system of form, but in point of harmony of Tint! nothing can exceed them. The rich flesh of a voluptuous female form, set off on [the] side by the grey tint of a warm sky and a rich furred purple robe half covering the others, united to the ground by reflections of its various tones, warm & cool — nothing can be finer. It yet affects me like tones of an organ. On the right hand are Paris and Mercury in fine brown, keeping [aloof], relieved & united by a rich sunny sky; opposite are Venus & Minerva.

Some attract by picturesque arrangement, some by colour, some by light & shadow, some by form, not considering that all these are but requisites, different modes of conveying intellect. Raphael never let either for an instant predominate at the expence of the other essential point. In Raphael the natural feeling of human beings predominates and touches the cord of every man's heart. When ever either requisite predominates at the expence of the natural feeling, in so much as it wanders from the natural feeling, so much does it cease to affect human nature generally. It may apply to the feelings of particular men — to the antiquarian, to the scholar, &c., but the feelings of such men are the acquired feelings, the result of education and not of nature. A perfect picture should apply to all of course, but the natural feeling is the great object. Excellence here will secure a man the hearts of mankind, tho he be deficient in every other requisite.

All sensations conveyed by inanimate objects must surely be inferior to those excited by human features.

The learning of Poussin[5] was not the learning of Nature, not

5. Lord Kinnaird owned Nicolas Poussin's "Bacchanalian Dance," now in the National Gallery.

the learning of the refined beauties of form & expression, but the learning of the habits, the customs, the notions of the Ancients — it was the learning of historical research. Homer & Shakespeare were the most learned of all men, that is, in that in which learning is only valuable, Nature. All other learning is a means, a requisite, to set off, adorn, improve, the learning of Nature. Every fault will be excused if that feeling is true, while no learning, no acquirements, no knowledge, will interest if that be deficient.

Tom Jones is a delightful novel. It lets you into all the little follies and amiable weaknesses of Nature. It shews you that the most virtuous, the most pure, the most innocent woman may have little imperfections, little vanities, little natural feelings, without corrupting her heart. It sends you into the World prepared for it, and renders you more satisfied with human Nature. No doubt the scope, the view, the intentions of Clarissa Harlowe and Grandison are greater, higher; the consequences of vice are there shewn to be so dreadful that you shudder at them and inwardly thank God if you have no just reason to expect such consequences. They exhibit such a refined knowledge of Nature, such an exquisite insight into human character; they hold up so strongly the danger of persisting. Tom Jones paints to you that salvation may be attained by abstaining in time; Clarissa Harlowe that destruction must ensue by persisting. Richardson always separated vice from virtue, & rendered the one always contemptible by associating it with contemptible qualities. Fielding has mingled both, and undoubtedly reconciles us more easily to vice, by shewing that many fine qualities may unite with it. You relinquish Fielding with hope, but Richardson leaves you in a gloomy trembling, a pathetic agitation, a hopeless horror — you regard your own failings with fright and promise amendment in terror. Fielding painted men as they are; Richardson as they ought to be. The characters of Fielding are the result of observation, those of Richardson of imagination & observation united. Fielding is the Hogarth of novelists & something higher, while Richardson may be called without exaggeration the Raphael of domestic life.

March 3. Those that neglect Nature are to be pitied, poor fellows. What beauties, what delights do they miss. Today, while I was painting my child,[6] every time he rested, every time he put himself in an attitude, it was beyond all description. Dear little innocent laughing cherub, ἀλίγκιον ἀστέρι καλῷ.[7]

No Roscius,[8] no prematurity of talent without experience, without intercourse with the World, could produce such a play as Othello. As men get older, as they know more, in that proportion does Othello get more interesting. The way in which the dagger of doubt is first planted in Othello's mind, open, unsuspicious, & honorable, is so true to life! The progress & the termination, with all its affecting varieties from his love, is beyond all praise. Who that has known the agitations of any violent passion, when what delighted becomes insipid, what roused the fancy & fired the blood, is passed with indifference and disgust, and the agony doubled by the consciousness that what moves not ought to move and that the former feelings of enthusiasm were feelings worthy to be nursed and fit to be fostered, can see Othello bid adieu to the "tranquil mind," [9] bid adieu to all that fired him from infancy, "the neighing Steed, and all the pride & pomp of glorious war," [1] without having a cloud of melancholy obscure his peace that a spirit so noble, so great, should suffer suspicion to fix itself in his soul, without at once investigating, without making his doubts known, and giving his fair wife an opportunity to establish her virtue. The progress of his blurred intellect, of his fumed brain, is finely pourtrayed; aware of his former confidence, her innocence, her loveliness, her shrinking modesty darts into his heated fancy; he seizes her accuser by the throat, swears vengeance if he prove false! The wary villain laments his honesty and still pushing Othello's feelings to the most dreadful stretch, asks

6. The son of BRH's landlord, Perkins, was a model for "The Judgment of Solomon" (see I,231).

7. *Iliad*, VI,401; Hector's son Astyanax is thus described, "like a fair star."

8. William Henry West Betty (1791–1874), the popular boy actor who played Shakespearean roles such as Hamlet while in his early teens; he was known as "the young Roscius."

9. *Othello*, III,iii,348.

1. *Othello*, III,iii,351–354.
> "Farewell the neighing steed, and the shrill trump,
> . . . and all quality,
> Pride, pomp, and circumstance of glorious war!"

him how he would be satisfied? Would he grossly be the supervisor, and quietly behold her? The bare notion of such a sight, the bare fancy of beholding the woman we love, on whom we have thrown our affections and to whom we owe the most rapturous moments of life, the pander to another's passions, causes such contemptible Ideas of ourselves, and such confused & racking associations, that Othello groans forth "death & damnation! O!" [2] & he then bids adieu to affection and in the boiling agony of agitated torment, bids his "bosom swell, with its fraught, for 'tis of aspicks' tongues." [3] Iago begs him to be content — experienced wretch, knowing nothing so stimulant to passion as advice to conquer it, the cause being unsettled. Othello answers in the foaming fury of a disordered imagination, fired by suspicion, with a sort of eclipsed reason, "blood! Iago, blood!" [4] conscious that he can only regain his peace by the assertion of his power, by annihilating the objects of his revenge; Desdemona meets him, determined to amuse by her presence, makes him forget all. He weeps that such a creature, to whom he had garnered his heart, should be guilty — it really breaks one's heart. Even when he & Iago are plotting her murder, he keeps reminding him of her perfections, her accomplishments, her gentleness, and concludes by acknowledging in pathetic terms the "pity of it." [5] When Emilia meets her after her accusation, Desdemona says she's half asleep with that sort of lethargic agony that dulls & mists the faculties in excessive grief. What a Picture of Nature is her bed room — undressing, singing a melancholy ditty, and at intervals talking & humming the burden, their conversation easy, natural, unaffected; men of rank have arrived from Venice. Is it not likely, grieved as she may be, that her mind would relieve itself by reverting to them, as a little fresh & innocent topic? She talks of them and what she knows of their connections at Venice, that there is a lady who so loves one that she would walk barefoot to Palestine to touch his nether lip. [6] How likely is all this; how relieving! how reposing! how natural! how unaffected! no gigantic

2. *Othello,* III,iii,396.
3. *Othello,* III,iii,449–450.
4. *Othello,* III,iii,451. "O, blood, blood, blood!"
5. *Othello,* IV,i,206.
6. *Othello,* IV,iii,38–40.

forebodings, no unnatural apprehensions — a simple conversation in a simple manner, in the bed room of a Lady undressing by her maid. O Shakespeare, Shakespeare, thou spirit of Nature, thou interpreter of her thoughts, thou representative of her feelings. What regular, methodized, marble hearted unity writer would have ventured on this!!! The maid withdraws and Desdemona is left to repose on her pillow till the entrance of her Lord. He comes in still haunted by the Fiend that has possessed his faculties, unconscious of all around him, occupied by his own dishonor & the lascivious guilt of his wife. He begins abruptly, in a mournful, melancholy tone, "It is the cause, it is the cause!" [7] He hangs over her as she sleeps in dewy breathing forgetfullness, kisses her, weeps, and is almost bereft of his resolution by her sweetness, her innocent look, her heavenly composure, her breathing & blushing beauty. Disturbed by the light and his motion, she wakes! Who does not fancy her turning round and putting her delicate hand on his; with the purity of an angel [she] asks him if he will "come to bed." [8] Deep must have been his suspicion and rooted his revenge to resist such a creature! but the more innocent, the more pure, the more lovely she appeared, the more horrid her guilt & her hypocrisy must have seemed to his disordered Imagination.

What follows is too horrid to detail. He murders this fair creature! and exhibits a fatal example of suffering doubt to take possession from mere suspicion, or any circumstances however strong to strengthen it without sifting them to the bottom and laying all open without passion or fear. March 5.

I read this play at Breakfast without ceasing. I pushed through it with a disordered fury & agitation that I never before experienced. My heart beat, my frame perspired, I wept for Desdemona, cursed Iago, pitied Othello, with all the acuteness of reality. I do not remember ever to have been so touched, so completely knocked up with agitation.

P. S. When Othello recollects he has no wife!!! "Methinks," says he, "it should be a huge eclipse

Of Sun & moon, and that the affrighted globe
Should *yawn* at alteration." [9]

7. *Othello,* V,ii,1.
8. *Othello,* V,ii,24.
9. *Othello,* V,ii,99–101.

How true! after the Death of a Mother or wife, the whole World seems dark, as if the Inhabitants were moving about in silence without uttering a syllable, in an eclipse! The globe yawning too! What a conception! as if jaws as big as the globe! had, after having been closed from all eternity! began slowly to unclench and gaped in silence to the utmost stretch, with a sort of gurgling mutter! like the bubbling of the whole ocean! — and then shut again with a clenched closeness *for ever!!* so dreadful was the deed! so unusual, so unnatural *the consequences.*

When the whole cause opens on Emilia's mind like the breaking of day, with the heat of a first perception she exclaims "Villainy! Villainy! Villainy!" [1] conscious herself but careless & forgetting that *she* only perceives.

When Iago promises to kill Cassio, he begs him to spare Desdemona, well knowing that when once a man's passions are roused, the most assured method of making [him] commit the deed you want is not to advise him to it directly, because you may exceed his passion, but to advise him not to do it, which falling short of his heat, will excite his imagination to push him beyond.

Women make every allowance with the greatest generosity and benevolence for the imperfections and vices of men, but severely judge and cruelly censure weakness in their own sex.

"She therefore to encourage hir people against the enimies, mounted up into an high place raised up of turfs and sods made for the nonce, out of the which she made a very long and pithy oration. Hir mightie tall personage, comelie shape, severe countenance, and sharpe voice, with hir long yellow tresses of haire reaching downe to hir thighes, hir brave and gorgeous apparell, also caused the people to have hir in great reverence. She ware a chaine of gold, great and verie massie, and was clad in a lose kirtle of sundrie colours, and aloft thereupon she had a thicke Irish mantell: hereto in hir hands (as her custome was) she bare a speare, to shew hirselfe the more dreadful." Hollinshed, 496, 4th Book, Hist. Eng. Vol. 1st.[2]

"Amongst many other Britons there was Edol, Earl of Gloucester or (as others say) Chester, which got a stake out of an hedge,

1. *Othello*, V,ii,190.
2. A description of Voadicia [*sic*] in Holinshed's *Chronicles of England, Scotland, and Ireland*, 1807, I,496.

or else where, and with the same so defended himself and laid about him that he slew 17 Saxons and escaped into the Town of Ambrie, now called Salisburie, and so saved his own life." [3] [*Six illegible words.*]

The Directors have again judged — 300–200 — are given but they withold 100 — and the 100 for landscapes, and purchase Westall's vicious stuff for 400[4] — really is most cruel, capricious, tyrannical conduct. Is it no violation of duty, of virtue, to entice young men to make efforts and then disappoint? What right have they — but no, they do not seem to be the only persons who care little for their respectability or character!

"After this, Siward, noble Earl of Northumberland, died of the flux, of whom it is said that when he perceived the hour of Death to be near, he caused himself to be put in Armour and set up in his chair, affirming that a Knight and a man of honor ought to die in that sort rather than lying on a couch like a feeble & faint hearted creature, and sitting upright in his chair, armed at all points, he ended his life, and was buried at York. The said Siward, Earl of Northumberland, was a man of giant like stature, and thereto of a verie stout and hardy courage. His son Waltief was an infant not out of his cradle." Holinshed, [I], 750.

The Normans had their upper lips & cheeks shaven, whereas Englishmen used to suffer the hair of the upper lips to grow at length.

March 10. The first thing is to settle the characteristics of Man as a species, distinguished from Animals. This being settled, you have ascertained the distinguishing marks of his Nature — the various characters, form, and face, must be the result of observation & experience. This is the grand requisite.

The seat of refinement or vulgarity is the mouth, with the various passions, characters, & feelings that come under the head of either. [*Thirteen sketches of heads.*] Of firmness & manliness

3. Holinshed, *Chronicles*, I,561.
4. In the British Institution's exhibition of 1813, Edward Bird received the first prize of 300 guineas for "The Death of Eli" and John James Halls the second prize of 200 guineas for "The Raising of Jairus' Daughter." The directors of the Institution purchased Richard Westall's "Elijah Restoring the Widow's Son to Life" for 400 guineas.

is the nose & chin; of intellect, forehead; because the same mouths & chins become feminine by changing the nose, & the same nose, chin, & mouth become weak by changing the forehead. [*Ten sketches of heads representing infancy, boyishness, youth, manhood, age, animals, idiotism, brutality, and the feminine.*] There are distinct characteristics in Man and Woman. In infancy, Manhood, & Age are periods of Man & Woman.

There are distinct characteristics in Animals. Mingle the characteristics of either, and the association of the character of that being or of that class from which the characteristic is taken will be associated with the mark selected.

Infancy — flat forehead, feeble hair, fat cheeks, sunken nose, belly & limbs pulpy, cornea & pupil of eye filling nearly the white.

Manhood — forehead divided by the nose risen, jaw set, cheek bone firm, &c., limbs muscular, tendonous, and bony, &c., hair elastic, bushy, & vigorous, &c., &c.

Age — nose dropped, mouth sunken, a little open, tongue becoming too large, bald, hair scattered, eye dull, skin wrizzled, &c., &c., &c., round shoulders, limbs shrunken.

Woman (γυνή delicieuse) — pulpy cheeks, lips full, mouth small, eye brows arched, eyes beaming, rich & watery, forehead flat, nose refined, rather inclined to sink in middle, hips broad, knees inclined inwards, the whole air a palpitating, shrinking, blushing, breathing timidity.

Animals — no forehead, exposed nostrils, eyes inclined downwards, mouth large, split in middle, jaw immense, teeth apparent, feet flat, &c., &c. [*Fourteen sketches showing the combination of these qualities in the same face.*] Perhaps the way to ascertain the character is to exaggerate characteristics & see to what they lead — thus [*twelve sketches of heads*].

March 15. A day never passes but I feel the blessing of having investigated so thoroughly every difficulty in Joseph, Dentatus, & Macbeth. I could not have and never can again have more difficult subjects — subjects requiring greater effort. When it is considered that I attacked such subjects little better than a raw youth from my Father's counter, the difficulties I experienced were surely nothing but what were natural.

The age of miracles is ceased. All that is to be required cannot be attained without acquiring. Ignorance must be conquered by research. The only gift from nature is the capability of conquering it; the only way to conquer it is by putting this capability in action, and the proof that it is conquered is the result.

"Nature gives no man knowledge." I cannot sketch a foot, a limb, a head, or any[thing] without instinctive reference to those pictures; by knowing the body in one position you acquire the feeling for it in others.

When Health sparkles in the eye & blood circulates through the limbs, when the body is active, young, & interesting, the consequences of vice are not felt because they [are] not reflected on. The mind is capable of enjoying variety, which calls it off from its own reflections. We are interesting to ourselves because we are interesting to others, but what if disease or old age o'ertake us in our progress? Can there be a more lamentable or effecting sight than a lovely woman with a form & intellect capable of rendering a man blest, debasing both and destroying her happiness by carelessness & vice? Deprived of her beauty by disease or misfortune, driven for consolation to her own reflections, where, alas, no consolation can be afforded, such a sight have I witnessed! such a creature did I know! — young, lively, beautiful, with a comprehension of singular acuteness, and yet careless, vain, & vicious. It is now 8 years since I first knew her and 5 since I last saw her till now, but what a change. Her liveliness, her beauty, her form gone! — no longer sneering at religion, with a bold & impudent temerity, which gave (even wicked as it was and much as one pitied & sighed at her levity) a beauty & an interest to her air — alas, how changed; — her drawing room of elegance & voluptuousness changed to one of darkness & disease — instead of the rich, thrilling, delightful laugh, instead of the playing bend of her fine form, and the subduing, bewitching, enchanting smile, I beheld an expression of sorrow, I heard an acuteness of sigh, & surveyed a sadness of air that touched my heart strings. O God — . . . [*The next six lines are heavily scratched out*]. . . . I retired melancholy & musing. A life of virtue, a life of goodness, would have now calmed her agitations and soothed her sorrow, but what satisfaction could she have in reflecting on her past life, when reflection could only bring the remembrance of time squandered! an intellect perverted! a form prostituted! A God angered & inflamed!!! Industry, virtue, & piety are the only means of *present* enjoyment, and the only true sources of *future*.

[*The next five lines are heavily scratched out.*]

Experience soon shews what can & what cannot be done, what to be satisfied with and how far to go, & when to leave off. Many excellencies are destroyed from wishing [to] exceed them, when to exceed them is impossible, yet this inherent, characteristic propensity, to exceed the excellent, is the true cause that excellence is at all approached. A man of such feelings entangles himself in mountains of difficulty, yet when he comes out, he comes out with greater power & greater confidence. He may be crushed — let him; he is crushed not tamely, waiting his hour like the majority of the insipid world, but struggling to enlarge the bounds of our ability, to expand the sphere of human exertion, and to make man think higher of himself & his Creator. March 19, at Breakfast.

Thank God this week has been a week of hard, severe, vigourous application. My Picture is advanced, my mind easy with that elastic spring that an approving conscience gives it. All methods of study are absurd, all plans. The only method is to study as hard [as] Nature will allow, to finish at once, to think conclusively; a sincere & determined desire to do this will produce the effects that mathematical regulations, eight hours [of] classes & vows, which are but excuses, to a wish to place dependence on any thing but ourselves, struggle for in vain. A rooted determination to get on is the best exciter and the surest stimulation. March 28.

We are certain of nothing but human feelings, which have always been the same from the age of Homer to the present hour. All systems of Philosophy, all metaphysics, must be continually changing because attempts to discover the cause, the nature of [the] mind must vary from its impossibility, and these Philosophers, these metaphysicians continually treated Homer as if unworthy. A Poet forsooth! mere fancy! but what does it prove?

What does it prove? What [do] we know of them & their systems? Passed like a shadow into contempt. What does this prove? That Homer applied to the feelings of the heart, & principles of human actions, which [are] never varying. What he built [was] on an iron foundation, and that he will survive & has survived when they, having set forth their own whims on no principle but caprice, must meet the fate that usually attends it.

As an instance of Shakespeare's truth — an old Friend of my Father's died from mere age and exhaustion. A witness was relating to me the manner, and said just before his death, with a quiet and composed countenance, he began playing with his fingers and the sheets. "Nothing could be finer, Sir," said he, "than the way he went out of the world." "No, Sire, when I saw him fumble with the sheets and play with the flowers, and smile upon his fingers' ends, I knew there was but one way, for his nose was as sharp as a pen, and he babbled of green fields." Henry V.[5] April 1st.

Sacred to the memory of John Eastlake,[6] who fell a sacrifice to the vigour of youth at the commencement of an intended enterprise to penetrate into the mysterious interior of Africa. Beginning to rival his illustrious predecessors, Ledyard[7] & Parke,[8] he relinquished the fairest prospects and the dearest connections, submitted cheerfully to the severest trials that he might be inured to the expected difficulties, and left his native Country, England, inflamed with thoughts of his noble undertaking with ever his habitual energy, his intensity of application, his unceasing perseverance & his extension of view that had he lived, had time matured his power and steadied without weakening his fire, advanced the rank & enlightened the ignorance of his time, warm with success & admiration. This Tablet is erected by those who

5. *Henry V*, II,iii,14–18. "After I saw him fumble with the sheets, and play with flowers, and smile upon his fingers' ends, I knew there was but one way; for his nose was as sharp as a pen, and 'a babbled of green fields."

6. The youngest brother of Charles Eastlake. He died of fever in Sierra Leone in 1812, six months after leaving England to explore the interior of Africa.

7. John Ledyard (1751–1788), Asiatic traveler; he died at Cairo at the outset of African explorations.

8. Mungo Park (1771–1806), African explorer, killed by natives on an expedition to the Niger.

admire his talents, laud his aspirations, & glory in his illustrious destruction. Hail & farewell.

I dined on Friday last with a man of Genius, William Hazlitt.[9] His child [1] was to be christened, and I was desired to be there punctually at four. At four I came, but he was out! his wife ill by the fire, nothing ready, and all wearing the appearance of neglect & indifference. At last home he came, the cloth began to cover the table, and then followed a plate with a dozen large, waxen, cold, clayy, slaty potatoes. Down they were set, and down we sat also: a young mathematician, who whenever he spoke, jerked up one side of his mouth, and closed an eye as if seized with a paralytic affection, thus [*a sketch*]; an old Lady of Genius with torn ruffles; his Wife in an influenza, thin, pale & spitty; and his chubby child, squalling, obstinate, & half-cleaned. After waiting a little, all looking forlornly at the potatoes for fear they might be the chief dish, in issued a bit of overdone beef, burnt, toppling about on seven or eight corners, with a great bone sticking out like a battering ram; the great difficulty was to make it stand upright! but the greater to discover a *cuttable* place, for all was jagged, jutting, & irregular. Like a true Genius he forgot to go for a Parson to christen his child, till it was so late that every Parson was out or occupied, so his child was not christened. I soon retired, for tho' beastliness & indifference to the common comforts of life may amuse for a time, they soon weary & disgust those who prefer attention & cleanliness.

As I was going to bed last night, my Picture had an imposing and a grand look. I felt impressed by it.

I began life with a determination to seclude from Society and devote myself to my Art, but a little experience shewed that he who wishes to paint to the feelings of Men & Women must ascertain them by intercourse. Many important feelings, many notions, many new ideas, have occurred to me in Society, and in consequence too of my being there. April, 1813.

9. James Northcote introduced BRH to Hazlitt (1778–1830) in 1812 (William Carew Hazlitt, *Memoirs of William Hazlitt*, 1867, I,209).
1. William Hazlitt, Jr. (1811–1893), who became a barrister and registrar in the court of bankruptcy.

Tho' one loses time by one's follies & vicious pursuits, yet one gets a knowledge of the World, of character, of human feelings. Tho' my vices have cost me many a pang, yet they have also given me many a new idea. To be sure, this is rather a plausible excuse, but I mean it not as an excuse, but rather as a mere observation. So it is — it is the truth, and that's all.

Michel Angelo, Milton, Phidias, seem to have been beings who carried their feelings to a higher World. Raphael was confined to this. Shakespeare could dive into boundless space with divine & steady wing or descend to the minuteness of this, with exact & scrupulous pertinacity. It puzzles me how to class these men, how to ascertain their respective value. To enter into the feelings of human beings, to ascertain their characters, to make them think & act as they would think & act is the result of a fine faculty impregnated by experience, but surely to attempt describing Worlds & beings unseen & unknown can only be the consequence of an elevation of soul, which tho' not so strictly intellectual, that is, tho' not so strictly — mind — in the power of distinguishing right from wrong, is of course higher; it is a pure effort of imagination.

But human beings will not be so interested with creatures of which they know nothing, either from experience or Nature, as with a detail of their own feelings; therefore Raphael & Shakespeare have more the approbation of men than Michel Angelo & Phidias, tho they rank higher in the estimation of the few. The greater men are those that unite the two, Homer & Shakespeare, who apply to the uncultivated or the refined fancy, who melt with pity or love or inflame by terror or sublimity, who can detail the feelings of this World, or attempt the sensations of the other. April 20.

April 25. I felt this morning an almost irresistible inclination to go down to Greenwich and have [a] delicious tumble with the Girls over the hills. I fancied a fine, beamy, primy, fresh, green, spring day (as it was), a fine creature in a sweet, fluttering, clean drapery, spotted with little flowers, a slight, delicate, muslin, white scarf crossed over her beating bosom, with health rosing her shining cheeks, & love melting in her sparkling eyes, with a soft warm hand & bending form ready to leap into your arms, confiding & loving! After a short struggle, I seized my brush with a spasmatic effort, knowing the consequences of yielding to my disposition, & that tho' it might begin today, it would not end with it.

May 4. Surely the character of Satan is a character of the greatest human interest, for what could be more interesting than to see such a tremendous *human* being, ambitious, heroic, failing in a great attempt, too proud to submit, burning to revenge, yet longing to regain his glory, if it could be obtained by any means but submission, stung by conscience, lamenting his folly & wickedness, with a bursting heart. There is something interesting about the failure of Satan — it is mingling human character with angelic power.

There are three great points of hindrance to the advance of the higher walks in this country: the perversion of the Royal Academy, the neglect of the Government, and the prejudices of the People, but perhaps the best answer to all these objections is — paint a fine Picture, paint a fine Picture. He that fails always attributes it [to] any cause but his own incapacity, and to him that succeeds, all is light & cheerful; every thing is conducted as it ought. The faults of this or the failings of that are but human imperfections; we must take things as they are & make the most of them.

Nothing can prove in a stronger degree the truth of association excited by figure & feature than fine ideas repeated by one possessed of neither. Why do we laugh? because the feeling excited by the idea is not continued by the action intended to express it.

When an ugly, gaunt, bony, ungraceful, angular figure utters a melancholy, pathetic sentiment of love, his modes of expression are so totally incongruous, so totally inharmonious, the feeling excited by the one is so compleatly contradicted by the other, that laughter or pity, instead of tenderness & sympathy, must be the result — vice versa. Repeat a boisterous, comic notion with a melting air, what more absurd? The action & expression therefore excite the association of the idea intended to be conveyed; if they did not, any idea might be expressed, and any action or expression might accompany them. This proves its truth.

This was excited by seeing that poor wretch Coates[2] last night —never was there a more melancholy exhibition of human infatuation. May 7.

[*A sketch of Coates, marked "The gallant gay Lothario! This is exactly one of his exquisite actions when talking to Calista."* [3] *Also a sketch of "B. R. H. in his Youth, 1807."*]

"More money," says Payne Knight, "has been spent on Art in England than any other Country." What does this prove? More men have been spent in fruitless expeditions than would have conquered Europe. All this only shews the miserable management of the means, in those who possessed them.

The agonies of disappointment, the agonies of sickness, the agonies of any agony on Earth, are nothing in comparison with the agonies of idleness. The timidity, the cowardly feeling, it excites, the restless, tormenting, piercing pang, the excessive pain of mind and aking of conscience I suspect are nothing but the stings of a mind preying on itself and rotting in sloth that has been accustomed to the fiery delight of perpetual effort. When I am idle, I have hardly courage to look any one in the face. I slink through the streets as if haunted. When industrious, when up early & to bed late, I feel my breast broaden, I rear my head high, and stride like Juno when she strode from Lectum to Gargarus.[4]

Sir Joshua's exhibition opened.[5] The first impression on my mind was certainly that of flimsiness. They looked faint, notwithstanding the effect was so judiciously arranged. Sir Joshua's

2. Robert Coates (1772–1848), known as Romeo Coates, who had an undistinguished career as an actor from 1810 to 1816.

3. Calista and the "gay Lothario" are the lovers in Nicholas Rowe's *The Fair Penitent* (1703).

4. *Iliad*, XIV,277–293. Lectum is a promontory in Troas, the end of the mountain range Ida which includes Gargarus as one of its highest summits.

5. After an inaugural banquet attended by the Prince Regent on May 8, 1813, the British Institution opened its exhibition of some hundred and fifty works by Sir Joshua Reynolds. This was the first exhibition of a noncontemporary artist; because of its success, the directors annually arranged similar important exhibitions of Old Masters borrowed from private collections (Whitley, *1800–1820*, pp. 205–206).

modes of conveying ideas were colour & light and shadow; of form, the third part, he knew nothing. The consequence was he rested when he had attained the effect without intruding form, for if colour & light and shadow be not directed by form, the effect even cannot be given as it ought, for what is effect but the leading prominences of objects, the result of a combination of smaller parts, so that the true effect is putting the result of this combination exactly where it ought. Sir Joshua saw where it ought to be put but had never acquired the power of putting it rightly by a careful & laborious investigation & mastery of the smaller parts, like Michel Angelo, Raphael, [*an illegible word,*] & Rubens. The consequence was he hinted to his eye & untrained hand, and with great labour & bungling, modeled out his feelings with a floating richness, an harmonious depth, and a gemmy brilliancy that was perhaps encreased by his perpetual repetitions, and which renders him as great a master of colour as ever lived. Of poetical conception of character as it regards Portrait, he had a singular share. He could elevate what he saw if he still kept the elements of what he had before him, but if left to his imagination wholly, he could do nothing, and what is as extraordinary, his poetical characters have a meaner look than his Portraits. His Portraits have the elevation of Poetry and his history the meaness of individuality. His Ugolino is but a poor starved beggar — is that the leader, the Hero, the chief? his Beaufort a grinning low life wretch, his Satan the devil of superstitious ignorance, his King[6] nothing but a floating mass of mellowed vermilion and yet too stolen and the remaining characters the meanest of the mean, without dignity, without grace, without expression, without even sentiment, yet as an example of colour & effect, what can be finer? It is unrivalled. It is painted with a crimson velvet brush dipped in racy cream. And in female beauty, how delightful are his Portraits, their artless simplicity, their unstudied grace, their chaste dignity, their retired sentiment command us, enchant us, subdue us, while his children! his inimitable, unimitated children, who can approach? Raphael's children have the

6. BRH apparently refers to the following pictures in the Reynolds exhibition: "Ugolino and his Children in the Dungeon," "The Death of Cardinal Beaufort," and "King Lear."

sedateness of age, Rubens' the plumpness of peasants, Titian's no
doubt the elegance of nobility, but none, none have that exquisite
sprightliness, that unthinking playfulness, that quizzing importance, full of tricks, full of fun, assuming the airs of men, tricked
& flounced with feathers & trains, while their blue eyes and laughing little mouths belie to us their attempt at thinking, and divert,
delight us at their delusions. If he had poetry any where, it was
in his children, and his infant Hercules is a specimen that here
he could be great, that [he] could give a child the grandeur of
men, tho' he could not give men [the] sublimeness of Heroes. Sir
Joshua Reynolds was certainly an extraordinary man. He raised
the Art to a pitch of beauty, he knew what *was* to be done, tho'
he had not *done it* his lectures testify. The exhibition does great
credit to the Directors of the British Gallery. It will have a visible
effect on Art; it will raise the character of the English School; it
will stop that bigotted, deluded, absurd propensity for Leonardo
Da Vincis & insipid Corregios, and as men who shared Sir J's
friendship and been soothed by his manners, it does credit to their
hearts as men. Lord have mercy on all the poor flies at the next
exhibition. I advise them to keep out of the way; bird lime will
lose its violence and bees wax its importance; we shall be able
to take root in magilp. We shall have Glaziers, habitual agents
of monopoly of putty, and chandlers complaining for virgin wax.
The Dead Sea will [be] drained for Asphaltum and India ransacked for lac Lake! When men of property set their faces
against the tales & impositions of Picture Dealers, there is indeed
some hope.

As a specimen of it, Colburn overpowers all.

The Powers of this Zerah Colburn[7] are certainly miraculous.
At six years old, his Father overheard him while playing at his
feet tell how many 5 times 13 were; he looked at him with astonishment, and asked him some other questions, which he answered
with as much facility. He then asked him how many 13 times
ninety-three were, and was instantly told. He tried the result on

7. Zerah Colburn (1804–1839), the American mathematical prodigy, born in
Cabot, Vermont. His father exhibited him in England and France from 1812 to
1816. The British Museum owns a chalk study of Colburn made by BRH.

paper and found he was right. He told me he never can describe his feelings at this moment. It was in a wild wood in America, where he had encamped to enclose some fresh land. His boy was born in this wood, a child of 6 years old. Doing this had the air of supernatural interference. From this moment his powers gradually developed, and extraordinary ones they certainly are. It is an evident faculty from Nature, a faculty of great & refined power. It acts like a natural power; it can be accounted for, which is the great thing; it is not like an unintelligible gift; it is a probable, natural, common power, which every one has in some degree, carried to the highest perfection, so that there is no saying where it may end. It will grow with him, and expand as he expands. Good heavens, others may rise with similar powers in other things and leave those who have acquired excellence by human methods in hopeless gaze.

I was less satisfied with Sir Joshua today. Surely you may say life has been passed in a futile manner if after forty years' practice a well painted cheek or a sparkling forehead is the result. Surely to Men who are not Painters, it must appear a trifling employment. What human passion, what human excellence, what human action has he transmitted? Does your breast expand, does your heart beat, do you tremble with terror, melt with devotion? Give me the sublimity of chaos, give me the terror of Hell, give "Hail, horrors, hail, . . . and thou profoundest hell receive thy new possessor." [8] Thence many a league he rides audacious; all unaware he meets a vast vacuity. Plumb down he drops, ten *thousand fathom deep* and to *this day* down had been falling, had not a cloud, instinct with fire & nitre, *hurried him as many miles aloft!* [9] Here is something to spend a life for! But I must own in walking round the room and perpetually coming to the same thing, I felt a sort of contempt for a man who could pass forty years in painting cheeks, noses, & eyes, with no object but individual character, and no end but individual gratification.

Mrs. Siddons is another instance of his power to elevate a Portrait as the Tragic Muse, and his incapacity to elevate an imaginary muse in Garrick.

8. *Paradise Lost*, I,250–252.   9. *Paradise Lost*, II,929–938.

Sir Joshua from ignorance of the forms of objects always painted with hesitation.

Payne Knight says he raised himself gradually by undertaking at first whatever was offered.[1] The fact was he undertook at first what was offered, and the easiest, and after painting 30 years, he found he must do some thing more than sleeping girls to secure a reputation. He attacked great works totally unprepared. Whereas, had he at first wrestled with the highest difficulties, he would have received a foundation to build on for the remainder of his exertion. I am convinced perpetual intercourse with women either of body or mind enervates & weakens the mind, habituates it to trifles.

Examined today a Negro I had to sit. Found all the marks of brutality more strongly than ever.

Milton exhausts human means in describing a grand Idea, and yet leaves your imagination to finish it.

While Patronage remains in the hands of any body, it will always be liable to be conducted with partiality, with tyranny, with caprice. The only effectual Patronage is when directed by one, & by a Prince or a Minister! One who knows when he has Genius and when he has not, and when he has, gives it its full scope, happy in its development, and not envious.

June 22. Yesterday gloated with delight on a fine Rubens for 2 hours, perfectly painted. Nothing could go beyond it — that exact mixture of sharpness & softness. The hand of Christ was perfection in every requisite. In going this morning to the Reynolds gallery, they looked careless, slobbering, unfinished, in short, they are only beautiful sketches. Sir Joshua's mind triumphed over the ignorance of his hand. He knew effect, but his means of attaining it were inadequate; his breadth was emptiness.

June 23. Went down to Elgin's to consult about feet. Felt impressed by their beauties as much as ever. The Artist seems to have been sure of his means and wielded them as he pleased.

"Far off his coming shone."[2] This conception is a complete

1. Knight wrote the introduction to the exhibition catalogue.
2. *Paradise Lost*, VI,768.

illustration of sublimity. Surely this requires more pure poetry of conception, independent of all acquired materials, than the expression of human beings, the result of experience. The one is innate, the other acquired, tho' the faculty to acquire it is innate also, yet it must be tried before it can act, whereas the other acts from its own unpremeditated efforts, and cannot be assisted with such facility by Nature. This, I think, is the principle to criticise Michel Angelo & Raphael.

Things I might have said but did not.

Campbell,[3] Poet, said he never slept but two hours in the night and was always stupid in the day in consequence. I thought of telling him I supposed he slept very soundly the night before.

Fuzeli said to me once at Johnson's that People generally went to Church in proportion to their profligacy. I had it on the tip of my tongue to say I wonder he did not go every day.

Michel Angelo's genius could not be so effectually asserted by the appearances of nature. His assertions were not so palpable; of course his fancy must have acted from excitement, but when it did, it had more to supply by its own internal power than Raphael's; human expressions are more frequently met with, are more palpable.

July 9. I do not recollect feeling greater pleasure than when I read of the capture of the Chesapeake, American Frigate.[4] I turned my eyes to Heaven & thanked God. When the Guerrière[5] was captured, I recollect dwelling on it a whole morning, in sullen disgust. I felt as if I had been grossly insulted. I felt indignation & detestation at Dacres[6] for not sinking — such were the feelings of every one in the Kingdom. But I hope we shall yet regain our glory. I feel the honor of my Country more acutely than my own. I recollect from infancy seeing French Frigates sailing into Plymouth Harbour, dismasted, and running along the Sea Shore,

---

3. Thomas Campbell (1777–1844).
4. During naval operations of the War of 1812, the British frigate *Shannon* captured the American frigate *Chesapeake* on June 1, 1813.
5. The American frigate *Constitution* captured and burned the British frigate *Guerrière* on August 19, 1812.
6. Captain James Richard Dacres (d. 1853), commander of the *Guerrière;* he was acquitted at a court martial, October 2, 1812, investigating the surrender of his ship.

cheering till my throat was parched. People bred up in London have not those feelings so strongly.

Nothing cuts so acutely as the recollection of time neglected or wasted from folly & idleness.

It is impossible to bear one's wretched imitation of nature but in her absence; the moment she comes in competition, down sinks your effort, dry, husky, feeble, flat, wretched.

July 22. I was at the Wellington fête[7] last night and affected extremely. It was a grand scene. Under the bust of Wellington stood a British Grenadier with the flag of the 100 Regiment, 2nd Battn. and the Baton of Marshall Jourdan.[8] I was peculiarly interested at the sight. The associations were pathetically grand, the retrieved character of the British Army, the perseverance of Lord Wellington against the sneers, the contempt, the forebodings [of] the Nation, the glorious reward for his perseverance — these were the feelings excited by his bust & trophies. While the rich dresses of the Visitors, the variety of character — here was the Turkish Ambassador, then came the Russian, then followed the Duke of Sussex[9] in a Highland Dress, then the Marquis of Wellesly, here a group of beautiful creatures with sparkling eyes, some exhausted reclined in groups to converse, while the Hussars, with their golden tassals and rich boots, their warlike heads, and dark mustachios, with a sort of martial condescension were bending down to whisper to lovely women, whose graceful, floating feathers would intermingle (as they held up their head) with their rough sweeping horse hair. As day dawned the groups in front were lit up by its silvery light, while those within were still engoldened by the deep yellow effulgence of the lamps. The crimson, golden, beaming dress of the Soldiers, the satinny, creamy, feathery lightness of the delicious women "whose bright eyes rained influence," [1] gave it an air of chivalrous enchantment or fairy land — to my dying day I shall never forget it.

7. A festival in honor of Wellington's victory at Vitoria, held at Vauxhall July 20, 1813. This was the decisive battle of the Peninsular War.
8. Jean Baptiste Jourdan (1762–1833), marshal of France, who surrendered at Vitoria. Wellington sent his baton to the Prince Regent (Philip Guedalla, *The Duke*, 1931, p. 239).
9. The Duke of Sussex (1773–1843), George III's sixth son.
1. "L'Allegro," ll. 121–122.

It is astonishing the difference of Raphael from every other Painter. Turn from him to another and it is instantly perceived. He considered his heads as small Pictures — no part empty, all full, yet not confused, never predominating.

The materials of Raphael are human feelings. These he wields, as others wield colour or light & shadow. If he wanted repose, he put a human expression of repose; if truth, if energy, if he wished to rouse the attention or excite the passion, it was by human features & human faces. Rembrandt's repose was mysterious vacuity, his points of interest voluptuous colour, &c., &c., and so on every other Painter. Raphael's materials are the most interesting, because his mind was most interesting. He ranks then as the most affecting because his materials are the most affecting, which he chooses the oftenest to express the most affecting conceptions.

Painters have but one moment — never consider that if he (of a figure) moves he would not be so, but so. He will never move. You must therefore often violate Nature for the harmony of your whole. People have [*several words are illegible because of a blot*] with what it would be if [*the blot obscures several more words*] with what it is. July 30.

I knelt down last night surrounded by the works of Raphael, and prayed God fervently & from my soul, to grant I might be as great or greater before I left this World, to enable me to supply his deficiencies, and rival his beauties. O Almighty God, grant it, grant it. Amen, with all my Soul.

Perhaps there is no expression in any poet that creates a sublimer feeling than the "va sublime" [2] of Tasso. Homer's ἀπείρονα γαῖαν, ἅμα πνοιῇς ἀνέμοιο[3] and Milton's "sails between Worlds & Worlds with steady wing" [4] do not create such a calm, sedate, consciousness of power, such a conviction of superiority, such an indolent relinquishment without fear of falling, as Tasso's. You see him drive on in one even direct line, "from his Kingly state inclining not," [5] gradually diminishing his glorious splendour, its beaming effulgence lessening, till it becomes a point, and then

2. Torquato Tasso, *La Gerusalemme Liberata*, Canto 1, Stanza 14, l. 3.
3. *Iliad*, XXIV,342. A description of the sandals of Argeïphontes, which bore him over "the boundless land swift as the blasts of the wind."
4. *Paradise Lost*, V,268.
5. *Paradise Lost*, XI,249–250. "He kingly from his state/Inclin'd not."

vanishes, still leaving his brightness in the eye of your mind, till that also dies away, and leaves you wondering at the glorious, dreamy apparition that has passed.

A sketch, possibly of Patience Smith, dated July 29, 1813.

My Breast swells at the idea of compleating my Solomon. O God, thou who has never deserted me for one moment, support me through and bless me afterwards; grant I repeat, grant, grant, O merciful Father, that no sickness may check me, or misfortune overwhelm me before it is concluded; grant me strength of mind to bear my wants, and conquer, effectually conquer, the difficulties of my Art. Grant my mind may be adequate to any calamity or any effort, grant I may create a feeling towards public encouragement, and grand taste. O God, thou knowest the most inward feelings of my Soul; thou knowest the prime wish & object of my existence. Realize it, O God, before I die; realize it I humbly pray thee, thou awful, thou great Being. Listen and assent. O Almighty, grant I may deserve by virtue & industry what I presume to ask. Amen, Amen, Amen.

August 3. My Soul yearns to see the Vatican & Capella Sistina. My enthusiasm for Michel Angelo & Raphael hourly & daily encreases. O great illustrious immortal pair, may I be worthy to meet thee in a purer existence! My frame trembles at the idea. I feel the want of kindred spirits — there is not an Artist to whom I can pour out the enthusiasm of my soul, who will listen & participate. Wilkie's mind & broad humor [*the rest of the sentence is obliterated*].

> The noble heart that harbours virtuous thought
> And is *with child of glorious great intent,*
> Can never rest, untill it forth have brought
> The eternal brood of glorie excellent.[6]

Just looked into Ariosto. There appeared instantly a racy spirit, a feeling for natural incident that you find not in the stateliness of Tasso. A Knight lost his helmet in a fountain and as he gropes for it, up starts another Knight out of the water. It has such an entertaining, novel air that I felt delighted, after dwelling as I have been on Tasso's Gerusalemme.

> He was a man,
> That liv'd up to the standard of his honor,
> And prized that jewel more than mines of wealth.
> He'd not have done a shameful thing but once,
> Tho kept in darkness from the World, & hidden
> He could not have forgiven it himself.
> Orphan. Otway.[7]

6. *The Faerie Queene*, I,v,1–4.
7. Thomas Otway, *The Orphan*, II,ii,206–211.

August 4. Spent the greatest part of the morning at Sir Joshua's. Derived the greatest benefit. Some of his expressions exquisitely refined, graceful, & delicate. The greatest men in the Art all concealed the Art itself by making natural objects its vehicle. Sir Joshua often & nearly always makes it its own vehicle. His breadth is often emptiness, his shadows often blank spots of darkness, his colours masses of yellow, without form or meaning, but as to colour, his touch, a careless, scraggling splash that evinced neither knowledge of the part painted, or power in the hand that expressed it, tho a dawning feeling was laid open ignorantly as it was conveyed. Yet in spite of such deficiencies, such was his fashionable air of attitude, such his grace, such his feeling for the beauty and artlessness of children, that one is captivated & delighted & enchanted. His very ignorance of form gives a novelty to his powers that prevents him ever being common place or insipid. He acquired a rich surface by his repetitions that to a painter is delightful.

Michel Angelo is greater than Raphael because his characters are more elevated. Raphael improved Nature in his characters. Michel Angelo immortalized it, raised it at once to sublimity in his Profets.

His Profets are a higher order of beings than any characters Raphael ever executed. They are standards of sublime elevation. Raphael never executed any character of beauty or sublimity that can be referred to as standards. The greatest man is he that can do both, but beauty, expression, or grace, tho' they sting the heart with exstatic sweetness, never take such a hold on the imagination, never warm the breast, expand the feelings, awe, oppress, & weigh down the faculties with such strength as sublimity. There is a vastness, a greatness, a power, a majesty, an encircling thunder, that soars round the Profets of Michel Angelo, while Raphael's mild loveliness seems accompanied with the delicious strains of an Angel's harmonious harp. Beauty, grace, & loveliness fire the imagination with passion, and warm the breast with anticipated rapture, but sublimity unconnected with any human passion, oppresses by its immensity. "The thing of rage with rage does sympathize." [8] Your heart beats, your breast expands, not from the anticipated pleasures of fiery appetite, but the glimmerings of a superior existence, of a higher power, the pleasures in the pure, unpolluted pleasures of intellectual imagination, the raptures of love infuse into your nature (the first time felt) and with all things "the spirit of amorous delight" [9] but these pleasures are peaceable, quiet, amiable, tender, melting; the pleasures of sublimity are those that few minds can bear without breaking. They are the delights of immensity, infinity, gigantic strength, deafening roars, & superior beings. Raphael brought from Heaven the beauty, the loveliness, the sweetness of Angels; Michel Angelo the power, the sublimity, the Thunder of God!

August 8. Walked to Hampton Court. Tho Michel Angelo could not do what Raphael did, what he did was of a higher kind.

Raphael's women did not strike me yesterday in so lovely [a] manner as before. They are full of naïveté, simplicity, & artlessness, but they are not beautiful.

August 9. Saw by accident Rubens' Luxembourg.[1] What glittering, tawdry impotence in point of character & expression, after dwelling, as I have been lately, on Raphael's purity — it disgusted one. Except Mary looking affectionately at her new born infant, which is very sweet, all are fat, disgusting beasts. Yet what power in arrangement, what painting, I daresay, what colour. One only laments the perversion of such powers.

How inadequate is allegorical painting. It is, I think, upon the whole an excuse for impotence of mind.

If any thing would drive me mad, it would be idleness. The horror, the agony, the dwelling distraction I suffer then is beyond all conception. For my own peace, comfort, & tranquillity, I am forced to work.

Raphael had such a decided comprehension of every thing. Every thing in him is clear, intelligible sense—no useless, sense-

8. *Troilus and Cressida*, I,iii,51–52. "The thing of courage,/As rous'd with rage, with rage doth sympathize."
9. *Paradise Lost*, VIII,477. "The spirit of love and amorous delight."
1. Rubens' "Luxembourg" pictures of the life of Marie de' Medici have never left France. BRH must refer to a copy of "The Birth of Louis XIII at Fontainbleau."

less dashes of pencil. Every touch in him is a touch urged, influenced by his intellect.

The Cartoons are certainly his finest subjects and his finest works. His composition is perfect, compleat, settled, the Master in every line.

August 13. The first object in composition is to please the eye. Composition is the means of conveying the story to the mind; all individual objects must be sacrificed to this; if a mass is wanted for harmony, for breadth, for repose, for attraction, a mass must be had. The naked form if ever so exquisite then must yield. If the form be not broad, flat, or ponderous enough for the situation, other materials must be selected, and as drapery is the most pliable of all materials, drapery is usually chosen. This was Raphael's principle and sound it is in every point. The eye must be carried on a plain surface, as it were, from one thing to another; then holes may come in to give value to each mass. All the means of contrast may be used — in composition, in fact, all nature is your material, her you use as it suits your purposes. Raphael's great excellence being expression, and the head taking little as to room, being not large enough for a mass, and too small to be of importance, he could always put heads in any part and supply its deficiencies as to breadth by masses of other materials beneath it; therefore he was never obliged to sacrifice his main excellence, for the sake of composition, while those who make their greatness to depend on the form alone, will find themselves obliged often for the sake of filling a picture, to cover that on which they have placed their reputation. Raphael therefore has always the advantage of being able to shew the most interesting part of man, his face and expression residing in the features and expression being his great excellence. He was by his principles enabled to shew his great excellence always by a means which individually unconnected with expression, is the most delightful. The effect of Raphael is irresistible, in conjunction with his means.

[*The next three pages of the diary are largely devoted to Italian exercises. Haydon copied stanzas 11–16 of Canto VII of Ariosto's* Orlando Furioso *and commented on the verb forms.*]

Always recollect your first impression of every thing; recollect your feelings when you were first vicious, when you first transgressed the laws of God. If the 2nd transgression do not affect you so acutely as at the first, and if the first impression was the right one, depend on it you are familiarized to vice. Fly, stop, hesitate, before you are totally benumbed.

> True be it said, whatever man it sayd,
> That love with gall and hony doth abound,
> But if the one be with the other wayd,
> For every dram of hony therein found
> A pound of gall doth over it redound.
> That I too true by trial have approved
> For since the day that first with deadly wound
> My heart was launcht and learned to have loved,
> I never joyed houre, but still with care have moved.[2]

But yet there is a sweetness in the very gall (except it be the gall of jealousy), the misty, gleaming, poisonous feeling of your mistress's sweetness and bending voluptuousness, which in the midst of all the akings of love, deliciously floats before your fancy, with a steaming, burning, honied luminousness, is delight, but in jealousy! O God, the "lover's hell indeed," [3] — the cutting, razory agony, the fuming, blurred stupor, the contemptible feeling that another has enjoyed her on whose beating breast and pulpy shining lip you have tasted the sharp sweetness of melting rapture and sighed your soul to a higher existence, excites such dreadful, intense, acute pain, such a weighing down of the faculties, such an overwhelming, dreary grief, as nothing in this world or in any world that ever was or ever will be can equal — no punishment that the most malicious demon could discover after years of thought and ages of experience can ever approach the torment of this racking hell. The more vicious the object of attachment, the more liable are you to this torture, as if God had held out the calm quiescent delight of virtuous confidence as a reward to a virtuous love, and caused the racking torture of

2. *The Faerie Queene*, IV,x,1–9.
3. *Paradise Lost*, V, 450. "The injur'd lover's hell."

jealousy to punish him who was foolish enough to expect faith from her who had violated her faith to another.

Whatever is right, *do.* I am convinced perfection is to be attained. If a man have a full perception of it, be determined, suffer not procrastination, indolence, or vice to interrupt, say they *shall* not, and their influence withers, say I *will* do it, and then take all the requisite trouble, and it *will* be done. I never yet recollect a fault in any work of my own that need have been there and that I might not have corrected if I had acted as I ought. If men would but exert all their virtuous power as well as their vicious, vice would never have a moment's chance.

Turner's notion needs only to be examined to be refuted; he mistakes copying literally for imitating freely.[4] No man can add to the stock of knowledge but by imitating others; keep the same road, proceed on the great principles on which they proceeded, the principles of truth and Nature, and you may proceed further, you may carry them to a greater extent [than] those who, fatigued with the difficulties of the great road, caper off in the bye paths or attempt to attract attention by cutting little roads where sound minds would disdain to cut them.

Another Michel Angelo would not be worth much, but another man with Michel Angelo's mind would be worth something, for he would not copy the touches, but proceed on the principles, be animated with [the] same fire, and by the benefit of his predecessor's experience & faults, carry this noble Art a greater length by more extended notions.

August 26. The great difficulty is to find a woman of exquisite susceptibility, curbed & directed by principle. Many there are who tremble with love at every pore but whose very feeling is a

4. Sir George Reid writes: "[In 1805 Turner] painted the 'Shipwreck' and 'Fishing Boats in a Squall' . . . , seemingly in direct rivalry of Vandervelde, in 1806 the 'Goddess of Discord in the Garden of the Hesperides' (in rivalry of Poussin), and in 1807 the 'Sun rising through Vapour' (in rivalry of Claude). . . . This spirit of rivalry showed itself early in his career. He began by pitting himself against his contemporaries, and afterwards, when his powers were more fully developed, against some of the old masters, notably Vandervelde and Claude. During these years, while he kept up a constant rivalry with artists living and dead, he was continuing his study of nature, and, while seemingly a mere follower of the ancients, was accumulating that store of knowledge which in after years he was to use to such purpose" (*Britannica,* XXVII, 476).

cause of their vice, whose susceptibility renders them liable to be affected by every one of beauty or intellect. Happy is he who can find one that will be satisfied with his attentions, and lock up her heart against the attentions of another, after having yielded her hand to him. God in heaven grant I may find one such, who would encourage & participate in my efforts for grandeur, who would solace & refresh me after the day's fatigue with her gentle & tender endearments, who while my arm pressed her slender and bending waist, would feel delight as we walked before my Picture, at the success of my day's struggle and sweetly smile approbation from her sweet mouth, and sparkle love from her lustrous eye, who would shrink with horror at cruelly trifling to prove one's affection by rousing a needless jealousy, but rather feel agony at giving a moment's uneasiness, or an instant's pang. Let me but find such a creature susceptible of the tenderest, the most exquisite trembling love, and the purest virtue, the strongest understanding, and the gentlest & most affectionate heart, one with a soul for grandeur, and yet a relish for domestic duties, and I am her slave, her devoted, enraptured, impassioned lover while existence lasts.

I begin to be weary, to be heartily weary, of vice. No faith can be expected from any woman who has broken her faith to another, and even if she is faithful, there is always an agonising, stinging doubt poisoning your felicity. There may [be] "glowing pleasure" in guilty enjoyment, for fear of discovery, from apprehension of detection at the moment, & snatched in the hot, icy fury of passion, yet surely the confidence, the rapture of legitimate pleasure with a lovely creature, pure & depending, is a million times more exquisite. Then consider the distraction of violated duty, the agony of consequences, the horror of ruin, the fear of having been the dupe of intrigue, the dreadful pang of deceiving a good man, and the agony of discovery and being obliged in honor to marry a woman who has perhaps been the whore of half the Town. Talk not of a life of pleasure, if this is pleasure. No man is more contemptible than a man of the Town, no character more despicable than a man of intrigue, the man who never feared the face of God or Man, yet let him get once entangled in an intrigue with a woman of loose habits, and he instantly becomes timid, cowardly, despicable, abhorring himself, fearing every eye, dreading every hand, shrinking at every blast, with his eyes on the ground as if he dreaded to meet the terrific, steady glare of the eye of God! open from all eternity, and to all eternity! fixed with an intensity of eager enquiry gleaming with an internal sort of scintillation, as if it emitted sparks! — irresistible! unmerciful! eternal! inexorably severe! to deceive which, impossible! to escape, hopeless; firmly fixed as if it had rooted to its situation and blazing at every additional discovery with the fierceness of a heated furnace.

August 24. The nature of the materials of sublimity, namely, size, noise, darkness, light, infinity, & eternity, are not in themselves more powerful than the nature of the materials of the pathetic, namely, the affections & passions, love, filial & maternal regard, &c., &c. Pure sublimity is totally unconnected with Earth, supra limen[5] in fact. Pathos refers entirely to the feelings of its inhabitants. There are instances of pathos that partake of the nature of sublimity, when they tend to lift one out of the world either by making themselves superior to it, or by alliance with the other, superior to it by despising its allurements or its miseries. This approaches to the sublime.

But it is absurd to say the nature of the materials of sublimity have an imposing air and contribute to their effect, independent of the ability of the wielder and not the feelings of Nature — of the lover, the husband, the Sister, the Father, the Mother, the child, equally piercing of themselves independent of the ability of the user, and do they not contribute to the effect if applied to, as much as the materials of sublimity? No doubt of it. Cannot a blockhead, by telling any one a Father let his child drop into the river and saw it struggling in Death without being able to help it, will not a blockhead, I say, be able to affect any human creature as strongly as another who was to describe a gigantic being ascending to Heaven in a tempest of Thunder? Do the materials, namely, noise, height, size, contribute more to sublimity than the materials Paternal feeling, innocence, Death to pathos?

5. "Above the threshold."

Are not the materials of the one just as likely to pierce the heart as the other is to overwhelm the imagination, independently of the genius of the teller, or independently of their connection with reality? Surely so. Therefore if the materials of the one are just as imposing as those of the other are piercing, and if sublimity of character in a man of genius always ranks higher in the estimation of [the] World than pathos, it does not arise from any accidental quality in the materials he uses, but in the superior power of the user in conjunction with his superior materials.

The materials are more overwhelming than those of pathos, but they do not contribute more to overwhelm the imagination than the materials of pathos do contribute to pierce the heart. They are more powerful than the other, but it requires also more power to wield them; therefore the sublime genius is a greater genius both from his own power and his materials.

Pathos applies to the heart, of which all can judge, but sublimity to the imagination, of which all are not judges, because all have not cultivated their imaginations. Sublimity means something raised above this World, either applied to sentiment or scenery; pathos something that peculiarly belongs to this World, its passions & its affections.

August 25. Is not the power of describing scenes and characters above this World greater than detailing scenes & characters in it, which is the result of experience, and tho the elements of the other are laid in this World, yet passing through the Artist's mind, they are raised & elevated above it.

What is there important in size, in greatness, more than in any strong exciter of feelings? Are not murder, Death, equally strong in themselves, and is it any dereliction from a man's Genius to choose such subjects for its exercise? On the contrary, are not the greatest works of Genius in the World those where the subject, the power, the material, were equally strong, imposing, & terrific? What is Macbeth? what Agamemnon? what the Iliad? what a stronger exciter than Murder? what than War? And were Shakespeare or Eschylus or Homer considered unpoetic because the very nature of their materials & subjects were per se strong, terrific, exciting? The universal voice of mankind will answer "certainly not," because tho their materials were so powerful, yet the greatest skill is required to manage the most powerful materials to prevent them becoming too powerful, to prevent them degenerating into bombast & absurdity. I believe the capability of wielding strong materials is always considered a proof of power. Does the choice of sublime subjects supply talent & impose? Why are we not imposed on by Claudian, by Statius, by Blackmore?

August 30. The pathos of Lear is razory, piercing, agonizing, but yet it is the pathos of a "poor, weak, despised, old man." [6] You feel horror & detestation at the cruelty of his fiendish daughters; you weep at their base heartlessness. When Lear says, "I pray unbutton this," [7] his breast swells so, nothing can be more acute, but it is merely human, it is tied, pinned down to this World. Whereas the pathos of Milton, united [with] sublimity, pierces while it overshadows. Lear's conduct, to Cordelia, is capricious & wanton. You feel a great contempt, tho mingled with pity and even in his acutest sufferings a slight dawning comes over your feelings, as if he deserved such return; then again at the conclusion, when Cordelia is reconciled & flies to her dear aged Parent, the mingled feelings of forgiveness, the association of anger & injury, from a Father to his child, and the piercing tho delightful pang of reconciliation, when each forgives the other, is melting, amiable, tender. It gives a calm, beamy, bathing freshness to your brain; you feel as if the storm had broken up, and clouds of grief & misery, dispersed, were scattering & splitting at the effulgence which shone from the smiling face of rising Hope. Then the associations are not vicious; they are pure, delicate, paternal. Tho they are human beings, the associations are Heavenly, because the affections of our nature, the finest affections are excited; whereas in Milton's angels, there is a feeling of vice, of diabolic ingratitude to God, which tho it adds to the overwhelming power, detracts from the purity of enjoyment.

6. *King Lear*, III,ii,20. "A poor, infirm, weak, and despis'd old man."
7. *King Lear*, V,iii,309. "Pray you, undo this button."

August

　　　　His form had not yet lost
All her original brightness, nor appeared
Less than arch Angel ruined.[8]

You see me here, you Gods, a poor old man,
As full of grief as age.[9]

　　　　　　and th' excess
Of glory obscur'd, as when the Sun new risen,
Looks through the horizontal, misty air,
Shorn of his beams, or from behind the moon,
In dim eclipse, disastrous twilight sheds,
On half the nations, and with fear of change
Perplexes monarchs. *Darken'd* so yet *shone*
Above them all th' Arch-Angel; but his face
Deep scars of thunder had entrench'd, and care
Sat on his *faded* cheek, but under brows
Of dauntless courage, and considerate pride
Waiting revenge; cruel his eye, but cast
Signs of remorse and passion, to behold
The fellows of his crime, the followers rather
(Far other once beheld in bliss), condemn'd
For ever more to have their *lot in pain;*
Millions of spirits for his fault amerc'd,
Of Heaven and from eternal splendors *flung,*
For his revolt, yet *faithful* how they stood,
Their glory wither'd; as when Heaven's fire
Hath scath'd the forest oaks, or mountain pines,
With *singed* top, their stately growth though bare,
Stands on the blasted heath. He now prepar'd
To speak; whereat their doubled ranks they bend
From wing to wing, and half enclose him round
With all his peers. Attention held them mute.
Thrice he assayed, and thrice in spite of scorn
Tears such as angels weep burst forth; at last
Words interwove with sighs found out their way.[1]

8. *Paradise Lost,* I,591–593.
9. *King Lear,* II,iv,275–276.
1. *Paradise Lost,* I,593–621.

Certainly there is a dreary, melancholy grandeur, a fine over-whelming association, with ruined greatness. You see millions of heroic angels, faithfully adhering to their leader, wither'd, dusky, singed, scarred! — the consequences of their dreadful defeat. You see them drawn up, in endless line, illumined by the gleaming fiery flame of glimmering hell, and the recollection of their former glory, when virtuous, weighs down your faculties, when you reflect on their present misery. You admire their faith, their firm-ness, their adherence; you lament with their ingratitude, their infatuation, but it is the faith of bad minds, and yet, such is the power of their qualities, that it is only on reflection the perversion of their powers and the justness of their present state have any strength to cool your enthusiasm. You weep with Satan, at their hopeless, endless prospect, yet you must acknowledge the justice.

Satan! grand, terrific, revengeful, daring Satan! What terms can express the admiration, the enthusiasm, the grief, the de-testation of thy diabolic and tremendous Soul. Rebellion seems sanctioned by such a Leader, and fit for such followers in their blaze of enthusiasm. You would glory to be of such a band, and it is only when you recollect the attempt and consider against Whom, that you tremble at your temerity and suffer your feelings to evaporate with almost an unwilling sulleness. To the energy of perseverance, to the firmness of an unsubdued mind, dark gran-deur of crime surrounds them like an atmosphere and adds a terrific vigor to their fiery desperation.

Certainly it must be acknowledged that tho' the Devils never break out in absolute impiety, yet upon the whole, one's moral feeling is weakened. Their enthusiasm seizes daring minds; you would rather dwell with such grand fellows than hymn with "evertuned harps." [2] You ought not to feel so, but do you not?

Surely before any man of Genius throws his powers into any subject, he ought to consider its tendency. He ought not to rouse your enthusiasm, in favor of that which your principles forbid; he ought not to envelop crime with noble tho' perverted senti-ments, with pathetic, sublime feelings, rather making you lament the misdirection than detesting the intention of the director, and often indeed, too often, rendering you blind to their wickedness,

2. *Paradise Lost*, III,366. "Harps ever tun'd."

and in the enthusiasm of the moment forgetful of every thing but their perseverance, their energy, their noble unconquerable spirit. You sink into their souls and reverence their presumption as these qualities of mind will always excite admiration. Why not mingle then with fallen virtue or noble ambition? Why mingle feelings, the very best feelings of our nature, with characters without principle, without virtue? so that you cannot admire but at the risk of your morality, and the effect of what, if united with virtue, would be irresistible is really weakened by being linked with vice? Rather than detest Satan, or rejoice at his agonies, when the sight of the Meridian Sun recalls to his fiery mind from "what height fallen," [3] you sympathise with him, you lament such noble qualities should have such a termination. Is there a moral here? Does it send you from him warned by his example, or do you not turn from Satan rather animated by his splendid daring, his gigantic attempt? It is indeed a question.

No man ought to select crime to exercise his powers on, without debasing it by failure & misery in the end. Satan is to be punished eternally in the end, but still he triumphs for a while, and hell is not disgustingly horrible but sublimely terrible, a place where souls of great sensation would like rather to wander than fear to dwell, and which would rather encrease the sum of human means of pleasure, if when melancholy, one could sail amid such beings and enjoy for a time the luxury of sublime terror in such a dreary, fiery, hopeless, and tremendous situation.

It may be answered, "But Milton's punishment is not bodily torment but the racking agonies of conscience." Still, they are agonies of superior Souls, but surely his object was to shew how great qualities may be misdirected, and therefore the moral is as forcible to those possessed of great qualities as if they had been merely ferocious & demoniac. You see their grand feelings bursting through their diabolical ones, and is not the piercing reflection that great qualities have led to ruin instead of to glory by the vice of the possessors just as likely to serve as a warning as great qualities having led [to] ruin by the vice of others? Surely more so.

Is not Satan punished by misery of mind? Does not every

3. *Paradise Lost*, I,92.

fresh sin revolt only on his own head? "Of worse acts, worse miseries must ensue." [4]

August 31. Perhaps the most effectual way of interesting all human beings is to make human beings the agents of sublimity as well as pathos, as Shakespeare has done.

"Immenso negli espedienti, sempre inclinato ad intraprendere [le] cose difficili, ed a tentare pur anco le impossibili, *deciso di non abbandonare mai all' [azzardo] cio che poteva essere condotto dalla prudenza, risoluto di tutto osare quando il consiglio era inutile.*" I Romani nella Grecia. Barzoni.[5]

September 4. I thank thee, O Almighty God, that my blood rushes to my heart with encreased vigor at the contemplation of what I have to conquer. I undertook Solomon without being fully aware of the nature of my undertaking, just as I plunged into Macbeth, but my spirit, thank God, rises in proportion to my difficulties, as it did then. It must be done, & finely, or I am ruined. This is the way, this is the contest, this is the struggle, this is what I am by nature adapted for, and O God, spare my eyes, my health, and my intellect, and if Atlas were to roll the World on my shoulders, I'd bear it or be crushed.

O God, bless my exertions, limited as they must be, to conquer Italian. Let me know it perfectly, and speak it fluently. Let it not interrupt my duties, and grant me strength of intellect & health of body for all my wishes, for Jesus Christ's sake, Amen — with all my Soul, Amen. In thee I trust from the bottom of my heart.

"Il ne faut," disoit il, "employer les sculpteurs et les peintres que pour conserver la memoire des grands hommes et des grands actions. C'est dans les batiments publics ou dans les tombeaux, qu'on doit conserver des representations de tout ce qui a été fait avec une vertu extraordinaire pour la service de la patrie." Fenelon.[6]

September 10. I do not recollect a week since I began the Art of greater exertion than the one past. I thank God for it & that I

4. *Paradise Lost,* IV,26. "Of worse deeds worse sufferings must ensue!"
5. Vittorio Barzoni, *I Romani nella Grecia,* 1797, p. 5.
6. BRH's reference to this quotation is illegible but was identified by Professor Herbert McArthur as *Télémaque,* Book 10 (*Oeuvres de Fénélon,* Paris, 1835, III,75.)

have had resolution & energy sufficient & have painted & drawn night & day without intermission.

"The mental disease of the present generation is impatience of Study, contempt of the great Masters of ancient wisdom, and a disposition to rely wholly upon unassisted genius and natural sagacity." Rambler, number 154.[7] The wits of these days have discovered a way to fame which the dull caution of our laborious ancestors never attempted.

A certain action being requisite to the expression of any particular feeling, and the feeling always predominating and consequently always exciting the action of the part requisite to express it, the part in action from perpetual excitement will take the shape caused by the action and the association of the cause of the action will be excited by the shape produced by the action itself requisite to express the feeling. This is the principle of all characteristic expressions.

Find out the characteristics of all the passions and [how] to express any character that has tendencies to any one particularly. Mark gently the characteristics of that passion and the association of the tenderest passions of the being must be excited.

Inherent character of intellect or idiotism lies in the Scull, the passions & weaknesses in the face, the power of motion in the form. Class every thing; find out the character of particular human characters, of all characteristics of Women, of those of animals of all descriptions; find the distinctive marks of strength in form, of agility, of indolence, of beauty; consider all these as the materials to express your conception and as points to impress human feelings; wield them, combine them, mingle them as your fancy dictates or your reason enjoins — on the same principle of simplicity as marking the muscles of a limb to express its action at a given point, the association of intention to that point is excited, so the characteristics of any given expression marked, excite the association of the feelings intended.

Faults after 3 days' absence [*three illegible words*]. Executioner's legs too thick; body not full enough; Black's head too big; the Picture must be fine or I am ruined.

There is an absurd notion that compleat grandeur of form is

7. Samuel Johnson, *The Rambler*, Number 154, September 7, 1751.

vulgarity; slenderness, slimness is what all want. Man is composed of body and mind; therefore he performs the functions of his body to gratify the suggestions of this intellect. If the muscles, the causes of motion are not full, compleat, he cannot compleatly realize the intentions of his creation; therefore in Painting higher qualities of character, you must compleat the creature by giving a body, tho Nature seldom unites the two exactly.

October 10. One of the great fundamental principles of form is that the opposite lines of a contour should never be the same. Any antique that approaches this defect may safely be always considered as not of the finest age or by the greatest artist, because in the finest age, viz., the age of Greece, it is never seen, not even the hair's breadth approach to it. They were aware of it because they always avoided [it] in a decided manner.

October 28. Great Talents are always feared, Superiority always hated. Fear urges men to attack the object, either openly or secretly. Let those that have great talents endeavour to make men bear their inferiority by sweetness, gentleness, & benevolence, which will give them no cause or excuse for enmity and render their powers grateful instead of hateful to their companions.

Every man has his little circle. Many men comprise many circles, many circles contain a number; therefore do not willfully displease any one, because you will infallibly create more enemies than that one by so doing, and nothing displeases more than an overbearing manner, an insolent assumption, fierce consciousness of the talents God has given you. The meaner man may assist you, the meanest man may injure you. There is no occasion to be servile any more than insolent — suaviter in modo, fortiter in re[8] will enable you to attain your object, without hurting the feelings of your fellow beings.

[*The next page is devoted to Italian exercises.*]

October 29. I think the great reason of the superior manner of the Nobility is their elevation in rank above others, so that in

8. "Suave in manner, courageous in action."

whatever company they fall, they are at ease. Who is not polite, witty, affable, when he fears no competition? When he thinks he descends, when he is among those who are ready to laugh, and who feel honor at being noticed?

As I looked at the different animals today at Pidcock's, who were so different in character, so decidedly divided by impassible bounds, I could not help asking, "are not Men equally as distinctly separated & confused by natural powers or natural deficiencies?" Surely they are.

I hope in God to complete before I die a book of form, beginning with the exact proportions of European & quadruped — the gradations — beginning with the simple elements of drawing and going gradually on to the most refined systems.

October 31. Some one remarked that any Man could become a general in a month — what absurdity. What are the qualities that [are] requisite? A clear conception and energetic decision, the result of an instant & luminous conception, a power of wielding at once his materials to complete his own plans, or to frustrate that of his antagonist's, an unconquerable spirit, not daunted by any difficulties, a frank affability without degenerating into familiarity, an unceasing activity, a self command. Are these qualities attainable without Nature's assistance? Nonsense.

It is not I who am extravagant, but it is you who want comprehension. What is wild in my idea? Is it wild to wish the halls filled, the palaces painted, is it wild to wish that the Academy should be made subservient to the real purposes & intents of its foundations, is it wild to wish the Patrons on a scale, & the Nation should acquire taste? If this then is to be wild, then were Lorenzo & Leo wild and Pericles & Julius madmen. Romantic, wild, extravagant are always the epithets of envious imbecility on schemes beyond their power.

"You should not have began so large a work," said one, "so young as you are, because on a smaller scale your faults would not have been so perceptible." Oh you despicable wretch! So you would have had me begin on a scale which would have concealed my faults, and not have began works that would have shewn them to me till my old age, when it would have been too late to remedy them. Oh you poor, timid, wretched, foggy miscreant. Dec. 5.

Attend to the sensations of a thing first felt, if a second time you are less alive to its wickedness, be assured it is not that you are better informed & less timid but that you have disregarded the warnings of your heart when sensitive from innocence and suffered example to dull the acuteness of your virtuous perceptions. There are many feelings that to conquer the World agree to be right, but there are many also that the vicious & the vain think right to be subdued; the moral & the virtuous prefer to see indulged, cherished, and depended on. How are these poor wretches to be pitied, who drunk with the perpetual buz of crowds by night, and dizzy with the dying recollection by day, never know the blessedness, the holy silence of secret study, who never know the rapture of an intellect undisturbed, undistracted, eliciting by its own intuitive efforts trains of thought and visions of fancy in a ceaseless round of innocent and delightful peace, who never know the eagerness of a heart, whetted by absence from the object of its love, but who gratifying each feeling to surfeit, are fatted with all and not satisfied with any. Extract from a letter to my carissima fanciulla.

December 6. As yet this noble, this sublime art, has not ever received the patronage & assistance of the state; individual support is its only support. This can only go to a certain extent, and great & significant works to raise the character of the Nation and successfully contend with Italy & Greece, cannot ever be effected in succession without the Prince & the People reward Painters as Sculptors are rewarded, and Halls, Palaces, & churches are alike open to both. This is gradually affecting, and can only be decidedly affected by the artists giving such unanswerable proof of genius, as shall force attention, and not by sitting still, without struggle & whining over their neglect.

Why in God's name, why do you preserve the memory of great men in Sculpture and not in painting? Why? Surely the monotony of Sculpture can never interest the feelings or the imagination of men like Painting. In Sculpture you only erect to his memory, in

Painting you could particularize his acts and rouse enthusiasm withall.

You put [up] a Statue of the man and allegorize his virtues & his valour, while in Painting you realize his performances by selecting the most illustrious & rival reality by actual representation; then you see him not solemnly standing, but in all the energy of life enthusiastically acting — [these] are the feelings excited by the one.

War will always exist, not because men like to kill each other, but because the World will always praise & admire those who have courage to risk killing.

Nothing can shew more decidedly the superiority of Milton's Genius & judgement over Tasso's than his conception of the characters of the rebel angels. Tasso's are monsters fit only for Hell, Milton's are Angels worthy of Heaven.

> Millions of spirits for his fault amerc'd
> Of Heaven, and from eternal splendors flung
> For his revolt: yet faithful how they stood
> Their glory wither'd.[9]

> Tosto (says Tasso) gli Dei d'abisso in varie torme
> Concorron d'ogn' intorno all' alte porte.
> Oh come strane, oh come orribil forme!
> Quant' è negli occhi lor terrore e morte!
> Stampano alcuni il suol, di ferine orme
> E'n fronte umana han chiome d'angui attorte;
> E lor s'aggira dietro immensa coda,
> Che quasi sferza se repiega e snoda.[1]

How totally unsympathetic is this conception; disgust & horror are only excited; like the deformities of this World, they are monsters, not degraded angels. Whereas in Milton's, you weep, while you know and bend to the justice of their state — you see great minds & angelic forms, blasted, withered, ruined! This creates the melancholy sublimity of feeling, of great attempts without success; Milton too has his chimaeras dire,[2] but mark

9. *Paradise Lost*, I, 609–612.
1. *La Gerusalemme Liberata*, Canto 4, Stanza 4.
2. *Paradise Lost*, II,628.

the exquisite taste of their introduction — *they* belong to a part of Hell where the guilty are brought for punishment; they don't enter their Palace and hiss round them in debate. Milton never lost sight of this — that the Devils were Angels once; Tasso conceived them as if they had been Devils forever. Dec. 8.

[*The next two pages of the diary contain a series of quotations from such authors as Homer, Shakespeare, Spenser, and Milton.*]

And the Lord magnified Solomon exceedingly in the sight of all Israel, and bestowed upon him such *royal majesty* as had not been on any King before in all Israel.[3]

I wish to express in Solomon a fine youthful King of Israel, with delicate hands, clothed in gold, a sceptre, a crimson robe; his face, a luscious youthful love, mingled with profound wisdom.

> His fair large front, and eye sublime declar'd
> Absolute rule; and hyacinthine locks
> Round from his parted forelock manly hung
> Clustring, but not beneath his shoulders broad.[4]

December 24. I have succeeded to my own conception in the head of Solomon. I thank God humbly & sincerely for it. I painted on till three in the morning from ten the morning before. I was determined not to go to bed till it was done, and happily did I retire to rest when I had accomplished it. My model left me, exhausted, after 6 hours.

December 25. It struck me this morning in the same way. Once more I thank God from my heart and soul. Were I to die now I should leave the world more contentedly.

December 31. This year is now fast approaching conclusion. Upon the whole I have exerted myself with true energetic vigour. My mind is improved, & my powers of conception certainly more powerful & intense. When I conceive any thing now, it bursts into my brain like the breaking of day. My knowledge of art also encreased but not so much as it might have been. O God, when I reflect on the truly miraculous manner in which thou hast

3. 1 Chronicles, 29:25.
4. *Paradise Lost,* IV,300–303.

supported me and enabled me to bring my Picture to its present state, I bow down in gratitude & feeling. O God, may I always deserve such goodness, may I always deserve such unexampled mercy & protection. Amen, Amen, with all my soul.

[*About six lines are torn from the diary.*]

. . . gratitude. May I, O God, not be disappointed. Last year I remarked how little I was affected by the change of the year. This year I am less so; thus habit deadens all our perceptions.

I humbly hope, O God, for thy protection the ensuing year, for this year will make or mar me. Bless me, protect me, O God, I humbly entreat thee, with the most perfect confidence in thee I trust, in thee I trust. Amen.

The clock has struck twelve, and the year is gone forever. Alas! how many idlenesses might I have corrected, how many vices might I have avoided, how many moments might I have seized. The good that I have done only remains, but how much more might I have had to shew. I am retiring to bed pensive & thoughtful.

1814

January 7, 1814. I had not met Fuzeli for one year and a half till the other evening, and being left entirely to converse with Raphael and other delightful beings in the interim, without the shattering horror of his contaminating conceptions, I was more enabled to estimate him. He really shocked me. All his feelings & subjects were violent & horrid & disgusting. I returned home with an inward gratitude to God that I escaped in time, that I had purified my soul from the influence of his dark & dreary fancy.

January 9. I bought two prints after Michel Angelo. The first impression was certainly tremendous, but in a day or two it died away, and I returned to dear Raphael with renewed pleasure.

After all, grandeur of form is not interesting. Superhuman beings can only interest by action or expression; and what action or expression can they have which is not human? Therefore to make them interesting you must make them human, and if you do not do this, they are mere automatons. The feelings of the

335

heart expressed by a look are more delightful than all the grand forms that ever extravagance doated on.

Delicious, delightful, interesting Nature! The look of a lovely girl, glowing with love & heart, "celestial rosy red, love's proper hue,"[5] is more true & lovely than all the legs, arms, backs, breasts, or bellies, in ancient or modern art. My mind has taken a new & truer turn; I thank God for it from my heart.

An eye melting, piercing, shining, full of soul as it beams, is a more lovely object, a more intellectual object, than a great limb or a fine foot. The most interesting part of Nature is the face. All intellect & passion are conveyed by its features. The combination of form & feature is perfection, but a man is not to dwell only on form and tell her he is in the grand style. It won't do. Tell a story, talk a language, affect human beings. All human beings have hearts, but all human beings cannot relish those parts of the art as an art that can be acquired only by study. I am convinced from what I see that Michel Angelo had no permanent principle of form; he could not reject the superfluous from the essential; he burdened his figures with useless & ostentatious anatomy, with useless & subordinate parts — not always *useless* parts, for Nature has nothing *useless*, but parts that are not essential to the great motions, and in an abstracted figure need not be shewn. These parts he always abstracted, as in Angerstein's Lazarus,[6] &c., and all the Prints I ever saw.

Michel Angelo's forms have no refinement; they are heavy & not grand; they are the forms of Porters and Mechanics. Theseus of the Elgin Marbles is grand, and with all his grandeur & greatness you can see it is not the result of hard work but the harmonious combination of subtle Nature. He is a refined gentleman, a Prince, handsome & educated. Michel Angelo would have made [him] fierce, turbulent, & vulgar, more bulky but not more sublime.

To dress figures as if they were beggars is also in the grand style, not considering that Michel Angelo & Raphael generally

5. *Paradise Lost,* VIII,619.
6. Angerstein's "Lazarus" was painted by Sebastiano del Piombo, with Michelangelo's assistance (see I,163).

painted Saints, Popes, & Apostles, men professedly poor, but should Kings & Women be dressed with the same restriction? All dress should be part of the character, and you are not to tell me that yours is the grand style, and you must reject any but mere folds. I say no style will authorise absurdity, and there ought to be no style for every thing but the thing should regulate the style. Raphael's Attila[7] is a perfect example of dress; here are the brutal soldier, the peaceful Pope, the brutal King, & saintly Apostle, all dressed according to their respective characters. Would you wish them in the *grand* style, clothe them in rags & blankets.

I have been four years without receiving one sixpence from my professional exertions. I began this Picture without a farthing and have brought it to a conclusion, now & then assisted by my friends and now & then by disposing of my books & property supporting [myself]; those who have trusted me know that I payed them faithfully & honorably when I had the means, and they have given me credit, with the full conviction that when I have again the means I will be again faithful & honorable.[8] I always exerted myself to the utmost in my present Picture with the hope of its being patronised by & purchased by the B[ritish] G[allery]. Had I not been prevented by illness I should have been ready in time, but I am now ready, and I shall be pleased to keep it for exhibition next year. I do not write this because I fear my situation, but because I should prefer exhibition in the B. G. to any other, and because I shall be incapable of keeping [it] for exhibit there unless the Directors think proper to assist me. If they do not [*three illegible words*] but I hope they will not be offended if I yield it before the Public at another place, and

7. "Attila Turned away from Rome," in the Stanza d'Eliodoro in the Vatican.
8. "How Haydon contrived to live during the next two years [1813 and 1814] at first appears a mystery. But his own tradesmen gave him full credit, and for anything else he went to the money-lenders, who assisted him, though at the rate of sixty per cent. How he paid this interest was by the simple method of incurring a fresh debt to pay off the old one, till at length, his punctuality becoming known, his patronage was sought, and offers made to accommodate him at forty per cent. And this remained his normal rate for the rest of his life" (*Correspondence*, I,77 n.). At the end of 1811, BRH admitted that his debts were £616. 10s., £200 being due to his landlord (*Autobiography*, I,125). The death of his father on June 25, 1813 (unrecorded in his diary), erased all hope of an allowance, and he seems to have inherited nothing.

that if it meet with Public approbation, it will not weaken me.*

I congratulate the Institution most sincerely on their perseverance in purchasing; let them pursue with undeviating course this plan and it must ultimately advance the Art. They have but one thing more to do, and that is present the Pictures they purchase to the vacant Churches and every heart will beat with anticipated pleasure. If they do this, and this they surely will do, there will be nothing for the Students [to do] but qualify and produce, and if the production be sterling & legitimate for the Patrons to approve & purchase, however delightful it may be to the Directors individually to protect highly finished cabinet pictures for their own gratification, let me beg them for a moment to consider their character as Patrons and that the Institution will never realize the hopes of the People or the intentions of its founders but by great & significant encouragement, but by setting the example to other Institutions and other Patrons, by filling gradually the Churches & Public Buildings with sacred & sublime subjects, & solemn, sublime effusions, by giving Painters the same protection & assistance as Sculptors & Architects, and let them yearly make gigantic efforts which are despised and forgotten as soon as the Season is over.

The last two pages of Volume V contain a hastily written and frequently illegible recapitulation of Haydon's views that churches should contain pictures as well as statues, and that small paintings should not be exclusively patronized.

* I did. I sent it to Spring Gardens & sold it (Solomon) for 700 £.

Volume VI

JANUARY 1814—FEBRUARY 1815

Volume VI

January 26. This day is my Birth day.[1] My Picture is nearly concluded. When I look back and reflect that I have never received one sixpence professionally for four years, that I concluded Macbeth in the midst of the greatest want, that I began Solomon without a penny to get a candle in the evening of the same day to proceed with it, that I have brought this Picture too to a completion, that I have often had a model which I was unable to pay when I had done, till I had parted with some of my property — when I reflect that I have never known since Dentatus what peace of mind was, i.e., compleat serenity, that every head I have finished with a mind burthened with debt, with a bill approaching for which I was not prepared, or a dun coming for which I was not ready — I reflect & [re]collect the many apparently inextricable situations from which I have been extricated, surely I must think and I do feel that I am preserved for some great purpose, by my great & beneficent Creator, but that I am & must be first cleansed of my follies by the battles & troubles of life — (O God, pardon me if this be presumption, but grant, O God, it may *not be*). This feeling has cheered me in danger, & supported [me] in trial, this feeling has sent [me] to my duties with an unbending energy, & an expanding breast, has rendered me insensible & unconquered by failure, and enabled me to recommence and reattack with a light heart & a firm hand, vigourous & irresistible. O God, my Protector, to whose mercy I never applied in vain, O thou great & good Being, I bless thee from my Soul for thy mercies; still assist me, still protect me, still grant me health of body & vigour of mind & firmness of spirit to persevere till (if it please thee) I realize my great object; grant, O thou eternal spirit, that by my invincible perseverance, my perpetual effort, & my undaunted mind, I may give such a shock to the Art of my glorious country, that the

1. On July 7, 1821 BRH wrote, "So I was born on St. Paul's conversion! instead of the day after." The Feast of the Conversion of St. Paul occurs on January 25, the date which BRH observed as his birthday after 1821.

Nobility & the people may be roused, and high Art have that assistance & that protection, adequate to its difficulties and worthy of its grandeur. O God, assist me; O God, protect me; O God, realize before I die my great enthusiastic intentions; they are virtuous; in thee who has so mercifully directed me I trust, with delight & security. Bless my efforts, thou good, thou merciful Father. Amen, with all [my] heart & soul.

After all, what are the difficulties of life in comparison with the rapture of a successful effort to realize a poetical character? Who would change the difficulties of an historical painter for the luxuries of a Portrait painter? Give me one moment of the delight after succeeding in pathetic beauty or sublime majesty, and I'd bear all the miseries of want & debt. God spare me my intellect & health, and what shall subdue me?

Many complain of the cruelty of the World. God knows I have never found it so. All those who were my Friends in success proved themselves so in misfortune, and many who had not the privileges of intimacy came forward with the feelings of it. I have been peculiarly blessed with Friends who, conscious of my honor and admiring my intentions, have trusted to the one and promoted the other, with zeal & confidence.

January 28. Where necessity is the only object, men are nearly alike in their remedies at all times. I could not help observing on the Serpentine that the huts[2] they constructed were of the same simple form, the same plain unadorned awkwardness, of those in New Zealand or Otaheite.

February 6. I had a fine bit of human nature yesterday. An Artist called, and evidently affected by my Picture of Solomon, endeavoured to conceal it by censure. This was wrong, that was wrong, nothing was right, and then he reverted to his own habits, complained of his obstructions, excused his indolence, defended his irresolution, concluded all by languishingly affirming he was an unhappy fellow, because he knew so much that he could never be satisfied with his own efforts or those of another. Poor fel-

2. Since bathing was permitted in the Serpentine, BRH may refer to bath-houses. The boathouse had Gothic architectural decorations (Charles Frederick Partington, *National History and Views of London,* [184–?], p. 28).

low! How lucky Michel Angelo & Raphael knew so little or at least just enough, that they were continually struggling to know more, that with all their knowledge they never found it burthensome or an obstruction. How many excuses, how many specious shifts does Idleness put on. An entertaining lecture might be written on the various characters of Artists. One I know who never could meet with a good light, and therefore never began; another who always delayed that he might take a leap bye & bye; a third struck off into methodism; a fourth became an astrologer; a fifth etched all day for years because etching might be useful — I think I could venture to predict, from a drawing or week's habit, what any man could do.

February 6. When I reflect on the escape I had from ruin, from "entanglement" with an infernal woman, I shudder at my danger. Never was such a creature!!! Other women I have known had hearts, but this infernal, abandoned creature had no feelings but her own appetites, and if you refused to yield, your destruction was her object. Such was her corruption that every thing in Nature, light and darkness, solitude or society, beauty or deformity, every object that seeing, smelling, touching, or tasting could reach, were to her sources [of] licentious gratification. "The perfume of flowers has an amorous smell," she would say, trembling with passion; the richness of a golden evening, the silence of a woody grove, affected her vitiated fancy only as affording more refined means of lechery & lust. Nothing, however petty, however mean, however humane, however cruel, however terrible, however tremendous, or however sacred, but she would wield, if by such instruments she thought she could bend her objects to her appetites. It was her plan to discover your weakness, and sup till she ruined! — to ascertain your crimes, & hold you in subjection by threatening disclosure; to gratify your taste, [and] by gratifying *it*, make you gratify *hers*. She felt exquisite delight in making one ruined being the instrument of another's fate and then contrive they should all know it, when they were *irretrievably committed* but *not before*.

I have seen her at table, surrounded by such lovers, all nervous, agitated, & melancholy, all watching her looks, all in love, all jealous of each other, and yet knowing these were her only terms, and yet with such consummate art was this managed that she contrived to make her husband invite them! I have seen her smile like a beautiful devil and enchant the whole. The more difficult, the more pure, the more innocent, the more holy was the object, the keener was the anticipated pleasure, and the more delightful the triumph to conquer & enjoy. Her unconscious husband & her innocent children were the instruments of her vices! She could be charitable, innocent, abandoned, religious; one day a girl of sixteen, another a matron; she could faint at a picture, melt at music, or affect indifference for either. Her whole time, her whole occupation, her whole soul, were bent in discovering objects of pleasure, enjoying & ruining them! She would suck with poisonous delirium the balmy lips of a blooming youth, or bite, with keen & burning appetite, the disgusting sickliness of deformity.

This was the creature into whose power I was near falling. Attracted by apparent innocence, I became enamoured, but escaped without sin, tho with a shattered mind, that it was long before I recovered. I look back with horror and return thanks to God for my escape.

March 16. My eyes ill — written by Friends, I dictated.[3] The Institution has done an immense deal. They are entitled to the thanks of the country and the support of the arts; but still, without positive employments, the life of an historical painter must be one continued scene of danger & risk. Let me for a moment take a comparative view of the state of encouragement given to Portrait painters, Sculptors, & Architects, with that to Historical Painters. No Architect builds a house, no Sculptor makes a monument, no Portrait Painter paints a Portrait unless they are posi-

---

3. "I had finished my picture except toning, but my eyes were so affected that I could see no longer. Adams the oculist visited me, and came just as I was laying my head down, by the advice of a little apothecary, to have my temporal artery opened. Adams in his blunt way said: 'If that's done he will be blind. He wants stimulants, not depletion;' and he saved my eyes.

"I used at this time to dictate my Journal to my friends who successively called, so that nothing was lost" (*Autobiography*, I,165).

As surgeon and oculist to the Prince Regent, William Adams (1783–1827) was knighted in 1814. In 1825 he took his wife's name and was thereafter known as Sir William Rawson.

tively ordered, unless half the price of what they are to be paid is given them to defray the necessary expenses of their respective works. Thus their minds are at ease, & their bodies in comfort, & they work in security & delight. Whereas the English Historical Painter has no positive, certain demand; he risks his existence & reputation on great works, begun without the desire of others & continued without applause; begun at the instigation of his own enthusiasm for his noble art and his glorious country. Premiums are offered & rewards are given by the Directors of the British Gallery, but still this is limited & uncertain. A few only can have them, and there is still a risk that those few will not be they who deserve them most. All the historical works of the country, by which its reputation has been raised and its genius established, have resulted from the spontaneous, unprotected efforts of enthusiastic individuals. Hogarth adorned the Foundling [Hospital] for nothing; for nothing did Reynolds & West offer to adorn St. Paul's. Barry painted the Adelphi without remuneration, & Boydel as a patron brought ruin upon himself. What are we obliged to quote to refute the sneers of foreigners, when they ask us for our productions in the highest walk? Why, the works of those individuals who were forgotten by the nation & laughed at by the patrons, the works of those men, produced under the greatest possible obstructions and in the greatest possible want. For this is the fact; and the wonder is, not that those works are so bad, but that they are so well. Can any man pretend to say that had these men been fostered and encouraged, the powers of their genius would not have expanded with more vigorous strength? Had their works been ordered by Government, had money been advanced them at the commencement, how many difficulties must have been relieved, which obstructed their genius and burthened their powers. All the great works of genius which have been produced in other countries were the result of a liberal and enlightened patronage; there is no example on record except in England of any work of importance which raised the character of the country being began and compleated without private and public support. In England the works of the highest walk have been painted not only in spite of negative neglect but of positive obstruction, and yet these are the works which have rescued the country and the Artists from the stigmas of Dubous[4] and Winkleman and to which the country is obliged to refer when its genius is doubted.

Surely it's time that a change should take place in this system of things; surely it is but *fair* that English Historical Painters should have the same fostering, the same protection, and the same opportunity as the Portrait Painter, the Sculptor, and the Architect. And pictures are now bought, but still the option of buying or rejecting renders patronage uncertain, & purchase a chance. This, though it may do something, will never have an extensive influence & accomplish all. There must be no longer uncertainty; there must be no longer a risk of destruction; security must be perspicuous and payment sure; historical works must be clearly and decidedly ordered; then will the daring spirit and the gentler genius rush forward with equal vigour, the one safe from difficulties that burthen without oppressing his talents or daunting his iron strength; the other relieved from misfortunes which without invigorating would crush him and waste his powers in their bud. Should ever the Directors get permission to fill the Churches or the Halls, little good would be effected if Artists rush forward with works well studied and honourable to their talents dependent upon the accidental selection of those that have the power. There must be nothing accidental any longer in patronage. When once the Directors have the opportunity to fill the Public Buildings, they must issue their orders every two years, confining the size to fit the Building intended, but leaving the subject to the Artist himself. When this is *done,* all that can be *done* by patronage will be *done,* and if in twenty years, the Artists have not completely rescued their country from the accusation of the croakers and raise it up or above the glory of other countries, then indeed there must be some natural defect which no patronage can remedy and no power supply.

There are a set of Men who groan against the powers of the country in Painting, as there were a set who groaned against its genius as generals, but Lord Wellington, with a vigorous

4. Jean-Baptiste Dubos (1670–1742), author of *Réflexions critiques sur la poésie et sur la peinture*, Paris, 1719, 2 vols.

contempt of a great mind, overthrew the one; let the patrons give opportunity and Painters with equal energy [will] crush the other. There are various causes; some men doubt the genius of their countrymen because they doubt their own; some because they fear it, and know their own comparative insignificance; some from envy of success in others after having toiled for it in vain themselves, yet tho' the secret cause of an opinion should not influence its falsehood or truth, yet the motive of the deliverer must influence truth or falsehood of its application.[5]

March 27. You say we have to do with things as Poets with properties. No, things are [a] medium of properties, as words are your medium, but words in comparison with things are nothing. The one is artificial, the other native. You must translate words. Words are adopted by one Nation to express its wants. Poets of that nation express the conception of these words, but to a neighbouring nation who have adopted other words to express other wants, they are quite unintelligible. The Poet of a Nation is never properly felt by the Poet of any other, but the Painter speaks in the language of Nature. He needs no translation; he speaks by the thing itself. The Poet [speaks] by a patent means agreed upon by his Countrymen to mean the thing, whereas the Painter speaks what all can feel, the Poet only a few.

All[6] the absurdities with which Infidels incrust the law on Christianity never have or never will weaken the pure and impenetrable vein of truth that steadily flows through them in spite of all. Supposing that we had not been informed of their connection with divinity, the singular and wonderful superiority of a barbarous nation over other nations more enlightened and more advanced in science, in their notions of God, must have made a deep and uneffaceable impression. Here was a nation the earliest in which we have record in their most remote period believing in one God, here was a nation affirming their law was the institution of the Deity himself, affirming that what was incomplete then would be perfected afterwards by a system engrafted on the law, though superior to it, delivered by a being

5. The dictation, written by two of BRH's friends, ends here.
6. The dictation continues at this point.

whose birth they always suspected and clearly predicted. It is
certainly a strange and singular coincidence with their own
assertions of their divine connection that their law and their system should have survived the laws and systems of greater nations and superior men. It is certainly strange that these nations
great in Art and in Science from which we have derived all our
principles of Architecture, Painting, & Poetry, superceded in
their morality by a nation totally brutal and uneducated in these
matters. Why have not the religious systems of the Babylonians
and Chaldeans, the Assyrians and Egyptians, the Grecians and
the Romans, kept pace in stability with their systems of Art?
Why? The answer is obvious. Because the one was the result of
human powers that required not divine assistance and where
human powers unaided availed but little, how futile, how
absurd, how feeble were their attempts. Here they were inferior
to an inferior people, aided by the inspiration of God, here
their attempts have been completely obliterated by the law on
Christianity, which from the beginning of the World asserted its
divine origin, has triumphed over obstruction, or has triumphed
over every difficulty, increases in blazing brightness and iron
strength as it proceeds, and finally will overspread the World
like a mighty flame, unquenchable and irresistable.

March 28. I intreat the rising students, whether in Edin-
borough or in Leeds, in Bath or in Bristol, in Liverpool or in
London, to ground themselves fundamentally in art, to root out
every difficulty thoroughly and clearly, to consider high art as
that species of Art only which will give consequence and rank
to their country. I entreat the Patrons to consider it also of that
species of Art most worthy of their protection; not to neglect the
inferior branches but to give the higher walk its comparative
importance by effective & positive reward. I beg them to reflect
that without protection, demand, and encouragement, Historical Painting will only gleam with the uncertain sunshine of a
cloudy day, instead of blazing with the heated intensity of a
summer noon. I beg them to follow the system of the Director of
the British Gallery to encourage and order pictures for the
churches and halls within their influence, and let not every

Corporation confine their liberality to Portraits of the county members, but let them ornament their immense walls with Historical Pictures, with subjects from their own History. Is there any thing unreasonable in this request? Do they not give these opportunities to Sculptors & to Architects? Why should the Historical Painters be neglected? Is not the Town Hall the most splendid room in its respective City, and why should it not be ornamented in a style worthy of its magnificence?

As to the people being ignorant of these matters, are they more ignorant than the people of other countries? Certainly not. The people of all countries are equally ignorant and look up to the Educated and refined part for moral instruction.

April 1. Such is the fame of this grand country that was all animated being again to be immersed in darkness & in deluge, the brightness of its glory would shine like a gigantic meteor on the roaring wave & point to the spirit of the waters amid the dreadful silence where England lay.[7]

April 30. The above observations were written by Friends who accidentally came in when I was laid up in my eyes. I am now, thanks to the good great God, again well and able to continue them myself.

My object is not my own aggrandizement on the ruins of others, but to reform & direct those who have the means of aggrandizing the Art. Let me but see a desire in the Academy to foster instead of crush, let me but see a feeling in the Directors to patronise great works for their Halls & their palaces, instead of cherishing little ones for their parlours & drawing rooms, and that instant will I forget & forgive all my own paltry oppressions and back them with all my might & mind. It may be thought presuming in [one] so young to talk so highly; it may be so, but I deny that I am presuming. I speak with the freedom I have a right to assume. Conceive of the soundness of my principles. Talent is not hereditary. The rank of the Directors entitle them to our respect, but if they assume the character of Patrons of Art, when talent alone enables them to prove their

7. The dictation ends here, and BRH continues.

capability, they must be directed by those who know their road & are able from habit & study to inform them.

May 4. O God Almighty, permit me on my knees to thank thee for thy mercies; the great work to which two years of anxious study was devoted is finished, exhibited, sold, & has succeeded.[8] O God, it has given that shock to Art that I so anxiously prayed it might give at its commencement; it has roused the people; it has affected the Artists; it has excited the nobility. O God, grant its effect may succeed beyond example, and shew them the value, the beauty, the morality of the higher species of Painting. For thy infinite mercies, for thy unheard of goodness, no expression of my soul can convey a full and adequate feeling. I would kneel till my knees rooted, I would bow my head till I had bent it to my feet, to express my heart's gratitude and

8. BRH exhibited "The Judgment of Solomon" at Spring Gardens, where it was well hung in the Water-Colour Society's exhibition. A notice in the *Examiner* of May 1, 1814 (pp. 286–288), probably written by Robert Hunt, the regular art critic, asserts that the light and color of the picture have "the vivacity without the flutter of Rubens," and that "the regular simplicity of composition has a striking similitude to the style of Rafael, so distinguished for composition. . . . We will not scruple also to add, that not even Rafael has surpassed [Haydon] in the grand object of Art—the portraiture of the heart, or, as it is commonly called, expression." The two old counselors "bear some resemblance to and equal the best of Rembrandt's figures." The picture was purchased for 700 guineas by Sir William Elford, a banker of Plymouth, and his colleague, referred to variously as Mr. Tingecombe by BRH (*Autobiography*, I,169), Tichincombe by Farington (VII,245), and Trigcombe by Miss Mitford (L'Estrange, II,20). His name actually was J. W. Tingcombe, as is shown by his signature on two letters to BRH attached to the diary. The British Institution also awarded the picture a premium of 100 guineas (*Autobiography*, II,847).

Later owners included Edward Prideaux (*Annals of the Fine Arts*, 1819, 4:278), Sir Edwin Landseer (*Autobiography*, I,201 n.), and Louisa, Lady Ashburton (*Correspondence*, I,269 n.), but "the present Lord Ashburton has no knowledge of it" (George, p. 62), and it is assumed to be lost. Miss Rhoda Welsford, of the Courtauld Institute of Art, informs me that it was included in the sale of Lady Ashburton's property, conducted by Phillips, Son, and Neale; "the picture in question was included as Lot 1481 in the eight-day sale, started on September 18, 1911, of the contents of Melchet Court, Near Romsey, Hampshire. It was hanging in the servants' hall, was catalogued as 'Unknown [Artist] —large gallery painting unframed—The Judgment of Solomon,' and was bought by a Mr. Jenkins for £1.10s."

No engraving was ever made of the picture (*Correspondence*, I,269 n.), but sketches from BRH's diary of "The Executioner & Heads in Solomon" are reproduced in *Correspondence* (I,78), and the Tate Gallery owns a black chalk "Study of the head of a youth, for the picture of 'The Judgment of Solomon,'" reproduced in *Autobiography* (I,144) and by George.

my soul's sensation. O God, still support me. Great trials are yet coming, but grant the worst may be over. Grant me such modesty, such propriety, such delicacy in my prosperity, such a feeling for my enemies as not to exult but rather to relieve them by my kindness when I meet them. Let my whole behaviour be so magnanimous and good that I may not need adversity again to punish me. O Almighty, have mercy. One request more: spare my life till I have reformed the taste of my Country, till great works are felt, ordered, & erected, till the Arts of England are on a level with her Philosophy, her heroism, & her Poetry, and her greatness is compleat. Spare my eyes; invigorate my intellect; grant me capacity to discover my faults, and energy to correct them; strengthen every requisite that I have, and supply those I have not. Grant my next effort may be greater, and grant I may succeed; grant every fresh struggle may remedy the errors of [the] preceeding one, and when thou callest me hence, let it be perfecting the talent thou has given me; let it be doing my duty to my Art & to my God. Amen, with all my heart.

[*The next two pages contain twelve preliminary sketches for "Christ's Entry into Jerusalem," the last two closely resembling the finished picture.*]

May 7. My Canvas up & ready. God in his mercy support me & grant me power to cover it with excellence and to advance the great cause.

May 16. My Sister came up to see me. There is something so pure & correct, so unassuming & unsinful, so delicate and lady like in her manners & feelings, in her air & thoughts, that she has done great good to my own mind & habits. Really the contrast with the women in London is palpable, and it has shewn me the beauty, the value, the comfort of virtue in so striking & forcible a light, that the thought, the mere perception of vice, grates against my soul.

May 17. Heartily sick of idleness & relaxation. My Picture is sketched in, but I have been running about, unable to apply myself from weak eyes & delicate state of health. I am now better refreshed & getting stronger. God grant me power to advance well, steadily, rapidly, and enthusiastically in my dear, dear Art.

It is strange that all the Pilgrimages to Rome should never have produced a Michel Angelo or Raphael! There is a certain idle, regular, talking habit they all get into, a certain neglect of all the decencies & cleanliness of life, a certain systematic, mannered nonsense that a man depending on and urged by Nature disdains to suffer. Why should you light your own fire? Why should [you] wear a dirty shirt? Why should your room be filthy, your chin unshaved? Will this make you conceive finely & execute with power? Will this give you fancies, judgement, & taste, & feeling? Alas, alas, the productions of such habit are futile & vain, useless & trifling; a few years [and] they dwindle & sink into that oblivion, the just reward of the folly.

Wilkie & I left Town May 26th, 1814,[9] for Brighton in order to embark there for Dieppe and then push on to Paris.[1] After a pleasant voyage, we landed at Dieppe, and certainly the contrast between the two Countries was extraordinary. The high caps, rich crossed shawls, their lively black eyes, struck amazingly. The Women are beautiful but [of a] stern nature, the children with exquisite features, but not rosy. The French appear to me active, ingenious, unwearied people, polite yet persevering in an object with politeness, bowing, smiling, yet keeping their object in view.

The conscripts we saw — a miserable set of galley slaves in appearance, squalid, little, and bony. Some of the officers handsome. Two men after an appearance kissed each other heartily.

The town of Dieppe old & gothic & fine like Vanderheyden's[2] views in Holland. A great proportion of Women. Climate mild. Shops open airy, & every thing looking elegant. The French Sailors noisy, awkward, theatrical; boats dirty & rusty. The Inn clean, neat, & comfortable.

9. According to Wilkie's diary, he and BRH left London on May 25, 1814, and reached Dieppe on May 26 (Cunningham, I,389–390).
1. With Paris in the hands of his enemies, Napoleon abdicated on April 11, 1814, and was sent to Elba on April 20, where he remained until February 26, 1815. Paris was therefore open to travelers, and the Louvre, still containing Napoleon's spoils from galleries and churches of conquered countries, was a Mecca for artists.
2. Jan van der Heyden (1637–1712), Dutch landscape painter.

May 28. Nous partimes de Dieppe pour Rouen dans un Cabriolet. Le chemin fut très bon, très large, avec les arbres des pommes, fut fleuris sur chaque coté. La Campaigne etoit fort riche, et les maisons de manufacture, et les chateaux des Gentilhommes etoient très beaux, bien batis, et très fort avec les briques; en un mot, Je n'ai jamais vu en Angleterre plus de bonheur dans les peuples, plus de proprieté dans les habits. Les habits des femmes etoient très picturesque; ses bonnets très hauts et blanche comme la neige, ses jupes rouges comme les roses, et aussi bien que ses coiffures allumées par les rayons du Soleil, presentent aux yeux du Peintre une etude la plus belle du Monde. Je ne suis pas encore etonné aux ouvrages des Peintres d'Hollande; ils ne dessinoient que les objets toujours devants leures vues, et dans les villes la meme brilliance, la meme richesse, la meme couleur que les Francois voient toujours. Rembrandt et tous les grands Maitres toujours voyoient aussi — ils copioient exactement la chose qu'ils virent, et si chacun copioit les exactement, il pouvoit faire des beaux tableaux. Le tems est fort beau, l'air et le souffle tres doux. Les fenetres et les portes sont toujours ouvertes, et les habitans n'ont pas froids. Nos allâmes à la comedie;[3] les acteurs etoient tres bons, un peu extravagants, mais plus mieux que seroient les acteurs en Angleterre dans une ville de même grandeure. Nous vîmes aussi "la place aux v[e]aux," ou La Pucelle etoit brulée par le Duc de Bedford; il y a une Statue de la Pucelle, et sur les pieds etoient les mots (presqu' effacés), "Liberte, Egalite, et Fraternite," les ruines de les marques de la Revolution et du tems de la terreur. Le postilion avoit été tiré dans la conscription. Il fut à Paris quand les Russes y entrent, mais il fut envoyé chez lui quand elle etoit abolie par Le Roi Louis dix huitieme. Il me dit avec une expression de fureur que l'Empereur fut un tyran sanguinaire. Un beau jeune homme, à qui Je parlai pour un moment à l'hotel ou nous restâmes, me demandoit que pensoient ils les Anglois quand l'Empereur etoit à Moscou. Je lui dis, et il me repondit avec enthousaisme que l'armée Françoise ne fut pas

---

3. Wilkie wrote in his diary for May 28: "Went to the theatre in the evening; saw a play, and an after-piece, the latter being the same as Colman's 'Love laughs at Locksmiths'" (Cunningham, I,391).

vaincues par les vilains Russes, mais par les neiges. Les Cossaques, il dit, etoient laids, avec une barbe longue, &c. Tous les peuples sont polis. Le postilion passa la maison ou demeuroit sa mère; son frère etoit à la porte, et il lui faisit ses compliments avec un grace qu'on ne voit jamais en Angleterre que dans les mannieres des personnes de qualité. Les filles vous parlent avec un "oui Monsieur" qui est très beau, très naif; les yeux vous regard, à meme tems avec une expression plein de suavité, et de douceur. J'aime La France, elle est un beau pays, et Je n'ai rien vu de degouter dès mon entrée ni dans les choses pour manger, ou dans les modes. Dans le theatre il y etoit pres lès loges "un cabinet des hommes," et sur l'autre coté, "un cabinet des dames." Mon Dieu! Les dames delicates, tremblantes, d'Angleterre, que penseroient-elles de cette coutume? Les maisons à cafe sont très nettes — mais dans notre hotel la salle publique pour dames etoient sales. La cathedrale fut très grande, baties par les Anglois.

There is a strange inconsistency in the French character. No people reconcile the most contrary feelings with such ease. One moment they pray "dans le presence de Dieu;" they next jest; one moment they laugh at the grimaces of a Merry Andrew, and the next weep with tender sighs for the death of their Friends or their Fathers. Their houses, their rooms, their beds, every thing they do, and every thing they say, display the same want of arrangement and thought.

At the Cathedral we saw them at confession. There was a silence, a mystery calculated to impress the mind deeply; in the evening Wilkie shewed the Landlord's boy a sketch of it; "ah, ah, la confessional," said [he], "des bêtes, des bêtes." This plainly shews it was not the general feeling.

While this was going on in the Church, out side was cricket, and later men roaring & running, and even to give one the feeling of gaity, while under all was awe & silence, lit up by a silent, golden setting sun.

The view above Rouen was truly delightful — a large extended plain, the venerable old gothic city toning the colored Seine, winding with glassy richness through, spotted with little islands. We have not seen any fine luxuriant trees; the country

"Une jeune fille de Rouen," May 28, 1814.

is barren of trees, and not being divisé, has to my English eyes a barren look, tho full of corn; never did I see so much corn — acres without end.

At Equi,[4] ou nous dinons, Je rencontre un vieux prêtre. We got into conversation about the various revolutions France had suffered, and never shall I forget his look when as I was expressing my sentiments in an English manner, he looked with horror at me, and asking me to speak lower, we walked away. He took me to his house with satisfaction in his face. Here was a perfect French family. By the fire sat the Grandmother, old, bowed down with age, the Mother an old French Lady in a lace cap, smiling as she spoke, with an elegant, accomplished satisfaction, delicate, reserved, yet free & open. His wife, a fine youth, and two little children concluded the group. If I spoke of the King Louis XVI, a pang, an acute pang, seemed really to seize all; their faces really had a look of habitual sorrow. He told me he had lived there during the whole "tems de la terreur" & suffered horribly. He had packed up all, if the Allies had come this last time, but "Dieu remercie," he escaped. All the people were relieved, said he, but the Soldiers, "ils ne sont contents."

I never saw a family of more kind feeling. They seemed delighted to see an Englishman. They called in all their acquaintance; in slipped one, then another, then he wispered to go to such a one, &c. He took me upstairs and shewed me a cabinet of stuffed birds, &c. In the midst of all his execration of Buonaparte and his air "pour les Anglois," he looked at me gently and asked me if he [had] not done great mischief to England. I said no, and that we were but more vigorous and more powerful than [when] we entered. Il fut etonné. The people seem pleased and not pleased. They are glad to get [rid] of Buonaparte's oppression, and yet they regret that they have lost also with it their military grandeur. One moment they curse him — comme un tyran sanguinaire — the next — but he was [a] great genius. They would have liked him had he behaved with common decency; what a Kingdom had he lost!

4. According to Wilkie's diary, the travelers left Rouen on May 30 and dined at Aqui (Cunningham, I,393). The name thus Anglicized is Ecouis, a village midway between Rouen and Magny.

June

I spoke to an Austrian Cuirassier at Rouen who was at the Bataille de Leipsig & Dresde.

At Rouen the colours of the dresses, the deep tone of the Church, the solemnity of the priests, yet shine to my feelings like a golden dream.

We left Rouen in a Cabriolet in high spirits and slept that night at Magny, and the next morning again proceeded and arrived at Pontoise to breakfast. About two we entered Paris by the Rue St. Denis, after having passed over the field of Battle. Never was a more infernal enterance to any city than that of St. Denis to this. The Gate of St. Denis is very grand, but the first appearance of Paris to a stranger is that of inextricable confusion, houses, figures, carriages, men, women, & children, all huddled together in dirt, mud & filthiness.

We drove to Hotel Villedot which was uncomfortable & extravagant. After paying, as all must pay, for a little experience, we got lodgings in Rue St. Benoit,[5] Fauxbourg St. Germain, and became settled. The dreary, neglected look one feels in a great city without a Friend was never more acutely felt by any young tyro from his Parents' wing in London, than by me, till I had honest lodgings.

The next morning[6] I went down to the Louvre before breakfast and enquired of a National Guard at what time it opened. With the manners of a Gentleman, he told me every thing I wished, and at ten down we went.[7] Certainly my sensations were very grand as I approached this celebrated Gallery. I darted up stairs through all obstructions, and was in, instantly, but I must own it disappointed me. It is too long — it has too much the look as if one was looking in at the wrong end of a spy glass. From continually imagining what the Transfiguration[8] must be, of course I formed a fancy very different from what it was. The consequence must always be what it was with me — the first

5. At No. 6, belonging to M. Lenoble (Cunningham, I,397).
6. June 1.
7. Wilkie's diary and letters show that a Mr. Sewell accompanied them from Brighton and went to the Louvre with them (Cunningham, I,389, 397). BRH referred to him as "Sewell, our Lincolnshire friend," in his entry for June 29, 1841.
8. Raphael's "Transfiguration," now in the Vatican.

glance made it look small & rather insignificant. There appeared a want of power in the mode of expressing, and a want of beauty in the female heads. Corregio opposite[9] certainly does injury to Raphael in sweetness. Neither Raphael or Titian or any artist that ever lived since the ancients have expressed the form with such feeling & knowledge as Rubens; his taste of design is vulgar, but his knowledge of the organization was profound. His hands of women rank as high in organization as the face of the Venus de Medicis. Tintoretto looked dashing & careless, spotted & unfinished. Of all men that ever lived, for sensitive, trembling, sweet sensitiveness, Corregio is the most extraordinary. There is a magical, refined, almost imperceptible beauty. He has realized those fleeting, momentary expressions, which scarcely have existence, and yet affect us with their beam. He has caught them & kept them, with a harmony, a poetry, a refined delicacy, an enchanting grace; his nerves had been the strings of an Angel's lyre, and the dreams of an Angel had been his fancies. The only man that exceeded my feelings is Corregio — Reynolds surely studied him, and the same system & harmony of colour & the same look & surface that Reynolds carried to excess, is apparent in Corregio. No one in England is aware of Corregio's power; he is a most extraordinary man, and in Raphael you can trace, you can see his advice, his assistance, his struggles, but Corregio you cannot trace to any human stimulus; you know not when he altered or when he improved; you know not what gave him this hint or what gave him that. There are his works. You feel that they are exquisite, and you feel the part he has expressed is in Nature, and was neglected by all before. Corregio gives me such sensations that I never think of him without having a musical harmonious strain undulate over my brain.

Paris is a filthy hole, and the Palais Royal a pandemonium in the midst of it. It is a beautiful palace in the midst of the city and is a fine enclosed square, the alleys full of shops, and the houses full of gaming and brothels. After nine never was such a scene witnessed! The whole is illuminated, the walks & gardens which form the Square full of villainy & depravity,

9. Correggio's "The Mystic Marriage of St. Catharine" (*Correspondence,* I,271), still in the Louvre.

stuffed full, that as you enter you feel a heated, whorish, pestilential air flush your cheek & clutch your frame. The blaze of the lamps, the unrestrained obscenity of the language, the indecency, the baudy, bloody indecency of the People, bewilder & distract you. Such is the power & effect of this diabolical place that the neighborhood, like the country around the poison tree of Java, is mad by its vice and infected by its principles.

The Country round Paris is vast, dreary, & melancholy — old chateaux, dilapidated — and Paris itself has the look of misery in the People & splendid despotism in the princes.

June 10. I went to the Theatre Vaudeville & saw Cupid & Psyche. Wretched singing, and by the company it seemed a very inferior affair. As I was crossing the Thuilleries and saw Buonaparte's triumphal Arch towering darkly against the twilight sky, I could not help stopping & thinking how little good all his industry had done to the World or himself. All his monuments will serve now but to remind one of his folly, & his vice, his cruelty & tyranny.

June 11. Made an excursion to Vincennes, Belle Ville, & Pantin. As I approached Vincennes, where D'Enghien was murdered, I felt certainly exceedingly affected. There was something severely terrible in the look of the Castle surrounded by a deep moat, a draw bridge, small windows, grated, and an iron railing on the top for the prisoners to walk inside, gave one an idea of state tyranny, that nothing in England excites the slightest association of. How little do we know of such fear and apprehensions. The Governor was a fine, soldierly, polite fellow, who had lost his leg at the battle of Wagram. He gave me permission to make a sketch of the tower, and afforded me every convenience; after staying a short time and asking as far as I might venture several questions about D'Enghien's murder, to all of which I got indirect replies, I took my leave, and drove to Belle Ville, and the heights of Chaumont, which were so well defended by the Ecole Polytechnique. The heights of Chaumont are certainly admirable positions, and must have cost the Russians many men. The vineyards had [been] injured here, and the cottages I entered literally stripped of furniture, which had been burnt for firewood by the troops. In Belle Ville, as I approached Pantin, marks of the obstinancy of the battle became apparent. Many houses were absolutely bored with musket shot, and several had their corners & roofs beat in with cannon shot. At Pantin I entered a Gentleman's private house belonging to M. Le Grand, and here indeed were specimens such as I hope never again to witness — a beautiful house, furnished in an elegant manner, absolutely reduced to a shell, to bare walls. In the Parlour, horses had stabled, and their dung was yet on the marble floor. All the windows and cupboard doors had been wrenched off to burn; the paper of the rooms had been torn down; the wainscot had been beaten in with the butt end of muskets here & there, in order to see if valuables were concealed, and the glasses shivered to atoms. Many of the fruit trees in the garden had their stumps cut, and the garden itself, fitted up to be sure in French taste with statues of Shepherds & Shepherdesses, was trampled on, and in a state of perfect desolation. "Vous êtes Anglois, sans doute," said the shrewd old Frenchman who shewed me the House. "Oui," said I. "Ah, you fight for the *good* cause," said he, looking cunningly at the ruins about us. "Yes, I do," I answered, "but recollect," I told him, "that you had given Europe the same sort of proof of a *good* cause, and you amused yourself at Moscow, and now they amuse themselves here." "Ah, cela est vrai, Monsieur — la sorte de la Guerre. But," said [he,] "it is not the French people who have been guilty of such conduct but their Governors." "Then why do you suffer yourself to be duped by such Governors? I'll tell [you] what," said I, "if your Nation were a little more attentive and a little more interested about the conduct of your Governors, and took more interest in your national affairs & constitution, you would not be at the mercy of every rascal who choosed to struggle for the lead." "It is all true, Sir," he said, but I saw he hardly apprehended me.

The garden walls and houses throughout Pantin were beat to pieces by cannon shot. The man shewed me one which had entered the garden wall, knocked a wooden bust all to pieces, and indented a wall opposite, quite spent. All the houses along the road to the Fauxbourg St. Martin were shattered & dilapidated, many without a single window left. The People were busy repairing, singing gaily, as if it was a good job, and we met many carts returning with beds & bedsteads and household furniture, which in the confusion had been carried into Paris. In Pantin every crack & corner that was capable of defence bore marks of murderous fighting.

I returned to Paris about five, highly interested with my jaunt, & by the same route as the allies entered. I was shewed the house where the Emperor had his head quarters till he made his entry — at Pantin — it was a nice house at the end of the Village. The Country was very sweet and much richer in trees & woods than that on the side of Mont-Martre.

In the evening Wilkie and I went to the Royal Academy,[1] and never did I witness such a dirty set of rooms, filthy, and the people worse.

At Vincennes, as at Rouen, a fine Church was turned into a Work Shop. The Castle was at present filled with powder. The Governor in asking me if I wanted any thing or if I preferred another room, opened a suite of elegant apartments with true French magnificence & vanity.

June 12. Today was the fete de Dieu,[2] a grand fete of the Catholic Church. The streets were hung with tapestry, and altars erected at the different grand points in the streets. Every thing was gaity & bustle out of doors, tho every thing quiet and comfortable within.

As this was the first Sunday on which the Shops had been shut since the revolution, it was therefore a remarkable Sunday, and we arrived just in time to see the effects in religious matters of that tremendous convulsion. Last Sunday the people were at work, the Shops were open, the inhabitants dirty & dissipated. Today the shops were shut, the people happy & clean. No one can conceive the difference unless they had seen it.

There appears to me a great deal of good sense in the King's ordering Sunday to be kept, and commencing with the grand

1. Wilkie recorded in his diary that they went to the Académie Vivante in the Palais des Beaux Arts on June 11 (Cunningham, I,407).
2. The festival of Corpus Christi, falling on Thursday, June 9, 1814, was transferred to Sunday, June 12.

fete de Dieu, so that the People, who are distracted after *Spectacles*, may have one to reconcile them to the change.

I asked the Guarde Nationale at the gate of the Thuilleries if we could go up, as we were Anglois. "Certainly," he answered, and up we mounted into the Salle des Mareschaux, round which were hung their Portraits. Here we waited & walked about, until we heard that Louis XVIII [3] was coming, and saw him, Duc D'Angouleme[4] & Dutchess,[5] walk through to go to Chapel. The King looked smilingly & happily. We shouted, "Vive le roi" as did all the rest heartily, and we all kept repeating it till he passed by. On his return I had not so good a view, being careless about it, but his reception was more flattering than at first. I staid looking about the room, and saw several of the mareschals come out, Augerau[6] & Moncey.[7] I could not help thinking, as I have often before thought, how strange it is that the world suffer themselves to be guided & governed by so few. The generality of men do not attain greatness because they do not aim at it, not because they are incapable of attaining it. Perhaps this is a question. Those arise only who have the capacity. It never perhaps occurs to those who have not. Is it not strange that men with bodily powers & mental too should suffer themselves to be trodden down by little creatures, whom they could have crushed had they willed it? How our powers are checked by an imaginary principle!

In the evening Wilkie and I went to the Cirque Olympique, and there we saw an English, a sweet English Woman, unaffected, natural, interesting, full & finely formed. O Heavens, this is the first time I have felt my heart warmed by the sight of a Woman since I entered France. The manners of the French women are fascinating, but I have never seen one yet without a beard, which destroyed the effect of their sparkling eyes. As

3. Louis XVIII (1755–1824), King of France, brother of Louis XVI.
4. Louis-Antoine de Bourbon (1775–1844), duc d'Angoulême, nephew of Louis XVIII.
5. Marie Thérèse Charlotte (1778–1851), duchesse d'Angoulême, daughter of Louis XVI.
6. Pierre-François-Charles Augereau (1757–1816), duc de Castiglione, marshal of France. His desertion of Napoleon in January 1814 contributed largely to Napoleon's defeat.
7. Jeannot de Moncey (1754–1842), duc de Conegliano, marshal of France.

to their forms! — really, really, skeletons wrapped in lace &
muslin & fringe. Never did I see the superiority of my dear,
darling Country[wo]men so decidedly manifested. God, there
was some appearance of suppleness & contour. [*Three sketches
of typical French and English women.*] This was the exact difference. Look at the sweet air of my sweet countrywoman and
say, gentle reader, say whenever you read this, which you'd
rather kiss?

June 13.[8] Went to Gerard's,[9] the Painter's, and was certainly
very much affected at the Portraits I saw there. Buonaparte 10
years ago. Good God, what a [picture!] Heavens, a horrid yellow
for a complexion, the tip of the nose tinged with red, his eyes a
watery, dull, fixed, stern, tiger like, lurid fierceness; his lids red-
dish and his mouth cool, collected, & resolute; his mouth [*four
illegible words*] his eyes & forehead shewed a capability of conceiving. Never in my life do I recollect being so horridly
touched. All the other heads in the room looked like the heads of
children in comparison. Josephine was [in] the middle, looking
interesting & good natured, and Maria Louisa on the other side,
young & full. Murat[1] was in the outside room, with Lannes[2] with
his wife & fine interesting children. Setting aside every consideration of Buonaparte's cruelty, there is something melancholy in
the recollection of the height from which he has fallen. There
are moments when one forgives one's bitterest enemies and
laments rather than revenges their cruelty or conduct. This was
precisely my feeling on contemplating the portraits of these men,
the product of the French revolution. There was Lannes, a gallant Soldier, who lost his life at Aspern.[3] I had read of his being
killed; I had known [of] his power of electrifying the Grenadiers
at an assault. I felt regret & interest in his heroic character, and
his wife with six sweet children by his side gave a loveliness, an
amiability, that was quite Hectorian. How could they suffer

8. Wilkie's diary supplies the date (Cunningham, I,409).
9. François Pascal Gérard (1770–1837), portrait painter to Napoleon and
later to Louis XVIII.
1. Joachim Murat (1767–1815), King of Naples.
2. Jean Lannes (1769–1809), duc de Montebello, marshal of France.
3. Lannes was mortally wounded during Napoleon's defeat at Aspern-Essling,
Austria, May 22, 1809.

Buonaparte to deceive & sacrifice them all, one after the other, is to me extraordinary. Maria Louisa had given Gerard an easel with her cypher, and as his wife told us this, she said with a sigh, "tres aimable." Poor Maria Louisa! married to the Emperor at the time of his highest glory. Who knows what thoughts & anticipations swelled her youthful bosom? Who knows her dreams of future greatness & future grandeur, to be the empress at 19 of the Hero of the World. At so young an age to be so elevated, was to all affecting, but at so young an age to be elevated with every prospect of greatness, and to suffer nothing but agony & distress — here is the moral! She is gone, her son no longer a monarch, and her husband in exile, in contempt. O God, if ever the hand of Providence was writ in the affairs of this World, it has been visible in the conduct and conclusion of this man's career.

As to Gerard's Art, he has certainly in his Portraits the power of making a strong likeness, but there is no feeling in his character or colour, — wretched, smooth, green, & blue mud & filth, flimsy & varnishy things. I felt sick, heartily sick, and disgusted at such mawkish marble, at such hard, square vulgar ivory. Let me banish it from my memory at once.

France at this moment and Paris in particular is most interesting. So many remarkable events have happened, so many people are alive that have seen the beginning and the end, that the recollections of the commonest beggar, or the most unlettered mind, are full of novelty and subject. "Ah," said an old respectable man to me yesterday in the Palais Royal, "this is indeed a Sunday, and makes one quiet and composed after the turbulence of twenty years."

In the evening I went to all the gaming houses in the Palais Royal. They are certainly worth seeing. What is considered a heinous offence in a man in England is thought nothing of in a woman here. The scale of virtue & vice is altered. There the question is are they guilty of crime if what they do is not considered such? — but then you must come to what is crime morally considered or what is not. If the happiness & ties of Society are split, if virtuous pursuits are neglected, if families have a greater chance of being rendered miserable than happy by gaming — gaming is not so laudable a study as many other things essential to human existence. I think that the consequence of any pursuit carried to excess should be considered, and if carrying any pursuit to excess would be vicious or ruinous, as much as you advance on the road, so much you approach to vice or ruin, in the degree. This applies more particularly to gaming. The expressions of disappointment, of agonizing disappointment, of silent, piercing, acute abstraction, of a dreamy, cold, perspiring vexation in some, of a long drawn leer of chuckling pleasure & yet suppressed triumph in others were apparent, were so apparent that no man could mistake what was passing within. Young women were wandering about, losing at one table and gaining at another, and old men & their wives alternately winning, failing, and then blaming. Never did I see such a scene. Certainly it was a scene of miserable, heated, midnight vice that without the extacies of voluptuous abandonment, had all the consequences of that excess. They looked jugged, fagged, worn out creatures, whose whole lives had been passed in one perpetual struggle of opposite passions. Gain was their wish, to this all was sacrificed. Their dress was neglected, they were dirty, & had all the look of dissipated filth. Hardly a word was spoken and [the] only thing that disturbed this hot, secret, & silent scene, was the tinkling of the money and the smart crack of the stick as the gamer wacked it into his bank.

June 14. Wilkie and I went to [the] Jardins des Plantes, and we were exceedingly delighted. There were some remains of Roman magnificence in suffering wild beasts to wander about at ease in spacious yards, without confinement or restraint. The collection of birds [and] insects were beyond any thing of the sort I had ever seen.

I declare to Heaven, that the more I think of Gerard's dreadful fac simile of Buonaparte, the more I feel as if all that approached him were destined to be his victims. Oh, that cruel, bloody, glassy eye, that looked you through without mercy, without feeling!

So infinitely various is nature, so mishapen and so absurd in form are many insects & animals, that we could not help fancy-

ing as we looked at them that they were the produce of un-
methodized chance, tho' to him that studies them, they have
all the plan & clearness of arrangement. God forgive me for this
fancy — evil may come into the mind of God or man, so it pass
unapproved.

The Skeleton of Kleber's murderer[4] is kept, the bones of his
right hand black from the burning — he was impaled. An old
Soldier was devoured last year by the bear in descending for a
five frank piece a Gentleman had dropped the preceding day,
and ever since they have called the bear by the man's name!
Instead of feeling horror, they think it a good joke!

June 16. Saw the King and the Dutchess of Angouleme at
Chapel. The King has not a foolish head, but a keen, acute eye.
I expect great firmness from his look. The silence was so intense
that you could hear the lamps burn, with a sort of gleaming
flutter.

June 17. Went to Versailles. The Chateau has a look of ruined
splendour, and the Town of desolate devastation. Painted ceil-
ings faded! Crimson tapestry torn! Golden friezes brown with
age, and every thing wearing an appearance as if a thousand
years ago there had been a nightly tournament, and that since
it had sunk & withered under the stroke of a mighty enchanter.

The Palace of Versailles in its glory must have been a gleaming jewel. Invention seems to have been racked to find excuses for
new habitations. I wonder they did not build a room for the
King's right hand and a room for his left, a room in short for
every action of his body and every conception of his mind. The
opera house was vast & melancholy, ruinous & dark. Here Maria
Antoinette sat the night of her marriage, young, lovely, & blushing! Here were assembled all that was beautiful, and all that was
splendid, to bewilder her youthful sense, and left her dreaming
of uninterrupted happiness and undisputed dominion. Her evil
genius hovered over all, and with demoniac chuckle revelled at
her approaching misery; had she been endued with immortal
acuteness, she would have heard his devilish laugh, as the music
died on the wind or undulated on the waters. I dwelt on the

4. Soleyman, a Syrian fanatic (see I,200 n.).

place in which she had sat with mute abstraction. What had passed since that night! to a female the happiest of her life! that night of young, inexperienced, delighted anticipation! Good God, in every congratulation of an adoring friend, a deep sigh might have been heard from her Angel; to every exclamation of blessings on her marriage, a satanic, evil laugh echoed through the vaulted ceiling from her spirit! His gigantic wings already flapped a gentle soothing air that entrapped, as it deceived, & soothed as it destroyed her! Peace to her soul, young & beautiful creature!

During the revolution, a little wing was made a barrack of [soldiers] and bore evident marks of their ferocity.

At the end of the great Park is Great Trianon and Little Trianon, built by Louis XIV. In Great Trianon Buonaparte occasionally resided, and here in his study were marks of recent habitation. When at Trianon, this was the study of Buonaparte, "the disturber of the poor World's peace." It was simply but conveniently fitted, with desks at every book case. On the one which he more used than the others, were two candlesticks and four smaller ones for other purposes. The place where he leant was rubbed; the chair where he sat was worn; the books behind were mostly military, Campaign to Egypt, Returns of the Army, & Histories of the Different Nations. On another desk was a candlestick with a shade for reading. The fire place had a look of recent use; the tongs and poker were black. The next room was his bath and while he bathed his Mameluke Rostan[5] always stood at the door outside, as there was a stair case close to it.

The Pictures were wretched, as they mostly [are] in the Palaces here. The whole Palace was elegantly & luxuriantly furnished. The gardens were formal & disagreeable to me. Versailles' gardens, the admiration of all France, I must own are studied & affected. How any human eye can look at the sweet, unaffected beauty & simplicity of the English garden at Petit Trianon and then prefer the stiff pedantry of the other, is to me a wonder. Of its kind, certainly Versailles' Gardens are fine —

5. Roustan, or Roustam Raza (1780–1845). At the age of six, he was kidnaped from his native Georgia and enslaved in Cairo to be trained as a mameluke. The Sheik of Cairo presented him to Napoleon, and Roustan became his confidential valet.

open & expansive, and when the jets d'eau are playing must be delightfully refreshing, but you are wearied with such preconceived art.

The roads in France are tedious beyond expression — long, endless threads, paved, jolting, & noisy.

Little Trianon was delightfully fitted up for Maria Louisa. This was the favourite palace of the poor Queen, and after the murder, was let to a Restaurateur.[6] On a large Picture at Versailles we saw 175 put on, which had remained there since the revolution & was placed when the Convention meant to sell the furniture of the Palace.

June 18. I set off by myself this morning to Rambouillet, the hunting seat of the Kings of France. It is a curious old Palace, two towers and joined by modern Architecture. I was exceedingly affected at going through the Chambers of Maria Louisa. Here she had been but lately; here she came on foot, the last league, with her child, when the Allies entered Paris. The rooms were precisely as she had left them. Her toilet was elegant; solitary by her bed stood her pianoforte, and her little boudoir was sweet & retired. The Servant told me she was exceedingly low & silent, and walked incessantly in the walks & grounds. She scarcely eat any meat for the last six days, & was exceedingly afflicted when she finally left the place. The crown of France seems to be an unfortunate temptation for an Austrian. She was very amiable & sweetly dispositioned, and what has she known but misery since at 19 she became Empress of France. I so well know the artificialities that swell the bosom of all at that age and at every age. I so well know how often at the very instant we imagine & dwell on our happiness that agony is approaching, that from my soul I feel for this young & unfortunate creature.

From her chambers, in melancholy mood, I passed to his, which were splendid & luxurious, and never shall I forget my sensations as I entered his salle de repos secret. Here was a compleat illustration of this extraordinary man's feelings. It

6. Wilkie wrote: "The house of Petit Trianon had been let out to a traiteur during the time of the Revolution, and had received considerable damage from the parties that used to frequent the house and gardens. But this seemed now to be entirely repaired" (Cunningham, I,418).

was a small room, with a satin couch & pillows under an arch. The room was decorated & over this arch was painted Austerlitz, Marengo, & Friedland. On each side were the arms of the states tributary to France, and under each were groups of warlike arms & instruments. Here he used to retire when exhausted, or when he wished for extreme & silent reflection. Here as he lay on his luxurious couch at ease, he was reminded of his former actions, and as he cast his eye down his walls, Austria, Prussia, Italy, and all his tributary states would fan his fancy or stimulate his mind to arrange new conquests. Here I stood, as it were, in the very midst of his soul. Here was his private, secret, sacred closet, painted & arranged by his own orders and for his own particular gratification. This was the stimulant to a Conqueror's appetite. What indecencies are to a debauchee, these mementos are to a tyrant. Here he lay in dim twilight, reveled in associations of dominion, and visions of conquest. Here perhaps he lay & fired his mind to the gigantic enterprise against Russia. He never arose but with his mind filled with bold designs, his blood fevered, his brain in a blaze! I almost trembled to look round & reflect that I stood in the secret sensations of one that made the world shake, that had first been the admiration, then the terror, at last the detestation of the Earth. It was singular, interesting, and dreadful. I enjoyed the full luxury of meditation. The Conductor seemed amused at my appearance of intense abstraction, and never spoke till I recovered my perceptions.

The Garden à l'Anglois was very fine, much finer than & cleaner and better kept than any I had seen. The forest was immense, and [in] the old Tower at the top was a room where Francis 1er died. I returned to Versailles after a short repast, and the next morning,

June 19, set off with Wilkie for Malmaison, St. Cloud, & Paris. The road was picturesque, hilly, & variegated. Tho' paved, it was a sort of cross road, and from the top of the hill, we had a beautiful view of Versailles. A M. Richard had a villa in the neighbourhood, and in passing by the park gate, we met his English steward, who had almost forgotten his language. He told [us] at present the Aldobrandini family had got it, and that if we asked for M. Etatte at Malmaison we might see it, as the House was shut up. By enquiring at the Palace, we were admitted to her, she was English, but could scarcely understand or answer me. As Josephine was but lately dead,[7] the house was closed, and we could only see the Picture Gallery. The collection was the best I had met with out of the Louvre. There [were] many exquisite specimens, and one of Titian in finer preservation than any Picture of his I had ever seen. The state of this delicious picture compleatly proves that the skies & back ground, which come forward & are blue, have been rubbed, for here was a sky, retiring & yet rich, in perfect harmony. All the Titians in the Louvre are ruined in comparison with this, Pietro Martyre[8] not excepted. Here were some statues by Canova, which raised my opinion of his powers immensely. They were fleshy & soft, and his feet defined with the feeling of the Venus. His hands & wrists were very bad. In the middle of the room was a small statue found at Necropolis, near Alexandria, some fresco paintings from Herculaneum, wretched affairs, a green tin box, one of them to hold the manuscript, like this [a sketch]. A fine Ostade & Wouverman & Paul Potter & Cuyp, and a Picture of Pietro Carloni[9] that gave me a higher opinion of him than any that I had ever seen. The man had strict orders not to suffer any sketching or to leave any one alone. This compleatly proves that in France, private collections are as difficult of access as in England, and that their boast of easy admission is confined to their public galleries.

We then drove to St. Cloud, which we could not see, as the Comte d'Artois[1] was there for his health, but I do not wonder at Buonapate's preference of St. Cloud. It is beautifully situated, and the trees higher & more full of foliage than any I had observed in France. We returned to Paris highly amused with our jaunt.

7. Empress Josephine died on May 24, 1814.
8. Titian's "Martyrdom of St. Peter Martyr," returned to the church of Santi Giovanni e Paolo in Venice but destroyed by fire in 1867.
9. Doubtless an error for Giovanni Andrea (1590–1630) or Giovanni Battista Carloni (1594–1677).
1. Charles Philippe (1757–1836), comte d'Artois, brother of Louis XVI and Louis XVIII; he ruled as Charles X from 1824 to 1830.

June

Every where do you meet with the consequences of the gigantic wars that have desolated Europe. There is scarcely a waiter at a coffee house or a coachman of France that has not served as a Soldier, been in a battle, or received a wound. On going to Rambouillet, I took up a fine youth, [who] was going to join his Friends, and had been wounded at Chaumont. He was just nineteen, delicate & slender. He came from Chartres and told me he had sat off with 60 companions from the same town, and that he was the only one alive. He belonged to the grenadiers of the foot guard! "Grenadier," said the coach man, who had been wounded at Fleurus, and looking at me with a shrug, said, "his whole army, Sir, was like these boys at last." Poor youth, he had been stripped by the Cossacks and had wandered into Paris, half naked & bleeding. Here he told [me] if it had not been for the benevolence of the Princess of Moskwa, Ney's[2] Lady, he must have died. She took him into the house with many others, gave him soup, and as he was nearly well, had presented him with 40 francs, got his discharge, and had clothed him from head to foot, to send him to his Friends, to whom she had written when he was out of danger. He really wept as he told me. He said if Buonaparte had reigned longer, he would have murdered all the World, and then made war upon the animals. He said at the beginning of the battle, he was frightened, & trembled to see his companions falling about him, torn & cut.

As I came back I took in a Chasseur who had served in Spain, and complained horribly of his sufferings. This is a way in France. At every step you meet with nothing but Soldiers, or those that have been so, wounded, or maimed, or worn out in the Service. The present army are literally boys, and the Veterans that remain have a ruined look. The contradictory state of the minds of the people is singular. They hate Buonaparte, and yet they glory in his Victories. They will tell you stories of his genius & execrate his government in the same breath; talk of him as a conqueror, they fire with enthusiasm; speak of him as King, they curse & detest him. They would have liked the fame without the trouble & suffering.

2. Marshal Michel Ney (1769–1815), prince de la Moskova.

371

They like the King who is returned, and yet they would like too to have Napoleon as their General. A young officer told me when the Emperor spoke to them as they were going up a hill against some Russians, "Doucement, mes camarades, douce-ment." He damned the Corps Legislatif, and he said the Emperor told [them,] "Je vous abolirai, Corps Legislatif, and Messieurs Senateurs, prenez garde de vous memes." He said he had been betrayed, and concluded with a low voice, saying if he was but now here, Louis XVIII was but a boy! He was a compleat specimen of French versatility. His chest was ornamented with fleurs de lis, and Napoleon eagles he still kept with a lingering fondness on his coat. "You are still Napoleon at your heart," to which he winked assent.

At Versailles I saw Hamlet *traduit* and rendered fit for the French stage.[3] Ophelia was murdered,[4] and Hamlet literally rendered a blubbering boy. "Oh ma mere, mon pere." Ophelia is with Hamlet entreating by her affection to be more composed, when his Mother enters. Here, as he is talking, he sees the Ghost. The impression on the audience and the effect on me was certainly dreadful. I shall never forget it and it has shaken my orthodoxy as to the admission of the Ghost. It was truly terrific to see Talma's[5] terrible look, and the stupified amazement of his Mother & mistress. There was some cause for their amazement, when nothing was seen. Hamlet in the next scene brings out an urn that contains his Father's ashes. Here was true French whine & affectation. Tho when his Mother again returns, and he makes her swear she knew nothing of her husband's murder, and brings her to touch his sacred ashes, there was an awful silence and a severe agony throughout the House. The Translator has compleatly lost Shakespeare's exquisite feeling of a "grief within

3. Wilkie's diary dates the performance June 17 (Cunningham, I,419). The translation was actually an adaptation made by Ducis and widely differing from Shakespeare's text. For variant editions, see Mary B. Vanderhoof, "Hamlet, a Tragedy Adapted from Shakespeare (1770) by Jean François Ducis. A Critical Edition" (*Proceedings of the American Philosophical Society*, February 14, 1953, 97:88–142).

4. Ophelia dies in none of Ducis' versions. Gertrude, however, kills herself in the versions of 1809 and 1813 but was murdered by Claudius in earlier versions.

5. François Joseph Talma (1763–1826), French tragic actor.

that passeth shew"[6] by making his Hamlet's grief all shew! and nothing else.

June 20. Went to Catacombs.[7] Singular & solemn.

June 21. To the Temple where Louis XVI was confined, but it was pulled down & no vestige of the place remaining in the Garden.

June 23. At the Theatre Francais last night, when the King in Hamlet said,

> Laissons à l'Angleterre et son deuil et ses pleurs
> L'Angleterre en forfaits trop souvent fut feconde,[8]

the whole House burst forth in applause of the most tumultuous fury. This was mean & paltry, and was only the effusion of impotent malice for having been well beaten. It was the mouthing of a beaten boy, who lies on the ground afraid to rise from the experience he has had of his adversary's strength. The people about us looked at us, but we were so high we did not hear distinctly what had been said. Had I distinctly heard it, I would have certainly said something. There was some row beneath us and I suspect from English men opposing.

June 25. It is curious to observe in the Louvre those Pictures which have the most effect. Breadth, brightness, & size & depth bear down all opposition; greyness, Teniers, has no chance, or Rembrandt, brownness, as little. When I was looking [at] Champaigne and saw good drawing, expression, & colour well finished, I could not help wondering he had escaped a reputation, but this is reputation, is it in parts — whereas Rubens, without beauty, without conception of character, without fine touches in form, without grace, has obtained and will ever keep, a splendid reputation. The reason is what ever he felt, he felt as a whole. It was his gigantic comprehension in the lowest parts of the art that

---

6. *Hamlet,* I,ii,85. "I have that within which passeth show."
7. "The catacombs at the Barrière d'Enfer," according to Wilkie (Cunningham, I,421).
8. Ducis (1809), III,ii,106–107 (Vanderhoof, "Hamlet," p. 133).

gave him a reputation over those who had many of the higher individual requisites in a greater degree.

Went to see Talleyrand's[9] Pictures — very fine. They were hung in the room where the Peace was signed.[1] In his bed room was the Times newspaper.

Vandyke looked black; Teniers dirty; Rembrandt brown; Rubens overpowered all near him by the vigour & purity of his traits. In his bed chamber also were portraits of all the sovereigns of Europe. This was *his* delight, too. The House was comfortable, elegant. At the corner was a restaurateur, and bills were stuck directly under the drawing room Windows.

June 27. Studied Titian's Pietro Martyre with profound attention. Indeed to the Italian School you must turn for all the refinements of the Art. The expression of the executioner's head is truly wonderful; he has cut his victim down, and feels all that grating as if a razor had touched his heart; it can hardly be described — not in a brutal manner, but with a sort of ah! as if he felt for every cut.

The compleat, exhausted, languid, and yet penetrating look of the monk is sublime. He is dying; he is mortally wounded, and yet gives a last look of helpless superiority, as if a burst of thunder had crashed out with his last look. The management is fine, but the principal light by no means palpable. Expression is "all in all";[2] every thing must & does sink after a little time, however attractive, by expression.

Paul Veronese looks certainly flat and unsubstantial; Rubens, full, vigourous, & vast. His power of handling is dashed, terrible, overpowering. His feeling of a whole as to masses & composition has given him, and will ever give him, a reputation in spite of his want of grace, beauty, expression, poetical conception of character, or any of the great requisites of Art. Surely there must be something extraordinary in a man who can obtain & keep

9. Charles-Maurice de Talleyrand-Périgord (1754–1838), prince de Bénévent, statesman.
1. The First Treaty of Paris, signed on May 30, 1814, sought to establish lasting peace in Europe after Napoleon's first abdication and arranged for the Congress of Vienna.
2. William Cowper, "Table Talk," l. 542. "Manner is all in all."

a splendid Fame in spite of such deficiencies. Tintoretto, strawey, rushed, & careless, without the solidity of Titian or Rubens; Titian full of sweetness, feeling, & sensation.

The present French Artists have immense knowledge, but their taste is bad. They know not how to avail themselves of it — how to marshal, order, & direct it. The principles of costume are excellent. The things they introduce are the very things that ought [to be] & nothing more or less. They belong to that people, only. I hope to avail myself of this principle. I shall go back greatly enlarged in every thing. I have gone regularly down the French, Flemish, & Dutch Schools, and this day have began the Italian Schools. In Baroccio there is a marble look as if his Pictures were [made] with veined marble.

June 28. Saw Gobelin tapestry of Raphael's works — gave me an exact idea of their size, and some of their breadth, colour, & character.[3]

> Vive Buonaparte
> Vive ce grand conquerant
> Ce diable de Buonaparte
> A bien plus de talents
> Que votre Henri quatre
> Et tous ses descendants

This verse the French officers have added.

Spent the day at the private library of the Institute, copying the dresses of the Ancient Egyptians, from the great Work published by Napoleon;[4] exceedingly useful. The French expedition to Egypt has been proved a great delight to the learned, by the exposition of several cities, which no single Traveller could explore before. The consequence to us Painters is a complete series of the costumes, features, & manners of the inhabitants, copied from their temples, still perfect & uninjured. They are worth the sacrifice they have made.

3. Wilkie recorded that he and BRH saw the Gobelins on June 30 (Cunningham, I,428).

4. *Description de l'Egypte, ou recueil des observations et des recherches qui ont été faites en Egypte pendant l'expedition de l'armée française,* ed. E. F. Jomard, 20 vols., Paris, 1809–1828.

July 3. My dear Wilkie set off this morning for England; in spite of Wilkie's heaviness of perception and total want of spirit as to gentlemanly feeling, his simplicity & honesty of manner, his good sense and natural taste endear one to him. I feel low at his departure, tho' I shall soon see him.

Wilkie and I came to France at a very interesting period. The effects of the revolution were not over; the shops were all open on a Sunday. The next week, "l'ordonnance du Roi" made its appearance. Of course it was a subject for amusement to this light, airy, elegant people. The Sunday after it my Landlord, who is a Turner, seemed to feel rather awkwardly at not working; the second Sunday he seemed relieved, and the third he brushed his coat, went to Church, and in the evening took a walk with his femme & petite. I have no doubt he would as lustily defend the comfort of the order now, as he would have ridiculed it at its commencement.

July 4. Saw the Cartoon Raphael, the original cartoon for the School of Athens — exceedingly fine.[5] Not remarkable for drawing but for breadth and a whole. The heads of the boys talking to Archimedes beautiful, the hands finely sketched, the whole composed in a masterly manner, and with true feeling. It was really delightful to see something in this way after the insolent imbecility of the present French pictures. Some Spanish Pictures also, two very fine Murillos and a fine sketch by Velasquez.

When a man finishes so highly as to lose Appearance of touch, he gets entirely rid of all association of Idea, because a touch is the result of an Impression on the mind, expressed rapidly by the hand. Rubens ranks high because his works are all thought, not refined or elevated, but thought of some sort or other. There is nothing material, nothing laboured; his thoughts are expressed as they occurred, without hesitation. This is the reason of the delight his works give.

July 6. Left Paris in the Diligence for Fontainbleau in company with six ladies. Finding I was an English man very shortly, they all attacked me. "England was too rich for the happiness of

---

5. This cartoon is now in the Biblioteca Ambrosiana in Milan.

France." "Oh oui, oh oui!" Paris was betrayed, one Lady swore to it, and said Marmont had been paid 3000 francs; "Pardon, Madam," said the other, "3500. I know it, too."

Peace was then discussed, and Peace would be the ruin of France!!! and had been the salvation of England!!! "Sans doute, sans doute," said they all, twirling their little ruffles, and darting their little black eyes at me with such little, coquetting, impudent triumph & sweetness that one could not resist letting them have it all their own way. There is such pretty little affectation in every thing a French woman does or says, that tho' you cannot esteem it, you would not like to see them without it. Every little creature has her ridicule, and away they go, tripping & mincing their steps as if they trod on needles. "Are your Ladies pretty?" said one, the prettiest among them.

After taking leave of these creatures, I secured a room and sallied forth to see the Chateau, which I found gorgeous beyond description. Napoleon's bed was hung with the richest green Lyons silk, with painted roses of richest crimson, satin of the purest white, with golden stars on the covering of the foot stool; behind or inside was a magnificent mirror, which reflected the bed, and the ceiling was one immense mass of gold & silver. In the private Salon of Josephine was a sofa, from the Grand Senior, silver net work with gold flowers. No Arabian tale, or Caliph of Bagdad, or Sultan of the Turks, & no Monarch of Babylon, or Emperor of India ever exceeded in their palaces the gorgeous splendour & voluptuous magnificence of these apartments.

The man who shewed me had lived with Napoleon 10 years; he talked of him with mournful respect. He told me his conduct was always polite & affectionate to Maria Louisa; he shewed me all the rooms he occupied latterly and told me he saw him with[in] ten minutes after he had signed his abdication, and that he had not the least appearance of crying; he behaved with courage & firmness throughout, and the only time he could discover by his appearance was the morning after he had tried to get into Paris and found it taken. When he returned to Fontainbleau, he was pale, agitated, & shaken, and this man observed it as he waited on him from his carriage. In an hour or so he recovered, and never after did he shew the slightest symptom of alarm. I strolled out in the evening to see the Imperial Guard on foot parade. There were 2500 of them here; the remainder of the 8000 were quartered in the different villages. More dreadful fellows I certainly never saw. Their appearance really impressed me. They have the look of thorough bred veterans, a disciplined banditti, without the irregularity but with all the depravity; desperate indifference, & blood were burnt into their veteran faces; black mustachios, gigantic caps, a slouching air, and a ferocious expression are their characteristic marks. Conducted by the talents of Buonaparte, what would have become of the World if they ruled it? Principle and intellect would have vanished from its surface, & morality & virtue [would] have been crushed. A sight of his guards would cure his admirers.

In the court yard during the evening I got into conversation with some of them. They told me how they cried when he left them, and one said when the Standard bearer was ordered to bring him an Eagle, he turned away his head, as he delivered it to the Emperor, he was weeping so profusely. Colonel Campbell [6] cried, as well as the Prussian & Austrian Commission, but not the Russian. "Did the Emperor cry?" said I. "Non," said a Grenadier, "Bougre, il etoit toujours firme!"

While dinner was preparing, I took a stroll through the Town. In one retired street I saw a Nun standing at a door. I went up to her and asked if it was a nunnery. She said it was not, but that if I would walk in I might be interested. I followed her up stairs and found it a hospital, and all the wounded and sick in the nicest possible order & cleanliness. Higher up I entered a room in which a Nun on her knees was reading prayers to those who were in the most dangerous state. Some were sitting up with pillows at their backs, others too weak for such an effort were lying on their backs, without strength to move or look, repeating in long tremulous sounds the prayers; some crossed themselves with anxious devotion, and all were so intensely occupied & silently abstracted, that our entrance was unregarded, and no one for an instant turned his feverous eye towards us. We retired calmly, & I, deeply affected by the solemn quiet of the scene. Below I again went in, and here, the sick being in a state of recovery, regarded

6. Sir Neil Campbell (1776–1827), who escorted Napoleon to Elba.

me with a look of eager debility & pallid anxiety; on every side a dozen sparkling eyes watched & met me. In the medicine room down stairs, I observed French names on all the bottles. "We put them in Latin," said I. "Yes, but for us to understand they must be in French," she answered. "We never call in a Surgeon unless it be a broken limb or a case of great danger." As I was going away, I felt awkwardly as to what I should give her for her trouble, and putting my hand into my pocket, and then taking it out, at seeing her; she perceived my embarrassment, and with the sweetest air, held out her hand, with "for the poor, perhaps, Sir." The French women are full of such delicacies of manner.

At nine o'clock the drums of the Imperial [Guard] beat their round, with a stormy crash and unity, as if all were actuated by an impulse of one. It set the mind immediately alive, and every association of battle & war crowded, till images were obliterated by their number.

Again do I touch the Shores of Old England.[7] My sensations were grand. Never did she stand higher, or on a more glorious point. As I approached her sacred shores, and France vanished from my view, I felt as if my journey had been a dream, as if it was ages & centuries behind the mighty barrier of the ocean that rose like a huge wall & intercepted all sight. I regret Paris, I feel melancholy at leaving the delightful gaity, *"si aimable, si naive."* I have seen many, many virtuous women, good wifes, the tenderest Mothers mixed with a polished sensibility that touched one's heart. Their manners are exquisite, but in the men there is a careless ferocity of feeling that stamps them. A Frenchman will tell you of a murder as a joke, an Englishman with a natural horror, because War is never felt in England, and murder [is] as strange. A Frenchman would kill a man by accident, and not regret it, but talk of it with an affected lamentation, while the satisfaction of the Devil would illume his eyes. The great business of the Continent is fighting — this is their last finish to the tournure of a Gallant Youth, to be interesting, to be desirable, the bloody air of a campaign must infuse its effect, and then his education is compleat. A Frenchman always assumes more than

7. BRH's authorization to embark from Calais, attached to the diary, is dated July 17, 1814.

he has any right to, an Englishman never half as much. There is a noble simplicity about the English, as if they were unconscious of any thing, while the Frenchman is invested with such pompous pretence as if he was inspired by Heaven and despised all those who were less happy.

The French are a gay, volatile, brave Nation, with a great deal of the ferocity of a Tiger, but thank God, without the strength. They have no radical judgement, no broad capacity of thinking deeply. They have no general knowledge.

The morning I left Paris I called on Denon, and had a long and instructive conversation with him. He thought the early Egyptians negroes, and that they had been driven out by a different People because on all the temples he had seen a hero killing a negro, where battles were the subject. But why should the Negroes have been the Inhabitants of Egypt because Heroes were represented killing them? Is it on record of a whole Nation being extirpated by another so compleatly as to superseed it? Why may not the Heroes be the real inhabitants triumphing over their neighbouring enemies? This appears to me the most likely conclusion.

When I defended Lord Elgin's conduct at Athens, because the Turks destroyed them, he affirmed the Turks destroyed nothing!!! He shewed me bits of the Pyramids & Statue of Memnon, bits of the rocks at the Cataracts, and Stones of the Desert, which were horribly yellow.

The French in surrendering their city saved their lives, and the first impulse urged them to thank Marmont, but recovering their senses, and finding their reputation injured, they swear they were betrayed, and Paris should rather have been burnt. This is the boasting of cowards.

Oh how the honest simplicity of the English character affected me at entering England. Never shall I forget how seriously and affectionately two men cautioned me against the danger of leaning carelessly against the machine by which they were landing horses on the quay. "Two days ago, Sir, a poor young fellow was squeezed as flat as a cake, I assure [you]," said they, with a look of real concern. From being in France and continually hearing the French talk of murders and horrors, with a bloody politeness and a ferocious elegance, a chuckling sneer, or a witty indifference, I looked at them with a species of wonder at making so much of a young man being squeezed to Death! But then in England, his connections & family ties are always associated, the agony of his Mother, the tears of his Sister, the sympathies of his children, or the distraction of his wife, their wants & their sufferings, his unhappy fate, & their miserable distress, appear to an honest English heart, as sources of pain & causes of unconcealed grief.

I do not wonder at the Nations of the continent having a contempt for the English, when they only know them from external appearance. Of all Nations on Earth, I think the air of the English is the most awkward, both in Men & Women; the Women with exquisite figures, plump bosoms, destroy the effect of both by a clodhopping clumsy role, as if they wished to be remote from affectation, no doubt, but as if they were indifferent to appearance. The Men with the noblest chests and finest heads have an unexpressive cut in comparison with the Nations of the continent, that must have given these military nations a notion as if all the inward qualities of the Soul were wanting. But O God, the qualities of England's soul are always in reserve for grand occasions, and ever veiled when they would be needless.

To stroll amidst lascivious women, to attract the gaze of the idle, or the wonder of the ignorant, are not objects that can expand the bosom of England, or dilate her form, but let the World be in danger [of] despotic oppression, or bloody ravagement, let the Widow be in want, or the infant be starving, look then at England's heroic stature! Her eyes sparkle, her form encreases, her whole air & attitude assume the undaunted courage of a Hero, the mercy of a Christian, & the power of a God. The World relieved & her duty effected her gigantic grandeur, her heroic virtues are gradually lost in her natural simplicity of her external appearance, adequate to the common duties of life, and lie in secret, nourished but not extinguished, till great occasions again rouse them & the World are again in want.

In every French Soldier there is a look of hatred, rapine, & blood, while the rosy generosity of an Englishman's face soften the horrors of his profession and take off the ferocity of look. All that elegant, martial politeness in the Soldier, of which we have so much read, is gone, nearly gone. Twenty years' robbery & murder, tyranny & despotism, have given the Soldiers, the Officers, a look & a feeling of disciplined lawlessness and methodized depravity that makes one shudder.

July 20. I met a Young Couple going to France to settle, ignorant of the language, ignorant of the manners, young, thoughtless, & just married. The Woman, a sweet young creature beautifully formed, full of interest, of heart, of feeling & innocence, resolved to follow her husband, who had, from what I gathered, been unfortunate and was resolved to try his fortune in other Countries. I felt immediately affected by their story, and assisted them by advice and directions when they arrived in France. They thanked me with honest gratitude, and the sparkle of her sweet eyes, shewed the purity and artless sensations of her heart.

They are just gone. Each shook me heartily by the hand, each wished me health & happiness, I looked out of the window as they walked away, and caught a glimpse of her sweet form, springing lightly, with a sort of clinging hilarity to her husband, which seemed to insinuate, "my love, rely on my devotion," and before they could make another stride, the projection of the street hid them from my view. Peace & happiness go with them! They are gone — to combat & fight in the struggles of life, in health and adequate to its fatigues, and in vigour and able for its misfortunes. Never may I again meet them "in this dim spot." [8] This sensation is romantically melancholy and sweet. Farewell, you innocent & tender creatures, happy in each other's affection, & content in each's love, farewell.

There is something drearily melancholy, solitary, when we all separate to our respective duties, and yet the sensation of meeting again after long & successful effort, is perhaps more delightful than the pain of separation is acute. All the sensations of life to me are pleasures. I can always sublimely abstract in trouble & enjoy the sweets of acute meditation. I do not know whether the fatigue after pleasure is not more painful than the fatigue of misfortune. All the strongest qualities of the mind are called into

8. *Comus*, l. 5.

action by difficulties, & the pleasure of resistance is an adequate support for all.

I am glad to see the military now keep their heads as they deserve, and take their places by the side of the Navy. Captain King,[9] who commanded the Jason Frigate, told me today on the Pier, that old Blucher,[1] as he stood looking towards England from the quarter deck of his ship, muttered to himself, as the tears trickled from his eyes, "that's a fine Country." Capt. King said he was convinced he did not know he was observed or heard, for no body but himself was immediately near him. Capt. King repeated, "He really cried tho' he tried to conceal it, Sir." He was sailing in the Jason to Ostend, and leaving England perhaps for ever. Glory & peace to his heroic old Spirit!

August 18. Began my Picture in reality. My heart swelled as I touched it.

August 19. Proceeded with vigour & encreased delight, my mind filled with the great examples of art I had seen.

[*A sketch of Christ's entry into Jerusalem.*]

"And a great Multitude spread their garments in the way; others cut down branches from the trees and strawed them in the way. And the multitudes that went before and that followed after, cryed, saying, 'Hosanna to the Son of David! Blessed is he that cometh in the name of the Lord. Hosanna in the Highest.' And when he was come into Jerusalem, all the city was moved, saying, 'Who is this?' And the multitude said, 'This is Jesus, the prophet of Nazareth.' " [2]

[*The next three pages of the diary contain quotations from Isaiah, Matthew,* Paradise Lost, *the* Iliad, *and the* Aeneid.]

Siècle de Louis XIV, Voltaire. Tome 2, Page 123. "Les genres dont les sujets se renouvellent sans cesse, comme l'histoire, les observations physiques, et qui ne demandent que du travail, du

9. Captain the Hon. James William King. The *Jason* was frequently used to convey distinguished visitors between England and the Continent.
1. Prince Gebhard Leberecht von Blücher (1742–1819), Prussian field marshal.
2. Matthew, 21:8–11.

What ignorance of the animal! —
So much is the mind able
to conceive and to find when uninformed
by Practice & investigation!

A preliminary sketch for "Christ's Entry into Jerusalem," August 1814.

jugement, et un esprit commun, peuvent plus aisément se soutenir; et les arts de la main, comme la Peinture, la sculpture, *peuvent ne pas dégénérer, quand ceux qui gouvernent ont, à l'example de Louis XIV, l'attention de n'employer que les meilleurs artists.* Car on peut, en Peinture et en sculpture, traiter cent fois les mêmes sujets; on peint encore la sainte famille, quoique Raphaël ait déployé dans ce sujet toute la supériorité de son art, mais on ne serait pas reçu à traiter Cinna, Andromaque, l'Art poétique, et le Tartuffe." [3]

If employment from the Government is only necessary to make great Painters, why are not the Painters of the *siècle* as great as those of Leo Xth's? They were encouraged with the same magnificence. They had the same opportunities. They had the same field for the exercise of their fancy. This has always [been] the way with literary People. They only see the means & never the mind of Painting, because the vehicle of thought is imitation. Imitation to them is the end & whole of the Art.

The hand of Painting is certainly of more importance to him than the hand of Poetry, but only in as much as it is more beautiful per se. You must write your thoughts, as you must paint them, but painting your ideas no more degrades the conception than writing them. Does Voltaire mean to say that because the same subject can be a hundred times repeated in Painting it can be always repeated with equal power? Does he mean to say that government can, when they please, order Holy Families and obtain them when they order them, as they obtain & order shoes for the Army? All subjects in Poetry & Painting are inexhaustible, if they apply to any human vice or virtue, characteristic or feeling, and it is only from the narrow field on which Cinna, Andromache, l'art Poétique, or Tartuffe are planned. If it is impossible to repeat them, it is impossible to repeat with equal success any effusion of talent that was written & applied to any reigning folly at the time, but it is not impossible to write & repeat the subjects of tragedies & poems, which apply to any unalterable principle of human weakness & human sentiment. It is not impossible to repeat any subject, and as often as a Man of Genius ap-

3. Voltaire, *Le Siècle de Louis XIV*, new edition, Chapter 23, "Des Beaux Arts" (Amsterdam, 1764, II,222–223).

pears, and he that would not venture to repeat them is not a Man of Genius. Does he mean to say that because Holy Families have been repeated they have all displayed equal genius with Raphael? Besides, it is not true as a simple fact, that L'Art Poetique cannot be repeated. Were not Boileau's a repetition of the Ars Poetica of Horace?

There is an ignorance throughout this whole sentence of Voltaire's confused view, a taking a mean for an end, which is extraordinary. Bowpeep[4] near Hastings, Sep. 1814.

[The next five pages of the diary contain a repetitious and unfinished draft apparently of an article on the necessity of an artist familiarizing himself with great works of the past.]

O God, grant my eyes vigour to execute & my conception purity, poetry, & vivid intensity to conceive the character of my blessed Saviour. Grant it, grant it, O God, I humbly pray thee. Amen, amen, with all my Soul. Sep. 16.

Genius can only have its full scope where, though much may have been done, more remains to be done, where models exist chiefly to shew the deficiencies of art, and where the perfect idea is left to be filled up in the painter's imagination. Where the stimulus of novelty and of necessary exertion is wanting, generations repose on what has been done for them by their predecessors, as individuals, after a certain period, rest satisfied with the knowledge they have already acquired.[5]

But this is precisely that state at present, and ever has been, and ever will be the state of the World, were 100 Painters greater than Raphael born at this moment, still more would remain to be done when their careers were over. Do you mean to say that Nature has been exhausted? that there is no longer any thing to be done, that nothing new, nothing great can any longer be attempted? Futile, vain, imbecile assertion, the product of dis-

4. Now St. Leonard's (Dorothy Hewlett, *A Life of John Keats*, New York, 1950, p. 109).
5. This paragraph, cut from the *Champion*, is attached to the diary. It is from Hazlitt's article entitled "Fine Arts, Whether they are Promoted by Academies and Public Institutions," in the issue of September 11, 1814, p. 295 (reprinted, with minor variants, in Hazlitt, XVIII,42–43).

appointed irritibility, of morbid vanity, & of conscious weakness, of deep rooted indolence, of that blurred & envious wretchedness the result of disappointed failure, of just aimlessness enough to know what ought to be done of that, & just perseverance enough to attempt and relinquish it. Alas, poor unhappy spirit, thou goest about the world & breathes thy blasting breath on every shoot of promise & every department of mind, from Art & Science to politics & Buonaparte, but shooting roots of Painting shall spread their [*an illegible word*] threads & in spite of the spittle & venom, with which thou demon like hast befrothed the earth in hopes to wither her when beneath the ground or to shrink her budding beauties when above it.

We shall conclude with offering some remarks on the question, — Whether Academies and Institutions must not be supposed to assist the progress of the fine arts by promoting a wider taste for them.

In general, it must happen in the first stages of the arts, that as none but those who had a natural genius for them, would attempt to practise them, so none but those who had a natural taste for them would pretend to judge of, or criticise them. This must be an incalculable advantage to the man of true genius, for it is no other than the privilege of being tried by his peers. In an age when connoisseurship had not become a fashion; when religion, war, and intrigue occupied the time and thoughts of the great, only those minds of superior refinement would be led to notice the works of art who had a real sense of their excellence, and in giving way to the powerful bent of his own genius, the painter was most likely to consult the taste of his judges. He had not to deal with pretenders to taste through vanity, affectation, and idleness. He had to appeal to the higher faculties of the soul; to that deep and innate sensibility to truth and beauty, which required only an object to have its enthusiasm excited; and to that independent strength of mind, which, in the midst of ignorance and barbarism, hailed and fostered genius, wherever it met with it. Titian was patronized by Charles V. — Count Castiglione was the friend of Raphael. These were true patrons, and true critics: and as there were no others (for the world in general merely looked on, and wondered) there can be little doubt, that such a period of dearth of factitious patronage, would be the most favourable to the full developement of the greatest talents, and the attainment of the highest excellence.[6]

6. Like the last quotation, this is also a cutting from the same article in the *Champion,* attached to the diary.

Do you think that there were no pretenders, no men who had desires without talents, who from longing to be painters sunk to be critics?

Why must it in general happen in the first stages that none but those who had a natural genius for this would attempt, and none but those with a natural taste would judge them? Is not the World pretty nearly alike in all times? Was it not as vicious as at present, and why should [it] have been more pure in matters of art? Did War & intrigue occupy the minds of the great more than *now?* Surely not, for they *had* not wars so vast, so important, so pregnant with human rights. As to the assertion that only those minds of superior refinement interfered, two simple facts will give the direct contradiction. The Soderini at Florence, who thought David's nose too big, Michel Angelo immediately ascended with some dust in his hand, and pretended to chisel the nose less by letting fall some dust at the same moment. The Soderini deceived, cried "exquisite, exquisite; it has now life." [7] Now here was a pretender to taste, a man too the principal Patron & Magistrate of Florence, Michel Angelo's greatest encourager, for whom he painted the Warriors in the Arno. Now I venture to think this is a proof that minds not very refined, not only interfered but patronised as well. Again the Cardinal at Rome who bought a Cupid for an antique, which was buried by Michel Angelo and executed as well,[8] and when he discovered his error, grew tired of the work and exchanged it. I do not mean to say that it would not have been better for Michel Angelo & Raphael had there been no pretenders, but I mean to shew an absence of smatterers were not the cause of their greatness, but there was no absence, and that nothing extraneous, no state of the World will either make Men of Genius or obstruct them. That their greatness is & always has been the consequence of their own intuitive vigour, which made the state of Society or the circumstances of life as much contribute to their success as if they had happened on purpose; the reverse is never asserted or believed but by those

7. The anecdote, according to Vasari's "Michelagnolo Buonarroti," concerns Piero Soderini, the gonfalonier of Florence (Vasari, IV,59).
8. According to Vasari, Cardinal San Giorgio bought this statue (Vasari, IV,50–51).

who have desires without ability and who are willing to attribute their own failure to any cause but their own want, and the success of their great predecessors to any consequence but their own powers. Genius now & always will be hailed with as much enthusiasm as ever, and a direct appeal to innate feelings of mankind would be rewarded with as much feeling as in the time of Raphael & Michel Angelo.

So far from war & intrigue occupying exclusively the minds of the great, those who may be supposed to be most occupied in such matters, were men of the greatest taste, and the greatest Patrons, Julius II, Leo X , & Charles Vth. Count Castilione was a mere man of taste; he never employed Raphael, he merely admired him. There you are — selection is your own reputation.

The diffusion of taste is not, then, the same thing as the improvement of taste; but it is only the former of these objects that is promoted by public institutions and other artificial means. The number of candidates for fame, and of pretenders to criticism, is thus increased beyond all proportion, but the quantity of genius and feeling remains the same, with this difference, *that the man of genius is lost in the crowd of competitors* who would never have become such, but from encouragement and example; and that the opinion of those few persons whom nature intended for judges, is drowned in the noisy decisions of shallow smatterers in taste. The principle of universal suffrage, however applicable to matters of government, which concern the common feelings and common interests of society, is by no means applicable to matters of taste, which can only be decided upon by the most refined understandings.[9]

You always attribute to second causes. Public Institutions do not harm the Art, it is the want of men of Genius to direct them that occasions their defective influence. A Man of Genius lost in the crowd!!! My heavens, what an assertion, as if a million of imbecile candidates & ten million of smatterers could obscure a man of Genius!!!!!!! It is the want of men of Genius, & not the encreased number of candidates, or judges, that cause the decay of Art. Whose fault is it that the People who crowd to Somerset House[1] become indignant before a "Guido & a Dante"? The fault of the Exhibition *per se*, or of the *Pictures* that fill it?

9. Continued from the preceding quotations from the *Champion*. The italics are BRH's.
1. Where the Royal Academy held its exhibitions.

I doubt whether Corregio is a melancholy instance of want of encouragement. He that was selected to paint a great Public Cupola[2] could not want much encouragement, or be very unknown. No rewards would make a Corregio, of course, but if your plans were adopted, another Corregio would not be likely [to] have his reward.

It is throwing down the barriers which separate knowledge and feeling from ignorance and vulgarity, and proclaiming a Bartholomew-fair-show of the fine arts —

"And fools rush in where angels fear to tread"—

to vanity and avarice — it is leading astray the youth of this nation by fallacious hopes, which can scarcely ever be realised; — it is beating up for raw dependents, sending out into the highways for the halt, the lame, and the blind, and making a scramble among a set of idle boys for prizes of the first, second, and third class, like those we make among children for gingerbread toys. True patronage does not consist in ostentatious professions of high keeping, and promiscuous intercourse with the arts. At the same time, the good that might be done by private taste and benevolence, is in a great measure prevented. The moment that a few individuals of taste and liberal spirit become members of a public body, they are no longer any thing more than parts of a machine, which is usually wielded at will by some overbearing, officious intruder; — their good sense and good nature are lost in a mass of ignorance and presumption, their names only serve to reflect credit on proceedings in which they have no share, and which are determined upon by a majority of persons who have no interest in the arts but what arises from the importance attached to them by regular organization, and no opinions but what are dictated to them by some self-constituted judge. Whenever vanity and self-importance are (as in general they must be) the governing principles of systems of public patronage, there is an end at once of all candour and directness of conduct. Their decisions are before the public; and the individuals who take the lead in these decisions, are responsible for them. They have therefore to manage the public opinion, in order to secure that of their own body. Hence instead of giving a firm, manly, and independent tone to that opinion, it is their business to watch all its caprices, and follow it in every casual turning. They dare not give their sanction to sterling merit, struggling with difficulties, but take

2. Correggio decorated the cupolas of two churches in Parma—"The Ascension of Christ" in San Giovanni Evangelista and "The Assumption of the Virgin" in the Duomo.

every advantage of its success to reflect credit on their own reputation for sagacity. Their taste is a servile dependent on their vanity, and their patronage has an air of pauperism about it. They neglect or treat with insult the favourite whom they suspect of having fallen off in the opinion of the public; but if he is able to recover his ground without their assistance, are ready to heap their mercenary bounties upon those of others, — greet him with friendly congratulations, and share his triumph with him.

Perhaps the only public patronage, which was ever really useful to the arts, or worthy of them, was that which they received first in Greece, and then in Italy, from the religious institutions of the country; when the artist felt himself, as it were, a servant of the altar, when his hand gave a visible form to gods or angels, heroes or apostles; and when the enthusiasm of genius was exalted by mingling with the flame of national devotion. The artist was not here degraded by being made the dependent on the caprice of wealth or fashion, but felt himself at once a public benefactor. He had to embody by the highest effort of his art subjects which were sacred to the imagination and feelings of the spectators: there was a common link, a mutual sympathy, between them, in their common faith.[3] — Every other mode of patronage but that which arises either from the general institutions of the country, or from the real unaffected taste of individuals, must, we conceive, be illegitimate, corrupted in its source, and either ineffectual or prejudicial to its object. Positive encouragements and rewards will not make an honest man, or a great artist. The assumed familiarity, and condescending goodness of patrons and vice-patrons will serve to intoxicate rather than to sober the mind, and a card to dinner in Cleveland-row or Portland place, will have a tendency to divert the student's thoughts from his morning's work, rather than to rivet them upon it. The device by which a celebrated painter has represented the Virgin teaching the infant Christ to read by pointing with a butterfly to the letters of the alphabet, has not been thought a very wise one. Cor-

---

3. Hazlitt's footnote: "Of the effect of the *authority* of the subject of a composition, in suspending the exercise of personal taste and feeling in the spectators, we have a striking instance in our own country, where this cause must, from collateral circumstances, operate less forcibly. Mr. West's pictures would not be tolerated, but from the respect inspired by the subjects of which he treats. When a young lady and her mother, the wife and daughter of a clergyman, are told, that a gawky ill-favoured youth is the beloved disciple of Christ, and that a tall, starched figure of a woman visible near him is the Virgin Mary, whatever they might have thought before, they can no more refrain from shedding tears, than if they had seen the very persons recorded in sacred history. It is not the picture, but the associations connected with it, that produce the effect. Just as if the same young lady and her mother had been told, 'that is the Emperor Alexander,' they would say, *'what a handsome man!'* or if they were shewn the Prince Regent, would exclaim, *'how elegant.'* "

reggio is the most melancholy instance on record of the want of proper encouragement of the arts; but a golden shower of patronage, tempting as that which fell into the lap of his own Danae, and dropping prize medals and epic mottoes, would not produce another Correggio!

Very excellent, very excellent. Truth itself, tho' I wish the last part had been left out, which alludes so palpably to myself.

The diffusion of taste is certainly not the same as the improvement, but whose fault is this? The fault [of] the Public Institution or of the bad Pictures shewn in it, supposing the others be good Pictures? Would it not improve at the same time? You attribute the bad taste diffused to the Institution, founded to diffuse [*an illegible word*] of the Work which the Institution [*about four illegible words. A sketch has been drawn over them.*] Hastings. Sep. 17.

I walked last night on the Sea Shore. The Stars were out in steadfast gaze. On the right the light of an autumnal Sun set still warmed with golden tone the horizon. On the left the Sea was beating in on an extended shore, with angry surf, & the crescent moon hung in the midst, the Queen of all, like a lamp in heaven, & glittered on the restless waters. As I looked at all in this silent scene, the Stars seemed to shoot out with an encreased intensity. The Moon gleamed forth with stronger rays. I heard a voice through the stillness of the evening, a solemn cadence, utter from [on] high, "Oh miserable mortal, thou who risest & passest like a flower's scent! Thou who now contemplatest us, remember that we have always shone since creation, that the Sea has roared, & rose & fell, the Stars have glittered, with steady continuity, the Moon has been born, been full, & declined while generations of men & Kingdoms & Empires have risen & fallen & decayed. We have witnessed all, and we shall witness your passing off, as we witnessed the passing off of your Fathers." It ceased, and left me mute in excrutiating abstraction. I beheld the same Sun & Moon & Stars that were beheld by the Egyptians, Chaldeans, Syrians, & Babylonians. The moon is monthly renewed, the Sun & Stars rise & set, the Sea flows; the Spring refreshes what Winter destroys, but the feeble wretched frame of Man only as Earth can have but one spring, one summer, one autumn, one winter, & then return from whence it sprung, old, feeble, decayed, putrid! Why should inanimate nature without the power of deduction & invention, be thus [*an illegible word*] that matter only be reanimated, & must that divine gift of thinking not be reanimated too? Impossible! Impossible to conceive, that the Power which created us with such palpable inferiority in stability to the Earth, the Sun, the Air we live in, should not recompense the agony we feel at our palpable weakness, by a ressussitation after Death, more stable, more firm than the renewing of the Sea, the monthly reanimation of the Moon, & yearly refreshing of the Earth. It must be! My God, if it is not! The idea of annihilation can not be born — it splits one's faculties.

September 24. I cannot help being amused when I reflect sometimes at my own restless spirit. What incessant raging & craving activity I have undergone for these last two days! The first thing in the morning I bathed in a stormy sea, for it blew a gale, and amidst the breakers, where I was almost suffocated with surf & foam, & beat down upon the sand by a gigantic wave, I dived through it and reared my head on the other side, "breasting the Seas," [4] as it raised me to the top, & then sunk me with a long sweep into the valley between. How my heart beat with real enthusiasm when I was on the top of a wave and saw another coming as if to overwhelm me (however there was no danger; it only requires firmness & skill). The first wave left me & passed with roaring dash in upon the shore; the other caught me up & passed on like the other. I felt like a God. Ulysses himself never behaved more like a Hero.

After dashing about I got ashore — was carried in an immense way & left dry. Before I could recover another fellow came roaring in and almost drowned me in bubbling spouts. Covered with sand, bruised with stones, & tired with perpetual ducks in the face, I hobbled up to dress. Here the bracing qualities of the Sea soon made my body burn, & I went into breakfast with an appetite like Hercules. The moment I had done, I saddled the Horse myself, as the Landlord was not in the way, and rode twenty miles before dinner, then spent an hour spiking eels, then I dined and then set off to Hastings on foot to buy some-

4. *Henry V*, III, Prologue, l. 13. "Breasting the lofty surge."

thing. I was upon [my] return as full [of] strength as ever, ready for another twenty miles or 40 if required.

Never did I receive so much benefit in so short a trip. My eyes, thank God, are recovering & nearly established. I hope in God to return to Town in full vigour for another campaign. It is a long time since I painted any thing, but I have been to Paris, seen a great deal, thought a great deal, and had I not come down here before I began seriously, I know well enough I should have been knocked up before I got through. Imprudent excess in work injured my system, not so much injured, perhaps, as disordered my system. I should never have been at all ill, had I worked with more regularity and [not] too much at a time, but it is my disposition. All my illnesses & sufferings were owing to it, and perhaps, when Age will have weakened my strength, my Death will be brought on by some such cause. I am now *able* to recover. The time must come when I shall cease to be able, and then the curtain will draw up and unveil what is now hid, with iron rigidity & eternal silence! May my exertions here render me worthy of a sublime opening. God grant it, Amen.

May the curtain be lifted by beautiful spirits, to divine sounds. May my Soul be welcomed, with undulations of millions of harps, & millions of voices. May I take my seat in the midst, and may the rumbling of distant thunder signify approbation & reward!

All this is of a piece with: They must have had better models; They must have had better colours; They must have had better lights; They must have had more encouragement. What matter where, says Satan, if *I* be still the same,[5] who was not much in the habit of suffering age or situation to check his perseverance.

The age was more adapted and the climate was clearer, and then up starts a Man of Genius and confounds them all.

The only period when public encouragement from the Institutions of the Country is when the Institutions are fitted & the thing has been done. This much is not the lot of Britain, but in this a Man of Genius would raise himself above the level. Canova. The Art of Italy is [in] a state of exhaustion as to encouragement, but yet Canova shines.

5. Identified by Professor Samuel N. Bogorad as *Paradise Lost,* I,256.

October

September 29. Hastings. I this day received communication from the Mayor of my native Town that the Freedom of it had been voted me by the Commonalty.[6] I do not ever recollect being so acutely affected at any success as at this. It sunk deeply into my heart, made it beat, and my cheeks flush & eye fire, as it beamed across my mind. God grant this honor may rouse my energies of body & mind to the greatest possible vigour. God grant that my next production may shew me worthy of such distinction. God grant that the example of my Native Town, and my own, may be an aera in the Arts of my glorious country. The Record is put in on the other page.

October 8. London. There is not a more pitiable object than an old Man whose faculties are just sinking into imbecility, but whose passions or malice gets more intense as his powers of gratification or revenge get more incapable.

I am returned to town full of health, thank God. At Hastings I lived in a farm house and amused myself with sketching & studying the habits of pigs, ducks, chickens, & geese. I mastered all their characteristic feelings. I used often to think, when they came regularly to be fed, and expressed their wishes by their restless dumbness, how tremendous was their fated limits!

[*A sketch of a man's head.*] A character upon the coach from Hastings, exactly like him. He had been a rifle man at the Battle of Talavera, and when the French entered, hobbled out with a corporal of the guards, who was also wounded. A Spaniard rode by on two mules; they begged a lift, which was refused. "I say," said the Corporal, "Rifleman, is your rifle loaded?" "I have never looked," said he, "since the battle, but I believe it is." "*Touch up* that fellow," said the other. "If it will go off, to be sure I will," said he. "I clapt my rifle to my shoulder when I found it was loaded, & down came my gentleman, Sir. We were so wounded we could not mount, so leading the mules till we came to a deep ditch, we put them in, & slid off the road on their backs. We found 300 dollars in a bag, tied to the neck of one, & away we trotted without stopping till we came to Elvas. We often drink (for he is alive, as well as me) success to the 300 dollars."

6. On September 26, 1814, Henry Woollcombe, mayor of Plymouth, wrote BRH of this honor, in recognition of "The Judgment of Solomon."

This fellow was a complete rascal. He told me stories for his villainy, as proofs of his cleverness, which made one's flesh creep! He was coming to Town for employment, and if he could not get it, he was ready for any villainy for a living. If I wanted to murder a rival, to way lay, to gag, to rob an enemy, this would be the man. Keen from nature, and active from habit, full of courage & daring, he was adapted for a leader of Banditti. He once led the way and brought off 56 prisoners, like himself, by digging under the wall of his prison. They chose him as commander, and he conducted them after a march of peril to Lisbon, where Lord Wellington presented him with 56 dollars for his bravery (it was mentioned in the papers). He was one of those singular beings who with ambition to rule a certain class, was conscious of an inferiority to command all, while he directed with tyranny like a despot, to those under him, he would submit, when he felt his incapability, to those above him. He had a feeling, & knew those who shewed higher intellect, but would advise any one, even his officer, if his inferior.

I called on Northcote[7] yesterday, who is a Native of Plymouth, who instead of congratulating me on my freedom, shewed me an old book to prove to me his grandfather had been *mayor* 200 years ago. This was a sweet touch of human nature!

Let every man remember that if he succeeds one year, the effects of his success will induce people to find unexisting beauties in his next Picture during its progress, and that if he fails, it will urge them to discover unexisting errors. In the one case let him not be flattered to unbounded hope, nor in the other to helpless despondency — exposure to the Public generally proves the fallacy of both, and all these shrink from their former opinions. Let a man confide in his own strength, with a wary circumspection, & an exulting energy.

In Titian (from want of power in expressing the passions) there is certainly in his historical productions too much a look of Art. His figures are too much under the influence of arrangement. Their arms & their legs, their hands & their feet, fall too exactly

7. James Northcote (1746–1831), R.A., who worked as an assistant in the studio of Sir Joshua Reynolds, about whom he wrote and published a memoir. He was commissioned by Boydell to paint nine pictures for the Shakespeare Gallery but is known primarily as a portrait painter.

into their proper places. This entirely arises from weak expression, which not seizing the mind so as to absorb it, leaves it at liberty to perceive the skill. Now in his Portraits he is exactly the reverse. There he is all nature & Soul; thus mingling their truth, their characters seize your faculties, and obliterate the colour & arrangement.

October 28. I saw Kean's[8] Hamlet last night, and totally disagree as to its being his worst part. The fact is we are ruined by the ranting habits of the stage. We are so used to noise, declamation, & fury, that was Nature herself to act it, she would appear tame. They complain Kean is insipid in his soliloquies! Absurd — what is the impression from his whole acting? Is it not of a heart afflicted youth, who silently "wanders for hours in the lobby," [9] in despairing desolation. At *these times* in *Nature* would he soliloquise, & how would he do it? Would he rant? Would he stamp? Would he thunder? Oh no, he would reason quietly; he would weep at his Father's name, & in half suppressed sighs & bursting agony, lament his Mother's marriage. Was not this then the progress, the system, of Kean? It is impossible one who feels the parts of passion so justly should not feel as justly the parts of secret soliloquies. To me his whole conception & execution of Hamlet is perfect. You see him wander silently about, weary, in grief, disgusted; if he speaks, it is not to the audience; if he feels, it is not for applause. No, he speaks because impelled to utter his sensations by their excess. He weeps because his faculties can no longer retain themselves. The longer he acts, the more will he bring the World to his principles, and the time is not far distant when his purity, his truth, his energy, will triumph over all opposition.

November 8. I thank God from my Soul, that the head finished this day is an immense advance in my Art, more soft, more fleshy, and nothing of that strawey touch so apparent to my feeling in every one of my other Pictures. O God, I thank thee from the very bottom of my heart. Spare my eyes, O God, till I have done

8. Edmund Kean (1787–1833), who achieved his popularity as a Shakespearean actor in 1814.
9. *Hamlet,* II,ii,160–161. "You know, sometimes he walks four hours together/ Here in this lobby."

all my power can do, till I have reformed the Art & taste of my Country, Amen.

November 19. In spite of our fogs and our tasteless Government, in spite of all the obstructions in Earth, we will be the greatest historical Painters of the World. I never go to bed but with fresh aspirations; truly may I say, as Nelson said, that a radiant glory shines inward in my brain and urges me onward in my glorious path. I never wake, but that the conviction of my great duty is my first perception. I never lie my head on my pillow but I breathe a silent prayer to my great Protector to bless my exertions, to enlarge my capacity, & realize my views, to grant I may be good & great, a reformer of my Country's taste and an honor to humanity.

My success this year has certainly shaken my enemies to the center, but it is quite extraordinary, not the number, but the nature of my enemies. Those who professedly stand out as Patrons of Genius, both the Academy & the Institution, have both attempted to blast my views & crush my Intentions. Payne Knight has pursued me with the malignity of a Demon, never answering me like a Man, but stabbing my Principles a year after my attack, in a preface to Sir Joshua's exhibition, then sneering in the Edingburgh on Northcote's book,[1] and then going before the Exhibition opened with the Princess of Wales, a thing he never did before to that exhibition, and trying to damn the Judgement of Solomon, telling her not to look at it, it was distorted, it was bad. Was this noble & like a Patron, like one anxious for the advance of high Art? Shameful, pitiful conduct, but in spite of all such enemies, I shall triumph, God but give my eyes & intellect [strength].

I believe out of both I have not a single man who does not heartily wish me success, and I believe the greatest part of the members are convinced of the hopelessness of attempts to check me. At the Gallery there was some reason for using me ill. I had exposed one of their body, but at the Academy, there was none. I was an eager, enthusiastic student, devoted to my Art, & secluded from Society, to a class of Art too they professedly wanted,

1. BRH's name is not mentioned in the unsigned review of James Northcote's *Life of Sir Joshua Reynolds* in the *Edinburgh Review*, September 1814, 23:263–292.

& yet they put a Picture on which I had spent two anxious years in the Dark, ran it down to my Patrons, ridiculed in Public. I was almost ruined & should have been had I [not] gained the prize the year following with this very damned Picture. There was no excuse. The act stands out as a wanton act of meaness, because they had put my first Picture, only 1 foot less, in a conspicuous situation, as an unprincipled piece of cruelty, without heart or feeling, without conscience or remorse. Against such a system of things was I not right to make a stand? Certainly. By having exposed their treatment of Wilkie and united him in my own, a sensation has been excited, and the Public will be more on the watch and they more on their guard.

"You'll have no easy job, let me tell you," said a man with a wise nod & look, as he put a glass [of] wine to his mouth, and his face & his belly bore ample proofs of good eating & indolence. "You'll have no easy [job] in your next Picture." This was said with that knowing sort of acuteness, as if its difficulties were unknown to me & as if his superior sagacity would deter & influence. Alas, thou poor, deluded being, thou who hast talked of the grand style for 30 years and never made one step towards attainment, thou who hast been affected at every rugged check and every paltry obstruction, thou who preferr'st thy wine & thy beef, thy arm chair, and thy snuffy sleepiness, it is natural for you to suppose difficulties ever frighten instead of rouse, ever bewilder instead of fire a man's faculties.

Let me, O God, be ever on the watch against such habits. Let me ever be wary of small things till they become great, for all habits are but an accumulation of imperceptible indulgences, till the mass is too great to shake off & not great enough to annihilate. Thus a man you see with sense enough to wish but not strength enough to execute.

November. I do not think Raphael's Women have each the characteristics of the head of a class. They are not Cordelias or Gonerils or Beatrices. They have all one general air of loveliness. They exhibit the combined points of interest as Women. They are tender, gentle, & sweet, inclined to love. They have what we all sympathise with, because their qualities are those that make Women delightful, but yet he never distinguishes them as Nature distinguishes them. They are nothing but gentle, tender, & sweet. They are never daring or vicious. They are never fascinating jilts or lovely intriguers. They have never the ripening beauties of opening youth or the glowing mellowness of maternity. They have general qualities but not particular, distinctive marks of character, the result of habit or organization. November 24.

[*Two sketches, one in the manner which he says is typical of Raphael, of "Maria Foote, 1814, Lady Harrington, aged 17,"* [2] *and the other of a scowling woman, saying, "Could I have believed that I should have had a mere drinking, vulgar husband. Oh, had any body told me this. I shall go mad."*]

[*A sketch of a handsome young man.*] This is the head of a young dog, with just manner enough, just sense enough, just music enough, just verse enough, just figure enough, just impudence enough, to seduce a thoughtless, unsuspecting, sweet girl, & desert her. Nov. 1814

December 1. It is always a disadvantage, I think, to choose a subject for an epick poem so far within the range of history that it is known; events occurred & conclusions were brought about without the apparent interference of supernatural agency. In such subjects the ground is not prepared by habitual associations. The supernatural agents are intruders, and it is an effort of the mind to reconcile their introduction. The Enchanters of Ariosto, the Gods of Homer, & the Angels of Milton are a part of the belief of the period to which the poems refer, but this cannot be said of [the] machinery of Tasso or Camoens.

December 2.

La reine se ranime à ces tendres accents;
Ainsi l'éclat du jour colore, vivifie
La jeune fleur des monts par l'orage flétrie. [3]

2. Maria Foote (1798–1867), actress. She retired from the stage in 1831 and married the fourth Earl of Harrington (1780–1851).
3. Lucien Bonaparte, *Charlemagne; ou l'Eglise Délivrée*, Canto 7, Stanza 22.

December

. . . et quand l'aurore luit,
Du palais et des tours la masse confondue
     Disparaît à sa vue.
Une épaisse forêt la reçoit dans ses flancs:
Ces bois virent jadis sa pompe souveraine;
Lorsqu' auprès d'un époux, les cors retentissants
Guidaient de cent chasseurs la poursuite incertaine.[4]
Oui malgré la clameur d'un aveugle univers
Les premiers des livres sont ceux de la nature
Et ceux qui les brisent appartient aux enfers.

Lucien Buonaparte appears to me to want that intuitive, keen, lucid power of first conceiving a subject and then bending all his incidents (and none more or less) to elucidate it. Lucien Buonaparte, from his poem of Charlemagne, appears to me to want that keen intensity of internal light, which enabled Homer, Shakespeare, & Milton to select or reject, to arrange or bring forward, the images of their mind and the incidents of their memory, to elucidate the plan & develope the stories of their inventions. His Poem is overwhelmed with episodes; the heart beating human interest one felt when Armélie was rejected & Adalgise restored to Charles' favour, is suffered to die away & be forgotten. Charles when he appears is surely the Captain, but not so much from desert as favour. His deeds would surely not entitle him to it, and he appears so seldom that one is more interested for Roland, who was murdered at Roncevales, than for the Hero with all his Piety, heroism, & Stature. Surely an opportunity has been lost, for a fine underplot, in the intrigues, acts, & passions, of the two women & their parties, while the grand scheme of restoring the Church was in progress. There are many original touches. The book of L'enfer is the best & pushed through with great genius & as original as it almost can be after Homer, Virgil, Dante, & Milton, & Tasso have racked their minds on it. Here and there are imitations that annoy one & excite a feeling of imbecility. He has feeling, one of the constituent parts of Genius, but he has not in an equal or superior degree the directing spirit without which

4. Bonaparte, Canto 5, Stanza 31.

feeling & taste & even invention or judgement can do little, for it is a combination of all that constitutes this spirit.

The World & Posterity will never do a man justice who yields any scheme from disgust. Never relinquish any plan in disgust at ill treatment; the world will never sympathise with you. Each man is full of his own troubles, whereas if you persevere through, the World will not forget your having conquered your disgusts. Make yourself remarkable by your talents & the common properties of your Nature will then be elevated into virtues. Suffer your disgusts to subdue you to failure, and then your common failings will be censored as vices.

Notwithstanding Buonaparte is down, his influence & his system, which is before the world, will do & has done an irreparable injury to Liberty. It will shew monarchs how much they have in their power, what controul they can have over the minds of their own subjects from infancy to manhood. Lancaster & Bell's system of education,[5] tho doubtless a benefit to Society & a great blessing in thus distributing knowledge & thereby correcting vice, yet it will take off the fiery edge of Nature. Man will be better regulated, and there may be less crime, but they will also be more humble, more obedient, more awed at the great, & more terrified at Majesty. I am convinced that the principles of this System are those of submission to power. Boys will be educated with a notion of the infallibility of Kings, & brought into Life with a horror of opposition, that a hundred years will have prepared the minds for slavery & submission.

[*A letter from William Prance, dated November 3, 1814. As secretary of the Plymouth Institution, he informed Haydon of his election to honorary membership in that society as a tribute to "The Judgment of Solomon."*]

There is no pleasure so delightfully calm and gratifying after the buffets & ingratitude of enemies as to find little kindnesses acknowledged by innocent and artless people.

5. Joseph Lancaster (1778–1838), founder of the "Lancasterian system" of education, used at his free school for poor boys, in which older students drilled the younger ones as monitors. Lancaster took some of his ideas from Dr. Andrew Bell (1753–1832), who originated a system of mutual tuition while he was superintendent of the male orphan asylum in Madras. The "Madras system" was adopted in many schools, including Christ's Hospital.

December

I have lately been amongst Actors & Actresses. I never refuse invitations that will afford me opportunity of seeing human nature in all its varieties.

Those who have once violated any of the great principles of Society & live in the practice, however surrounded with splendour & luxury, can never rid themselves of the aking whisper of conscience. I have been introduced to a Lady adopted or kept by a rich [*a word is scratched out*]. Not being a Woman of information, her thoughts in solitude are irksome. She is surrounded by every pleasure, by gold, silver, & precious stones; every want is anticipated, every wish gratified, but yet to whom does she owe these? To her own vigour of mind or body, to the honorable exercise of her faculties, which would make her glory in its acquirement? Oh no. Her invisible & keen & restless monitor tells her with a bitter laugh she is a slave! She feels it, she knows it. The scrutiny of sound understandings she shrinks from. She surrounds herself with the basest flatterers, unidea'd girls, who look with rapture on a silver ewer & bow in adoration to a diamond necklace. Having lost her own liberty, she takes refuge in enslaving others. Being a slave to her keeper, she makes those around her slaves to her. Alas, I looked at her with pity as I dined off her silver plate & drank from her golden goblets, and saw her smile with delight at every flatterer's incense. She met my silent investigating look & blushed! It spoke volumes to me! She was pensive the whole of dinner and listened to my remarks about an hour with a shaken frame. She then suddenly seemed to burst out with an internal flash, and fled from thought in the most violent gaiety. At her side dangles a lover, one who professes affection but whom, I verily believe, is in hopes of replacing by marriage his shattered fortunes. "But he can never marry her," said I, "while her —— lives." "Oh no," said one of her Young Ladies, "but he is an old man, he *can't live long!*" The greater the obligation, the greater the burthen. Death only can relieve her from the painful favours of her benefactor. What a lesson to both is this little history. The Man to whom she owes all, now when she wants nothing, is a burthensome intruder!

December 31. The last night of 1814, a year to me in which I have suffered the extremities of misery, sickness, & want, & enjoyed the greatest success; in which I have enlarged my mind by seeing another Country, & studied the productions which the World have for 300 years looked up [to] with reverence & delight. O God, thou who has always watched, protected, & urged me onward in my path, accept from my heart the enthusiastic effusions of its gratitude. In the midst of sorrow thou cheered me by thy spirit; in the extremity of want, thou relieved me by thy influence; thou still whispered me to be wary in success, & saved me from its dangers by higher views & deeper impulses. O God, from my soul I bless thee for thy goodness. I bless thee that my enthusiastic views time has hardened & envigorated. I bless thee for the strength thou hast given me, to act on the principles of my boyish purity, & God, let all the good & great visions of my youth be realized before I die. Grant I may reform & rear the Art of my glorious Land; grant my exertions during the next year may make a great stride to their accomplishment, & grant each ensuing one may tend to compleat what the previous one approached. O God, have mercy on me, spare my eyes & my intellect, & continue my strength of mind & vigour of body to resist every vicious inclination, & accomplish every great, good, & glorious wish, for Jesus Christ's sake, my Saviour, my Redeemer. Amen, Amen, O God.

1815

January 4, 1815. The World are always willing to suppose that he who has any faculty more intensely strong than themselves must have others as intensely weak. "Thus they lay the flatt'ring unction to their Souls" [6] as a soother to their own incapacity.

Oh, the bitter agony of being the dupe of an artful Mother, who, throwing her daughter perpetually in your way, engages you from benevolence to be civil, and then obliges you from honor to marry one you don't love, you don't respect, you don't [feel] intimate [with]. You find out too late that you are a dupe, by the insolence of her, when to be obsequious is no longer necessary. Children arise, difficulties come on, and to relieve yourself

6. *Hamlet,* III,iv,145. "Lay not that flattering unction to your soul."

& your wife, pecuniary obligations are requisite. Perhaps she can afford them, perhaps she does in her infinite condescension.

Oh the agony of a Husband, a dupe of an artful woman, to marry a girl he doesn't love, conscious that he is one & yet despising as he does the Art of her who has duped him, obliged [to] borrow money of the blaster of his hope. I saw him play about his wit with a bitter smile, while his heart sunk, his stomach weakened, & his voice failed. She sat by with an air [of] smirking insolence, and smiled at his futile efforts to forget his degradation, while she held the net invisibly, embarrassed him, and enjoyed his trembling struggles to forget his being gone. It was a painful sight!

I would never marry any woman as a point of honor, but in seduction.

January 7. When once a Woman has tasted the dram of public applause & admiration on a stage, the pure crystal of domestic life is lifeless & insipid. Actresses get the energy & spirit of men. Their minds are constantly on the stretch; they have regular active duties to perform. I don't wonder that after having once known the sweets of exertion, they should shrink from the horrors of ennui and prim propriety. They get an independence of thought, a fearless, swinging security of action that marks them. Actresses seem to know they are not held in pure estimation, & have a fiery sensitiveness to insult that one risks offence, every word.

I repeat, if fifty children were at the same instant to see the same thing, would they be all equally impressed? No, certainly, they would be all impressed according to their respective capacities to receive impressions, generally, and would be impressed with that one thing, according to their capacities to receive the impressions of that one thing. Why should not human beings have organs to do in intellect as much as they have organs to do in body? Can a hand walk? Can a foot hold? Can not some walk better than others, cannot some grasp stronger? Why cannot a hand walk? Because it is organised from nature to grapple. Some men are impotent; will accident, habit, or any impressions change their defectiveness? Why? because they are without the power from Nature. If the body has particular organs for particular purposes, has not the mind? If defectiveness in these particular organs renders the being incapable to do that for which that organ is meant, will any education supply the want? We know human faculties by the result. There are particular powers called judgement, wit, imagination. If they are essentially distinct, why should there not be distinct organs for them? Why are some without wit in spite of all cultivation? Why are some full without effort? There seems to be some cause [for] all this.

Painting is the effect of objects, Sculpture the objects themselves.

To insist on the details of objects because they exist in the objects themselves, is like insisting on the stones of a tower seen ten miles off in a Picture because it must be built of stones individually. You cannot make out more than what you see at such a distance. Why should [you] make out more than the effect on objects that are nearer?

Raphael wanted that comprehensiveness in representation that he had in expression. The consequence is all his representations are equally detailed, prominent, hard, & unfeeling; by [the] side of Corregio, who felt every part, idea, & representation with equal intensity, Raphael looks hard & German.

At the moment of execution, one suffers agony, at the impossibility to compleat the idea; the imagination fired at the moment goes so much beyond the efforts of the hand that not till days afterwards, when fancy has cooled & Nature is absent, do you begin to relapse into approbation. I never was satisfied with any effort till I had forgotten what I wanted to do.

January 17. In all daring attempts, nothing should be left to chance, but what cannot be attained by human skill & arrangement, and the probability is they will be [the] cause of a man's elevation instead of destruction.

January 18. Certain delightful qualities in a Woman are usually attended with certain tendencies to vice. If you love the one, you must put up with the other & risk your peace. If you will not risk your peace by marrying the one with such delightful qualities, you may secure your tranquillity by marrying those of decent inanimateness, without gaity or playful fascination, but with fire side, stocking-mending moping, and hot plain work, breathy stench.

January 24. It is evident the reason that flesh finished smoothly has a hard appearance at a distance. The Skin is by no means a smooth surface when examined, but full of pores & lines & roughnesses. This atmosphere & distance melts into a mass agreeably soft, but the same reason that Ivory at an equal distance will look hard, makes flesh look soft. The pores of Ivory are not discoverable; distance & atmosphere flatters the surface of that which even when examined has nothing to interrupt it. Thus the little there is is flattered & united to a more intense degree. It is beaten together, as it were, compressed. Rembrandt's Picture looks like Nature, Vanderwerf's[7] like Ivory, on this principle, because leaving nothing for distance to do what it did do, was an injury.

The most detestable women are those without taste, without imagination, without feeling or delicacy or breeding, & who have a hot, fiery, red haired appetite, as racy as a monkey's and almost as rank.

January 31. In Miss Edgeworth's Stories, the Art is too apparent. The follies or vices of the Actors bring them too regularly to ruin to act as an example. They act in circumstances arranged for them, and do not produce circumstances by the development of their own characters.

In the left hand corner, I'll have a penitent, abandoned daughter, pale, lovely, blushing, trembling, shrinking, yet entreating with her fair hands pardon of her Saviour, protected by her Mother, who in the agony of apprehension, is clasping her, yet has a gleam of hope & smiles through her tears, encouraged [by her] pure & virtuous sister, who gently presses her shoulder & smiling at her to give her hope, at the same time feels pain for her viciousness. Christ must regard the poor penitent with a look & smile of mild & exquisite, angelic benignity, pointing to Heaven with his hand.

I thank God for the conception of this Christ & I pray him

7. Adriaen van der Werff (1659–1727), Dutch artist.

to grant I may execute it with intense exquisiteness. Grant it, O God. Amen. February 3.

February 5. Sunday. I arose full of aspirations & glowing elasticity of imagination, the result of a week vigorously & successfully passed, in which I have strained my faculties & body to the greatest stretch without injury or weakness. O God Almighty, I bless thee for this from my heart. O grant me strength of mind & body to realize all my views before I die & take me before my power is gone, take me before the imbecility of age has numbed my sensation, & deadened my conception, but thy will be done. To thy merciful & unexhausted goodness I trust with blushing confidence.

Good heavens, what a character! [8] She imagined all her letters were burnt. She imagined she was safe. She could now talk of her Husband & her children, when she thought there was no proof against her, but my own assertions, but by mere accident, three or four of her letters were mislaid. I subjoin one[9] given me at the time she fancied I did not misunderstand her and her manner & air had changed to one of fearless licentiousness, tho nothing was said. It was an extract from Chateaubriand, and she added 4 lines, which she underlined. It was too palpable, but it was too late. My honor had been roused, & the more she advanced, the more I was terrified.

She thought to flatter my vanity!

She forgot the worthiest of men and the future respectability of five children, when her appetites were concerned. Now she was all sensitiveness & delicacy & purity & insulted virtue!!! I have more respect for Messalina herself, who disguised not her vices, than this devil of vice & corruption, iced over with snowy reserve. I believe in the History of human depravity this creature would take the lead. Never was such a woman. Other women I have known had hearts, however lecherous, but this infernal, abandoned creature had no feelings but her own appetites, and if you refused to yield, your destruction was her object. In my most dreadful state of depression, when she saw she was in my power,

8. BRH had already described this "infernal woman" in his diary for February 6, 1814 (I,343).

9. The letter is no longer attached to the diary.

she asked me if ever I read "The Sorrows of Werther." [1] I said no. "Take it home," says she, "but promise to read it *through.*" I took it home & began, but it affected me so horribly before I got half through, that self destruction once or twice glittered to my blurred intellect. Such was her corruption that every thing in Nature, light and darkness, solitude & Society, beauty or deformity, every object that seeing, smelling, touching, or tasting could reach were to her sources of licentious gratification. The perfume of flowers, she would say, trembling with passion, has *an amorous smell!* The richness of a Summer evening, the silence of a woody grove affected her vitiated fancy only as affording more refined means of lechery & lust. Her system was the most dreadful under Heaven. It was when once the mind was corrupted to her purposes, to make the commonest expressions, & the most innocent words a vehicle of vice.

[*Four lines are scratched out.*]

. . . but yet what harm was in this if *you* reported it. Yours must have [been] the vicious mind to put such construction on her thoughtless words, & how could *she* mean impropriety in the presence of *her child?* By this infernal plan, she could intrigue in her husband's presence, as I have witnessed. To a third person who *heard,* nothing could appear but to the lover who *saw,* every thing. She felt exquisite pleasure in making one ruined being the instrument of another's fate, and then contrive they should all know it, when *the last* was irretrievably *committed,* but *not before.* I have seen her at table surrounded by such lovers, all nervous, agitated, trembling, & melancholy, all watching her looks, all in love, all jealous of each other (which gave her exquisite gratification), all submitting, for these were her only terms. I have seen her smile like a beautiful Devil & enchant the whole [company], and yet with such consummate art was this managed, that she contrived to make her husband invite them! It was a part of her art to discover your weakness & sap till she ruined! to ascertain your crimes, to hold you in subjection by threatening disclosure, to gratify your taste & by gratifying *it,*

1. Johann Wolfgang von Goethe's *Die Leiden des jungen Werther,* first translated into English in 1779.

make you gratify *hers*. The more difficult, the more pure, the more innocent, the more holy was the object, the keener was the anticipated pleasure, the more delightful the triumph to conquer & enjoy! She could be charitable or unfeeling, abandoned or religious, one day a girl of sixteen, the next a Matron. She could faint at a Picture, melt at Music, or affect indifference for either. Nothing, however petty, however mean, however good, however infamous, however cruel, however terrible, however tremendous, or however sacred, but she would wield, if by such instruments she thought she could bend her objects to her appetites.

(Note. Once she thought I was religiously inclined, she called & took me to hear a Sermon at the *Magdalen Chapel!* Another time when I had absented myself and was endeavouring to shake her off, in the midst of prayer at St. James Church, I saw this Devil right opposite to where I always sat! The moment she caught my eye she sat down apparently overcome, & I shook & buried my face in my hands.)

Her whole time, her whole occupation, her whole soul, were bent on discovering objects of pleasure, enjoying & ruining them! She would suck with poisonous delirium the balmy lips of a blooming Youth, or bite with keen & burning appetite the disgusting sickliness of deformity! This was the creature into whose power I was nearly falling. Attracted by her apparent innocence, I became enamoured; & tho by a mere accident I escaped without vice, yet with my mind so shattered, my peace so disturbed, my health so affected, & my habits so ruined, that it was long, long, before I relapsed with tranquillity into my habits of application, and longer, still longer, before I erased that impression she had burnt on my aking soul. Damnable, devilish vice, what misery is concealed beneath thy artful, pathetic, interesting mask. Whatever pleasure the vicious enjoy, they are not happy. How they shrink at the fear of detection; how alive are they to every word, however innocent, which their phosphoric souls kindle into meaning. With a guilty person, you risk offence every instant. Often in the midst of a wanton laugh a footstep has made her start! and instantly her face resumed its *reserve*. The fears that Religion excites are the fears of doing wrong, the horrors of

Vice, the dread of having done it. There may [be] "glowing pleasure" [2] in guilty enjoyment, from fear of discovery, from apprehension of detection, snatched at the moment, in the hot, icy fury of passion, on a luxurious sofa! by a silent fire! in a winter evening, silent, secret! — yet surely the confidence, the rapture of legitimate pleasure with a lovely creature, pure & depending, is a million times more exquisite. Then consider the distraction of violated duty! the agony of consequences! the horror of ruin! the fear of having been the dupe of intrigue! the dreadful pang of deceiving a good man, & the torment of discovery, & being obliged to marry a woman in honor who had perhaps been whore to half the Town. Then the acute intense pain of jealousy, the overwhelming weighing down of the faculties, the contemptible notions of oneself, the dreary grief this suspicion excites that nothing in this world or in any world, that ever was or ever will be, can equal, no punishment that the most malicious demon could ever discover after years of thought & ages of experience could ever approach the torture of this racking hell. The more vicious the object of attachment, the more liable are you to this torture, as if God had held out the calm quiescent delight of virtuous confidence as a reward for virtuous love, & caused the racking torture of jealousy to punish him, who could be weak enough to expect faith in her who had broken her faith to another! Talk not of a life of pleasure, if this be pleasure, no man is more contemptible than a man of the Town, no character more despicable than a man of intrigue. Let him who never feared the face of God or Man, get once entangled with a woman of vicious habits, and he instantly becomes timid, cowardly, despicable, abhorring himself, fearing every eye, dreading every hand, shrinking at every blast! With his eyes on the ground as if he dreaded to meet, the terrific, steady glare of the eye of *God!* open from all eternity & to all eternity! fixed with an intensity of eager enquiry, gleaming with an internal sort of scintillation as if it emitted sparks! — irresistible! — unmerciful! — eternal! — inexorably severe! — to

2. Identified by Professor Herbert McArthur as John Dryden and Nathaniel Lee, *Oedipus,* IV,i,3–5.
> "A malicious joy,
> Whose red and fiery beams cast through your visage
> A glowing pleasure."

deceive which — impossible! to escape — hopeless! — firmly fixed as if it had rooted to its situation, and blazing at every additional discovery with the fierceness of [a] heated furnace. There, there are the horrors of vice! That I have felt them I am thankful, because I know the delights of virtue.

[*A sketch of the "demon" whom he has been describing, dated "Nov. 1812" and labeled "Exactly her moments of her vicious torture" is attached to the diary.*]

Her husband, her children were the unconscious instruments of her pleasures. There was nothing in existence, all nature, animate or inanimate, but she would bend to her purposes. Exactly like her.

It makes me shudder whenever I see it by accident.*

* It was from the momentary expression of this devil that I got the expression of the wicked Mother in Solomon — 1812, June. B. R. Haydon, 1825.

Volume VII

FEBRUARY 1815 — OCTOBER 1816

The first four pages of Volume VII contain sketches, a phreno-
logical chart, and memoranda; the only one of significance is as
follows: "April 5th, Lent young Landseer my Anatomical Drawings, John Bell on the Bones, Anatomy of a Lion, Plates, &c."

Volume VII

FEBRUARY 1815—OCTOBER 1816

"Magnum iter ascendo, sed dat mihi gloria vires." Propertius.[1]

February 10. I commence this new Journal on my dear Sister's birth day.[2] God protect & honourably & virtuously settle her. I pray him to bless her intellect & encrease its power, to bless her health, & to open her mind to the purity, the truth & value of his Divine Religion, to conduct her through all the temptations & troubles of life with honor & virtue. Amen. *Magnum iter ascendo sed dat mihi gloria vires.*

My mind & powers of hand are certainly encreased as *they ought,* but it is a satisfaction to find they have not gone back. My jaunt to Paris afforded me the most essential benefit. I saw what the World had so long admired. Conclusions were more readily drawn & deductions more easily made. The principles which I had before ascertained in my own Country were here established. I saw what Fame had so often reported. I did not spend my time in making useless copies or dwelling in indolent inertness on favourite works. I ventured to compare one man with another & both with Nature. I studied the character of a new Nation. I enlarged my feelings & stored my mind by visiting places recently remarkable by great events.

An Artist's faculties should spend as much time in studying human Character as human works. He should store his capacity with general knowledge, instead of daudling over a reputed Picture. Let him glance his eye down the whole room, and ascertain which works *strike,* and then investigate *why,* & establish a code for his future practice, & begin a work of his own, & put the principles he has ascertained into it. Here will be an effort; his faculties will be active, and he may & must add something to the already acquired knowledge of the World.

1. *Elegies,* IV,x,3. "I climb a steep ascent, but glory gives me strength."
2. FSH, in a genealogy of his family prepared in 1872, recorded that BRH's sister Harriett was born on February 8, 1789.

February 11. My dearest Sister, as I prayed most sincerely yesterday, has had an offer which will settle her independently & virtuously.[3] O God, I thank thee for thy mercy, thy goodness, thy blessing; bring it to a happy conclusion, I humbly pray. Grant she marry him & do all the duties of a Wife affectionately & steadily, and grant he may make her a virtuous and affectionate husband. O God, in thy mercy grant it, and let no untoward incident prevent their marrying or mar their happiness when they are married. Amen with all my Soul.

I knew not the acuteness of the cord that held me to her till now. Dear, dear Girl! It has always been my object to guide her acute intellect to virtue, to stimulate it to higher objects, than the usual objects of women. I am sure I have succeeded. I am sure she will be & is a treasure for any human being on Earth. Dearest Harriett, my interesting, my darling Sister, you are going from my influence and controul, to the more mysterious influence of a husband. Your name will be changed, your affections will be of a deeper cast, your dear mind will receive finer impressions. I now feel my heart cut at the idea of losing you; tears fill my eyes at the thought of you. How many innocent sweetnesses did we enjoy in childhood. We always loved each other. If I was chastised you always cried, if you were ill I always soothed you; we have grown up from the fondling innocence of infancy, to the intense feeling of mature affection, without one pang from disagreement or one agony from mutual distrust. We both felt the lacerating pang of separation for the first time when we lost our dear Mother in a strange Inn, on a strange heath, by night, & no friend near us, when we were young & tender & susceptible. I am depressed at the thought and feel as if a string of my heart would be torn out, when you leave me. God protect you, my sweet, my dearest Girl. One o'clock in the morning, February, 1815.

I had a most singular dream. I dreamt Wilkie and I were both climbing a high wall, immensely high, at the top of which were sweet creatures smiling at us & welcoming us. We could scarcely

3. On August 2, 1815, according to FSH's genealogy, Harriett Haydon married James Haviland (1788–1869), M.R.C.S. Bridgwater records show that he was elected mayor of the Borough for one year on November 9, 1848. Their five children were Harriett, Anna, Alfred, Orlando, and Edgar Haviland.

keep our hold, it was so perpendicular & slippery; when all of a sudden Wilkie let go, & I saw him wind & curve about in the air, and felt all the horror that his body must be dashed in pieces. After a moment's grief, I persevered and reached the top, and there found Mrs. Wilkie & his Sister,[4] lamenting his Death.* February 15th, 1815.

Why should God have made a sign in Heaven? Would the World now, those who did not see it, believe it? Certainly not. Would there not have been thousands of reasons to prove it could not be, that God would not think it worthy, that we were mere atoms in creation and unworthy such notice? How has he acted? Gave us a code of moral laws, which it is necessary to follow strictly to feel, told us if we adhere to them, we cannot fail to believe them, and a man who struggles to follow them will find there be left to every man's virtue to be received.

[*Two cuttings follow, giving Napoleon's proclamations, dated March 1, 1815, to the French people and the army, on his return from Elba, and a description of Napoleon during his exile.*]

Emile was a young french Surgeon, a true specimen of his Countrymen, fierce & elegant, blood thirsty & devoted to Napoleon, seeing only the glory of France in war & battle. He had seduced the wife of his Friend & boasted his children would bear his Friend's name. When he spoke of Napoleon his frame shook, his face became pale, & tears started into his eyes. "Whatever differences you have amongst yourselves," said he, "you unite if threatened with invasion. You have a character." Later, "Imaginez vous quand l'Empereur embarqua à Fréjus[5] personne ne disoit 'adieu, mon Empereur, adieu, mon general,' mais tout le monde guarda un enorme silence."

* How odd. It is like an omen of his dying first. B.R.H., 1844.

4. On August 30, 1813, Wilkie's mother, Mrs. Isabella Lister Wilkie, widow of the Reverend David Wilkie, and his sister Helen joined him in London at 24 Lower Phillimore Place, Kensington (Cunningham, I,385). "Helen Wilkie, the painter's only sister, married, after Wilkie's death, Dr. William Hunter, Surgeon-Major in the Coldstream Guards" (*Paintings and Drawings by Sir David Wilkie*, [*exhibition*] *16th August–21st September 1958*, Edinburgh [1958], p. 17).
5. On April 28, 1814, for his banishment in Elba.

When Napoleon's Statue was taking down,* a Russian Officer looked up & said, "vous etes bien grimpé en la haut, mais nous ferons vous descendra toute suite." Emile was standing amongst them in melancholy quiet with his arms folded, when looking round to him he said, "Prenez garde qu'il ne vous ecrase pas dans sa chute!" He never spoke of Napoleon without trembling and tears starting in his eyes. He had kept all his proclamations, and pasted them in a book. He was engaged in [a duel] with his Friend from a most trivial joke. On separating to go home, his Friend asked him to accompany him. "Are you afraid," said he. "Afraid! Sacre nom de Dieu, you shall see that tomorrow." "Ce soir," said Emile, "s'il vous plait." The following morning they fought. In the interim my Friend called on his Mistress, to console her & soothe her anxiety — "I fear you are uneasy." "Oh non, non, Monsieur, Je vous assure. Je suis si accoutumée à ces choses qu'il ne me donne pas de la peine." *She* was a French Woman, & Emile a French Man. This is an answer & will account for all. When my Friend was in doubt to leave Paris or not, he asked Emile, who was smoking a segar with melancholy musing, what he should do. "You had better go, perhaps, but yet, Sacre nom de Dieu, if you stay you will see the Napoleon *mount his horse!* Oh, that's a sight! — Bougre — ah!"

The prospects of the World are at this moment dreadful. If there was any hope of his reformation or any prospect that adversity had calmed his passions for rule, I should be delighted to see such Genius at the . . .

[*The sentence is incomplete. On the next three pages of the diary and on two later pages Haydon copied part of the description of the Battle of Poitiers from Chapters 160–166 of Lord Berners' translation of Froissart's* Chronicles, *describing the gallantry of Lord James Audley. Haydon painted this subject in 1836.*]

Genius has always a mixture of presumption & Modesty — of Presumption in comparing with others, and modesty in comparing its own efforts with its own conceptions.

* From the Colonne Vendome.

April

Three Thousand Guineas for a Picture appear a great sum! [6]
— but has it produced him a single Commission? No Great Town
steps forward & orders an Historical Picture for its hall, as it does
a monument for its Church. It is never thought of. I do not complain, I only wish to shew the singular state of Public feeling.

April 8. There is nothing like the sight of a lovely Woman!
Nothing so subdues one, so controuls one; I feel the influence [of]
her eyes if they wander down my form just like electrical air from
a point. I sat by one this morning at a lecture of Spurzheim's,[7]
and without one atom of appetite or passion felt an affectionate
desire to put her sweet arm round my neck and nestle my own
cheek on her lovely bosom — with pure heartfelt softness. She
looked so gentle, so delicate, so soft, so yielding, that one's manly
feelings of protection were roused, and one's gentle emotions of
tenderness were excited.

The principle implanted by Nature that the feelings of consciousness as to manhood should be encreased by gratifying the
other Sex, often pushes us to the gratification without reference
to the object for which that sensation was given.

April 9. "Fear ye not me," saith the Lord; "will ye not *tremble
at my presence,* which have placed the sand for the bound of the
Sea by a perpetual decree, that it cannot pass it, and tho the
waves thereof *toss themselves,* yet can they not prevail; tho they
roar, yet can they not pass over it." Jeremiah, Ch. 5, 22 V.

Religion settles at once whether there is such a thing or not
as vice. "Thou shall not murder." [8] Murder therefore is wrong,
and it is the will of God that it shall not be done, &c. Without
religion we know nothing. Once believing revelation — there is
no occasion to split your brain with metaphysical doubts.

April 10. God grant I may make the woman in the right hand
corner of my Picture[9] the finest thing ever seen in the world, in

6. In 1811 the British Institution bought Benjamin West's "Our Saviour
Healing the Sick in the Temple" for three thousand guineas (Whitley, *1800–
1820,* p. 189. See I,213).
7. Johann Christoph Spurzheim (1776–1832), German phrenologist and
popular lecturer.
8. Exodus 20:13. "Thou shalt not kill."
9. The kneeling Canaanite woman in "Christ's Entry into Jerusalem."

expression, colour, drawing, beauty, & grandeur & exquisite softness. I have set my soul on doing it, & so help me God, I'll try.
Amen.

The great Thing in representation is substance. As the eye can
only take in a part of any object, where the surface of that object
ends and another begins is where the object is drawn, defined by
a *line*, but there is no line in Nature. The thing is defined by its
receding from sight and by another thing appearing on the
boundaries of the first thing; real imitation then, & real Art, as
far as imitation (and Art is imitation, either imaginary or Natural) is concerned is distinguishing objects by their contrast
with each other, by their mutual relief, and not by positive line.
All Art, the Florentine & Roman celebrated for their line, is imperfect, because it is only line. The border of the contour of the
ending of any [of] the objects must be perfectly correct, but not
definable by line; it must be one substance ending on another &
must be definable by the relief of another substance.

April 10. I painted a Portrait of a Friend, a long promise!
Then did I miserably feel the different sensations after conclud-
ing the one to those after a day's work on my Picture. The one
was all the timid, mean sensation of a face similist[?]; the other
all the swelling, bursting glories of realizing a [host] of visions of
imaginations. I feel the beauties of individuality as much as any
one, the sharpness and softness of flesh, the delicacy of touch, and
calm sweetness of breadth & melting, racy flush of colour; but if
all these tend to elicit a mean character, of what value are they?

They go on perpetually sewing the seed, raising the crop, and
then suffering [it] to take its chance without care, that they may
have the delight & novelty of raising a new one. There is at this
moment more talent in this Country than any Country in Europe.
The right encouragement is giving employment to it. What is
their object in wishing to have *sketches*? Is it ultimately to employ those who exhibit the best? If so, why not employ those
who have already given proofs of their ability, who have already
the attention[?] of their favour, who by their fostering have
sprung above the ground with healthful promise, and only want
a continuance of warmth to compleat a Summer ripeness. Envy

of that very reputation to which they have contributed to raise him! The favourite of this Year is only a favourite in as much as he is subservient to knock down the one of the last, and will be himself the year following ran down by a new one. Thus they go on, praising & talking, and if they are suffered to persevere will not only leave Art ultimately worse than they found it, but with talent incompleted and genius extinct[?], with amiable feelings cut, & noble darings blunted.

Why are they continually requiring *proofs* of talent? They are like those Parents who would wish to keep their offspring perpetually in infancy that they might always have the pleasure of despotic guidance, and never have their authority weakened, or their reason doubted by the risk of superior capacity in those to whom they have given existence. Their object is to get the notoriety of nourishing Genius, and as much envy is excited amongst them as in any other human pursuit. Payne Knight was envious of Lord Mulgrave bringing forward Wilkie & I, as a man could be, and from his darting at a young man lately and telling him he would stand by him if he exerted himself, is a proof of his anxiety to protest. From the first moment of my appearance in Public, Payne Knight attacked me and my whole system, in the grossest manner, and then the Directors refused me the prize for Macbeth, and set their faces against great Pictures, and the year following advised great Pictures to be put into their halls, and in the same preface, attacked me for painting them. What is the meaning of this exquisite boggling and fogginess? Macbeth was distorted the Public thought, so they were right. Poor Knight, the moment he saw Solomon, said "distorted stuff!" Poor creature, he imagined because Macbeth was so Solomon must be so, and having no judgement of his own decided from theories[?] of another production he thought was convincing[?]. Now Solomon was as unlike Macbeth as one thing was unlike another, and the Public said so, and he found his mistake in a day or two, for in spite of his going with the Princess, a thing he never did in his life before, and trying to damn it by taking her attention from it,[1] its reputation rose, it sold, and my glory & my triumph were complete. Poor Knight still rankling with spite, again sneered in

1. See I,398.

the Edinburgh review;[2] but he is unworthy of notice. I shall succeed in spite of such despicable beings, and the very animosity I
excite is a proof of the consequences I am assuming.

In God I trust, who never forsakes him whose motives are
pure, great, & for the Welfare of his fellow beings. In God I
presume to trust, because I have always trusted, and always been
rewarded for so trusting. Out of what inextricable troubles have
I escaped by his mercy? What difficulties have I surmounted by
his goodness & support? I will do all I can do as far as my own
talents & powers are concerned, & leave the consequences to him.
O God bless them, grant I may accomplish the great object of
my being & live to see my enemies convinced & assured of the
value of my object. Grant I may reform the taste of my Country,
grant I may [place] its fame in Art, on a pitch with great Nations
of Antiquity, grant I may [be] good, great, & an honor to the
World, for Jesus Christ's sake, Amen.

For thy mercies already bestowed, accept my acute gratitude.

April 14. Ne quittez jamais vos affaires pour votre plaisir; mais
faites vous une sorte de règle qui vous donne des temps de liberte
et de divertissement. Voltaire, Louis XIV.

April 15. Beware of those Women whose propensity & delight
is to correct the errors rather than love the good qualities a man
may have — a pretty life he will lead who marries one.

The reason I think there is such envy among men of Genius
is an Instinctive feeling that genius is purely from Nature. A man
of great genius must be envied by those of less because no effort
can supply their own deficiencies.

I am sure I pity those who with knowledge & feeling for what
they ought to do, have not energy to do it, who pass their lives in
longing struggling, stung by Conscience or cut by remorse.

April 15. My perpetual sicknesses from weak eyes greatly break
in upon my habits. It is a long time before I recover my regularity

2. Knight reviewed *The Works of James Barry* in the *Edinburgh Review* of
August 1810 (16:308–309). See I,259.

of application. Without employment I am the most wretched of wretched beings, preying on myself, like the knawing of aqua fortis, irritable, unhappy, capricious, & gloomy, & no demon who holds a poor quivering wretch over the flames, so that they may alternately in their rolling scald & wrinkle his skin, and then roll off & give him time to feel, on the burning end of a red hot arrow headed fork, and who now & then pitches him up, and catches him on the points before he falls, or throws him to a malicious companion, who pierces him through the heart, or sticks him through the brain, and holds him up, his legs & body writhing from one side to the other, like a tumbler, and who, as he puts out his tongue for agony, is caught by the tongue by the other, who waits with his burning fork, and then they lift him, hanging by his tongue, and each puts his fork through his swollen tongue, frothing with the gurgling drag, and when the other's fork is fixed, the first jirks out his fork, and the poor being hangs from the fork of the latter. All this agony of body but feebly expresses my agony of mind without employment.

April 16. What a delightful moment is that of declaring a passion which has long possessed one to a pure, delicious girl, who owes to you her first excitement. In a silent evening, accidentally alone with her, the flutterings of heart, the longings for disclosure, the trembling approaches! The heaving & bursting of her beautiful bosom, hardly concealed by a snowy slip of lawn, which takes the form of its undulations! She sits — you venture to sit near her! You slip gently from the edge of your own chair to the edge of hers, which you affect to conceal! and which she affects not to see! an involuntary sigh; you put your arm on the back of her chair without daring to touch her lovely shoulder — awed, for fear of offending, "for terror in a beauty," you dare, agitated & shaken, with a chattering of teeth and circulating wrench of sensation, to touch her soft hand! She withdraws it not! Your fears instantly vanish, and the liquid flow of a drinking poison oozes through your veins! You raise it from the full thigh on which it rested, and drag in your abstraction some of the muslin that covered it. You press with a start of passion the gentle, helpless hand to your full & burning lips! Your floating eyes meet hers, looking out under her black locks with lustrous tenderness. Down sinks her lovely head under your heated cheek, and you feel her heavenly breath, breathing quickly into your neck! With a languid turning, as if to slow, Angelic music, as if both were bathed in an atmosphere of love, in a broken, tremulous, trembling voice, as if coming through honey, you try to utter, but cannot! You move your lip gently to meet hers, but are unable to reach it, buried as it is in your neck. O God! with the look of an Angel flushed! at the mercy of love! balmy, lovely, languid, heated, she turns up her exquisite mouth, & as you kiss it, your lips cling, with a lingering at every little separation. Your sweet breaths mingle, and you suck extasy till your brain is steeped in steam! You press her with an intensity of grasp. She suffers all, trembling, depending, smiling. Does not this speak all a man would wish? No cant, no dropping on knees, no speaking to Fathers, or consulting cold blooded, brutal brothers — not even a word to her dear self! Perhaps a noise — the Servant with candles! She starts up, with her hair each side of her forehead, and with a dreaming sort of distraction at having been kissed by a Man!

These are the sweet sensations of life. At tea with the family, not a word spoken to each other, hardly venturing to treat her with common politeness; when unwatched, when the rest are occupied, a stolen look, and an exquisite smile from her exquisite lip, assures one of approbation of her sweet recollection. What ages of doubt, of fear & pain, does *this* obliterate. One bounds home like a deer, and rushes to rest that one may dream in misty dozing.

April 20. The more I reflect on my nature, the more I am convinced of my adaptation to great difficulties. I am once again without one farthing! I have paid off the greatest part of my debts — but the price I got for Solomon was so inadequate that my jaunt to Paris & my expences for Models since have swept off the greatest part.[3] So far from being depressed, my breast broadens at

3. The last page of Volume VI contains an account of "Expences of Models for Christ entering Jerusalem" for August, October, and November 1814, totaling £14.3s. One model, Borwood, charged a shilling an hour. The rates for other models, such as Salmon, "Gipsey," "A Fine Jew," and "5 Grenadiers, for a group," are not given.

with candles! — she starts up, with her hair each in of her for[e]head, and with a dreaming sort of delicacy at having been kissed by a man!

: These are the sweet sensations of life — At tea with the family — not a word spoken to each other — hardly venturing to treat her with common politeness — when unwatched, when kisses are occupied — a stolen look — and an exquisite smile from her exquisite lip — assures one of of approbation of her sweet recollection — what ages of doubt, of fear, ʼtwere does this obliterate — She bounds home like a deer, and undresses that one may dream of misty dozing ————

Maria Foote, April 16, 1815.

the contemplation of conquering. I look upon all difficulties as objects of contest & stimulants to action.

I have two hundred pounds to pay the twenty-first of next month. As yet I have not a sixpence towards it, but in God sincerely I trust, who has always relieved me. Let me but be successful in realizing my conception & wishes in my day's labour, and what shall subdue me but extinction?

O God, assist me, enable me to bear up without flinching against the whelming of the approaching tide, let my breast divide it, and let it rush by without carrying me off the footing I have already attained. Support me, assist me, thou great & merciful Being. Grant I may thoroughly & effectually reform the taste & Patronage of My Country.*

April 20. O God Almighty, permit me first to bless thee for thy innumerable mercies during life; for Thy protection, for thy goodness in relieving me from apparently inextricable difficulties, for raising up Friends, & blessing me with success when on the brink of destruction & on the borders of ruin. They are again accumulating; to thee I again cry. Enable me, O God, to conclude grandly & magnificently my present Picture of Christ's triumphant entry into Jerusalem, in spite of all obstructions, however great. Grant its effect when finished may compleat the feeling Solomon has began, grant it may shew the Nation the value, the beauty, the morality, of the higher species of Painting, and rouse the Patrons and the Public to a just sensation of its defective support. O God, let me not die in debt, call not me hence till I have paid all I owe with honor, call me not hence, I humbly entreat thee, till I have accomplished the great object of my being, till I have reformed the taste of my Country, till the views of its Patrons are enlightened, and great works are felt, ordered, & erected, till the Arts of England are on a level with her Philosophy, her Heroism, & her Poetry, and her greatness is compleat. Spare my eyes, invigorate my intellect, grant me capacity to discover my faults & energy to correct them, strengthen every req-

* O God, thou didst support me, thou merciful Protector. January 4, 1818.

uisite that thou hast blest me with, and supply those thou hast
not, and, O Almighty God, if it be permitted for a human being
to conceive the human form & features of the Great Redeemer of
Mankind, spread thy sacred influence over my faculties, instill thy
essence into my being that I may conceive with the most intense
clearness, and execute with the most awful power, in feature &
in form, the virtues, the feelings, & the Divine relation of my
blessed, blessed Saviour. O God, in *this* grant I may preeminently
succeed. Let me live till then. Grant I may contribute as far as
my Art can contribute to advance the morals of the World and
the great interests of Christianity, and when thou callest me
hence, let it [be] in the act of perfecting the talent thou hast
given me, let it be doing my duty to my Art and to my God.
Amen, Amen, in humbleness & gratitude.

April 21. I met two melancholy instances of the fate of life.
My sweet Gipsey Girl,[4] whom I had not seen for two months,
passed me in the Street. I knew her lustrous black eye, which
looked up as usual with its accustomed sparkle, but she shaded
her face, and seemed conscious of something she was ashamed of.
I went up and to my infinite horror, her lovely features were
totally disfigured by the small pox! She told me with true female
chagrin, she had caught them in the natural way, and as she
blushed & felt pain at my presence, I left her. Poor girl. 3 months
ago she used to dart in with romping vivacity, full of health, &
conscious beauty & grace; now she slunk by me in trembling pain!
As if this evening was destined to melancholy sights, I called on a
Friend. The Servant shewed me into a Parlour, and giving me a
chair, walked down to her Master. As I sat musing, the door
slowly opened and a delicate, slender creature, who had the
remnants of beauty still glimmering on her faded cheek, enveloped in a black, long veil, which she held under her chin with
her bony hands, that still were graceful tho fleshless, her back was
almost bent and her lovely bosom almost shrunk, her hair was

4. Patience Smith, the model for the young mother in "Solomon" and for
Jairus' daughter in "Christ's Entry" (*Autobiography,* I,162). A. C. Sewter con-
jectures that she is pictured in the sketch reproduced at I,314, and that she also sat
for some of the studies in BRH's album of drawings in the British Museum
(*Journal of the Gypsy Lore Society,* July-October 1944, 3rd Series, 23:69–71).

carelessly, as it were, straggling over her polished forehead, as if the thought of personal appearance was now absorbed by contemplation on her near approach to another existence! As she advanced, she perceived me, and was retiring. I instantly rose and begged I might not retard her, and offered her my assistance. She took my arm and tottered towards the other door. As she was thanking me and going out, we both like a flash of lightning recognised each other. Good Heavens, this was a young Lady, whom I had known; young, plump, active, & beautiful, dying in Consumption! I could scarcely refrain from tears, as I touched her feeble hands & shook them. "I am sure you don't know me," said she, "Mr. Haydon," attempting to smile with her parched lips, which almost cracked with drouth as she moved them. She had not strength to speak or to bear questions, so she withdrew like a spirit, and looked a friendly & eternal farewell, with her yet gentle eye, into which some tears had started, as a crowd of associations & once happy remembrances shone to her fancy. Dear Soul — how strange such few years should have produced such changes. Old age & disease! What terrific enemies ye are to human vanity! I remember her tho' never in violent spirits, always sweet, lively, & interesting. I have walked & whispered to her & poured out the overflowings of a heart excited to feelings of gallantry, by having a gentle arm within my own, or feeling the soft pressure of her bosom. I have ridden with her, and curbed my horse by degrees that we might loiter behind, and enjoy the beauties of a Summer evening, or a golden sun set. I was then 17, gay, volatile, & boyish. Death was then to our young thoughts in long perspective. She, alas, is now almost arrived at the end of it. I went home & spent the evening in mournful meditation. There are moments when all the beautiful periods of one's existence crowd to one's fancy in melancholy remembrance, when as if permission was given to our guardian Angel to turn the mirror that reflected them to our minds, that they might for a moment obliterate the rugged impressions of trouble. There is something extremely interesting in sickness. I think I should love my wife more tenderly then than at any other time, so keenly was I affected at this young creature's state that my nerves were most sensitive, like the strings of a violin richly & newly rosined!

which speak harmony at the slightest touch. I looked at every thing with a double interest. I felt the humming of silence in my brain! and the racy thrill of sensation throughout my frame, mixed with melancholy wishes to be quiet, reflective, & secret. I went home & mused till midnight, hating the noise even of a dropping cinder!

April 22. Why is any thing more unaccountable in the mind's acting on the brain, than the will acting on the muscle?

April 27. An old Friend whom I had not seen for fifteen years called on me today. We were school fellows and parted in the gaity of Youth, he to go to India, and I to pursue my Father's business. We now again met, but he was so altered I did not know him. He has returned with all the cursed consequences of that Climate, a liver complaint & feeble. After a burst of recollections of our youthful follies, which delighted us both, he invited me to Breakfast. I went and there we indulged in gay remembrances till we were convulsed with laughter. Our old Master was dead [5] — we paid a tribute to his kindness, and then calling up our school fellows, found one killed in a duel, a second in action, a third died abroad, & a fourth on the King of [*The name of the kingdom is omitted*] a fifth another, till gradually sinking into the sorrows of life, we came to our own. He had married & 8 days after his beautiful wife lost the use of her limbs, & has been a cripple ever since. She remained at Calcutta, he was come home. The tears started in his eyes as he talked of her. We shortly after parted and really we both cried as we mutually squeezed each other's hands. Elias Dunsterville[6] at school was the Soul of us all, full of fun, fond of Acting, well read in plays, he would quote for an hour, open hearted & generous; he would share any thing he had, if it would contribute to the general gaity of all. Boys are not able to discriminate. I found he now wanted soundness of judgement, which had not encreased with his other good qualities, but I love him & remember him with pleasure. Peace go with him.

5. Since the Reverend William Haynes (or Hayne), master of the Plympton Grammar School, did not die until 1816, BRH doubtless refers to his earlier teacher, Dr. Bidlake (see I,242).

6. On March 8, 1838, BRH wrote: "Dear Elias Dunsterville is dead."

April 29. This week has really been a week of great delight. Never have I had such irresistible, perpetual, & continued urgings of future greatness. I have been like a man with air balloons under his arm pits and ether in his soul. While I was painting, or walking, or thinking, these beaming flashes of energy followed & impressed me! O God, grant they may not be presumptuous feelings. Grant they may be the fiery anticipations of a great Soul born to realize them. They came over me, & shot across me, & shook me, & inspired me to such a degree of intensity, that I lifted up my heart, & thanked God.

May 1. I went to the exhibition[7] again and am just come home, worn out in eyes, mind, body, & Soul, hot, murky, horrid, & weary.

May 2. Went to the Institution to see the Vandykes & Rembrandts lit by lamps. Was amazingly impressed with the care, the diligence, the compleat finish of the works of these great men. Came home & looked at my own Picture. It must be done so, and there's an end. The beauty of the Women, the exquisite, nosegay sweetness of their looks, their rich crimson velvet, & white satin, & lawn, & muslin, & diamonds, with their black eyes & peachy complexions, & snowy necks, & delicious forms, & graceful motions, & sweet nothingness of conversation, bewildered & distracted me. What the Nobility have in their power to enjoy in this World! What has not the Prince? The finest Women, educated, elegant, & accomplished. But they seem not happy; they seem not to relish that which we feel exquisitely. They want the stimulus of action of a scheme. Their minds preying on themselves, seek refuge in novelty, but that alone from its nature not exciting hope or fear or enthusiasm, the usual feelings of faculties in action. They become used & weary even of that for which they sacrifice principle & honor to pursue.

May 5. The Directors are always guiding Youth but never think of rewarding maturity.

7. At the Royal Academy or the British Institution. "This — the first exhibition of Old Masters held in England — was composed of Flemish and Dutch pictures, borrowed from the most important private collections (Whitley, *1800–1820*, p. 247).

May

I used to suffer great pain at the bad passions of Wilkie, at his envious, unenthusiastic disposition, but alas, being now thoroughly hopeless of any ardent feeling towards me, I pity his pale meaneses and heartless, dry-lipped shrinkings.

There's not a more horrid feeling in the World, than that after having been out all day roving about at Exhibitions (which I always do every first week in May), to return and see your own Picture, standing in a solitary manner, untouched & neglected. Tho I improved in mind probably and benefitted in health, yet the acute agony of an idle, unemployed day makes one unhappy.

I have passed this day at the Institution again, studying Rubens & Rembrandt with the greatest attention, & have derived the greatest instruction. It is only by studying their beauties & discovering their defects that one can hope to surpass them. The Artists complain, the Directors wish to run the Masters against them; why complain? If it be true, let them exert themselves, and try to run against the old Masters. I am no Friend to these groanings, they are all excuses for Idleness.

Tho' I do not approve of the conduct of the Directors in thus shutting the Institution against the living Artists at the full Season of the Year, yet I cannot but be grateful to them for affording me such advantages of study and such means of improvement, and tho' I grievously suspect the Vanity of shewing their own Pictures that they may see their names in the Catalogues, &c., &c., &c., &c., to be the predominant feeling. Let every man scrutinize his own principles of action. Will he always find them quite pure?

I really do not know a more detestable feeling than that monopolizing feeling generated in Corporate bodies. Any other Society of whatever nature is always considered an enemy. Every thing the Institution has ever done has been reviled, with the most acrimonious severity. Every Picture brought forward in the Style of any of its Members has always been considered an attack on that Member. I would not belong to them for the whole World. The Academicians, to be sure, are pretty fellows to scrutinize the purity of principles. I never think of belonging to the Academy but I feel as if I should instantly become from a healthy looking, pure, wholesome being, a yellow, jaundiced, poor, shrivelled creature, as if I had been dipped in a bilious puddle.

[*A sketch of Vandyke's "Charles I on Horseback," lent to the exhibition by the Duke of Marlborough, and now in the National Gallery.*]

The Colour of Charles's Portrait is very fine toned & Titianesque, but the great principles of motion & form are grossly defective. The haunch, the fetlocks, the shoulders are all out in form, badly understood & frittered away in paltry little bits without sense or intelligence. The head & character of Charles's head are very fine & Gentlemanly, but the way he sits no horseman sits one moment, but to stretch his limbs for an instant. Nothing can be more awkward than the straight, stiff limb poked out for a position to rest in, a position in which he could not remain for over 5 minutes.

In point of feeling for effect the great requisite to make others feel, nothing can be finer. The whole is like the deep toned roar of a Cathedral organ, in the glimmering of a Summer twilight. Colour, light, & Shadow, & form are the means. Under form I comprehend the principles of motion & causes of action [and] expression. Of course form is the most important part of the means of conveying ideas. The head & face are the principle parts. Intellect & feeling is more intelligibly expressed by the head & face & features than by any other parts. Many defects in limb & body will of course [be] overlooked if the head & face be fine & true, but tho' the limbs & body are inferior parts or were instruments of the head, yet to complete truth, they ought to be all equally correct & expressive. You must divide the World into scientific & natural critics, those whose eyes & minds are qualified by Study, & those whose only qualifications are a feeling heart & a sound capacity without study or acquirement. They can tell whether the expression be true or the story told, whether the colour be harmonious or the proportions be incorrect. All these [are] general points, for which a natural organization are requisite to understand. I have always found any error in harmony, in proportion, in truth & in expression, to be instantly perceived by such people. Therefore Artists are too often content if the feelings of such people are affected no *matter how.* But they must recollect that tho' the expression be true to please those who feel, the parts that compose the means must also be right to gratify those who understand.

[*Five sneering profiles, labeled "Owen."* [8]]

Pauvre Academicien! Ne soyez pas au desespoir. An Academician's face while he was looking at Rubens — actually! I watched him, I studied him, I dwelt on him in silent contempt!

I intend to begin by an immense mass, & gradually diminish it till it comes to the ground.

"Well," said an Academician,[9] "this will destroy us all, Mr. Haydon." "Destroy us," said I, "God forbid. I'll answer it will rouse me." "Well, I believe," said he, "this is the right way of taking it." Poor, miserable, half begotten creature — and had he just found that out?

Nothing in my opinion shews the mean feeling & the paltry talent of the Academy more compleatly than the way they have taken up the present exhibition of fine works of the Institution; instead of being fired to excel, they are excited to decry, instead of doing justice to the genius of the great men who have painted, they set about insinuating mean motives to those who have collected them. From my heart & Soul I despise them & their paltry Souls, & God grant that no infatuation may ever come over my feelings to make me disgrace myself by joining them.

May 6. Why does not Payne Knight put forth his reasons for doubting the originality of the Elgin Marbles?[1] Shall a mere

8. One of these sketches of William Owen, "made by a friend of our's, a clever fellow," is reproduced in the *Annals of the Fine Arts* review of the *Catalogue Raisonné of the Pictures exhibiting in Pall Mall* (1816, 1:196). The review was reprinted in the *Examiner*, October 6, 1816, pp. 635–637.
9. Identified as Thomas Stothard (*Autobiography*, I,205).
1. BRH delivered a lecture on the Elgin Marbles in 1840; he quoted (*Lectures*, II,237), with slight inaccuracy, the following opinion, which he said that Payne Knight wrote: "Of Phidias's general style of composition, the friezes and metopes of the temple of Minerva at Athens, published by Mr. Stuart, and since brought to England, may afford us competent information; but as these are merely architectural sculptures executed from his designs and under his directions, probably by workmen scarcely ranked among artists, and meant to be seen at the height of more than forty feet from the eye, they can throw but little light upon the more important details of his art" (*Specimens of Antient Sculpture, Aegyptian, Etruscan, Greek, and Roman:* selected from different collections in Great

connoiseur's opinion be put against the opinion of an Artist? Shall the idle, superficial, conceited, vain glance of a dilettante be of more value than the deep investigating principles & practiced search of the Artist? Posh! Shall a dabbler in Gypsum grounds & a learned bungler of Pliny,[2] shall a secret sneerer of the Art in the Edingburgh review, & a pretended public Patroniser tell me they are not pure? What does all this prove? Why, what all artists knew long since, that Mr. P. Knight knows nothing of Art, either from feeling or Practice. When an Artist knows & feels & can prove the system these divine productions are built on; when he sees this system running through them, both great & little, like a code of laws, when he sees the most exquisite execution & most principled composition, when he sees & knows & can prove the greatest of all difficulties is here accomplished, the union of the truth of Nature with the highest ideal beauty. What can he feel against a cold blooded, selfish, revengeful connoiseur, who dares to doubt the purity of such effusions? That my opinions may not be considered as merely the result of enthusiasm, let me explain why a deep knowledge, facilely executed, is a proof of originality. When the mind is uninformed, how little can the eye see, or the hand execute? And if the mind ever thoroughly comprehends, without practice the hand is nerveless & the eye sees in vain. Knowledge may be feebly executed, tho truly, but when knowledge is firmly executed, as well [as] easily, it argues two things: first, that [the] Artist possesses the knowledge and secondly that practice has rendered him skilful in executing it. There then are the two great tests of originality in any Work. In the Elgin Marbles, the Composition, that is the arrangement of objects, to express the end in view as a whole, is perfect. The science of the parts that compose these objects individually [is] profound, and

Britain, by the Society of Dilettanti, 1809, I,xxxix). This essay, like all others in the book, is unsigned; it ends with a reference to Greek coins "from the cabinet of Mr. Payne Knight."

2. In his first letter "To the Critic on Barry's Works in the *Edinburgh Review*, August 1810" (see I,213), BRH attacked Knight's misunderstanding and ignorance of Pliny in contending that Greek artists painted only small pictures (*Examiner*, January 26, 1812, p. 62 n.).

the execution of these parts to express the conceived Idea, of the end of the object, particularly as referring to the said whole [is] easy, vigourous, & powerful. The whole, the result of genius in the conception, arrangement, & industry & perseverance of execution. Sculpture conveys its meanings by form; light & shadow is the consequence of the form, & cannot be considered as the cause or a part of the language. Men & Animals are the principal organs of a Painter or Sculptor's conceptions, and the conception generally [of] some powerful event, by which the passions or feelings of Men or animals are excited. The passions or feelings when excited are expressed by the features & form as instruments of the passions or feelings.

The Bones are the foundation of form, & the muscles & tendons the means of moving the bones, as the passions excite or the feelings dictate. The bones, the things moved, & the muscles, the things moving, are all covered by skin, and the great business of the mechanism of the Art, is to shew the true effect of the causes of the motion, acting beneath, shewing above the skin that covers them. When the mind has informed itself thoroughly of the means, the eye may easily perceive the effect of the means thus acting, & when any passion & feeling is wished to be expressed, the means that express them will by the Artist thus qualified be as complete in form & as true in effect as Nature, and the idea thus represented will be doubly effectual, by the perfection of the means of its representation.

Genius enables a Man to conceive events & the passions likely to be called out, & practice & study enables him to execute by the above means the passions he has conceived. The next thing is, what is his great characteristic distinction of that form that contains the highest intellect as opposed [to] the form that contains none? Standing erectly — the causes of this are physical formation; the physical formation must be ascertained & always visible. When I see & can prove this great principle in every figure however small in the Elgin Marbles, is a Connoiseur, a mere man of doubtful taste, to tell me or the public that works with such marks of Genius & Science are doubtful productions! That the Nobility should suffer themselves to be led by such blurred, infatuated, envious, & prejudiced intellects! Dr. Clarke[3] too has joined the hue & cry against Lord Elgin — Dr. Clarke, who took away all he *could* take away, and sneers at Lord [Elgin] because he had the power to take & did, thank God, take away more, Dr. Clarke! who first says the Turks destroy nothing, and then speaking of a Temple of Corinth with the most interesting sang froid, mentions there having been sixteen columns, but that the Dirdar Aga had destroyed 4 of them.[4] The cause of all this is paltry envy. Lord Elgin is envied by his fellow Nobility because he did what they had never courage to do before him. He is hated by the French because he finished what they had begun & were interrupted in finishing, but by all true lovers of their Country's Art, by all Painters, Sculptors, & Architects of this & all generations, he will be loved, adored, & reverenced. To him I owe every principle of Art I possess & to his energy & vigour & perseverance, the Country will ultimately owe right notions & firm principles that will extricate it from the perversion of truth & dereliction generated by the Royal Academy.

For if any were excited incompatible with the feeling, the body would do what the mind meant it should not do (and which is always the case in spasmatic affections). Science of the parts, then, is a complete knowledge of what muscles are exerted & what movements are the consequences of the passion or intention, and the unscientific spectator, without knowing why, if the thing be truly done, feels the result in his own brain like the harmonious roar of an Organ, from the scientific touch of an accomplished musician. If the Spectator feels thus from the Elgin Marbles, & the Artist can prove the cause, so that the Artist must have the knowledge, and then can shew the exertion to be easy, so that

3. Edward Daniel Clarke (1769–1822) LL.D., traveler and antiquary, author of *Travels in Various Countries of Europe, Asia, and Africa.* 6 vols., 1810–1823. Concerning excavations in Athens, Clarke wrote: "Among English travellers, the Earl of Aberdeen is particularly distinguished for his liberality in encouraging works of this kind: the more laudable, in being opposed to the lamentable operations which another British Earl, one of his Lordship's countrymen, was then prosecuting, to the *utter ruin* of the finest works of Antient Greece" (Part Two, Section Two, 1814, p. 465 n.).

4. "The destruction that has taken place [in the Temple at Corinth], of *four* columns out of the *eleven* seen by *Wheler* and *Chandler,* had been accomplished by the Governor, who used them in building a house; first blasting them into fragments with gunpowder" (Clarke, *Travels,* p. 735).

practice must have given him power. No other proof is necessary, for their authenticity & originality.

The obstinacy & ignorance of English Connoiseurs in high Art is a basis of perfect ridicule on the Continent, and Heaven knows well it may!

All the objects animate & inanimate of Nature are the means of conveying the conceptions in Painting or Sculpture. Composition, that is, the arrangement of these objects for an end, of which every object is a part, and then the parts these objects are composed of individually, so that each object may be truly expressed, and then the power of representing these objects truly by imitation — are the mechanical acquirements requisite before a thought is ventured. Then when an Idea is conceived, composition develops the idea by the arrangement of objects, and science develops the objects by an exposition of the parts that compose them; — but then composition has principles of its own. Expression, composition, colour, light & Shadow, may be all reduced to one principle — bustle & repose & the gradation from one to the other — bustle excites attention & repose relieves it. In composition the greatest quantity of objects will excite the greatest quantity of interest, in expression the most intense, in colour the brightest, in light the strongest, & shadow the deepest.

[By] his language is Man as a species distinct from Animals. Not men as distinct from each other. What then is the great characteristic distinction of man, as distinguished from Animals as a species? This ascertained, your means of representing by form the being which is your organ is ascertained. The various movements, expressions, or beauties of this being, in limb, in action, or repose, or as influenced by the common principles of his Nature is thus your language, with respect to his feelings or passion, and as influenced by the common principles of life, with regard to the [principles] as to its individual composition as matter.

Flesh is soft, bones are hard. Flesh in repose will be affected by a substance harder than itself against which it may be pressed, and its shape altered. Bone never will, and its shape never can be altered but by its own movement. All angles, such [as] arm pits, & all joints that can be extended or compressed, will when extended give flesh greater room, & when compressed less. So flesh compressed into a smaller space or stretched to a larger, must, being soft, be wrinkled or stretched. Thus all wrinkles are requisite to shew the consequences of action or repose, &c., &c., &c. These [are the] common probabilities of the substance of Man's body, & these the Greeks [showed] in the Elgin Marbles. Every expression of intention by form & feature, & every variation of form produced by the slightest variation of motion in consequence of the variation of intention can be proved to exist in the Elgin Marbles. Every shape of each part in consequence of inherent formation, every shape in consequence of momentary muscular action, every beauty of execution, [*an illegible phrase of about six words*] every variety of motion in consequence of professional practice can be proved to exist in the Elgin Marbles. And yet a Connoiseur of known bad taste, tho' of considerable talent & ingenuity to make the worse appear the better reason, doubts their originality. I think we need no longer to doubt his judgement. This is harsh, but is [it] not truth? The last time I honored Mr. Payne Knight by exposing his mistakes of Pliny, I was told he was a Patron of Art & a Director of the British Gallery. These were given as reasons why I ought not to have ventured on exposure — these were my very reasons for doing it. Had he been an unimportant man without influence, his absurd notions should have been passed over, but being what he was, it was my duty to destroy them. Surely I did it without heat or presumption.

May 10. I was never so struck with the identity and reality of Rembrandt as today. The things made me start. They seemed moving, speaking, sparkling, burning with life & vigour.

"There is a Providence that shapes our ends, rough hew them how we will." [5] Let me not be vain to think this applies to me, but can I think it otherwise when I recollect those who used me so ill & triumphed & trampled over me, who refused me admittance as an associate and conducted themselves with insolence when they met me, who saw me oppressed, in want, in misery, and imagined I was ruined? Can I imagine otherwise when two years

5. *Hamlet*, V,ii,10–11. "There's a divinity that shapes our ends/Rough-hew them how we will."

after Sir G. Beaumont & I quarrelled & I carried myself so high to Sir G. as frightened even my enemies, that I go by invitation to Sir G.'s this evening and there meet one of the very Academicians who hung Dentatus in dark! What his astonishment & feelings were I need not attempt to explain. My triumph both as to my independence of mind regarding him & Sir G. was compleat. God grant this may not too much puff my pen up, but really my success this Year is great indeed & my sensation seems delightful.

May 13. The great business of life is to enjoy oneself [without] any sensuality, but there are several modes of enjoyment. Some enjoy themselves at the moment and suffer from the consequences, while others conquer the urgings of the moment, which is enjoyment too, after the contest is over, and feel real delight in the result. There is no real enjoyment in life but acting on principle, or there is no real pleasure if the pleasure be not on principle.

I came home from the Elgin Marbles melancholy. I almost wish the French had them; we do not deserve such productions. There they lie, covered with dust & dripping with damp, adored by the Artists, admired by the People, neglected by the Government, doubted by Payne Knight, because to doubt them is easier than to feel them, & reverenced & envied by Foreigners, because they do not possess them. What new idea of the perfection of Art God Almighty has pleased to inspire this Man's imagination with — Heaven knows! But I begin to believe with Soame Jennings[6] in his "Origin of Evil," that these beings who delight & exist in miseries, the diseases, the follies of Man, and as Johnson said in his Review, perhaps some of these mischievous creatures induced Jennings to write an essay on evil that he might revel in his absurdity, and I have not the slightest doubt the descendants of the same branch of little demons are now enjoying the success of their whisperings that like ignes fatui have set visions before the eyes & have bewildered the imaginations of Payne Knights to doubt the beauty of the Elgin Marbles. Poor man, there

6. Soame Jenyns (1704–1787), author of *Free Enquiry into the Nature and Origin of Evil* (1757), reviewed by Samuel Johnson in numbers 13 (pp. 171–175), 14 (pp. 251–253), and 15 (pp. 301–306) of the *Literary Magazine* for 1757. It was published as a book in 1759.

is nothing more miserable than to think men are the instruments of organizations or infatuation or fancy. Whatever takes away from the power of reasoning on differences & seeing distinctions & arriving at conclusions deprives a human being of half his dignity. When I go to the Chapel at Newgate & see chained convicts all brought in, creatures who for the benefit of Society are obliged to be confined, I imagine I see so many beings acting from irresistible formation, like wood that irresistibly ignites from friction or snow that irresistibly becomes water from melting. When I see round a Minister's Table creatures & clergymen who sit destined to cringe & flatter & fawn, the propensity to do which was even then to gain what Nature had denied them the power of doing without, when I see a poor Connoiseur who pretends to taste, without feeling, I no more wonder at his doubting the Elgin Marbles than at a cow bellowing, a frog croaking, a thief thieving, a Courtier fawning, an author investigating the origin of evil which can't be investigated, or Payne Knight doubting the Elgin Marbles, which can't be doubted. All this, after all, makes one [*the sentence is unfinished*].

Why should nature create unhappy beings with a propensity to pretend to that for which she with willful maliciousness the next moment unqualifies them to ground their pretensions? Why should she create a man with a desire to be a connoiseur, without at the same time giving him the real power to be one? Why should she create some with the desires of ambition without the abilities? Why does she not create a frog with a desire to roar like a lion, or a cow to race like a Hunter? No! It is only with unhappy man she plays her freaks; on him she exhausts her invention, on him she revels. She limits the will of the animal to the power, but she suffers the will, the wishes, & the ambiguities of Man to inhibit his ability, to desire often what he cannot do, & to do often what he cannot feel.

No other professions are cursed with connoiseurs but Poetry & Painting. There are no connoiseurs in War, in Physic, in Surgery. No man will trust his limb[?] to a connoiseur in Surgery; no sweet Girl in Consumption, with her lovely bosom wasting & her sparkling eye sinking, would believe in her recovery if a Connoiseur was her adviser; no Government or General would admit a Connoiseur in to a council of War. The professor's tactics of every other profession on Earth, who devote their lives to it, are supposed (& justly) to know more than those who fill a vacant day with wandering gabble or casual glance. Connoiseurs never existed in finest periods of Art. They are beings who rise like flies from carrion, in the decay & rotteness of its Works. To know one Master's touch, or another Master's peculiarity, instead of to feel a beauty or recognize an expression, are the great points & criteria of a Man's capability. They are curses to living Artists because their very origin & nature instigates them to value only the dead. Poor Painters & Poets are the beings who are supposed to be the mere mechanism of these creatures' thoughts.

And yet the direction of the public taste and the direction of the native genius in Art is to be left not to those who have spent their lives in the study, but to those who take it up for their amusement to fill an idle day and afford chatter for a dinner.

Genius in Poverty is never feared because Nature, tho' liberal in her gifts in one instance, is forgetful in another, but Genius in affluence alarms the *amour propre* of those whom Nature has made rich, and yet made foolish. They cannot bear a Man to rise by the native vigour of mind to that pitch of independence which they have inherited, because they were born & not because they've deserved it. Hence the preaching that want is requisite to stimulate talent, that competence is only necessary, that Milton got but ten pounds for Paradise Lost. This might be impartial & candid in the Painter to say, the person to be paid, but looks rather suspicious from the Patron, the Person to pay him.

As I sat amidst the ruins of Athens this evening, piled on each other as if shaken by an earthquake, and on every side caught glimpses of the living groups, the presumption of a Connoiseur in daring to doubt these inspired productions came across my feelings with the most intense disgust. These are the works of Art he doubts the beauty of! These are the productions whose excellence he affirms not to see! Now when the united testimony of artists & men of taste have born down his absurd surmises, he says with cold blooded sarcasm they *may be* original but they are such fragments that half their value is gone, and would he have them sacrilegiously restored? No doubt of it, no doubt of it. Remember this — thou art not perhaps insensible to posthumous reputation. Remember, Mr. Payne Knight, the fame of the Elgin Marbles will encrease with our knowledge and treble with time. Remember that when all thy works are sunk into oblivion, Priapus[7] & all, thou will be only recollected by thy presumption in disbelieving their beauty. If to such fame you aspire, you shall have it. Thy name shall be mentioned by posterity in conjunction with these immortal works, but it shall be with contempt, with sneers of indignation. I cannot speak of such a cold blooded being without having my frame shake & my lips become pale. Either he has no judgement or you, you curb your sensations to cloke meaner passions. Envy of Lord Elgin in the possession of such works — you have a collection yourself of paltry bronzes, remarkable for nothing but rusty antiquity. The breathing nature, the unaffected majesty, the naked simplicity of the Elgin Marbles must have struck you at once. Not even the Louvre can be compared to these in style, and there are few after this we suspect that dare expect the honor.

Either you do see the beauties of these exquisite works or you do not. If you do not, you are to be pitied, but cease at once to undervalue what you do not feel — but if you do, & affirm you do not, that you may cloke the envy of another's possessions under a fastidiousness of taste, you deserve to be detested by all, and you have my detestation from the depths of my soul. You cannot suppose I can feel any very great delicacy of sensation towards your mistakes; you have hung on me during my career with the malignity of a demon; you have sneered at my views & endeavoured to blast their success. It was you who, without generosity enough to admire the enthusiasm devoted to his Art in his exposure of your mistakes, who influenced the Directors to refuse me the prize. It was you who went to the private view of the pictures at Spring Gardens (a thing you never did in your life before or since) and ridiculed Solomon to the Princess of Wales.

7. Knight's first published work was *An Account of the Remains of the Worship of Priapus Lately Existing in Isernia; to which is added a Discourse on the Worship of Priapus, and its Connexion with the Mystic Theology of the Ancients* (1786). After severe attacks on the book, Knight attempted to buy up all the copies.

May

It seems to me that I feel & think & invent more in May than in any other month.

May 19. I saw Miss O'Neil [8] in Isabella. Really there was no bearing it. I sat with the tears trickling over my cheeks like a woman. Never tell me the feelings of a youth are half so intensely strong as those [of] a man of experience in the World's troubles. What does a boy know of the passions of the World, what does he know of that mysterious depth of love, after connection with a creature on whom your soul doats, & a child is the result? Oh God, when Biron came in to her and she screamed & fell on the floor & rushed up to him & felt him & looked at him & dwelt on him & seemed eager to devour him, what my heart felt! I entered into the essence of her very being. I sobbed with remembrances. It touched a cord of my own sensitive heart, that the World will never be acquainted with. Thus it is, you are born with the feeling, as with the capacity; exercise of both more finely tunes each. You must more easily comprehend what you have previously comprehended, as you must more intensely feel another's agonies if you have previously suffered them.

May 20. For the first time in my life, I have [been] obliged to borrow money of a money lender. A Friend [9] went first & asked him to do it. He consented & appointed me the next morning. I went & shook at the degradation as I entered the door. He received me with a sort of sob, and said with a jirk of his finger, "walk in there." I went in & took up the Paper to conceal my agitation; his Wife came in & began to talk, with the airs of a Person used to see people in want. I bore it silently. He entered! As I had seen him in the passage, his features were not perceptible. He was now a little, low fellow, with red eyes, his lids hanging down over his pupils so that he was obliged to throw his head back & look at you through the slit, as it were, his eye lids

8. Eliza O'Neill (1791–1872), tragic actress. She played Isabella in Thomas Southerne's tragedy *The Fatal Marriage* (1694), produced at Covent Garden Theatre May 18, 1815. In 1819, she married William Becher, M.P., later a baronet, and retired from the stage.
9. Identified in BRH's "Vita," the first draft of his *Autobiography,* as John Varley (1778–1842), a landscape painter who suffered many financial difficulties. Of course BRH had borrowed widely from his friends before this time (see I,228), and according to FWH had patronized moneylenders (see I,337 n).

made. I could not speak to him, so he began, "Well, Mr. Haydon, you want to borrow [a] hundred pounds." "Yes. I will give you a bill endorsed by a Friend so that you will be secure." He hummed & said he had respect for my talents but that he feared he could not do it. I really blazed with indignation; he had induced me to come by promising to do it, and now drew back to see what further I could offer. I begged pardon for troubling and left him, cursing my stars to be so insulted. My Friend saw him in the evening, & told me the only way was to carry the bill at once and not explain & ask him at once what he would cash it for. I did so. He now said, "Sit down, Sir." I sat down. He was shaving. "You see, Sir, I never like to deal with Gentlemen. I only do business. I have no objection to cash the bill, provided you will take some goods of me." "Certainly," was my reply. "Walk up stairs in the Front room & look about you. Choose what you like & let me know." I went up, & found a room full of every thing on earth — Pictures, books, shirts, leather breeches, shoes, hats, jewelry, &c., &c. A rascally sketch of Rubens was placed [so] as to catch my eye, *knowing my love for him.* I saw it at once. I went down & told him I liked that sketch. "Well, what you'll give?" "What d'ye ask?" "Twenty guineas." "It's mine," said I. His little skinny lips drew back & smiled. He became gracious. He could not conceal a little degree of nervousness at such an imposition, but he soon recovered. He talked of my nearsightedness, begged to look at my glasses, tried them on, asked me to try on his, enquired where I got mine, & then wondered with affected interest, *& yet real abstraction,* that I should be nearsighted as well as he. "Well," said he, "draw out the bill for 122.10, that is, including the interest, and it shall be paid you tomorrow." "At what time?" said I. "*My* time is *your* time," said he. "½ past Seven in the Morning," I said. "Yes."

I left him — he attended me to the door — & returned home to finish the drapery I was painting. I did finish it before dinner (nothing now obstructs me I am so used to harrassings — I finished the two arms of the Woman by snatches of an hour at a time, & they are the best things I've done, thank God). This morning I called again. He now seemed unwilling & took the bill with a sulky air; however, after reading it over & over & over again, he made out the draft. "Don't call for it by [*sic*, for *until*] the afternoon," said he; "by that time more money will be paid in for me." "It will be paid *then?*" said I. He laughed inwardly with a malicious pleasure at my simple question, knowing himself to be worth 100,000 pounds. Thus this man has accumulated his wealth, cashing bills, & then if the drawers are tradesmen & can't take them up, he makes them give property, such as hats, breeches, & books, &c. He then cashed other bills for other people, never taking more *than the regular interest,* so that he is always safe, but making them take a book or Picture worth ten pence for 20 or 30 Guineas. His house is respectable & to cover all this he is a wine merchant!! What degradation will not a lover undergo to attain his mistress? What degradation will not I suffer (except dishonor) to attain the highest point in my noble art?

What agonies did I first suffer at my first want. I who never knew what it was to stretch forth my hand without having it filled, I who never borrowed a sixpence, till driven. The question was this, should I give up my views & render useless my knowledge in Art by sacrificing to a false pride? *No.* I resolved to go on, knowing my integrity, trusting to my talents & my God to finally extricating me & enabling me to pay all with honor, with the pleasure of reputation & greatness arising from the degradations. Had Sir G. Beaumont treated [me] with common feeling, I should never have wanted, but enough of this.

I am not in want from extravagance but from being disappointed of my pay after sacrificing every thing to deserve it. My Father's means failed when in the middle of Macbeth. I finished it by selling my cloaths, my property, my prints, expecting honorable treatment when all was done. I was disappointed. I began Solomon with this accumulated weight. I was obliged to borrow to go on with it. What I got for that did not pay all; it cleared half of that Picture's expences & the remainder of Macbeth's. Consequently I am again in want & I must again borrow or paint Portraits, which is still a greater degradation. O God, thou who has never forsaken me, in thee I trust with all my heart & soul & mind. Enable me to proceed in spite of all; grant I may bring this Picture of Christ's entry into Jerusalem to a grand & magnificent conclusion in spite of all. Grant me every power requisite for its conception & execution, & energy of mind & body to bear up & conquer every difficulty arising out of the greatness of the attempt. O God, thou knowest my heart. Grant I may live to reform the taste of my Country, to deserve thy mercy & my Country's fame. In thee I trust, with all my Soul. Amen, Amen, Amen.

I remembered in the agony of want, I once rushed to a pawn broker with my watch & found myself in the midst of wretches of the lowest cast, before I was aware, some selling their under petticoats, some with their husbands' coats, some with their shoes, & now & then came a hand through a hole with a silver spoon, which was taken & paid for, the seller never seeing & never seen! What with my furious passions & my agonising wants, I often wonder I kept my head. The Master where I had dined regularly, seeing my uneasiness & suspecting the cause (as I had [been] trusted for a week), took me aside & told me not to be uneasy, "he relied on my principle," & I might dine there till I could pay. He trusted me during the whole time of Solomon's painting! With what delight did I pay him! Two years did Mr. Seabrook,[1] Rupert Street, receive me with a smiling face & an open hand, without one complaint, one surly air, & one shade of disrespect, as if I had paid him like a Nobleman. My throat choaks as I write it! — must I not think, O God, I am under thy merciful protection to be so assisted? Pardon the presumption, but I must.

May 23. I Breakfasted with Wordsworth[2] & spent delightful two hours. Speaking of Burke, Fox, & Pitt, he said, "You always went from Burke with your mind filled, from Fox with your feelings excited, & from Pitt with wonder at his making you uneasy, at his having had the power to make the worse appear the better reason. Pitt preferred power to principle," he said.

I have now no harrassings for a Month. How I worked after I paid Saturday's bill, as if two weights of iron were taken off my hand; tho' it never crushed, it always excited me to bear up against it; such is my elasticity from Nature.

There [is] no sect, or philosophy, or religion, or law, that has

1. John Seabrook, proprietor of John o' Groats' Tavern, 61 Rupert Street, Haymarket. He retired by 1817 (see II,111) and became proprietor of the Abercorne Arms, Stanmore, Middlesex (Pigot).
2. William Wordsworth (1770–1850), poet.

so much contributed to the public good as the Christian faith. Bacon.[3]

The most painful age is the age between maturity & Youth, when with all the boyish feelings, you have not sufficient character of manhood to indulge in them, without losing the little reputation which your dawning beard begins to give. When once a man, any nonsense is excused. Thus it is with reputation of every kind, when once established, your freaks are excused as proofs of amiability, which before would have been censured as marks of weakness.

The great wish of Mankind are objects of pursuit. Some furnish themselves & some are content to be furnished by others. This is the reason why men of Genius are so obeyed by Mankind, not from any principle of obedience, but because it can furnish men still with objects of excitement, according to their own capacities to be excited. They then act from their own principle or motive tho contributing to the principles of another.

I like amazingly Voltaire's impudence, supposing that Bacon, Locke, & Newton were blind & infatuated beings, as to Religion, tho' having such immense intellectual power in other matters, because he imagined [himself] to be possessed [with] such amazing perspicuity of perception in these matters & that whoever differed with him must be wrong.

The just ridicule with which Voltaire treats the superstition of some Religion is applied by his pupils to all. The Religion that demands of the votaries to run nails into their bums is put in comparison with that which demands of them to examine themselves whether they repent them truly of their sins, to give alms to the poor & Fatherless & the orphan & the Widow — to be meek in spirit & pure in heart!!!

May 27. I have worked this week intensely & advanced my Picture delightfully, my eyes strong, my mind in fine tune, prac-

3. This apparently is BRH's translation of: "Nulla omnibus saeculis reperta est vel philosophia vel secta vel religio vel lux aut disciplina, quae in tantum Communionis Bonum exaltavit, Bonum vero Individuale depressit, quantum Sancta Fides Christiana" (Francis Bacon, *De Dignitate et Augmentis Scientiarum*, Book 7. *The Works of Francis Bacon*, ed. J. Spedding, R. L. Ellis, and D. D. Heath, New York, 1864, III,13).

tice encreasing my powers of hand, & application encreasing my practice. Have I not cause to be grateful to God? I have; I am; & will be ever so.

Last night expired in extreme agony from a short illness Richd. P. K., E.,[4] supposed entirely from a fright he received in consequence of wandering accidentally into the King's Mews and unexpectedly seeing the grand figure of Phidias from Monte Cavallo,[5] shortly to be opened there. This figure is two & twenty feet high and it so overpowered all the feelings & brought all his former foolish arguments about size so vividly to his conscience, that he drooped from that moment, and died in extreme torture. During his delirium he never spoke; others seeing his fatal state in his last struggles he attempted to utter with great earnestness, finding he could not he made signs [*four illegible words*] brought him, but before he could commence the pangs of cancer & Death seized him, & he had not even time to seek to repent, tho' it was evident he did do so, however incapable he might have been to express it. We hope, sincerely hope, this will be a warning to all remaining Patrons not to suffer pride to blind the reasons, to understand by this fatal end of one of their colleagues to repent & ere death, as it always doth, can seize & put an end to all plans of reform.

My Landlord, who was brought up from low life to his present situation, one of comparative gentility, never washes his hands in a basin & on a stand, but goes regularly down to the kitchen and does it at the pump, which he actually seems to relish. His wife, who was a servant when first married to him, was proud of a parlour and appearance, but before two years were over, the parlour was kept for friends, and he and she kennelled into a little fusty shop room, with an old broken rug, dusty & kitcheny. They oftener dine in the kitchen than the parlour, and their whole delight seems to be in perpetually cleaning things, and never enjoying the consequences. Such is the effect of early habit.

May 30. I was in company with young Betty.[6] He is a boisterous, good natured youth, but in spite of all his gaity & fun, his

4. BRH is satirizing Richard Payne Knight, Esquire, who lived until 1824.
5. See I,113.
6. See I,294.

gaity was the gaity of despairing remembrances. His situation is certainly the most melancholy & the most singular in the world. His fame when a boy was certainly never exceeded by any one; not even Buonaparte had ever a greater share of public attention for the time. Columns & columns of the Public Journals criticised & lauded him. The Nobility, the Ladies, & the Prince doated on & devoured him. I remember when he was confined with a cold, a bulletin was obliged to be put in the windows to satisfy the enquiries of all the fashion & beauty of the World. Poor fellow! When grown to man's estate, without feeling or capacity or sense, he attempted again to excite the applause of the World, but alas, the novelty was over, faults were no longer pardoned, because Youth was no longer an excuse for them. He was now criticised as a man, & he sank like "an exhalation of the evening, never to rise again!" [7] All his future life seems embittered, in spite of his noisy boisterousness to conceal it. He talked of his past blaze with a melancholy sigh, and drowned recollections as they crowded into his mind, and flushed his cheek, with a sort of gasp that allowed the wine to rush down his throat as he put the glass to his mouth to drink it. His chief amusement is driving his friends about in his curricle to make their calls, while he sits on the box with as many capes as he can carry, and if the Servant mistakes him for a Coachman, his delight is unbounded and he will repeat it for a month! He amused us with mimicking the cries of hounds, & the chuckling of Turkey cocks, but as to sharing a sensation from a passage of Shakespeare, it was useless to attempt & hopeless to expect it. He avoided all discussion that would have exposed his intellect, and roared down every attempt at thinking with a noise that made us sigh.

He is a melancholy instance that fame not acquired by gradual improvement is a sort of innovation that cannot last. He said he remembered dining with Fox & Sheridan at the House of Commons, but it was a dream, he remembered only the fact.

Instead of finding out ingenious reasons why modern times are not calculated for grand Art and allowing ingenious excuses for them, rather supply the deficiencies of modern [art] by in-

7. *Henry VIII*, III,ii,225–227. "I shall fall/Like a bright exhalation in the evening,/And no man see me more."

genious remedies. Let us exert our faculties to remedy the defects, rather than excuse the errors of modern government. What trifling nonsense is this with regard to the Climate? Surely if the Painter can paint in spite of the Climate, the Patron might encourage. If it be damp, let stoves be erected, and with 50 per annum let a man be hired whose whole occupation should be to dust & preserve the Pictures.

Because after a few years the Public would neglect them, what argument is this? We may as well argue because we are mortal, because human works & human efforts & human prospects decay from the principles of our nature, why should we do any thing? Of what value can our little trifles be in the silent vastness of eternity? Let the Public neglect them, let them still hunt the butterfly novelty of the spring. Why should this fear prevent us supplying our Country when it is deficient? We do not do it to gratify the people, but to honor them, not for their amusement but instruction. We do it because it forms a component part in the greatness of other nations, & because without it our greatness will not be comparable to theirs.

June 13. I had a cast made yesterday of Wordsworth's face.[8] He bore it like a philosopher. Scott[9] was to meet him at Breakfast. Just as he came in the Plaister was covered over. Wordsworth was sitting in the other room in my dressing gown, with his hands folded, sedate, steady, & solemn. I stepped in to Scott, & told him as a curiosity to take a peep, that he might say the first sight he ever had of so great a poet was such a singular one as this.

I opened the door slowly, & there he sat innocent & unconscious of our plot against his dignity, unable to see or to speak, with all the mysterious silence of a spirit.

When he was relieved he came into breakfast with his usual cheerfulness, and delighted & awed us by his illustrations & bursts of inspiration. At one time he shook us both in explaining the principles of his system, his views of man, & his objects in writing.

8. This life mask of Wordsworth is now in Dove Cottage, Grasmere.
9. John Scott (1783–1821), editor of the *Champion* and later of the *London Magazine*. BRH apparently met him in 1813 (*Autobiography*, I,161).

Wordsworth's faculty is describing all these intense feelings & glimmerings & doubts & fears & hopes of Man, as referring to what he might be before he was born & to what he may be hereafter. He is a great Being, and will hereafter be ranked as one who had *a portion* of the spirit of Homer, Virgil, Dante, Tasso, Shakespeare, Chaucer & Milton, but as one who did not possess the power of wielding these feelings to any other purpose but as referring to himself and as wishing to make others feel by personal sympathy. This is, in my opinion, his great characteristic distinction.

We afterwards called on Hunt, and as Hunt had previously attacked him & has now reformed in his opinions, the meeting was interesting. Hunt paid him the highest compliments, & told him that as he grew wiser & got older he found his respect for his powers & enthusiasm for his genius encrease. Hunt was ill or it would have been his place to call on Wordsworth. Here again he really burst forth with burning feelings & I never saw him so eloquent as today.

I afterwards sauntered along to Hampstead with him with great delight. Never did any Man so beguile the time as Wordsworth. His purity of heart, his kind affections, his soundness of principle, his information, his knowledge, his genius, & the intense & eager feelings with which he pours forth all he knows affect, enchant, interest & delight one. I don't know any man I should be so inclined to worship as a purified being.

Last night I was at an insipid rout and certainly the contrast was vivid. The beauty of the Women was the only attraction.

In speaking of Lucien Buonaparte's Poem,[1] I said the materials were without arrangement as referring to an end. "Oh, I don't care for that," said he, "if there are *good things* in a Poem." Now here he was decidedly wrong but he did not say this with reference to the Charlemagne because he thought little of it, but with reference to my idea.

Wordsworth is original surely on this principle — he has one part (& perhaps the finest) of the genius of the great but he has

1. *Charlemagne, ou l' Eglise délivrée,* an epic by Napoleon's brother Lucien Bonaparte.

not all. He has not the lucidus ordo;[2] he does not curb, direct his inspirations for a positive moral, but leaves them to be felt only by those who have a capacity to feel with equal intensity. The moral is not obvious, only the feeling; but he that can feel the feeling will feel the moral too.

June 14. My feelings, my heart, yearn & are sick for a sweet woman on whose bosom I could lay my head & in whose heart I could confide. I would marry her from any class of life if she had elegant & tender feelings, but alas, I have seen so much of the weakness of women, or perhaps their vices, that I often sigh with agony that we can call these delicate creatures ours, but not *their appetites.* My love, my enthusiasm, my reverence for a woman of susceptibility & virtue is unbounded; to women I owe the change of my taste since Macbeth; their loveliness & softness & beauty have worked a reformation in my Soul, have expanded my sensations, & softened the fierceness of my Nature. Could I but meet with one! But even if I could, I must yet sacrifice my feelings till their gratification will not interrupt the great object of my being. How many feelings am I obliged to curb with iron grasp till that be accomplished.

At a house where I visited, a most elegant, lovely servant opened the door; an exchange of feeling took place in our eyes. When she came in nothing could be more graceful. The Mistress & family talked of her kindness of heart, elegance of manner, and said she had a mind above her situation. This affected me. I longed for her to be pure & virtuous, but alas, the next time I went a hang[?] of the head & smile of intelligent meaning gave indications of an easy conquest. I was melancholy, as I have often been, at such disappointments, to me at least when I had highest views, than corrupting their hearts [*the rest of the page is torn away*].

People find fault with Wordsworth for speaking of his own genius; to be sure they do! The World always find fault with a man of genius for speaking of his own genius [*the rest of the page is torn away*].

2. Horace, *Ars Poetica,* l. 41 ("clearness of order").

Mr. Philips,[3] a member of Parliament, called and seemed much delighted with my Picture. After a little time he said with apparent feeling, "I have no doubt from your long devotion to historical painting, it is probable you may not be quite easy in pecuniary matters. I intend to have a picture of you, and if you will allow me to present you with 100£ in advance, you will do me great pleasure." [4] I was really quite affected at such conduct. I frankly told him my situation; he seemed more confused than I was. Three months ago I was pennyless, with a bill coming due of 225£. I have paid that bill. I have now another friend start up, and from his kindness am enabled to go on in peace & ease. O God, thy kindness to me is unvarying & steady. I have always trusted in thee, & will always trust & never, oh never, was I disappointed, thou Good & Merciful being. Grant I may accomplish my great object, grant I may live to see it, but O grant that my life or Death may equally contribute to it. Spare my eyes & intellect to the latest gasp of existence. I pour out my gratitude, thou great being.

His face was the picture of delicacy of feeling, of elegance & benevolence. I never saw any man who impressed me so much at entrance.

Last November Soane said, "You owe me 15£. Suppose I make it fifty!" Really the benevolence I have met with, I believe, is unexampled, as well as the malevolence, but perseverance, industry, & reliance on God was never yet disappointed. On God I rely & in him I trust with a keeness of sensation I cannot tell. May I always deserve such protection. When I think of my early Friends who deserted me without one shadow of reason & are now courting me again, can I help feeling contempt? If I contrast them with this good amiable man — But I must check such feel-

3. George Philips (1766–1847), of Sedgley, near Manchester, elected M.P. for Ilchester, Somersetshire, on November 24, 1812. He was created baronet in 1828.

4. On August 19, 1815, Philips sent BRH £100 again. BRH wrote on this letter, which is attached to the diary: "Two months ago, he advanced me one hundred without my application and now trusting to his character, I applied at once from [*sic*, for *for*] another — he returned 100 without a moment's hesitation. I have not known him two months — were any of my early Friends so kind or considerate? Alas, no."

ings & do. I lament their want of heart & their mistakes of my character. Peace go with them.

I have felt indeed the blessings of ease of circumstance this last week. I have kept my Model late & long, & dwelt & worked, with silent, uninterrupted intensity. O God, let me not know again the horrors of being harrassed, not that I fear or shrink from any horror on earth that I must meet in my path, but that I wish to put forth my powers unburthened & unchecked to their full capability. Thou knowest I have never yet done this, because I have always been obliged to leave things incomplete from necessity. But O God, if it be thy Will that I must be further tried in trouble, I submit; grant me only health & confidence in thee. Let me only attain my great object at last. In thee with all my Soul I trust. Amen.

June 19. Went to the Gallery[5] between four & five to consult, before I compleated my day's labour, & derived the greatest Instruction. Returned home & worked till dark with delight. Sir George Beaumont sat & saw me put in the sleave of the Soldier. He seemed to take great pleasure. What a singular character he is. He is now doing exactly again what he did before. He expressed a wish to have a Picture of me, just in the same undecided manner. He presented me a beautiful sketch of his, which is rather a sort of promise I shall be a *longer favorite than before.*

I begin now to have a taste of the real delights of my Art. I hope I approach that time when the hand will be thoroughly obedient to the conception.

June 22. Went again to the Institution and studied intensely. One feels the beauties of great works a great deal more when you see them at the time you are making similar attempts yourself; you enter into all their feelings, you imagine all the feelings of the Artists, you recognise the same views of Nature as you have seen yourself, and you see their attempts at imitating what you perhaps [have] been trying the same day. The sympathy is delightful. How did I enter into Rembrandt, how drink his excellence, how did I profit by his beauties! How did I recognise ef-

5. The British Institution's exhibition of old masters continued. BRH uses the names *British Institution* and *British Gallery* interchangeably.

fects of shadow on arms, gradations of colour, softness, & tones which I have seen in Nature often, and which "lie in my mind like substances." [6] I shall go to work again tomorrow with God's blessing fired to the most extraordinary effort. I will rival and if possible exceed them; possible it is, because they are but mortals, and great & beautiful as their efforts are how feeble by the beauty of Life.

What a wonderful creation is the World! how beautiful in ornament, how intensely deep in principle, how simple in arrangement. How singularly delightful that the elements requisite to our physical being should afford materials for the exercise of our intellectual faculties.

If God spare my eyes & intellect, exceed them I will, because I will add beauty & grandeur of form & expression to their colour & surface & tone. Time shall shew this is not the vanity of impudence but the consciousness of *Power*.

Rembrandt is not vulgar tho his characters are mean; there is such a refinement in his surface & colour.

June 23. What times these are! [7] How often lately has my mind been haunted by Buonaparte. First there was his advance to Moscow, then the burning of that city, then his retreat, then his recovery, then his abdication & dethronement, all of which actually sank so deeply as to disturb me. Then we were quiet for a few months. Then he escaped from Elba. Then our associations were again up; the bad & malignant spirits of the Country again rejoiced, the World again trembled. Now comes the great battle

6. Wordsworth, *The Excursion*, I,136–138. "Deep feelings had impressed/So vividly great objects that they lay/Upon his mind like substances."

7. The Battle of Waterloo was fought on June 18, 1815. BRH did not mention it in his "Vita" nor write in his diary the entry for June 23 as printed by Taylor (*Autobiography* I,211–213), which contends that he was one of the first persons in London to learn of the victory, since he received his information from a courier bearing the news to Lord Harrowby on June 23. A writer signing himself "H. F." contributed an article to *Notes and Queries* (5th series, October 28, 1876, 6:344) in which he showed that the news of Waterloo was generally known in London on June 21. He had examined the holograph of BRH's *Autobiography* (now lost) and stated that the handwriting of this description differs from that of the remainder. Other discrepancies between the holograph and Taylor's version led H. F. to believe that the passage had been tampered with or that BRH himself might have written his account from memory some twenty-five years after the event.

& up rises Wellington, having beaten him fairly, no Saxons deserting, no frost, nothing the cause but superiority of Generalship & superiority of courage. This battle will do him more injury in the opinion of the World now & hereafter than any thing that has ever happened. He has measured swords with Wellington & British troops, & now he will be able to account how his Marshalls were beaten before.

How singularly success operates on our minds. When he was at Moscow, and it was burnt, one thought of him as a tremendous being. When he abdicated one felt a contempt. When he escaped and rushed to Paris, you imagined him like a comet. Now he is again beaten, one knows he will yet struggle, but yet one's apprehension is gone. Really, one cannot think of Wellington (on whose Genius I always depended, as my Friends know) & the British Troops without tears. Their constancy & firmness, his genius & prudence, the way they have gallantly worked their way to their present splendid reputation against the prejudice of Europe & the insolence of the French. Now will the Imperial Guard say again, "Napoleon n'etoit jamais battu"? I believe not. Even the French, vain & impudent as they are, must now acknowledge it. If the Allies do not now think us too powerful in influence & negative our efforts by coldness, his destruction approaches, and the French will, I trust, be effectually punished. Have not the efforts of the British Nation been gigantic? Think of her Naval Victories — St. Jean,[8] St. Vincent, Nile, Copenhagen, Trafalgar, then of Vimeiro, Talavera, Fuentes D'honoro,[9] Salamanca, Vittoria, Orthes, Pyrenees. Think of her treasure in coalescing Europe, & now again this battle of La belle Alliance compelling all. Think of her Glories in India, and her subduing all the Colonies of the World. To such Glories she wants but the glories of my noble Art to make her the grandest Nation in the World, and this she shall have if God spare my life. Grant it, Amen.

When Men want to depreciate Genius by faint applause, they praise them for possessing the negative qualities.

How this Victory pursues my imagination! I read the Gazette four times without stopping. I then tried to work, but the Horse-

8. St. Jean d'Acre.
9. Fuentes de Oñoro.

guardsman Corporal Salmon was in such perpetual irritation to go & enquire more about his regiment charging, and I myself was little better, that I was obliged to let him go. Away he went. I never saw him till late the next day. I read the Gazette again, the last thing [before] going to bed. I dreamt of it & was fighting & waking all night. I got up in the morning in a steam of intense feeling. I read the Gazette again, ordered a Courier for a month, called at a Confectioner's shop, & read all the Papers till my stomach aked. The more I think of this glorious Conflict, the more I glory in it.

Every passion, every feeling that could rouse the energies of our Nature were called into action in this tremendous shock — one Nation excited to the most violent passion from mortified vanity & disappointed ambition, the others roused to revenge by the insolence & ingratitude of their opponents; one enraged at having lost the fruits of twenty years' victory, furious to regain their glory, the other firmly determined to compleat their own by the annihilation of their enemies. It has all the skill of modern improvement and all the sanguinary personality of ancient combat. It was a specimen of the character of each chief. Buonaparte's attack was brilliant & daring without prudence, & Wellington's a combination of both. Wellington will truly be considered by Posterity as the Saviour of the World's intellect, for the age would have been brought back to ignorance & barbarism had the Demon succeeded in his despotic system. Great & Glorious Man, I remember when he first went out to Portugal, sneered at, laughed at, & ridiculed, by all, abused as rash when he was daring and spoken of with contempt when he was prudent; how calmly, how quietly, in how dignified a manner did he bear their short sighted taunts. Even the Ministry who sent him out were never fully aware of his capacity or his views, cramped his means, and neglected his succours, and it was only by proving how much he could do without means that they gave him means to do more. My heart beats when I think of him. I only fear he has not a sympathetic heart, and he is not capable of feeling the sensations he excites in others.

Had he been beaten in this last affair, all his former glories would have been of no avail. This feeling perhaps in the Public,

457

however ungrateful, is the true stimulant to exertion, while any thing remains to be done. "To have done is to hang in monumental mockery like a rusty mail." [1]

I heard Lord Mulgrave say at Table in 1808, that he would prove a second Marlborough. All who were intimate with him knew his power.

I have heard he is now exceedingly affected at losing so many friends. He says nothing but seems exceedingly touched. I shall be happy if it is so. This is only what he wants to render him interesting.

But what had Marlborough to contend with equal to this? Princes did not then fight for their Thrones, a People for its rights, and the World for its existence.

June 25. Read the Gazette again; I know it now actually by heart. Dined with Leigh Hunt. I give myself great credit for not worrying him to Death at this news. He was quiet for some time, but knowing it must come bye & bye, so putting on an air of indifference, "Terrible Battle this, Haydon." "A glorious one, Hunt." "Oh, certainly." To it we went. He was dished about Wellington & had not a word to say. Knowing as I do Hunt's heart to be good, I attribute his leaning again to the French entirely to his disappointment in the conduct of the allied Princes, because when the allied Princes promised better things, surely no man defended in a stouter manner than he did, even against his own brother in the Examiner. He said Buonaparte had risen from middle life, with all its vigour & experience, & there was no excuse for his tyrany, whereas the Allies had been educated in despotic notions and every excuse might be made for them, joined as it was to a natural incapacity; he is now disgusted at them and fancies Buonaparte may be the means of producing something better because he is not so powerful as he was formerly, to push his victories to the extent he did, so that he may work an improvement in others and be even under its influence himself; but here is thy error, my dear Hunt. Do you imagine his heart can be effected by any influence, do you imagine he is not aware victory

1. *Troilus and Cressida*, III,iii,151–153. "To have done is to hang/Quite out of fashion, like a rusty mail/In monumental mock'ry."

would at once rouse the French Nation, and when roused, do you imagine they will again know where to stop? You wish an end to be brought about by a means, which if brought about by such a means, would substitute a consequence more dreadful to human liberty and more destructive to human intellect than the object you wish to get rid of, could ever effect. Buonaparte's system had all the energy of the Genius of a Demon; theirs, the weaknesses, the stupors, the gloated blurrings of slothful imbecility, which might have improved by brighter minds & more acute intellects, while his diabolical system pressed intellect into its service, and the brighter the mind & the more acute the talent, the more dreadful the tyranny, & the more horrible the influence. The great object of *his* being was to sap youthful susceptibility & divert mature capacity to make one infatuated being the instrument of another's destruction, till he was the dreaded Deity of this lower World, and all its inhabitants trembled at his name & went in terror at his power. Skillful in nothing but wielding artillery, and ignorant of all instruments but muskets & shot, their great creed submission to Napoleon's will, which oozed into their very marrow with their Mothers' nourishment, and his awful name the burthen of every ditty that lulled them in the cradle, or the first word that trembled on their innocent lips, intermingling in their boyish amusements, striking their imagination in every Public building, & intermingling in the most awful acts of solemn devotion, by seeing its initial blaze round the statue of their crucified Christ. Any people, however sound, might have been influenced by such a system, but what can any man say to the effect of such a system operating on the French, on the French! — vain, insolent, thoughtless, blood-thirsty, active, & impetuous by Nature, so susceptible as [to] have the little reason always blinded by the bubble of Glory held before the mind's eye, a People who are brilliant without intensity, have courage without firmness, are polite without benevolence, & tender without heart; tall, fierce, & elegant in their looks; depraved, lecherous, & blasphemous in their feelings; mingling the most disgusting offices of Nature with the most elegant duties of Social life. Good God! This is the being & these are the people who are to be the instruments of liberty! Into their hands power is again to be placed, because they wielded it with such moderation before! *Their* character is to be a guarantee for Europe's repose. *Their Character!* celebrated for its fickleness, who have violated every treaty & invaded every kingdom, whether for a Friend —

Misfortune was to alter him too. Yet he was much altered certainly. At the very time you thought he will [be] affected by adversity, he was guilty of the grossest tyranny, arresting people in violation of the Constitution which he had sworn to keep.

It was pretended he was the head of the cause of talent. Yes, of that species of talent, who are too idle to exert it for the benefit of themselves or their country and who, with the powers of genius are suffering the penalties of imbecility, act in malignant hatred of all those who obtain by a virtuous exertion of their own the respect & admiration of the World. These are the creatures among whom Buonaparte was the God, envious of all rank, to which they had spirit to aspire or energy to gain; they beheld with delight Kings humbled & nobility overturned; it was a gratification to see those mortified whose station they envied and whose capacity they knew to be inferior to their own. Hence they looked up to Buonaparte as a scourge for those who had obtained their hatred only because they were higher; hence he was the advocate of Genius & the organ of liberty, who was the bitterest crusher of both; hence the French were to enlighten the World. The French! if the World is to be enlightened, let us not be indebted to the French! So despicable is their character that no terms should be made with them; they are not to be considered like any other Nation.

June 28. Sir George Beaumont [called] & settled about the Picture he wishes me to paint for him[2] & paid me 50 Guineas in advance. The Academicians who envy this conduct of Sir G. as it relates to me, are beginning to affirm I must have been submissive. Pitiful fellows, they cannot conceive how a man who has

2. This picture was never painted. On an unpublished letter from Sir George Beaumont, dated May 30, 1816, which is attached to the diary at a later page, BRH wrote: "Sir George gave me a Commission last year for 200 Gs. and advanced me one hundred. This year I proposed (as he first mentioned having seen Macbeth and liked it better), I proposed his taking it at the 200, to which he at last agreed, so there is an end of this, & I really believe he wishes me well." Sir George wrote: "If you can in any way subdue the violence of Macbeth's action, of which you are now sensible yourself, I shall be glad."

conducted himself with spirit to these People can escape without ruin & imagine because I have been successful, I must have acted as they must have acted to have obtained the same result. No. I have not deviated one wit from my principles of Art, nor will I to my death. Sir George has made the concession to me. I told him I would not paint less than life. He consented & said he had no wish I should. Was I to behave pert & uncivil when a man of his rank behaves with such politeness to me? Surely not. The fact is, the Academy hoped my destruction and urged me on as they thought blindly in the contest, by saying "Go on, Haydon, you are the Champion of Artists' rights." I did go on because it was a part of my own system & I was conscious of my own power. Did they imagine I did not see through their motives? Poor fellows. Many times to try them did I affect more violence about it, to elicit their notions, and how have I laughed to see the Woodcocks caught in their own springes[3] they were setting for me. They thought I was young, inexperienced! I played off my age & youth against their weakness. Ha, ha. They felt not the fire I felt within my own breast, they knew not the urgings that lifted me above the earth and convinced me that my first great step was to assert my own dignity, to oppose the Patrons in their errors as to my character, and shew them theirs by my power. At the very time these poor creatures were urging me on in my presence, they were saying at table, behind my back, "He thinks his talents will carry him through; he is mistaken!" — and yet to me, "Depend upon your talents, Haydon. I have no doubt of them." Honorable Gentlemen! I knew all this — & more! Amiable Friends! disinterested Painters! in a word — Academicians!!!

June 29. Went to Gallery again & studied with mute thought. Rembrandt's light & shadow is certainly on too confused a principle for large works. Ostade[4] has not that massy breadth you see in Teniers. Teniers *might* have been a painter in large, Ostade never.

"The British are the only Nation who never know when they are beaten," say the French. The misfortune is also they never

3. *Hamlet,* I,iii,115. "Springes to catch woodcocks."
4. BRH refers to Adriaen van Ostade, since Isaack van Ostade was not represented in the British Institution's exhibition.

461

know what they have done; they are equally insensible to the extent of their misfortune or the value of their success.

June 30. Went to Hampton Court to study the Cartoons and to ponder upon a National subject. I mused in a hay field till the sun had set and twilight was coming in saffron silence.

[*The next seven pages of the diary contain random notes for allegorical and historical pictures. Many of the sentences are unfinished and rough pen and ink drawings obscure much of the writing. On three more pages well drawn pencil sketches of heads from the Cartoons are attached; the second, of an old man, is labeled: "Sketched in horror for fear of Discovery — great facilities for study in this Country, where Artists are obliged to be in a fright at the footstep of a despicable Cicerone!!!" The third, of a young man, is labeled "From Ananias, June 30, 1815. Exquisite, amiable, bland, delightful Raphael."*]

July 8. The incidents in Homer are so simple and follow each other so naturally that one cannot help wondering they are at all interesting — a quarrel of chiefs about an interesting Girl, a battle & one man killing another.

I never read Homer without longing to run somebody through for a week afterwards. I remember once darting up & seizing a pole in my room & dashing it through a study of Wilson the negro on a colossal scale, saying to myself, "bite the earth, you κορυθαίολος[5] dog!"

Such is the consequence of my habitual application that any interval between the doing of one thing and another thing is excrutiating torture. Constant exertion of mind is my only happiness. I should think the nature of my mind to be extremely active and any ennui from a moment's rest must give it pain.

[*The next two pages contain an unfinished draft of an article on the necessity for public support of painting, as well as of sculpture.*]

July 11. There is something to me infinitely imposing, sublime, & overwhelming in the present degraded state of France & Napo-

5. "Moving the helmet quickly," an epithet applied to Hector, for example, *Iliad,* II,816.

leon Buonaparte. English troops in the Champs Elysees! What a change! What a punishment for their presumption, what a glory & reward for our forbearances. When one thinks of the efforts of England during this long, long contest, wherever they went, in Egypt or in India, by Land or by Sea, the British Standard gleamed like a meteor before them, to their terror, discomfiture, & disgrace! Point out in the history of the World such a series of continued persevering & glorious efforts. One's imagination is oppressed with their brightness, one's faculties dulled by their remembrance. Perhaps in this glory may be the seeds of ruin & commotion, perhaps the effort may have been so great & the strain so violent that it may be long before the [country] may attain solidity, peace, & real prosperity after it. But let her be ruined if she must fall. Can she bring destruction on her head in a nobler way than by a glorious struggle for the liberty & intellect of the earth? No. Who would not be whelmed beneath the ruins of such a result?

Is it not a disgrace to the Public bodies of a Country that the leading Historical Painters are obliged to exhibit their works like wild beasts, to advertise like Quack Doctors, and parade men about the streets with poles, to the awe, fear, & apprehension of the keepers of the Lotteries? With all the noise & reputation that Christ Healing the Sick gave the Painter,[6] such reputation indeed for the time that the usual address about the weather was forgotten, and "have you seen the Picture?" became its substitute — with all the reputation, I repeat, has it ever obtained him a commission? No, no, no, not even if his years are prolonged beyond the days of Methusalem or longer, if the present system of things remains.

Why should this Country be fit for works of a less scale than others? Is its intellect more inferior, is its rank on a lower scale, are its actions less glory, are we really the People [*the sentence is incomplete*].

July 14. My old School drawing Master called on me yesterday. He appeared uneasy, and, as it were, had an air of mortification about him. He offered his remarks with a sort of fear and yet

6. Benjamin West.

a wish to retain his old consequence, mixed with acknowledge-[ment] that it could not be, but as I appeared inclined to attend to him as much as ever, I could see his features lighten. He put his hand on my shoulder, and expressed raptures at the parts that pleased him. I then told him an anecdote of his begging me to observe that the shape of the eye was so & so, &c., which I had ever thought of since the time he recommended [it]. This delighted him, and he took his leave of me with his self love not at all injured, and as high in his own estimation as ever. I would not have mortified him for the World. I felt for him & sympathised for his feelings, tho Heaven knows never was a more impracticable brain & heart.

July 15. Saturday. Painted this whole week with intense application. Finished my corner figure. Painted yesterday till I had excrutiating pains in my optick nerve from continued staring.

July 18. Lost this whole day by the neglect of a model. I went on without her, but alas, what miserable stuff one does without Nature. Never was I in finer feeling, never was the sky brighter, never were colours in a finer state, and all this was useless, owing to the caprice of a black eyed houri. It is impossible to express the disappointment one feels as he [has] been obliged to suffer the inspiration to go off without having made the utmost use of it. I passed the day in fretful misery, cut to death at this interruption.

July 19. It is a melancholy thing to see one makes so little improvement. Drawings I did two years since are just as well as any thing I can do now.

Perhaps I yesterday found more the value of Nature from attempting to paint without her.

July 24. Made a cast in the evening of Wilkie's face, with Wyburn, our Paris Friend.[7] Never had such fun, as Wilkie lay on

7. Although BRH did not mention him at the time of his visit to Paris, Wilkie's diary shows that they called on Wyburn on June 24, 1814, and saw him on numerous occasions during the following days (Cunningham, I,424–429). Two letters signed B. [?] Wyburn are attached to BRH's diary, one from Paris dated March 8, 1816, and the other from Grand Mont Rouge, dated June 30, 1816. The first is inaccurately printed in *Correspondence* (I,300–301); FWH read the sig-

the ground looking like a Knight Templar on a monument, with his features battered out. We quizzed him till we roared. All that he could do was to tack his hands to express his participation, for we gave him leave to laugh if *he could.*

July 25. Spent the Evening with Hunt looking over some of his finest drawings by Raphael, Michel Angelo, &c.

August 6. All my old Friends who remembered me a rosy boy just come to Town but always felt my genius, drank tea after 9 years separation. Scott came in, and we all spent a happy, happy evening. One had been in the Spanish War, another had been to India,[8] Scott & I had been to Paris, the last tho' not least, and we all listened & Participated in turns. We got into such a humour for laughing from repeated funny stories that the Table shook. When they departed & I came back & felt the silence, where wit & humour & jollity were just before, I relapsed into a muse, a painful muse of why is variety necessary to our enjoyments? Why must we separate to relish meeting? Why must we sleep to relish waking? Why must we &c., &c., &c., because this life is but a life of duty & not of pleasure, a life of effort to be worthy of a better!

What a delightful sight it is, after a shower of rain, to see the dear Women tripping along and tucking their drapery round their lovely hips, now & then giving one a glimpse of a lovely ankle & part of a full leg.

August 15. Note of Ten pounds, Bank of England, sent to G. Whiteway, who has the care of Solomon.[9] Put into the Portland Street Post Office.

The Business that has been carried on by my family for 60 years is now sold, & I have no longer any right to a habitation in my Birth place. There is something melancholy in this, to be cut off as it were from dwellings of my Ancestors, and the scenes of my youthful associations, but this life rolls on — one thing succeeds another and obliterates the last.

nature "F. Wyborn." These letters indicate that Wyburn was a wealthy dilettante, particularly interested in metaphysics and astronomy.

8. BRH's friend Du Fresne went to India in December 1808 (see I,38).

9. "Solomon" was exhibited with little success in Plymouth, Exeter, and Bath; in June 1815, BRH arranged a second exhibition in London, which failed to pay the expenses of the hall (Farington, VIII,6–7).

Made a bet with Ballmano[1] of a dozen that Boney is in St. Helena 2 years hence. He bet of course he would not be. August 15, 1815, Tuesday. Scott witness.

August 20. My Darling Sister, according to my earnest prayer when I first commenced this Journal, is married.[2] God in Heaven protect her, and grant those seeds of virtue & good sense with which she teemed, may now ripen to a full maturity.

August 23. How the least proposition for Public employment sets one's imagination teeming with subjects.

Who can ever want amusement in this World while a human character exists?

One man I knew, who having failed in his early schemes from his own debility perhaps as much as any thing, passes life in sour groans at all the World. If Beautiful Women walk with an air of consciousness, he fancies it is contempt at him; if a Carriage rolls by, he imagines it sneers at his want of fortune in not being able to keep one. "Phash," said he, "let us turn up this lane," with absolute grimace as if his blood was curdled milk & his spirits steeped in vinegar. The most laughable of all was one day when it rained in torrents when he wanted to go somewhere. He walked up to the window, and turning round to me with a face ready to burst into fretful tears like a child, and the most ludicrous expression of chagrin, "did you ever see any thing like it?," as if it was on purpose to plague him.

To dare all for the risk of Success, without providing something against the chances of failure is not daring but *risk.* We are not gifted with a power of prophecy, we cannot foresee, we know the uncertainty of human calculation. With this conviction is not a man grossly deficient in Wisdom who never calculates or provides for failure? He is not so likely to ensure success finally, and as soon as his method is known, destruction can be more certainly entailed. While he who is thoroughly conscious of the imperfections of mortality is more likely to attain Success, by providing against the possibility of Misfortune after having so provided than risk, because [the] result must always be risked.

1. Robert Balmanno (1780–1861), contributor to periodicals.
2. See I,416.

September 8. I think a complete answer may be made to the objection of Christ's saying "he came to bring a sword." [3]

He is giving his Disciples an account of his doctrines, his principles, what they are to do, & what they are to expect. He says don't be surprised at the difficulties, don't be shaken at the apparent dreadful consequences of my coming — Father will be against Wife, & Brother against Sister, &c., &c.

My Mind is gradually filling in the contemplation of the head of the Great Redeemer. God grant I may succeed in it. I shall make him a pale, handsome, melancholy being; black, soft, lustrous eyes, shining with love, nose & mouth quavering with compassion, eyes looking out beyond this World, purity, a look of suffering without pain.

There is no taste in Christianity, that is a selection of the beauties of Nature. Christianity is a religion professed to give hope to the wretched, comfort to the miserable; it forbids not the elegancies of life, the enjoyment of the beauties of Nature, of Art, of Poetry, & of science, but to instruct the educated is not its object; it is to console desponding, dying misery, and to shew even the Genius that there is a higher feeling than even the feelings of taste. The elegancies of life may sooth & soften, but they afford no hope, no dependence; faculties are precarious, fortunes may be ruined, a lovely being on whom you have placed your passionate soul may be diseased & die, but looking to the Great, Immortal, eternal being, is depending on what can never change and what can always afford assistance & relief. The greatest happiness in this World is a conviction (and acting on that conviction) of the immediate interference of Providence. I do not mean that a fear of the beauties of this life, from our conviction of their fallibility should weaken our enjoyment of them. I only mean that a feeling of dependence on the Great being should make us feel grateful for any enjoyments of life.

September 8. I yesterday met an old Schoolfellow, dressed in a dirty coat, shoes rusty for want of blacking, filthy white stockings, unshaved chin, pale face, & a smirking smile of conceited

3. Matthew 10:34. "Think not that I am come to send peace on earth: I came not to send peace, but a sword."

humility on his countenance. From seeing me dressed like a Gentleman, of course he imagined I must be a fop, I must be idle, I must have, in short, every vicious quality he attached to a good hat & a genteel appearance. I asked him what he was doing. As he squirted tobacco juice from his yellow teeth & eyed me with a sort of shaking of the head & presumptuous elevation of the chin, "Why I served my time to a Plumber," imagining I should think it a degradation. He seemed determined to shew me his superiority of view & that he gloried in his pursuit. He seemed to feel it an inferior object, & without having the real humbleness of mind that knows its situation, he seemed to claim praise for the strength of his intellect in bearing his humble station and claim superiority over me who would not submit to exalt myself by such humility. Such characters I despise & took him to task immediately. "What right have you," said I, "to suppose I am vicious, idle, & puppyish? Because I regard my personal appearance, do I attribute a disposition in you to pick pockets, or pimp for girls, because your external appearance excite such suspicions?" He blushed at this, asked me home, & begged I'd not be angry. As I felt inclined to see the conclusion of the man, I followed & entered a large old house, with workshops; in the front parlor sat a pleasing, canting little woman. It was Saturday night. There was no carpet in the parlor; the floor had just been washed & was damp. A little dirty smutty Girl held by her Mammy's apron, her Mammy, or *Mississ* as my Friend called her, was dressed in a brown stuffed, awkwardly made gown, a blue checked apron. She seemed a sort of upper servant & was very big with child, her hands dirty, her fore finger worked to death with needle pricks, her hair neglected, her face not clean. "*Mississ*, my Friend Ben Haydon you have heard me speak about." "Pray sit down, Sir. Saturday night, all confusion, Sir. Just washed the parlour, Sir; hope you will excuse it, Sir." The Bible lay by her side, & a few books in a case I examined. I found them Hawker's Sermons,[4] Spiritual Assistance, &c., &c. I found they were *serious people*. Was asked to Tea — agreed to stop. Madam or Mississ seemed to look at me with a certain interest that made me regard

4. Robert Hawker, *Sermons on the Divinity and Operations of the Holy Ghost* (1794) or *Sermons on the Divinity of Christ* (1792).

her in turn. She then looked at her own appearance, & seemed awkward. I went out in the Shop & found much edifying conversation about sheet lead & casting & melting & gained [a] great deal of information.

At Tea Mississ was quite shined up. Her face was washed, her hair curled. She paid particular attention when tea was poured out. "Now, my Dear," said she. He stood up & poured forth a long grace, & sat down, eying me with the same conceit as much as to say, "see how *holy I am*." I found him canting, conceited, grovelling, & affected. "Look, my Dear, do you think so, dear me, Sophy." At the same time I could see she *feared* him — mean in his desires, & yet conscious that the World esteemed them so, alive to another's success, & unhappy at his own meaness, claiming to himself honor for his degraded inclinations, & yet convinced that others were more honorable & more entitled to approbation. Methodism was a cloke, & Religion a shelter. I left him wondering at one's want of Judgement when young in selecting Friends. At School he was remarkable for attention to his book & good memory, but always for a surly, prim propriety — afraid of wearing out his shoes at cricket, avoiding all risks of displeasing the Master, cunningly learning more than his lesson to get above others, & then impudently boast[ing] of it, when he was too far ahead for others immediately to overtake him; without taste or feeling, he was a sort of boy whom nobody knew where in Heaven he came from — no House or Home, no family, no Sisters, no friendly communication or interchange of visits. Some times in waiting for him out side a long, silent alley, he would come out with a sort of mystery, and we should see a little mysterious Woman open the door for him & caution him to be home in time.

When he was in his Shop, he explained [to] me the principles of his business, told me that as the world grew wiser, new inventions superseded the old ones, that individuals suffered, that formerly all pipes were cast, but now the latest pipe was only used, that he had gained much by selling cheaply to the Trade. "That was my advice, Love," said Mississ. "Yes, Sophy, I know it," said he.

In the course he asked me if I was in want of Lodgings, that he had an elegant *first*, which he would let me cheaply, that there was an old lady over head, but she made no noise, and I should hardly know she was alive. I walked up following Mississ; Master closed the rear. This elegant first was full of cobwebs, unfurnished & dark. In the little dressing room they particularly shewed me the conveniences of a lead sink they had made, how water could be easily got without trouble, and how it could be easily thrown away. This was a fine bit of professional feeling. I enjoyed it. He then took me up in his garret work shop, where the sun shot through burning tiles, but I could not stand this. He seemed to glory in all the feelings of a journeyman. When he washed his hands to come into tea, he did it in a leaden bowl & used a towel hung up in the shop for the men, and which all the men used after him, and dragged its heavy ruffness over their smutty & soapy faces.

"What sort of a boy was I?" said I to him. "Very idle, very idle. I remember I soon got ahead of you. However boys in general are idle. Sometimes," said he, with an air of suppressed pleasure, "you find boys who are fond of their books — & *I* was *one*."

The Bricklayer came while we were at tea. "Look, my Love," said he, "this is an unseasonable hour. Every thing just cleaned & washed." "Hush, my love, don't anger Robert." "No, my Love," said he, & away he went with a lifted stalk on his heels to talk to the Bricklayer. "Pray Sir, are you married," said she. "No, Ma'am, I am not so happy." "Ah," said she, "They all said Robert said [he] would never marry." "& I daresay he would not, Ma'am, had he not seen you," said *I*, at which she simpered & wiped a crumb from off [her] lips with, God forgive me, her husband's red silk handkerchief, which [it] seemed he had left in his chair & which seemed to serve the whole family.

September 20. My eyes being again inadequate to intense application, by Adams' advice I set off for Brighton to bathe & brace up for the Winter. How sincerely I detest the weakness & diseases of this wretched frame. It is no use to grumble; this life is a life of trial; we must make the most of the blessings we have, and submit to the deprivation of those we have not. For this last year I have been obliged to yield after study; my eyes gave in, and 4 months have I lost in idleness & pain of mind, wondering & musing till they recovered. This is the consequence of foolish excess during the conclusion of Solomon. Once more, no morbid complaints. They are weak & must be made strong, & there's an end.

In the Coach was a pleasing man of a bilious habit, who always smiled after he said any thing, with a pleasing expression. The rattling of the Coach prevented me hearing what he said, but I thought it must be something clever, from his own expressive self approbation. However, never was any thing more inane when I listened, and yet always this pleasing smile followed every thing. He was what a *certain class* of females would call a very delightful man, one who would sit for hours & look at his legs, make a profound observation on the wonderful improvement lately in the manufacture of thread, or the astonishing facility with which they made needles, who, unable to conclude on any thing would tumble head over heels three times & *half*, if his Physician told him to do so precisely six & twenty minutes before he bathed in the warm bath, and pass the day in a perpetual fret, and be thoroughly convinced he had derived no benefit, if he had tumbled head over heels three times & three quarters 45 seconds more or less than the six & twenty minutes prescribed.

Such poor blackeyed, pretty teethed weakness soon tired me, so I did nothing but muse & abstract & left him to talk to the rest. About 14 miles from Town, we took in a healthy, breathing, sturdy old Englishman, who had a basket of grapes tied down awkwardly with a sheet of an old school copy, perhaps of his eldest boy. I saw through — he was going to see his children somewhere & was carrying his grapes to please 'em. He was a fine contrast to the other, answered his mawkish questions with a bit of thorough good sense, talked about the War, "damned all these yere Foreigners who took away all our gold," was convinced Old England would be ruined if she did not take care of herself, and "let all these yere rascals fight it out by themselves." This was exceedingly clear sighted. At Dinner he seized the [glass] and before drinking blew away the froth with such violence that he sprinkled the People opposite. He then begged pardon & drank till it was out.

I met him the next day. He shook my hand & swore I looked
better already. He was a fine, hearty, healthy headed old man
in affairs of the heart, had brought [up] a large family. "Jim was
at Sea, Tom in the Army, Bill, poor fellow, was killed in Spain,
my eldest daughter Mary, as fine a rosy girl as you'd see again,
is well married," said he, "has three children. I am going to see
'em & handpicked these grapes with my own hands & am going
to carry them." Three he had buried, and three more daughters
were all well, "thank God for it, better to pay the butcher than the
Doctor, you know, Sir," at which he looked at us both, clapped
his sturdy old thigh with his hands, & in his exultation of heart,
nearly knocked his grapes down. "Odds bobikins," said he, "I
had better put these yere grapes in the seat." The string came
off, the paper crumpled up & glided down, the jirking of the
coach kept him full five minutes tying it up again, during which
he forgot every thing but what he was about, & held his head
down & laboured at it till the blood filled his face & perspiration
bedewed his sun burnt old grey headed forehead. I watched him
with great sympathy.

The next morning I set out for Lodgings. I knocked at a door;
out came a pretty, lovely girl in a clean frilled bed gown, which
hung over her bosom & shelved off at the bottom (which was
frilled also), into the contour of her lovely shape. I was soon in
a fluster & as she shewed me the rooms, was burning to touch her
ripe lip, but her manner was so retired & proper, I dared not, had
not courage to approach. I promised to call again, but on second thoughts, as I came down to be quiet I thought I had better
go further on. At the next door out came a little, deformed, horrid
creature, who spoke almost unintelligibly. I liked her rooms and
took them, thinking highly of my own sagacity in thus preferring
age & ugliness, being quite sure of no interruption but to be
peaceable, retired, & comfortable. I passed the evening in musing
on the happiness of that period of life, when the passions are cool
& one's reason predominates. Ugly as the little creature was, I
was convinced she was amiable & innocent, & tho I had two or
three pangs of sensation as I caught her form & figure, I quieted
my feelings by thinking habit would deaden my perceptions. I
went to bed in a true, philosophic quiescence, thought I had

escaped disturbance, dissipation, & extravagance by escaping from the frilled bed gown, & resolved through life to act on such principles of self command. I put this resolve in practice immediately by abstaining from eating a luscious pear, which I was dying to eat, which lay on a plate under my nose, but which I determined not to eat, as it would be more prudent to keep it till the next day after dinner; and as he who would regulate his passions in great things must begin by regulating his appetites in small, I fell asleep astonished at my progress in my new code of conduct, & felt my heart sympathise towards my hump backed little landlady, as she cannot excite my feelings of propriety & prudence. Alas, how soon was I convinced that tho Nature makes beauty dangerous, she generally renders deformity cunning.

About three the next morning, I was roused by the whole house shaking and soon after heard the tremendous bump & the well known ring of a black smith's anvil & hammer. I buried my ears, nose, & eyes & head in pillows & blankets. Still the sound searched every nerve. I got up in a nervous ake, rolled my bed across the room, but all was useless, & totally unable to sleep or lie, I dressed & sallied forth. It was surely odd, I thought, I was not informed of the probability of this interruption round the corner & close under the back of my bed room. I saw these brown heroes thumping away with all their fury & totally unconscious how dreadfully they had irritated me. I called my little hostess in at Breakfast, & told her I was sorry I must leave her, as this noise was dreadful. I saw a sort of malicious pretence at astonishment on her features, & then expressing great sorrow at losing so nice a Gentleman, said I must pay [for] a week. To this I consented, & she seemed quite pleased. I have no doubt she got all her money by getting people in & then making them pay to get out again. There seemed a sort of consciousness in the maid servant as I came in, as if to say "ah, he's found it out." If I was a cynic might I not say, "alas! what security is there in this World," for if one endeavours to avoid the allurements of beauty, one is sure to fall a victim to the cunning of age! I determined in future to prefer Beauty & frilled bed growns with all their temptations to deformity however secure or age however experienced!

On passing the window the day after, I saw the bill up; in the

473

afternoon it was down. "Ah ha," thought I, "what poor victim hast thou now drawn in?" I prayed for him tomorrow at three. In the afternoon of the day following, the bill was up again! I smiled at the tale this little billet told & passed by sympathising with the unhappy Lodger's nerves. How strangely habit affects us.

I got nice rooms[5] that morning but after I got in I felt uneasy that there should be another on the upstairs floor. What business, I felt, has any other person to lodge here but me? I felt my own importance injured; when his bell rang I was angry & rang my own directly to let them see I would be attended to, tho I did not want any thing, as well as he. All this was owing to my having lodged alone in London, to my being the great object of attention in the house, to my bell being the only bell, to myself being the only one to attend to. I could not help laughing, but so it was, and now it is entirely passed off.

My Friend Mr. P. Hoare, who with all his little weaknesses, has been a kind & constant Friend to me, & who advised me to go on & backed my views when others sneered & tried to chill me, lives at Brighton. He was happy to see me, & took me to the characters & intellects of the Town. I was highly interested; the Geniuses of a Country Town were a new race of beings & I felt eager to examine them.

The first was an antiquary, a connoiseur, & a Parson, in all of which he shewed considerable talent, but never suffered his views to ripen, from a want of consciousness of the value of his own discoveries, or from a want of sense to see excellence was not attainable at a single effort. This defect blasted & withered his mind. His house was full of Pictures, unfinished, but in which something good was intended. Disgusted it was not accomplished, he flew to some novelty, & when equally unsuccessful there, again returned to his first attempts. He has past life in beginnings, & now finds had he devoted his powers to one thing & made as many efforts on one pursuit as he has made on several, the World would have been benefitted & he would have commanded praise as a duty from having accomplished something, instead of begging it now as a boon for having only began every thing. He was un-

5. At No. 1 Clarence Place. Sir George Beaumont wrote to him at that address on October 9, 1815.

happy & well he might be so, for he had a consciousness of his defects, & had no power to supply them. He was an amiable & good man. He was more versed in antiquity than any thing else, and even there he did not take his rank from the same timid unconsciousness.

The next was a *Parson* again, who was a great herald and who had written a fine tragedy, the passions of which hinged entirely on a dispute to a Barony. The third was an old Poet of 80. He painted from his poems, & his house was filled with Pictures the sight of which would have killed Raphael at 35.[6] He had married a young wife of 40 years younger than himself. She was very fond of Majors & colonels, gave gay assemblies & courts and suffered her inspired old greyhead to give vent to his effusions to the Muses without jealousy or a sigh.

Altogether I like Brighton amazingly. There is something extremely gay. It has all the elegance of St. James Street, backed by the roaring ocean, which gives a fairy, enchanted look to it. It looks of an evening as if all the Nereids had landed for a walk, so lovely so angelic, so rosy are the Darling creatures who parade its shores. Its splendor & elegance & fashion must give a Frenchman a high idea of our opulence, ease, & beauty — one of the proofs of weakness, perhaps, being proud of the common propensities of our Nature, that is, pluming oneself on what all have & all can't help having. Cynics are generally men who censure the World from either imagining the World has not done justice to their talents, or to excuse their own weaknesses. All groaners & croakers, & all those who love justice to the letter, the causes can generally be found to be neglect of the World from their own misconduct, or envy of the World, from their own insignificance. For my part, I like the World. There is more beauty & loveliness & happiness in it than misery. If I see another in Wealth & happiness, I never envy him. I always see him pass & like to see him use his riches well. I like to see a fine young Man of fortune driving tandem. Why should not he make a part of the composition? Without him & his tandems, a beauty would be out. I like to see lovely Women dress six times a day, notwithstanding the con-

6. Raphael was born on April 6, 1483, and died on April 6, 1520, having just achieved the age of thirty-seven.

tempt croakers talk of this. Is there a more innocent employment than dressing? If they are lovely, let them shew it to the best, let 'em shew their pretty feet & delightful forms, & glance their lustrous eyes. My heart leaps to see health & splendour; to be sure I always wish for Mahomet's powers in these matters, but I need be satisfied, if I — Oh lovely, dear, lovely, lovely Woman! Will I ever live a moment when I am useless to thee? No. Shall ever age & debility sink me to grey headed feeblness? Can there be a finer time to quit the World than when one has the keenest relish for its raptures? Who would ever live till all his pleasures are the remembrance of these delightful creatures? Who would exist when his only delight can be to sit and muse in glorious dreams, on the passed by beauties of his Youth? What! Is it cowardice to leave a spent World & risk an unknown one? when to wait might assure you reward? Is it cowardice to dart into a dark & bottomless abyss? It is not that one fears the troubles of this life but that one fears to live to a living decay. Why should I live till I crumble to uselessness & be kicked aside? Why not go when all are interested, when 20 hearts beat at one's sight & pity would bewail one's departure? I'll think of this.

September 29. Charlotte certainly never loved Werter. Would any woman that loved ever have talked to her lover to restrain his impetuosity of temper, which made him feel every thing as a passion which he liked? I have no patience with her. Nothing can be so cruel in a woman as attempts to reason a lover out of his feelings, to censure nature & disposition. Every woman that loves sympathizes & soothes her lover's violences, instead of talking to him with the icy tongue of moderation. Yet poor little thing, too, perhaps she is to be pitied, engaged to a cold blooded man of propriety, by the wish of a dying mother. It was her duty to endeavour to direct poor Werter's feelings, at the expence of her own. We never make allowances for women in such situations, and never give credit to concealed passion because it does not break through all bounds like our own. Women are brought up to conceal their emotions. We have not so much interest in doing so; no injury arises on our character at exposure. The reverse is the fact with Women of Character & rank in Life. Many times

476

when their hearts are cracking, they are obliged to be apparently cold and advise with timid firmness. Dear, dear creatures! What their air, their voice, their looks, their manner contradict at every word.

October 7. Sunday.[7] As I sat after dinner reclining and looking towards the Sea, which was calm & grand, lit up by a golden autumnal afternoon Sun, which hung just above the horizon and seemed scarcely able to approach it, not a cloud or a breath of air, or a human being was stirring. All was sunny, bland, and silent! It was so silent on Earth that the mind took refuge in seeking intercourse with spirits! I fancied I heard their whispers! and the floatings of their wings! I fancied I saw them like summer gossamers, sailing along, and as they crossed each other, smile with a recognizing loveliness that baffles expression! I thought of those that were dear to me & that were dead! Thus sat (I recalled to my mind) my dearest, dearest Parents! — generous, affectionate, & pious! Thus *they* sat, and talked of those who were gone before them, and thus I sit and think with tears of them! After dwelling with sweet remembrance till their influence came over me, like a melancholy dream, I thought of Death! of Creation! of God! of the World! of the deluge! of the Earth! changing its polarity, & the Sea finding a new level, rushing forward with a dreadful roaring & destroying all the works of man! Perhaps many Worlds have thus been destroyed. How insignificant for a moment did the applause of this World seem, compared with this scale of immensity! How trifling time with eternity! How feeble the buildings of Man, with Elements of the Creator! & so would reputation be insignificant if it ended here! but its effects, its hereafter consequences, the approbation of higher indestructible spirits — this is the delight! this is the exciter!

But what a stimulus, a glory, can one feel after having gloried.

October 30. Wilkie & I returned from Brighton,[8] where we had spent a very delightful time. A new sort of knowledge has

7. This word is inserted above the line, probably at a later date. October 7, 1815, was a Saturday.
8. An unpublished letter from Wilkie to BRH of October 14, 1815, mentions his hope of going to Brighton on October 16 or 17.

been opened to our minds by J. Douglas,[9] of Preston, relating to the ancient inhabitants of this Island. The Principle is this: — There are a set of Burial places, without Mounds over them, in which are found Urns of baked clay, lachrymatories, &c., known to be Roman. There are others with high mounds, in which are found skeletons, iron knives, spears, buckles. There are others in which are found Urns of unbaked clay, of a form wild & severe, in which ashes are found, brass spear heads, but *never iron*. These are found *under* Roman causeways. Roman roads have been *cut through them,* clearly denoting their previous existence. He wishes to establish a principle that these were the burial places of the most ancient Britons, the others were of Saxonised Britons & the first Romans.

As I came through my rooms and my Elgin drawings caught my eye, ah! thought I, those were glorious times when I did them. No weak eyes! No fear of cold! I could then sit for twelve hours without fear of damp upon the ground & draw & revel in delight as I proceeded. How changed at present — unable to do any thing intensely without feeling my eyes give in, shrinking at every gust of wind, fearing the blessed light of Heaven, nervous, irritable, wretched — God forgive me. I have torn up my strength by my paroxysms of application. My stomach is so debilitated from fasting & forgetting to dine that it infects my whole frame, & tho as yet I do not bear its marks in any paleness of feature, yet this is my dread. I hope in God by attacking it thus early I may attain my former vigour, and not finally break up till I have secured my own fame & my Country's Glory. O God, I humbly pray thee, thou who hast so mercifully granted all my requests, thou who never forsook me in want & trouble, support me & relieve me in decay of health, grant my mind may bear up against its attacks, as thou enabled it to bear up against the oppressions of my enemies, grant I may finally get out of my present weakness and be restored to all the blessings of my former vigour. Grant it, I humbly pray thee, Amen.

I am convinced it [is] not so much a decay as a derangement. I could formerly digest iron.

9. Identified in the "Vita" as the Reverend James Douglas (1753–1819), author of *Nenia Britannica, or A Sepulchral History of Great Britain* (1793).

November

November 6. I look back on my days of early devotion &
Study with melancholy enthusiasm — what glorious times! Alas,
what a contrast now. O God, that ever I should be obliged to
yield to anything! Here I sit with my hand trembling as I look at
my Picture & call to mind that it was in the same state precisely
three months ago. With what intensity was I proceeding! rapt,
abstracted, in ease of circumstances & peace, & then comes a
melancholy debility of sight, and stops me in the very midst! I
have no philosophy; I hate it; I am very wretched & I will complain. I had made a positive improvement; I had began to have
clearer views. O God, restore me to vigour, I humbly entreat
thee.

November 7. Passed an acute & miserable morning in comparing myself with Raphael. At my age he had completed a Vatican Room.

November 10. Got leave to mould some of the Elgin Marbles'
feet. Went to Mazzoni & began directly.

As I looked at the Lapitha who grapples a Centaur, I dwelt
on it with more intensity than ever. Its beauty, its divinity, came
over my soul like the influence of an angelic spirit, & totally abstracted from the World and its affairs, I caught myself actually
uttering a prayer to it! I never was so acutely impressed before.
I thank God my feelings are ripening & not getting cooler. Its influence came over me stronger & stronger & stronger till I could
scarcely bear it. It felt as if a supernatural being was directing the
beam of a burning lens to fire my soul. I hardly breathed. I
imagined the red & fiery point was burning my heart, & then, as
it were, suddenly sprung up in my feelings with an elasticity of
Spirit, as if one had slipped out of one's skin. All night its Divinity
has beamed to my brain — never was I so impressed with its inspiration. I would lay my head on the block to impress its beauties on the World. I would suffer every torture this instant if
suffering it would instill taste in the World's feelings.

Could I have believed 7 years ago, when I first saw them, I
should ever be blessed in being allowed to have casts? I got leave
today for a whole figure, I thank God, & hope now by having

their beauties impressed before my eyes, to burn them into my nature.

November 16. Pushed on the Workmen to mold away, for such is the uncertainty concerning these divine things, that I may be stopped, and now all those who have had leave to mold this year & have only talked begin to be roused at my doing it at once, and if I don't finish away in a day or two the whole place will be full of modelers and nothing will be allowed at all. Asked leave with fear & trembling to mold a whole figure — got it, to my astonishment! Told the men the value of expedition. They took fire at my urgings, & promised to work night & day. I at once began upon the exquisite lying figure & if (as I hope in God) nothing happens to prevent me, I will have a beautiful cast of this figure to dwell on all my life. How fortunate I am. I could hardly sleep last night. I dreamt I was at Rome & thought nothing of any statue & told them that our Elgin Marbles were the only true works of art. I dreamt about the Pope & Raphael & Heaven knows what, & awoke perfectly alive, like a fish just out of water.

November 17. Mazzoni, by great exertion, got the mold completed & off & home by four o'clock. Huzza! Rossi[1] called & asked if I had permission. I wished I had been there. I went down fully prepared for a row before it was over, expecting some one would go & cant & pretend it was injuring Lord Elgin's property, &c., &c., &c. As I had got so far, they should have fought through me before they should have stopped me. However nothing happened. Many artists came & gaped & looked unutterable things — "en avant" was my look to the molder. I thank God for my success. I hope I shall make a proper use of them.

My eyes better able to work. Got in a head from the lovely Maria.[2]

Just as I had expected, an order came down to put a stop to moulding yesterday afternoon.

---

1. John Charles Felix Rossi (1762–1839), R. A., sculptor of many monuments in St. Paul's Cathedral. He was BRH's landlord at 22 Lisson Grove, North, from 1817 to 1823.
2. Maria Foote.

November 19. Sunday. Last night I was introduced by Mr. Hamilton to Canova,[3] and was extremely interested. He has a fine Italian head, & when he smiles the feeling sent forth is so exquisite that one fancied music would follow the motions of his lips. As I heard reports of his not speaking with enthusiasm of the Elgin Marbles, I asked, "Ne croyez vous pas, Monsieur, que le style qui existe dans les statues d'Elgin est superieur à tous les autres connus?" "Sans doute," was his reply; "la verité, les accidents de la chair et les formes sont si vrais et belles que ces statues produiront un grand changement dans les Arts. Ils renverseront le systeme mathematique des autres." I was delighted & turning to Hamilton asked him, "n'ai je pas toujours dit la meme chose il y a six années?" "Vous verrez," continued Canova this morning when he called [on] me, "dans les statues de Monte Cavallo des divisions du ventre qui ne sont pas naturelles. Vous ne les verrez pas aux Grecs."

As I was determined to push him further, "Ne croyez vous pas, Monsieur, que si L'Apollon Belvedere etoit une figure en repose, ce ne sera pas d'une si grande reputation? Ne croyez vous pas que ce sera comme ordinaire? N'est ce pas l'esprit de l'action et ne pas la beauté inherente de sa forme qui attrape l'ignorant?" "Oui, peut-etre," said he. This I consider a great deal from a man who has passed 50 years without seeing the Elgin Marbles and must feel jealous of any attempt to make him yield to any reasoning that will lower the statue that has reigned at Rome. Mr. Hamilton told me he said to him that if the action was taken away the Apollo was a common figure. This is delightful. He behaved to me with great affection. He looked at my casts & appeared to take an interest in every thing I had done. He was feelingly & deeply impressed with my present Picture, & at the Gipsey's head in it he repeated "charmante, charmante." In shewing some drawings of hands, "parfaitement bien, vous êtes un brave homme." On one hand where I had marked things too acutely he said, "souvenez

3. Antonio Canova (1757–1822), the leading sculptor of the period. Pope Pius VII sent him to Paris in 1815 to superintend the return of Italian works of art and made him Marquis of Ischia for his successful efforts. He visited London primarily to examine the Elgin Marbles; his enthusiastic endorsement of their genuineness and beauty strongly influenced Parliament to purchase them for the nation.

vous bien, that two parts can never be marked with equal strength. There must be always a predominant one. Never cut up equally. Sharpness & softness constitute the principles of flesh." Tho convicted on my own drawing, yet these were my own principles & my heart beat as I recognised an Italian coming to England whose mind must have passed through the same train of thought to come to the same conclusions. Now indeed was the sympathy of Genius. He said the composition was plus belle. He told me all the copies from Praxiteles had the same flesh with [the] Elgin Marbles. He again lightened up as he mentioned them, and repeated they were worth coming from Rome to see. Mr. Hamilton said after we left him last night he had never heard him express himself so distinctly about the Marbles before, because he had never pressed him, feeling a delicacy, as he was connected with the Marbles. He told me he thought Rubens flesh too shining; owing to his power of touch, it was rather like porcelain. Titian & Paul Veronese were more perfect in flesh. He seemed to have great feeling for Colour, and I am convinced is a well grounded & great Artist. He deserves his reputation.

What a paltry set of beings are the R. A.'s, never to pay him any honor, but to vilify & pretend he is coming over here for work! He told me, he had all his life had too much work, & if he wanted work, he would not have given a colossal figure of Religion to St. Peter's.[4] "Come to Rome, vous y verrez la veritable democracie de l'Art," said Canova. I promised I would. One had a feeling about Canova as if he was, as it were, a descendant of the great. His opinion was an opinion formed at a place where every thing great & good & grand in Art had nursed it; it was coming from head quarters, and I cannot help saying I felt extreme delight in finding principles and conclusions which I had attained from observation on Nature in England, sanctioned by Canova, who had drawn them from both Nature [and] Art at Rome. Our minds had, [as] it were, passed through the same train

4. William Michael Rossetti wrote that in 1815 Canova "contemplated a great work, a colossal statue of Religion. The model filled Italy with admiration; the marble was procured, and the chisel of the sculptor ready to be applied to it, when the jealousy of churchmen as to the site, or some other cause, deprived the country of the projected work" (*Britannica*, V,205).

of feeling & thought; we had observed the same effects, & came to the same conclusions, tho 500 miles asunder.

At my sketch of the Dead Child he was even affected. He mentioned what he thought in the contour a little defective. I told him in making studies from Nature, I always copied every thing that I might adapt it as I pleased in my Pictures, but I liked to be sure of Nature, that I might have some thing to refer to. "Vous avez raison," he said.

November 20. Dear Maria* sat again today and tormented me as I painted, with her lovely archness & wicked, fascinating fun. After sitting some little time, she insisted with that sort of irresistible, insinuating "now do," which makes resistance useless when from the mouth of a beauty, she insisted she could paint the hair better than mine, & taking the brushes out of my hand, with a delicate apprehension and graceful shrink as she touched the paint, for fear of her black silk, just put on for the first time, flounced four times to the knee, taking my brushes, she dabbled a lock over the forehead, & then laughed with a rich thrilling at her own lovely awkwardness. I looked at her as she leant over, my hair & cheek accidentally grazed the silk that covered her exquisite bosom — I could have eat her bit by bit — but her Father[5] had trusted her to my honor, & I would have split with passion rather than ventured to have touched her hand. She sat for three hours, with perfect good humour, sometimes singing sweet airs with a honey voice, sometimes mimicking ballad singers, with a comic simplicity that was exquisite, & sometimes asking my opinions on different things, and wondering at a new idea put into her mind with a lovely smile. Her face & form & air & manner are perpetual exciters of "lovely fancies & all heavenly things." Sweet, sweet Girl. She found some pretence to go shopping in Bond Street, tho I taxed her that it was only to shew her new flounces to the Bows, which she denied with a blush. Peace & happiness for ever attend her.

* Lady Harrington. 1835

5. Samuel T. Foote (1761–1840), manager of a theatre in Plymouth in which Maria Foote appeared as Juliet in 1810. He later managed a hotel in Exeter.

Her Father was the second son of a Clergyman. After a life of dissipation, he went on the Stage. His Brother married one Sister of two Sisters, & Maria's Father, being on a visit, contrived to interest the other. He married her without her being aware either of his profession or temper. I believe to her surprise she found him manager of a Country Theatre, and tho her connections were genteel and she herself a very interesting little Woman, yet the prejudice in the Town was so strong that no one visited the Wife of the Manager, tho infinitely better educated than any one in Plymouth. My dear Mother, whose heart & feelings were always alive, protected & received her. She became almost an inmate in our family; but at the assemblies no one spoke to her. Officers only danced [with her] or noticed her. Finding without a crime she was suffering the penalties of vice, she became indifferent to character altogether. She had not strength of mind enough to retire within herself; being fond of the Theatre, & her husband's situation enabling her continually to attend it, she became infected with a wish to act, hoping to make up in the flattery of applause the aking pang the cruel neglect of her sex had excited.

November 27. Dined with Hamilton to meet Canova. Spent a delightful evening.

November 28. Spent the whole of this day shewing Canova the Duke of Devonshire's[6] &c., &c. Called at Turner's. He exclaimed "grand Genie" as he looked at his Pictures. He had seen a Picture of Northcote's at Guildhall of Wat Tyler & he asked to see him. We called about half past three, took him quite by surprize. He was in all his glory of filth & beard. After we left him Canova [said], "Je prefere ses Tableaux au Cité." It would have been better for Northcote had he never called, I doubt not. Indeed I saw that Northcote would have given all he was worth on earth to have had something important to shew him. He kept bringing out wretched Portraits & at last, conscious what a figure he cut before such a man, he looked up as he spoke, with a twist of his body and a mortified insignificance in his face, his whole air, as

6. The sixth Duke of Devonshire (1790–1858), bibliophile and collector of coins and pictures.

it were, assuming a withered littleness, "we can only paint portraits here." Poor fellow, I would not have had thy wealth if at
the expence of thy feeling at that moment. What are all my wants
& harrassings? I would bear twenty times as much, give me but
the sweet consciousness of having done my duty to my Country's
taste, of having never sacrificed it for paltry interests, of bearing
pain & want & hunger & blindness, rather than yield a step on the
road, which I am born to tread on, even if all the miseries of
Earth wait to clutch me at its end.

November 29. Met Canova at the Elgin Marbles. He was delighted to see me. He pointed out all the beauties exactly as I could
have wished. "Come e sentito" he kept saying as he put his hand
with the dash of experience on all the principle beauties of the
body. On better acquaintance he is a facetious, unaffected, delightful man. "When they get a mold of this figure (meaning the
Neptune), how they will be astonished," said he, "at Rome." Of
Fuzeli he said, "Vi sono due cose — il foco e la flamma in Arte.
Raphaello a il foco e la flamma, qualche non hanno che la
flamma." Capitally true. I had actually said this to Scott some
time since.
    "If any Sculptor," said Canova, "had made such Statues be-
fore these were seen, 'sono troppo veri' would have been the cry."
Canova said at Table the characters of Raphael & Perugino were
neither Greeks or Romans but "veri devoti."
    As I am now without a single sixpence in the World, having
spent all I had left at Brighton, and as I knew the blessings of
ease & peace in pecuniary matters, as to my progress, I determined to state my state to Lord Mulgrave & ask his assistance till
I had got through with my Picture. I therefore wrote him telling
the whole, that even in the middle of Macbeth my means failed,
that I persisted through that Picture till I finished, expecting my
reward, that owing to the misunderstanding between Sir George
& I, I was disappointed & that this was the cause of all my wants,
that at the beginning of Solomon I had not a sixpence in the
World, that the Man where I had dined, seeing my uneasiness &
knowing I had [been] trusted for a week, told me not to be uneasy, & had allowed me to go on two years without paying him, by

which means I was able to finish Solomon, that I did not fear a recurrence of such wants, but that I was convinced tho' they did not crush, they interrupted me, that had I had less difficulty I should have had less faults, that I would never yield an inch of the ground I stood on, and I laid my circumstances before his Lordship, as he had always interested himself in my favor, that 300 would completely relieve me, and it should be returned at the end of my Picture with gratitude. To this I received the following answer: [*a letter from Lord Mulgrave, dated November 18, 1815, regretting that it would not suit his convenience at the present time to make the advance that Haydon asked.*]

December 3. [*Two anatomical sketches, with the muscles numbered.*] In the Torso,[7] 1 is a roll of the obliquus muscle in consequence of the space between the ribs & the Ilium being lessened by the body pressed on that side. As much as it contracts on one side, it extends on the other; a muscle being flexible, is influenced in its shapes by action or position. Of course it must stretch on the one side as much as it folds on the other. Now there is very little difference in the Torso. Behind 2 is the Scapula, [which] is drawn forward by the position of the arm; its muscles are not in action. 3 is the scapula, [which] is rather drawn back by the arm's action. The muscles then are farther in action. Let such a body be a God's or a devil's, it [will] have muscles & they must be liable [to] the consequences of action or repose. No. 2 could never be marked so strongly if No. 3 is not stronger. They must be dragged & their projection lessened. If No. 3 is right *as it is,* the power & shape of No. 3 in such action could never [be] so like No. 2 in that action. The actions differ. One is more in use than the other, & yet both have similar strength in marking! Both then must be the same action! or in repose? or both must be in action that causes similar projections. No, this can be proved — not. They are in actions that are not of similar strength, but of totally dissimilar, consequently they cannot have similar exciting cause, and if they cannot have similar exciting cause, they cannot be similarly excited, and the Figure on which the two Scapulae are in opposite actions, and on which the muscles that belong to

7. See I,28.

them are in equal projection, as if in similar actions, must be untrue & absurd; consequently the torso in its back having two Scapulae in different actions, & yet the muscles belonging to them having similar projections, is an untrue & absurd back, and the Artist must have [been] deficient in the great & unalterable principles of life, and yet the Artist that made such a back could not have been ignorant of the great principles of life, but must have been influenced by a delusive principle of giving grandeur & rant. Let him mark muscles in repose as strongly as they are marked in action in common life, but let him mark his muscles in action proportionately vigourous, or there will be no distinction. No. They would be then too gross. Why, then, your principle is a gross one. The Theseus is as grand as the Torso without the affectation, because no principle is violated — there is a being whose action varies & whose consequences vary with the action; both are true & all are grand, simple, & eternal. The Torso & the Apollo are Marbles, Statues; the Theseus, the Lapithae, & the Neptune living Gods.

I think Racine in his Iphegenie has lost an opportunity of shewing the deep secret struggles of passion against the consciousness of duty, in Achilles, when he becomes acquainted with the fate of Iphegenia, to whom he was betrothed. This decides his inferiority to Shakespeare, who would never have suffered such an opportunity for truth to pass without exhibiting it. The character of Achilles is passion for Glory. He had preferred Death before Troy to an inglorious ease with his parents. When he was told that the oracle has said the Greeks should never proceed to Troy if Iphegenia was not sacrificed, what would have been his first sensations? "Shall I then lose my field of Glory if she be not? Yes — why, then, let her! But yet shall I suffer a lovely Girl to be murdered, merely because I risk losing an opportunity of distinguishing myself, one to whom I am betrothed, who is, in fact, my wife, & who has more claims on my protection because she has not the full right of wife? But yet shall Troy rear her guilty head unpunished merely from my weak passion for a woman? No. Troy shall fall. Iphegenia must be sacrificed. Must I submit to fate? Die I must, I know. Is it not more glorious to save this tender creature & rush to Troy in spite of oracles &

Priests? Yes. Troy shall yet fall; Iphegenia shall now be saved."
Rushes out — in a short time — shouts & shrieks should be heard
— messengers or soldiers struggling in in terror, relate what had
passed, how Achilles rushed to the Altar at the moment, &c., &c.,
&c.

What an opportunity to exhibit the glorious struggles in a
great breast, those secret whisperings of self, which gleam across
the mind and are concealed beneath the smile of — As I read it
my heart beat as I approached this crisis, and I was miserably
dissappointed in find[ing] common place chit chat.

December 5. Death puts an end to all hopes of amendment.
Frailties are then pardoned, & virtues only remembered. The
only reason why frailties are censured is from the hope of reform-
ing while the Man's alive.

The Marbles from Arcadia[8] are fine compositions, with a few
exceptions, but more violent. They have not the subdued elegance,
the polished air, the infinite skill of the Elgin Marbles. They are
executed by some provincial Artist after the Parthenon must have
made a noise all over Greece. The Temple was built by Ictinus;
it is described in Pausanius.

I like Racine's Phedre better than Iphegenie. There are more
touches of Nature & passion.

[*The next page of the diary contains a rough draft of ideas
elaborated in the next three paragraphs.*]

The Engines in Fuzeli's Mind are Blasphemy, Lechery, and
blood. His women are all whores, and men all banditti. They are
whores not from a love of pleasure but from a hatred, a malignant spite against virtue, and his men are villains not from a daring
desire of risk, but a licentious turbulence of moral restraint; with
the look of demons, they have the actions of galvanized frogs,
the dress of mountebanks, and the hue of pestilential disease.
Such a monstrous imagination was never propagated on lovely
woman. No. Fuzeli was engendered by some hellish monster, on

8. The frieze, now in the British Museum, from the Temple of Apollo Epi-
kourios at Bassae, near Phigaleia in Arcadia.

the dead body of a speckled hag, some hideous form, whose passions were excited & whose lechery was fired at commingling with fiery rapture in the pulpy squashiness of a decaying corpse.

Can the purity, the truth, the chastity, the beauty of the Elgin Marbles or Nature please him? Would it not be an insult to their excellence, would it not at once blast their fame & excite doubts of their divinity if they excited delight in Fuzeli's corrupted fancy? To be sure, never were higher comp[limen]ts paid to the Elgin [Marbles] than to have two such minds deny them as Payne Knight's & Fuzeli's, the one teeming with Priapism & the other with hell.

The greatest geniuses are those who with a feeling for the perfection of another & a higher World, have a full understanding of the imperfections of this. Wellington is a perfect genius as a general, because while faced with the romantic conception of rescuing Spain, he always remembered it must be done by men, & men must eat, because food was requisite to animal life; without food animal life ceased to be nourished. He therefore, in the midst of his highest feelings, never forgot biscuit & beef. Thus ideal beauty in Art is the highest feeling; ideal beauty in form is beauty of man. Men are composed of parts, heads, hands, feet, legs, & thighs. These heads, hands, feet, thighs, & legs are all moved by certain things called muscles, which in their actions to move head, hands, feet, thighs, & legs, make certain markings on a skin that covers them, and produce certain contours externally which develope agility, beauty, & perfection. You may feel perfection in form when it is produced, but you must produce it by *determining* the parts & causes that compose it.

As external form depends on internal organization, a thorough knowledge of external organization is necessary. If you do not know the essence from the accident, how can you reject the one from the other?

In England every thing must be done by a Man's self. I soon saw when I began life no one would employ me in large Pictures, so I resolved to employ myself. I soon saw no one would give me opportunities, so I resolved to make them. Now this government will not make a "Ministre des Arts," so I will make [one] myself.

489

[*The next three pages, endorsed by Haydon "Fragment of Elgin Mem. 1816," have been inserted into the diary. See Appendix D.*]

"What right has Mr. Haydon to expect [to] become an Academician without submitting to the same regulations as others," said an Academician to a Friend of mine after a good dinner & plenty of claret. "He might have been one if he liked long ago." Why, I tell you the right. He did submit to put his name down & to go through the regulations of the Academy, and you disgraced him by refusing to let him in, and you shall now submit by way of vanity. "We don't fear any refractory Students," said Carlisle. Don't you? Then why does it occupy your mind? Why, tell me so? God only grant me eyes, Intellect, & health, & I'll bring you all on your knees.

Do you suppose I'll submit to enter, just to keep up the farce of the Academy? One historical painter is quite enough for the purposes of the Portrait painters.

December 16. What a tremendous character is the Cumaean Sybill of Michel Angelo, a being purged from the passions of the world, grown old & experienced, to a settled age, old without being withered, bent without being weak, a creature that would smile on beauty as on a rose, & look through its future life with the mental eye of inspiration. The Cumaean Sybil looks as if it came from a desert, the silence of whose solitude was never broken but by her own footsteps or breathings. She seems as if she had never spoken since the Divine Essence chose her as the first organ of his Influence, as if she for ever pondered, as if she had never been young, would ever be old, & would never die, as if her form had become dry, nerveless, wrinkled, yet vigourous, powerful, & firm. The whole conception of this character ranks Michel Angelo with a God! Raphael's characters strike us from their truth, Michel Angelo's from their poetry & power to realize what his imagination conceived. She looks as if she would survive the destruction of the World, without an alteration of feature!

Feeling will enable you to feel a result, but feeling alone will not enable [you] to produce one. After feeling a result, to produce on others, you must exert your understanding & practice your hand. This is the progress of genius, and tho by feeling without practice or reason you may produce a feeling of your feeling in others, yet the feeling produced will not be so compleat as when the means of conveying the feeling are perfect. The moment you attempt to produce a feeling alone, you begin immediately to exert your understanding.

Why & wherefore, how & what, one perpetually asked one self. When the why, the wherefore, & the how & what are answered, your understanding is stored with the reasons, and your feeling being tutored, you can make others feel. The first requisite step is a capacity of feeling a result. The next an understanding to ascertain the means of producing in others what you have felt yourself, and the third the feeling again to tell you when you have done what you felt you wanted to do.

The understanding being thoroughly stored with the principles of every feeling felt, & the hand thoroughly ready from habit to express the feeling by the principles, the feeling can no sooner feel than the understanding at once supplies the principle & the hand at once executes, till at last, feeling, understanding, & hand go so instantaneously together, as not to be perceived in their separate departments by the possessor, and all resolve themselves into feeling which was at first the instigator & then becomes the director. The Vulgar, the idle, and unlettered seeing a result produced by the Artist the moment it is felt, conclude that feeling alone was the cause of his doing it, ignorant what effects of the understanding & hand were at first requisite before they could so completely obey the feeling, as to be identified with it.

December 29. The two previous glories came in one week, Scott's fine burst of enthusiasm[9] and Wordsworth's sublime sonnets.[1] It is impossible to tell how I felt, after the first blaze of joy,

9. On the preceding page of the diary cuttings from the *Champion* on BRH's defense of the Elgin Marbles are attached.

1. On December 21, 1815, Wordsworth wrote to BRH, enclosing three sonnets, one of them addressed to BRH (*Letters of the Wordsworth Family*, ed. William Knight, 1907, II,63–64). With Wordsworth's permission, BRH published the sonnet in the *Champion* of February 4, 1816, and the *Examiner* of March 31, 1816.

> "High is our calling, Friend! — Creative Art
> (Whether the instrument of words she use,
> Or pencil pregnant with ethereal hues)

feeling as it were lifted up in the great eye of the World, and feeling nothing more could be said of one. I relapsed into a melancholy sensitiveness, and my heart yearned in gratitude to God as my protector, my divine inspirer, on the great Spirit who had led me through the Wilderness, who had first my Soul fired when a boy, ignorant of my future prospects or probable fate. O God, oh thou great, good, merciful being, thou knowest the first Sunday after my arrival in London, to commence my great march, I went to thy Temple and on my knees prayed to thee to bless, inspire, & protect my exertions, to grant that I might reform the taste of my Country, & be at the head of my Art before thirty, to grant no obstructions might check me that I might subdue all human difficulties & render those more than human of no avail, to grant that I might sacrifice my being with rapture, if sacrifice was necessary and if it would attain the great object of my heart. O God, true to my hope, thou hast never deserted me, still has sent a shining beam to direct me. Often in misgivings hast thou shot across my brain in fiery letters "go on," and then I have felt as if a supernatural being inhabited my Soul, as if something living lept in me. For thy mercies accept the purest gratitude that ever issued from the heart of a human creature. I have succeeded grandly, let me not be puffed up and lessen my efforts. Still must I succeed & compleat my undertaking, to its completion. Still assist me. Grant, oh grant I may compleat it before I die, or if not, grant my death may be effectual to its completion. Let me have a clear conception of what I must do and all I must do, and supply me still with every great requisite both in my intellect, my body, & my soul, & I will yield my breath with raptures whenever thou in thy infinite wisdom thinks fit to take me. Amen, with all my Soul.

Demands the service of a mind and heart,
Though sensitive, yet, in their weakest part,
Heroically fashioned — to infuse
Faith in the whispers of the lonely Muse,
While the whole world seems adverse to desert.
And oh! When Nature sinks, as oft she may,
Through long-lived pressure of obscure distress,
Still to be strenuous for the bright reward,
And in the soul admit of no decay,
Brook no continuance of weak-mindedness —
Great is the glory for the strife is hard!"

December

My feelings are keen & cutting, nervous, alive, & trembling. To live and see all my little virtues acknowledged by the World, my industry felt, my devotion understood & estimated, never have I done what I ought to do, but that is between myself & my Creator. What I have done is sufficient to excite the applause of the World, but not my own. What I may do I humbly hope will deserve the remembrance of both.

This year has been to me a year of glorious retribution, without any effort of my own. My distresses have been redressed, my genius felt and acknowledged, my enemies humbled (O God, let me never deserve humbling). I now want nothing but eyes, and O God, grant them, grant my eyes may no longer be inadequate to compleat my Picture, grant them strength, enable me to proceed day by day, with firmness, intensity, & vigor. Grant I may conceive & execute for the awe of the World the head of my blessed Saviour, and when the work is finished, let it excite the feelings of Mankind, let it advance the interests of Christianity, let it elevate the glory of my Country. Oh let it prove to the World the power of its Genius, its virtue, its perseverance. O God, humbly do I pray to thee, sincerely do I trust in thee, and faithfully do I depend on thee, thou good, grand, & merciful Being. Amen, in heart cutting feelings.

Oh, my sweet, sweet V——, had I but thee to communicate, to participate, to share, had I but thy lip to press with kisses pure at all this glory — I complain not, I submit.

December 30. In all feelings arising from such causes, the heart turns at once to some beloved being to share the triumph — to Woman, with all her gentleness and loveliness, to that creature depending on your protection, living by your efforts, who grows, as it were, by your caresses, whose delights of life have been owing to your devotion, whose pains have been soothed & miseries lightened by the purity of your love & kindness of your constancy, whose highest ambition is your approbation, and highest delight your happiness, who has no cause to envy, for she is content with the reflection of your splendour, who in the midst of exquisite enjoyment seems only pleased in as much as she contributes to your own. This is the true Woman. This is the creature

493

To warn, to comfort and command
And yet a Spirit, still and bright
With something of an Angel light.[2]

But alas, I have none such, none to pour my soul in. I have
no bosom that beats only for me. I look now at the empty chair
and see no more the graceful loveliness that has filled it, that
heavenly figure, those full exquisite thighs pressed out by the
chair, with silk drapery that covered without concealing their
delicious shape, while two lovely ankles came tapering out beneath that gave a lightness, a fairy lightness to the rich lengthened
beauty of her figure. Oh my sweet, dearest V——, how would
thy bosom have beat as I laid my cheek on it and told thee my
glory, in the intervals of study. The solitary chair unoccupied!
silent! still! seems to speak to me, to tell me by its look, to remind
me by its appearance, as the fits of flame from the winter fire light
up & flush upon it through the darkness, what lovely form has sat
on it & inspired me. It seems as if an Angel had gone with all its
brightness and left the World in an huge eclipse. Oh! why were
we ever [*the sentence is incomplete*].

As one advances in life the greatest difficulty is to manage the
feelings of those Friends with whom you were once on an equality
in situation, and who remain stationary while you blaze by and
leave them in desponding gaze. They cannot bear your presence,
and take refuge in insulting you in order to regain their own estimation. Many painful sensations have I experienced from conduct
of this sort & many painful struggles have I had to curb my
resentments.

December 31. The last night of this wonderful year, to me a
year of glorious retribution. The whole year develloped, perpetual consequences of the success of the previous one. January,
March, August, Sep., Octo., Nov., Dec. — seven precious months
at this precious time of my life was I wandering about in weak
eyes, unable to apply myself a moment, & three the year before,
make nine, nearly a whole year lost, in consequence of imprudent
excess during the latter part of Solomon, when I painted sixteen
hours a day six days without ceasing. I hardly slept, and such was

2. Wordsworth, "She was a phantom of delight," ll. 28–30.

the rage of passion for work that it resembled the lecherous fury of a Lion rushing about the woods unable to find its mate, when burning for coition. Could my strength have lasted, I should have gone mad. My reward was a month unable to do anything at that critical time, and an irreparable injury, I fear, to my constitution. Regular hours of application are more conducive to continuance, tho' I look back on this effort with a burst of feeling I can't describe. Tho' I have not painted so long yet upon the whole my mind by perpetual efforts has been strengthened. I think it has given me the practice of internal deduction. I made a study of a head & found my hand improved. Thank God. I close this year in humble hope that at the conclusion of the next, my present great Picture will be well near a conclusion. O God grant it, grant no longer weakness of sight may check or harrass me. In thee I trust, Amen. *Finis.*